HOODED AMERICANISM

*The History of the
Ku Klux Klan*

DAVID M. CHALMERS

D1268101

DUKE UNIVERSITY PRESS   Durham 1987

Library of Congress Cataloging-in-Publication Data
Chalmers, David Mark.
Hooded Americanism.
Reprint. Originally published: New York: F. Watts,
c1981.
Bibliography: p.
Includes index.
1. Ku Klux Klan—History. 2. Ku Klux Klan (1915–
History. I. Title.
[HS2330.K63C5 1987] 322.4'2 86-29133
ISBN 0-8223-0730-8 (alk. paper)
ISBN 0-8223-0772-3 (pbk. : alk. paper)

HOODED AMERICANISM

DATE DUE			
AUG 17 2005		JUL 1 2003	
DEC 2 2 2005			

To Dexter Perkins, Scholar and Teacher

CONTENTS

Preface: Media Hype and Poor-Boy Politics   xi

1. *A Quick Look behind the Mask*   1

2. *The Klan Rides, 1865–71*   8

3. *The Birth of a Nation*   22

4. *The Klan Revival, 1915–21*   28

5. *The Eyes of Texas*   39

6. *Mayhem and Martial Law in Oklahoma*   49

7. *The Razorback Klan*   56

8. *Louisiana: Black Sheets among the Bayous*   59

9. *Mississippi: Fiery Crosses on the Levee*   66

10. *Georgia: The Klan Tabernacle*   70

11. *The Heart of Dixie*   78

12. *Oregon: Puritanism Repotted*   85

13. *Success and Schism in the Tarheel State*   92

14. *Klansmen in the Carolina Piedmont*   98

15. *The Price of Success*   100

16. *The Ten-Dollar Special*   109

17. *Gold-Rush Days in California*   119

18. *Pikes Peak or Bust* 126

19. *In Defense of Inland America* 135

20. *Twisting the Klan's Shirttail in Kansas* 143

21. *Bad Luck in Minneapolis* 149

22. *Border-State Klans* 152

23. *Klan Castles in Indiana* 162

24. *Mighty Ohio* 175

25. *The Fighting Illini* 183

26. *Badger Games in Wisconsin* 190

27. *White Robes on Woodward Avenue* 194

28. *National Politics* 198

29. *The Championship Fight in Madison Square Garden* 202

30. *Anticlimax: The Nineteen Twenty-four Election* 213

31. *From Canada to the Rio Grande* 216

32. *Every Man for Himself in Florida* 225

33. *Attempted Dominion in Virginia* 230

34. *Riotous Doings in Penn's Woods* 236

35. *Methodists and Madness in the Garden State* 243

36. *The E-ri-e Was a-Rising, and the Gin Was Getting Low* 254

37. *Defending the Puritan Fathers* 266

38. *The Klan International* 279

39. *Marching on Washington* 281

40. *Decline* 291

41. *Nineteen Twenty-eight, a Year of Perils and Promises* 300

42. *The Depression Decade, 1929–39* 304

43. *All Dressed Up But Not Going Anywhere: The Colescott Era* 319

44. *The Hooded World of Dr. Green* 325

45. *The Death of the Dragon* 335

46. *Laissez Faire, Violence, and Confusion in the Late Fifties* 343

47. *The New Frontiers of the Nineteen Sixties* 366

48. *The Long Hot Summer* 375

49. *Declining Power* 386

50. *Bad Times in the 1970s* 397

51. *Confrontation, Poor-Boy Politics, and Revival* 405

52. *Death in Greensboro* 416

53. *The Enduring Klan* 424

Acknowledgments 439

Bibliography 441

Index 465

PREFACE:
MEDIA HYPE AND POOR-BOY POLITICS

Although it is in Europe, the Middle East, and Latin America that terrorist groups count as a political force today, the United States is the home of one of the world's oldest such organizations, the Invisible Empires of the hooded Knights of the Ku Klux Klan. The Klan is seldom out of American newspaper headlines. Klan leaders are guests on talk shows and are interviewed on network TV by Barbara Walters and Tom Snyder, featured on the evening news and various newsmagazine shows, reported on regularly by journalists who are syndicated by the *Los Angeles Times* and *New York Times* services, and profiled in *Penthouse, Oui, Esquire,* by Harry Crews in *Playboy,* and in an hour-long PBS special. A black sociologist interviewed Georgia and California Klansmen in connection with a baseball story in the twenty-fifth anniversary issue of *Sports Illustrated.* At a recent Klan rally in Florida, the igniting of the flaming cross was delayed twenty minutes at the request of a TV news crew so that the ritual could be shown live on the eleven o'clock news. When Klansman and talk show celebrity David Duke announced that his California realm would patrol the Mexican border against illegal aliens, only eight Klansmen, but more than a score of news and TV cameramen, showed up.

As the Klan becomes more active, so does its media coverage. A hooded Klansman, a flaming cross, a pretty blond child in miniature Klan robes are of surefire public interest. The picture goes into the news section of the daily paper, and there is a Klan story in the Sunday supplement. For the reader, there is a touch of mystery, a thrill of danger—and excitement. Guided by the Klan-watching authorities of the Anti-Defamation League and the Southern Regional Council, the press has learned to be cautious about the Klan's own membership estimates, which often run from the tens to hundreds of thousands. For the unwary, the turnout of spectators at a Klan parade or rally can be similarly misleading. Does it represent support or approval, or curiosity? Wouldn't any of us go if there were to be a cross-burning just down the road or outside of the town in which we lived?

Like others who have written on the Klan, I get calls from editors, journalists, wire services, researchers for "The McNeil-Lehrer Report," students, and network TV for comment on "the Klan revival." I used to reply to members of the media that *they* were the Klan "revival." This would be followed by a startled pause and a good two-way discussion of the distinctions between news reporting and publicity.

Over time, I have come to believe that I was being somewhat unfair to the media. The Klan does receive disproportionate attention, but that exposure is not an important factor in current Klan revivals. For the most part, the Klansman is not a devoted follower of the local press or the evening news. He is likely to have copies of Robert Shelton's *Fiery Cross,* David Duke's *Crusader,* Bill Wilkinson's *Klansman,* or the National States Rights Party's *Thunderbolt* on his living room table, rather than *Time* or *Newsweek.*

The Klansman is distrustful of the leadership of his community and country and is no more trusting of the media, which he believes is run from New York, controlled by the Jews, and part of the conspiracy against him and his kind. While the media may overplay the Klan, it is a distrust of those very media that helps to produce Klansmen. In the growing economic uncertainty and social confusion of the 1980s, at least a stratum of the small-town, working-class South has reacted by linking racial integration, communism, crime in the streets, the inflationary squeeze, and job uncertainty into an emotional package, summed up at all Klan rallies in the threatening words: AFFIRMATIVE ACTION.

In at least portions of the American South, where the Ku Klux Klan is still part of a great tradition, confrontation with black "justice and job" marchers in the streets has produced soldiers for the Klan ranks. In the cycle of Klan growth and decline, a sort of revival is under way, nurtured by social uncertainty, racial change, confrontation, and poor-boy politics.

HOODED AMERICANISM

1

A QUICK LOOK BEHIND THE MASK

In 1923, H. L. Mencken and George Jean Nathan, the recognized high priests of criticism of the American scene, described the Ku Klux Klan for *Smart Set,* their journal of satirical sophistication. In what none of their avid followers would have mistaken for praise, they flayed every organizational aspect of the national life. Sparing no one, majority or minority, they connected the newly reborn Invisible Empire with all that was ludicrous and unwarranted in a society which they felt represented the bumptious mediocrity.

Not a single solitary sound reason has yet been advanced for putting the Ku Klux Klan out of business. If the Klan is against the Jews, so are half of the good hotels of the Republic and three-quarters of the good clubs. If the Klan is against the foreign-born or the hyphenated citizen, so is the National Institute of Arts and Letters. If the Klan is against the Negro, so are all of the States south of the Mason-Dixon line. If the Klan is for damnation and persecution, so is the Methodist Church. If the Klan is bent upon political control, so are the American Legion and Tammany Hall. If the Klan wears grotesque uniforms, so do the Knights of Pythias and the Mystic Shriners. If the Klan holds its meetings in the dead of night, so do the Elks. If the Klan conducts its business in secret, so do all college Greek letter fraternities and the Department of State. If the Klan holds idiotic parades in the public streets, so do the police, the letter-carriers and firemen. If the Klan's officers bear ridiculous names, so do the officers of the Lambs' Club. If the Klan uses the mails for shaking down suckers, so does the Red Cross. If the Klan constitutes itself a censor of private morals, so does the Congress of the United States. If the Klan lynches a Moor for raping someone's daughter, so would you or I.

The Klan, in approvingly reprinting the piece in one of its own journals, *Dawn,* recognized itself, even though it missed the barbed touch which the description contained. Except for the first nights of playful pranks and mystic initiations in Pulaski, Tennessee, during the early days of Reconstruction, the Knights of the Ku Klux Klan have not been noted for their sense of humor. The grim defense of a society under attack in the twentieth century, has been a highly serious affair for the wearers of the hood and mask.

The Klan was born during the restless days after the Civil War, when time was out of joint in the South and the social order was battered and turned upside down. As a secret, nocturnal organization, operating during lawless times, the Klan soon turned into a vigilante force. To restore order meant returning the Negro to the field—just as long as he didn't do too well there—and the prewar leaders to their former seats of power. Those who felt differently would have to go. And so the masked Klansmen rode out across the land. Where intimidation was not sufficient, violence was used. The Klan raided solitary cabins and invaded towns, preferably at night, but in the daytime where necessary. Although Klansmen were occasionally hurt, the death toll of Negroes and Republicans probably ran close to a thousand.

Although soberer leaders set up a centralized, hierarchical organization for the purposes of better co-ordination and control, their success was limited. The local dens proved uncontrollable and continued to operate for private as well as political ends, even after Imperial Wizard Nathan Bedford Forrest formally disbanded the Klans in 1869. Changing conditions and martial law finally combined to bring the Invisible Empire to an end by 1871, but the memory of the Ku Klux Klan remained as one of the treasured folk myths of the South.

In the twentieth century, Thomas Dixon and D. W. Griffith lit a candle to its memory with their epic *The Birth of a Nation,* and an Alabama fraternalist, Col. William J. Simmons, fanned the flame into a major brush fire after World War I. The reborn Klan's internal adhesive was fraternalism. Its greatest selling point was the protection of traditional American values. These were to be found in the bosoms and communities of white, native-born, Anglo-Saxon Protestants, whether in the small towns or transplanted into a newly minted urban America. The changing world of the 1920s, which saw postwar restlessness and new waves of immigration combined with the Prohibition-accented erosion of both the small town and fundamentalist morality, brought the Klan millions of recruits. The Invisible Empire was soon a factor to be considered in the communal and political life of the nation from Maine to California.

Although it first caught on in the Southeast, where Georgia was its citadel and Atlanta its holy city, the Klan was a national phenomenon. It picked up its first genuine Klan senator in Texas and almost got the governorship. It whipped and elected throughout the state, but its particular center was Dallas where the appearance of Imperial Wizard Hiram Evans, a local dentist made good, drew 75,000 of his brothers-beneath-the-robe to Klan Day at the state fair. In Oklahoma a brash and bumptious governor who used martial law after literally hundreds of incidents of violence, was impeached and dropped from office. In Arkansas the Klan was so politically powerful that it held its own primaries to decide which brother to support in the regular Democratic ones. Klan violence in California was as brutal as anywhere in the South, and in the town of Taft, in Kern County, the police and best citizens turned out to watch an evening of torture in the local ball park. When an anti-Klan candidate won the Republican primary in Oregon, the Klan jumped to the Democratic party and helped capture the governorship and enough of the legislature to outlaw all parochial schools. In Colorado, the Klan, with business support, elected two U. S. Senators and swept the state. When the Grand Dragon, a Denver doctor, was accused of having forced a high school boy into marriage by threatening him with castration, the governor appointed the Klan leader aide-de-camp, as a show of confidence.

Under D. C. Stephenson, Indiana Klansmen elected a senator, the governor and the legislature, and in one small town went down to lynch the Pope when the rumor got abroad that he was coming on the train from Chicago. In Wisconsin the Socialist rank and file responded to its lodge appeal and its anti-Catholicism. The quarter-of-a-million-man Ohio Klan did battle with alien invaders in the Mahoning Valley and the Pennsylvania Klans had some impressive riots in Lilly and Carnegie. The Klan was organized in every county of New Jersey, although it felt most at home among the Methodists of Asbury Park, while in New York the Klan's anti-booze crusaders patrolled the Merrick Road on Long Island and met mightily from Poughkeepsie to Binghamton and Buffalo. Part of the Klannish National Guard had to be disarmed in Rhode Island. Klansmen and Irishmen spent their summer nights rioting in central Massachusetts and in Maine the Invisible Empire helped boost Owen Brewster into the governorship.

The national organization of the Invisible Empire was still authoritarian and hierarchical, but the Klan of the 1920s, like that of Reconstruction, was marked in practice by anarchic local autonomy. Although Imperial Emperors, Wizards, Kligrapps, Giants, and Kludds dreamed, paraded, klonvokated, and clashed over power at the center of the hooded Empire, it was at the rim in thousands of communities across the nation that the Klan lived and mattered—as a mystery and a presence, and as a disruptive and eventually self-destructive force. It was here, at the rim, that the real saga of the Klan unfolded. It took place among the black lakes and bayous of Louisiana's Morehouse Parish and the yellow clay hills of Illinois' "Bloody Williamson" county. The white robes of the Ku Klux Klan trailed through Ben Lindsey's juvenile court in Denver, LeRoy Percy's Greenville in the Mississippi Delta and the fairgrounds of New York State from Chemung to Suffolk County, and across the editorial pages and headlines of William Allen White's Emporia *Gazette* and Julian Harris' Columbus *Enquirer-Sun.*

At the 1924 Democratic National Convention the Klan was almost as much of an issue as picking the presidential candidate, and a year later, the Klan paraded down Pennsylvania Avenue over forty thousand strong in the nation's capital.

And yet, by the beginning of the great Depression, the Klan's power and glory were almost gone, its strength spilled out like water on a bottomless sand road. It was not the Klan's principles which had been responsible, for had it selected its members more carefully and grown more slowly it might have found a permanent place in the lodge world of America. Rather it was the combination of violence, politics, and exploitive leadership which destroyed the power of the Invisible Empire. The leaders of the Klan were out for money and ruled irrationally and dictatorially in its pursuit. The fight over the spoils wrecked the organization in nearly every state and practically every community.

Politics helped do the job of destruction. The Klan's ambitions as well as its promise to lead the defense against the changes taking place in a twentieth-century America, propelled it into the political arena. There not only could it not deliver, but it found its unity split asunder on the sharp rocks of existing party factionalism and alignment.

The very dynamics of Klan organization dictated violence, which initially brought respect and members, but eventually created revulsion. The godly came to realize that the Klan was not. Terror went too far, the extremists ranted too loudly and the leaders were too immoral. The affluent and civic-minded came to realize what a divisive force it actually was in a community. When a young woman whom the Klan's most dynamic northern leader, Indiana's D. C. Stephenson, had kidnaped and assaulted gave a full deathbed testimony, it cost the Klan thousands of members.

By the time of the Depression, the Klan, numbering no more than one hundred thousand members, was held together by mystic fraternalism and concentrated primarily, though not wholly, in the South. Where in the 1920s Klansmen had banded together against Catholic and alien, now in the thirties they discovered communism and, soon afterwards, the New Deal. Anti-Semitism was also on the rise. Then, in the mid-thirties, organized labor pushed its way to the fore among the enemies of one-hundred-per-cent Americanism. Klan organizers were told to lay off Roman Catholics, Jews, and Negroes and concentrate on the invasion of the South by communism in the form of the CIO's Steel and Textile Workers Organizing Committees.

Nothing, however, revived the grandeur and power of the 1920s. While the Klan was an active force in numerous communities in the southeastern part of the country and often had high-placed friends, not even the flurries of national interest aroused by the Shoemaker flogging murder in Tampa, Florida, and the appointment of former Klansman Hugo Black to the Supreme Court, revived its power.

In the late thirties, Hiram Evans, the one-time roly-poly cut-rate dentist who had seized the Klan from its founder almost twenty years before, retired. The Imperial Wizardship passed into the hands of Jimmy Colescott, a former veterinarian from Terre Haute, Indiana, and a veteran of the Klan wars. A major recruiting drive plus violence in the industrializing southern piedmont failed to change things much. This, combined with bad publicity over joint meeting with the German-American Bund, World War II, and a federal tax suit retired Colescott and the Klan.

At the end of World War II, the Klan was revived in the hands of its last great leader, Atlanta obstetrician Dr. Samuel Green. The Klan had its usual officeholding friends in Georgia, but it was increasingly parochial. Although it emphasized klannishness, which it defined as mixing with those who have the same ideas, its dynamics of speech, heritage, and organization led it into violence. However, despite its parades and cross burnings, its mystic initiations on Stone Mountain, its warnings, night raids, and floggings, it failed to gain any of the respectability and, outside of Georgia, the power it had held in the past. And it was beset by opposition as never before. The national and state attorney generals, the FBI, and the Bureau of Internal Revenue kept their eyes upon the shrunken Invisible Empire which was forced to close down its few remaining non-Southern branches. Below the Mason-Dixon line, state officials and local communities pressed it further with denunciations, antimask laws, and grand jury investigations, even though trial juries were still reluctant to convict.

With the sudden death of Samuel Green in 1949, the movement splintered badly. Independent Klans proliferated. No leader emerged as sufficiently strong to either unify or restrain them. They engaged in endemic violence and many Klan leaders and followers ended up in jail.

The 1954 decision of the Supreme Court striking down public school segregation gave the Klans a new spur to action. Although it brought neither unity nor social approval in the South—where resistance took the more respectable channels such as the staunchly middle-class White Citizens Councils—the resulting turmoil did create an environment in which the Klans could operate. New names such as those of Asa Carter, the pistol-packing ex-radio announcer; John Kasper, the Ivy League segregationist; and the Rev. Jimmy "Catfish" Cole, who tangled with North Carolina's Lumbee Indians, flashed like comets across the Klan skies. Anti-Semitism became increasingly important as the professionals such as *Common Sense*'s Conde McGinley peddled their wares among the wearers of the white robes. The Jews and Supreme Court Chief Justice Earl Warren's "communist conspiracy" offered useful answers for the otherwise inexplicably growing Negro-rights movement. Dynamite was becoming an increasingly popular instrument of protest. Even so, the Klan tended to be less of a resistance than a status movement for some of those left insecure or unrecognized by society.

After a tapering off in the late fifties, the Klans sprang into action again with the campaign of Negro lunch-counter demonstrations, freedom rides, sit-ins, and, later, protest marches of the 1960s. The increasing pressure of integration, the growth of the equal-rights movements and the shift of its focus to the city streets of the South, fueled a growing interest in the Klan. Nocturnal cross burnings and mass meetings began to draw larger turnouts in Alabama and Georgia than had been seen for a decade. The Klans found a new leader in Robert Shelton, a Tuscaloosa rubber worker. Although Alabama's United Klans outstripped the loosely formed Georgia federation, it did not bring unity or come up with a definite program. However, the

Klans were becoming more truly the resistance movement they had always claimed to be.

The decade of the 1960s was a difficult time for the Klans as integration moved slowly forward and mass civil rights movements yielded to black power. When Klansmen struck back violently in Florida, Georgia, Alabama, Mississippi, and Louisiana, they gained some strength and support but helped bring about legislation for federal voting rights, public accommodation, and racial protection.

The 1970s seemed to narrow the future even more. The black marchers were gone from the city streets, but were taking their places in the schools and factories, legislatures, city commissions, and even Southern police forces. Klansmen seemed even more likely to end up in jail. With the conviction of the Klan dynamiter, the Alabama Attorney General judicially solved the deaths of the four teenagers in the bombing of Birmingham's Sixteenth Street Baptist Church, one of the most notorious murders of the 1960s. It seemed that the Klans could keep few secrets from the law. However, it was revealed that the FBI had uncomfortable secrets of its own. J. Edgar Hoover terminated the FBI's covert program of Klan disruption, but a controversy grew about proper police—as well as Klan—behavior.

As the 1970s ended, Klan fortunes were somewhat on the rise. Bill Wilkinson's tough new Invisible Empire Klansmen confronted black "justice and job" marchers in northern Mississippi and Alabama, and a handsome, young, college-educated Klansman, David Duke, was trying to give Klandom a new image via the college campuses and national television. Behind the revival lay a growing blue-collar job anxiety, produced by a troubled economy and what the Klan charged was governmental favoritism toward black people. As the Klansmen saw it, the problem was not one of keeping the blacks down, but rather giving white people an equal chance.

There was an armed clash in Decatur, Alabama, and an anti-Klan rally in Greensboro, North Carolina, left five dead at the hands of Klansmen and American Nazis. Perhaps the lesson that the revival was to teach again was that the Ku Klux Klan was part of an enduring tradition, an available vehicle for the social and racial anxiety of at least part of a stratum of American society.

2

THE KLAN RIDES, 1865–71

The little market center of Pulaski (locally called "Pew-laski") in Giles County, Tennessee, was named after the dashing Polish count who crossed the ocean to help fight for American independence. According to generally accepted belief in the Volunteer State, the freedom-loving young nobleman had once journeyed through middle Tennessee. As a result, he not only gave his name to the land but had left behind other lasting reminders. To be of a good family (and in small Southern towns everyone is of good family, except those who are not) bearing a Polish name obviously meant proud descent from Pulaski or his aristocratic entourage.

Unfortunately, history fails to bear out the legend. Young Count Casimir Pulaski did indeed have a passionate attachment to rebellious struggles for freedom. At the age of twenty he and his father led a doomed attempt to fight off foreign partition and domination of their homeland. After a heroic and ultimately vain effort, Pulaski fled to Turkey and eventually to France. Friends at court placed him in touch with Benjamin Franklin and in 1777 he journeyed to America to offer his sword to George Washington and the Continental Congress. His exploits as a cavalry commander were marked by unalloyed bad fortune, and some said bad judgment. In October of 1779, at the age of thirty-one, he wiped away all stains of failure by his death at the head of his men, leading an ill-conceived cavalry charge against the British positions at Savannah. Unfortunately his short and heroic life never permitted him opportunity to visit the unsettled wilderness area of middle Tennessee which was to commemorate his name, and perhaps his spirit.

In December of 1865, in Pulaski, near the Alabama border of Tennessee, six young men decided to form a club. They were mainly college men and had been officers during the late War for Southern Independence. Their problem was idleness, their purpose amusement.

They might have taken almost any name, "The Jolly Six" or "The Thespians," and followed a completely different path, but someone suggested the Greek word for circle, *kuklos,* and with its fine alliterative and mystical possibilities, their path was set. They met in secret places, put on disguises, and had great fun galloping about town after dark. They engaged in much horseplay, for which purpose the secret initiation was the focal point of their activities.

They soon discovered that their nocturnal appearances had an unexpected effect and they capitalized upon it. Ghastly, ghostly figures who claimed they had not had a drink of water since the battle of Shiloh and who lived in hell and had ridden twice around the world since suppertime, frightened the initially credulous Negroes. To the Southern white, to take a phrase from S. F. Horn's history of the first Ku Klux Klan, the time was "rotten-ripe"[1] for the development of the Klan as a means to control the newly freed Negro and his Northern friends. At first there was no thought of violence, but this soon changed.

The Klan was attracting attention and was spreading. There was a loose allegiance to the mother-Klan in Pulaski but no over-all organization, and no discipline or restraint. In April of 1867, representatives met in Nashville, at the Maxwell House, and turned out a flavor more to their liking. With much talk of unity of purpose, concert of action, proper limits, and authority to the prudent, a constitution or *prescript* was drawn up. The weak, innocent, defenseless, and oppressed, the Constitution of the United States, and all constitutional laws were to be upheld. Gen. Nathan Bedford Forrest, lately of the armies of the Confederacy was elected Grand Wizard, and his Empire divided into realms, dominions, provinces, and dens, headed by Grand Dragons, Titans, Giants, and Cyclopes, and composed of Ghouls.

The Klan, thus drawn, was a combination of discipline and irresponsibility. Each den was governed by rigid rules but in practice was sovereign in its own affairs. As a self-appointed police organization, it regarded itself as the enforcer not the breaker of the law. It was police, judiciary, and executioner. Its purposes and the "needs of the times" justified its actions, and no sense of guilt lingered. The oath to secrecy had superior jurisdiction over the *"tyrannus useages"* of Reconstruction courts and committees, and so the gentleman was not put in the position of prevarication. And the gentleman did belong; the Klan had many former Confederate officers, including a

[1] Stanley F. Horn, *Invisible Empire* (Boston, 1939), p. 21.

number of generals, and drew from among the best citizens in areas in which it rode.

Nevertheless, as the Klansmen themselves boasted, they were a "rough bunch of boys." The method of the Klan was violence. It threatened, exiled, flogged, mutilated, shot, stabbed, and hanged. It disposed of Negroes who were not respectful, or committed crimes, or belonged to military or political organizations such as the Loyal and Union Leagues. It drove out Northern schoolteachers and Yankee storekeepers and politicians, and "took care of" Negroes who gained land and prospered, or made inflammatory speeches or talked about equal rights. It assaulted carpetbag judges, intimidated juries, and spirited away prisoners. It attacked officials who registered Negroes, who did not give whites priority, or who foreclosed property.

The Klan was active in nine states from Tennessee and the Carolinas to Mississippi, Arkansas, and Texas. However it rarely if ever touched the large cities and the tidewater, coastal, delta, and black-belt areas. The Klan generally operated in the piedmont, upland areas, usually (with the exception of Florida, Tennessee, and some sections of Alabama and Mississippi) in the part of the South where the Negroes formed a lesser percentage of the population. Although the Klan was initially composed of, and led by, the better citizens, it represented a cross section of the population. It rode where the economic distinction between the Negro and white was less pronounced, where society had been less hierarchical before the war, where the Negro had been less respectful of the whites ("the pore no'count white trash") whose status was less differentiated from his own.

The invisible but very apparent order was founded in December 1865, but it did not spread throughout the South until 1867, the year in which the Radicals in Congress displaced the state governments set up by Lincoln and by Andrew Johnson. Under the presidential programs for reconstruction, the reins of government had been passed back to white citizens in each state, once they had given evidence that they realized that the war was truly over. These new Southern governments accepted the emancipation of the Negro but accorded him only varying degrees of limited citizenship, always excluding the ballot. The inequalities and restrictions placed upon the freedman by these Southern "black codes" upset many Northerners. So did the eruption of race riots in Memphis and New Orleans that looked primarily like occasions to massacre the Negroes. Bitter disagreements with

President Johnson, concern over the return to public life of so many former rebel leaders, anger over the Southern rejection of the Fourteenth Amendment, concern for the Negro, and for the future prospects of the Republican party, led the Radical majority to reject the Southern version of reconstruction. Dividing the former Confederacy into military districts, Congress decided to start over again.

In every state but Tennessee, the Democrats were removed from power, their constitutions invalidated and their leaders disfranchised. In the Volunteer State, Parson William G. Brownlow, the Knoxville editor and ex-Methodist minister was already in the governor's mansion. He had been a leader of the eastern Tennessee unionists and after imprisonment and then exile, he had returned to the state in the wake of the Union armies and added the phrase *"and Rebel Ventillator"* to the name of his Knoxville *Whig*. In the other states Congressional Reconstruction meant the establishment of new governments, headed by Southern white antisecessionists, whom the ex-Confederates called "scalawags," or former Northern officers.

It was this overturn of governments that made the Ku Klux Klan an important force in Southern life. In practically every one of the states in which the Klan rode, it sprang or expanded into active life with the advent of the new Radical governments of 1867 and 1868.

On the heels of the Congressional Reconstruction Act and Parson Brownlow's somewhat belated conversion to Negro suffrage and a mixed state militia, the call went out to all of the Klans to send delegates to the great secret convention in Nashville. The closeness with which these events followed each other seems much more than coincidental. Thomas Alexander, the later historian of the Tennessee Klan, has guessed that the purpose was to prepare the Klan for the coming political struggle for control of the South, and the evidence seems to bear him out. In Tennessee, Georgia, and South Carolina at least, the ex-Confederates—or Conservatives as they were often called —first sought to win over the new Negro voters. While they did not approve of enfranchising the Negro, many of the leading planters and businessmen were willing to make the best of it—if they could count on at least making something of it. In South Carolina, where Negroes were actually in the majority, the Democrats formed themselves into a Union Reform party and sought the support of discontented Republicans and freedmen alike. To this end Reform party orators, like the Populists a generation later, spoke out for Negro rights, and a number of the freedmen were picked as candidates for local office.

Might South Carolina and other areas of the South have developed genuine—or even approximate—peaceful, biracial democracy had such efforts succeeded? The answer never saw light. The Negroes voted Republican by large margins, and after these elections the Klan forces mounted up in Tennessee, Georgia, and South Carolina, as they had elsewhere in the South. In all cases the dates of the Klan explosion corresponded to either the establishment of the new Radical governments or the failure of these Democratic efforts at biracial political harmony. Henceforth it was to be war between the Klan and Radical rule.

It was not, however, a struggle of massed armies and big battles. The Civil War had been fought through once, and no one was really ready to try it a second time. The North knew that it had won and hoped to avoid having to actually use troops to rule the ex-Confederates, who in turn were not at all interested in forcing them to do so. Altogether, there were not enough regular army forces stationed in the South to have taken on a single corps of the old Army of Northern Virginia during the war. Most of the soldiers were in Texas and the rest were kept in camp, off the streets and out of the countryside. When hard-pressed and frightened Radical governors requested troops, they were more than likely refused.

The Radical regimes of the newly reconstructed Southern states ruled because Congress had decreed that they should, and, in the final analysis, would prevent their armed overthrow. Apart from this, the Reconstruction governments had to fashion their own support. They could not rule by force and fiat, but rather must win elections and convince legislatures. In most cases, the number of disfranchised ex-Confederates did not constitute a very large portion—albeit a vital one—of the population. It was not that there were fewer votes, but rather, in an anything but solid South, Reconstruction had enfranchised the Negroes and greatly increased the number of voters.

The new Radical administrations built up their own strength and followings, and where their various military organizations ended and the political ones began was often difficult to determine, although what happened varied from state to state. In South Carolina, for instance, the duties of the militia seemed to be primarily intimidating those freedmen who showed signs of weakening in their support for the Radicals. In Alabama, Governor William Smith shared his poor white followers' dislike of the freedman and did not attempt to organize his own military force. In North Carolina, Governor Holden, who had led the losing Jacksonian and antisecession wing of the

Democratic party before the war, recruited a rough, violent, counter-insurgency force in the western mountains which he used for anti-Klan duty in the piedmont.

If the Negro in politics meant continued Radical rule, then to change things meant disposing of Union and Loyal Leagues and the militia. The purpose of the Klan in upcountry South Carolina, according to that state's prime historian, Francis Simkins, was to secure the "political impotence and social subordination" of the Negro. To this end the night riders particularly attacked the Negro militia and Negro suffrage as the two institutions through which the freedmen exercised their citizenship. And so militiamen were whipped, their officers murdered, and Negroes frightened away from the ballot box or into promising to vote Conservative.

The Northern governor of Florida gave up his attempt to organize a militia when the arms he had procured for it disappeared from the locked and guarded cars of the train that was carrying them from Jacksonville. Arkansas' young governor, Powell Clayton, a former Union officer from Kansas, had a similar misfortune. When the War Department and the governors of the North did not heed his appeals for help, Clayton arranged for the purchase of ammunition and several thousand secondhand Belgian muskets in Detroit. However, while the steamboat *Hesper* was taking on wood twenty miles below Memphis, she was attacked by a troop of masked Klansmen who boarded her from the steam tug *Nellie Jones* and tossed her precious cargo into the muddy waters of the Mississippi. The Arkansas Radicals did put together a force of about 2000 men, however, which they used against Klan dens in the state.

In most cases, the militia proved ineffectual against the Klan and its very presence often served to provoke white fear and ire, and Klan attack. In Union County, South Carolina, where a group of Negro militiamen had wantonly killed a one-armed Confederate veteran, the vengeful Klan took them from jail and sent them to join their victim, but the murder of the white veteran was perhaps the only piece of overt militia violence during the Klan era. This points up the conclusion that the night riders were striking against the Negro as a citizen, rather than a lawbreaker. And few Negroes, even militiamen, banded together to fight back or even protect themselves. From the general record of race riots in the South during Reconstruction, it was probably just as well that they did not.

Almost any unpleasant incident or show of Negro resistance was likely to provoke an outbreak of violence. Favorable accounts of the

Florida vigilantes have pointed out that the Negroes often outnumbered the whites and that they were in the habit of congregating, holding armed parades, and generally making not only a nuisance but a threat of themselves. It is probable that the freedmen were urged on with inflammatory talk of rights and even violence, but carrying out the latter seemed to be the almost exclusive prerogative of the native whites, operating either from ambush or boldly in the open. When the Negroes occasionally emulated their tactics or gathered together with the prospect of doing so, the outraged white community turned itself into an enormous posse and the Negro leaders went into hiding or fled the county. The Klan-led riot in Meridian, Mississippi, in 1871, was fairly typical. A group of Negro leaders was put on trial for making inflammatory speeches and disturbing the peace. Other freedmen gathered as a show of support or force to protect their own. Someone, Negro or white, drew his pistol and took a shot at someone else. In a few minutes there were numerous dead and dying Negroes and but one injured white. The bulk of the Negroes took off for the woods, and their leaders, whose trial had been the occasion for the gathering of forces in the first place, were taken out of jail and hanged. Those in hiding, in this case, were left unmolested, although in the mid-seventies in Mississippi they would be hunted down and shot. Unless there were federal troops at hand, the safest thing for Negroes to do was to hide during periods of Klan activity or after outbreaks of violence. It was reported that in some regions of South Carolina, more than a majority of the Negroes slept in the woods during the Klan's active winter of 1870–71.

Although Klansmen occasionally sortied out across the moonlit countryside to punish criminal behavior, they most frequently called upon Radicals, Union and Loyal Leaguers, Republican candidates, and Northern schoolteachers. The purposes were clearly to destroy the basis of Negro political effectiveness by driving out its leaders, white and black. The particular opposition to schoolteachers seemed based on the reasoning that the Negro was not capable of learning anything other than political insurrection and insolence toward whites, and in the years before the war, teaching a Negro to read had been a serious crime. In eastern Mississippi the new institution of public schooling had to face the added problem of economic depression. During a period when times were hard and Reconstruction had made labor uncertain and elevated livestock theft to a common profession, the farmers were called upon to pay taxes for a new school system which they feared might eventually mingle white and Negro children. The response was a veritable reign of terror which saw schools burned and teachers whipped, tortured, murdered, and driven out of the state.

Whenever the Klan was getting organized in a state the inevitable Tennessee Klansman, usually General Forrest himself, coincidentally appeared to take care of some railroad or insurance business. In North Carolina, Georgia, Alabama, Mississippi, and probably in Arkansas, Forrest was on hand at the proper moment, and state Grand Dragons were usually ex-Confederate generals such as George W. Gordon in Tennessee and John B. Gordon in Georgia. However, despite the Nashville Convention and attempts at co-operation and co-ordination, the Ku Klux Klan remained an anarchic, localist organization, whose membership, discipline, and method varied from state to state and locality to locality.

In Nashville and Memphis, Tennessee Klansmen faced down municipal police in open daytime parades. On the other hand, although the Alabama Klan was probably sired by the Tennessee night riders, only once, in Huntsville, did it put on a massed drill similar to those in which the Volunteer State men delighted. However, the Alabama Klansmen were always ready to join with their Mississippi brethren who competed with similar though even less disciplined local vigilantes such as the Washington Brothers in Leake County, the Knights of the Black Cross in Lawrence, and Heggie's Scouts in Holmes, Carroll, and Montgomery counties. In South Carolina, the Klan could seldom even count on countywide co-operation among its members, while in Florida there was always doubt as to whether it was actually the Klan at work at all. Although the mystic syllables "Ku-klux" were on people's lips everywhere, most night riders were unwilling to concede that they went by any other name than the Young Men's Democratic Clubs.

Politically the Klan seemed to have a considerable effect. Republican margins of victory were substantially cut in middle Tennessee between the spring and fall elections of 1868, and when the Republicans made some gains in North Carolina's Caswell County the same year, it was a sign for a sudden increase in Klan violence. During the governor's race early in the year, the Republicans carried all seven of the principal Klan counties in Georgia's upper cotton belt. By the time of the national presidential election, the Klan had managed to substantially rearrange things. In Oglethorpe County, eight months before, the Republicans had received more than 1100 votes; in November they got 116. In Columbia County they had fallen from 1122

to a single vote, as the Democrats swept all but two of these former
Republican areas with no more votes than had carried them down to
defeat the previous spring.

Although other organizations such as the Knights of the White
Camelia pursued an oath-bound duty "TO OBSERVE A MARKED DIS-
TINCTION BETWEEN THE RACES" in the South's black-belt cotton areas,
the Klans seldom rode there, and the racial bitterness and unrest
were usually less severe. The planters preferred to control and use
the Negro vote, rather than prevent it, and unlike the white yeomen
in the piedmont and upland areas they depended on rather than competed with black labor.

In Tennessee, the Klan spread from Pulaski's Giles County to the
middle and western parts of the state. North Carolina's Klan reached
its high point in Alamance, Caswell, and Orange counties, north and
west of the state capital at Raleigh. The hooded knights of South
Carolina were also centered in the piedmont, in the nine counties of
Spartanburg, Laurens, Union, Newberry, York, Chester, Fairfield,
Lancaster, and Chesterfield. Although Reconstruction sat less heavily
on Georgia than many another Southern state, the Klan was there too,
in the upland counties along the northwest Alabama border and in
the upper cotton belt between Atlanta and Augusta. In Florida the
Ku-kluxers—or the Young Men's Democratic Clubs—rode in the
sparsely settled though heavily Negro north-central area, particularly
in Jackson County where over one hundred and fifty Negroes and
Republicans were killed during Reconstruction. The eleven counties
from Fayette through the hill country along the Tennessee River and
Tennessee border and the upper coastal plain and eastern piedmont
regions contained most of Alabama's hooded horsemen. Mississippi's
night riders sortied out in the eastern part of the state along the middle
Alabama border. Those of Arkansas were not centered in any particular locality while the Klan's somewhat more limited east Texas operations seemed practically unnoticed in the general carnage which
Texas historian W. C. Nunn described in the state.

Ryland Randolph, Exalted Cyclops of the Tuscaloosa Klan and
editor of the *Independent Monitor,* which became the official spokesman of the Alabama realm, explained the origin of the night riders.
They had come, he wrote, from "the galling despotism that broods
like a nightmare over these southern states." This consisted of the
disruption of the accustomed life, the presence of troops, and "a per-
sistent prostitution of all government, all resources, and all powers,
to degrade the white man by the establishment of Negro supremacy."

To Randolph, as to his Southern brethren elsewhere, Radical government based upon Negro votes and the disfranchisement of many whites, was a revolutionary situation that had to be combated.

It is not possible to understand the events of Reconstruction and the saga of the Klan without accepting two facts. They are that the Negro composed a large and often majority portion of the population and that the dream and the dread which troubled many Southerners was black insurrection. The formerly dominant whites throughout the South continually lived with fears that their fair land might well become another Santo Domingo. With the defeat and confusion of society which had been the contribution of the late War Between the States, the danger seemed possible and pressing. In the eyes of the white Southerner for whom slavery, curfew, the patrols, and a prewar garrison state had kept the Negro docile, controlled, off the roads, and quiet at night, the new Negro organizations were surely the instruments of plotted violence. The very meetings of the Loyal Leagues, and their ritualistic secrets, the discharge of firearms, and the "going about at night" betokened intended mayhem to the alarmed whites.

The South, stamped with the characteristics of a rural society based upon pride, honor, temper, and the exploitation of the soil and a captive people, had neither been particularly peaceful nor well policed before the war. Now—in a region marked by defeat, exhaustion, economic depression, rumor, and a revolution in its social relationships—disorder and insecurity were prime characteristics of society. Although much of the reigning disorder was white, the Negro was restless and his unwillingness to accept a completely servile status was taken as insolence. Under these circumstances it mattered very little that such fears had small basis. The historian Vernon Wharton has written that "the Negroes, largely unarmed, economically dependent, and timid and unresourceful after generations of servitude, would offer no effective resistance to violence."[2] Despite inflammatory speeches, Northern leadership, extension of the suffrage, some officeholding, and occasional political power, membership in the Loyal and Union Leagues and state militias, and sporadic support from federal troops, there seems little evidence that the Negro considered or threatened insurrection. Nevertheless, victory after victory, riot after riot, violence after violence failed to lodge a recognition of this in the Southern consciousness. A world in which the

[2] *The Negro in Mississippi, 1865–1890* (Chapel Hill, 1947), p. 90.

traditional white leadership was dispossessed and the freedman walked abroad, insolently and without restraint, was to many Southern eyes a perilously criminal disorder.

In many of the portions of the South where the Klan rode, the grievance and the gain were economic and social as well as political. Although the Klan leaders were usually men of affairs, the ordinary Klansman in the piedmont regions was more often than not a poor dirt farmer, fearful of the Negro as an economic competitor. Negroes were flogged for refusing to work for whites, or for prospering, or leaving their farms. In the Klan counties in northwest Georgia and Alabama, for instance, the whites usually comfortably outnumbered the Negroes and there was little if any Negro or carpetbag politicking. Here the big problem was the unsatisfactory social relations between white and Negro. In an area that was poor and not unaccustomed to violence, the major dividing line between the races had been swept away with emancipation and enfranchisement. There is substantial evidence of Negro lawlessness in the Georgia hill country but in addition to lynching for rape, a traditional procedure which was not the product of the war or Reconstruction, the Klan whipped for sass, insolence, and theft. Here and elsewhere, industrious Negroes who improved their farms also received attention from the Klan.

Others suffered because they violated the racial mores. The Klan punished Negroes who associated with low white women. White prostitutes in South Carolina accused of receiving Negroes were tarred and driven away. A Negro was killed and his daughter whipped because she "had caused embarrassment" to a white family by bearing the child of one of its members. Another Negro girl was beaten for "breaking the peace" between a wife and her husband.

Many of the poor, ignorant, illiterate South Carolina men, who later confessed in open court, pleaded that they had only joined the Klan to avoid becoming its victims. Their night riding had been crudely conceived and crudely carried out, with none of the dash and disciplined planning that marked much of the Klan activity elsewhere. Generally speaking, however, the leadership, if not the rank and file, represented some of the best elements in society, with the younger men usually the most venturesome. Acts of violence were usually applauded by the conservative press and justified then, and afterwards, by the always allegedly bad reputation of the victims. In North Carolina, where the Klan did not respond to General Forrest's call for disbandment, it was particularly the young men of good family who continued to carry out its blood-letting.

By 1869, the Klan was both increasingly successful and in serious internal trouble. A secret, masked society, composed of autonomous units, dedicated to the use of force, operating in unsettled times, proved impossible to control. The better citizens were dropping out and the quality of membership in many of the states was declining. In January of 1869, the Imperial Wizard, Forrest, ordered the dissolution of the order and the burning of all of its records and appurtenances. His explanation was that the Klan had become perverted in some localities and that public opinion was becoming unfavorable to masked orders. The testimony of the strong-willed, uncompromising Alabama Klansman, Ryland Randolph, that the Klan had fallen into low and violent hands, backed him up, and there was much of the same feeling reported from Mississippi.

Most Klans followed instructions, and activities were apparently liquidated in Tennessee, Georgia, Alabama, Mississippi, and Arkansas. In a number of these states important strides had been made toward the restoration of prewar white rule, and the more responsible leaders were willing and perhaps a little eager to call off the Klans. Elsewhere in the Carolinas there was still work to be done, and the possibilities of masked opportunism continued to create and maintain new formations. Although Forrest could truthfully tell congressional probers that the order no longer officially existed, it remained for the Federal Force Act, martial law, mass arrests, confessions, and a rather surprising number of convictions to join imperial disbandment and growing disapproval in bringing the Klan to an end by 1872. By this time, as Walter Fleming, the able pro-Southern historian wrote about Alabama, the Klan had done its work successfully. It had kept the freedmen quiet and gotten rid of "alien" and "aggressive" leadership among them. It had stopped incendiarism and generally toned down the Negro, normalized relations, and established law and order. In other words, although Radical control lingered on for a while longer, its revolutionary social and political drives had been blunted. The eventual return to "normalized relations" had been initiated, even if not yet fully achieved. Other organizations were to function in the declining yet bitter days of Reconstruction, and violence smoldered and flared, but it was not masked and did not ride at night.

The Southern states, under Radical Reconstruction were a defeated and occupied territory. Under these circumstances the Klan was fighting the kind of war of resistance that is now expected, if not demanded, for the preservation of national respectability. The conditions of the occupation were neither greatly onerous nor everywhere of equal restrictiveness, but perhaps a question of degree cannot be substituted for a question of principle, even though more people were actually voting than ever before. Why should not the Klan and the general populace which supported its resistance be similarly honored outside the South? As long as federal troops and military rule were thrust upon the ex-Confederate states, and as long as normal self-government was refused and outsiders—with or without carpetbags—placed in power, this was an occupation.

Usually under such circumstances all organized violence, whatever its real motives, is justified as political. It is curious, then, that in the case of the first Ku Klux Klan, things have been somewhat reversed with the political and social counterattack against Congressional Reconstruction being explained as the necessary effort to prevent crime and uphold law and order. This paradox stems from the central role of the Negro in Reconstruction and the story of the Ku Klux Klan. The weakness of klannish and much of Southern reasoning is that it assumed that they and their kind were the South. The carpetbagger did not belong, the Radical white was a scalawag who did not count, and the Negro was neither a man nor a Southerner. The saga of the Klan as the hero and great folk legend of the South stems partly from the fact that the night riders appealed to a sense of excitement, adventure, mystery, and violence. The Klansmen were aristocrats, they were heroes, and they were a hell of a bunch of fellows. The high estate of the memory of the Reconstruction Klan also stemmed from the fact that it was the action of white Southerners who believed that the color of the South was and had to be white. The resulting view of the Klan as a regulating force for protection in lawless times captured the hearts of those who rode and of future generations of Southerners.

The Klan *was*, in Southern eyes, primarily a law-and-order organization. Gen. Nathan B. Forrest, Imperial Wizard, Ret., of the Invisible Empire, also partially retired, testified to this before hostile yet respectful congressmen and senators. What had created the Klan? Forrest explained that it was the ". . . insecurity felt by Southern people . . . many Northern men [were] coming down there, forming Leagues all over the country. The Negroes were holding night meetings; were going about; were becoming very insolent; and the Southern people . . . were very much alarmed . . . parties organized themselves so as to be ready in case they were attacked. Ladies were ravished by some of those Negroes. . . . There was a great deal of insecurity . . . this organization was got up to protect the weak, with no political intention at all. . . ."

Who then were the weak? They were the formerly dominant white Southerners now concentrated in the Democratic party. Their aim was not "political"; it was merely to restore law and order, that is: things as they had been before. Government was inordinately corrupt and often as incompetent. Time was out of joint. The old, stable, hierarchical social order was gone, the bottom rail on top. The Negroes were not only voting, they were a good part of the electorate. They were organizing politically and militarily. In General Forrest's phrases, they were "holding night meetings; were going about; were becoming insolent." The Southerner feared Negro lecherousness, Negro violence, Negro insurrection, and Negro dominance.

Most of the time the Klan rode to prevent future rather than to stop present and punish past actions. To perhaps a majority of Southerners, the Negro and white out of their places and—worse yet—reversed, was social disorder and lawlessness. If the plight of white womanhood seemed to loom large in the explanations, despite vagueness in the statistics, it is because the new position of the Negro constituted a threat to the vitals of white Southern civilization. The woman not only stood at the core of his sense of property and chivalry, she represented the heart of his culture. By the fact that she was not accessible to the Negro, she marked the ultimate line of difference between white and black. Not only was any attack on white womanhood a blow against the whole idea of the South, but any change in the status of the Negro in the South thereby also became an attack on the cultural symbol: the white woman. Therefore, though rape was bad enough in itself, it was impossible to assault either the Southern woman or the South without having implicitly levied carnal attack on the other. To the white Southerner, the Ku Klux Klan was a law-and-order movement because it was directed at the restoration of the proper order.

3

THE BIRTH OF A NATION

In 1877, President Rutherford B. Hayes withdrew the last of the federal army of occupation from the South. With government again in the hands of native-born white Southern Democrats, or Conservatives, there were no mass pogroms against the Negro, nor were the freedmen purged from the voter rolls and more rigorously cordoned off into a segregated corner of Southern life. Violence there was, but on a scale commensurate with the frontier conditions which still existed in the Southern minds and much of the Southern countryside. If mobs still broke into jails or scooped up suspected evildoers from their piney woods shacks and dispatched them with the blazing torch or more merciful fusilade, it was not the doing of an organized movement, and until the 1890s their victims were as likely to be Southern-born white as colored. Gangs and unreconstructed bushwhackers still existed, but there was no need for calling of the Klans to redeem a captive homeland. If the baser sort rode out at night it was not as Klansmen. In the newly redeemed South there was little question of the Negro "not knowing his 'place,'" and he was generally left undisturbed in it. Indeed, for the business-minded Redeemers who believed in railroads and industrialism and nailed the flag of the creditor to their masts, the Negro was a great convenience on Election Day. His vote was essential to ward off the numerous debtors and discontented agrarians. And so, through need and *noblesse oblige,* the Bourbons extended their paternal protection to the Negro.

In the 1890s the embittered agrarian Populists sought to breach the battlements. They made a major effort to build a poor man's alliance of all of those, white and Negro alike, who wanted business and the wealthy to pay their share, the corporations regulated, and aid given to the poor farmers. The Bourbons raised the cry of white supremacy as they herded the Negroes to the polls for the last time to vote for their conservative landlords and employer-protectors. The Populists saw themselves cheated out of office by fraudulent manipulation of those very Negro votes that they themselves had gone so dangerously far to win. Both sides now agreed that the Negro was a source of trouble and had to be removed from political life. In most states of the Deep South, the disfranchisement and segregation of the Negro began with a vengeance in the 1890s. Populist leaders like Tom Watson, who had pleaded with Negro and white that they were both together in the same economic ditch, now climbed up out of that ditch into the statehouses and the national legislature over the body of the Negro. In North Carolina, where a Negro-Populist-Republican alliance had actually won control of the state and placed undue numbers of Negroes in public offices, white men joined in a holy war to toss them out. Red-shirted horsemen rode the highways by day, where Klansmen had once launched their nocturnal raids, and North Carolina returned to the grasp of the white masters. In Wilmington, Atlanta, and many other Southern cities, the inflamed passions that had been used to separate the Negro from the mainstream of Southern life touched off mob assaults upon the now friendless Negro.

It was in this world that young men of the twentieth-century South grew up. In the rough and receptive conditions of the *fin de siècle* South, the saga of the Ku Klux Klan as the savior of an oppressed people during the dark days of Reconstruction remained the treasured folk heritage.

This was the world in which Thomas Dixon, Jr., grew to manhood, scratching his way up from the lean days of Reconstruction to shining brilliance at Wake Forest College and then on to the new graduate school at Johns Hopkins where he made friends with another young Southerner, Thomas Woodrow Wilson. Where the Virginian followed a meteoric path upward, first through the theory, and later the practice of politics, Dixon succeeded in everything and followed through on very little. He left Johns Hopkins for a try at the legitimate stage but returned to the law and politics in North Carolina. He was elected to the legislature before he had reached the legal age to vote, and almost made speaker. However, politics was disillusioning, and so he resigned in favor of the Baptist ministry, a calling in which his flame and his oratorical ability made him a great success. He moved upward from Goldsboro to Raleigh, then to Boston, and finally New York. John D. Rockefeller talked of building him a great tabernacle, but Dixon found the pulpit confining and this time he moved on to the lecture platform. Here again he was immensely successful, but reaching out for an even greater audience, he turned to literature. His account of how his native Carolinas were twice redeemed from black degradation, told in *The Leopard's Spots* (1902), was a sensation. The sequel, *The Clansman, an historic romance of the Ku Klux Klan,* published in 1905, far outdistanced it. The plot was a sheer, sweet, sticky, cotton-candy love story. Ben Cameron, the heroic young Confederate colonel was being tended in the prison hospital by Elsie Stoneman, the lovely sister of his captor, the equally young Union officer, Phil Stoneman. Phil, in turn, fell in love with Ben's darling sister. With the war over, surely love would find a way. However the devil *ex machina* entered in the person of Phil and Elsie's father, Congressman Stoneman, an enormously malevolent copy of Thaddeus Stephens. Stoneman was determined to punish the South for its transgressions. The instrument of his hate and madness was to be the Negro, and for Thomas Dixon this meant turning the South into a great carnal Valhalla. Dixon's portrait of the crazed venomous Stoneman was a compelling one. His Abraham Lincoln, apart from his excessive proneness to debate the position of Negro inferiority, caught the humanity and the trials and sadness of the martyred President. Dixon pictured him as the last protective bastion standing between Stoneman and the defenseless South, and the President's difficulties with the stern, hateful Stanton were great drama in the midst of melodrama. The Negro was a brute, and Reconstruction a tragedy beyond all bearing. The Negro was not a citizen and an equal, not even a child as yet unprepared. He was a semisavage descendant of an old and degenerate animal race. "For a thick-lipped, flat-nosed, spindle-shanked negro, exuding his nauseating animal odour, to shout in derision over the hearths and homes of white men and women is an atrocity too monstrous for belief," Ben Cameron's father told the evil Stoneman. But Stoneman would have it no other way. And so it began, with rapine in the seats of government—and in the hearth-temple of Southern worship:

"We have no money . . ." she pleaded, a sudden glimmer of hope flashing in her blue eyes.

Gus stepped closer, with an ugly leer, his flat nose dilated, his sinister bead eyes wide apart, gleaming apelike as he laughed:

"We ain't atter money!"

The girl uttered a cry, long, tremulous, heart-rending, piteous.

A single tiger spring, and the black claws of the beast sank into the soft white throat and she was still.

With Lincoln, the Great Protector, dead, was there no one to deliver the South? No one but the South itself, in the form of the Ku Klux Klan, led in the Carolina uplands by its Grand Dragon Ben Cameron. Though the despoiled girl had thrown herself from a cliff, the retinal image of her assailant lay ready in her eyes to guide her revengers. The redemption of the South was on its way! "The old club-footed Puritan, in his mad scheme of vengeance and party power, had overlooked the Covenanter, the backbone of the South. This man had just begun to fight!" In the end, God's justice is done, Civilization saved, and the South redeemed from shame.

The Clansman was just too good to be hidden between the covers of a book and so Dixon successfully adapted it for the stage. He himself took the lead in one of the several touring companies and tried to organize his own movie company to do it in color. Dixon never got it going, but Biograph's talented young director, D. W. Griffith, had been saving his money to set himself up to do greater things. The idea of filming *The Clansman* excited him. In a world of short slapstick quickies produced for the fifteen-cent-admission nickelodeons, Griffith set out to create a masterpiece. There wasn't enough money to finance such an extravagance and so Dixon reluctantly consented to accept 25 per cent of the profits in the place of his $10,000 asking price. Griffith took Dixon's scenario for *The Clansman* and added bits from the author's other books. But this wasn't enough and so the young director dipped further into American history.

The first half of the picture told about the arrival of the first bondsmen, how the New England slavers profited from the trade, and how the Negro lived a not unhappy life on the Southern plantations. But the twin spirits of abolition and secession were rising in the North and South. The war came, with its battles: Gettysburg, Petersburg, Appomattox; and its heroes: Lee, Grant, and, particularly, Lincoln.

With a skill that was to shape the creative techniques of the industry, D. W. Griffith restaged the history of the nation as his ace cameraman, Bill Bitzer, took it all down on film. Working without a detailed script, writing and rehearsing his players on rainy days, and always desperately short of funds, he created an epic. Panoramic battle scenes copied after Matthew Brady's famous photographs, the shifting camera's eye, close-ups, medium and long shots, expanse and detail, contrast and symbolism, the cameolike iris of the destitute family expanding to show the devastation created by Sherman's army, one image contrasting with another, created the excitement and the pathos of the war between brothers. Against this setting, Griffith told the perilous, tangle-beset romances of the young lovers and of the prostrate South.

The special score, written for a thirty-piece pit orchestra, wove in Negro spirituals with passages from the classics. Most of them were from Wagner and each of the principals had his own theme. It was full of memorable scenes of battle and of the returning soldier, of Mae Marsh as the little sister who threw herself over the cliff to die rather than yield her honor, and of Lillian Gish as Stoneman's daughter besieged in the cabin by the lust-crazed freedmen. The tension became unbearable. An orchestral passage from *Die Walküre* heralded the assembling of the Klansmen. A bugle blast from the pit brought the audience shouting to its feet as the hooded horsemen rode to the rescue. The orchestra matched passages from "The Hall of the Mountain King" to the galloping of the horses' hoofs, as the scene shifted back and forth between the approaching Klansmen and the pale heroine in the cabin surrounded by frenzied blacks.

No wonder the picture was a sensation, with sellout crowds paying an unprecedented two-dollar admission to watch the unmatched two-hour-and-forty-five-minute epic. At first Griffith used the novel's title, *The Clansman,* but when Reverend Dixon saw a preview showing in New York, he called out to Griffith that the title was too tame, it should be called "The Birth of a Nation."

To the Kentucky-born Griffith and the North Carolinian, Dixon, the picture was no more than fair. To many indignant viewers and nonviewers, such as Harvard President Charles Elliott, Jane Addams, and Booker T. Washington, it was inflammatory. Protest mounted. It was egged in New York City, protested by riot in Boston, and nearly banned by the Massachusetts legislature. In most major cities of the North and West it ran into censorship difficulties, despite packed houses wherever it was shown. In the South the reviews were triumphant. Dixon and Griffith were initially puzzled over how to successfully fight back the opposition, but Dixon had already laid the way for a telling counterstroke. He called upon his friend, Woodrow Wilson, now President of the United States, and a showing was arranged in the White House for the Chief Executive and the Cabinet and their families. When it was over, the Southern-born President was much moved. "It is like writing history with lightning," he said, "and my only regret is that it is all so terribly true." Then, with the aid of Dixon's old North Carolina friend, Navy Secretary Josephus Daniels, an interview was arranged with the Chief Justice of the Supreme Court. Justice Edward White was reputedly not a man much interested in social pleasantries, and Dixon got right to the point. He wanted the court to see a picture about the Ku Klux Klan that President Wilson had highly praised. At the mention of the Klan, White's manner changed:

"You tell the true story of the Klan?"

"Yes—for the first time—"

White removed his glasses, Dixon recalled, pushed his book aside, and leaned back in his big swivel chair. His strong lips contracted and then relaxed into a curious smile. He leaned toward Dixon and said in low tense tones,

"I was a member of the Klan, sir. . . . Through many a dark night, I walked my sentinel's beat through the ugliest streets of New Orleans with a rifle on my shoulder. . . . You've told the true story of that uprising of outraged manhood?"

"In a way I'm sure you'll approve," Dixon replied.

"I'll be there!" the Chief Justice announced firmly.[1] Word of official approval smoothed the path and the picture opened triumphantly in New York. Before it was retired to the art theaters and film clubs, *The Birth of a Nation* grossed almost eighteen million dollars.

With the book and movie doing so well, why not a revival of the Klan itself? When *The Clansman* first appeared, Dixon was urged to take the lead in some sort of a Klan revival. Correspondents suggested such titles as "The Aryan League of America," "The White Heart League," and the "Sons of the Clansmen," but though he was alarmed about the future and the peril of miscegenation he replied that such suggestions were premature. When the revival did come, ten years later, it was not Thomas Dixon who led it.

[1] Eric Goldman, *Rendezvous with Destiny* (New York, 1953), pp. 228–29.

4

THE KLAN REVIVAL, 1915–21

The stories of the Klan's rebirth differ. There were those on the inside who claimed that it was suggested by Griffith's picture. Colonel Simmons, its founder, maintained that he had thought for twenty years of creating a fraternal order that would stand for "comprehensive Americanism." He spoke variously about childhood stories and fancies, about an illness and a vision: "On horseback in their white robes they rode across the wall in front of me. As the picture faded out I got down on my knees and swore that I would found a fraternal organization that would be a memorial to the Ku Klux Klan."

William J. Simmons was born in the little central Alabama town of Harpersville, in 1880, and grew up on his father's farm. His father had given up doctoring for a spell as a mill owner, but when the floods of 1886 washed away his wealth, he returned to the practice of medicine. He died not too many years afterwards, and young William had to abandon the dream of becoming a doctor, but his father and life on an Alabama farm had initiated him into the love of place and heritage which has long been a major factor in Southern life. A part of this, in a society less than two decades removed from the tumultuous days of Reconstruction, was the Ku Klux Klan. "My father was an officer of the old Klan in Alabama back in the 60s," he later told an interviewer. "I was always fascinated by Klan stories. . . . My old Negro mammy, Aunt Viney, and her husband, used to tell us children about how the old Reconstruction Klansmen used to frighten the darkies.

" 'Why, dat Klansman was shore twelve foot high,' I heard Aunt Viney say to Uncle Simon.

" 'Go 'long with you, Viney,' said Uncle Simon. 'Dat Klansman was twenty foot tall, on his hawse!' "

When he was eighteen, Simmons enlisted as a private in the 1st

Alabama Volunteers to fight against the Spaniards. The title of colonel, which he later liked to attribute to his wartime service, was still a thing of the future. Released from the army, inspired by patriotism and Americanism, too poor to study medicine, he turned to the career traditionally open to talent, the church. It was not a happy choice but it was a useful one in developing his talents. The ministry did not pay. He rode circuit and was given only backwoods districts in Alabama and Florida, never the big churches, such as Mobile or Montgomery for which he yearned. He developed his oratory and his eloquence, and gave popular lectures at revival meetings on "Women, Weddings, and Wives," "Red Heads, Dead Heads, and No Heads," and the "Kinship of Kourtship and Kissing." And he went deeper and deeper into debt on his $200 to $300 yearly stipend, each year attending the church conference with hopes that this would be his year to get the "big" church. The bishops of the Methodist Church South, however, recognized their man. The call was missing, and they failed to move him upward.

After twelve years, the 1912 Alabama Conference voted to deny him a pulpit because of inefficiency and moral impairment, and he was pushed out to tread the secular path to fame and fortune. First he tried his hand as an ordinary salesman. His detractors later said that he had been a garter salesman and a poor one at that, but he soon found his calling in the attractive commercial field of fraternal organizing. Here was proper employment for his talents, and he rose to the youngest colonelcy of the Woodmen of the World, in command of five regiments. Within two years, he later boasted, he was out of debt and was earning $15,000 a year as a district manager. In addition, he belonged to several varieties of Masons and to the Knights Templar. He was a post commander and a national aide-de-camp of the Spanish-American War Veterans, and was a member of perhaps half a score other organizations, including both the Congregational and Missionary Baptist churches. "I am a fraternalist," he was to explain whenever anyone asked his profession.

During all of this time he dreamed of founding his own fraternal order based upon the Ku Klux Klan. When an automobile accident laid him up in bed for three months he worked out all the details, which he duly copyrighted. It remained only to pick the time. In the fall of 1915 the right moment seemed at hand. With *The Birth of a Nation* scheduled to open in Atlanta, Simmons sprang into action. He gathered together nearly two-score men from various fraternal orders, including two members of the original Klan and the speaker of the Georgia legislature. They agreed to found the order, and Simmons picked Thanksgiving Eve for the formal ceremonies.

When the members gathered at Atlanta's Piedmont Hotel, Simmons had a surprise prepared. The ceremonies were to be held on Stone Mountain, an immense, striking, granite slab, rising from the earth sixteen miles outside of Atlanta. The late-November nights are cold in northern Georgia and some of those present refused to go, but fifteen piled into the hired sight-seeing bus which Simmons had waiting at the door. Using flashlights they picked their way to the top of Stone Mountain, and, under Simmons' direction, his shivering company gathered stones to make a crude altar and a base for the cross of pine boards which Simmons had brought there that afternoon. He touched a match to the cross which he had padded with excelsior and drenched with kerosene. Then, "Under a blazing, fiery torch the Invisible Empire was called from its slumber of half a century to take up a new task and fulfill a new mission for humanity's good and to call back to mortal habitation the good angel of practical fraternity among men."

When *The Birth of a Nation* opened a week later, an Atlanta paper carried Simmons' announcement of "The World's Greatest Secret, Social, Patriotic, Fraternal, Beneficiary Order" next to the advertisement for the movie. And so, with an assist from D. W. Griffith, Colonel Simmons' "HIGH CLASS ORDER FOR MEN OF INTELLIGENCE AND CHARACTER" was launched.

Within a short time, Simmons had ninety followers to whom he sold membership, raiment, and life insurance. The Ku Klux Klan was incorporated as a "purely benevolent and eleemosynary" institution, intended to be not unlike the Elks, the Masons, and the Odd Fellows. Despite the crudeness of its early advertising—A CLASSY ORDER OF THE HIGHEST CLASS—it drew good, solid middle-class members. Among the first were Robert Ramspect, future congressman from Georgia, and Paul Etheridge, lawyer and long-time member of Atlanta's Fulton County Board of Commissioners of Roads and Revenues. In its initial stages, the Klan was not a night-riding organization but merely a fraternal one which stressed 100 per cent Americanism and the supremacy of the Caucasian race. It was Protestant rather than anti-Catholic, and to favor "keeping the Negro in his place" was little more than the meaning of the term, Caucasian. In these characteristics the Klan was not unlike the multitude of other fraternal organizations to which Colonel Simmons and his new Klansmen were accustomed. The word "fraternity," in its most common usage, had long since come to mean the exclusiveness of the in-group, rather than the commonality and brotherhood of mankind.

When America entered the war in 1917, Simmons and the Klan found a purpose and a role. The nation had to be defended against alien enemies, slackers, idlers, strike leaders, and immoral women, lest victory be endangered. The Klan accepted the challenge. Simmons was not asked to join the elite government-sponsored American Protective League, but as a member of the lesser Citizens' Bureau of Investigation he entered the fray. Klansmen in Georgia and Alabama secretly kept tabs on local goings on and reported back. It was all very exciting. Warnings against evil-doing were posted. Robed Klansmen intervened in a shipyard strike in Mobile, hunted draft dodgers, and occasionally marched in patriotic parades. Public sentiment seemed favorable. By 1919 the Klan had several thousand members, whose dues were naturally Simmons' wages of entrepreneurship. Secrecy had become its pattern.

To have garnered only several thousand members after five years of work, was not, somehow, tapping the full potential of as big an idea as the Klan. There was much more money in it than Colonel Simmons had touched thus far. His talent lay in the realm of fraternal ideas and rituals. As his whole life was to show, he lacked the ability of generalship to execute his logistical ideas, the capacity to master a situation and achieve victory in the end. In reality, his was not a fighting spirit, and under pressure he tended to retreat. Gutzon Borglum, sculptor of mountains, student of men, and once high in the inner circles of the Klan, assessed Simmons as a dreamer who tended to surround himself with weak men.

Perhaps realizing his limitations and yearning for success, Simmons, the mystic, looked for apostles to spread his gospel. They came in the persons of Edward Young Clarke and Mrs. Elizabeth Tyler. Together, they were the Southern Publicity Association. Clarke had drifted from newspaper work into fraternal salesmanship, and then went on to become a not very successful publicist. He was slim, graceful, with a mass of curly dark hair. The eyes behind his horn-rimmed glasses looked cultured, and his nervous intensity passed for drive and intellectuality. Bessie Tyler was a large woman, with blue eyes and auburn hair. She favored black, from her patent-leather pumps to her broadcloth cape, and her definiteness and decisive manner of speech gave her an air of forcefulness. Clarke was running a Harvest Home Festival in Atlanta and Mrs. Tyler had handled the "Better Babies Parade." They were attracted to each other, and they saw a future in it. Their business venture was the Southern Publicity Association. They handled fund drives for the Anti-Saloon League, the Theodore Roosevelt Memorial Fund, and Near East relief. The accounts differed on who found whom first, but Simmons was in need, and he had what Clarke and Mrs. Tyler considered to be a potentially good thing going. "He was a minister and a clean living man," Mrs. Tyler later told the newspapers. "After we had investigated it from every angle, we decided to go into it with Colonel Simmons."

The expenses of mass recruitment and high-class publicity would not be small, but Klan affairs were stagnant and if they could get things going it would be worth the 80 per cent they asked. As the colonel later remembered it, Clarke seemed insightful as to the nature of the movement that he was about to join. "I have lots of friends among the Jews and Catholics," Clarke told him. They had helped him in drives such as the Red Cross, and he could not afford a break with them unless the price was right.

In June of 1920 the contract was struck. Clarke was to be in full charge of recruitment. His department was to receive eight dollars of the ten dollars paid by each recruit it brought in, plus two dollars from the membership fee of those who were signed up by the already organized Klans. Mrs. Tyler explained that their hopes had been modest and primarily directed toward the South. "But the minute we said 'Ku Klux,' editors from all over the United States began literally pressing us for publicity." The news value of the Klan initially caught them all by surprise. When Simmons and Clarke refused to pose for a press photographer, he rigged up his own costumes after those he had seen in *The Birth of a Nation* and hired Negroes to pose in them for two bits a man. The picture sold like wildfire.

The Klan was doing better than anyone had dreamed. Fraternity, secrecy, and white supremacy were not enough. A broader program of action was necessary and Simmons, Clarke, and Bessie Tyler responded to the need. From the lip-service to the traditional racial values of the white South, the Klan shifted into a pyrotechnically aggressive defense of one-hundred-per-cent Americanism.

Upon being introduced to an audience of Georgia Klansmen, Colonel Simmons silently took a Colt automatic from his pocket and placed it on the table in front of him. Then he took a revolver from another pocket and put it on the table too. Then he unbuckled his cartridge belt and draped it in a crescent shape between the two weapons. Next, still without having uttered a word, he drew out a

MCCC LIBRARIES
Tutorial Services
College Hall 1st Floor
Free. No appointment
necessary.
Visit early and often!

TO RENEW ITEMS:
Online: http://bit.ly/mc3renew
Your account PIN is:
Email: circdesk@mc3.edu
Phone: 215-641-6596

ITEMS CHECKED OUT

Title: Hooded Americanism : the history of
 the Ku Klux K
Call number: HS2330.K63 C5 1987
Date due: 3/1/2013,21:30

Title: Sheehy's emergency nursing : princi
ples and pract
Call number: RT120 .E4 S54 2010
Date due: 3/1/2013,21:30

HOURS
Mon-Thur: 7:30am-9:30pm
Fri: 7:30am-5pm
Sat: 10am-4pm
Sun: 1pm-5pm

Check us out on Facebook!
facebook.com/mc3libraries

3 months

bowie knife and plunged it in the center of the things on the table. "Now let the Niggers, Catholics, Jews, and all others who disdain my imperial wizardry, come on," he said. The Jews, Mrs. Tyler told newspapermen during a shopping trip in New York, were upset because they know that the Klan "teaches the wisdom of spending American money with American men." To be for the white race, she continued, means to be against all others. Clarke suggested sterilizing the Negro. Simmons explained that the Japanese were but a superior colored race. Never in the history of the world, the Klan believed, had a "mongrel civilization" survived. The major theme, however, was the rich vein of anti-Catholicism, which the Klan was to mine avidly during the 1920s, and it was this more than anything else which made the Klan.

To the Negro, Jew, Oriental, Roman Catholic, and alien, were added dope, bootlegging, graft, night clubs and road houses, violation of the Sabbath, unfair business dealings, sex, marital "goings-on," and scandalous behavior, as the proper concern of the one-hundred-per-cent American. The Klan organizer was told to find out what was worrying a community and to offer the Klan as a solution.

Simmons' conception of the Klan as a special secret service bustling about spying on radicalism and questionable patriotism and generally reliving its wartime grandeur, was translated into a more enduring system of societal vigilance. The Klan was brought to Muncie, Indiana, by leading businessmen to cope with a corrupt Democratic city government. It entered Tulsa, Oklahoma, and Herrin County, Illinois, to put down bootlegging. When a newly formed Klan chapter would write to Atlanta for suggestions as to what to do first, the response was almost unvaryingly to "clean up the town," an injunction which usually came to rest its emphasis on the enforcement of the small-town version of the Ten Commandments.

By the summer of 1921, almost a hundred thousand Klansmen had paid their money and stepped across the mystic threshold to take their chances in the Invisible Empire. Clarke, in his newly created role of Imperial Kleagle, or chief of staff, sent a small army of recruiters fanning out across the country. The nation was divided up into regional sales districts or domains, each headed by a district sales manager, the Grand Goblin. Each region was divided into state realms, headed by King Kleagles, under whom the ordinary Kleagles, or recruiters, worked. To aid them the national and state organizations sent out lecturers, usually ministers, to spread the more exalted parts of the Klan gospel. Of every ten-dollar initiation fee (Klectoken), four dollars went to the Kleagle responsible. The King Kleagle of the state realm got one dollar. The Grand Goblin got fifty cents and the rest went back to Atlanta: two dollars and fifty cents for Clarke and Mrs. Tyler, and two dollars for Simmons.

The newly recruited Klansman, with or without sheeted regalia (two dollars for costs and three to four dollars for Klan headquarters), belonged to a provisional Klan, headed by the appointed Kleagle. Only when the region had been thoroughly combed for members did the Klan chapter receive a charter. With it came the right to elect its own officers and, subject to veto by a new hierarchy appointed from Atlanta, conduct its own affairs. As subsequent history was to prove, that chartered independence was often too long in coming and even then too greatly subject to interference.

Wherever possible, Clarke selected his salesmen from among members of other lodges, since they would be likely to be skilled in the world of ritualism and fraternal dynamics. He particularly favored Masons because of the size of their own order and because the chances were they would not be overly friendly toward Roman Catholicism. Many Masonic leaders bitterly denounced and fought the Klan both for its divisive effects within their lodges and because they disapproved of its violent intolerance. However, the rank and file turned to the Klan by the thousands, and the Scottish Rite Masons and Orange Lodges were particularly rich hunting grounds.

The usual Klan pattern was to approach the local Protestant minister. He would be offered a free membership and urged to take office in the to-be-formed local, either as its chaplain (Kludd) or higher up in the leadership structure. Hundreds upon hundreds did join, and in some areas constituted a major portion of the local officialdom. Others left their flocks for the wider Klan calling as either organizers or speakers. Almost all of the national Klan lecturers were ministers. Usually the presence of a Klan in a town was announced by a Saturday night parade of hooded horsemen down Main Street, a cross blazing on a nearby hillside, or a sudden appearance in the midst of the Sunday service. Robed in white, masked, they would divide into three columns and march silently down the aisles congregating in front of the pulpit to present a purse of thirty-five or forty dollars to the minister. If their appearance was not completely unexpected or unwelcome, they might file into the front rows that had been left vacant, while the minister or one among them propounded the principles of the Klan and read from the Twelfth Chapter of Romans, calling upon them to present their bodies, through the Klan, as "a living sacrifice, holy, acceptable unto God." Or, having made the donation, they might march out again while the church choir sang "The Old Rugged Cross" or "Onward, Christian Soldiers."

By the late summer of 1921 the Klan was a flourishing concern. In the first fifteen months of the Clarke-Tyler regime, approximately eighty-five thousand members had been added, worth, at ten dollars a head, over three quarters of a million dollars. Naturally expenses were high, but since the Klan was a benevolent and charitable enterprise, taxes were not a worry. Colonel Simmons' share was $170,000. In token of his past devotion during the lean years prior to 1920, the Klan rewarded him with $25,000 back pay and a $33,000 suburban home, which he named Klan Krest.

While Simmons puttered about with the ritual, made platform appearances, and dreamed of the great University of America that he intended to build in Atlanta, Clarke tended to business. The Kleagles pressed their recruitment for the Knights of the Ku Klux Klan, Inc. The Gate City Manufacturing Company of Atlanta, Georgia, was established as the sole manufacturer of Klan regalia. The Searchlight Publishing Company assumed control of the growing Klan publications and printing, and a realty company owned by Clarke manipulated the Klan's real estate holdings, mainly in the direction of Clarke's pocket.

But as the Klan grew, so did its problems. Klan violence was increasing and with it, demands that someone—the law, Congress, the Justice Department, the Postmaster General, or the President—do something about it.

In September of 1921 the New York *World*, which was to make a profession out of snapping at the skirts of the Klan, opened a running exposé which was syndicated throughout the nation. Not to be outdone by the revelations of the *World's* ex-Kleagle, Henry Peck Fry, Hearst's *Journal-American* charged into the fray. They had a different, more exotic kind of an ex-Klansman, C. Anderson Wright, an ex-World War I aviator who had interested the Klan in incorporating his languishing flyers' organization into an aeronautical branch of the Invisible Empire. It soon turned out that he wasn't going to be getting much money or support and that Clarke intended to use the Knights of the Air as a recruiting dodge without airmen in it. While Anderson and the *Journal-American* described the internal gossip and financial manipulations of the Klan in Atlanta, Fry and the *World* concentrated on its activities in the field. In October, the *World* finally climaxed its campaign with an impressive tabulation of Klan violence.

President Harding and the Justice Department decided that the Klan was exclusively a state problem but pressure for congressional action mounted. According to a resolution introduced by a Massachusetts congressman, the hooded order had been guilty of violation of the First, Fourth, Fifth, Sixth, and Thirteenth Amendments, in that it had outraged religious freedom and the prohibitions against illegal seizure, trial, punishment, and involuntary servitude. In addition to illegalities and brutalities, the Klan had not been paying its income taxes. The Rules Committee of the U. S. House of Representatives agreed to hold hearings in October.

Edward Young Clarke was scared. It was easy enough to shrug off the *World* articles but Congress was something else again. And further, the *World* had come up with embarrassing information that was already causing considerable unrest in some Klan circles. In 1919, the stories went, Clarke and Mrs. Tyler had been arrested, somewhat less than fully clad and sober, in a police raid on a house of questionable repute. They had been found guilty of disorderly conduct, and fined five dollars. Now that the event had come to light, inspection of the records revealed that the appropriate page in the police court docket had been removed. Clarke claimed that there had been no wrongful deed done, other than on the part of his wife who had been the malicious instigator of the raid. However, this explanation was hardly designed to strengthen the image of the Klan as the protector of the home and basic morality. Some of the field representatives of the Klan demanded that Clarke and Mrs. Tyler be dismissed, and were fired themselves for their pains.

Clarke had become terrified over the impending congressional investigation and announced his resignation. Bessie Tyler was furious. She denounced Clarke as "weak-kneed" and managed to stiffen his courage to the point that he decided to stick it out. To add strength to the claim that the Klan was itself the real victim of persecution, a fake attempt was arranged upon the life of Mrs. Tyler. But these were only a sideshow; the future of the Klan was in the hands of Congress and Colonel Simmons.

The hearings before the Rules Committee lasted little more than a week. They were a rambling, rather than a probing investigation. The committee heard testimony about Klan finances and organization, a good deal of internal gossip, and some details of Klan violence. The imperial cashier testified that Simmons was very bad about keeping records and that the Klan's monetary affairs were quite confused. Then it was time for Simmons himself to testify.

The Imperial Wizard of the Invisible Empire made a pleasing impression on the stand. His appearance was that of a politician of the old school and the Old South, a colonel of the fraternal volunteers. He moved his tall frame with dignity. He wore a Prince Albert coat and a stiff-necked collar, the kind where the whole of the necktie is looped with stately dignity around it. His vest was crossed by a gold chain weighted down by dangling fraternal keys. His vest pockets bulged with fountain pens and a large case for the spectacles which perched on his long, thin, prominent nose. His complexion was sandy, his lips thin but firmly composed, and his red hair was beginning to recede noticeably.

Having informed the committee of the perilous state of his health: tonsilitis, which, combined with laryngitis, had developed into bronchitis and threatened pneumonia, he settled down to defend the Klan. Parrying all questions with good humor and rhetoric, he told of his efforts to build his fraternal order and how he had remained steadfast against adversity and treachery. His only intent had been fraternal and benevolent. The strange ritual and titles of the Klan were standard in the lodge world. No, he didn't think that Clarke was getting too much money. Of course the Klan maintained a monopoly on its regalia. Why let someone else profit from it when the income would help the Klan? Was he being imperialistic in his use of power within the Klan? No, he explained; was it imperialistic for a father to command his own child? As for investigation, he had always welcomed it. The oath and ritual of the Klan were copyrighted and a matter of public record.

On the vital topic of violence, he always disclaimed knowledge and sought to disassociate himself and the Klan. Because a few had acted wrongly, the whole organization should not be punished. The Klan, he claimed, with some justification, was blamed for all masked crimes and a myriad of unrelated wrongdoings. He didn't believe that the Klan was involved in the incidents for which it was denounced, but if any Klansmen were, they were violating the principles of the order.

On the third day of hearings Simmons showed strain, speaking hoarsely and rocking unsteadily on his feet, as he told how he had suffered from treasonable action within the Klan. Caesar had his Brutus, he declaimed, Washington his Arnold. "If this organization is unworthy, then let me know and I will destroy it, but if it is not, then let it stand," he orated. Turning to the spectators he announced his desire "to call upon the Father to forgive those who have persecuted the Klan." With the conclusion of his peroration, he swayed and sank senseless to the floor.

The Klan had come off better than many of its leaders had expected. Simmons maintained later, that it was because Congressman D. W. Upshaw had introduced a bill which threatened to extend the investigation to all other secret societies. Most probably, however, the committee had been seeking information rather than legislation. How anyone expected the national government or Congress to handle the Klan was never clear. Then, too, the Klan situation was both too vague and yet too alarming, for cautious politicians to willingly tackle. When the committee chairman, Congressman Philip Campbell of Missouri, was defeated at the next election, many able politicians nodded knowingly.

It was the newspaper series, particularly that of the New York *World* which seemed to have had the greatest impact on the Klan. It had all been priceless publicity, and the *World*'s acceptance of the Klan's highly inflated membership claims did not hurt. The series increased *World* sales by a hundred thousand. It increased Klan sales by ten times that number. The press had seen only the commercial motives of the founders and violence of some of the members. It had missed the appeal of the Klan and this made many Americans distrust the attacks in the press. E. H. Loucks, in his seminal study of the Klan in Pennsylvania, suggested that what New York attacked, rural America, with its belligerent inferiority complex, would stubbornly support.[1] At any rate, with new members coming in by the thousands, Simmons reported that many of them joined with facsimile coupons which they clipped from the *World* and other papers carrying the series. "It wasn't until the newspapers began to attack the Klan that it really grew," he reminisced years later. "Certain newspapers also aided us by inducing Congress to investigate us. The result was that Congress gave us the best advertising we ever got. Congress made us."

[1] *The Ku Klux Klan in Pennsylvania* (Harrisburg, Pa., 1936), p. 23.

5

THE EYES OF TEXAS

The Lone Star State was the first chartered self-governing realm within the Invisible Empire. Its story falls into several fairly definite periods. The high quality and social level of its initial recruits in 1920 was followed by a degeneration into violence in 1921 and 1922, as the membership climbed. In 1922 the Klan temporarily solved the internal crisis induced by its own lawlessness, by focusing on politics, although its night riding continued into 1923. The stunning success of local candidates and the election of Earl B. Mayfield as the first Klan member of the United States Senate were its high point in Texas, and the Klan's power was probably past its peak by the time of Hiram Evans' triumphant Dallas home-coming in the fall of 1923. The Invisible Empire was the main issue in the 1924 election which saw Ma Ferguson and Dan Moody sweep into the governor's mansion and the Attorney Generalship on anti-Klan platforms. This heralded the rapid decline of its power as Texas became one of the most anti-Klan states in the Union.

It was the usual pattern of racial unrest, hard times, and nostalgia which offered the Klan its foothold in Texas. It first disembarked at Houston in the fall of 1920 and took advantage of the sentiment for the past rekindled by the annual reunion of the United Confederate Veterans. Simmons was there, juicy ripe with patriotism, and the very name of his companion and aid, Nathan Bedford Forrest III, conjured up past devotions. A select number of leading citizens succumbed to his offer of the exclusive opportunity to "maintain forever the God-given supremacy of the white race," "commemorate the holy and chivalric achievements" of their "embattled fathers," and protect the "sacred rights, exalted privileges, and distinctive institutions" of the civil government. When the Klan held its own first night parade, Houston blacked out her lighting system and policemen kept the streets clear for the marchers, all ghostly garbed by a local

Jewish-owned overall factory for $1.50 per. The Klan's first recruits literally constituted a Who's Who of business, the professions, and patriotism.

Within a year, the picture had changed greatly. Membership was soaring to peak in 1922 at probably over two hundred thousand Klansmen. A string of able Kleagles, under the direction of former Houston ice-cream salesman, Grand Goblin George B. Kimbro, Jr., busily worked the territory. Members were coming in as fast as they could pay their ten dollars and be naturalized into the order. Cyclopes, more and more supplied from the pulpits of rural churches, who would have to run the Klans, had no time to examine and pass on applicants.

By 1922 the Realm of Texas had been organized under its first Grand Dragon, a Protestant Episcopal minister Dr. A. D. Ellis of Beaumont, and divided into five provinces with their headquarters in Fort Worth, Dallas, Waco, Houston, and San Antonio. The Grand Titan of Province No. 2 was an affable, outgoing, dentist, Hiram Wesley Evans, who had been Exalted Cyclops of the state's largest Klavern, in Dallas.

The Klan that was first making the headlines in Texas, though, was neither Houston's Sam Houston No. 1 nor Dallas' No. 66, but Dr. Ellis' Beaumont Klavern. There, in the oil, lumber, and agriculture-rich land near the Louisiana border, the Klan reaped its biggest headlines and its first setback. Beaumont No. 7 not only went in for the whip, tar, and feathers, but after they had worked over a local doctor accused of performing abortions, they officially delivered a four-thousand-word explanation, complete with poem, to the local papers. Although the resulting outcry forced Klan headquarters in Atlanta to go through the motions of lifting the Beaumont's charter, local conditions remained a bit noisy and the next year the Jefferson County sheriff was discharged, despite his plea that his Klan membership had not interfered with his unavailing efforts to apprehend the wrongdoers. Later testimony was to maintain that the mayor and district attorney of Beaumont were also Klansmen and that the latter had a habit of communicating with juries by giving the Klan sign and making reference to "red-blooded Americans" when Klansmen were on the stand.

The Klan was a supersecret organization, masked and mysterious, with a tradition of violence for which a generation of legend had achieved a high measure of social approval. The attainment of its avowed goals, which were to protect God, Country, Home, Womanhood, the South, and White Supremacy, was of paramount urgency. The fact that the Klansmen were backed not only by their own masses but also by so many in high office, resolved doubts of propriety and fear of retribution. In Waco, the mayor and the Board of Police Commissioners were Klansmen. So were the county judge of DeWitt and most of the jurors. So were the sheriffs of Jefferson and Austin's Travis County, and scores upon scores of others. When a newspaper charged that the city and county officials of Dallas were Klansmen, no denial was made. When the McLennan County sheriff's attempt to halt a forbidden parade led to a riot in which a man was killed, the leading citizens of Lorena, where it took place, signed a complaint against the sheriff.

And so it went. In Denton the Klan took two Negroes from jail and flogged them. A Negro bellhop in Dallas was flogged, KKK was branded on his forehead with acid, and he was dumped in front of the hotel. A warning, signed KKK, sent striking Negroes back to the cotton fields of Corsicana at the old rate of fifty cents a hundred pounds. When a Negro dentist was kidnaped and whipped, the resulting rumors of retaliation and racial warfare brought the Klan out, armed and badged, to patrol the streets of Houston.

But only a small portion of the Klan's defense of morality and society was directed at the Negro. A white man in Timson, who had recently separated from his wife, was taken out and beaten. So were a Brenham man who spoke German, a divorced man in Dallas, a bank cashier in Bay City, a lawyer from Houston who annoyed girls, and another attorney who participated in Negro lawsuits and sometimes won. A woman was taken from a hotel where she worked in Tenha, stripped, beaten with a wet rope, and tarred and feathered, over the disputed question as to whether her second marriage had been preceded by a divorce. Waco police arrested three masked and hooded Klansmen, with the molded, feathered tar still warm upon their victim, and the grand jury presented no indictment. Jewish-run businesses were boycotted, Mexicans carefully watched. Ex-Governor Ferguson's daughter wrote of coming out of the Paramount Theatre in Austin and seeing two men, tarred and feathered, running up Congress Avenue with a jeering mob at their heels. They had been released at the river, she learned, and told to run to the newspaper offices and then get out of town. The Klan in Dallas was credited with having flogged sixty-eight people during the bloody spring of 1922, most of them at a special Klan-whipping meadow along the Trinity River bottom. One unfriendly tabulation of affairs in Texas credited the Klan with over five hundred tar-and-feather parties and whipping bees, plus other threats, assaults, and homicides.

It would be wrong to maintain that the people of Texas were not alarmed by these developments, and that some at least did not attempt to take preventive measures. A number of outspoken district judges ordered investigations and some sheriffs and city officials attempted to prevent Klan parades. Although the Klan boasted that a grand jury in Wichita Falls brought in no indictment, the judge sent three Klansmen to jail for refusing to answer questions. The mayor of Dallas demanded that the Klan disband. Forty-nine members of the state legislature petitioned a silent governor for an antimask law. Chambers of commerce, American Legion posts, DARs, the Texas Bar Association, and others denounced the Klan or wrote to the Justice Department for action. The Masons struck out resolutely against the Klan, and the Grand Master traveled all over the state trying to stem Klan inroads in his lodges. The Houston *Chronicle* editorially told the Klan: "Boys, you'd better disband," and an anti-Klan citizens' league was formed in Dallas.

Early in 1922, with the papers full of tar-and-flogging parties in Dallas, the national headquarters of the Klan had become concerned. Hiram Evans came back from his new office in Atlanta to talk things over with the boys. It wasn't that the officers back at the palace objected to frightening Negroes away from the polls. This was old stuff and everyone agreed that it was a good idea. The particular issue that had caused question was the castration of a very fairskinned Negro doctor who had been accused of consorting with white women. The Houston Grand Titan, H. C. McCall, argued that a little bit of violence was good for the Klan. "Come off it," he told Evans. "That kind of stuff went on when you were here in charge of things." McCall had previously taken the lead in fighting for the "2% of rough stuff," and at that time Evans had stood with him. According to later congressional testimony, Evans himself had been a party to the acid branding of the Dallas bellhop. Obviously, Atlanta was in no position to put down violence within the ranks.

The initially high respect for the Klan had turned to fear, and now fear was beginning to turn to anger. Serious opposition without and dissension within were rising, and the sharp edge of ridicule was beginning to cut away at the Klan's pride. According to a story in the ever hostile New York *World,* a crowd of four thousand Klansmen had been waiting the arrival of Colonel Simmons to address their Fourth of July celebration. The colonel was quite late, and so several Klansmen filled in. Finally, with a broad self-confident smile, the chairman asked if there was an anti-Klan speaker who would dare to come to the platform. To his surprise, a young law student from the University of Texas made his way to the stage. Having examined, extemporaneously, the Klan's monopolistic claims to patriotism, its professed concern for free speech, and its wordy protection of white supremacy, he finally got around to Klan morality. "Klan speakers say they stand for chastity of womanhood and all high ideals," he told them. "I stand for it and practice it," he continued, "but there are thousands of you Klansmen who don't."

In the spring of 1922, the Klan found a more respectable unifying outlet for its energies and its power. It turned to politics in a big way. In the primary campaign for the governorship, three of the candidates were Klansmen. Former congressman and one-time mayor of Texarkana, R. L. Henry, took a trip to Atlanta to seek endorsement from the Klan's national officials. Believing that this settled things, he "uncovered" and ran openly as a Klansman. His competitor beneath the robe, State Railroad Commissioner Earl B. Mayfield played a more subtle and effective game. He quietly made the rounds within the Texas realm itself and, before Henry knew it, had won the support that counted. The local leaders liked the idea of Henry drawing off the anti-Klan fire and they were impressed with Mayfield's railroad and business connections. Atlanta approved, and the word went out that Mayfield was the chosen candidate. In the first primary he led the field and a furious Henry ran last.

The Klan was ecstatic. Brown Harwood, the new Grand Dragon, sent out a letter to all Klansmen, rejoicing over the triumph of "the native-born white Protestant Gentile." The election, he explained, meant safety for the soil of Texas on which Protestant blood had been shed in wresting it away from the priest-ridden tyranny of Mexico.

In the Democratic runoff, Mayfield defeated former Governor Jim Ferguson with the particular aid of his fellow Klansmen, anti-Fergusonites, the Anti-Saloon League and the women's vote. The Klan swept the lower house of the Texas legislature, elected judges and other officials, carried everything before it in Dallas County, where it celebrated wildly in the streets.

But not all Texans accepted Klan victories silently. It was widely claimed that any candidate but Jim Ferguson could have beaten Mayfield, and a call was issued for a state-wide meeting to "name a real Democrat to oppose the Ku Klux Klan nominee." George

Peddy, a young assistant district attorney from Houston was selected. The Republican party withdrew its own candidate and endorsed Peddy. The months before the final election became not only a battle of the stump and ballot but of the law court. The Peddy supporters sought to have Mayfield ruled off the ballot on the grounds that his Klan oath meant he could not be a Democrat. The Mayfield people tried to remove Peddy on the grounds that his participation in the Democratic primary meant he couldn't be anything else but a Democrat. In a welter of suits, investigations, and confusion, it was not clear whether either could legally be permitted on the ballot. However the Klan controlled the Democratic party election machinery, and in most places Mayfield went on the ballot while Peddy's name had to be written in by the voter. Mayfield, the Democratic-Klan candidate was victorious, with 264,000 votes to Peddy's 130,-000. Although his opponents contested the election before a U. S. Senate Committee, Mayfield eventually took his seat as the first genuine Klan senator.

Governor Pat Neff, whom the Klan listed as "favorable," was re-elected. Most of the state's nineteen congressmen tried to take a straddling position, though bluff John Nance Garner spoke out against the Klan in no uncertain terms. He was re-elected, but he lost areas, including his home county of Uvalde, that he had always carried before. In San Antonio, a Republican won over a Democrat, who was Jewish, in a supposedly safe Democratic district.

The election of 1922 was the high point of Klan power in Texas, and it initially seemed that the diversion from violence to politics was the saving of the Klan name and unity. However, despite continued election victories in Dallas and the seventy-five thousand faithful who rallied there to greet Imperial Wizard Hiram Evans' return for Klan Day at the state fair, opposition was mounting throughout the state. Klan violence was stirring up much popular anger. In Goose Creek, an oil town near Dallas, a woman recently separated from her husband, was ill in bed. A visitor had brought her a basket of fruit and while her daughters and neighbors' children were playing about, a throng of hooded men burst in. While the terrified children screamed, the woman and her visitor were carried off. Both were beaten with a flail. The woman's hair was hacked off and crude oil was poured over the man and his wounds. The citizens of Goose Creek were alarmed and angered. Suspects were arrested but the sheriff and the district attorney at Dallas were Klan-elected and not inclined to push things further. After five months, as the result of investigators sent in from Houston, twenty-five Klansmen pleaded guilty and were fined. What aroused the public ire even more was the revelation of the reign of terror which had been chalking up practically a whipping a week over the preceding eighteen months.

At almost the same time that the Dallas floggers were coming to something a little less than justice, violence was erupting elsewhere in the state. Finally, however, Texas and its citizens were beginning to fight back, and by 1923, some district attorneys were beginning to prosecute the Klan successfully. The credit was due primarily to Lt. Gov. T. W. Davidson, the Texas Rangers, and to increasingly resolute juries. The essential element seemed to be that Governor Neff be out of the state. On the night of July 2, 1923, a railroad worker, Otto Lange, was sitting on the porch of his Burleson County home with his seventy-year-old mother and his little daughter. When he resisted the Klansmen who had come to get him, his mother was clubbed with a pistol and a stray shot hit his daughter in the hand. Another bullet killed Lange. Acting Governor Davidson sent the Texas Rangers in to investigate, but when Governor Neff returned home the case was apparently forgotten. Four months later, when Governor Neff went off to Washington to attend a Prohibition luncheon with President Coolidge, Davidson sent in the Rangers again. As the Klan was assembling to greet Evans in Dallas, Davidson presented evidence to a grand jury about the night riding that had not only killed Lange, but for no discernible reason had flogged a Baptist preacher, the town marshal, and a local doctor. With the governor sojourning frequently in other parts, Davidson was able to have the Rangers investigate floggings in Port Arthur, in Wichita Falls, and Amarillo, and was finally able to start getting jail sentences.

But Davidson was not the first to actually see Klansmen convicted and off to prison. In the little town of Taylor, just north of Austin, a traveling salesman named Burleson liked to take out a local woman when he was in town. Someone apparently didn't think it was a good idea, and so Burleson was kidnaped, chained to a tree and flogged, beaten on the head with pistol butts, tarred and feathered, and dumped in the public square. Dan Moody, a young war-hero district attorney prosecuted the Klansmen involved, including a local minister and the chief of police. He secured several convictions and sent one man to prison.

The 1924 elections were for the most part fought on the Klan issue. Although Dan Moody, at the age of thirty-two, had the attorney general's nomination sewed up, the Klan put up a full slate, from local constable to Supreme Court justice. The major contest was over the Democratic nomination for governor and the Klan rallied its forces behind Felix D. Robertson, a World War I major and Texas National Guard officer whom the Klan had elected police judge in Dallas.

In the first primary, five candidates split the anti-Klan vote. In the runoff an unusual opponent but a familiar name was squared off against Robertson. It was a woman, Miriam Amanda Ferguson. "Farmer Jim" Ferguson had been impeached as governor in 1917 for showing himself somewhat exceptional financial favoritism. Although he had run unsuccessfully against Mayfield for senator in 1922, his impeachment was interpreted to bar him from purely state office. However, from the time of his removal from the governorship, Farmer Jim, one of the most compelling orators in Texas history, had campaigned for vindication and office. In 1924 he had a new wrinkle: he would run his wife for governor. Miriam Amanda was a quiet, austere woman, probably the least likely person ever to seek public office, and this sat well with the voters. She was no "political woman" but the "heroic wife" fighting for her "maligned" husband. And she had another excellent advantage: the first letters of her given names spelled "MA." Between her appearance of probity and Jim's experience, oratory, and following among the poor farmers, they made a good candidate. The usual Ferguson campaign pattern was a joint appearance. Ma would ask for the vindication of her husband and the good name of her family, and promise to be the governor of all the people. Then Jim would take over and blast the Klan's violence and its "Grand Gizzard" and "longhorn Texas Koo Koos." Someone lent Ma an old-fashioned sunbonnet for a picture whose wide circulation led to the adoption of "Put on Your Old Gray Bonnet" as a campaign song, and "A Bonnet or a Hood" as a slogan. ME FOR MA, AND I AIN'T GOT A DURN THING AGAINST PA, and TWO FOR THE PRICE OF ONE badges and posters plastered the state. The band wagon was rolling and people were jumping on. Practically all of the best-known political leaders of the state, including the lawyer who had once prosecuted Jim, joined in. It was not that most of them liked the Fergusons. Given any kind of a choice they would have gladly opposed Farmer Jim, for his veniality and his appeal to hatred of the Jew, the Negro, the well-to-do, and the educated would not have been too much out of place on the Klan platform. However, circumstance had made him the opponent of the Klan, and at least he opposed mob law and stood up for visible government.

The Klan was bountifully financed. It had the support of many pulpits, the Anti-Saloon League, a block of some two-hundred-thousand Klan votes, and the hope of gaining the adherence of those who disliked "Pa" more than the Invisible Empire.

The Klan praised itself for having insured the defeat of Al Smith and the eventual nomination of John Davis at the National Democratic Convention. Therefore, when Davis spoke out against the Klan during his presidential campaign, it was hurtful front-page news in the cities where the Klan had looked for its strength. Klansmen were dropping out and denouncing the order as political and dictatorial, rather than fraternal. When the Dallas *News* came out for Ma it was another bad blow. In desperation the Klan appealed for Jewish votes and modified its opposition to Catholicism, dropping all but the "jug" from its former "Jew, Jug, and Jesuit" cry.

The weather was clear and perfect on Election Day. The Klan precinct workers were well organized and on the job, with cars ready to take voters to the polls. It seems safe to assume that the Klan got out all of its votes, and on a vacant lot in Dallas a float, with GOOD-BYE MA in big letters, stood ready for the victory celebration. Within hours after the polls closed, however the anti-Klan ticket was piling up its margin. Robertson polled an impressive 337,000 votes but Ma beat him by 100,000. The sweep was almost complete, as other anti-Klan candidates came in by even greater margins. Although Klan strength had declined in the Texas cities, the Klan still carried the Dallas, Fort Worth, and El Paso counties and split almost even in Houston's Harris County. As the returns began indicating the anti-Klan victory, it seemed that all Dallas was out in the streets, Klansmen stunned and silent, while joyous anti-Klan forces whooped it up for "Ma" in a carnival-like atmosphere.

The November election was an anticlimax. The Texas Republican party had long been outspokenly against the Klan and had been the rallying point of the abortive anti-Klan move at the National Convention at Cleveland. Nevertheless its candidate for governor, the law school dean from the University of Texas, now kept silent on the Klan. Jim Ferguson denounced Dean George Butte as "a little muttonheaded professor with a Dutch diploma" who took orders from the Klan "the same as Felix Robertson did." In the November election the Republicans added the Klan vote and much of the business community to its usual tally. It did well in the "German" counties around Austin and picked up the support of a number of Democratic papers including the Dallas *Times-Herald* which had supported Robertson in the Democratic race. But Ma was not to be turned back.

With Klansmen still scraping NO MA FOR ME stickers off their windshields, the victorious Democrats settled down to the business of cleansing the party and the state. After the primaries, Klan supporters had been removed from their positions of authority in the party. When the legislature met, all important posts were put in the hands of those opposed to the Invisible Empire. Ma had campaigned for an antimask law, publication of membership, and the loss of tax exemption by churches used for Klan meetings. The actual law passed was less severe. A bill proposing the death penalty for hooded assault was turned down, but a strong antimask law was quickly approved. Ma Ferguson rooted Klansmen out of state office and the attorney general, Dan Moody, appointed a strong anti-Klan man as head of the Texas Rangers.

The general revulsion against Klan-preached hatred and brutal floggings, plus the enforcement of the laws, and political defeat, had crumbled Klan power. Scores of thousands dropped out. Those who would talk about it, explained that they had been forced to join to hold their jobs and they apologized for having belonged. Fort Worth's attractive new Klan auditorium had been burned by incendiaries the year before and now attempts were made on the Klan's Beethoven Hall in San Antonio. The blazing electric cross atop the Klan building in Houston was taken down and the building sold at auction. By 1926, the Dallas, Houston, San Antonio, and Fort Worth Klans were in the hands of Klan receivers. A former Grand Dragon of Texas estimated that the Dallas chapter was down from 13,000 to 1200 and that membership throughout the whole realm was less than 18,000. Not a province in Texas, he reported, could pay its help. Later in the year Dan Moody gave the people of Texas the choice that they had not had in 1922 and 1924 and wrested the governorship from "Ma." Though Jim Ferguson tried to label the thirty-four-year-old attorney general as a "Klene Kut Ku Klux Klansman," it would not stick.

In 1928, Senator Mayfield claimed that he had long since broken all Klan connections. He politically championed Al Smith and pulled in support from Jim Ferguson, but the people of Texas decided to send Waco Congressman Tom Connally to the Senate instead. When Mayfield later ran against Ma in the 1930 gubernatorial primaries, he could do no better than seventh, and all candidates with histories of Klan support faced trouble with the voters.

6

MAYHEM AND MARTIAL LAW
IN OKLAHOMA

Oklahomans like to do things in a hurry, and Oklahoma was a boomer
state for the Klan in the 1920s. The Goblins and Kleagles slipped in
early, and by the end of 1921 there were as many Klansmen in the
Sooner State as there had been in the whole Invisible Empire six
months before.

Oklahoma had been a state only about thirteen years when the
Klan's organizers first came. Its population was a mixture of immigrants from the South and pioneer West, transplanted Indians and
Negroes, the poor, the wealthy, the weak and the strong, the hard-
put farmer, the oil worker and owner, and the bustling, boosting,
civic-minded businessman. The newness of things and the great and
sudden riches in the oil fields still gave Oklahoma a frontier appearance and feeling. Graft and corruption, gambling, prostitution, and
drunkenness were overt. Prohibition had added the highjacker as well
as the strained note of morality. The law often seemed inoperative;
governors paroled and pardoned too much, and the vigilante tradition of privately administered law and morality was no stranger. As
elsewhere, the war heightened animosities, and encouraged the busy-
body. During the war, a group of Wobblies were flogged "in the name
of the women and children of Belgium." There was a public lynching
in Tulsa shortly after the war and in 1921 the Negro district was
burned after a race riot in which more than thirty Negroes were killed.

This was an atmosphere in which the Klan could work, and it first
appeared as a reformer. In September of 1921, Klansmen kidnaped
a local editor and took him along on a parade through Shawnee and
Tecumseh. He was there, they told him, to carry a warning to bootleggers, gamblers, joyriders, corrupt lawyers and bail bondsmen,
lenient judges, and men who lived off their own wives or fooled
around with those of others. In El Reno a Negro porter was whipped

for being "too free" with guests at the hotel. A mail clerk was taken from his home and tarred and feathered. In Enid a man accused of beating his wife was whipped and told to pay off his mortgage and leave town. More than a score of Negroes were also forced to depart. Not only were the Negroes bootleggers, dope heads, and hold-up men, the mayor told the American Civil Liberties Union, but Enid had ten policemen and fifteen hundred Klansmen. In the light of this, he felt that there was no point in making an investigation. "You might condemn the method," he explained, "but the results were entirely satisfactory to our city of twenty thousand. If it was the Klan, it has made our best citizens their best friends."

Having told the sheriff of Tulsa to get rid of roadhouses, bootleggers, and obnoxious resorts, the Klan proceeded to lend him a hand. Within a short time the membership of the Klan and police forces were fairly well integrated, with relatively devastating results for organized gangs and vice in Tulsa. This growing record for the enforced reform of wrongdoers brought the Klan general vocal approval. Its membership soared to almost ninety thousand. One person in twenty probably belonged to the invisible order, and the vice president of the University of Oklahoma was Grand Dragon for the state. From opposition to graft and organized crime the Klan had turned almost immediately to moral reform, and then into politics. After local victories in Tulsa and elsewhere it became involved in state politics. In the Democratic primary for governor, the Klan lined up behind the state school superintendent and his antiparochial school issue.

The winner, however, was the vain, affable, impatient mayor of Oklahoma City, Jack Walton. Hard times on the farm, not the Klan issue, carried Walton to victory. The postwar deflation had undercut the wartime commodity prices and pressed particularly hard on Oklahoma's toilers. Joining with the traditionally strong Socialist party, leaders of this depressed majority formed a Farmer-Labor Reconstruction League. In the Democratic primary of 1922 and the subsequent election, its support, plus that of Klan-fearing Catholics, gave Walton the governorship.

Jack Walton had come to Oklahoma from Indiana and Missouri, just before statehood. A contractor and civil engineer, he settled down in Oklahoma City and soon entered politics. At forty-two, Walton was a big-boned, square-built man with an oval face, ruddy complexion, and a Roman nose. With a quick sympathy for the underdog, he lined up with labor and talked friendly with the Socialists. As mayor of Oklahoma City he made a good record. Boisterous and hot-headed, Jack Walton was a young man in a hurry and he believed in his star. He wasn't very strong on economics and the philosophy of government but he liked to get things done. He liked to do them himself and do them big, and he liked them frenetic. He campaigned with a jazz band, and to celebrate his inauguration in 1923, he threw a barbecue to which over a hundred thousand people came.

Once Walton was installed in the governor's mansion, his problems began. Although the legislature passed an impressive parcel of bills to aid the farmers, labor, and the schools, and to regulate business, the Farmer-Labor Reconstruction League was vaguely uneasy. Walton sold his modest frame house to buy an expensive one in a fashionable suburb and installed a butler. He seemed too suddenly affluent and there were rumors that he had taken money from the oil interests. He tried to disassociate himself from the League, and when he did yield to pressure and appointed a League leader as head of Oklahoma A & M, there was a furious outcry. Nothing he did seemed to please anyone. Having antagonized the League, he was still too radical for the Klan, even though, at least for a while, he secretly became a member.

But while the governor contended with his former friends as well as his growing list of enemies, the Klan was busy. An Oklahoma City crowd of nearly thirty thousand cheered as an airplane with a crimson cross outlined on its wings wheeled over the city amusement park during a Klan ceremony. Klan floggings now numbered in the hundreds, and perhaps the thousands. In Atoka and Balk Knob, Klan posses beat I.W.W. and union organizers and announced their intent to break up any attempts to form a farm labor union. In Ardmore, Klansmen who allegedly killed a bootlegger in a raid on his home were found not guilty. On the whole the Klan was less concerned with crime than personal behavior and, many said, private vengeance. In Enid the musical societies reportedly placed a stipulation in all contracts that the performers were to be subject to approval by the Klan. The Klan went to work on a lawyer in Cushing who spoke against it, a Negro in Tulsa who attempted to register other Negroes, a man in Jenks who had opposed a school bond issue, a man who had deserted his wife and the woman with whom he had taken up, Okmulgee girls and young men caught riding together in cars, men involved in business controversies who were accused of hauling illegal liquor or immoral women, a man who took money from a sister-in-law, and one who quarreled with his wife. The usual victims were not Jews, Negroes, Roman Catholics, or aliens, but white native-born, Protestant citizens, women and youths as well as grown men.

E. Y. Clarke had offered Oklahoma Klansmen a special order for those who liked a little "rough stuff," and a number of Klans such as the one in Shawnee had special whipping squads. While the police stood by, men were kidnaped from the streets of even the largest cities to be carted off and flogged. Petit juries refused to convict Klansmen. Victims were afraid to report their whippings to local officials who were often members of the Klan. Night after night, in places like Okmulgee and Tulsa, victims were taken out and flogged. As the mayor of Enid had described it, when the Klan first came to town, "You elbow your best friends and you do not know whether or not you are rubbing up against a Klansman or not. Our watchword," he commented, "is 'Keep your mouth shut tight and keep out of the hands of the Klansman.'"

In the summer of 1923, Governor Walton assumed the center of the stage. A committee from Henryetta had come to tell the governor of the growing violence there, but before they were able to explain the details, Walton interrupted. "I've heard enough," he announced. "Mob violence is going to cease in Oklahoma; within five minutes the order will be given to place Okmulgee County under martial law." There were some arrests but few results, and martial law was soon terminated. Then, in August, Tulsa police questioned a Jewish rooming-house operator suspected of selling dope. He was released and by apparent prearrangement, snatched up from the street by the Klan and taken to the outskirts of town. He was stripped, whipped, and his genitals were beaten to a pulp. As soon as he was able to travel, his son put him in the back seat of a car and drove to the office of the governor in Oklahoma City. Afterwards Walton gave the order and the troops were on their way to Tulsa.

The Tulsans were furious. It might be necessary to take stern actions in a rural area such as Okmulgee, but Tulsa was a modern up-to-date metropolis. Martial law was not only insulting, it was bad advertising for the first city of the state. The Tulsan might have accepted a civil investigation, but the troops in Tulsa, never! And this attitude did not change when the governor's military court of inquiry sentenced four admitted floggers and started taking evidence on over a hundred other floggings in the county, many of them in the Klan's favored "whipping pasture" just outside of the little town of Alsuma. When city authorities refused to co-operate, the militia took over from them. The mayor complained to Washington that the National

Guard was being used unconstitutionally, but the Secretary of War replied it was a state affair. Habeas corpus was suspended, and when the press protested, military censors were placed in some newspaper offices. Protests mounted throughout the state. Then, the night before a grand jury was to open an investigation of him, Walton proclaimed martial law over the entire state.

Walton had gone too far, and in the eyes of a good part of the state, it was the governor not the Klan that stood guilty in the dock. When the grand jury attempted to meet to investigate charges of financial misdeeds against the governor and his administration, it found guardsmen with machine guns barring its path. When the legislature tried to assemble to impeach the governor, soldiers also turned them away. The governor had called a special veterans' bonus election, and the opposition managed to add a proposition permitting the legislature to meet in special session without waiting for a call from the governor. Both sides filed legal briefs, hurled charges, and armed. Walton threatened to call out all the state militia, plus seventy-five thousand volunteers, if necessary, to keep the polls closed. Walton's supporters flocked into Oklahoma City and both sides had thousands of men under arms. "There may be bloodshed," Walton threatened, "but there will be no election."

The state had come to the brink of civil war, and most people held Walton responsible. Newspapers ran NEITHER KLAN NOR KING on their mastheads, but, of the two, "King" Walton seemed to be the greater menace. Where the Klan broke the laws, Walton seemed to many to be intent on overthrowing constitutional government entirely. His old radical friends of the Farmer-Labor Reconstruction League were not willing to forgive his "treachery"; his handling of the state administration had been of questionable wisdom and honesty, and the press was in no state of mind to be lenient.

The courts upheld the legality of the legislative initiative proposal. Walton did not interfere, and the election endorsed it by a majority of almost three to one. There was now nothing Walton could do to prevent his impeachment and removal. When he offered his resignation in exchange for an anti-Klan bill, the legislature refused. The most vital and immediate task was to be rid of Walton, then it could handle the Invisible Empire.

Walton made no defense, declaring that he could not expect a fair trial from the Oklahoma Senate. All that he had done, he claimed, was to fight the hooded Empire. The Senate found him guilty of campaign-fund irregularities, manipulation of state payrolls, suspension of habeas corpus, use of the National Guard to obstruct the meeting of the Oklahoma City grand jury, and general incompetence. On the misuse of his pardoning powers, the vote against him was unanimous.

With the apparent removal of Walton from the political scene, the legislature next turned its attention to the Klan. Though the hooded order was numerically powerful and exultant over Walton's impeachment, it was not able to stay its own partial proscription. When it tried to water down the antimask bill, the Klan could not even control the votes of its own legislators. The admission by the Imperial Wizard, Hiram Evans, that he had sent large sums of money into Oklahoma for propaganda purposes, further weakened the Klan position. Dozens of bills were introduced and the law which finally emerged prohibited public wearing of the mask and slightly upgraded penalties for masked misdeeds.

Almost immediately after his removal from the governorship, Jack Walton sought vindication and a return to power, by running for U. S. Senator. All the signs seemed to indicate that he would have been defeated in the Democratic primary had not the Republican leaders of the Klan seen a wonderful opportunity in his candidacy. On the eve of the primary, the Klan gave its unwelcome endorsement to Walton's popular, front-running rival. As calculated, it was a political touch of death, and Walton won the nomination. Having helped the Democrats pick their weakest candidate, Grand Dragon Jewett led his Klansmen into the Republican party. With the support of the Klan, plus all of those for whom the name of Walton was anathema, Okmulgee oil millionaire, W. B. Pine, won easily in November, even though the Democratic ticket carried the state.

With Walton now defeated, the Democrats were on the whole rather hopeful to be rid of the Klan. Despite the success of Pine, its support was becoming a political handicap. Candidates for state-wide office found it wise to denounce the hooded order. When the local Klan met after the election in a downtown office building in Henryetta, United Mine Workers surrounded the building, and the besieged Klansmen had to wait until dark to slip away.

By the time elections rolled around again in 1926, the Klan had continued its downward descent. It had been years since there had been any night-riding violence, or big, publicly secret meetings with a blazing cross at the pitcher's mound in the local ball park. Membership was down to less than twenty thousand and there was conflict within the ranks. The Klan office building in Tulsa had gone, and in

Oklahoma City the Invisible Empire had moved to a cramped one-room office. At a meeting of the Democratic State Central Committee, only ten out of seventy-seven counties reported Klan activity.

The Republican party, which had courted it so warmly two years before, was backing away under Democratic attack. In 1924, it was all "Kitty, kitty, nice kitty, come to the G.O.P., but now it's scat," the Democrats needled. Senator J. W. Harreld, fighting desperately, explained that many Klansmen were good fellows and that the Klan had once been a useful moral force, but he was now through with it for good. Although both candidates for governor had had Klan ties, the Republicans were on the defensive and the Democrats swept the election.

The presidential candidacy of the wet, Catholic New Yorker, Alfred E. Smith, stirred up but failed to bring back the Klan. Imperial Wizard Evans circularized all former Klansmen, and the new Grand Dragon of Oklahoma preached the anti-Smith cause on a Friday-night radio program. Although the Klan exerted what pressure it had to prevent a pro-Smith delegation going to the Democratic convention, it just did not have the power. Those Klansmen who held office kept very carefully in the background, and almost all of the anti-Smith campaign fell to the hands of the Protestant churchmen, led by an Oklahoma City Baptist minister. The party went for Smith at the convention, but split in the election, and Hoover carried the state. However this presaged no revival. The Oklahomans had long since come to the point where they were intent on handling their own business, including politics, Prohibition, and, where necessary, anti-Catholicism, without the help of the faded Invisible Empire.

7

THE RAZORBACK KLAN

The third bastion of the Klan's great Southwestern empire was Arkansas. By the end of 1922, the Klan was active throughout the state from the Red River cotton bottoms near Texarkana to the northern railroad town of Harrison in the Ozarks. Although it did not rival Texas and Oklahoma in the degree of violence, Arkansas Klandom had its share of action in its early days. In Smackover, what amounted to a pitched battle left one man dead and many others wounded. In Harrison, Klansmen helped supply the membership if not the leadership of the local vigilante committee which settled a strike on the Missouri and North Arkansas Railway. An accused bridge burner was hanged from a trestle, dozens of strikers and sympathizers were flogged, and others, including a Methodist minister who stood up for them, were forced to leave town. In the prosperous little farming town of Nashville, an old man was kidnaped and whipped, and a companion who sought to protect him was shot and killed. Near Hot Springs' health-giving waters, three men went to jail for shooting up a Klan law-enforcement meeting and, in a series of raids, officials and Klansmen smashed stills, and arrested 140 Prohibition-law violators. After the murder of a farmer in Wilmott, Arkansas, a Klan-sponsored Louisiana-Arkansas Law Enforcement League patrolled the border to catch evildoers, and Arkansas Klansmen often joined hands with their Louisiana brethren in Morehouse Parish. The signs carried in a Texarkana parade summed up the way the Klan in Arkansas looked at things:

LAW AND ORDER MUST PREVAIL.

COHABITATION BETWEEN WHITES AND BLACKS MUST STOP.

BOOTLEGGERS, PIMPS, HANGERS-ON, GET RIGHT OR GET OUT.

WIFE-BEATERS, FAMILY-DESERTERS, HOME-WRECKERS, WE HAVE
 NO ROOM FOR YOU.

LAW VIOLATERS, WE ARE WATCHING YOU. BEWARE.

GO JOY RIDING WITH YOUR OWN WIFE.

THE SHERIFFS OF BOWIE AND MILLER COUNTIES HAVE MORE DEPUTIES THAN CARRY COMMISSIONS.

WE ARE KLANSMEN. WE ARE KLANNISH. WE STICK TOGETHER. WHY SHOULDN'T WE?

WE STAND FOR OLD GLORY AND 100% AMERICANISM.

WE INVITE ALL 100% AMERICANS TO JOIN US.

HERE TODAY. HERE TOMORROW. HERE FOREVER. WATCH US GROW.

With the Klan gaining strength every day, it was soon involved in politics. It elected its members and friends to local office and to the House of Representatives in Washington. The center of Klan strength was in Arkansas' capital city of Little Rock, where the Klan swept practically every office in 1922. Governor Thomas C. McRae was not a Klansman, but his "friendly neutrality" and his appointment of a Klansman as his secretary were sufficient to gain him its support. Although there was some overt opposition to the Klan, the political leaders of the state kept tactfully silent.

These were the lush years for the Klan in Arkansas as its membership climbed to probably more than forty thousand. In the Fourth of July "Komme-moration" parade in Little Rock, in 1924, there were close to ten thousand marchers. The Klan endorsement was accounted so valuable that the Klan conducted a number of its own primaries to decide which friend or Klansman it would support in the regular Democratic one. However, despite a large number of Klan office-holders, opposition was growing within the Democratic party and state administration. Retiring Governor McRae threw the weight of his administration to Tom J. Terrall, a reportedly former Klansman, whom the Invisible Empire bitterly opposed. In Pulaski and St. Francis counties the official Democratic organizations denounced the Klan, and the victory of most of its other state-wide candidates did not compensate the Klan for the election of Terrall.

A major portion of the Klan's problems were internal. Its forays into politics were divisive rather than unifying, for disappointed candidates refused to withdraw and groups of Klansmen continued to support them. Even more devastating was the conflict which raged around the Grand Dragon, J. C. Comer. As a result of his part in the coup which ousted Colonel Simmons in 1922, Judge Comer became an intimate friend of the new Imperial Wizard, Hiram Evans. His influence was such that he was able to maneuver his wife-to-be into control of the Klan's women's auxiliary. But the judge's deviousness and imperiousness, plus Commander Robbie Gil Comer's regal ways, did not sit well with the local constituency. By 1924, the opposition was so strong that Judge Comer had lost practically all control of the Little Rock Klavern which he had once headed. A faction within the Klavern even tried to remove him from membership. When this failed, the dissidents withdrew and formed their own "Independent Klan," and competed with their former brothers-beneath-the-robe in state elections.

Although he turned his attention more and more to the national affairs of the Women of the Ku Klux Klan, Judge Comer clung to his Grand Dragonship in Arkansas. It was, however, a leadership more and more without followers. Despite its victories in the 1924 elections, the loss of the governorship and the schisms in Little Rock accelerated the decline of the Klan. Within little more than a year, total paid-up membership had fallen to about ten thousand. Politicians now ran for office on the claim that they had not been or were no longer members. In 1928, Senator Joseph Robinson was nominated for Vice President on the same ticket with the once-damned Romanist Al Smith. With Arkansas' favorite son stumping the state and nation for religious tolerance, the Klan's day in the Razorback State was over.

8

LOUISIANA: BLACK SHEETS AMONG THE BAYOUS

Although it never achieved the degree of state-wide power that the Klans of Arkansas, Oklahoma, and Texas did, no portion of the Invisible Empire became more notorious than the Louisiana realm of the Ku Klux Klan. A promotional office in New Orleans did not do well, but the great oil and cotton center of Shreveport in the northwestern corner of the state soon became the throne city of local Klandom. From there it spread out into the piney woods and hill country along the Arkansas line and down through the rolling farm country and prairies toward the Gulf-coast border with Texas. Initially, the Louisiana Klansmen behaved as any self-respecting Klansmen would be expected to act. They held initiations and parades, raided stills, and threatened neighbors but generally did little that might have attracted much attention outside of the state.

Then, in September of 1922, the Washington correspondent of the New Orleans *Times-Picayune* presented himself at the Justice Department with a letter from the governor of Louisiana. Governor John M. Parker had been elected two years before on a mild reform platform promising to clean up corrupt politics and work out some sort of regulation of the oil and gas interests. He now found himself confronted with a much more serious problem. In Morehouse Parish on the Arkansas border, the Ku Klux Klan had abducted five men and presumably killed two of them. The pro- and anti-Klan factions were arming and on the verge of civil war. The courts and police were in the hands of the Klan, the telephones and mail were being watched, and strangers searched and spied upon. The governor had not only lost all control over that portion of his state, but had also become distrustful of the security of his own mail and telephones. When the Democratic governor of a Southern state has to ask a Republican Administration to help preserve law and order, conditions are indeed serious.

Morehouse Parish lies in the region of northern Louisiana where the pine ridges fall off onto the yellow mud of the cotton flatlands of the Boeuf River and Bayou Bartholomew. The most important factor in the recent history of the parish had been the rivalry between the newly prosperous, industrial, ridge town of Bastrop with its tall-chimneyed pulp mill, its yellow-brick courthouse and whitewashed Baptist Church, and the old cotton center of Mer Rouge with its plantation houses surrounded by live oaks laden with Spanish moss. It was an enduring conflict, marked by bitterness over the location of the railroad and of the county courthouse, bond issues and mill taxes, newspaper rivalry, the rising bourgeoisie versus the old plantation way of life, morality, and now the Ku Klux Klan.

Not only did the good burghers of Bastrop join the Klan but so did the workers whom the discovery of oil and gas, and the new carbon plants in the clearings, attracted to the parish. Rough and rootless, the latter were a turbulent element, restless in their crude bunkhouses or unpainted shacks, unsatisfied by the single movie in Bastrop and the general shortage of prospects, liquor, women, and diversion. Leonard Cline, a perceptive reporter for the Baltimore *Sun*, wrote: "It must have provided a real thrill to go scooting through the shadowy roads in somebody else's flivver, to meet in lonely dingles in the pine woods and flog other men, to bounce down the fifteen-foot declivity where the ridge ends and swoop at twenty-five miles an hour through the flatlands around Mer Rouge, through phantasmal Lafourche swamp with its banshee live oaks waving their snaky tresses in the moonlight. It was perpetual Halloween. And even if one didn't care much for church, and took one's shot of white lightning when one could get it, and would pay a dollar any day for five minutes in a trollop's arms, it was reassuring to know that religion approved and sanctified one's pranks. It made one bolder."[1]

The Klan appeared in Morehouse Parish late in the year 1921; within six months the postmaster, sheriff and his deputy, prosecuting attorney, and police officers were members. Gossip said that Pastor Sloan of Bastrop's Baptist Church was a member and he did not deny it. Captain J. K. Skipworth was the Exalted Cyclops. Old Skip, in his gray coat with his Confederate veteran's pin in the velvet collar, liked giving orders and the sense of importance and power it brought—much more satisfying even than having been mayor of Bastrop back before the war.

[1] Leonard L. Cline, "In Darkest Louisiana," *Nation*, 116 (1923), 292–93.

Although Cap'n Skip was the head of the Klan, the real leadership, according to the Justice Department men who came to investigate, was Dr. B. M. McKoin. McKoin lived in Mer Rouge, which was not at all as well under control as Bastrop. There was trouble with gambling, drinking, and playing around with Negro girls. Dr. McKoin opened up a campaign against crime, but it wasn't going too well, and the general attitude of antipathy for the Klan in Mer Rouge was deplorable.

Dr. McKoin decided that conditions and the absence of respect ought to be dramatized. He went out on a rural call one night, inexpertly pumped some shots through the back of his Ford car, and came back to town saying that a criminal gang had tried to kill him. The Klan put the blame on a planter's son, Watt Daniel, and his friend, Tom Richards, a garage mechanic. They had been saying belittling things about the Klan and had actually been caught spying on one of its meetings. Masked men seized Daniel and Richards in broad daylight, and took them out in the woods. They were accused of having shot at Doc McKoin but were turned loose after being warned about their general misconduct.

This, however, was not to be the end of things. What was needed, the Klan realized, was a more impressive lesson, for Watt and Tom were still talking. On August 24, 1922, most of the population of the parish had been to a barbecue and baseball game in Bastrop, organized to interest them in a new bond issue for good roads. Afterward, the cars going back to Mer Rouge came upon an unexpected obstacle. An automobile was turned across the road, apparently having engine trouble. When the cars stopped, they were surrounded by masked Klansmen carrying shotguns. The Klansmen had commandeered the ferry and closed all roads between Bastrop and Mer Rouge; since midafternoon, they had blocked all communication. Innocent automobiles coming into town had been turned back or rerouted at the barricades. Cap'n Skip ordered the telephone girl in Bastrop to stop all messages between Mer Rouge and Bastrop, and when she refused, the lines went dead. A spotter in white robes went down the row of cars halted at the barrier. He came to one car and pointed to Watt Daniel. "That's the man we want." As women screamed, Daniel, Richards, their fathers, and another man were seized by the masked figures in black robes, who blindfolded and hog-tied them and heaved them into the back of a waiting Ford truck.

The captives were taken to a clearing in the woods. The elder Daniel, seventy, and one of his companions were tied to trees and lashed with a leather strap. Watt Daniel managed to get loose trom the ropes that held him and tried to fight his way through to his father. In doing so, he grabbed the mask of one of the floggers and ripped it off. He recognized the face framed by the torn borders of cloth and called aloud the name of the Klansman, as the others overpowered him. His friend, Richards, either heard the name or recognized the now-unveiled Klansman. It was to cost them both their lives, for their captors carried them deeper into the woods. Late that night the three older men were released, but there was no word of Daniel or Richards. In the two towns of Bastrop and Mer Rouge, men armed and gathered in the streets. In Bastrop there were reports over the next days that "they" were on the way from Mer Rouge, and Old Skip deployed his men around the courthouse, checked the mails and the telephones, and examined everyone for identity and arms.

It was in this atmosphere that Governor Parker had sent his message to Washington for aid. The Klansmen in Bastrop boasted that they knew the identity of the federal agents and talked of "taking care" of them as they had of Watt Daniel and Richards. But while one group of agents deliberately drew attention to themselves, another, working quietly, had gathered a considerable amount of information. In November, Governor Parker and his attorney general went to Washington to consult with President Harding and the Justice Department, but the national administration felt it did not have jurisdiction to go further. Local Louisiana officials and congressmen claimed that law and order did prevail in the state, and the legislature was not interested in Parker's proposal for the public registration of Klan members. Governor Parker denounced the Klan at the Governors' Conference in Hot Springs, Virginia; in Chicago; and in various cities of his own state, but the Klan seemed scarcely daunted. "Lyncher John and Dago Cocacola [the governor and attorney general] have been transformed by the witchcraft of Romanism," a pro-Klan minister wrote in a Leesville paper, and in a meeting near Baton Rouge, the Klan initiated a thousand new members. Along the northern border, men kept their weapons close at hand and the night riding of the Klan continued.

The attorney general was ready to act, but to do so he had to have the bodies of Watt Daniel and Richards. The federal investigators had reported in September that the corpses had been cast into one of the deep lakes in the parish. However, with conditions as they were, no one had been so bold as to search the lakes and dispute with the garfish and alligators for their prey. Finally, toward the end of the fall, Governor Parker sent in a company of infantry to protect the dragging of the lakes. Late one night, a large charge of dynamite was exploded in Lake Lafourche. A few hours later, two badly mutilated bodies, bound with bands of rusted wire, were found floating on the surface. Who had set off the explosives, no one knew, and the rumors said that the attempt had been to destroy the evidence rather than to reveal it.

The bodies were hideously mangled. The victims had first been flogged and then some sort of torture machine had crushed and splintered all of the bones in the still-living bodies. Afterwards the pulped corpses had been mutilated and dismembered. Only the torsos had floated to the top of Lafourche's dark waters, but they were positively identified by various fragments of clothing.

With the courthouse in Bastrop heavily guarded by infantrymen and machine gunners sent in by the governor, a grand jury held its investigation. Dr. McKoin, who had quietly slipped away to brush up on his medicine at Johns Hopkins in Baltimore, gave up his fight against extradition and voluntarily returned. The much discussed "torture machine" was identified as the cleated wheels of a large road-grading tractor which had been driven over Daniel and Richards. Klansmen identified themselves and testified about Klan floggings but denied participation in this particular affair. Klansmen and the attorney general raced to see who could first get to crucial witnesses. Numerous people identified the Klansmen who had taken part in the abduction. Alibis were offered, challenged, maintained. The time sheet of the principal suspect was tampered with to show that he had been at work on the night of the murder. Klan supporters claimed that Daniel and Richards were not dead and showed scrawled notes allegedly signed by them which had been sent from various parts of the country. There was expert testimony that the bodies had been in the water for only a short time. Old Skip told his cohorts to "be good" while the heat was on. Two successive grand juries, whose membership contained known and alleged Klansmen, refused to indict anyone, reporting only that the parish needed a new jail and repairs on the courthouse roof.

The best that Governor Parker could do was to hold open hearings on Klan night riding and to push for conviction of some of the suspects on various minor misdemeanors. Old Skip got off with a ten-dollar fine for raiding a still. As something of a national celebrity, he gave little speeches to neighboring Klan rallies and took a group of his Klansmen to Atlanta to support Simmons against the new Imperial

Wizard, Hiram Evans. A number of the Morehouse Parish Klansmen involved in the Daniel case left the state, most of them migrating to the little town of Marfa, in Texas' Rio Grande Valley. Governor Parker continued to denounce the Klan and refused to promote several district judges because of their membership. In Morehouse Parish, he appointed a Jewish sheriff. The publication of the names of Klan members was proving increasingly embarrassing to them. In the city of Lafayette it led to a minor mutiny in the National Guard when an officer's name appeared on the list. In the state generally, Klan-supported political candidates were not doing well.

In the state elections of 1924, the Klan was an important issue. Local candidates were forced to take a stand, and in the race for governor none of the three hopefuls were on the Klan's side. The two leading candidates, a Roman Catholic from the French parishes to the south and a Protestant from Baton Rouge, promised legislative action against the Invisible Empire. This left the third contestant, a young lawyer from the North named Huey Long, out in the cold. Huey doggedly campaigned on economic issues and his opposition to entrenched wealth, trying to ignore the embarrassing Klan question which could cost him votes in the northern and central parts of the state. Although he did not favor the Klan, his silent attempts to straddle led many to accuse him of being its candidate. The future King-fish finished third, and Henry Fuqua, the Protestant from Baton Rouge, won in the runoff.

The first order of business was the Klan. Uncle Henry Fuqua had won on a campaign platform of the end of strife and the unmasking of the Klan. To this end, even a great many of the Klansmen themselves willingly co-operated. In the interests of harmony, the leadership in the legislature was deliberately divided. An active Klansman became the speaker of the house; the presidency of the senate went to a Roman Catholic. Within a week after his inauguration the governor's bills were introduced, and they became law in less than a month.

There were three bills in all. One required the annual filing of membership lists by all such organizations. If any member attended a meeting of a society which had not turned in such a list, he was committing a crime punishable with imprisonment. A second bill prohibited the wearing of masks in public on occasions other than Halloween, school affairs, minstrel shows, and Mardi Gras. The final one listed as felonies a long string of crimes, including simple threat, if committed by the wearer of a mask. Although half a dozen Klan senators forecast retaliation, war, and the destruction of liberty if the registration bill were passed, the antimask and felony bills gained assent with no more than two or three votes in opposition. The floor manager who steered them through was an avowed Klansman from Millikin.

The national headquarters in Atlanta was furious. All of those who had voted for the bills, including two Grand Titans and the speaker of the house, were expelled from the Klan. This in turn caused mass dropouts among members particularly from the Monroe and Lake Charles Klaverns. Other Klansmen hastily quit during the period of grace at the end of which all members of the Invisible Empire would have to have their names publicly listed.

The Louisiana Klan was busy reorganizing itself to face its new circumstances. The conduct of realm affairs was placed in the hands of a triumvirate of Klansmen, including Judge W. C. Barnette of Shreveport, who had defended Old Skip and the Bastrop Klansmen. Together with the national headquarters in Atlanta, they concocted a plan. On the proscribed registration day at the end of December of 1924, the Klan officials filed lists of the members of its fifty-nine male and thirteen female chapters. In each case only the names of the officers were listed. All other Klansmen had been secretly assigned to membership rolls in Atlanta and other states. Though the Klansmen sometimes rode at night or paraded through their capital city of Shreveport, the Klan's device had much unintended truth to it. Klan membership and power had shriveled. The people of Louisiana were weary of the Invisible Empire and the memory of the victims of Morehouse Parish. In 1926, when the wet, Catholic Edwin Broussard came up for re-election to the U. S. Senate, the joint opposition of the Klan and the Anti-Saloon League could not turn him back. Ambitious Huey Long read the winds of the future and turned his back on the Klan prejudices to build political friendships by rallying his dry, Protestant followers for "Couzain Ed." The big thing abuilding in the state of Louisiana was the Kingfish; the Invisible Empire of the Ku Klux Klan was a thing of the past.

9

MISSISSIPPI: FIERY CROSSES
ON THE LEVEE

The story of the reborn Ku Klux Klan in Mississippi was not as lurid as that of her neighboring realms to the west. Here, as elsewhere, the Klan was a town phenomenon, and it spread through the centers of population from the black prairie and the clay hills to the piney woods towns of the south and the brown hills and Mississippi delta.

The best account of the Klan and what it meant in Mississippi comes from William Alexander Percy's classic of Southern life, *Lanterns on the Levee*. The Percys were old-line, aristocratic, big planters in Washington County in the heart of the delta. Although the newly infiltrating red-neck farmers from the clay hills viewed the planters with ill-concealed populist and evangelical suspicion, the delta of the Percys' had been a reasonably orderly world. Dominant white and subordinate Negro, Jew, Italian, Irishman, Chinaman, Dane, and Syrian lived comfortably together. Drunkenness, lechery, Sabbath-breaking and gambling were more a matter of personal judgment than sin, and the Masons had a Roman Catholic member.

The better citizens read uneasily and scornfully about the revived Klan, but its first appearance in Greenville surprised them. In the spring of 1922 there were advertisements that a "Colonel" Camp would hold a meeting in the courthouse to organize a Klan chapter. Obviously there had to be Klansmen about, so it was decided that former Senator LeRoy Percy, William Alexander's father, should be there to reply to the "colonel."

On the night of the meeting, the room was packed with tense citizens, most of them armed, all of them suspicious. The Klan speaker got right down to business. Who had killed President Garfield? A Catholic! Who had assassinated President McKinley? A Catholic! Who had recently bought huge tracts of land opposite the military academy at West Point and overlooking Washington? The Pope!

Convents were, in reality, brothels and the confessional was a place of seduction! Arms were being stored in church basements as the Pope got ready to seize the government. Klansmen must rise to the rescue!

However, to the surprise of the Klan "colonel," it was Senator Percy who rose. Speaking to an approving home-town crowd, his irony was devastating, and he buried the Klansman's case in a withering barrage of ridicule. As the roaring crowd shouted approval of a resolution condemning the Klan, Colonel Camp scuttled for the door. A Roman Catholic deputy sheriff provided him escort to his hotel.

But despite this initial, never to be overcome setback to its reputation, the Klan prospered and spread in Greenville and elsewhere in the state. And, as in Greenville, it divided and soured the communities into which it came. Friendliness and easygoing relationships yielded to suspicion.

Klansmen kept watch for the bootlegger along the Mississippi River and guarded the southern Gulf Coast against the rum runners, but their role tended to be that of informants for the federal Prohibition agents rather than participants in direct action. But the Klan was the Klan, and the black lakes of Morehouse Parish were only a short way across the river from the Percy home in Greenville. The Percys went armed, as did many others in Mississippi, and locked their doors at dusk. One rainy night a rough-looking man came to the Percy mansion and insisted the senator come out and give him help with his stalled car. The arrival of company led the caller to change his mind about his need for aid, and the younger Percy afterwards always believed that his father had been marked for violence. He went downtown to the Klan offices to announce in no uncertain terms that harm to the senator would mean the death of the local Klan leader.

The primary role of the Klan was the defense of state and society against the menace of Roman Catholicism. There weren't many Catholics about but the very scarcity seemed to emphasize the subterranean nature of the peril. The Klan first set down its roots among the Masons of Mississippi where the atmosphere was not always uncongenial to anti-Catholicism. Much of the initial leadership of the Klan came from the upper circles of state Masonry, supplemented by ambitious local politicians. Catholics lost their jobs, saw their businesses boycotted and their elections opposed.

But not all Masons, or Protestants, were anti-Catholic, for there were those among the common folk as well as the planters who resolutely opposed the Klan. Some of the most respected men in the state took the lead. Although Percy was the most active, the venerable John Sharp Williams, newly retired from the U. S. Senate, hurled his potent shafts into the Klan. In 1923 the Invisible Empire supported the idol of the piney woods folk, James K. Vardaman, when he lost his fight to succeed Williams in the Senate, and it failed again in its attempt to defeat long-time Vicksburg congressman, John W. Collier.

Things were looking up by the next year, and the high point of Klan influence in the Magnolia State was probably reached when the Democrats gathered to pick their delegates to the National Convention in Madison Square Garden. A minority of the seats were given to non-Klansmen, including Senator Pat Harrison who was to deliver the national keynote, but it was a Klan delegation bound together to vote as a unit.

After 1924 the Klan was beginning to decline. In Greenville, the local Klan put all of its strength into an effort to elect a Klansman as sheriff. As usual the Percys led the opposition. It was a markedly bitter contest. No one could tell who was Klan and who was not, and the outcome was in doubt. Several hours after the polls closed, a sweating, red-faced man came rushing up to the Percy mansion where the senator was playing bridge on the porch. "We've won! We've won!" he cried, with tears pouring down his face. "Alexander's elected! God damn the Klan!" A deliriously happy crowd, singing as it went, marched by torchlight to the mansion. The senator made a speech, but, as his son recalled, everyone was too happy to listen. He realized it, stopped, and had the kegs brought out. Everyone drank and danced; the banker's wife whirled around with the hottamale man. It was a party to be long remembered, the Percy chronicler recorded, while the "Ku Klux neighbors stood on their porches watching . . . and prophesying Judgment Day."

Although the Percys, Greenville, and the delta were far from representative of the tides of men and events that marked the state, Klan influence continued to slip away. A bishop told the conference of Methodist churchmen that membership in the Klan was outdated for the clergy. A Texas lawyer took over from the home-town, Canton, Mississippi boy who had been Grand Dragon since the chartering of the realm. From his suite in the Henry Memorial Building in Jackson, Grand Dragon Wankan reorganized his Klaverns—"to drop out the undesirable material from the mass mobilization days"—and further hastened the decline of his forces. His big issue was predictably the Roman threat. The Klan, he announced, would seek a delegation to the 1928 Democratic convention committed to oppose the nomination of Al Smith. In his fight against anything short of outright resistance to the party's inevitable nominee, he denounced those who sought to compromise the issue with an uninstructed delegation. This brought him into conflict with the major powers in state politics, Senator Pat Harrison and Governor-elect Theodore Bilbo. Governor Bilbo, himself a one-time Klansman, was to help defeat the forces of prejudice and keep the state for Smith in the national election by passing about the story that Herbert Hoover had danced with a Negro woman while administering flood relief in Mississippi the previous year.

By this time the Klan had become so unimportant that when an unmasking law was suggested, an editorial in the Jackson *Daily News* could sum up popular feeling in the phrase "Don't kick the corpse."

10

GEORGIA: THE KLAN TABERNACLE

One of the major themes in the history of the Ku Klux Klan in the twentieth century has been its long-lived relationship with the state of Georgia. The Klan was reborn there in the fertile mind of Colonel Simmons and consecrated on the top of Stone Mountain, which for almost fifty years has been sacred soil for the Invisible Empire. It was in Georgia that Simmons picked up his first disciples, recruited his salesmen, and officered and staffed his armies. Although his successor, Hiram W. Evans, the Dallas dentist, introduced his Southwesterners into the command strata, Klan leadership has traditionally been strongly Georgian. Despite an expansive foray into Washington, D.C., during the middle twenties, Atlanta was the capital of the order. It was here that the Klan expanded from its first headquarters in the loft of the Georgia Savings Building and Edward Young Clarke's Southern Publicity Associates office above the never sleeping eye on an oculist's window, and moved upward in the world to the Imperial Palace on Peachtree Street. The hotels of Atlanta filled with Klan potentates who came to attend Klonciliums and Klonvokations, and the streets of the state's towns and hamlets bore the sound of tramping feet and the swishing robes of hooded marchers. It was here that Emperor Simmons dreamed of founding his Klan university to teach the principles of one-hundred-per-cent Americanism, and it was on the lonely roads and sylvan glens that the Klan took up the lash as its primer.

For fifty years, Imperial Wizards have come to Atlanta to take up their reigns. Cities and towns have borne or resisted the Klan, celebrated it with fish fries and chicken dinners, sheltered its Klaverns or banned its processionals, cheered it or turned in revulsion from it. The Klan has dwelt in Georgia for half a century, won elections and lost them, seen its ranks thin and its almost constant procession of powerful friends in high office waver. And through the years, Georgia has been its tabernacle.

Almost from the beginning of its expansion in the early twenties, the Klan undertook a vigilante role in Georgia. A Klan parade in Columbus warned against loafing, thieving, and prowling by either black or white. Lebanese and Syrians were ordered to leave Marietta. Members of the Atlanta Board of Education, who opposed firing all Roman Catholic teachers, received warning letters. In Columbus the mayor's home was dynamited when he refused to remove his "blue-bellied Yankee" city manager, but after a beating at the hands of "persons unknown," the city manager got the message and left town.

On the whole, Klan violence in Georgia did not reach the general crescendo of that in the brasher Texas and Oklahoma realms, although local epidemics of flogging in the mid-twenties matched those anywhere else in the Invisible Empire. The frontier tradition of direct action has long lingered in the South, and has gained added strength as one of the entrenched folkways of race relations. In Georgia, the will to violence was fueled by the bitterly anti-Catholic and anti-Semitic campaigns of the one-time Populist great, Tom Watson. The lynching of the Jewish factory owner, Leo Frank, after his exoneration of the rape-murder of one of his employees, helped shape and prepare the way for the Klan. Despite this heritage, the Georgia Klan seldom directed its violence toward Jew, Roman Catholic, and Negro. They were objects of its semantics, but its direct action was visited primarily on its fellow white, native-born Protestants. The main role of the individual Klaverns, however, was their lodge function. When Colonel Simmons and their other leaders talked tough, it was directed more at the Southerner's picture of himself as "one hell of a fellow," than sounding a call to action.

Politics, however, was a major outlet and use of Klan power. From the very beginning the Ku Klux Klan gathered important recruits and friends. In Atlanta prominent lawyers, members of the city council and the school board were Klansmen. Paul S. Etheridge found that being the Imperial Klonsel and then chief of staff of the Klan did not interfere with his re-election to the Fulton County (Atlanta) Board of Commissioners. The editor of the Klan's official newspaper was also a member of the state legislature. When the House of Representatives in Washington investigated the Klan in 1921, Georgia Congressman William D. Upshaw and Senator Tom Watson rose to Colonel Simmons' defense.

Although Governor Thomas W. Hardwick praised the Invisible Empire when the New York *World* asked for his response to its exposé, he demanded of the Klan that it unmask and cease its violence.

The Klan leaders went to confer with the governor and pretended agreement. Instead, they rallied their speakers and legions to help former state Attorney General Clifford Walker beat him in the 1922 elections. With Walker as governor there was not going to be any trouble about who would call on and comply with whom. At the National Convention of the Klan, Walker promised that if the organization got into any trouble he would not report it to the newspapers or the electorate. "I am not going to denounce anybody," he told the assembled Klansmen, "I am coming right here to your leaders and talk to you."

Along with the new governor, the state superintendents of education and agriculture were friendly with the Klan and drew its backing. The Klan was also close with the elder Richard B. Russell, the much respected Chief Justice of the Supreme Court of Georgia, and Klan leaders conferred with Walker and Russell on state policy. However, in 1924, when Russell wanted to run for U. S. Senator, the Klan dissuaded him by arguing that it was already supporting incumbent Senator William J. Harris.

In the 1924 elections, the Invisible Empire was interested in even bigger game than a U. S. Senator. The state of Georgia had been generally conceded to the forces of presidential hopeful, Senator Oscar W. Underwood of neighboring Alabama. However, Underwood had been outspoken in his opposition to the Invisible Empire. A few days before the primary, candidate William Gibbs McAdoo, Woodrow Wilson's son-in-law and wartime Secretary of the Treasury, came to speak in Georgia. During a public appearance in Macon, one of the state's top Klan leaders rose to question him about his position on religious freedom. McAdoo replied that he stood "four square on the Constitution" and the First Amendment but did not mention the Klan. The answer was satisfactory, and the Klan threw its strength behind him. The Underwood people calculated that this meant forty thousand Klansmen plus their families and friends, and it was enough to carry the state.

At the Democratic National Convention in Madison Square Garden after a dramatic internal conflict, Georgia delivered the crucial votes that beat back the plank condemning the Klan. Georgia stood firm for McAdoo for one hundred ballots, but with the national Klan working for Calvin Coolidge wherever it could, many Georgia Klansmen switched over, led by M. O. Dunning, who had asked the crucial question of McAdoo in Macon.

But even before 1924, a tide of opposition had been mounting against the Klan. There were probably three particular factors involved in Georgia: violence, the bitter internal struggles constantly going on within the Klan, and the development of a critical, often crusading press, which gave leadership to a growing popular reaction. Almost from the beginning, Klansmen were fighting Klansmen, and the prize was clearly loot rather than principles. During 1921–23 suit after suit hit the Klan as it was constantly in the courts over the probity of its leaders and the possession of its treasury. The ousting and defection of dissidents, the questionable history and behavior of Edward Young Clarke and Mrs. Tyler, and the deposition of Colonel Simmons by Hiram Evans cost the Klan loyalty and respect. When Evans' chief public-relations man, Phil Fox, shot Simmons' lawyer, William S. Coburn, and escaped the death sentence with a plea of paranoid insanity, the image of the Klan was not enhanced. Atlanta was particularly unenchanted, as a reporter for the New York *Times* put it, with being the tub in which all of the dirty linen of the Klan was washed.

In the struggles between Simmons and Evans, one of the principal sufferers was Atlanta's Nathan Bedford Forrest Klan No. 1 which for the most part sided with the loser. The mother Klan of Klandom was suspended and then reorganized (by Nathan Bedford Forrest III), but lost several thousand members in the process. Meetings of insurgent Klansmen called by Clarke and by Simmons said worse things about the Klan than any outsider did.

In Macon, 1923 was the year of an epidemic of Klan floggings. At least six men and women were kidnaped and beaten. The night riders clashed with the police, who eventually set up a special round-the-clock "antiflogging squad" of motorcycle officers to answer all calls for help. Washington sent in investigators, and Governor Walker himself offered the militia. When the Klansmen, led by a local doctor, were finally captured, the testimony was not helpful to the Klan, even though the jury refused to convict.

Among the things brought out was that the state capitol building had been used for Klan initiations, and the ties between the visible government and the Invisible Empire had begun to trouble many people. A former woman legislator attacked the governor for "hanging his hood and nightie" in the state capitol. In 1924 the Atlanta *Constitution* broke the story that Governor Walker had traveled secretly to Kansas City to address a closed meeting of Klan bigwigs on the topic of "Americanism." He had covered such vital points as the "threatened destruction of America and Americanism" by the encroachment of Jews and Catholics and by the way in which a "gang of Roman Catholic Priests" had taken charge of the Democratic convention. When the press pushed him, Governor Walker admitted having given the speech. Although he had joined the Klan, his role, he maintained, had always been an inactive one. In his speech, Walker had accused Woodrow Wilson's private secretary, Joseph Tumulty, with having discriminated against Protestant churches during the war. When the irate Tumulty suggested a Protestant tribunal of the governor's own choosing as a court to hear proof of the charges, Walker, whom the press dubbed "Kautious Kleagle Kliff," made no reply.

Some portions of the state and some of its leaders had resolutely opposed the Klan, and their number was growing. The Invisible Empire did not do particularly well in Savannah. In Albany, the mayor and city council denied the Klan the use of the municipal auditorium. Ex-Senator and Governor Hardwicke continued to run for office on anti-Klan platforms. Editor James C. Williams of the *Herald-Journal* helped to keep Greene County unfriendly. Andrew Erwin, editor of the *Banner-Herald* and twice mayor of Athens, fought the Klan as editor, public official, and in a memorable speech at the Democratic National Convention.

The chief antagonist of the Klan in Georgia was Julian Harris, editor of the Columbus *Enquirer-Sun*. Columbus was a typical small Southern city. Its citizens accepted the traditional sectional fundamentalism which vaunted superiority of the white race, the Protestant religion, and the Democratic party. In 1921 there were about five hundred Klansmen in Columbus, operating with the endorsement of the city officials, and holding their meetings in the armory above police headquarters. In that year, Julian Harris bought into the local paper for the purpose of speaking out for racial understanding and justice, and for honest government. The son of the beloved teller of the Uncle Remus tales, Julian Harris, had turned his back on the big metropolitan press of the North and Europe to come home to Georgia.

His was the only paper in Georgia to carry the *World*'s series on the Klan and to send a reporter to Dayton, Tennessee, to cover the Scopes trial. His was also the only paper to print the protest of the University of Georgia students over the attempted appointment of pro-Klan Chief Justice Russell as chancellor. The *Enquirer-Sun* lost circulation; Harris' friends cautioned him, and the Klan sent him warnings, but when hooded marchers paraded past his building carrying signs announcing that America was for the gentiles and that "Rome works while Protestantism sleeps," Harris and his city editor dashed out on the sidewalk to take notes.

The *Enquirer-Sun* took the popular booster slogan, "It's great to be a Georgian," as its keynote. "Is it great to be a citizen of a state which is the proud parent of a cowardly hooded order founded and fostered by men who have been proved liars, drunkards, blackmailers, and murderers?" Julian Harris asked on his editorial page. "Is it great to be a citizen of a state whose governor is a member of and subservient to that vicious masked gang, and whose officials are either members or in sympathy with it? . . . Is it great to be a citizen of such a state? Is it great to be a Georgian?"

When Rev. Caleb Ridley, an Atlanta minister and sometimes chief chaplain of the Klan, was picked up by the traffic police, Harris wrote about it in an editorial entitled "The Drunken Kludd." When a Prohibition officer killed a bootlegger, Harris called it putting out a fire with gasoline. When a group of legislators introduced an anti-evolution bill, he blistered them as "thirteen midget-minded imitators of King Canute." He denounced Calvin Coolidge for appointing Klansman M. O. Dunning as Collector of the Port of Savannah. He satirized the "liquid test of statesmanship" followed by many Protestant churches and called Georgia "the Empire State of Illiteracy." When a mob openly lynched a lunatic and no attempt was made to do anything about it, he asked if this made his readers feel "that it was great to be a Georgian."

The *Enquirer-Sun* printed news of the Negro community, brought in good wire-service coverage and worked on its page make-up. A number of other papers, such as the *Madisonian,* the Dalton *Citizen,* the Americus *Times-Recorder,* the Cobb County *Times* and the Cartersville *Tribune-News,* were beginning to follow Harris' pattern and speak out on the Klan. In 1925, Julian Harris and the Columbus *Enquirer-Sun* won a Pulitzer prize for public service.

By 1926 the Georgia Realm of the Ku Klux Klan was decidedly on the wane. Hiram Evans had moved his headquarters to the nation's capital in Washington, D.C., and Klan officialdom had followed him there. The deposed Emperor Simmons' imperial home had been sold and the once-proud Imperial Palace on Peachtree Street was tenanted only by a night watchman.

However, the Klan was greatly interested in the state elections that year. An impressive list of its members and friends were up for election. Senator Walter George had voted for American adherence to the World Court, and Judge Russell and the Klan had decided to oppose him. Governor Walker was retiring after two terms. Klan *Searchlight* editor, J. O. Woods, who had run for the state legislature on a platform demanding more rigid inspection of convents and institutions run by religious orders, wanted to succeed him. And there were many others of the hooded order out on the hustings. The eventual results were disaster for the Klan. Every candidate it supported, lost. George won, as did Supreme Court candidate, Judge J. K. Hines, who openly lambasted the Klan during the campaign. J. O. Woods came last in the primary.

But although its state-wide political power declined, the Klan still rode at night in many communities. In Toombs and nearby counties the night riders had been spreading terror for almost two years. They picked both men and women as their flogging victims and more than one murder resulted. When local juries failed to convict, the Klan marauders became sufficiently emboldened to kidnap and flog one of the lawyers who had assisted in the prosecution. Both Governor Walker and Grand Dragon Forrest denounced this particular episode. Forrest found the floggings to have been outrageous and therefore not the actions of Klansmen, while the governor threatened martial law unless action was taken.

The lines against violence were generally tightening in the state. In July of 1927, a pair of floggers were rewarded with a year's sentence on the chain gang. In Stephens County, near the South Carolina line, a score of such episodes had taken place over a four-year period. In the case that finally brought retribution, the lash had been laid on for sixty-one strokes on the back of a woman who was charged with "immorality and failure to go to church." When her fifteen-year-old son responded to her screams, he too was beaten. The man who held her head and directed the floggings turned out to be the principal of the Stephens County High School, superintendent of the Baptist Sunday School, and moderator of the twenty Baptist churches of his association.

Such episodes had long since come to subtract from, rather than add to Klan strength in Georgia. And so the Klan continued to slip in 1928. The liquidation of its assets proceeded with the sale of its office building in Atlanta, and in 1928 the Klan's stand in national politics cost it additional members. With Forrest rallying his depleted forces to man the barricades against the candidacy of Al Smith, a number of Atlanta Klansmen were reportedly expelled for refusing to pledge against Smith, and others indignantly resigned over being asked. In its empire state, the Klan's gutted candle flickered weakly, though it was far from burned out.

11

THE HEART OF DIXIE

The story of the Klan in Alabama closely followed the pattern of Georgia, apart from the latter's role as the site of the national head-quarters. There was the same early connection with Klan personages and affairs, the initial night riding, the capture of the largest city, the movement into state politics, and the unsuccessful opposition of a major leader, the acceleration of violence in rural counties, the growing opposition led by firm-willed local newspaper editors, and the subsequent decline. But, of course, there were many differences. Alabama is Alabama, and her story was her own.

Both Emperor Simmons and Hiram W. Evans, his successor as Imperial Wizard, came from the same farming and lumber region in central Alabama though they probably met for the first time in the Klan's Imperial Palace in Atlanta. Alabama appeared in the records of the twentieth-century Klan in 1916, when an organizer sent to capture the encampment of Confederate veterans there absconded with his collections. The resulting court case, the first in what was to be a long tradition, was handled by an efficient young county prosecutor, Hugo Black, whose name was to wander in and out of Klan affairs. Black next showed up, not as a prosecutor or a Klansman, but as a defending lawyer of a Klansman. In 1921 the daughter of a Catholic-hating former Methodist minister changed her religion and married a Puerto Rican. The irate father shot the priest who performed the service, and lawyer Black helped convince the jury that this constituted justifiable homicide.

The Klan had picked up a few early wartime recruits in Alabama and generally kept an eye on things. After the war it expanded its surveillance. It backed up an official antivice campaign in Anniston and worked over a Roman Catholic druggist in Sylacauga. The Sylacauga Klan decided that it would be a good idea if the druggist and all the Jews and Catholics got out of town, while the Birmingham Klavern reportedly pressed employers to fire their Roman Catholic workers. The Klan was particularly active in Birmingham's Jefferson County. From a double flogging in the summer of 1921, it had moved on to reportedly more than a score of victims in 1922. Included among its victims was the city health officer who had offended by his "too Kaiser-like" behavior in office.

The response in Birmingham was an outburst of protest. The better citizens, led by their ministers, merchants, and the local bar association, pressed for an antimask ordinance, and a defensive "Law Enforcement League" was temporarily formed. Although the city commission passed an antikidnaping law, it refused to make it unlawful for masked men to gather in public places. The reason was quite apparent. In September of 1923, Birmingham's Robert E. Lee Klan No. 1 staged a monster rally to celebrate its seventh anniversary. A city park was leased and invitations were sent out across the South. After a day of picnicking and games, and a parade through downtown Birmingham, an audience of nearly twenty thousand Klansmen and twice that number of spectators watched two thousand new members march eight abreast to take their oaths in the flickering light of burning crosses, and be sworn into the Invisible Empire. Local political leaders were not interested in opposing so powerful an organization, and it is generally accepted that at this ceremony the rising young politician and inveterate joiner, Hugo Black, became a member.

The Klan remained in a minority in the state. It failed to gain political control in the other major cities of Montgomery and Mobile and in a large number of rural counties. But in Birmingham, the iron and steel center of the South and the largest city of Alabama, the Klan had become entrenched. Of the approximately thirty-two thousand voters in Birmingham's Jefferson County, the Klan was generally credited with fifteen to eighteen thousand. Many of the local judicial and political officials and police officers were Klansmen.

Against this, Alabama's senior and nationally respected Senator Oscar W. Underwood stood out in loud and bold opposition. Campaigning hard for the presidential nomination of the Democratic party, whose spokesman he had been in the Senate during the administration of Woodrow Wilson, Underwood waged ceaseless battle against the hooded order. Although the rank and file of Klan members were increasingly bitter and Klansmen elsewhere fiercely condemned him, the Alabama leaders hesitated to tangle openly with him. Underwood was an esteemed leader, and his candidacy was a matter of considerable state pride. Unsuccessful opposition would result in a dangerous loss of prestige. Although Klansmen were reputedly in the delegation, Alabama remained loyal to him at the National Convention. For 103 ballots, the roll call in Madison Square Garden began with the Alabama delegation, in top hats, casting "Twenty-foah votes foah Oscar W. Underwood."

With Underwood's failure to win the nomination, the Klan came out in open attack. His Senate term was to run out in 1927, and as the time approached he put off announcing his candidacy for re-election, and finally withdrew. The Klan crowingly took credit and was probably right. The New York *Times* reported that he had quit in utter disgust.

The Klan in Alabama reached its greatest power during the years 1925–26. It drew regular dues from at least fifty thousand members and occasionally from perhaps as many more. This strength was concentrated in Birmingham and in the central portion of the state. The word went out that membership was to be a requirement for jobs after the election, and applications flooded in from police, firemen, and all levels of municipal and county officeholders. The Thursday-night meetings of Robert E. Lee No. 1 were swamped. It seemed clear that Klan favor would be necessary for all hopeful candidates and one of those who saw the signs of the times was Hugo Black. He solicited and received the support of Grand Dragon James Esdale, and, with the latter's consent, formally resigned from the Klan in order to be safe from hostile charges of membership.

In the 1926 elections Hugo Black was sent to the U. S. Senate and Klansmen Bibb Graves and Charles C. McCall were elected governor and attorney general. Imperial Wizard Hiram Evans journeyed from Atlanta to attend an exultant secret celebration. Amid much horseplay and verbal violence against Negroes and Roman Catholics, Graves and Black expressed their appreciation for Klan aid and accepted gold-engraved lifetime passports to the Invisible Empire.

But the very success of the Klan proved its undoing. It controlled the votes and jobs in Birmingham, and its influence and power reached into the top offices of the state. Businessmen were putting TWK placards in their windows to urge that the faithful and the fearful "trade with a Klansman." The Klan was feeling its oats. Grand Dragon Esdale particularly overreached himself. When the new Attorney General McCall announced that Esdale was to be appointed assistant attorney general the protests were furious. Governor Graves, who had been cooling to Esdale's increasing demands for patronage and power, offered no support, and the whole thing was eventually dropped. Success was just not turning out well for James Esdale and the Klan. The Birmingham *Age-Herald* published reports of Klan speeches, including one by Esdale, advocating whipping for opponents of the Invisible Empire. Esdale and Attorney General McCall sued for libel, but the defendants hit upon the interesting tactic of calling upon each member of Birmingham's Robert E. Lee Klan to take the stand. When the court upheld this line of defense, the Klan lost interest. It now shifted to a different approach.

In August of 1927, the lower house of the Alabama legislature proposed laws to silence the press. Fines for libelous criticism of state, city, or local officials would run as high as $25,000, and to make sure that the charges would stick, the attorney general could try the case in any county he wished. A further provision was to make the law retroactive to cover the preceding twelve months. The opposition to what was quickly known as the "Graves-Klan Muzzling Bill" was led by a legislator from anti-Klan Montgomery. It was a close fight. One bill lost by a tie and a second was defeated only by clever parliamentary maneuvering in the Senate.

With the growth of its connections and power in the state, the reports of Klan night riding had assumed alarming proportions by early 1927. When Klansmen took someone out and flogged him, they usually told him to be quiet about it afterwards—and sometimes to leave the state—and wisdom usually dictated that he heed their warnings. The number of people who were secretly kidnaped and flogged in lonely wooded clearings will never be known. In 1927 the Birmingham *News* guessed that scores, perhaps hundreds, had felt the lash over the past five years, mainly for possession of slot machines and sale or possession of liquor.

A few brave editors told the people of Alabama what they thought about it, and a curious set of circumstances led the attorney general to take action. Word was coming in of floggings in Jefferson, Blount, Talladega, and Randolph counties around Birmingham, and in Butler and Crenshaw counties in the south. A naturalized citizen was whipped because he married an "American" woman, so were a white divorcee, a young girl for keeping the wrong company, a Negro farmer who refused to sell his land, and many others. Editors like Victor Hanson of the Birmingham *News* were speaking out, but the man who really gave vent to the feelings of an increasing number of Alabamans was Grover Cleveland Hall of the Montgomery *Advertiser*. A new and well-established outdoor sport had taken over in "the Chivalrous South," he commented. There was a time in the

South when you couldn't lift a hand against a woman and get away with it. Now, when there was a bit of idle gossip against a woman, the Southerner had a new approach: "We bend her over a barrel, or a log, or tie her to a tree and beat the hell out of her—we new Southern gents."

Beginning with his first editorial entitled, "The glove of the beast —will the state pick it up" editor Hall waged a campaign for law enforcement and the end of violence. The police, the governor, and state officials showed a touching concern over the sale of liquor; why didn't they do something about violence and upholding the dignity of the state? Why, he asked, were the press, the politicians, and the pulpit so silent? More than a hundred floggings had been reported to the attorney general in one three-year period. Why was nothing being done? The big need was to unmask the Klan which would cut down on violence and make punishment possible. The Alabama papers and the Alabama Klan were drawing nationwide attention, and Editor Hall received a Pulitzer prize that year.

It was this burst of indignation in the press which had led to the "muzzling" bills in the legislature. Those who supported the bills were not necessarily favorable to or influenced by the Klan. What they were in many instances objecting to was the unfavorable publicity that was thus being given to Alabama, and this was their means of doing something about it.

Nor was the opposition to the Ku Klux Klan lodged solely in a small segment of the press. The politicians and people of Montgomery were also in the forefront. The city had long had an antimask ordinance, and in the spring of 1927 it beat back a Klan campaign, directed by Grand Dragon Esdale, in the mayoralty election. A Montgomery man had led the fight against the Graves-Klan Muzzling Bill, and at the same session of the legislature, a law was passed making masked violence a felony.

Other legislators were beginning to bestir themselves, and county judges were less reluctant to call grand juries. However, with so many friends in high places, Klansmen were not alarmed. There seemed little reason to believe that state authorities would prosecute and juries convict. The cast of characters who were involved in the break-through was a most unlikely one. Klansman Bibb Graves was one of the most successful politicians in Alabama's history. A former state adjutant general he had been colonel of an Alabama regiment during World War I. He was a "practical" politician who built his following on a "friendship and favor" relationship with local leaders throughout the state. Klansman Charles McCall was also a veteran and had gained some renown as an amateur boxer while in the A.E.F. Exalted Cyclops Ira Thompson was a former A.E.F. captain and a prominent lodge and churchman. Klansman L. A. Nalls was a Baptist minister.

Governor Graves formally sent Attorney General McCall to investigate a flogging in the southern Alabama farm county of Crenshaw, only to find to his displeasure that McCall's sense of duty led him to do just that. Word now trickled in of some forty floggings in the county, including those of a divorced farmer and the divorcee with two children whom he had married. The Klan had worked over both of them, and after the whipping Reverend Nalls offered her a consoling sermon: "Sister, you were not punished in anger this evening; you were punished in a spirit of kindness and correction, to set your feet aright and to show your children how a good mother should go." A collection for her was taken up among her floggers and the resulting three dollars and fifty cents were given her along with a jar of Vaseline for her wounds.

McCall soon found that his greatest obstacle to successful prosecution was Governor Graves. The governor ordered a special investigation made, but then refused to let his attorney general see it. McCall managed to get a copy of the report anyway. He found it among the papers seized from the safe of the local Klan leader, Ira Thompson. Along with it was a letter to Thompson from Grand Dragon Esdale promising that the co-operation of the governor, "which had been so nobly lent in the past," would be solicited to end the embarrassing proceedings. McCall finally resigned from the Klan with a bitter letter denouncing its criminal actions and its interference with justice. Governor Graves cut the requested money for prosecution expenses down to approximately fifteen dollars a case and went off to Washington to speak at a law-enforcement convention. When the local jury started handing down acquittals, McCall withdrew personally from the cases. Amazingly enough, however, the juries began to convict, and finally several floggers drew sizable prison terms. Exalted Cyclops Thompson admitted that he just "couldn't control" the members, and Reverend Nalls fled to Texas.

With Klansmen actually being sent to jail, past victims were becoming more willing to testify and the effect of it all on the prestige of the Klan was devastating. Klaverns, such as that in Tuscaloosa, disbanded. More and more civic leaders were denouncing the Klan and calling on Governor Graves to disband it. By the end of 1927, the power of the Klan was crumbling.

The campaign against the nomination of wet, Catholic, Tammany-ite, New Yorker Al Smith was not sufficient to counteract the disgrace into which the Klan had fallen. Senator Black, whose Klansmanship had probably been dictated by political survival rather than intense conviction, campaigned for Smith in Alabama. Although it was with no sense of exultation, the state went narrowly for Smith by eight thousand votes. Klan strength fell to an estimated six thousand members in 1928 and to probably half that the following year. Membership in the Klan had become a liability for most, and the story was told of one municipal officeholder who had been elected with Klan support, arranging to have a cross burned in front of his house to restore his reputation.

12

OREGON: PURITANISM REPOTTED

Superficially, Oregon was an unlikely recruiting ground for the Invisible Empire of the Ku Klux Klan. The population was 97 per cent Caucasian with, as one commentator described it, not enough Negroes to man a Pullman car.[1] Eighty-five per cent of the people were native-born, and most of the others came from Canada and northern Europe. Illiteracy was almost nonexistent. Roman Catholics numbered no more than one in twelve. However, Oregon was opened up to the Klan by a combination of inherited anti-Catholicism, isolation, the wartime tradition of suspicion and inquisitiveness, Prohibition, management-labor conflict, and superior salesmanship. The bulk of the Oregonians had come from the Mississippi Valley, and before that from New England. They had brought with them a suspicion of Rome which remained undiluted in the parochial small-town life of Oregon's valleys and broken, hilly coastal plain. The wartime concern about the behavior of one's neighbors combined with the demands of small-town morality to create an atmosphere of suspicion, which the noble experiment of Prohibition did nothing to alleviate. A special feature on the Oregon scene was the Federation of Patriotic Societies. Formed of the representatives of various lodge and fraternal orders, such as the Orange Lodges, the Knights of Pythias, and the Odd Fellows, it had developed during the war as an instrument to counteract the strength of corporate power in Oregon. As the Klan unpacked in Oregon, the railroads and utility companies and the Federation of Patriotic Societies still eyed each other with at least a degree of uncompromised wariness.

The Klan moved across the border from California early in the spring of 1921. As usual it looked about for a local issue and found it in the lax enforcement of Prohibition. Within a week after he had called his first meeting to outline the philosophy of the Klan, Major

[1] Waldo Roberts, "The Ku-Kluxing of Oregon," *Outlook,* 133 (1923), 490.

Luther Powell had signed up 100 members in Jackson County, including most of the local enforcement agents. A high-powered evangelist turned a local revival into a recall movement against the sheriff, and with support from the W.C.T.U. and several churches the Klan was in the law-and-order business. It tried it out on a convicted Negro bootlegger who was warned to depart from town by the device of pulling on the rope around his neck until his toes just barely dragged on the ground. Next, a white salesman who was suing a reputed Klansman was similarly made aware that his presence was not desired, and the same communication was presented to a Negro citizen the next month. Anti-Catholic evangelists and Klan organizers followed in the wake of meetings held by a former Catholic nun. Crosses were burned on the hillsides around Medford. Politicians, including the mayor, hastily got on board, even though the city council had banished parades to surrounding towns by passing an anti-mask ordinance. If the Seventh-Day Adventists had not been brought to the polls by fear of a threatened compulsory public schooling bill, the sheriff would have been recalled.

The Klan pattern in Oregon was now set. First, under the auspices of some Protestant church, an "escaped nun" would tell of her ordeal. Next, the Klan's anti-Catholic and patriotic pamphlets would be slipped into cars and under doors. Then, a fire-branding evangelist or Klan lecturer would whip up feeling against "the Roman Octopus which has taken over control in the nation's capital." Finally, with a local pastor or two leading the way, the Klan would recruit its legions. Within months after its first appearance, the Klan was active throughout the state.

In southwestern Oregon, anti-Catholic lecturers announced that "this is a white, Protestant and Gentile man's country, and they are going to run it." A United States flag was nailed to a Roman Catholic church steeple in Marshfield and a local editor was boycotted as a Papist when he tried to refute anti-Catholic stories. In Eugene, the Klan waged a successful war to prevent the University of Oregon students being corrupted by the opening of a Newman club. The Klan elected city officials in Eugene, Tillamook, and in Astoria near the mouth of the Columbia River. At Condon, in eastern Oregon, a new Congregational minister turned out to be a Klansman. He remodeled the parsonage so the Klan would have room to meet there and formed a boys' club which soon raised its fee to twenty dollars and became a Klan chapter. He took so many Klansmen into his congregation that the others had the devil's very own time in ousting him. When they finally succeeded, he transferred his local Klan business to a downtown office building under a Church of Christ sign.

Klan activity did not go without challenge, as forums and congregations in some Protestant churches rejected it. The Knights of Columbus in Albany offered rewards if Klan accusations could be proven to an impartial non-Catholic jury. Minutemen and Citizens' Leagues were formed to combat the Klan in Yamhill County and Condon, and Klan headquarters in Condon was shot up by unknown gunmen. When the Medford authorities, including its avowed Klan mayor, refused to investigate the three "practice" lynchings, Governor Ben Olcott asked aid from Washington. The Justice Department reported that no federal statute was involved, and so the governor pushed his own proceedings which ensnared leading local citizens, including the ex-chief of police.

Throughout the state the Klan issue spread suspicion, launched boycotts, and divided communities into bitterly antagonistic factions. Yet despite what was taking place, Lawrence J. Saalfeld, the historian of the Klan in Oregon,[2] has pointed out, the press of Oregon said scarcely a word, even on events which were widely reported and discussed outside of the state. Saalfeld estimates that although the Klan had become the major force in politics and was behind the compulsory public school issue, 80 per cent of the papers in the state never mentioned it. Governor Olcott told the Governors' Conference, in 1922, "We woke up one morning and found the Klan had about gained political control of the state. Practically not a word had been raised against them."

Klan politicking, as well as Klan power, centered in Portland, where the driving force was Fred Gifford. A transplanted Minnesotan, Gifford, had worked for Southern Pacific Railroad and the Pacific Telegraph and Telephone. He was the business agent for the Electrical Workers' Union for a while, but left this to become a general superintendent and labor fixer for the power companies in Portland. When the Portland Klan decided to reduce the take to Atlanta and fired its two Kleagles who were squabbling over initiation fees, Gifford assumed leadership. In a short time he was the Grand Dragon of Oregon and the top Klan leader west of the Rockies.

Gifford was not an orator, but he was an able organizer and manipulator. From behind his desk in the Pittock Block in downtown Portland, he ran Klan affairs and tried to run everything else in Ore-

[2] Lawrence J. Saalfeld, "Forces of Prejudice in Oregon, 1920–1925." Unpublished Master's Thesis, Catholic University of America, 1950.

gon. Politicians came seeking endorsement, and orders went out to his growing Klan Empire. The newly organized Capital City Klan in Salem protested his authoritarianism and his handling of the money. Many Klansmen withdrew, but a big Armistice Day rally and field day at the state fairgrounds concealed the split in the pandemonium of bands, colorful uniforms, paraders, and flaming crosses.

According to the best estimates, actual Klan membership by the spring of 1922 was fourteen thousand or only about 2 per cent of the population of the state. It surely continued to climb after the Klan's political successes of that year, and estimates of its ultimate size ran upward from twenty-five thousand. Over half of the Klan's early strength was centered in Portland which was also the home of its affiliate for nonnative born but otherwise one-hundred-per-cent Americans, The Riders of the Red Robe.

Initially, Gifford and the Klan worked along with the Federation of Patriotic Societies. There were sufficient numbers of Klansmen in the member lodges to place Gifford on the board which regularly endorsed candidates for public office. However, conflict developed when the federation refused to let Gifford increase his power by bringing the Klan into the federation. In addition, Gifford and the Klan appeared to have close ties with the big utility corporations which the federation opposed, and the Klan supported men friendly to the utility companies for membership on the Public Service Commission. Gifford's response to the opposition was to split the federation and take over a rival, more conservative, Good Government League, gathering to it many of the lodges which had belonged to the federation. These formed the base of Gifford's political machine. With it he dominated Portland politics.

When Governor Olcott spoke out against it in the spring of 1922, the Klan marked him for political elimination. In the Republican primary, Olcott squeezed through after several days of doubt with less than five hundred votes. The Klan's hesitation over what to do next was solved when the Democratic candidate, Walter Pierce, came out in favor of a compulsory public school bill much favored by Klansmen and many of the fraternal orders of Oregon. The Scottish Rite Masons, the Orange Lodges, and others had long supported a law making public education compulsory for all children between the years of eight and sixteen, and such a proposition had been placed on the ballot by initiative for the 1922 election. The bill, similar to ones introduced in Michigan, California, Oklahoma, Washington, Texas, and parts of Canada, formed a fine rallying point. The Klan now had a new candidate and a battle cry: ONE PUBLIC SCHOOL FOR ALL EIGHT GRADES.

The Episcopalians, Lutherans, Presbyterians, and Seventh-Day Adventists joined the Roman Catholics in opposition to the bill, but the tide was running the other way. The normally ruling Republican party was badly split. The Klan whispered that Governor Olcott was a Papist, and he could hardly make the fact that he was not into a platform issue. The general noncommittal line taken by the press made things more difficult, as did the fake advertisements which the Klan bought in the name of a nonexistent Catholic Defense League. With over two hundred thousand votes cast, the Klan-supported Democratic candidate won by thirty-one thousand, and the public school bill slipped through by fourteen thousand.

By all outward signs, 1923 was to be the year of the Klan in Oregon. Although not many actual Klansmen had been running, the candidates it backed were widely successful, particularly in Portland's Multnomah County. The Klan helped pick the president of the state senate and the speaker of the house. In the latter instance, it was widely held that K. K. Kubli's initials were probably his greatest asset.

As events turned out, the Klan had power, but not control. It had a hand in introducing an array of bills including those providing fines and imprisonment for the wearing of religious or fraternal insignia in the schools, eliminating Columbus Day as a state holiday, prohibiting the importation of sacramental wine, discontinuing chaplains at state institutions, cutting state aid to charitable institutions, and taxing sectarian ones. Despite Grand Dragon Gifford's very visible lobby in Salem, the bills were blocked or emasculated, particularly in the lower house. Meanwhile, in the governor's mansion, Governor Pierce seemed ungratefully stingy in his distribution of patronage, and some disgruntled Klansmen made an unauthorized effort to recall him.

By the time the 1924 elections approached everything was in a disturbing degree of confusion. The Klan and the federation wrangled over whose friends should supply fire apparatus to the city of Portland, and the Klan-favored city commissioners had turned out to be somewhat less than universally satisfactory in office. The struggle for control of the national Klan in Atlanta spilled over into local Klan affairs, with a covert Simmons' faction opposing Gifford who had sided with Evans. The outspoken *Capitol Journal* ran a series of exposés on the Klan, and many Salem ministers had become fed up with the antagonisms which the Klan seemed to continually create.

When the Exalted Cyclops of Portland told an audience in the Salem armory: "the only way to cure a Catholic is to kill him," there was angry protest.

The race for the United States Senate made no small contribution to Klan division and decline. Both Mayor George Baker of Portland and House Speaker K. K. Kubli wanted to run against Senator Charles McNary. Each had support among Klan leaders and rank and file. Gifford, who had been supporting Mayor Baker, decided that his candidate couldn't win and switched to McNary, who had been careful to avoid bad relations with the Klan. The result was a bitter battle for support, which raged within Klan ranks and Klaverns.

Senator McNary had spoken out strongly against the Klan when he came home in 1922 to campaign for Olcott and the Republican ticket. However, faced with the need to be re-elected in 1924, McNary's instinct for survival brought him to feel that the battle against the Klan had best be fought by others. Although he announced himself opposed to appeals to racial and religious prejudice, he was apparently willing to accept Gifford aboard his growing band wagon.

In the May primaries, all of the Klan-supported candidates in Portland were defeated. In the meanwhile there was increasing disaffection within the Klans of Oregon over the fact that while Gifford was prospering, Klan enterprises were not. As always, the organization of the Klan had meant the proliferation of auxiliaries, degrees, and commercial ventures so common to the fraternal world. The Klansmen who had bought stock in Gifford's Skyline Corporation of Oregon, saw neither the erection of the planned Klan skyscraper nor an accounting of their money. The same thing happened to the funds collected for the W.C.T.U.'s children's farm near Corvallis. The Klan Kommunity Kitty, which was to replace the insufficiently discriminatory Community Chest, never really got organized. The Loties, or Ladies of the Invisible Empire, had objected to being dominated by Gifford and his aides. When a Klan official from Atlanta bustled into a Lotie meeting and demanded that the Mother Counselor hand over the charter and merge with the National Women of the Klan, he had to be rescued from enraged Loties who beat him with their fists and pocketbooks.

Intramural quarreling became endemic. The Salem Klan not only accused Gifford of fraud but also added Catholicism to the list of his mortal sins. In an exchange of charges of corruption, Gifford excommunicated Oregon's original Klan organizer Luther Powell, who later went north to Washington and then to Alaska to carry the Klan gospel. Gifford's Chief of Detectives, Rev. Keith K. Allen left for Vancouver in order to form a chapter of the Catholic-hating Royal Riders of the Red Robe, and the chief Klan editor turned to writing his "Confessions." An organizer from Atlanta tried unsuccessfully to get things going again in 1925 and 1926, with falsely glowing claims of a Klan revival in the Columbia River Valley. In the 1926 senatorial elections the Klan helped its favored candidate, Frederick Steiwer, win the Republican primary by spreading the word that it was supporting his opponent. The Oregon School Bill was finally laid to rest when the U. S. Supreme Court upheld a district court ruling declaring it unconstitutional. As the Klan declined after 1923, the rest of the Oregon press joined the Corvallis *Gazette Times,* the Portland *Telegram,* the Salem *Capitol Journal* and the *Eastern Oregonian,* the Pendleton *Tribune* and the Oregon *Labor Press* which had continuously fought the Klan. The ministers of Salem had come to oppose the Klan to the extent that they refused to offer guarantees to Billy Sunday, at least partly on the ground that he had endorsed the Klan Kreed. The verdict of the Catholic historian Saalfeld that the Klan died at its own hand in Oregon, seems valid.

13

SUCCESS AND SCHISM
IN THE TARHEEL STATE

After an uncertain start, the North Carolina Klan achieved stability under the leadership of Judge Henry A. Grady. With its night riding usually unreported and its political activities relatively minor, the Klan's role was primarily that of a fraternal lodge which stressed its own version of Protestant morality. It was perhaps this very quietude that disturbed Imperial Wizard Hiram Evans and the leaders of the national Klan. The controversy that blew up when they forced Judge Grady out of his Grand Dragonship, in 1927, rocked the Tarheel realm and became a major issue in state politics.

The Invisible Empire spread quickly and quietly in North Carolina, gathering its greatest following in the southeastern and central portions of the state. Initially, as often happens with secret organizations, there was some confusion as to the lines of command. Things got straightened out when popular, handsome Judge Henry A. Grady, newly elected to the Superior Court of the state, took charge. His membership in the Klan was one of Colonel Simmons' proudest triumphs, and the Klan founder talked of Grady taking over the administrative headship of the order. When the struggle between Simmons and Evans threatened to completely disrupt the Klan, the judge was a member of the court-approved board which oversaw the transference of undisputed control to Evans. From 1922 to 1927, as Grand Dragon of North Carolina, an officer in the Klan's national cabinet, and a member of the high court of his state, Judge Grady was one of the chief ornaments of the revived Ku Klux Klan.

The hooded order was not free from opposition and attack in the Tarheel State. Early in 1923 a bill was introduced in the state legislature which would have required the registration of membership and banned masked parades or wrongdoing. The opposition immediately tried to table the bill without debate, but after a heated battle it was passed and sent to the Senate. Representative R. O. Everett, an able legislator from Durham, was one of those who pushed it through. He had originally been opposed to it, he explained, until the head of the local Klan told him that he had better not change his mind if he wanted to remain in office.

In the Senate, the fight was hotter. Senators Armfield and Johnson from Duplin County's cotton, vegetable, and Klan-producing farmlands in the southeastern part of the state led the fight against the bill. Rivers Johnson, who was to figure prominently in the Klan story and who later became dean of the state Senate, played the major role. He spoke, he said, on behalf of "twenty-five thousand red-blooded North Carolinians who are members of the Ku Klux Klan. . . . Invisibility is the force of the Empire," he proclaimed, describing the Klan as an organization standing for "Protestant Americanism, free speech, free press, white supremacy, and the support of all law." In the last superior court term in Duplin County, he testified, twenty-five of the twenty-seven men convicted had been brought to justice through the good offices of the Klan. The enemies of the Klan were the Knights of Columbus backed by the A.P. and some parts of the press!

One of the papers which he surely had in mind was Josephus Daniels' Raleigh *News and Observer*. And it was Daniels who most clearly reflected the general philosophy behind the bill. It was hostility to the Invisible Empire but one based on general dislike and Klan behavior elsewhere. The Mer Rouge affair, rather than the doings of the Klan in North Carolina, seemed to have been a precipitating factor. Some of the best people in the state joined the Klan when it got going in Raleigh the previous year, Daniels reported. Their belief had been that a few masked parades would frighten the criminals and build respect for law and order. Racial and religious feeling had not been involved. These better citizens who soon saw that they had been mistaken about the nature of the Klan, had dropped out. The main purpose of the proposed law, Daniels summed up, was preventive. It was intended to forestall lawlessness rather than punish it. In an interview for the *News and Observer,* Thomas Dixon, the author of *The Clansman,* commented on the commercialism of the modern Klan and upon Mer Rouge: "There can be but one end to a secret order of disguised men. It will grow eventually into a reign of terror which only martial law will be able to put down." Senators favoring the bill declared that it would show that they did not intend to permit the growth of an Invisible Empire to uncontrollable strength without its membership being known.

Before packed galleries, the Senate took up the various measures directed at the Klan. Every favorable reference to the masked order was applauded, and the Senate substituted a bill favored by the Klan which preserved the secrecy of membership and the general use of the mask.

Josephus Daniels had not been right when he editorialized that the Ku Klux Klan had attempted little or no "regulation" in North Carolina. In 1922 the Greensboro Klan delivered a fugitive Negro assailant to the sheriff and secured the arrest of a white man who had walked off from an affair with a Winston-Salem girl. A Negro state farm expert was kidnaped and flogged by Columbus County Klansmen who had also visited three other townsmen. A band led by the chief of police took two white Lumberton women to a Negro churchyard and flogged them for the mistreatment that one was accused of giving to her sick husband. In a little town near Raleigh, a country storekeeper was warned to leave the county after becoming involved in a neighborhood school quarrel. When he failed to do so, his store was dynamited. Testimony offered in the legislature gave indication that the Klan was also trying its hand at improving things in Washington, Durham, and Duplin counties.

As always, the Klan was talking tough. The next year in Ahoskie the Klan boasted that it was planning a "welcome" for two wealthy Negroes who had had the insolence to take a Pullman to New York. The minister of the Southside Memorial Baptist Church in Raleigh preached a sermon, entitled "Automobiles, Women, and the Ku Klux Klan," in which he upheld flogging and called upon the Klan to prevent immorality. The Klan conducted a "clean-up" campaign that year in Raleigh and was believed to have had a hand in replacing the chief of police. The Klans were busy in the piedmont region in central North Carolina, and when the realm split apart in 1927, information came to light of night riding in various parts of the state, as well as a large number of unreported floggings in Raleigh's Wake County.

No one indicated that Judge Grady was involved. He himself had spoken out strongly against flogging, and he apparently tried to prevent violence as well as generally hold down the Klan's role in politics.

In fact, the national Klan leaders came to feel that Judge Grady was too restraining an influence on the development of Klansmanship in the state of North Carolina. Grady himself was veering toward support of an antimask law because it was a good way to keep the Klan from either getting into trouble or being blamed for what others did. Possibly he had come to agree with that wing of the Klan in North Carolina which opposed mass membership and sought a highly selected and elite group. Any such move would have certainly conflicted with both the political power and the commercial possibilities which remained dear to the heart of the national officers.

Judge Grady managed to run afoul of both. In July of 1926, he had dismissed the first vice president of the North Carolina Klan, over the latter's involvement in politics. Shortly afterwards, Evans appointed the dismissed Kailiff as the state agent for the Klan-run Empire Mutual Insurance Company, which was one of the Imperial Wizard's pet projects. This incensed Judge Grady, and he refused to permit the former Kailiff to operate within the North Carolina Klans.

Then, early in January 1927, national headquarters sent its Grand Dragon another unwelcome gift. The Invisible Empire was pushing a package of four bills for which it was seeking passage in the various state legislatures. The proposed bills would forbid intermarriage between "whites and blacks," punish derogatory remarks made by Roman Catholics about non-Catholic marriages, prohibit contracts concerning the religious education of children, and banish the Knights of Columbus. In the case of the last bill, the national headquarters suggested to Judge Grady that he have it introduced by someone not connected with the Klan, preferably by an active member of the American Legion.

Judge Grady refused. The law against miscegenation was already on the books. The others, he felt, were "silly, unseemly, and unconstitutional." With a flowery letter of praise and dissatisfaction, the Imperial Wizard fired his Tarheel Grand Dragon. Saying, in effect, "You can't fire me, I quit," Judge Grady released their correspondence to the press.

It all caused a great sensation. The first word was that sixty-six of the state's eighty-six Klan chapters had decided to quit. Two members of the legislature, Senator Rivers Johnson of Duplin and the Reverend Oscar Haywood, Representative from Montgomery, introduced a bill outlawing secret membership organizations and the public wearing of masks. What made this turn of events particularly spectacular was that Reverend Haywood was a former national Klan lecturer who had been fired from the Calvary Baptist Church in New York City for his Klan exhortations, and Senator Johnson had led the pro-Klan forces against the Milliken bill during the 1923 legislative session.

Despite the newspaper stories, only a small number of individual Klans, including those of Raleigh and Wilmington, decided to turn in their charters. Most Klans affirmed their loyalty to Evans and his program. In making their decisions, many of them bitterly denounced their former leader. The Kinston Klavern voted to change its name from the Henry A. Grady Klan, to remove his picture from the wall, and to ban the song, "Let the Fiery Cross Be Burning," for which the judge had been responsible. Up in the Blue Ridge Mountains, in the northwestern corner of the state, Goshen Klan No. 73 of Calypso blamed Judge Grady's action on the Knights of Columbus. "We have scoured Goshen and Bear Swamp for illicit distilleries and watched our stores and streets for bootleg liquor for the past few years," its spokesman announced, "until now Calypso is one of the cleanest little towns in North Carolina. . . . All the Catholic gold in the universe can't buy our manhood and our liberty."

The Johnson-Haywood anti-Klan bill swept through the state Senate, where the Milliken bill had died in 1923. This time galleries were treated to no fiery debate but were offered a different kind of drama. Without either debate or a single dissenting vote, the bill was sent off to the House. With the Reverend Haywood handling it there, quick passage seemed certain, but even in this brief period the Ku Klux Klan had marshaled its forces. Former congressman, H. L. Godwin of Dunn, took over the leadership of the Klan lobby, and Washington sent in a group of its top strategists. Telegrams poured in on the House members. Unlike 1923, no one defended the Klan on the floor of the House. Instead the arguments were that the law would violate the freedom of assembly, that it would be harmful to other groups, such as the Moose and labor, and that the legislature should not become involved in what was obviously an internal feud within the Klan. Having tied up the bill with technical parliamentary maneuvers, the North Carolina House of Representatives killed it. Just as it was doing so, almost within the shadow of the capitol, eleven Klansmen, including a local doctor and a deputy sheriff, were going on trial as part of a mob which had flogged a one-armed storekeeper, and his Negro helper, for selling liquor and carrying on with women.

The biggest problem that the Klan faced was to regroup its shattered forces and recoup its strength, which, judging by Rivers Johnson's estimate, had probably fallen below eight thousand. At its peak the Klan's cohorts may have numbered more than six or seven times that many. With the Raleigh Klan disbanded, headquarters operations were shifted to Charlotte. Plans were being talked of to defeat Judge Grady, state auditor Baxter Durham, and other "turncoats" when they came up for re-election. In October of 1927, when Senator George of Georgia spoke at the anniversary celebration of the Revolutionary War victory at Kings Mountain, Imperial Wizard Hiram Evans sought to get on the program. Although unsuccessful, he came anyway and spoke afterwards. The faithful of North Carolina, led by the Kings Mountain Klan, put out their best effort for their Imperial Wizard and turned the ceremonies into a Klan demonstration.

With the state's Democratic party badly split over Al Smith in 1928, the Invisible Empire sought to increase its own still-low prestige by vigorously opposing the New Yorker. Alabama's Senator Heflin, America's leading anti-Catholic, was brought in to speak, and later a full-time Klan lecturer was sent in from Washington. Although Herbert Hoover won in North Carolina for reasons of which the Klan unquestionably approved, there is little sign that the Klan itself was directly responsible. Some of the counties where the hooded order had been strongest stayed with Smith while others went for Hoover. Although the stuff of which Klansmen were made was still apparent, the Invisible Empire continued to become less and less visible in North Carolina.

14

KLANSMEN IN THE CAROLINA PIEDMONT

The last of the ten realms chartered in 1921–22, during the reign of Colonel Simmons, was South Carolina, but there is scant detail of its history. This may well substantiate the general feeling on the part of historians that the Invisible Empire was of negligible force and importance in the Palmetto State. And yet, it was not the policy of the Klan to charter a state until its recruitment policy had borne at least a fairly lush crop of members and fees. Most of the components of Klandom were there: hard times on the farm as well as racial unrest and ill-enforced Prohibition. Although white supremacy has been one of the dominant battle cries in South Carolina politics, and its native sons Ben Tillman, Cole Blease, and their successors have taught the South Carolinian to hate, the menace of the immigrant and the alienation of the old Jewish and Roman Catholic families was absent.

Still, the Klan mixed opposition to those things Catholic, Jewish, socialistic, and foreign, with its exaltation of white supremacy, while its Grand Dragon called for war on vice, particularly of the alcoholic variety. In 1923, Senator James R. Bellamy from coastal Beaufort introduced bills in the legislature which would require the registration of membership and prohibit public wearing of the mask. He praised the old Klan, but likened its revival in the 1920s to the later degeneration of the Reconstruction one. His bills, he explained, were to protect the basic American freedoms from the Klansmen.

However, Bellamy was prevailed upon to withdraw his proposal for the registration of Klansmen and legislative attention focused on the antimask bill. When Senator Holland from Florence defended the Klan as the preserver of the ideals of home, womanhood, and one-hundred-per-cent Americanism, the Charleston delegates pointed out the difficulty of defining one-hundred-per-cent Americanism, and the dangers of leaving it up to the Klan. In the end, however, the bill was voted down.

The next year, long-time Congressman James F. Byrnes decided to run for the U. S. Senate, and when he made the runoff he was rather hopeful about his chances. Although now an Episcopalian, Byrnes had been brought up a Roman Catholic. The afternoon before the election, a circular appeared, signed by ten of his boyhood neighbors, praising his youthful Catholicism and his service as an altar boy. Copies of the circular were distributed by the thousands in the areas where the Klan was strong and active. When the results of the election came in, Byrnes had lost by a narrow margin.

For the most part the Klan of the twenties, like its Reconstruction ancestor, operated in the coastal terraces and Carolina piedmont and made relatively little headway in the coastal plains. Its name was in sufficient disrepute in Charleston that a losing candidate in the 1923 mayoralty election tried to get votes by picturing himself its victim. Upstate, however, people were more respectful, and led by the Wade Hampton Klan No. 50 of Columbia and Greenville's Poinsett Klan No. 26, the Invisible Empire strutted its stuff in the piedmont. When it paraded, it bore aloft on its banners the traditional slogans of Klan iconography: THE LITTLE RED SCHOOL HOUSE, FREEDOM OF SPEECH AND PRESS, SEPARATION OF CHURCH AND STATE, PURE WOMANHOOD, and WHITE SUPREMACY. When Imperial Wizard Hiram Evans toured his South Carolina realm in 1926, he gave two public addresses under the sponsorship of Charleston's Klan No. 1, and then moved about the state to take the cheers of the faithful. Rallies of the various Klan provinces were held for him at Sumter, Marion, and Spartanburg. In May of that year, the unsympathetic mayor of Columbia was defeated by a local doctor, said to be a Klansman, who campaigned against the twin menaces of liquor and prostitution.

However, with the traditional values of Protestantism and white supremacy unchallenged in the state, South Carolina Democracy stayed loyal to Al Smith and the party in 1928. The Klan came to South Carolina in the 1920s as it did to the South and the nation, but, in the Palmetto State, society seemed too orderly to need another order superimposed on it.

15

THE PRICE OF SUCCESS

For the top leaders of the Klan, the price of success was to be very high. The initial storm broke about Clarke and Mrs. Tyler. Many members had not liked the prominent role of Mrs. Tyler in what was supposed to be a man's organization. The newspaper revelations about the financial and personal relations between Clarke and Mrs. Tyler hurt the public image and the private sense of propriety of many Klansmen.

A month after the congressional investigation, four of the top Northern regional sales managers met in Washington to compare notes. Clarke and Mrs. Tyler would have to go, they decided, and they set off to headquarters in Atlanta to make their decision known. "Boys, I love you, and I know that everything you are saying is true," the Imperial Wizard told them, repeatedly promising that he would get rid of Clarke. When it finally became clear that Simmons had no intention of making any changes, the unhappy Goblins gave the story to the press.

For the next month, it was seldom off the front pages. The dissidents claimed that the charges of immorality against Clarke and Mrs. Tyler brought the resignations flooding in. Clarke, they said, had padded payrolls and misappropriated funds, was holding unlawful sway over an ailing and disintegrating Simmons, and had perverted the Klan into a vehicle for the dissemination of hate and prejudice. When Clarke and Simmons dismissed them from the Klan, they refused to accept it. When Clarke swore out warrants against them for larceny and slander, they countered with suits for malfeasance. When Clarke got a vote of confidence from the mother Klan in Atlanta, the rebels displayed anti-Clarke telegrams which had been sent from all over the eastern seaboard.

By the spring of 1922 the turmoil had temporarily subsided. The various law suits had been dismissed and the protesting Klansmen had silently departed the realm. Mrs. Tyler also resigned, blaming need of rest and the illness of her daughter, and Simmons himself was becoming less and less active. He had been unwell for a considerable period of time, and the rumors persisted that the nature of the illness was alcohol. In June, after much coaxing by his wife, Simmons took a six months' vacation from Klan affairs, leaving Clarke as Imperial Wizard, pro tem, to mind the store.

Clarke had come to rely for aid more and more on the shoulders of Fred Savage, an ex-New York detective, now the chief of staff of the Klan, and Hiram Wesley Evans. Evans was a roly-poly, glad-handing, cut-rate dentist from Dallas, Texas. He was an inveterate joiner and lodge man, with a fine capacity for intrigue and manipulation. Mrs. Tyler used him to combat an anti-Klan movement among the Masons in Texas, and, paying off his debts, brought him to the imperial headquarters in Atlanta. Former cotton-mill superintendent L. D. Wade had been one of Simmons' original immortals. He was found by the police in an embarrassing circumstance (the top Klan officials were always getting trapped in embarrassing circumstances) and Evans succeeded him in charge of the party secretariat. From this key post Evans began to entrench his power and to spread rumors against Simmons. In the late fall of 1922, the Imperial Wizard returned to his desk and launched into the preparations for the first annual Klonvokation of the Klan. Still content to leave most of the Klan's affairs in Clarke's hands, he assumed that some administrative changes would probably be the answer to his Empire's growing problems.

Other people had other solutions. To a group of the bright young men in the Klan ranks, several things were clear. In Simmons' weak hands and Clarke's greedy ones, violence and scandal were hurting the Klan. Both men would have to go! The young turks met in Atlanta's Piedmont Hotel, the night before the opening of the convention. The conspirators were Hiram W. Evans (the Texas dentist turned imperial official), Klan investigator Fred Savage, Louisiana's H. C. Ramsey, and the Texas and Arkansas Grand Dragons McCall and Comer. An invitation was sent over to the private railroad car of David Stephenson, asking the rising light of the Northern Klan to join them. Here was a group of ambitious men, men on the make, the new territorial magnates of the Klan.

Most of them had worked together; only Stephenson was an un-predictable outsider, and they eyed him warily. There was general agreement that Colonel Simmons was not the right man to be running things and that the state realms were not getting proper help from the Imperial Palace. There was some talk of blackmailing Simmons into resigning, but that was put aside. In order to smoke out their real plans, Stephenson suggested putting the problem up to the convention. As he had hoped, Judge Comer revealed what the others had in mind. Their plan was to kick Simmons upstairs with, perhaps, $500 a month, and give the real power to Evans. Stephenson, still feeling out his ground, suggested that the figure be moved up to a thousand. The others agreed. How could the whole thing be carried out? Stephenson and Fred Savage were appointed to call upon Colonel Simmons. Evans announced that if necessary he was going to have the Texas delegation attack Simmons' character from the floor. Stephenson demurred. The Klan was a valuable property, and he did not want it damaged. The others were forced to go along with him. Everything had now come to depend upon the success of the mission to Simmons.

Stephenson and Savage arrived at 1840 Peachtree Street at about 3 A.M., and woke Simmons who had been out drinking with some of the boys until only a short time before. They told him that they wanted to talk about convention affairs and he invited them into the library. Their first question took him by surprise. Had he, they wanted to know, decided whether or not he was going to allow his name to be brought forward for renomination? There was a ring about this that the Imperial Wizard did not like. He replied piously that he had nothing to do with it himself. He wasn't interested in politicking. His only thought was for the Klan. However, he added, if the Klan wanted it, he would have to serve. Then, perhaps aware of the seriousness of the growing internal discontent, he told them that he did plan eventually to add a top administrative officer, while he himself did the creative work and generally kept an eye on things.

Did he, they asked, have a candidate for the new post?

Yes, but he hadn't talked to him about it yet.

Who was it?

Judge Grady of North Carolina.

The nominations were to take place at 10 A.M.—only a few hours off—had he considered any other candidate?

Absolutely none!

And if Judge Grady were not available?

Simmons shrugged his shoulders and guessed that in such a case he would have to carry on as before.

What about Evans, they suggested?

No, he replied, he didn't think that that was a good idea.

This was the crucial moment for the conspirators. Simmons had closed the door and they now had to open it by force. They spoke with great agitation and urgency.

Don't let your name come before the Klonvokation, Stephenson and Savage warned Simmons. There would be men present who were out to cause trouble. These men were plotting to besmirch the Imperial Wizard's name from the floor of the convention.

"The moment your character is attacked," Savage counseled, "there is going to be somebody killed. I have got men placed and have given them orders to shoot and kill any damn man that attacks the character of Colonel Simmons." This would mean a roughhouse, the destruction of the Klonvokation, and the crucifixion of the Klan at the hands of the press, Savage concluded.

This was obviously serious business and plausible enough to be true. Before Simmons could think of a reply, the plotters presented their plan. To "preserve the harmony and peace and wonderful carrying on of the Klonvokation as we have it, let's beat those birds, and give them a message in which you refuse to allow your name to come before them to succeed yourself," they pressed. Just for emergency purposes, wouldn't he name Evans?

Simmons was not a strong man, and he grasped at what appeared to be a way out. Evans did know the workings of the office and could fit in in an emergency, he conceded.

"Good!" Savage said. "All we want to do is meet the emergency and to avert this crisis, and Dr. Evans will fit in temporarily until you can get a man to suit you."

Relieved, Simmons agreed.

Triumphantly, they almost pushed things too far: "Then you name Dr. Evans as your successor?"

Simmons was not to be caught by this. "I do not," he said.

Having beaten back this peril, Simmons was still a bit reluctant. As a veteran of church conferences and lodge wars, his suspicions were up. Now that he had committed himself, he was having second thoughts about the wisdom of having done so. His argument was that the membership did not know about his plan to separate the offices of Imperial Wizard and Emperor. Although he agreed with his callers that he had the power to proclaim it, he insisted that he had to submit it to his cabinet first.

They rounded up the cabinet and just before the Klonvokation was to meet, Simmons presented the proposed separation of offices.

The members of the cabinet were carefully surprised and refrained from any real effort to dissuade him. And so Colonel Simmons went before the First Imperial Klonvokation of the Knights of the Ku Klux Klan assembled and, unknowingly, decreed his own defeat.

The delegates eagerly declared Simmons Emperor for life, but the play was not yet over. For the past year, E. Y. Clarke had been the power behind the throne running Klan affairs and he had much support, particularly in Atlanta. But Clarke was more interested in wealth than office. He felt in need of rest from the already heavy responsibilities and mounting personal attack. A show was made of tendering him the Imperial Wizardship, which he turned down. Instead, he accepted the title of Imperial Giant, or Past Imperial Wizard, with hero's cross, life membership in the Klan, and a renewal of his sales contract. Hiram W. Evans was then acclaimed Imperial Wizard. A Texas dentist, an Indiana coal dealer, and a New York water-front detective had combined to wrest control of his beloved child from Emperor Simmons.

What had the shift meant to the conspirators? Fred Savage continued as the chief of staff. Kyle Ramsey moved up from Secretary of the Louisiana Klan to the same position with national headquarters. Within a short time, H. C. McCall, the former deputy sheriff of Houston, Texas, was sent to Washington as envoy from the Invisible Empire to the United States of America. Judge Comer's wife-to-be became the head of the national women's auxiliary when it was established later in the year. D. C. Stephenson, the young Klan hero of the North, got the free hand he wanted in Indiana, plus the control over twenty-two other states, in a subempire stretching from the Mississippi Valley to the Atlantic Coast. When squeezed, the fruits of office made a heady wine.

But the game had not yet been played out. Simmons was still powerful and had agreed to only a temporary relinquishment of control. E. Y. Clarke was still a source of embarrassment, and he continued to control the golden stream that flowed into Atlanta. In March of 1923, three months after Evans had assumed control, Clarke's contract was canceled "for the good of the order."

Edward Young Clarke was in no position to protest. The cancellation was permissible according to the contract and Clarke's own position was seriously embarrassed. He was a high-strung and nervous person, given to despondency. His alter ego, Mrs. Tyler, who had supplied a good portion of his backbone, had withdrawn completely from Klan affairs and was getting married. Simmons was no help.

Clarke's position was made absolutely impossible by the fact that he had just been indicted for violation of both the Volstead and Mann acts. In the latter case, it turned out that he had paid the fare of a pretty Houston girl, sister of a convicted bank robber, to come to New Orleans to assuage his loneliness. It was curious that this indiscretion of two years before should so fortuitously come to the attention of the Houston grand jury, but anyway it was hardly fit advertisement for the would-be protector of morality and American womanhood. Clarke got off with a fine, and Evans was able at last to disassociate the Klan from Clarke's more than tarnished reputation.

The last remaining obstacle to the new master of the Invisible Kingdom was its founder. Colonel Simmons had agreed to what he had thought was only a temporary arrangement. Soon the Emperor came to feel that things weren't what they should be. True, Evans talked about setting up a great white throne in a special throne room where Simmons could meet visitors, but nothing ever seemed to happen. The land on which Simmons had planned to build his great American university, he discovered, had been sold. People around the palace seemed cool toward him, and the sight of Evans sitting behind *his* desk and not getting up to make room for him, disturbed Simmons.

The answer was not long in coming. Casually thumbing through a newly printed copy of the Klan Constitution, as approved at the Klonvokation, he discovered that important changes had been made. The article establishing the authority and general prerogatives of the Emperor had been left out, as had the section reaffirming his property titles. To Simmons' protestations, Evans only laughed. On the face of it, there seemed to be nothing that the outraged Emperor could do. "Let's get the money, Colonel," was Simmons' report of what Evans had said.

Simmons was angry. If Evans had corralled the men, he, Simmons, would turn his attention to the women. The question of a women's auxiliary was becoming increasingly important to the Klan. The problem was that the Klan leaders had not been able to turn their attention to it. There were already a number functioning anyway, and some had even sent delegations to lobby for recognition by the Klonvokation. Simmons walked into the vacuum, took the White American Protestant Study Club of Oklahoma and dubbed it the official Klan auxiliary, Kamelia. Evans responded by forbidding Klansmen to have anything to do with the ladies of Kamelia. What Simmons had to say to the press about Evans, was not complimentary.

Simmons' next move was to lay siege to the Imperial Palace. Early in April, Simmons got a court order giving him control. With only a moment's warning of what had happened, two officers, loyal to Evans, managed to hide important papers and $107,000 of Klan cash. After ransacking the palace, the infuriated Colonel Simmons installed his own officers and charged the Evans loyalists with larceny. Evans dashed back to Atlanta from Washington. Suits and countersuits, charges and countercharges filled the air and the press. The mother Klan of the Invisible Empire, Atlanta's Nathan Bedford Forrest No. 1, and the Georgia realm including the *Searchlight,* generally rallied behind Simmons. The rest of the leadership in the realms and domains, whose members flocked into Atlanta, supported Evans, although a group of Klan heroes from Morehouse Parish, Louisiana, led by old Captain Skipworth, arrived to bolster the Simmons forces.

The issue, however, was to be decided in the courts. After much wrangling and litigation, an out-of-court settlement was announced. Simmons had turned out to be the exclusive owner of the Klan ritual, regalia, constitution, and charter. Even the name was his. It was all personally copyrighted. The settlement specified that Simmons would step down as Emperor. In return for his copyrights, he would receive his monthly $1000 as a pension for life, and after his death it would go to his wife, Bessie. Evans was to cease his opposition to the women's Klan which Simmons had been privately organizing and would promise neither to interfere nor to set up a competing organization. As for the Klan proper, a new Imperial Kloncilium, divided between Simmons and Evans men, would choose an executive board or Klan cabinet. Those finally selected were J. C. Comer of Arkansas, Paul Etheridge of Atlanta, Charles Orbison of Indianapolis, Nathan Bedford Forrest III of Mississippi, the sculptor Gutzon Borglum, and the Klan chaplain, Caleb Ridley. When they met, only Ridley took the Simmons side. Evans was clearly in.

Simmons and his remaining cohorts were soon dissatisfied with their share of the settlement. They had received little profit compared to the thousands that flowed into the main Klan and they were making little headway with Kamelia. After much grumbling, some of it public, Simmons burst into print accusing Evans of squandering Klan moneys. Evans immediately sued for libel. With Simmons' approval, a receivership suit against the national headquarters was filed by D. M. Rittenhouse and other dissident Philadelphia Klansmen. Evans' next move was to start work on an official women's order over which the Simmons faction in Texas sued him and the Texas

Grand Dragon for being monopolists in violation of the Texas anti-trust law. In November 1923, the on-again, off-again Rittenhouse suit was turned down in court, with the judge ruling that the charges of waste and mismanagement were in reality only an inside fight of a few hundred against the rest of the order.

But even then the Klan was not permitted to retire from the head-lines and enjoy its gains. When Evans rose to power in Atlanta, he brought with him the former city editor of the Dallas (Texas) *Times-Herald*, Phil Fox, who moved up from imperial speech writer to edi-tor of *The Knight Hawk,* and chief public-relations man for the Klan. During the Rittenhouse litigation, Evans apparently fueled Fox's hot temper to the boiling point. The explosion took place when Fox shot Simmons' attorney, William S. Coburn. Fox escaped the death penalty on the plea that he was a dangerous paranoid and thus not responsible for his actions. (He went to the penitentiary with a life sentence of which he was to serve a decade before parole and pardon by friendly Georgia Governors Eugene Talmadge and E. D. Rivers in the 1930s.) In a public letter to a silent Calvin Coo-lidge, E. Y. Clarke rhetorically called for a presidential dissolution of the Klan; Simmons agreed, and both he and Clarke attempted to organize new Klanlike competitors.

Surely, Evans must have felt, enough was enough. He banished Simmons and Clarke for their treasonable activities, and, in February 1924, announcement was made of what the Klan hoped was a final settlement. In return for severing all contact, ceasing all harassment of the Klan, and giving up Kamelia, Simmons was to exchange his monthly $1000 for a lump sum of $146,500. From Florida, Simmons announced that he had settled for only $90,000, a discrepancy which was accounted for a year later when Simmons sued his go-between, an Atlanta real estate man, for having made off with the difference.

This final settlement marked the departure of Simmons, and Clarke, who received nothing, from Klan affairs. Their litigation was over, their power and following spent, and their dreams of great new orders of fraternal horsemen in flowing robes, pouring money into their coffers, were beyond realization, full of bitter nostalgia rather than hope. Both Clarke and Simmons dropped off in retirement. Sim-mons spent many years in a little suburban home in Atlanta, passing his days in the lobbies of downtown Atlanta hotels, telling of the days of glory and treachery; finally he moved to Luverne, Alabama, where he died in 1946.

After two years of conflict, conspiracy, law suits, and publicity, the internal affairs of the Klan seemed momentarily at rest. Imperial Wizard Hiram Evans held unchallenged sway. However, the great internecine battle had cost the Klan dearly. As always, it had fattened the lawyers, but it had done more than that. Although Klan ranks were still swollen and expanding, the fight for control had discouraged many Klansmen and had generally weakened the Klan's reputation and power. The charges and countercharges of illegality, immorality, and profligacy, as well as the general mercenary tinge of the contests had disillusioned many members. Not only were Simmons adherents expelled, but many Klan chapters voluntarily disbanded. The press had had a fine time playing up the details of the buying and selling process that was going on. "Ku Klux Klan on the Auction Block," the unfriendly Memphis *Commercial Appeal* headed an editorial, and the La Grange (Louisiana) *Reporter* expressed the hope that the Klansmen would be so busy doing in one another that they wouldn't have time to mob any outsiders. The sources of Klan weakness were great, and they had not been helped by so public a display. The order was never to be free of schism, and, for a benevolent nonprofit organization, too many people were making too much money. For a defender of morality, there was too much immorality too openly displayed. For a secret terrorist organization, or at least one dedicated to creating awe and respect, there was something incongruous about it always settling its own affairs in the courts. Over the long run it would turn out that too many of its secrets had been spilled, and too much of the Klan's public reputation lay soiled upon the ground.

16

THE TEN-DOLLAR SPECIAL

Despite its continuous internal battles, the tide in 1923 was still running in favor of the Klan, and with so many converts flocking in, it was not yet to feel the effects of those rushing out. The Invisible Empire probably contained between two and three million hooded knights, with more galloping in all the time. What were the reasons for this awe-inspiring power? Why did the Empire spread so quickly outside of the South which had enshrined the legend of the first Klan? Throughout the nation, irrespective of section and sectionalism, the Ku Klux Klan was primarily emotional rather than rational, defensive rather than constructive. The feelings stirred up by World War I had not yet abated. Peace does not come because men suddenly declare it. The war was an emotional binge fed on whipped-up passions. It was sustained on the home front by enforced conformity and an increased awareness of one's neighbors. Rumor and apprehension became the food of everyday life.

The heightened patriotism, which men had felt within themselves and, where necessary, enforced upon others, still lived after the guns were silent. Those who came back from the battle fronts and those who remained at home were restless. The intensified habit of violence which had been created, expressed itself in a crime wave, an outbreak of race riots, and the social restlessness upon which the Ku Klux Klan fed. The Invisible Empire provided what amounted to an almost approved channel for its expression.

The static position of the Negro had been upset by military service and a growing migration from the farms into the cities and the Northern factories. In both the South and the North the white man's attention initially focused there. During the war there were race riots in East St. Louis, Houston, and in Chester and Philadelphia, Pennsylvania. With the end of fighting in Europe, the crescendo mounted, while the number of lynchings remained high. Men took up arms against their colored neighbors in the nation's capital and in Charleston; Chicago; Omaha; Knoxville, Tennessee; Longview, Texas; and Elaine, Arkansas, in 1919. The story was repeated in 1920 in Duluth, Minnesota; Independence, Kansas; and Ocoee, Florida, and again the following year in Springfield, Ohio; and Tulsa, Oklahoma. There were rumors everywhere, and other flare-ups were narrowly averted.

Concern soon shifted from white supremacy to a more national nativism. Its traditional harbingers—immigration and hard times—were there. A new wave of predominantly Catholic, Slavic, and Mediterranean immigration hit America as the wartime prosperity was falling off and economic recession was taking hold. Fear of the foreigner was reinforced by disillusionment with the results of the war, and alarm over the menace of Bolshevik subversion.

Although the Klan revival slightly preceded the rising vogue of anti-Semitism, there was always enough around to get involved with things. The Klan was a movement designed for native-born, white Protestants of northern European descent. This left the Jew out, and if he was on the outside, then he constituted a problem and probably ought to be treated as an enemy. If the citizen was hit by hard times, the manipulations of the Jewish bankers in the Eastern cities were at fault. If the citizen's business was not doing well, then it was because of the competition from his Jewish competitor who was being aided by his clannish New York bankers. If he were alarmed over the cost of the war or the absence of peace, then it was either the fault of the international branch of the Jewish monetary conspiracy or the pushing, quarreling, Jewish immigrants who brought with them their communistic conspiracies from eastern Europe.

The mongrelization of the white race was a peril that men thought about, and the American middle classes and intellectuals read Madison Grant's *The Passing of the Great Race* and Klansman Lothrop Stoddard's *The Rising Tide of Color*. The Oriental was a menace, though the Ku Klux Klan gave him only minor attention. So was the Mexican. Klan, and popular, conceptions of race were amply broad and subject to local definition. In Macon, Georgia, the Klan ordered all Syrians to leave town. In Palataka, Florida, the word was that a Greek had been flogged, after a considerable struggle, for going out with a "white" woman, and Italian storekeepers in East Frankfurt, Illinois, were placed beyond the pale.

The Klan's main concern, however, was the looming danger of Roman Catholicism. It would be a mistake to read too much theology into this. Nativism has not, in America, been primarily an attempt to complete the Protestant Reformation. It has, in the main, been an antialienism, an opposition to different and hence, presumably, unassimilable elements in the society. Most Klansmen did not believe that they were opposing the Catholic because of his religion but because hierarchical control from Rome prevented his assimilation.

Still, the Klan's anti-Catholicism had many theological overtones. Members of the Baptist and Methodist churches and the Disciples of Christ formed the mainstay of the Ku Klux Klan, and their ministers provided it a continuing respectability and, often, leadership. The Pope provided an even better symbolic outlet for aggression and emotional release than the Jewish banker, alien radical, or leering Negro.

Some Klan ministers were so violent in their utterances that Klansmen in Pennsylvania and Michigan protested against them. For the most part the rank and file listened approvingly to revelations that Lincoln, McKinley, and Harding had been done in by the Knights of Columbus and that 90 per cent of the deserters in World War I had been Roman Catholics. The Klan's standard piece of campaign literature, when it ventured into political contests, was the famous forged "Knights of Columbus Oath." Copies of the alleged pledge, by which Catholic laymen promised to "hang, burn, boil, flay, and bury alive" all non-Catholics, were distributed by the tens of thousands all over the country. Although Klansmen in Oregon shifted uncomfortably in their seats when they were told that the only good Catholic was a dead Catholic, the members of the Invisible Empire were willing to listen to a good deal.

One popular story was that every time a boy was born to a Roman Catholic family, the father added a rifle and ammunition to his local church's arsenal. The Pope was accused of buying the strategic high ground overlooking West Point and Washington, and attention was called to the fact that the two antique cannons on the front lawn of Georgetown University were pointed in the direction of the Capitol. When the word got around in North Manchester, Indiana, that the Pope was coming in on the train from Chicago, Klansmen went down to the station prepared to take the defense of America into their own hands.

As the partaker in the least laudable aspects of Protestant fundamentalism and its puritanical morality, the Klansman found approved channels for the satisfaction of his repressed fleshy appetites. The Klan offered both participation in the physical punishment, often sexually oriented, of accused transgressors, and the traditional anti-

Catholic pornography. The "liberated" nun was an extremely popular attraction in Oregon and Ohio.

The success of the Ku Klux Klan in rallying its millions stemmed in good part from the fact that there was a conscious white Protestant America, and it believed itself under attack. The Klan spread in those areas of the nation where the "old American" stock was dominant. Eastern immigrant cities, such as Boston, New York, and Baltimore, were generally outside its periphery, as were Charleston's eighteenth-century cosmopolitanism. So too was most of the black-belt area of the Carolinas, Georgia, and Alabama. So were the Gulf Coasts of Alabama and Mississippi, stretching through Mobile and Biloxi to New Orleans and down into the French parishes. The Klan was quiet in west Texas as compared with its galloping strides in the eastern part of the state. The Rio Grande Valley went for the Klan candidate Robertson in the 1924 elections only because tough-talking Jim Ferguson impartially damned Mexicans along with Klansmen.

Although, occasionally, the Klan aggressively slugged it out with the newer stock American in the mining towns of western Pennsylvania, and in the mills and towns of Ohio's Mahoning Valley, the Invisible Empire tended to stay away from the enemy. The Klan ran into trouble in Buffalo, and kept, for the most part, out of Cleveland. It made a substantial foray into the motor city of Detroit where the waves of old and new American migration met head on, and dashed into Chicago, during the early days, only to withdraw again. The other cities of inland America it took by storm.

The underlying ethnographic pattern of the Klan's success was laid out by John M. Mecklin, son of a Scotch-Irish preacher in the hill country of Mississippi.[1] Mecklin left the ministry and the world of John Calvin to become a professor of sociology at Dartmouth, the kind of hard-nose iconoclastic teacher that only the best college presidents ever appreciate. In his perceptive early history of the Klan in 1924, he traced the movement of his fellow Rome-hating coreligionists. One stream moved down the piedmont plateau into the South. The other spread through the Ohio Valley and Great Lakes country into the Midwest and then across the mountains to what was to become the early Klan bastion of Oregon. Norman Weaver, the historian of the Great Lakes Klans,[2] drew the movement of these two

[1] John M. Mecklin, *The Ku Klux Klan* (New York, 1924), Chap. 2; *My Quest for Freedom* (New York, 1945).
[2] Norman Weaver, "The Knights of the Ku Klux Klan in Wisconsin, Indiana, Ohio, and Michigan." Unpublished Ph.D. dissertation, University of Wisconsin, 1954, Chap. 2.

pincers together in Indiana, Ohio, southern Michigan, and Wisconsin. Perhaps significantly, Indianapolis, the queen city of Northern Klandom, sat astride the old National Road, west, at the end of the limestone hills where the Southern and New England migration came together.

The Klan did well in the Mississippi Valley, spreading upward from its southern and southwestern bastions. The recruiters and sales representatives fanned out across the great American heartland and marched westward. Advance parties of Kleagles moved into the Sacramento Valley, central California, and Los Angeles, and from there swung northward to capture the native American state of Oregon. In the same manner that the continent itself had been settled, the Klan, after leapfrogging to the Coast, then began to fill up the land in between. The pioneer state of Colorado pledged its allegiance to the Invisible Empire, and imperial embassies were scattered about in the other mountain states.

The old-stock Americans were the nation's dominant majority, but they had a profound persecution complex. Their prestige and social power were not directly challenged by the immigrant influx, but now for almost a generation the new settlers who flocked to the shores of America had belonged to different ethnic and religious groups. The old fires of nativism had already been rekindled. To a highly fragmented, disorganized Protestant America, the Catholic constituted a tightly organized, disciplined, well-financed fighting force. The diverse legions of Protestantism saw themselves as being under attack, and this meant *America* in danger. Dominant though they were, they developed a defensive stance. Where the Klan could convince them of, or seize upon, this sense of being an embattled minority, its membership rolls soared. Colonel Simmons had sounded the tocsin. "What were the dangers which the white men saw threatening to crush and overwhelm Anglo-Saxon civilization?" he asked rhetorically. "The dangers were in the tremendous influx of foreign immigration, tutored in alien dogmas and alien creeds, flowing in from all climes and slowly pushing the native-born white American population into the center of the country, there to be ultimately overwhelmed and smothered."

The world thus endangered was that of the American village whose formal mores, and often actual values, were those preached from the Protestant pulpits. The Klan, as the aggressive self-constituted instrument of Protestant evangelicalism, was concerned with much more than defense against the immigrant and Rome. It placed special emphasis on morality, which meant opposition to the increasingly rapid erosion of small-town, heartland America. Roadhouse and urban sin were among the enemies, with their nonobservance of the Sabbath, and bootlegging, gambling, and carnal indulgence. E. H. Loucks, the historian of the Klan in Pennsylvania, summed up its role by pointing out that it did what the churches talked about. It had assumed the task, he wrote, of "the militant defense, fulfillment, and enforcement of Protestant America."

The Invisible Empire was, for the most part, motivated by a combination of idealism and reforming zeal. Its initial role was that of a reformer, and the symbols that it used were those of the "old-time religion." In almost every state the Klan was a champion of the "noble experiment" of Prohibition, and in areas, such as New Jersey and upstate New York, this was its greatest rallying cry. Most of the things which the Ku Klux Klan stood for and those which it opposed became unified in their focus upon a common enemy, the outsider-alien, as symbolized by the Roman Catholic Church.

Although these were primarily the values of the small town, the Klan, clothed in flowing white robes and a Reconstruction-era tradition and activated by Henry Ford's wonderful horseless carriage, was no stranger to the large metropolis. Although there were many cities where the Invisible Empire was made unwelcome and its Kleagles turned back disappointed, the Klan was a potent force in urban America. Its members paraded and elected from Portland, Maine, to Portland, Oregon. The Klan became the dominant issue in Dallas, Des Moines, and Denver and was a factor in the life of cities from Philadelphia to Phoenix. The Klan's anti-Catholicism attracted Milwaukee's socialists in droves, despite the denunciations by their leaders; while in Tulsa, the businessmen liked the hooded order because it opposed radicalism and crime.

The explanation for the Klan's urban strength is probably to be found in the degree to which the rapidly expanding cities were being fed by the native American stock from the country's small towns and rural areas. The average American city dweller in the 1920s was far from cosmopolitan, and the chances were that he was no more than one generation away from either the farm or the immigrant ship. The internal migrant brought his heartland values and his defensiveness with him to the metropolis. The sociologist Mecklin wrote that the urban dweller in Fort Worth and Dallas had largely come from obscure American towns and country places. Poorly educated and unsure of himself, he was a likely recruit for the Klan. "He is tossed about in the hurly-burly of our industrial and so-called democratic society," Mecklin explained. "Under the stress and strain of social competition he is made to realize his essential mediocrity. Yet according to traditional democratic doctrine he is born free and equal to his fellow who is outdistancing him in the race. Here is a large and powerful organization offering to solace his sense of defeat by dubbing him a knight of the Invisible Empire . . . the chosen conservator of American ideals, the keeper of the morals of the community."[3]

The nature of the psychic value which the Klan offered went far beyond night riding, reform, economic gain, or political advantage. It provided recreation and a sense of belonging. Probably the greatest strength of the Invisible Empire lay not in its creed but in its excitement and its in-group fraternalism. As Mecklin so well grasped, merely belonging to the Invisible Empire solved many of the Klansman's problems. This was much more important in the small town, where the lodge and the social organization have been a vital counterbalance to dullness and boredom of life.

The lodge nature and the ritual of the Ku Klux Klan appealed to the joiner. Its mass initiations, masks and robes, parades, picnics, barbecues, and other ceremonies, its field days, and its midnight cross burnings enlivened the life of the American village. For the payment of ten dollars, the Klansman could become a member of the mysterious Invisible Empire, the masked protector of the virtue of white womanhood, and of one-hundred-per-cent Americanism. He could participate in the sacred ritual that connected him with millions of others in fraternity and mystic power.

After kneeling in prayer in the lodge room or, whenever possible, before a blazing cross in the center of a white-robed circle of members, the would-be knight took his oath of allegiance. He swore obedience, secrecy, fidelity, and klannishness. He promised to cloak with silence all the behavior of fellow Klansmen, except in cases of treason against the United States, rape and malicious murder, and violation of the Klan oath. He also committed himself to uphold the American flag, Constitution, and those laws which were constitutional. He concluded that he would preserve the sacred constitutional rights and privileges of free public schools, free speech, free press,

3 Mecklin, *op. cit.*, pp. 107–8.

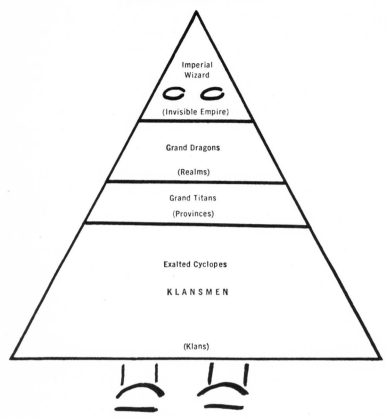

Imperial
Wizard

(Invisible Empire)

Grand Dragons

(Realms)

Grand Titans

(Provinces)

Exalted Cyclopes

K L A N S M E N

(Klans)

The organizational structure of the Ku Klux Klan

separation of church and state, liberty, white supremacy, just laws, and the pursuit of happiness against any encroachment.

Having covered everything, he crossed into the Invisible Empire. He was now a member of the lowest step in a great stairway of fraternity. Simmons had intended to build his lodge of four levels or orders, each characterized by higher rank, prestige, qualifications, and donations. He had never been allowed time to complete this ritualistic and philosophical edifice, and so its nature and nomenclature later went through a number of changes. In general outline there were four stages of Klankraft. They were K-uno, duo, trio, and quad, representing the plain, ordinary Klansman, Knights Kamelia, the Knights of the Great Forrest (named for the original head of the

Klan after the Civil War), or sometimes the Order of American Chivalry, and the Knights of the Midnight Mystery, the last intended for the aging Klansman who over the years had worked his way up the ladder.

The new Klansman found himself not only in a world of fraternal levels but also one of hierarchical structure, pyramiding organization, and strange names, almost always beginning with the mystical-sounding letters Kl. As a member of the Knights of the Ku Klux Klan, he gained access to its ceremonial language with its greetings and responses, avowals, and warnings. When two Klansmen chanced to meet, their fraternity could be quickly established and reaffirmed.

AYAK?	(Are You A Klansman?)
AKIA	(A Klansman I Am)
KIGY!	(Klansman, I Greet You!)
CLASP	(Clannish Loyalty A Sacred Principle)
CA BARK or	(Constantly Applied By All Real Klansmen)
SAN BOG	(Strangers Are Near, Be On Guard)

And so it went. In the proud days of the 1920s, it was a universal passport for the traveler. In the thirties and forties, in taverns in Hialeah Gardens, Florida, or the suburbs of Atlanta, cautious strangers might ask the fellow on the next stool, "Do you know a Mr. AYAK around here?"

A part of the Klan's mysterious language was its own secret Kalendar, with the years reckoned, sometimes incorrectly, from the birth and rebirth of the order.

Days	Weeks	Months
7. Desperate	5. Weird	12. Appalling
6. Dreadful	4. Wonderful	11. Frightful
5. Desolate	3. Wailing	10. Sorrowful
4. Doleful	2. Weeping	9. Mournful
3. Dismal	1. Woeful	8. Horrible
2. Deadly		7. Terrible
1. Dark		6. Alarming
		5. Furious
		4. Fearful
		3. Hideous
		2. Gloomy
		1. Bloody

If a Klansman were to receive a message reading:

> KIGY
>   ITSUB
> From one who traversed the Realm of the Unknown, wrestled the solemn Secret from the grasp of Night and became the Imperial Master of the Great Lost Mystery.
>   Done on this the Doleful day of the Woeful week of the Terrible month of the Year of the Klan LVIII and of the Year of the Reincarnation IX.

then he would know that Hiram W. Evans, *In The Sacred Unfailing Bond*, was sending him Fourth of July greetings for the year 1924.

The Klan offered a degree of mystery and a thrill of power greater than that of any other fraternal order and far outdistanced such contemporaries, and occasional competitors, as the newly founded American Legion. Whatever anyone else had, the Klan seemed to have it too, only better. With its highly accented sense of mystery, patriotism, communal guardianship, and nocturnal ramblings, the Ku Klux Klan gave to the Klansman the chance to live a second, more fulfilling life within the Invisible Empire. Where else could anyone get so much for ten dollars? It was this klannishness that underlay the appeal of the organization. In the 1920s the great fraternal lodge of America was the Ku Klux Klan, successfully acquiring and feeding upon the characteristics of a Protestant, gregarious, xenophobic, small-town subculture which extended from Maine to California, and which had been carried into the growing cities.

17

GOLD-RUSH DAYS IN CALIFORNIA

It was the legendary gold in the California hills which initially drew the attention of the Invisible Empire. From offices in the Walker-Auditorium Building in Los Angeles and the Pacific Building in San Francisco, Klaverns were soon organized from Calexico on the Mexican border to Santa Rosa, north of San Francisco. The centers of the Klan's most fervent activity were in Kern and Los Angeles counties, but wherever the Klan existed the quality of its recruits from the minister to the mailman, was impressive. The police chief of Bakersfield was a Klansman and so was the magistrate. So were the marshals, policemen, and sheriffs in Taft, along with the city trustees, county supervisor, and many businessmen and ministers. In Sacramento the Klan's organizer was a deputy sheriff and he reaped a rich harvest among the capital city's firemen, police, ministers, and public officials. A score of firemen and policemen belonged to the San Francisco Klavern.

The satellite communities that ringed the sprawling giant of Los Angeles formed the happy hunting ground of the Klan. Among the tidal ditches and canals of Venice, the Coney Island of the West, city hall practically doubled for Klan headquarters, while in Los Angeles itself, the sheriff and chief of police were among the members of the hooded order, and even the Catholic mayor of Los Angeles was reportedly solicited. The latter was obviously a mistake, for part of the Klan's mission in the forty-niner state was, as always, to guard against Roman subversion. The program of the Klan differed little from one part of the country to the next. In California as in Florida it counted on the oft-proven brew of white Protestant American fraternalism, the defense of morality, and opposition to drink and Rome, spiced with violence.

Klan recruiters were always on the alert to the dividends which might be reaped through a little bit of night riding. When it was reported that the suspected bootlegger in neighboring Inglewood was a Mexican rancher named Fidel Elduayen, it seemed a good opportunity to attend to both demons Rome and rum at the same time. At the next meeting of the local Klavern, plans were made for a raid to "put Inglewood on the Klan map." On the appointed night, the Klansmen surrounded the house and then burst in on their sleeping victims. The Elduayens denied being bootleggers and a search of the house revealed a disputed bottle of liquor but no still. The raiders bound the two Elduayen brothers and set off in unsuccessful search of a jail that would accept their captives.

Just as the prisoners were being borne off, disaster overtook the expedition. A neighbor had reported to the police that the Elduayen house was surrounded by masked men, and the night marshal arrived on the back seat of a commandeered motorcycle. When a masked guard stopped them, the marshal identified himself and demanded that the guard surrender. The mysterious sentry moved threateningly, and so Marshal Woerner shot him. Other masked men ran toward them. Woerner cried out to them that he was a policeman and held his flashlight so they could see his badge. When they failed to halt, he opened fire, which was returned, and two of the masked assailants fell. With the enemy too numerous and the situation clearly out of control, Woerner and his impromptu chauffeur hastily departed. The Elduayen brothers were set free later that night, but one man, who turned out to have been the local constable, lay dead, and his son and a deputy sheriff had been wounded.

With the case making daily banner headlines, the district attorney of Los Angeles raided Klan headquarters. The Grand Goblin, W. S. Coburn was taken by surprise. He asked if he might get his coat out of his inner office, and when the door was closed he seized what membership lists he could and jammed them into a hastily addressed envelope. Then, opening his door, he sprinted past the surprised officers and slipped it into the building mail chute. The men from the district attorney's office carried off the remaining files and records and studied them carefully. The case was now permanently anchored in the headlines. District Attorney Lee Woolwine denounced the Klan as "an unAmerican band of hooded cowards and outlaws," and a grand jury hearing was finally ordered. The Spanish-American War Veterans, the local heads of the American Legion, and the Pioneer Society denounced the Klan raiders. So did the Church Federation and the Ministerial Union. The city council passed a strong antimask ordinance, and the Eagles and Knights of

Pythias denied their halls to Klan meetings. Long Beach and Los Angeles resolved not to hire Klansmen, and district attorneys from all over the state were visiting Los Angeles to have a look at the captured membership lists for their counties. The Los Angeles grand jury was subpoenaing men whose names were on the Klan's lists, and investigations were underway in Kern County, where even more serious violence had taken place.

These were, indeed, perilous times for the Invisible Empire, even though Colonel Simmons announced from Atlanta that none of his men could have been involved in violence because the Klan stood for law and order. Resignations were flooding in, and so the beleaguered Klan sent its best speakers out through the state to rally the faithful.

In June 1922, the grand jury handed down indictments for kidnaping with intent to murder against thirty-seven Klansmen, including Coburn. To counter the prosecution's impressive evidence, the defense testified that the Elduayen home was a veritable bootlegger's den and applauded the defendants' courage in protecting their community. The presiding judge, who had opposed any investigation in the first place, told the jury to find the defendants innocent if they had been led by a police officer in pursuit of lawbreakers. The jury acquitted the raiders who in turn showed their appreciation by stopping by the judge's chambers to load up with his campaign literature.

News of the Inglewood raid and the subsequent seizure of the Klan's state records brought to light what the Invisible Empire had meant in other California communities. There were reports of Klan threats in Alameda, a kidnaping in San Bernardino, the flogging of a man in Fresno, and a literal reign of terror in Kern County. Twice before, the rich farmlands in the southern end of the San Joaquin Valley had returned to the lawless frontier stage. Once was when gold was found in the Kern River, and the other was at the turn of the century with the discovery of oil. Now for the third time, a new kind of wealth had brought new violence. In the summer of 1921, an itinerant Kleagle passed through the county selling law enforcement and the Protestant defense of American patriotism. Soon police officers, judges, politicians, ministers, and businessmen were joining and there were active Klans in the towns of Bakersfield, Taft, and Tehachapi.

Within a few months the Klan had launched a reign of terror. Men and women had been threatened, flogged, tortured, and forced to leave town. In the rough, bleak little oil town of Taft, where almost anyone who was anybody belonged to the Klan, a doctor and past president of the chamber of commerce was suing for divorce. He was lured from his house and taken to the local ball park. There, before thirty hooded Klansmen, his wife, and three other women, he was ordered to stop divorce action. When he tried to explain, his captors stripped him and hanged him until he was unconscious. Then they revived him and thrice flogged him into unconsciousness with knotted rope and wire whips. Then they cut his back, warned him against continuing the divorce action, revealing what had happened, or remaining in town, and left him on the ground.

Although some of the officers of the Bakersfield Klavern resigned over the episode, the terror was firmly established. Klansmen paraded, armed, and few people dared to complain. At least one victim who refused to leave town was twice flogged, tarred and feathered, and a Maricopa druggist was left on the road with fires burning on either side of him, to keep his coat of tar hot. Sometimes there were several victims in a single night. The Kern County district attorney investigated, and his men patrolled the roads, but it was not until the Inglewood affair that those authorities who opposed the Klan got the needed list of names. A grand jury reported that politics and "domestic troubles, jealousies, and other evidences of malice and hate" were at the bottom of the Klan's behavior.

While the trial of the Inglewood raiders was being prepared in Los Angeles, several Kern County Klansmen were convicted. Most cities passed antimask laws, some with considerable reluctance, and almost all of the Klan trustees of Taft were eventually forced out of office by a newspaper-backed recall election.[1]

The press in Kern County, led by Taft's *Midway Driller,* had fought the Klan from its beginning, and the major papers of the state joined in attacking the hooded order. Lists of Klansmen, which local district attorneys had obtained from the Los Angeles authorities, were being published in San Diego, Orange, Ventura, Santa Barbara, Fresno, and San Francisco counties, often accompanied by grand jury investigations, municipal antimask laws, and the firing of Klansmen. Prominent citizens, with their faces thus revealed, hastily resigned from the no longer Invisible Empire.

But each Klavern and community had to go through its own convolutions. The Klan had come to Sacramento only a short time

---

[1] For the Kern County story, see Sharon Lybeck, "The Ku Klux Klan in California." Unpublished paper, University of California at Los Angeles, 1961, in possession of Professor Harold Hyman, University of Illinois.

before the Inglewood raid. On Palm Sunday of 1922, the Klan made its first public appearance at Rev. William E. Harrison's Westminster Presbyterian Church at Thirteenth and K streets. Soon the city was full of stories of Klan meetings, initiations, and church visits. Observant reporters and the captured files in Los Angeles made the membership known. It included the usual prized assortment of public officials, ministers, police and firemen, and businessmen. The controversy over the Klan now became the first topic of conversation and debate in the state capital. The Grand Master forbade all California Masons to become Klansmen, and Governor William Stephens gave orders that employees and National Guardsmen must choose between the Klan and the state.

Since a similar local warning had already been given, the city manager of Sacramento felt justified in dismissing Klan fire- and policemen. However, the city council refused to back him up, and the suspended Klansmen were soon back on duty. It was only natural that the Klan should crow a little, and so Reverend Harrison and his colleague, Reverend W. A. Redburn, at the Wesley Methodist Church let their congregations know the facts of life. The Invisible Empire, Reverend Harrison pronounced, was doing more for the moral and spiritual life of the community than any other organization outside of the church, despite the un-American activities of the city manager, who was probably a Romanist. When his turn came, Reverend Redburn got right down to the real peril of Romanism:

> Nearly all the bawdy houses, bootleg joints, and other dives are owned or controlled by Romanists. A member of the Catholic faith may go to Mass in the morning and lie drunk in the gutter all day, Sunday or any other day.
>
> What would happen if I and the other ministers of the Protestant churches of this city, if we had sufficient money, would purchase a lot downtown and erect on it a building with barred windows like a jail and place in it twelve beautiful young women and keep them there, to be seen only by the pastors of our churches. Why, you would throw us in jail inside of twenty-four hours or run us out of town. But I want to tell you that this thing is going on in this city.[2]

However, what the press and the city manager of Sacramento

---

[2] The Sacramento *Bee*, June 12, 1922, quoted by Donald J. Merlino, "Sacramento's Cloak of Secrecy." Unpublished paper, Sacramento State College, 1961, p. 19, in possession of Professor J. A. McGowan, Sacramento State College.

were not able to do, the Klansmen soon did for them. By the fall of 1922 the Klavern was split wide open as Klansmen battled Klansmen, through the courts and newspapers, over where the money was going.

But 1922 was not solely a time of disaster for the hooded knights. It was election year in California, and, for the Klan, there was no problem of deciding whom it wanted. With their hated adversary, Lee Woolwine, the district attorney from Los Angeles, trying to move up to the governor's mansion, the Klan naturally supported his opponent. Not only was Friend W. Richardson sufficiently conservative to please the Klan, but he had the added advantage of being close to, if not a member of, the Invisible Empire. Whether or not he actually was a wearer of the robe was not clear, and the governor himself refused to comment during the election. According to reports from inside the Sacramento Klavern, the question was asked in meeting. "I just don't like to say as to that, Boys," the visiting state leader replied, adding, "I can say this—Richardson is all right." At this point one of the local leaders jumped up and asserted positively that Richardson was a Klansman. With Woolwine a Roman Catholic, the issue was clear: it was a dry, patriotic America versus the combined menaces of rum and Rome.

Although the Klan's endorsed candidate could not prevail against Hiram Johnson's hold on his Senate seat, Friend Richardson swept into office along with other candidates favored by the Klan. Among them was the judge who had presided at the Inglewood trial. Only then did the governor-elect choose to deny any affiliation with the Klan. However, with administration backing, Sacramento's Klan chaplain took over pastoral duties for the Senate, and local Klans in Sacramento and Roseville demanded that their legislators give support to the governor.

It would be difficult to say that the Klan had become a power in the state, though, for the affairs in Inglewood and in Kern County had turned its early surging tide. In 1923 and 1924 the Klan boasted of new members and turned out respectable thousands for an occasional big rally. Its night riding was minor and the Prohibition agent in Sacramento spurned Klan help on his raids. There were reports of anti-Japanese demonstrations, but Klan leaders claimed that they had no intention of disturbing Japanese farmers. Nativist sentiment was strong on the West Coast, but the Klan as the protector of the native-born, white Americans never gave the problem proper attention. It was not until 1923 that Klan papers became interested in the menace of alien land ownership and began publishing occasional articles. The next year Japanese correspondents stirred up public opinion at home by reports that Japanese farmers were being forced out of Sacramento and Sonoma counties, but Klan leaders denied any such intent. The issue that did move the Klan was Bible reading in the schools, and the Invisible Empire pushed hard for it. During a bitter organizing strike on the San Pedro water front, Klansmen picketed the I.W.W. headquarters.

In 1924, however, the state passed an antimask law, and the Klan's political influence continued on the decline. When the Imperial Wizard made his grand postelection tour of his western provinces, he found his welcome a weak one. San Francisco was particularly disappointing, the *National Kourier* complained, primarily because a hostile press refused him publicity and advertising room. Happily, however, the Klan journal commented, Oakland was more friendly. Although the people of the old German-founded town of Anaheim turned out its Klan trustees in a recall election in early 1925, suburban Los Angeles remained one of the busiest Klan areas.

The center of Klan activity, however, had shifted to Tulare County, between Bakersfield and Fresno. It was there in the county seat of Visalia, where the ranchers had once fought against the corrupt outside world represented by the railroads, that the Invisible Empire kept up the good fight against the dangers of corruption by Rome. The Klan remained active in California into the middle thirties, meeting in Visalia, San Diego, Long Beach, and a score of other towns, attending sunrise services, parades, picnics and memorials, and entertaining the visiting Imperial Wizard in the early thirties. The Klan was occasionally made welcome by mayors and city councils, but it was as a member of the lodge, rather than the political, world of California.

18

PIKES PEAK OR BUST

The success story of the western Klan was Colorado. The Invisible Empire was not able to rally behind a major piece of legislation like the school bill in Oregon, nor did it ever recruit an army the size of its legions in Texas, but it filled the seats of government, from city hall to the governor's mansion. Although its message was carried across the plains and mountains of the state, Klandom lodged itself in the narrow strip of land at the foothills of the Rockies, which contains Colorado's major cities. Its stronghold was Denver where, by 1925, one person out of every seven had pledged his allegiance to the hooded order. The Klan fought its way to control of the Republican party and swept municipal and state elections, captured the bench and appointive offices of Denver, dominated the lower house of the legislature, and sent two of its friends to the Senate of the United States.

The Ku Klux Klan first popped up in Denver late in the spring of 1921. Its announced purpose was to uphold "law and order" and it reminded people of Colorado's pioneer days and vigilante heritage, but the Klan had a new definition of the villain. The bad men no longer tied handkerchiefs over their faces and carried six-shooters. Now it was the good guys that went masked, while the evildoers lurked in the Jewish section along West Colfax Avenue, among the Negro and Spanish-American settlements north of Capitol Hill, and with the Italians of the Highlands and the Poles, German-Russians, and Austrians of Globeville.

Threatening letters, including one received by the mayor of Denver, brought a grand jury investigation and a spate of unfavorable publicity for the Klan which was operating under the name of the Denver Doers Club. Although there was no report of actual Klan night riding, its paramilitary Klavaliers drilled regularly, and a local broker went to jail for contempt of court because he believed his Klan oath precluded his giving testimony.

After the initial burst of public attention, the Klan concentrated on recruitment, keeping out of the headlines until it emerged as a leading force in Denver politics in the spring of 1923. It failed in an attempt to recall the able, young, and hostile district attorney of Denver, Philip S. Van Cise, but it did help defeat the similarly unfriendly mayor. Despite his claims to the contrary during the campaign, the new mayor, Ben Stapleton, was a Klansman. He used the extensive appointive power of his office, and soon members of the hooded order held most of the major offices of the city. This was particularly the case in the police and legal departments and on the various municipal benches. Whether or not there was any understanding between them, many of the business interests of Denver found the new turn of affairs to be highly satisfying. A recall election the next year failed to unseat Mayor Stapleton, and the Grand Dragon of the Klan in Colorado took public credit for Stapleton's victory.

The results were soon apparent. For nearly forty years a fight had been going on over the ownership and rates of the city's street railway system. Now, with Klansman Clarence J. Morley as city attorney, the case went hands down to the private transit corporation with a grant of perpetual right of way and a valuation that surprised even the company.

The Klan's great year in Colorado was 1924. After weathering Mayor Stapleton's recall election in Denver, the Klan expanded into state-wide politics. When the Republican party assembled in Denver's city auditorium to name its candidates, the Klan was firmly in control. Dr. John Galen Locke, the Grand Dragon, sat in a box in the rear of the building, supervising the proceedings. Klan candidates were put on the slate for practically every county as well as for most Denver and state-wide offices. City Attorney Rice Means was picked for the Senate, as was a friendly nonmember, Lawrence Phipps. Klansman Clarence J. Morley, now a criminal division judge in Denver, ran for governor, and Judge Royal Graham entered the lists against Ben Lindsey for judge of the children's court.

The Klan take-over in the Republican party was not without opposition. Many regulars were incensed over what they felt was the prostitution of their party. Clarence C. Hamlin, editor and publisher of the Colorado Springs *Gazette* and Republican national committeeman, denounced the divisions within the party that had enabled Klan candidates to win the nominations without a majority of the vote. Loyalty to the party and to President Coolidge did not require that the Klan's Republican nominees be supported in November, he announced. He was joined in his opposition by the Republican state chairman and by Philip Van Cise, the young war-hero district attorney, who had headed a "visible government" slate in Denver. Other prominent Republican leaders joined in discussions of a possible independent Republican ticket.

As the election approached, however, the two contestants were the Klan-Republicans and the Democrats. The most spectacular struggle, and the one that attracted the most nationwide attention, was for the $4000-a-year judgeship of the juvenile and family court of Denver. Ben B. Lindsey had been occupant of the post for twenty-four years and he did not consider it to be vacant.

Ben Lindsey had been brought to Colorado as a child, and when his father died he took over the support of the family. He studied law, went into Democratic politics, and was making quite a reputation for himself as a lawyer and a legal reformer. In 1900 he received a patronage appointment to the county court bench in Denver. One of his early cases concerned an immigrant boy charged with stealing lumps of coal from the railroad tracks. It was a routine affair and as Lindsey pronounced sentence on him there was a despairing wail from the boy's mother who, shrieking, battered her head against the wall of the courtroom.

His subsequent investigation into the poverty-stricken background of the family opened up a whole new field of awareness and concern for Lindsey. The upshot was that he got a juvenile and family court established which was given exclusive jurisdiction over youthful offenders. It was one of the first of its kind and it became the most famous. Judge Lindsey won international recognition as an expert on family and children's problems. He was "the kids' judge," and he got the legislature to pass more than a score of laws protecting their rights. In his heated struggles to change the environment which he felt was at the heart of their problems, he gained the animosity of press, clergy, and business. His campaigns against child labor and corruption, and for a better urban life made lifelong enemies of the utility companies and other powers of Denver. Both parties refused to nominate him. Attempts were made to remove him and to abolish his court, but he held on to his seat through three appointments and six elections for a quarter of a century.

In his pursuit of reform and in his zeal for his charges, Ben Lindsey made enemies. Some people believed that he encouraged crime by being too lenient, and that his methods were too unorthodox. Others felt that he had interfered with their legitimate business interests and pursuit of profit. Even for many who approved of his work, a quarter of a century was an uncomfortably long time to live with a Jeremiah in their midst. And to all of these was added a new antagonist, for he had been outspoken in his opposition to the Klan.

The campaign of 1924 was one of the bitterest and dirtiest in the history of the Centennial State. The Klan put up several hundred campaign workers plus most of the money. Klansmen packed the rallies of its opponents and turned them into near riots as the police refused to interfere. Crosses burned on neighboring hillsides, and the Klan held mass meetings on the mesas of Table Mountain just west of Denver. "They paid ten dollars to hate somebody," Judge Lindsey commented afterwards, "and they were determined to get their money's worth." He told of addressing one meeting at which a woman screamed in his face, "You cur, you dirty cur, you dirty cur." Having been responsible for over fifty laws for the protection of various rights for women, Lindsey was appalled by her hatred. "Madam," he asked, "why do you call me a dirty cur?" "You are not one-hundred-per-cent American," she screamed. "You are against the Klan."

The general election was a landslide for Coolidge, and for the Colo-rado Klan. Klansman Clarence Morley, who had deliberately stacked the juries in his court with Klansmen, was elected governor. So, too, were the Klan candidates for U. S. Senator, most state offices, and the lower house of the legislature. Only a few judgeships escaped the Klan grasp in Denver. One of them was the juvenile court. Four years before, Ben Lindsey had been elected by a twenty-five-thousand-vote margin. This time, although he ran that far ahead of the Democratic ticket in Denver, his margin was only several hundred, and the Klan moved to contest the results. For three years the case was to be in the courts, while the Klan and its friends maneuvered in the legislature to either abolish his court or to bring it under the appointive power of Klan officeholders.

There were a number of reasons why the Klan was eager to do this. For an organization which was pursuing all possible paths to power, possession of the children's-court records would have opened up the private lives of many of the city's most prominent families. The business interests which had fought Lindsey in the past now saw a chance to remove their troublesome gadfly, and the Klan knew a troublemaker when it saw one.

The degree to which Judge Lindsey could and would create trouble for the Klan was soon revealed. Less than three months after its great election victory, Lindsey had the Grand Dragon up before him on the charges of conspiracy and kidnaping. John Galen Locke was a large, heavy-set, affable man who looked something like a goateed version of Grover Cleveland. Although he had been refused membership by the Denver County Medical Society, he practiced medicine using his own small private hospital. He had been an early member and organizer for the Klan, and sometime late in 1923 was elevated to its top post in the state.

The Klan's success was exhilarating and Dr. Locke was carried away with a sense of power. When the son of a Denver hotelman was indiscreet, he was kidnaped and brought to the Grand Dragon's office. There, faced by the operating table and glittering array of scalpels and other surgical implements, the boy was given the choice of wedlock or never being able to father a child again. A minister was brought, and the wedding ceremony was held in Dr. Locke's office. The boy's parents protested and, since the case involved juveniles, it was brought before Judge Lindsey.

With the Grand Dragon now temporarily out of both jail and of the headlines, the business of the state of Colorado could proceed. Clarence Morley was sworn in as governor and used his inaugural address to call for a ban on undesirable aliens and sacramental wine. While the swells of Denver were packing the Arena for the horseshows, the governor graced the First Annual Ku Klux Klan Boxing and Wrestling Tourney being conducted in the Klan's newly acquired Cotton Mills Stadium. The tourney was immensely popular, with the home-town team from Denver University carrying off a good portion of the honors. The next week the governor made Dr. Locke, his aide-de-camp, a colonel of the National Guard Medical Corps, and recruiting and publicity officer.

John Galen Locke was good at getting publicity, but it always seemed to be the wrong kind. By the end of the spring he was under investigation by the Internal Revenue Service, and his two simultaneous court cases furnished daily fare for the newspaper-reading audience. The heart of the fight with the government was that Locke had never paid any income tax. The Internal Revenue Service figured that he owed thirteen years' worth and wanted to have a lock at both his and the Klan's bank accounts to see how much it should be. After many court appearances, Locke announced that his books were lost. The court fined him $1500 and sent him to jail for ten days to start remembering.

Of course it was Dr. Locke who was getting into all of the trouble, but the name and reputation of the Klan went everywhere that he did. Even in jail, the Grand Dragon found neither quiet nor solitude. A new controversy erupted over whether or not his National Guard appointment was legal, and when he sent out word that there was to be no violence while he was in jail, this also hit the headlines. His press was never particularly good in Denver, and the Rocky Mountain *News* commented tartly that although Locke did not see fit to pay his income tax, seventy-three thousand other people in Colorado paid theirs. However, this did not seem to faze his followers, for hundreds of them visited him in jail, and his cell was piled with gifts of tobacco, food, candy, and flowers.

All of the unwelcome publicity did not initially seem to hurt the Klan. The month before its Grand Dragon went to jail, the Klan carried six of the nine offices in the Denver municipal elections and was disappointed that it had not carried them all. The Invisible Empire numbered over sixty thousand Klansmen, Klanswomen, Junior Klansmen, and Riders of the Red Robe, and exercised more extensive political power than any other realm in the Empire. Non-Klansmen were removed from office whenever the civil service laws permitted, and the state's welfare program was nearly wrecked. When the state civil service commission turned down Governor Morley's appointment of fifty-two unsalaried auxiliary Prohibition agents, the Klan sought to abolish the system. Judge Lindsey narrowly escaped being reorganized off his juvenile court bench, by the state Senate. Having elected a Klansman as governor, the Klan's goal was to concentrate power in his hands by making most state offices appointive.

The Klan was riding high. Although temporary incarceration precluded the presence of Grand Dragon Locke, the First Annual Klan Picnic drew over a hundred thousand people to Lakeside Park. While the picnickers frolicked happily, the 100-man Imperial Band of Denver brassily serenaded them. Klan crosses burned on western hillsides and ex-Sister Mary Angel told over fifty meetings in Denver about the venereal sins of the Roman Catholic Church. In separate sessions "for men only," she exhorted them to steer clear of Catholic girls and told them lurid stories of convent sin, displaying little gingham bags—with drawstrings—specially manufactured for conveying the fruits of priestly lust to the furnaces. Although there were no reports of Klan night riding, one form of violence did come in the Klan's wake, and that was crime. Dr. Locke had selected a candidate for chief of police in Denver and the mayor duly ratified the choice. Vice and bootlegging flourished. Crime and violence were rampant. Soon this was too much even for the mayor. Without informing his chief of police, he conducted a vice raid and soon many Klan policemen were under suspension and investigation.

Despite Dr. Locke's cheery confidence, the troubles of the Klan mounted. A permanent state-wide organization, calling itself "The Constitutionalists," had formed to offer political opposition. Within the Invisible Empire, internal pressures were reaching volcanic intensity. Mayor Stapleton was seriously concerned over conditions in Denver, and Locke was trying to pull too many strings. In addition, the Grand Dragon's widely publicized troubles with the law were politically dangerous to those associated with him. They got in touch with the Imperial Wizard in Atlanta, and Evans agreed.

On the first of July, 1925, the Grand Dragon addressed a closed meeting of some twenty thousand Klansmen gathered at their Cotton Mills Stadium. With Evans' emissary in the audience, Locke announced that the National Klan requested the resignation of its Grand Dragon for Colorado. Although offering to comply, Locke brought the faithful to their feet, roaring in protest. He then pronounced the suspension of Mayor Stapleton, Senator Means, and the six other Klansmen who had sought his downfall.

The Invisible Empire was in serious trouble, for the Klansmen of Denver rallied to Locke. After two suspenseful weeks, Evans decided to go through with it. At a meeting almost twice as large as the previous one, Locke read a telegram from the Imperial Wizard about turning over all Klan funds and property to the parent organization. Locke's followers, who composed most of the Klansmen in Denver, talked of plans to turn themselves into a new Klan-like organization called the Minute Men. As both sides tensed, everyone waited for Dr. Locke to make a battle of it, particularly for the valuable Cotton Mills property. However, Locke had none of the fighting spirit. In a series of conferences with Klan representatives, for which Governor Morley was kind enough to loan his state house offices, Locke gave up all the assets except the Cotton Mills Stadium, which the courts later ordered the two factions to share.

Ex-Grand Dragon Locke never attempted to make anything of the Minute Men, but Klan ranks had been badly depleted. The Klan's chief Washington lobbyist, W. F. Zumbrunn, who had been handling the whole Locke affair, reported that thirty-seven Klaverns had remained loyal, including practically all of those in the western and southern parts of the state. The Klan reinstated the men whom Locke had suspended and reorganized its forces at a state-wide meet in Pueblo late in July, but with the loss of the Klans in Pikes Peak, Greeley, and Denver, the Klan had been deeply wounded.

The prestige of the Klan had not been helped either when the able Secretary of State, Carl S. Milliken, resigned in the middle of the conflict. Milliken had been one of the state's original members and, for a while, was number two man of the Denver Klavern. At the same time, Milliken's deputy was the son-in-law of the internal revenue collector who had gotten Dr. Locke into much of his trouble in the first place. Moved by integrity and belated political foresight, Milliken refused to remove his assistant. However, he did fire the one-time labor leader and now deputy state labor commissioner who had pressed him to do so.

The great debacle of the Colorado Klan took place in the early summer of 1925, but it was not until a year later that the political power of the Klan was put to the test. Klansman Rice Means, who was running for re-election to a full term in the Senate, led a Klan ticket in the Republican primary. Also rallied behind him were the Anti-Saloon League and his fellow Klan-elected senator, L. C. Phipps, who now headed the Republican National Senatorial Campaign Committee. In the opposition were the regular Republican leaders who were out to cleanse the party. Charles W. Waterman, counsel of President Coolidge's Oil Conservation Board, took charge of the fight. He himself was running against Means for the Senate. The Klan could only muster a third of its former might, and the antis swept the primary.

With anti-Klan slates nominated by both parties, the Klan issue might logically have been considered settled. This was not yet the case. It was too good to let go of, and both parties wanted to run on it. The result was that each attempted to hang the Klan label on the other. The feeling over the Klan was so bitter that it pushed the other issues, such as the sugar tariff, the world court, and Prohibition, aside. After a campaign full of confused maneuverings and angry charges, a highly mixed but strongly anti-Klan set of officeholders was elected.

The Ku Klux Klan was still to win one victory in Colorado, although it represented revenge rather than power. After its great sweep in 1924, the Klan charged that a number of the ballots in the predominantly Jewish precinct of Denver had been fraudulently marked for Lindsey. After a look at the evidence and the Klan's witness, the district court threw out the case. The defeated lawyer sued the Klan for payment of his fees and the plaintiff, Royal S. Graham, committed suicide rather than face an investigation by the state bar association.

Even this did not settle things. The Klan put up counsel for Graham's widow, and in 1927 the Colorado Supreme Court ruled in her favor. Since the lower court had dismissed the charges of fraud, Judge Lindsey had not needed to present his side of the case. Now, without permitting him to do so, the Supreme Court threw out not just the disputed ballots but the whole precinct. After a quarter of a century the nation's most famous children's judge was out of a job. The U. S. Supreme Court said it had no jurisdiction, and the verdict stood. On a vacant lot Judge Lindsey lit a "shame bonfire" destroying his files and records so that they might not fall into the wrong hands.

To many Coloradans, life seemed more peaceful without Ben Lindsey on the bench. He had only recently become an apostle of companionate marriage, based on birth control and easy divorce, which many mistook for wedding-less trial marriage. Within months after the Supreme Court's election verdict, he was disbarred from the practice of law for having accepted payment for his influence in a children's inheritance case. Under this triple cloud, he left for California. In 1933 the Supreme Court of Colorado offered to reinstate him as a lawyer if he would return and apologize for the case which had led to his disbarment. He refused, and the next year was elected to a superior court judgeship in Los Angeles by the largest number of votes ever cast for such an office. He served on the bench there until his death a decade later.

19

IN DEFENSE OF INLAND AMERICA

1

Although St. Louis was the headquarters city for the Klan's Mississippi Valley sales division and the Missouri realm became one of the largest in the Invisible Empire, it never really rated very high in the councils or the history of the Klan. Despite its growth to over a hundred thousand members, the Missouri Klan gained relatively little state-wide political power, and no powerful personalities or leaders emerged. Nevertheless, the hooded order became a major issue in Missouri politics and in the lives of countless small towns and communities within its borders.

There was relatively little reported night riding. A sixty-year-old Warrensburg farmer was whipped during the Klan's nationally bloody summer of 1921, and Missouri was lucky that this was all. Klansmen formed a rifle club in Springfield and generally went about armed. The only man to get shot, however, was a Klansman who managed to do it to himself with his own gun during a scuffle at a St. Joe meeting. Down in the southeastern boot-heel section of the state ruled by big planters and script-issuing merchants, white sharecroppers from Kentucky and Tennessee donned their masks and robes to drive newer Negro migrants out of the cotton fields. Violence lurked in the hands of Klan antagonists as well, for the shooting in St. Joe had taken place during the fight which followed the heckling of a speaker at the Klan's Crystal Theatre. A Klan display in a Kansas City store window was twice damaged by bricks, and Maxwellton Inn where the Klan held an initiation was bombed.

Generally speaking, Klan leadership and respectability tended to come from the ministry. Many Exalted Cyclopes, like the one in St. Joe, were ministers. Ministers addressed Klan meetings and a Klan evangelistic service was held in the House of Representatives Building in the state capital. In St. Louis, where the Invisible Empire claimed great support from local ministers, a sermon on the questions "What would Jesus say about the Ku Klux Klan? Would he accept their gifts?" concluded that he would have been a Klansman.

The Klan recruited and established Klaverns throughout the state, but its real strength lay in the western counties bordering on Kansas and Nebraska. The Klan's first major venture in politics was in the 1922 senatorial race. Both of the candidates were hostile, and so the Klan's leaders decided that the Democrat, James Reed, was the more dangerous of the two. Reed was a fiery individualist who had bitterly opposed Woodrow Wilson over the ratification of the League of Nations, which was a mark in his favor, but he was also an outspoken opponent of Prohibition and this would not do at all. Most of the Klan's twenty thousand votes in Kansas City were thrown against him, and he managed to squeeze through to victory by a very narrow margin.

It was in this same election that the ex-captain of Battery D of the 129th Field Artillery, now an unsuccessful haberdasher, was elected judge for the eastern district of Independence's Jackson County. During the hotly contested primary, Klan support was something to be considered, and at the urging of his supporters Harry Truman handed over his ten dollars. The accounts of what happened next do not agree. Truman's own story was that when he was told to promise not to give any jobs to Catholics he angrily withdrew and got his money back. A different version was that the future President did go through with his initiation although he was never an active member. At any rate, the Klan did not support him in the primary, and in 1924 the Invisible Empire, deeply involved in local machine politics, played a big part in defeating his bid for re-election.

Despite its battle against Jim Reed in 1922, the Missouri Klan generally favored the Democrats, but there were many in the party for whom the feeling was not mutual. In April of 1924, Missouri Democrats chose their delegates to the National Convention in Madison Square Garden and considered the adoption of an anti-Klan plank. In the pandemonium of the bitter all-night session that eventually watered down the resolution, the national Donnybrook in the Garden was clearly forecast. With Klan strength over the one-hundred-thousand mark, the Invisible Empire had become a force in Missouri politics and small-town life. Earlier in the spring it had been the dominant issue in numerous municipal elections which had seen victories for Klan-supported tickets in towns, such as Excelsior

Springs, Lee's Summit, Joplin, and Carthage, balanced by defeats in Poplar Bluff, Bunceton, and Anderson.

Although it showed strength in both parties, the Democrats were in a particular quandary over what to do about the Klan. The question was whether it was more dangerous to favor the Klan or oppose it. Congressman Harry S. Hawes of St. Louis, who led the antis, warned that the party would lose the state unless it took a strong stand against the Klan. Apart from reasons of conviction, Missouri had too many Roman Catholic, Jewish, and Negro voters to be thus slighted. The Klan's dominant concern with Prohibition and anti-Catholicism was particularly likely to offend Missouri's large German population. Nevertheless, in both the Democratic and Republican primaries, the winning candidates for governor bore the Klan endorsement.

In a highly charged election, the Klan's main support went to the Democratic candidate who ran nearly twenty thousand votes ahead of his ticket even though he lost the governorship by a small margin in the Coolidge landslide. Missouri presented the curious paradox wherein the Klan favored the national Republican ticket, while supporting a Democrat for the top state office. Whereas the national Democrats denounced the Klan and the Republicans remained silent, in Missouri it was the Republicans who took up the attack and local Democrats straddled where they could.

After 1924, Klan strength was declining. The once powerful Klavern in Springfield disbanded, and Klan support in Kansas City dwindled away. Recruitment could not match the losses, though for several years Missouri remained one of the most numerous realms in the Empire. Although its political influence was muted, the Ku Klux Klan continued to operate as a lodge organization, particularly in faithful St. Joe and in the western tier of counties where the Klaverns of the Invisible Empire offered cheer and Kompanionship into the 1930s.

2

The Ku Klux Klan crossed the Missouri River to enter Nebraska at Omaha, where Klavern No. 1 established its headquarters at Forty-first and Farnum streets. The Klan soon spread across the state, with its main strength in Platte River cities such as Fremont, Lincoln, Grand Island and North Platte. The five thousand members in Lancaster County, site of the capital city of Lincoln, numbered more than a tenth of the state's total. Anti-Catholicism was its usual stock and trade, but no night riding was reported, and the Klan, largely Republican, was not an important force in politics. The queen city of Omaha was never friendly to its enticements. During the early days, the mayor of Omaha forbade its public parades. In 1926 when it made a major effort in municipal politics, an anti-Klan candidate for sheriff overwhelmed the combined efforts of the Klan and the local political machine.

By the end of the decade, the Klan was still there and still uninfluential. The national Klan took a hand in the 1930 senatorial campaign in an effort to unseat George W. Norris, Nebraska's unbridled insurgent Republican, but its efforts were unavailing. For the most part, Klan power was something that Klansmen only dreamt about in their mystical citadels in York and Grand Island, as the Invisible Empire in Nebraska ebbed away.

3

The Klan faced active opposition in Iowa, but it grew anyway. The American Legion was an early and powerful antagonist. The Kossuth County Farm Bureau denounced it, and so did the Grand Master of the Masons. The city councilmen of Des Moines were hostile, and in 1923 the legislature passed a law against masked wrongdoing. In the small town of Goodall, high school students went out on strike against a substitute teacher whose husband was reputedly a Klansman, and in the farming town of Corning, seventy-five miles southwest of Des Moines, a Klan meeting in the middle 1920s touched off a first-class riot.

Despite these shows of disfavor, however, the Klan did well. It got started in Des Moines, the state's capital and largest city, and spread rapidly, particularly in the central part of the state. A number of ministers acted as organizers, and the head of the Des Moines Klan was the pastor of the Capitol Hill Church of Christ. Reverend C. N. Carpenter preached a sermon on "Why I Am a Member of the Klan," and caused a momentary sensation when he rhetorically challenged the Knights of Columbus to make its oath public. When the local K.C. leader accepted Reverend Carpenter's offered pulpit and quietly read the oath aloud, the excitement subsided. The Klan did not disappear from the headlines though, for the Des Moines *Register* carried daily front-page stories about Mer Rouge and the Simmons-

Evans fight for control in Atlanta. The tale of terror from the bayous of Louisiana had been particularly important in building anti-Klan sentiment in American Legion and legislative circles, but the Klan continued to expand and moved into local Des Moines politics in order to oppose those city commissioners who had been unfriendly.

Nineteen twenty-four was election year, and the Klan was busy. It threw its support behind the former state treasurer, who was seeking the Republican nomination for governor, and fielded a list of favorites in many sections of the state. Although W. J. Burbank narrowly lost out for the gubernatorial spot, the Klan's smoothly functioning precinct workers and poll watchers in Des Moines managed to carry Polk County for him and for almost all of the other candidates on its "blue ticket." Friendly officials also moved into power in numerous small towns such as Centerville and Marathon.

In the battle for the U. S. Senatorship, the Klan took a while to make up its mind. The Klan was Republican in Iowa, but the Republican incumbent Smith W. Brookhart was an undependable maverick who was supporting Robert La Follette for President. When La Follette attacked the Klan, this meant that Senator Brookhart was also unsuitable. Even though the Democrats were openly hostile, Klan leaders decided belatedly to muster what strength they could for Daniel Steck, the Democratic candidate. The vote was close, and a recount gave it to Steck. Brookhart contested the election, and the national Klan sent in one of its top operatives to size up the situation. Steck testified during the Senate hearing that he had no Klan connections and that as state American Legion Commander he had fought it since its first appearance in Iowa. Nevertheless, he chose as his counsel W. F. Zumbrunn, the Klan lawyer and legislative expert who had earlier helped seat a Klan senator from Texas. The Klan, reportedly, did its part by having its Indiana and Kentucky realms put pressure on the elections committee members from their states. Steck was seated.

Although other contests were more glamorous, the Klan did particularly well in Iowa school-board elections in the mid-twenties. Its success, if behavior elsewhere is any guide, meant that the employment of Roman Catholics probably became more difficult, and that there was added stress on school prayers, Bible readings, and patriotic observances. The degree to which Klan-favored boards were the center of conflict in their communities is shown by the intensity of the battles which were waged at the next election. The fight that drew the most attention was in Des Moines. The organization of the campaign fell to the mothers of Des Moines, and the way they rallied to their task was strong indication of the parental dissatisfaction over school affairs. The vote for the school-board elections in the spring of 1926 was the largest in Des Moines' history, and the mothers were triumphant. In heated campaigns, Klan-endorsed candidates were also knocked off the school boards in Dubuque, Perry, Creston, Centerville, and several smaller towns. For the first time in several years the Klan had no ticket in Davenport.

In everybody's capital city of Des Moines, the results tended to show the divisions along which Klan and anti-Klan sentiment split. In the parts of the city east of the gilded renaissance dome of the capitol building, where Swedish, Negro, and Italian settlements were encroaching on the homes of factory and office workers, the Klan did well. The upper-income, still-fashionable West Side of the city voted against it. Although the Klan-endorsed candidates for the school board lost, the Invisible Empire carried the home precinct of its municipal favorite, popular Commissioner John Jenny who was swept back into office along with the anti-Klan candidate for mayor, in the regular city election.

With the Klan weakening in Des Moines and other cities, people of Corning, near the old Icarian utopia in the southwest corner of the state, dealt with the hooded order in a direct fashion. When the Klan first appeared in the county the year before, opposition had been quietly organized. In July of 1926, the first big public Klan meeting brought it out in the open, and into the streets. Armed with pitchforks, hammers, and crowbars, an anti-Klan mob marched through the business district, took up positions on the outskirts of town, and turned back or stoned those who tried to get through to the meeting ground. Only the eventual arrival of the sheriff and the threat to call in troops quieted the disturbed town. The next year an Adair County judge ruled that the Klan had to pay city taxes on its headquarters because it was not primarily a charitable, benevolent, or fraternal organization.

4

As the Invisible Empire of the Ku Klux Klan fanned out into the inland heart of the continent, it came to the prairie cities of North and South Dakota. There was a lot to worry about in North Dakota, if one believed that the strength of America lay in her native-born, Anglo-Saxon heritage. Grand Forks, particularly, had come to seem an almost foreign town. As the largest railroad junction between St. Paul and Seattle, as well as the mill and warehouse center of a rich farm area, she formed the natural gateway into the state. A major portion of her population was either of Canadian or Norwegian descent, and foreigners of every description had come to dwell there. Although the Lutheran Norskis were at least better than the Roman Catholics and Russians who had flocked to the state, many old-stock Americans looked on them with suspicion, for in Grand Forks' compact "Little Norway" the language of the old country was still spoken and Prohibition too often ignored.

Although there had been no reports of night riding in North Dakota, Klan doings elsewhere were continually in the headlines. Klan violence, such as Mer Rouge murders and the floggings at Goose Creek, Texas, were reported in detail by the Grand Forks *Herald,* and it was probably these affairs which first stimulated anti-Klan action. In January of 1923, the senators from Bismarck's Burleigh County and from Richland County, to the south of Grand Forks, introduced a bill in the legislature to provide punishment for anyone over fifteen years old who appeared masked in public. "We don't want conditions in North Dakota to become such that a man must carry a pistol to be safe," the Richland senator explained.

To testify against the bill came Reverend F. Halsey Ambrose of Grand Forks. Reverend Ambrose was the pastor of the First Presbyterian Church in that city and was generally regarded to be the moving force, if not the Grand Dragon, of the Klan in the state. He spoke for more than an hour, defending the Klan and all of its works. There were thousands of members in the state, he proclaimed, all representatives of the highest American ideals. The mask was necessary to protect them against discrimination, and the exclusiveness for which the Klan was attacked was no different from that of the Knights of Columbus or B'nai B'rith. The real peril to America, he asserted, was not the Klan but foreign immigration which was pushing inland from both coasts. Unless it was stopped, the white Anglo-Saxon society would be overcome and smothered. Already two thirds of the people in New York City were foreigners and the Japanese were expanding on the West Coast, and 63 per cent of the men in America were eugenically unfit. All the while, true Americans like the Klan were being persecuted by unpatriotic conspirators such as the Grand Forks *Herald.* The *Herald* editorially pointed out that Reverend Ambrose's testimony had been full of bombast, coarseness, and contempt for the immigrant. It was a declaration, the paper said, of the superior virtue of the members of a particular group, whose identity was unrevealed, whose members were chosen by some undefined authority, and assumed the right to operate in the dark to regulate the affairs of society.

The success of the bill was initially in doubt, for political experts thought that some of the nonpartisan and independent senators might oppose it. Then a veteran legislator from one of the state's southwestern ranching counties jumped up to say he hadn't known much about the Klan until "this gospel sounder from Grand Forks stood before a crowd over at the courthouse and bragged about how they went around the country and imposed their will on people." His outburst touched off an avalanche which swept the bill through the Senate by a two-to-one margin. As if to underline the case for the bill, reports came in that a masked and hooded gang near Fargo had beaten a man and threatened his girl companion. The bill passed the lower house by a ninety-two-to-eighteen vote and was signed into law.

This rebuff, however, did not mean the demise of the Ku Klux Klan in North Dakota. Reverend Ambrose rallied its forces in Grand Forks and led them to a series of triumphs in local politics. In 1924, the candidates supported by the Klan did well in municipal elections and followed this up by capturing the school board after a bitter contest which brought out one of the largest votes in the city's history. Two years later, the Klan forces made a clean sweep in the city elections.

As Klan strength declined in the late 1920s, the Klans of the Dakotas were merged into a tristate realm headed by the mayor of the small Minnesota town of St. James. In both the Dakotas, the Klan opposed the nomination of Al Smith for President in 1928. Its favorite was Senator Heflin, the bitterly anti-Catholic senator from Alabama, and the Klan slogan, "Swat Smith and put Heflin in the White House," was prominently displayed on Klan materials circulated around both states. A projected visit to South Dakota by the Alabama senator did not materialize. When he did come to North Dakota in 1931, under the joint sponsorship of Valley City Klan No. 49 and Fargo's Kass Kounty No. 5, he was denied the New York Life Insurance Company's chautauqua site and had to make do with the Valley City municipal auditorium. The Klans of North and South Dakota continued to operate into the early 1930s, primarily in the counties around Fargo, North Dakota's largest city, and along the South Dakota-Iowa border. However, the secret order was beset by the usual internal dissension, and the earth shook not where it trod.

20

TWISTING THE KLAN'S SHIRTTAIL IN KANSAS

There was nothing restful about normalcy in Kansas during the 1920s, for labor troubles plus the Ku Klux Klan proved quite sufficient to keep life stirred up in the Jayhawker State. The Klan arrived in 1922, making its way north from its early bastions in Texas and Oklahoma and fanning out from its regional suboffice in Kansas City, Missouri. The Invisible Empire first struck fire in the railroad towns of Arkansas City, Coffeyville, and Pittsburg, near the Oklahoma line. There was trouble in the coal mines and on the railroads, and labor was becoming increasingly unhappy over the pro-management cast of the state's new industrial relations courts. With the railroad importing Negro strikebreakers, the Klan raised the banner of white supremacy and harvested its first waves of initiates. It soon met with opposition from Governor Henry Allen, the hard-nosed former editor of Wichita *Beacon,* who brooked no interference with his middle-of-the-road administration. When the Arkansas City Klan decided to march by the struck railway shops as a hint to the strikebreakers, Governor Allen threatened to remove the reluctant mayor if the parade was not halted.

The parade did not take place but Governor Allen, now thoroughly aroused, had his attorney general open proceedings to oust the Klan from the state. Specifically, the state maintained, the Klan was a Georgia corporation, illegally operating in Kansas for the purpose of stirring up civic dissension and creating religious and racial animosity. The subsequent testimony clearly confirmed this and showed how the Klan had spread out across the state. Following its usual pattern, the Klan would organize one area and then send the new recruits out to open up new territories. Until the individual Klavern was chartered it would conceal its Klan affiliation under some innocent name such as the Sunflower Club of Wyandotte, the Bourbon County

Industrial Association of Fort Scott, and the Southwest Trade Association of Caney. The witnesses whom the state called to testify were usually the business and professional men of Kansas' towns and cities. A large number of peace officers were also prominent among the lists of Klansmen, and one of them, the former police chief of Topeka, refused to testify because his Klan oath would not permit him to do so.

It was clear, as the investigation rolled onward, that the Klan was established in most of the communities of the state. At its high tide in 1924, membership ran close to the one-hundred-thousand mark. The Klan claimed that it was strictly a fraternal and charitable organization and therefore not legally required to seek a charter. The testimony, however, brought out what most Kansans were coming to know all too well. One out of every four people in Kansas was Jewish, Roman Catholic, or Negro, and they found themselves the particular object of snubs, boycotts, and harassment. The Klan appointed representatives in each ward in Kansas City to keep a watch on the behavior of their neighbors. The school superintendent in Arkansas City was requested to keep his staff Protestant. The superintendent in Kansas City was criticized for allowing Negro and white children to take part together in a school pageant. Klansmen stopped cars on the roads to search them for liquor and invaded homes in Emporia to make certain that no one was playing cards on Sunday. Word was received from Atlanta that a Jew driven out of the South had settled in Kansas and should be kept moving. The Klan sent warning letters to "misbehaving people" in Salina, policemen in Galena, and an editor in Columbus. In the town of Liberty, Klansmen kidnaped and whipped the mayor because he had refused them permission to use city hall for a meeting. Suspicion and fear beset individuals and divided communities.

There were those who opposed the existence of the Invisible Empire in Kansas. From the beginning, Governor Allen was among them, denouncing it as the "greatest curse that comes to a civilized people" and a "travesty upon Americanism." In a Coffeyville speech that Emporia *Gazette* editor William Allen White called a scorcher which would "burn holes in their nightie tails," he urged all citizens to oppose the Klan. The president of Emporia College took an anti-Klan stand, as did the state Lions, the bar association and the mayor of Kansas City, who publicly debated the hooded organization with a pro-Klan minister from Boston. But the political strength of the Klan grew. In the 1922 election it boasted that it had defeated Congressman Philip Campbell who had headed a probe into the Klan the year before. In 1923, Klan candidates made it in Pittsburg, Fort Scott, Wichita, Emporia, and Kansas City, as well as smaller towns such as Ottawa and Weir. As a shrewd journalistic chronicler of the Klan pointed out, calculating its voting strength was never simple for there were usually other influences involved. In Fort Scott, for instance, the winning candidate was not only a Klansman but also a former divinity student, a locomotive fireman, and a field representative for the Scottish Rite Masons.[1]

Although a clearly identifiable labor vote did help the Klan gain its initial election triumphs in towns such as Emporia, the Klan was no great friend to labor in the Jayhawker State. The Invisible Empire's announced intent to prevent "unwarranted strikes by foreign labor agitators" became a broad statement of policy, given the Klan's general belief that all strikes, being unwarranted, naturally had to be the product of foreign agitators. The Klan's state lawyer and one of its top leaders in Kansas was also the attorney for the Associate Industries, which was composed of such major corporations as the packers and railroads. The association actively fought labor and opposed such shocking notions as factory inspection and the minimum wage. During the 1924 election, Colonel Dean made no attempt to conceal his diverse clients, for in a single speech he managed to defend the Klan, attack the proposed child-labor amendment, and support the Republican candidate for governor.

The candidate Ben Paulen was not likely to object. During his rise up the political ladder, Ben had been known as a conservative. He was a friend of the Associate Industries, and the Klan had been responsible for his victory in the primary. Although he denied that he was himself a member, he always added "at this time." With the Klan lined up behind the Republicans, the Democrats decided they had little to lose by coming out against it at their subsequent state convention. Nevertheless, when a few Republican candidates did oppose the Klan, it endorsed their Democratic opponents. Once the endorsements were made, Klansmen were expected to support them. Two Democratic political workers were suspended from the Invisible Empire for "causing dissension" when they solicited Klan votes for their whole party slate. It seemed, in the late summer of 1924, that the Klan was on the march in Kansas and nothing could stop it.

But the Klan had not fully taken the measure of Emporia *Gazette*

[1] R. L. Duffus, "The Ku Klux Klan in the Middle West," *World's Work*, 46 (1923), 363–72.

editor William Allen White, the Kansas keeper of the nation's conscience. White was resolved that Kansas and the Klan should not be linked in the national eye. He had quickly taken the Klan's measure and mounted attack on the "moral idiots" who composed what he called an "organization of cowards." When Emporia's new Broadview Hotel played host to both a touring Italian musical society and a state convention of the Klan, White sent a reporter down for a copy of the guest register. A Klansman pounced on the reporter and the hotel manager took away the list. White's response was a short note to the hotel's director. Unless a copy of the register was delivered to the newspaper office, "the name of the Broadview never again will be printed in the *Gazette* except in case of police raids and similar events," he warned. The hotel complied; the *Gazette* named the two groups and printed the list of guests on the front page, leaving its readers the uncomplicated task of deciding who belonged to which. The Klan elected a mayor in Emporia and for a time no one in city hall would talk with the reporters from the *Gazette,* but by the end of 1923, White could note with pleasure that the mayor had appointed a Roman Catholic as chief of police with a Negro assistant.

When the Republican nomination for governor went to Ben Paulen who then overruled discussion on the anti-Klan resolution, White began talking of the need for an independent Republican candidate. He sounded out his old progressive friends for the undertaking, but none of them was willing to run, so White himself entered the lists. He did not expect to win. Again and again he told his friends that if he thought he had any chance to do so, he would have never made the decision. His intention was to try and keep a Republican beholden to the Klan, out of the governorship. The belated Democratic recognition of the Klan menace did not much interest him; he was out to purify his beloved party and his state. As a candidate he would be first-page news and could hope to draw crowds of listeners across the state. His intention was to make the people everywhere think and talk out loud about the Klan, and he hoped to be able to kill it with ridicule.

And so a middle-aged, rosy-faced, baldish man in a gray sack suit and a white campaign hat given him by a friend, rounded up the biggest independent nominating petition ever filed in Kansas. Then he climbed into his Dodge touring car and set out to defeat the white-robed hosts of the Invisible Empire.

He had no campaign headquarters, literature, or campaign fund. "Haven't any money and am too proud to beg," he explained, "so will have to get along without the usual fixins." For six weeks he toured his state with his son driving and his wife beside him, his white campaign hat and a few thousand buttons reading WHITE IS RIGHT. Each week he budgeted himself twenty-five dollars for expenses and, apart from this, stayed with his many newspaper friends. But there was nothing mild or pathetic about the Kansas "St. George," as the New York *Times* called him. He poured it on with his anti-Klan, antigang, save-the-state-from-the-bosses-and-bigots campaign. "The gang rule first came into the Republican party last May," he would tell his listeners and the flocks of correspondents who followed him, "when a flock of dragons, kleagles, cyclopes, and fuzzy furies came to Wichita from Oklahoma and held a meeting with some Kansas terrors and whambedoodles. They selected Ben Paulen to run as Republican candidate of the Ku Klux Klan . . . later the Cyclopes, Kleagles, Wizards, and willopus-wallupuses began parading in the Kansas cow pastures, passing the word down to the shirttailed rangers that they were to go into the Kansas primaries and nominate Ben Paulen." He labeled both candidates as Klansmen, and Colonel Dean, the Klan-Associated Industries lawyer, as the "August Horned Toad of the Invisible Empire." The crowds delighted in his homey metaphors and colorful expostulations, and showed little interest in the rumors, smears, and false letters which the Klan concocted against him.

Although White's almost 150,000 votes were only half of the total that elected Ben Paulen in Republican Kansas, he felt that his campaign had been successful. He had gone forth alone and harvested them, in the face of both parties and the Klan. And what was more important, he had been able to "clear up the atmosphere" by being able to "get out and spit in the face of the Klan."

And of great importance, he had helped save the election for the superintendent of schools and the anti-Klan Republicans who sat on the state's charter board. The re-election of C. B. Griffith as attorney general was particularly important, for the Ku Klux Klan had had no stauncher antagonist in public office. Griffith had conducted the investigation of the Klan and the suit to oust it from the state. When a thousand Klansmen paraded through the streets of Topeka, Griffith had unsuccessfully pressed the mayor to unmask them. At the Republican state convention he had introduced the resolution against the Klan which the presiding officer, Ben Paulen, squelched. Now, along with the anti-Klan secretary of state, he would sit on the charter board which would soon pass on the Klan's application.

In January of 1925, the state Supreme Court ruled that the Klan was not a benevolent but a sales organization, and as such needed permission to do business. Denied a rehearing by the court, the Klan turned to its friend, the legislature. Its device was a bill originally offered by the Shriners permitting such organizations to do business without a charter. Now, with Shrine senators prominent in Klan affairs, it was openly debated as a Klan bill, and finally passed. The attempt to rush it through the lower house brought a fierce debate. Legislators were threatened with business pressure. One of them announced he would oppose the bill because religious persecution had driven his ancestors out of France and he wanted freedom in America. A minister from Johnson defended the Klan with the assertion that 62 per cent of the public offices in America were held by Catholics. In the heat of the argument on the floor, he shouted out: "My people came here before your people came," although no one was quite sure to whom he was specifically speaking. The lone Catholic member in the House pointed out that in the district populated by his coreligionists, a Protestant had defeated a Catholic the previous year. The bill was eventually killed by a close margin. The charter board, as expected, then refused the Klan a charter, and the Invisible Empire turned to the federal courts. Late in the year a local judge enjoined all masked parades in the state. In 1927 the U. S. Supreme Court turned down the Klan's appeal, but William Allen White had long since pronounced the obituary on the Klan's power in Kansas when he editorially welcomed the news that "Dr. Hiram Evans, the Imperial Wizard of the kluxers, is bringing his imperial shirttail to Kansas this spring. . . . He will see," White continued, "what was once a thriving and profitable hate factory and bigotorium now laughed into a busted community."[2]

[2] Frank C. Clough, *William Allen White of Emporia* (New York, 1941), p. 157.

21

BAD LUCK IN MINNEAPOLIS

Nineteen twenty-three was the big year for the Ku Klux Klan in Minnesota. It was the year of its greatest reach for power and of its most crushing series of defeats. The leaders of the Invisible Empire in the Land of Ten Thousand Lakes felt confident enough in that year to both push its program in the legislature and to seek political power in Minneapolis. Neither the state nor the city of Minneapolis, however, were in a co-operative mood. In the place of the Klan's bill to prevent any noncitizen teaching in the public elementary schools, the legislature passed a bill to prohibit the public gatherings of masked crowds. Instead of being elected mayor, the Exalted Cyclops of the Minneapolis Klan ended up in jail.

In the early 1920s, George E. Leach became mayor of Minnesota's largest city. He had originally come in as a conservative, but his opposition to private control of a big power dam across the Mississippi led his backers to the conclusion that they had picked a tartar, who, they claimed, had driven away a Ford plant and headed the state toward Red control. Among those who rallied to oppose the mayor were the anti-labor Citizens' Alliance and Committee of Thirteen which had grown out of the wartime American Protective League and remained to oversee rectitude in municipal government.

The Klan in Minnesota had grown primarily within the ranks of other fraternal orders. According to a reporter for the Minneapolis *Daily Star,* most of the Klansmen in the city were Masons, while the state leaders included many prominent Shriners. Mayor Leach was a lodge man, but in the eyes of the Klan he was clearly an apostate one. Not only had he appointed a Roman Catholic as his secretary, but he also once dined with the Knights of Columbus. Further, under his administration, municipal police had been forbidden to join the Klan and an investigation was launched into reported Klan activity at the University of Minnesota.

The North Star Klan No. 2 discussed the problem at a meeting in its lodge room above the Public Drug Company on Seventh Street in downtown Minneapolis. The decision was that their Exalted Cyclops Roy Miner should run for mayor. Roy's professional experience, other than that of Klansmanship, was in merchandising fraternal regalia, but he responded to the call of duty. Next, Klansman Miner and his associates looked around for a campaign issue. Since the mayor's former backers had criticized the police for not stamping out gambling and vice, they decided that this would be a profitable line to pursue. Now the problem was to collect proper campaign materials. They found them in the city jail. A woman domiciled there claimed that she had been intimate with the mayor. Candidate Miner went to call upon her, and the Klan printed her story and distributed it about town.

A grand jury thought that the story was libelous. Farmer-Laborite Floyd B. Olson, on his way to the governor's mansion, handled the prosecution. The case attracted wide attention outside the state and Klan notables traveled to Minneapolis to witness what they anticipated would be a Klan exoneration and triumph. But such was not to be the case. The Klan's star witness, on leave from jail, admitted chronic drunkenness and the falseness of her claims of intimacy with Mayor Leach and other prominent men. The mayor, on the other hand, unco-operatively admitted nothing, denying the charges of protecting vice and gambling and personal attendance at wild parties. Despite the degree of latitude allowed in his cross-examination, Mayor Leach's testimony was not shaken. In his final summation, Prosecuting Attorney Olson dwelt on how the Klan and its principles were harming the Masonic order. The Protestant jury, which included a Methodist minister and several Masons and Shriners, brought back a guilty verdict and the five accused Klansmen went to jail.

One blow followed upon another. Milton Elrod, editor of the *Fiery Cross* and Klan troubleshooter in the Middle West, had been an unhappy observer at the trial. Now with Miner and the others convicted, there was nothing to do but cut them loose. To Roy Miner and the members of North Star Klan No. 2, this was hardly just, and they were furious. When they refused to surrender their charter, Elrod then huddled with prosecutor Olson to see if the banished rebels could be enmeshed in further trouble with the law.

Mayor Leach's re-election was not assured by the outcome of the case and the bitter wrangling among the Klansmen. Supported by the liberals and labor, he still faced strong and unplacated enemies, and a libel suit never helps anyone, even the victor. His remaining opponent was former state Senator William Campbell, who had been the second choice of the Invisible Empire, and now fell heir to the Klan vote. The most that Campbell was willing to say about it all, under fierce attack, was to deny that he was presently a Klansman. In the election, Mayor Leach won by more than five thousand votes; Campbell ran well, even though he carried only the silk-stocking Thirteenth Ward.

Although the unhappy events of 1923 marked the failure of the Klan as a political power in the state, they did not bring about its demise. Discredited in Minneapolis, the Klan managed to hold on to the loyalties of some of the native Americans who lived among St. Paul's many Irish and German Catholics. The Klan claimed strength in the Lake Superior port of Duluth and rallied and spread near the fundamentalist little town of Dawson in the rich farming country near the South Dakota border. Some critics described the Klan as a movement built on hatred of the Jew, Negro, and Roman Catholic. Other observers later remembered that the Klan had presented Bibles to Methodist churches, stressed "positive Protestantism," and made only infrequent use of the robes and other regalia at public meetings.

In July of 1930 five hundred Klansmen from all over the state gathered at an all-day picnic in St. Paul to install a new Grand Dragon for the now tristate realm of Minnesota and North and South Dakota. The chosen leader was Dr. C. E. McNaught, then serving his second term as mayor of the small southern Minnesota town of St. James. In addition to his political and Klan honors, Dr. McNaught also held office as Regimental Surgeon of the Patriarchs Militant, Grand Master of the International Order of Odd Fellows of Minnesota, and was member of nearly a dozen other fraternal orders. As a born joiner, even the fading Klan honors seemed a fit addition to his collection.

22

BORDER-STATE KLANS

1

The major power of the Tennessee Klan was concentrated in the western and eastern corners of the state. The Invisible Empire made its big political efforts in the Chattanooga and Memphis municipal elections in 1923, but was turned back in both cities, and the Memphis *Commercial-Appeal* won a Pulitzer prize for its reporting of Klan doings there. Although the Invisible Empire lingered on—never to leave Chattanooga—and remained a force to be considered in the 1920s, its power and glory were considerably dampened after these twin setbacks.

With her industry booming under the impetus of the war and the construction of a new International Harvester plant just afterwards, Chattanooga's population was to double and reach the hundred-thousand mark by the end of the twenties. Although a local physician headed the Klan and many of the better citizens joined, its strength came to be concentrated among the men who worked in the foundries, furniture plants, and textile mills south of the railroad tracks and in East Chattanooga. Klan No. 4's Committee on Moral Reform gave the authorities a list of over 100 suspected bootleggers, and liquor, immorality, and crime received Klan attention. However, the real enemies were the alien, Jew, Pope, and Negro. When the Klan took a hand in the 1923 municipal primaries, religious orthodoxy and anti-Catholicism were its major issues. The incumbent city commission was obviously unsuitable, for it contained two Roman Catholics, a Jew, and an undependable Presbyterian who, as head of the Department of Education, had permitted the hiring of several Catholic teachers. Out of a total vote of 12,000, the Klan-supported slate lost by only two hundred, but in reality it had been the author of its own defeat. Its aggressive campaign brought out the vote of its enemies. Jews, Catholics, and liberal Protestants, "who feared the mask more than the Pope," voted against the Klan's candidates. In the Churchville, College Hill, and East Eighth Street precincts, the Negroes, who numbered a third of the city's inhabitants, flocked to the polls.

The Klan's actual influence in the state was declining. The defeat in Chattanooga, the struggle for control in Atlanta, plus the details of violence in Louisiana and Texas were bad publicity, and much of the better element in town were pulling out.

Nevertheless, in Shelby County the Invisible Empire prepared itself for another battle. Set on a bluff above the east bank of the Mississippi, Memphis was the New York City, Chicago, Washington, D.C., and London for a large area of Arkansas and Mississippi as well as western Tennessee. The Klans had prospered in Shelby County, and in the fall of 1923 they sought to take control of the city of Memphis. Mayor Rowlett Paine and his principal antagonist opposed the hooded order while the Klan's favorite ran on an independent ticket. Despite the split in the opposition, the only Klan victory came in a city judgeship race when two antagonists to the Invisible Empire had so evenly divided the vote that the Klan's would-be magistrate won a minority victory. On the whole it was an impressive defeat for the Klan and one which the New York *Times* characterized as the most important "black eye" it had yet received in the South. The "bigger and better Memphis," which the Klan promised, was apparently going to try it without aid from the Invisible Empire.

Despite its losses, the Klan remained an important political factor in the state, though by no means a decisive one. Klansmen added their votes to the tide which washed wet Senator John Shields out of the U. S. Senate in 1924, and they worked for the re-election of Governor Austin Peay who had won their approval by refusing to support any anti-Klan moves. His appreciation was expressed the next year, the Klan claimed, when he capped its campaign against violators of the Sabbath by vetoing a bill permitting Sunday movies. For the most part, however, the Klan had reached its peak by 1923, and, in its subsequent decline, only the Klan's self-proclaimed "banner order" in Chattanooga had any appreciable life ahead of it beyond the 1920s.

2

The Ku Klux Klan spread its skirts over the Bluegrass State of Kentucky although many citizens battled it from the very beginning, and it gained less power here than in many of its neighbors to the south, or north. Circuit judges in Laurie, Pulaski, and Hopkins counties denounced the Klan, charged grand juries to investigate it, and refused to permit its members to sit on juries. In the major cities of Louisville, Lexington, and Paducah, the mayors opposed the hooded order by word and deed—and sometimes at a political price.

A Klan salesman from Tulsa, Oklahoma, tried to organize Louisville in the summer of 1921, but he ran smack into the opposition of Mayor George W. Smith and the Board of Public Safety. The Klan inserted full-page advertisements in the newspapers and, boasting of swelling ranks, sought to bring the national Klan chaplain in to speak. The city said no. The hooded order was a menace to the peace and the good understanding of the people of Louisville, the mayor announced, promising to use every lawful means at his disposal to halt it. He assigned detectives to check on the Klan and threatened to arrest anyone who attended its meeting. The Klan backed down and gathered instead in friendlier Jeffersonville, Indiana, across the river. In the Bluegrass capital of Lexington, Mayor Hogan Yancey opposed all Klan activity in his city and a Klan lecturer went to jail for speaking at an unauthorized meeting.

However, when a mayoralty candidate in the river port and tobacco city of Paducah ran on an anti-Klan platform, he was not rewarded with victory. Wynn Tully had taken the lead in getting the city to refuse permission for a public Klan rally. When he ran for mayor, he hoped to draw support from those who approved of his stand. Apparently not enough voters did, for Tully was the only Democrat to lose in what was otherwise a clean sweep for the party's ticket.

The Klan had first entered Kentucky from Ohio and swept along the south bank of the Ohio River from the multispired city of Covington, eastward to the industrial and warehouse city of Ashland, and westward to Henderson and Paducah. The Klan did best in the bluegrass counties of Kentucky across the river from Cincinnati. The John B. Castleton Klan of Covington was the oldest in the state, but Henry Clay No. 4 of Newport, its prestige enhanced by the endorsement of the local ministerial association, vied with it for recognition.

The Klan reached its greatest strength in 1923 and 1924 and became an important force in state-wide politics. When the hooded knights first appeared on the scene, Senator A. O. Stanley condemned both them and the Anti-Saloon League. The fact that he was up for re-election in 1924 did not tone down his stand, for he remained opposed to Prohibition and supported the anti-Klan resolution at the 1924 Democratic convention. He was hurt by a state bond drive and other local issues, as well as by Calvin Coolidge's national sweep, and the alliance between the Klan and the drys worked well, particularly in Kentucky's rural areas. In his own normally safe county of Henderson, Stanley lost by a thousand votes. After twenty-two years in public office as a congressman, governor, and senator, Stanley was beaten by a politically unknown Republican businessman from Louisville.

There were some areas of the state, however, which remained hostile to the Klan, particularly in the western coal-mining districts. John L. Lewis' United Mine Workers had come out in early opposition to the Klan, and the labor press denounced the Invisible Empire as a union buster and friend of the owners. During an attempt to proselytize the coal regions, Klan organizers had met with considerable opposition. The head of the U.M.W. in Central City was also the mayor, and though he denounced the Klan, he gave permission for it to meet, as long as it did so unmasked. In Mayfield, however, a Klan organizer felt it wise to heed the request of a committee of local citizens that he take the next train out of town. In the nonmining, bluegrass town of Paris, which had once been the site of the famous Cain Ridge revival meetings, local citizens boasted that this was a town where no robed Klansmen walked the streets.

Although the Klan had gained entree into Louisville, partly through the aid of the state's Court of Appeals, all was not well. In 1925, a bitter fight broke out over the handling of Klan finances in Louisville, and a few months later another group of Klansmen went to court for an accounting of the moneys which had been collected to construct a Klan building in Lexington. The dissidents claimed that all Klan-endorsed candidates had been defeated in the August primary, and that membership had dwindled from 1500 to less than 200. That fall, the Klan suffered a second municipal defeat. Two days before the election, the Louisville Republicans dramatically offered a thousand dollars to the Democratic candidate for mayor if he could prove he had never been a Klansman. Admitting that he had once worn the hood and robes, he withdrew, and the Republicans narrowly won over the badly split Democrats and their hastily named replacement.

The Klan approved when Kentucky went for Hoover in 1928, and Lexington's Fayette Klan finally got started on its disputed lodge building. The Klan lingered on into the thirties with its Lexington and Ashland Klaverns remaining the most active, but it never felt quite at home in Kentucky.

3

In West Virginia, as elsewhere, the Klan operated in the major centers of population. In the northern panhandle, thrust up between Pennsylvania and Ohio, Klansmen from the Mountain State rallied with their neighboring brethren. In Charleston, Clarksburg, and along the banks of the Kanawha and Monongahela rivers, the Klansmen met, marched, threatened, and voted. During the preceding decade, a stream of immigrants from southern and eastern Europe, mainly Italians, Poles, and Hungarians, had entered the state to work in the mines and factories of the panhandle and the Monongahela Valley. In Charleston, thousands of Negroes were drawn into the coal, gas, oil, and glass industries. This influx was sufficient to give the Klan a reason for being and something to say.

In the 1920s, the Klan wove in and out of the political affairs of both major parties. When it first appeared, the state refused it a charter, but it made itself at home, anyway. In the summer of 1922, a last-minute Klan intervention into the primary elections in Charleston was criticized widely, but the candidates it endorsed did well. However, the next year in the Ohio River city of Parkersburg, the Klan candidates for city commission were defeated and the mayor, whom it opposed, was re-elected. In the scarred, hilly, coal and gas county of Logan, famed home of the feuding Hatfields, a masked band of Klansmen accidentally killed a white woman while attacking a Negro cabin. In nearby Mingo County, the night riders threatened to use force to prevent the Negro prize fighter, Jack Johnson, from boxing there. The busy mining center of Clarkson, northward across the state in the Monongahela Valley, saw the Klan force the dismissal of a number of Roman Catholic teachers, while in nearby Grafton, the school board refused to hire any.

Almost from the beginning the United Mine Workers had opposed the Klan, and although union men sometimes joined, the hooded order was no friend to labor in the coal fields of West Virginia. Here, as in Kentucky, the Klan lined up on the side of the owners and sought to force striking miners back to work. The Klan sometimes acted as voluntary adjunct to the company-owned deputy sheriffs and the Baldwin-Felts Detective Agency, but it was an unnecessary role. Labor was generally on the losing side in West Virginia during the 1920s, and after a federal army put down a violence-tinged strike in Mingo and Logan counties the whole labor movement in the state was badly damaged.

Although West Virginia had generally gone Republican since the turn of the century, the Klan's presence sometimes proved upsetting. In Charleston's Kanawha County and in neighboring Fayette the Klan had been quite powerful, but in the mid-twenties a number of traditionally Republican cities went Democratic when the Republican officeholders gave the hooded knights too free a rein.

In 1924, John W. Davis, the handsome silver-haired son of the Mountain State, had been picked as the national Democratic standard bearer. Imperial Wizard Hiram Evans, who was presiding over the Klan's state convention, asserted that the Invisible Empire would not take sides between Coolidge and Davis. When Davis unexpectedly came out against the Klan, its Huntington leader, J. H. Humphries, reported that the Democrats would still get two thirds of the realm's vote. Humphries, who had once been president of the Bible-distributing Gideons, told why he expected Davis to hold the Klan's vote. He himself had fought the Klan, Humphries explained, but that was because he had not understood what the Klan stood for. "Now I know better and am proud to belong to it," he said, expressing the belief that Davis would soon follow the same path. Davis stubbornly failed to see the light, however, and the Klan helped hold the state for Coolidge.

In the mid-twenties it often did not pay politically to oppose the Klan. In the fall of 1925, the *National Kourier* reported that all Klan candidates in faithful Fairmont had won easily, and that in Republican Marion County a Republican judge who had spoken against the Klan had been beaten badly by a Democrat. For the most part, however, it was the Klan's Republican friends who won, and in the great anti-Al Smith election of 1928, the successful Republican candidate for governor was listed as one of the owners of the pro-Klan fraternal magazine *Fellowship Forum*.

4

The miniature size of Delaware and its Klan was no index to the passions which it stirred up. By late in 1922 the Invisible Empire had become quite strong in Laurel, a small timber- and box-producing town in the southwest corner of the state, and a local Methodist minister created quite a sensation by denouncing it. However, this was nothing compared to the response the Klan drew the next summer when it conducted an initiation ceremony near New Castle in the northern part of the state. Spectators gathered at the edge of the field, kept at a distance by hooded guards. At the completion of the ritual, a blank was fired as the signal to ignite a large kerosene-soaked cross, but the shot touched off more than anyone expected. The crowd on the outskirts surged forward onto the field, transformed, at the sound, into an unruly mob. Shouting "To hell with the Klan" and "Hurrah for the Irish," they dashed forward. A Klansman defending his flaming cross pulled out a pistol and fired. Other missiles filled the air. An automobile filled with departing Klansmen barreled through the crowd, knocking aside those in its way. In the wild battle between the mob and now outnumbered Klansmen, at least three men were shot and fifty injured. For hours afterwards, men roamed the streets of New Castle, hurling stones and sticks at the cars of suspected Klansmen.

Nevertheless, the Klan continued to operate in Delaware. Although it held occasional public meetings in Dover and other parts of the state, it was most active in the two rural counties of Kent and Sussex, which contained only a third of the voters but most of the area and Klansmen of the state. When the Democrats met for their state convention in the presidential election year of 1924, the Klan issue which had heated Madison Square Garden, was still intense. The big question was whether or not the Klan was to be denounced by name. The downstate delegates from Kent and Sussex were opposed. They were willing to follow the lead of the National Convention in accepting a resolution just as long as it did not contain the words "Ku Klux Klan." After much debate and indecision the resolutions committee finally knocked out the reference to the hooded order in an effort to bring party harmony. Such was not the result. When the watered-down plank on religious freedom was read, a delegate from the small farming center of Smyrna rose to demand that it be amended. "I will move to name the Klan and not avoid the issue," he announced. The convention was in an uproar. Everyone was up and shouting. The chairman, however, refused to permit the issue to be debated. When a degree of quiet had returned to the hall, he told them that since each delegate's mind was already made up, he would put the question. The vote was 140 to 55 against singling out the Klan by name. "Well, Kent and Sussex got their way," one embittered Wilmington delegate commented. "Now let's see them elect the state ticket."

5

Maryland was one of its least successful realms, but the Klan was there nevertheless. In 1922 a railroad man from Hagerstown, who reportedly mistreated his wife, was beaten and branded. When another Klan band tarred and feathered several more railroad men, four of the night riders were convicted and sentenced to seven years in the penitentiary. Governor A. C. Ritchie refused to let the Klan use Baltimore's 5th Regimental Armory for a lecture by Colonel Simmons, and a local tax court refused the Klan exemption on its ten-thousand-dollar lodge building, on the grounds that the Klan was a political organization. There was a riot in the Brooklyn suburb of Baltimore when Mrs. Helen Jackson, one of the Klan's stable of ex-nuns, spoke at the First Baptist Church, and an attempt was made to burn the former Presbyterian Church at Madison and Biddle streets, where Baltimore's Thomas Dixon Klan had its headquarters.

Despite this discouraging absence of hospitality, the Klan was doing sufficiently well for Frank H. Beall to resign as chief of the inspection division of Baltimore's City Highways Department to take over as Grand Dragon. Beall had been one of the Klan's original hundred in Maryland, its first Exalted Cyclops, and now, with the chartering of the realm in 1923, was the top Klansman in the state. That he had given up a safe city job to take the post was a sign of his faith in the future of the Invisible Empire as well as a certain credulity in regard to Klan membership statistics. At the Annapolis meeting that marked his inauguration, the Klan claimed that it had seventy-two chapters active in the state with a membership of thirty-three thousand.

The new realm of Maryland began its history with a resounding political defeat. Governor Ritchie was a wet. He favored modification of the Volstead Act, supported racing, and had appointed a Jewish judge. To compound all of this, the Roman Catholics liked him and he had been decided unsympathetic toward the new, growing order for native-born white Protestant Americans.

Although it made no public prediction of success, the Klan rallied in support of his opponent, and the state Republican party made things easier by not re-enacting their anti-Klan plank of 1921. Although neither of the contestants referred to the Klan issue, it was there. The Roman Catholic vote went for Ritchie as did that in Baltimore's heavily Jewish and usually Republican wards in the eastern and northern parts of the city. In the Negro areas of Baltimore and in traditionally Republican Montgomery County on the District of Columbia boundary, an unusually large number of people either voted for the Democrats or stayed home. On the other hand, the usual Democratic majorities in "the counties" on the Eastern Shore, where support of Prohibition was strong and the Klan reportedly active, were not forthcoming. Governor Ritchie overcame Maryland's one-term tradition in winning re-election by more than thirty-five thousand votes.

Although 1924 was the Klan's big moment in national politics, Governor Ritchie reported that it was not a problem in Maryland. It had been well organized when it went after him the year before but it was no longer as potent in his state. Still, the Klan continued active in the mid-twenties. Nearly a thousand Klansmen paraded through the streets of Annapolis prior to a Klan rally in August of 1924, and the next summer a big Cumberland Klorero drew Klansmen from all over, including a delegation which arrived in a special railroad car from the District of Columbia. A tarring and feathering near Frederick landed the participating Klansmen in jail, and in Havre de Grace the First Klan Church of Maryland was dedicated, under guard, having been burned out the first time.

In June of 1926, a bitter Frank Beall resigned as Grand Dragon. With a blast at national headquarters, he revealed the inner chaos which had chronically beset the Klan in Maryland. The national propagation department, he proclaimed, was "shamefully crooked" and "shockingly immoral." The Kleagles had been following the standard practice of whirlwind mass recruiting, followed by a splitting of the take with national headquarters. When Beall became Grand Dragon he discovered that membership claims were vastly exaggerated and the quality of those signed up was woefully low. To prevent errors of further hasty recruitment, he removed the remaining Kleagles and set himself to slowly and carefully building the Klan ranks. His aim, as he described it, was to "regain the lost confidence of the public."

This way of going about things was too slow for Atlanta, and in 1924 more Kleagles were sent in under the direction of a Klan salesman from West Virginia. They made a royal mess of things, and Beall had to cover a number of bad checks with payments from the realm treasury. He protested bitterly and agreed to stay on only when he was promised that this would never happen again. But it did happen again, and yet again. As the Kleagles moved in for the usual campaign "to take Maryland by storm," Grand Dragon Beall was tired of being the fall guy, and he was mad. His association with the Klan was terminated by mutual agreement, and he had delivered his valedictory to the press.

Although the Klan endured in Maryland, sentiment was of such a nature that when the Republican incumbent ran for re-election as U. S. Senator in the fall of 1926, he announced that he was both wet and anti-Klan.

23

KLAN CASTLES IN INDIANA

Booze, women, police, and public officials were for sale in Indiana during the 1920s as the rumrunners crisscrossed the state from Hammond to Jeffersonville and Terre Haute to Fort Wayne. Indianapolis, by geography and fate, was always in the center of things. However, though crime was an indigenous inhabitant, a good many Hoosiers were intent on tracing its tentacles back to the Mediterranean, Rome, and Africa. The story of the Ku Klux Klan in Indiana was a mixture of fear, personality, and politics. Like many things which men fear, the sense of alarm was often proportionate to distance rather than the closeness of the menace. Only thirteen men out of a hundred in Indiana were Negroes or Roman Catholics, but the tides of racial feeling, broadly defined—and people did broadly define it in the 1920s—were high, and the Ku Klux Klan did not have to pipe in the native American ethnic elixir in which it bathed.

The Pope was a popular enemy, and if he were not the bread and butter, he had at least long been the dessert of many pulpits in Indiana. In North Manchester a Klan lecturer reportedly alerted his listeners: "He may even be on the northbound train tomorrow! He may! He may! Be warned! Prepare! America is for Americans! Search everywhere for hidden enemies, vipers at the heart's blood of our sacred Republic! Watch the trains!" In the face of such an injunction, what else could the people of North Manchester do? The next day, more than a thousand strong they went down to meet the northbound train to Chicago. The one passenger who alighted was a ladies' corset salesman, and they gave him an uncomfortable half hour until they convinced themselves that he was probably not the Roman Pope in disguise, and put him on the next train out of town.

The second face of the Hoosier Klan was personality. The rise and fall of David C. Stephenson was the great success and horror story of American Klandom. The personable, shrewd, ambitious, Stephenson built a Klan Empire and practically annexed the state as an appendage to it. Behind his outer office full of henchmen, the bronze bust of Napoleon, the battery of eight phones—including a fake direct line to the White House, and his books on psychology and salesmanship, he pretty well ran state affairs from his suite in the Kresge Building in downtown Indianapolis. In an age when advertising man Bruce Barton could write a national best seller by depicting Jesus Christ as the world's most efficient sales executive, it was not completely beyond reason that the Klan's Indiana Dragon might aspire to the White House itself on a religious belief in salesmanship. At thirty-three he was "The Old Man" of Indiana politics. By the time he was thirty-six he was in the Michigan City penitentiary for life.

The third face of the Klan was politics. The Hoosier has always been a political animal, and there was no way that the Klan could have kept out of it, even if it had wanted to. For almost half a century the national parties had poured their money into Indiana, seeking to purchase victory in closely fought presidential campaigns. Hoosier politicians more often than not lifted their eyes toward the White House or lined up to doze unconcernedly, gavel in hand, in the Senate chambers. Only Colorado, Georgia, and Alabama equaled the bag of offices that the Invisible Empire made in Indiana, and perhaps only in the Centennial State was its political role as great. Even though it operated primarily in the Republican party, it was active among the Democrats. Spurred on by the Klan, Baptists in southern Indiana crossed over to the Republicans while Negroes sadly edged away from the party of Abraham Lincoln. D. C. Stephenson built a Klan political organization, which he called his "Military Machine." With it he Tammanyized Indiana and dreamed his dreams of high office. Klans there were in every state of the Union, but the Invisible Empire in the Hoosier State became a national legend.

The Klan crossed the Ohio late in 1920 and organized its first Klavern in the southern river town of Evansville. Joe Huffington, its first leader, didn't make much of it, and control soon passed into the hands of someone who did. David Clarke Stephenson stopped drifting soon after he arrived in Indiana. Born in Texas in 1891, he dropped out of elementary school, and moved about with a succession of jobs. He left a printer's typestick in Oklahoma to join the army and came out as a lieutenant, though the stories later had it that he had been a major. In 1920 he came to Evansville and went into the coal and veterans businesses. The essential Stephenson had already emerged; he was a salesman. It was all a matter of impression, he believed. You had to know the psychology of the thing. It lay in appearances. His figure ran to fat, but Stephenson groomed himself carefully and dressed conservatively and well. Men trust a man who is tangibly there, and Steve could speak with both the folksiness and the flowery phrases of the politician. There was nothing phlegmatic about his fleshiness or his ambition. He gave men a sense of confidence and anticipation, and it was infectious. The army had shown him what organization could do with a body of men, and he longed to hold the power himself. He had found the place, now all he needed was the proper cause to display his talents. When he mistakenly tried wet, Democratic politics, the Anti-Saloon League and the Republicans clobbered him. He was good-natured about it all, and, having learned his lesson, switched to dry Republicanism. He helped handle a Klan political campaign, and things went better.

There was a story that he took a trip to have a look at the Invisible Empire firsthand in Atlanta and came back feeling that things were being badly run but promising. He never liked Evans' Southern crowd and always stood a bit off from them, even when he helped the Imperial Dallas dentist turn the inefficient Colonel Simmons out to pasture. Anyway, Steve started getting things organized in Evansville, and in the first few months of 1922 brought the membership up to five thousand. He had found his proper calling, and when the Klan potentates gathered for the first great Klonvokation in Atlanta, he came by private railway car. For his role in the palace revolution that put Evans on Peachtree Street, Steve's share of the booty was twenty-three Northern and Midwestern states.

These were golden days for the Ku Klux Klan in Indiana. Every week brought thousands to be naturalized into Steve's expanding empire, for there was no nonsense about the careful selection of the kind of person to be initiated into fraternal klannishness. Steve was building a mass organization as the basis of a political machine, or better, a political tidal wave. In a growing hysteria of belonging, Klansmen and Ladies of the Golden Mask turned out by the thousands, and tens of thousands, and scores of thousands for meetings, parades, and field days in Hammond, Valparaiso, Fort Wayne, Crawfordsville, Jeffersonville, Winamac, and Kokomo. Faceless, sheeted men, with arms folded across their chests, marched through the torchlit nights of Indiana towns in seemingly endless columns, to the slow incessant roll of drums. Horses pranced, crosses burned. An enormous flag which stretched from curb to curb was paraded down

Kokomo's Main Street, gathering contributions to build a new hospital so that suffering Americans need not be turned over to the Catholic nuns.

Steve's inauguration as Grand Dragon, in July of 1923, was the occasion for the greatest single rally of the sons and daughters of Hoosier Klandom. Joined by the Imperial Wizard Hiram Evans, more than a hundred thousand Klansmen gathered in Kokomo's Melfalfa Park. The bands played, the ministers waxed eloquent, Evans gave his favorite "Back to the Constitution" speech, and the faithful lunched from block-long rows of tables. Then an airplane roared in from the south. It circled above the packed, excited Klansmen and came in to land on the waiting meadow. Clad in his silken purple robe, D. C. Stephenson eased himself out of the rear cockpit to be conducted to the speakers' platform. Raising his hand to still the crowd, Stephenson addressed his followers:

"My worthy subjects, citizens of the Invisible Empire, Klansmen all, greetings. It grieves me to be late. The President of the United States kept me unduly long counseling upon vital matters of state. Only my plea that this is the time and place of my coronation obtained for me surcease from his prayers for guidance."

When he had crowned himself and completed his plea for "Straight Americanism," he turned to go. This was Billy Sunday country and the Klansmen trained in religious ecstasies knew what to do. A shower of coins, rings, charms, pins, and pocketbooks fell about Steve's feet to show that his moment of glory had truly reached its climax.

Not all of the credit for the Klan's triumph of the will in Indiana should go to D. C. Stephenson, however. Indiana was equally deserving, for while Stephenson provided the organization and the leadership, it was the people of Indiana who listened and knew it was for them. The Klan grew in the proud hearts of the towns who boasted signs: NIGGER, DON'T LET THE SUN FALL ON YOU HERE TO-NIGHT, and communities like Mentone in the American county of Kosciusko, between the American cities of Warsaw and Sevastopol, which boasted that "With a population of 1100, Mentone has not a Catholic, foreigner, Negro, nor Jew living in the city. Practically every man in the city belongs to one or more fraternal organizations."

In 1865, when Indiana was not far removed from the frontier, and Washington Street in Indianapolis was the main avenue to the American West, the state legislature had made vigilantism legal. Now the Ku Klux Klan in Indiana, and similarly in Ohio, was using the statute to get its military formations deputized by county commissioners. More than twenty thousand Klansmen thereby became special constables authorized to carry weapons and detain suspects without warrants.

Duly authorized Klan Horse Thief Detectives raided bootleggers, gamblers, and disorderly houses. They developed the habit of stopping and searching cars on the highways to the point that motor clubs protested, took over control of adjacent highways when the Klan had meetings, and rode through the Negro district of Indianapolis, waving their revolvers, on primary day.

Merchants started putting "TWK" (trade with a Klansman) signs in their store windows. Boycotts against Jews, Catholics, and other outsiders were more successful in smaller towns, but even in the larger cities businessmen paid initiation fees to avoid trouble, advertised in Klan newspapers, and took greater care with their employment policies. Primarily, however, Klansmen were interested in being against, not for, things, and Klan department and shoe-repair stores, as well as two One Hundred Per Cent Restaurants, went broke.

Steve loved organizations and organization. Not only did he develop his private police force, but he fashioned his headquarters after the military model. In addition, his Military Machine was the best political organization anywhere in the whole Invisible Empire. Staffed by Klansmen with titles running from corporal to colonel, it kept watch on its fellow Hoosiers, Klansmen and non-Klansmen alike, on a block-by-block basis. The Military Machine gathered information on all candidates for office, passing it up to the top, where the decision was made as to whom the Invisible Empire was to support. Once it was decided and the word passed down the chain of command, Klan members were expected to give their support with bolshevik-like fidelity. Annotated lists of candidates were stuck into clothespins and tossed on porches or inserted in Sunday-school papers. If a candidate were "favorable," "neutral," or "unfavorable," it was so marked. If nothing appeared next to his name, the faithful knew he was actually a member of the Klan. Since the Democratic and Republican parties commanded almost equal strength, the Klan word and the Klan vote were often decisive.

And the Klan was more than a little interested in casting that vote. In 1922, even before Stephenson had his Military Machine in operation, the Klan helped defeat a veteran Jewish congressman as well as Catholic-tinged candidates for county and state office. The Klan's most notable effort was its role in sending Samuel M. Ralston, to the Senate. Ordinarily, the Klan might have been expected to support the Republican, but Albert J. Beveridge, the noted biographer and former Progressive Republican senator, was unfriendly. During the campaign he brought in Kansas' Governor Henry Allen who blasted away at the hooded order. Not so Ralston. In a talk at St. Mary's of the Woods, a Catholic women's college in Terre Haute, he spoke of the importance of religious liberty and the separation of Church and State. The Klan was delighted. Here was a man who was not afraid to tell the papists off to their very faces. Under the heading of WHERE COURAGE COUNTS, the passage from his speech was reprinted and distributed across the state. Backed by the Klan, and with usually Republican counties, like Putnam, Wayne, and Marion, going for him, Ralston won.

By 1923, Stephenson was ready. This was the year of Steve's great ceremonial at Melfalfa Park, the attempt to buy Valparaiso University, and the great schism within the Hoosier Klan. Even so, the way of the Hoosier Klan was not without some opposition. It was seldom as direct and personal as that of Col. Hiram Bearse, a much decorated regular army veteran who drove his tin lizzie into the middle of a Klan parade in Peru, Indiana, and then, monkey wrench in hand, offered to take on the whole Invisible Empire. Not only did the NAACP and the Roman Catholic Church look unfavorably on the Klan, but so did a state Episcopal Church conference. Notre Dame students rioted when local officials were named as Klansmen by a hostile newspaper, and opposition came from officeholders like Lou Shank, the iron-lunged ex-vaudevillian mayor of Indianapolis and the mayors of Gary, Lafayette, and East Chicago. Despite strong pro-Klan minorities within their ranks, the United Mine Workers and the Democratic party were anti-Klan. An occasional newspaper like George Dale's Muncie *Post-Democrat* took its advertising life in its hands and opposed the hooded order, and the first factional group was already departing the Invisible Empire to found its own Klan of the North. Within the Republican party there were occasional flashes of opposition in the disaffection of Negro leaders, the attempt by the mayor of Terre Haute to run for governor on an anti-Klan platform, and the resignation of the G.O.P. state chairman after his withdrawal from the hooded order.

All such opposition was of little avail. The Klan was on the rise, and no external force seemed able to stem the tide. If the much heralded Fort Wayne rally proved a dud, gatherings in Valparaiso, Kokomo, and elsewhere were enheartening successes. Steve's ambition knew no bounds. As a symbol of his success and the future that lay ahead for his growing Empire, he decided to complete Colonel Simmons' old dream of a Klan university. Valparaiso University had once been America's most successful example of a people's university. Operating without the frills of fraternal organizations and athletics, requiring no entrance examinations or formal graduation, Valparaiso, "Where Theory Squares with Practice," had educated thousands at not much more than a hundred dollars a year for tuition, room, and board. By the 1920s, competition from state universities, the rise of formal professional standards, plus a series of administrative crises, brought the once proud citadel of popular learning to the edge of extinction. At this juncture, the Klan proudly announced that it had come to the rescue. The Invisible Empire would raise a million dollars to pay off Valparaiso's debts and run it as a "one-hundred-per-cent American Institution," the Klan's Harvard.

The announcement touched off an explosion of editorial glee in the nation's press. *The New Republic* typically commented on the possibility of a campus featuring a "Mob Hall" and "Phi Beta Ku Klux Kappa men." Looking ahead to future ivy-bound traditions, the magazine commented that "It would be a bold yearling who would dare to lynch a professor within two blocks of the dining hall or light a fire in a synagogue on any day but Friday." But no one was ever to know what might have been, for the Imperial Wizard in Atlanta proved as unwilling as ever to see such a commitment of Klan funds, and the project was dropped to the intense ire and embarrassment of D. C. Stephenson. In 1925, Valparaiso was purchased instead by the Lutheran University Association and settled down to live a more traditional if less spectacular educational role.

The struggle between Hiram W. Evans, Imperial Wizard of the Ku Klux Klan, and David C. Stephenson, Grand Dragon of the Realm of Indiana, was over power. Into the conflict were poured the resources, skill, and prestige of the two men, and the life blood of the Klan itself. In the end when Stephenson made an impetuous, horrifyingly false step, his power and life, and perhaps that of the Klan itself, paid the forfeit.

Stephenson was discontented over what he considered the Klan's greed and shortsightedness. He had been pressing Evans to approach politics more systematically, rather than acquiescing in conflicting decisions brought about by local expediency in the various realms of the Empire. Accompanied by the sculptor of mountains and occasional Klan potentate, Gutzon Borglum, Steve attended the Imperial Wizard's secret strategy meeting at the New Willard Hotel in Washington. He came away disappointed. He found the Imperial Wizard and his Southern confederates to be politically small-minded, and the shouting multitudes, who hailed Steve when he dropped from the skies for his inauguration the next month, must have made a disturbing impression on the earthbound Evans.

Now, in the summer months of 1923, Stephenson and Evans grew further apart. With the seemingly never ending struggle with Simmons and other dissidents still dragging through the courts, much of the Imperial Wizard's attention naturally lingered there. In their conversations at Buckeye Lake, aboard Steve's new yacht on Lake Huron, and again in Cincinnati, Evans' thoughts, Steve later testified, turned to various ways of ending the Damoclean lawsuits. And again and again, Evans talked of violence and of ensnarement, the classic Klan method of disposing of unwanted sharers of power, and Stephenson may well have felt the brush of wings against his own shoulder. Addicted to a more than common desire for booze and sex, he and his boys followed a path that led through roadhouses and hotel rooms and made his new home in Indianapolis one of the bastions of high life in the state. If anyone were vulnerable to "having a woman tied on him," it was "The Old Man" himself.

Within months after his triumphal inauguration, Steve, while remaining a Klansman, stepped down from his Dragonship. This was only a truce, and it meant neither peace nor respite. Gathering strength within the order, by May of 1924, Steve was ready to take on Atlanta, and he had a convention of his followers elect him Grand Dragon of a newly autonomous Indiana Klan. Evans' officials met in Joe Huffington's room in Indianapolis' Lincoln Hotel and compiled the story of Steve's misdeeds, such as his drunken attempt to assault the manicurist and various other officials of the Deshler Hotel in Columbus, Ohio. They presented their evidence to Steve's home Klan in Evansville, which pliantly banished its once great leader. Stephenson sued Evans and Walter Bossert, the new Atlanta-selected Grand Dragon, for libel, and increased his charges when his beloved yacht was mysteriously blown up in the harbor at Toledo. Wrathfully he denounced them as "yellow-livered Southerners who hate everything that is pure throughout the state of Indiana."

And yet, despite the war that they all knew lay ahead, the contending factions temporarily glossed over their struggle to work together for the more immediate prize of political control of Indiana. With Governor Warren McCray being transferred from the State House in Indianapolis to the "Big House" in Atlanta on a mail-fraud conviction, and with other officeholders discredited by booze and gambling scandals, the prospects looked good for the Klan.

In the Republican state convention the Invisible Empire was so powerful that one newspaper described the proceedings as those of a Klan Kloncilium, and Stephenson was at the center of almost every decision. Nearly everyone who counted was Steve's selection. The November election followed much the same course. With President Coolidge leading the way, Klan-supported candidates were elected to office. The Klan's bag included sheriffs, court officials, district attorneys, school boards, most of the mayoralty races—including Indianapolis, Evansville, and Kokomo—a majority of the state legislators, and the governor. In return for his money and support, they had promised him allegiance and power, or had compromised themselves to the point that they could refuse him nothing. The new mayor of Indianapolis agreed to consult Steve on civic and police appointments, and Evansville's genial, bumbling Congressman Harry Rowbottom promised all of his federal patronage.

Most of the pro-Klan members of the lower house tended to follow Evans and Bossert. The senators and state and city officials belonged to Steve. Well might he look forward to replacing the ailing Ralston in the United States Senate as a prelude to even higher office. After all, how many young men in their thirties had already traveled so far, so quickly? With Steve in the Senate and the national eye, and the Klan increasingly influential within the Republican party, he might well be able to capture the nomination in 1928. From there it would be easy. With loyal card-carrying Klan Democrats crossing their party lines, as they were wont to do in Indiana, to vote for the flaming cross and 100-per-cent Americanism, the rest would be easy.

But for the moment, his stage was Indiana, and the scene shifted back and forth between the halls and chambers of the state house and Steve's Central States Coal Company office on the third floor of the Kresge Building. With his friend Ed Jackson as governor and a favorable majority in the legislature, the Klan had a first-rate opportunity to enact its desires into law. But this did not happen. The rival Evans-Bossert and Stephenson factions wrangled with each other, and Steve let his vision and his star become clouded by a meaner and more immediate desire for wealth and power. There are those whose nature turns them to intrigue, given the power; when it came to this, Steve was not very different from his hated antagonist Imperial Wizard Hiram Evans. A stream of lobbyists, office seekers, businessmen, and politicians coursed through "The Old Man's" office seeking deals, favors, and bargains. He lost his legislative attempt to cut himself into the lush patronage possibilities of the State Road Department, but he was not without influence in the awarding of contracts, did a profitable business in promises to pass and kill bills, and even saw his book, *One Hundred Years of Health,* temporarily adopted by the public schools. In the lower house, where the regulars were more influential, the Klan's program was presented in the form of bills to require that teachers be public school graduates and exclude religious garb for teachers in these schools. A state textbook commission was requested, and uniform textbooks were specified for public and private schools. Required Bible reading, credit for Bible instruction, release time, and the study of the U. S. Constitution were also asked. However, those bills which passed always seemed to die in the upper house where Stephenson's strength was greatest. There "The Old Man" built his power by directing the votes of his trusting followers against the "divisive" Klan bills in return for support on other issues from the opponents of the bills.

Probably the easiest bill to kill was one which would have abolished a minor position in the office of the state superintendent of public instruction. It was an action which helped lead to his downfall. The job he saved belonged to Madge Oberholtzer. Weighing 145 pounds at five feet four, Madge was on the plump side and not particularly pretty, if her pictures are to be trusted. At twenty-eight, she was unmarried. "The Old Man" in his middle thirties, was fond of women and usually moved in a faster set, but he liked Madge and she was flattered when he took her out. One night early in March of 1925, Madge came in early from a date and learned that Steve had been calling and wanted her to call him back. When she did, he sent over one of his bodyguards to escort her back to his Irvington house. Stephenson had been drinking and "forced" her to drink with him; then, against her will, Steve and his bodyguards hustled her aboard his drawing room on the train to Chicago. She was unsteady from her drinks and he pulled off her clothes and pushed her on to the berth. He attacked her and then began chewing all over her body. The next morning they got off the train at Hammond, on the Indiana side of the Illinois line and the Mann Act, and went to a hotel, while Steve's car was being driven up from Indianapolis. Madge got money from Steve to buy a hat but purchased poison, which she took. Thoroughly frightened, but confident that he could find a way out, Steve offered to take her to a hospital if she would marry him. Madge refused. During the long drive back to Indianapolis she was in agony, but they refused to stop and get a doctor. After keeping her for another night in the loft apartment above his garage while he tried to win her promise of marriage, Steve had her taken home. When she died several weeks later, her father charged "The Old Man" of Indiana Klandom with murder.

The defense questioned Madge's reputation as well as discrepancies in her dying testimony and maintained that she had died at her own hand, not Stephenson's. The defendant himself never took the stand, later claiming variously that he feared for his life from Klan assassins, and that he had been shielding the name of the woman with whom he had spent the night in question somewhere else. Still confident of his power in the state where he had liked to boast that he was "the law," he felt sure that his friends would come to his rescue. He had helped too many on their way up and knew too much to believe that they would dare desert him now. Even as the doors of the Michigan City penitentiary closed behind him and he began his life sentence for second-degree murder, he was certain that Ed Jackson, whom he had made governor, would set him free.

Madge's death and the well-publicized trial badly hurt the Klan, despite Evans' glee over Steve's conviction and the Klan's efforts to disassociate itself from its former star salesman. However, it was too large and too politically entrenched to immediately fade away. When Senator Ralston died, the governor appointed the Klan's sometimes legal adviser James Robinson to the seat for which Steve had waited. In numerous municipal elections in 1925, Klan candidates still did well. However, delayed disintegration was taking place. Further splits opened up within Indiana's politically volatile and heterogeneous Klandom. Investigations, growing newspaper opposition, criminal convictions, and the contents of Steve's "little black box" all played a role.

Indiana's senior senator, Jim Watson, was up for re-election in 1926, along with Robinson, and the Klan felt indebted to him. Watson was no Klansman, but he had been a friend in need when Mayfield, the first Klan senator from Texas had been challenged in the Senate, and he had kept quiet at all the proper times. The instructions from Atlanta were that the Klan should go down the line for Watson, and leading local Klansmen, plus the mayors of Indianapolis and Evansville traveled to Washington at Klan expense to talk it over.

The hooded legions of Indiana were willing to vote for a fellow Klansman, but the Democrats and anti-Watson Republicans, led by Grand Dragon Bossert, refused to violate their political consciences to vote for just a friend. When Bossert was squeezed out, Klansmen from the northern part of the state were mad. Hiram Evans himself made a quick trip to South Bend to forestall the revolt. The candidate of the dissidents was former state Prohibition director, Judge Charles Orbison, who led Indiana's Klan Democrats, but Evans got him out of the way by making him a national vice president of the Klan. The Republican state chairman tried to set the election issue for Klansmen and uninitiates alike by charging that "international bankers on Wall Street" were operating throughout the state to throw the election to the Democrats and the secret power manipulators of Europe. An investigation by the U. S. Senate elections subcommittee found no traces of Wall Street and instead presented a rollicking story of Klan politics and intrigue. For a whole day, former South Bend Cyclops, Pat Emmons, kept his listeners and the press amused as he commented wryly on Klan doings, including the story of how the Imperial Wizard of the Invisible Empire had to go to bed in his La Salle Hotel room while his trousers were being pressed for that evening's meeting. Watson and Robinson won re-election to the Senate, but it cost the Klan thousands of members.

For many of those in political and party office there was no painless way to sever association with the Klan. Stephenson was becoming increasingly restless in his closely watched cell in the Michigan City penitentiary. Governor Jackson was really in a most unenviable position, for it was becoming almost as dangerous to keep Steve in jail as it would be politically to let him out. The governor and the prison warden tried to keep Steve isolated, but in the summer of 1926 he sent out word to his friends to begin making public some of the contents of his much talked about "little black box." Grand juries and prosecutors were clamoring to question him, and a committee of the Indiana Republican Editorial Association, led by Tom Adams, publisher of the Vincennes *Commercial and Leader,* was pressing its own investigation despite party protest.

Finally in the summer of 1927, after a year of desperate threats and maneuvers to obtain a pardon, Steve authorized the release of his confidential files and talked freely. Affidavits and photostats bore

witness to agreements, signed by mayors, congressmen, and police
officials, to trade offices in return for campaign contributions and
aid. After thinking about it for several weeks, Governor Jackson
explained that the twenty-five-hundred-dollar check which he had
received from Stephenson had been in payment for a horse which
had since choked to death on a corncob. Although the horse was
thus unable to testify there were others who could. As a result of the
proliferation of investigations, scandals, and trials that engulfed the
state of Indiana, the Indianapolis *Times* got a Pulitzer prize, and a
score of prominent Republicans went to jail. The state party chairman was convicted of violation of the banking laws. When Mayor
Duvall of Indianapolis was convicted of concealing campaign contributions, he successively tried to turn the city government over to
his wife and his comptroller brother-in-law. For a time there were
four self-styled "legal" mayors, and all city business became en-
snarled in a welter of injunctions. A Muncie judge, rated as the best
Klan orator in the whole of Delaware County, was impeached by
unanimous vote of the assembly and narrowly escaped conviction
for his harassment of a local newspaper editor. Governor Jackson
himself was tried for attempting to bribe his predecessor, and he and
local party leaders were saved only by the fact that the statute of
limitations had run out. Other Klan friends, like the mayor of Evansville and most of his top aides were soon brought into court in various graft prosecutions.

Although Senator Robinson was elected to a full term on the anti-
Catholic wave of the 1928 presidential election, the municipal elections of 1929 marked the final political demise of the Invisible
Empire in the Hoosier State. At the peak of the Klan tide in the middle twenties, most cities had gone Republican; in November of 1929,
anti-Klan Democrats carried almost every major and most of the
minor cities in the state. For the first time in seven years, both the
Democrats and the Republicans were out from under the shadow
of the Klan, and could return to politics as usual.

Meanwhile, decade after decade, the great Klan salesman, D. C.
Stephenson, languished in prison. He was still protesting his inno-
cence, and friends still labored on his behalf. In 1950, a depression
and a war later, he was released on parole, disappeared, was found
working as a linotype operator in Minneapolis, and went back to
prison. In 1956, when he was released again—after thirty-one years
in prison—no one much cared.

24

MIGHTY OHIO

There was a time during the 1920s when it seemed that the mask and hood had become the official symbol of the Buckeye State. With a membership of close to four hundred thousand, the Ohio Klan was the largest in the nation. Nevertheless, despite a string of municipal victories, boasts and boycotts, platforms, parades, and riots, it never succeeded in massing its strength to seize state-wide office and match either the power of the Indiana realm or the reign of terror and fear created by the Klans of the Lone Star State.

Part of the trouble was that the Invisible Empire in Ohio failed to develop its own forceful leadership. The Klan probably first entered Cincinnati in the summer of 1920, about the same time that it sank its roots into Evansville in southern Indiana. The Klan grew more quickly in Indiana and its newly won Hoosier converts moved across the line into the Buckeye State. A Muncie man colonized Springfield early that fall, and the first Grand Goblin arrived from Indianapolis to set up state headquarters in Columbus. He was soon replaced by a local dentist, Dr. C. L. Harold, who turned his State Street office into the fee-extraction center for the state.

That fall D. C. Stephenson was given charge of a vast northern subempire as his reward for helping elevate Hiram Evans to the imperial throne. Building his own political power in the Hoosier State, he delegated recruitment and rule in his Ohio satrapy to one of his Indiana confederates. When Steve and the Klan came to a parting of the ways and his officials were exiled off to Iowa, Brown Harwood took over. For the most part, the Goblins, King Kleagles, and Imperial Representatives considered their function to be one of gathering members—and fees—and passing along the decisions of the various higher potentates. But the Ohio Klan was getting too large, its administration too complex, its politics too demanding, and its remarkably patient members desirous of self-rule. In the 1924 election, the

Klan leaders decided to support Calvin Coolidge for President and a Democrat as governor of Ohio. A complicated biparty maneuver such as this would need careful leadership and control. Clyde W. Osborn, a Youngstown lawyer, had shown the proper talent and zeal. Combining the skills of politician and administrator, he had been serving as law director for the Klan mayor of Youngstown. Evans liked him, and in 1924 the realm of Ohio was chartered, with Osborn as Grand Dragon.

As Osborn liked to describe it, the Klan entered Ohio fighting for the "submerged majority of Protestants." Since the turn of the century the number of Negroes had more than doubled, while the Eastern European and Mediterranean immigrants flooded into the industrial cities and towns of the state until one out of every six Ohioans had been born east of the Elbe or south of the Alps. By identifying patriotism with Protestantism and connecting the Roman Catholic Church with alienism and un-Americanism, the Klan drew in its members by the thousands. In an excellent unpublished study, Embrey Howson has described the Klan's membership as primarily middle class, representing a good cross section, but drawing heavily from the less successful white-collar classes and the fringes of the professions.[1] Many of the local Klan officers, and more than one half of its lecturers in the state were ministers. In one sizable Miami Valley industrial city, the Klan claimed that every Protestant minister belonged to the Invisible Empire. Although anti-Negro appeals were useful in cities, such as Springfield and Akron, it was the combination of Americanism and anti-Catholicism which sold Ohio.

The Invisible Empire soon spread across the state of Ohio with a Klan in each county plus the fourteen in Cincinnati's Hamilton County. It initially grew slowly in the proud old German-flavored city of Cincinnati itself, but gathered strength in the surrounding small-town counties of Ohio, Indiana, and Kentucky, for which Cincinnati served as the cultural and market center. In Cleveland, where the native-born white Protestant inhabitants of the nation's sixth-largest city constituted but a quarter of the population, the Klan never did well. Other immigrant cities, like the Great Lakes port of Toledo and the Ohio River steel center of Steubenville, saw only slow Klan progress.

However, in small-town Ohio, and in those big cities whose people had flocked in from the farms rather than from the immigrant ships,

[1] Embrey B. Howson, "The Ku Klux Klan in Ohio after World War I," unpublished Master's thesis, Ohio State University, 1951.

the Klan held mighty sway. In the Nordic town of Hamilton on the Great Miami River, Slav and Negro were segregated on the east side of town. Dayton staffed her industry with the skilled, native-born artisans, and in Springfield the farmers loafing about at the corner of Limestone and Maine gave evidence of a lingering rural flavor. Only 5 per cent of the population of Columbus was foreign born. They and the Negroes lived off by themselves in sections such as Bronzeville or the Italian district northwest of the state capital. In Akron, the Southerners had flocked from the hills to the rubber factories and industrial plants until they constituted more than half the city's population, and West Virginia Day became a civic fiesta. These cities became the centers of Klan activity, along with more rural Knox, Licking, and Muskingum counties. The Invisible Empire was equally strong in the Mahoning Valley southeast of Cleveland where the old and new American labor met face to face in Youngstown and the other industrial towns. By 1923, the Klans in Columbus and Akron reportedly numbered close to fifty thousand members each.

The life of the Invisible Empire in the Buckeye State was far from placid. Opposition from Cleveland's mayor and council, and the denial of permission to parade in Cleveland, or to use Akron's municipal armory, served as grounds for Klan cries of persecution. In Springfield, where race relations and city government had not been the best anyway, Negro voters flocked to the Democratic party when the Republican-dominated school board decided to segregate. Prominent Catholics hired a detective, and, on his evidence, the police chief raided the Klan hall and later charged a Klan funeral party with disorderly conduct. In the river city of Portsmouth, Klansmen marching to the laying of a church cornerstone were arrested for holding an illegal procession. Youngstown police similarly refused to permit a parade. In Steubenville, where the hostile Knights of the Flaming Circle had been organizing with Klanlike rituals, a mob assaulted a group of Klansmen, pulling them from their cars and beating them.

On the whole, this series of episodes aided the Klan. The attacks, its leaders cried, were, in reality, assaults upon Americanism and showed the real extent of the Roman peril. Opposition by police and city officials hastened the increase of the Klan's interest in local politics, and the violence in Steubenville brought Klan reinforcements pouring in from neighboring Ohio, Pennsylvania, and West Virginia.

By 1922, the Klan was already involved in senatorial primary and congressional races, and in the fall of 1923, it won impressive victories in Ohio's municipal elections. A last-minute campaign in Portsmouth defeated the mayor who had banned the Klan parade. Though anti-Klan mayors were returned in Springfield, Steubenville, and Ironton, and a judge whom the Klan opposed remained on the bench in Youngstown, the rest was velvet for the sheeted order. Klan-supported mayors were elected in Toledo, Akron, Columbus, Hamilton, Marion, Elyria, Newark, and in all five cities of the Mahoning Valley. The victors included Klansmen, Klan friends, and opportunistic politicians who read the signs of the times. In the city of Hamilton, it meant the first Republican mayor in a decade, and in many cases, Klan candidates won election to the school boards and other municipal offices. No wonder the Klan was jubilant. The Klan mayors of Mahoning Valley formed a mutual-aid organization to co-operate on police work, water, and "cleaning up" the valley. Col. E. A. Watkins, who had crested the Klan's Horse Thief Society police force, invited Klansmen from all over the country to Youngstown for Mayor Scheible's victory celebration, and Klansmen on the city council got so carried away that they presented a resolution asking the Klan to pay off the city debt of $600,000.

Emboldened by the municipal victories of 1923, the Klan looked ahead to the next year's state-wide and national elections. With the Klan operating primarily within the Republican party, Ohio Democrats took the lead in pushing for its condemnation by their National Convention. Although some officeholders, including Governor Vic Donahey, kept a discreet silence, the state committee adopted a strong anti-Klan platform. Since an anti-Klan former governor was running for the Republican nod, the Klan entered its own candidate, Joseph Sieber. Although he was politically unknown in the state, he ran second and polled a large number of votes. However, having failed to mass enough of its strength behind Sieber, the Klan now sought to keep the successful anti-Klan Republican from occupying the state house. This meant getting the somewhat undependable Ohio faithful to divide their ticket between Calvin Coolidge and Democratic Governor Vic Donahey. To organize this campaign, Clyde Osborn was appointed head of Ohio's newly chartered realm. Osborn later claimed that he wasn't much interested in the Klan's own fears and hopes, but he saw the chance as one to help elect a Republican President and make a little money on the side, and so he accepted. In the election, Coolidge and Donahey came through.

But the election returns were all but lost in the reports that came from Mahoning Valley. There, in the industrial complex which serviced the steel and metal producers of Cleveland, Pittsburgh, and Wheeling, old- and new-stock Americans had jarringly come together. When it was announced that a tristate meeting and parade would take place in Niles just before the national election, the antagonistic Knights of the Flaming Circle, which had been organizing in the valley towns, decided on a counterparade. Local businessmen petitioned the mayor to postpone the Klan parade, but nothing was done. Youngstown refused to send extra police and Governor Donahey said that he could not order in the National Guard until the peace was actually broken. The explosion of a bomb on Mayor Kistler's porch heightened the tension in the rumor-filled town. The day of the parade, the mayor went on vacation, leaving everything in the hands of Sheriff Thomas.

On the morning of November 1, Klansmen from all over northeastern Ohio began to arrive at the appointed field, north of town. Those who had to pass through the city from the south quickly ran into trouble. A large, noisy, determined crowd had begun to gather in the streets. Armed men were searching all cars, confiscating Klan robes, beating and occasionally shooting the drivers, and wrecking the cars. Sheriff Thomas managed to save a group of Horse Thief Detective Society men, who had come in on the interurban trolley, by marching them off to jail. Thus far, no one had been killed, but this was only a matter of luck. The sheriff turned to the National Guard officer, whom the governor had sent in as his observer, and requested aid. By midafternoon the troops began to appear, some of them Klansmen who had had to dash back to Akron from the rally to change uniforms and face the muster. Soldiers coming in from the south had heard reports of a massacre and rode in warily, with their machine guns ready for action. Though threats and hard feelings continued, subsequent investigation failed to bring either indictments or a count of the number injured.

With the exception of the Horse Thief Detective Society and the black-robed Night Riders of Bellaire that Doc Shepard brought to the Buckeye Lake Konklave in 1925, the Klan was not organized for violence. Still, it seemed to get its share. In addition to the Steubenville and Niles affairs, there was a skirmish between Klan and anti-Klansmen near Cleveland, and another one at a Cincinnati meeting addressed by Helen Jackson, the professional ex-nun from Toledo. In Toledo itself, two radicals, who criticized President Harding at a street meeting, were kidnaped and narrowly escaped lynching at Klan hands. Two Columbus men were stabbed after a dance-hall argument over the Klan. In Dayton, the Klan impartially touched off bombs at the Catholic University of Dayton and, to increase membership, in front of its own meeting place. In Alliance, a battle between rival factions of the women's auxiliary had to be quelled by police after one woman was injured.

Economic violence was also the way of the Invisible Empire in Ohio. Vocational klannishness was encouraged so that Klansmen might bring their custom to their brothers and avoid the establishments run by alien enemies. The Levy Department Stores were boycotted, and in Ashland the Klan had a big public meeting to tell the townspeople not to patronize any Jewish-owned store. Jewish- and Catholic-owned businesses were badly hurt in Klan strongholds, while in cities such as Marion, boycotting became a two-way street. In Columbus, where the Klan had distributed a list of "approved" businesses and went in for economic discrimination in a big way, the Budd Dairy Company was almost ruined by a spontaneous countersurge when it advertised its new soft drink in the Klan newspaper.

Perhaps the chief public concern of the Klan was the protection of the public schools. It was imperative that they be kept out of the hands of Rome and be kept moral. With as many as one quarter of the state assemblymen counted among its particular friends, the Klan sought aid from the legislature. The lawmakers had already turned down a bill that would have forced the Klan to reveal its membership; now they moved on to the consideration of more positive measures. The Klan, backed by rural legislatures and the Prohibition and utility lobbies, presented bills to require public schooling and to bar Catholic teachers. These, and a bill against interracial marriage, failed, but daily Bible reading did pass, only to be turned down by Governor Donahey as a violation of the separation between Church and State.

Rather than bringing unity to Protestantism, the Klan was often a divisive force. The minister of Galion's Peace Lutheran Church was asked to leave, after seventeen years, because he opposed secret societies, and a Presbyterian church in a Youngstown suburb was dissolved by its presbyter because the Klan issue had so badly divided the congregation.

Despite its many and violent contacts with the outside world, to its multitudes the real life of Klandom was the world of fraternalism within the lodge, and it was here that Klan failure was most serious. Klaverns were unmanageably large. As E. B. Howson has pointed out, membership often numbered in the thousands, and meetings tended to be more anarchic than fraternal, more likely to be swayed by emotion and oratory than by prudence and democratic procedures. Initially, success carried the movement along, but the fissures soon developed and widened. The violence which seemed to hover over the Invisible Empire hurt it in the long run. Quarrels took place over internal leadership, political endorsements, and money. Ohio members were resentful of the autocratic control of Klan affairs exercised by the predominantly Southern leadership. There was substantial feeling that the Buckeye realm was being milked. Ten million dollars had been collected from Ohio, and no one could say quite where it had gone. The Grand Dragons and their aides were living too high, with too many Klan-purchased automobiles and airplanes at their call. The Kleagles at Lima and Ironton disappeared with the treasuries, and there were continuous squabbles over commissions and fees.

The locals also used their moneys unwisely and faced building schemes unrealized and mortgages unmet. The huge Akron Klan squandered its resources on rifles for its drill team and a costly lot upon which the promised auditorium was never built. As internal dissension grew, the Grand Dragon appointed an unpopular minister to take control. When Gilbert Taylor, a former Huron County congressman and utilities expert, succeeded Clyde Osborn as head of the Ohio Klan, the trouble in Akron came to a head. With rival factions bitterly quarreling and banishing each other, the Akron dissidents made public the realm's financial records. Taylor claimed the remaining chapter funds for his faction of loyal supporters while the secessionists sought to transfer them to their newly founded Protestant Service League.

By 1925, the Klan was losing political ground in the municipalities it had captured in its great victory two years before. In Middleport, the announcement of an anti-Klan victory touched off a wildly happy street demonstration that lasted for hours. Only faithful Newark, near the Klan's Buckeye Lake stamping ground, and neighboring Lancaster gave the hooded order much to cheer about. In the next year's Republican governor's primary, the Klan-supported Secretary of State, Thad Brown, was narrowly nosed out. And the Klan gained no real pleasure from the re-election of Senator Frank Willis. It had only endorsed him because his opponent was the anti-Klan ex-Senator Atlee Pomerene. Willis himself, having voted for the World Court, was hardly better. As the Klan's destiny-marked troubleshooter, Jimmy Colescott, took over the Ohio realm, many Klansmen had come to feel that their political support was up for sale to the highest bidder. But, if so, bidders were becoming increasingly scarce. Early in 1926, the New York *Times* summed up the state of Klan prestige by commenting that the candidates who truckled to it in 1923, were cautiously indifferent to it in 1925. In 1926, many were eager to oppose it. In 1928, the *Times* guessed neither party would be likely to seek its aid.

25

THE FIGHTING ILLINI

By 1921, the Klan had established itself in Chicago under the name of the Southern Publicity Bureau. It was certainly made less than welcome by official Chicago, but it had money and zeal. It pushed its recruitment, using newspaper ads to answer criticism, and soon came to number an estimated eighteen chapters in the Windy City, with more downstate. By the summer of 1922, a series of initiation rallies drew Klansmen and spectators by the tens of thousands, and it was no uncommon occurrence for two, three, and four thousand aliens to be naturalized into the Invisible Empire at a single time. At mammoth events near Chicago, Joliet, Peru, Champaign, and Springfield, and at lesser meetings in Utica and La Salle, car headlights illuminated nocturnal Klan ceremonies and fiery crosses suddenly blazed forth over rented cornfields.

Despite its successes the Invisible Empire came under continuous attack. The weekly conference of Chicago's Baptist ministers denounced it, and various groups organized to fight it. In the summer of 1922, the American Unity League appeared on the scene, with a bishop of the Reformed Episcopal Church as honorary chairman. The conduct of affairs was in the hands of a determined Chicago attorney named Pat O'Donnell, who had conceived a novel way of combating the hooded knights. His method was one of logical simplicity: since the Klan thrived on secrecy, why not remove the veil of anonymity from its members? In his periodical, *Tolerance,* Pat O'Donnell began publishing long lists of Klan members. Now this was a rather horrifying and intolerant thing to be doing, and the Klan was considerably distressed. Although it claimed that the unwanted publicity had not been harmful, it must have looked at O'Donnell's plans for expansion into Indiana and New York with great trepidation. Although Klansmen suffered boycott and loss of jobs when their names were listed, O'Donnell was also having trouble. His staff of life was access to lists of Klan members, and this was a far from easy task. He got what he could from disgruntled Klan officials and private detectives, but his sources were untrustworthy and his material often inaccurate. Within a short time he was plagued with lawsuits brought by irate citizens, such as the Catholic undertaker whom *Tolerance* had identified as a Klansman. His most celebrated error was that of naming William Wrigley, the millionaire chewing-gum magnate, who wrathfully sued for damages. But even this was not the full extent of *Tolerance*'s troubles. In an ironic turnabout, the Invisible Empire planted an agent in the American Unity League, who managed to stymie its organizing efforts and dissipate its funds.

In Chicago, however, opposition mounted. Business establishments run by Klansmen as well as the *Dawn*'s printing plant were wrecked by bombs. Klansmen were barred from grand jury duty on the grounds that they leaked information. The city fire department, into which the Klan had made particular inroads, came under increasing scrutiny. A list of Klansmen who worked for the city was collected, and there was an aldermanic cry for the scalps of all of those whose names appeared on it. The chief of police sent out an order that no more meetings were to be held in city fire stations and the members of one engine company which the Klan had successfully proselytized were scattered among outlying stations. When two firemen were suspended on the ground that their Klan oath was contrary to the Constitution and therefore a sign of unfitness, they demanded a civil service trial, and the new Imperial Wizard Hiram Evans journeyed to Chicago to lend them support.

On the whole, the Klan did better downstate. It claimed the election of friendly mayors in Decatur and Paris, and in industrial East St. Louis, the Klan was organized on a precinct level throughout the city. Klan speakers, like the Reverend Samuel Campbell from Atlanta, instructed Klansmen on the "Duty of a Christian Patriot." The pastor of the First Christian Church of Mattoon explained that the Ku Klux Klan was the "masculine part" of the Protestant Church in action, and the Klan's weekly, *Dawn,* carried its message of racial purity, religion, and law enforcement to "true American patriots."

The summer of 1923 was rush season for the Ku Klux Klan in Illinois. Although Governor Len Small signed a bill which prohibited public masking and increased the punishment for masked crimes and violence, the Klan was doing well. In June, Illinois became a self-governing realm within the Invisible Empire, with Charles G. Palmer as Grand Dragon, and *Dawn* boasted that there were 287 chartered Klaverns in the state. Although the Klan was not unlikely to over-state its strength, both for reasons of enthusiasm and policy, there was at least a reflection of truth in the claim. During that great sum-mer of Illini Klandom, the members turned out by the tens of thou-sands for a succession of enormous outdoor Klan rallies at Joliet, Rockford, Springfield, Oak Forest, and Urbana. Zenith Klan No. 56 of Champaign-Urbana bought the old Illinois Theater, which seated over a thousand, to use as a Klavern, and when the Imperial Wizard Evans came to visit that fall, a mammoth open meeting was staged at the University of Illinois armory.

It was in the southern part of the state, however, that the hooded knights of Illinois reached their greatest power and achieved a degree of notoriety which challenged that of Mer Rouge, Louisiana. The town of Cairo, located where the mighty Mississippi and Ohio rivers join, gave the nickname of "Egypt" to the southernmost region of the state. For generations, the mountain people of Kentucky and Tennessee had peopled the yellow clay hills of Egypt, forming a back-water of rural, fundamentalist, old-stock America. When coal was discovered in the 1890s, a flood of foreigners began to pour in, some French and many Italian miners from Lombardy. By 1920 they made up a fifth of the population. The good citizens of Williamson County were concerned about foreigners, Roman Catholicism, saloons, and roadhouses, gambling, prostitution, and widespread public corrup-tion. In addition, an almost endemic struggle raged between the un-ions and antilabor mineowners. The brutal and unpunished massacre of almost a score of strikebreakers in 1922 had brought such un-favorable publicity that many people in Herrin felt that their com-munity stood on public trial.

The story of the Ku Klux Klan in southern Illinois is excellently told by Paul Angle in his *Bloody Williamson: A Chapter in American Lawlessness*. The Klan made its first public appearance during serv-ices at the First Christian Church of Marion. The evangelist, accord-ing to Professor Angle, looked at the three ten-dollar bills which the masked visitors had given him and then announced "That tells you . . . they stand for something good." And so the preachers of Williamson County became the convinced adherents and supporters of the Klan. As one minister later proclaimed at the funeral of a martyred Klansman, "O Lord, we have put our hand to the plow and we will not turn back. Thus shall the soil and soul of Williamson County be purged and purified."

The summer of 1923 was a period of church visits and great cross-lit ceremonials as thousands gathered to welcome new initiates to their ranks. The ministers preached of law enforcement, and told mass meetings that the county was going to be cleaned up. Conditions were bad in Williamson County, and Sheriff George Galligan was seemingly unwilling to do anything about it. The better citizens, led by their preachers and county officials, formed their own Law and Order League, which was soon absorbed into the Klan. Rebuffed in the state capital and in Washington, they found a man who would lead the great reform. He was a brash, aggressive former Justice Department agent named S. Glenn Young whom the Prohibition unit had recently felt it was wise to set at leisure.

Initially deputized by federal Prohibition agents, squads of Klansmen fanned out over the county in a series of raids on bootleggers and roadhouses. Three raids during the winter of 1923–24 put over a hundred establishments out of business and yielded hundreds of prisoners, whom the Klan herded to jail through the streets of Herrin and Benton. But although the raids gave support to the Klan's claims about the extent of crime in Williamson County, not all of the illegality rested upon the shoulders of the bootleggers. Dressed in a semimilitary uniform, wearing two forty-fives, and often carrying a machine gun, Glenn Young was always at the center of the trouble. Private homes were invaded and robbed and many men were roughly handled and abused. Frenchmen and Italians received so much attention from Klan raiders that the consuls of both nations protested. When Young was tried for assault and battery, he and his aides carried their pistols and machine gun into the courtroom and received a quick verdict of acquittal. This in turn brought the National Guard to begin two years of on-and-off duty in Herrin.

Even when the sheriff, with his new Klan deputies, finally bestirred himself to move against the illegal liquor joints, Young led his undeputized Klansmen on ever bigger raids. With both Klan and anti-Klan factions arming and spoiling for action, it came. The sheriff went to talk reason to an anti-Klan meeting at the Rome club, but when his Klan deputies also showed up, a riot was only narrowly averted. Later that night, a pro-Klan deputy was shot down in the center of town, and armed Klansmen took over Herrin. Learning that some of the antis were being treated at the local hospital, the Klansmen besieged it with blazing guns until the troops arrived again, at three in the morning. Bands of National Guardsmen and Klansmen, wearing homemade tin badges, separately patrolled the streets over that August weekend, while Glenn Young "arrested" and jailed practically all of the officials in town. Before the whole Klan episode was over, practically every prominent man in the county—judges, policemen, sheriffs, mayors, county supervisors, and state's attorneys —came under indictment for conspiracy, kidnaping, assault, malfeasance, riot, or murder. Guardsmen with fixed bayonets and emplaced machine guns became a part of the everyday life.

Glenn Young was cheered wherever he went. Prominent businessmen signed his bail bond. His coterie idolized him and the ministers praised him from the pulpit. However, the influential men who had hired Young in the first place were unhappy with the turmoil which had become part of their lives. When they privately told Young that they would no longer pay him his handsome crusader's wages, he had his gunmen shoot up the home of their spokesman. Young went off on a visit to encourage the Klan legions in East St. Louis, while back in Williamson County the Klan swept the April primaries. As the Klan's thousands paraded, prayed, dined, and flocked to a three-day Klantauqua, men kept their weapons handy and stocked up their arsenals.

Late in May, assassins overtook Glenn Young's now famous Lincoln touring car and riddled it with bullets. He was wounded in the leg and his new young wife was blinded by shotgun pellets. Klansmen quickly set up roadblocks and brought down the killer car with a volley of shots. Young emerged from the Catholic hospital, where he and his wife had been healing, leaning on canes and with all of his meager restraint gone. He wildly denounced Prohibition officials in neighboring counties and swaggered about with large armed escorts.

His trial date was coming up and both the state Klan and the federal government disclaimed responsibility for him. Tension tightened, and when Young finally left town for medical treatment in Atlanta, the state confiscated some thirty-nine thousand dollars bond which had been put up for him. In an attempt to bring an end to the growing feud, the men who had killed the deputy and touched off the initial battle were let out of jail. Immediately, the newly freed Shelton brothers, together with the sheriff and some anti-Klan deputies went to retrieve the murder car from the Klan-owned garage to which it had been taken. Their aggressive bullying led to a burst of gunfire which killed six men, mainly Klansmen and innocent bystanders. As Klansmen and sheriff's deputies mobilized at neighboring rallying points, the troops arrived and set up their machine guns again.

While the town seethed with tension, two things happened to make the situation even more dangerous. Glenn Young arrived back from Atlanta and Sheriff Galligan appointed the leading anti-Klan gunman as his permanent deputy. Despite the fact that Young had been expelled from the Klan, his support among the Williamson rank and file was undiminished, and he recklessly did his best to provoke a renewal of open battle. The respectable local Klan leaders paid him to leave town but he was soon back. Finally he and the sheriff's hired gunman shot it out at a tobacco store, killing each other and two bystanders. Perhaps forty thousand people jammed into Herrin to hear the ministers combine on his eulogy and to see him laid to rest in a specially built mausoleum over which relays of armed Klansmen were to long stand guard.

A community compromise was arranged under the evident possibility that unless it were done there would soon be no community. Sheriff Galligan went off into temporary exile, on full salary. A successful young evangelist was invited into town, and the people of Herrin gave themselves to him and to reconciliation during the course of six weeks of revival. The local Klan newspaper was forced into bankruptcy by its Klan creditors. Peace seemed to have settled over Williamson County.

Then, in April of 1926, the Klan swept Herrin's township and school board elections and was marshaling strength for county and state elections, which included the office of sheriff. Klansmen swaggered about town, Paul Angle reported, and the antis began readying their guns. On Election Day, John Smith, the Klan garage owner, challenged Catholic voters at the polls and was attacked by an anti-Klan precinct worker. Deputies separated them, and Smith went back to his garage, but the old enmities had been brought to the surface. Fist fights broke out in various parts of town, and carloads of gangsters carrying pistols and machine guns opened up on the Klansmen who barricaded themselves in Smith's garage. Then, as the National Guard moved in for the eighth time in four years, the raiders stopped to exchange fire with Klansmen lounging around the polling place in the Masonic Temple. When it was over, five men lay dead.

With the battles of Smith's garage and the Masonic Temple, the Klan wars seemed to come to an end in Williamson County. At a cost of twenty lives the Ku Klux Klan was able to tamp the lid down on open vice, gambling, and booze joints. In the process it trained a generation to the habit of violence, and drained away its own enthusiasm, idealism, and future.

To many people, the violent story of Williamson County only proved that the country needed the Klan. However, businessmen, politicians, and community leaders came to realize that they could not control the hooded order which had brought violence rather than righteous tranquility to their communities. But, while Klansmen and their antagonists filled the newspaper headlines, jails, witness boxes, and mortuaries, the Klan was wracked by intramural dissension. The struggle for control of the national Klan split the ranks of Illinois Klansmen, and Evans himself journeyed to the Windy City to explain his case against Colonel Simmons. During a big Klan rally in Aurora, Klansmen exchanged their hoods for aviators' helmets when, if the story is correct, two pro-Evans planes had to go aloft to block out a third aircraft which was dropping pro-Simmons leaflets. A schismatic Independent Klans of America did relatively good business, and Chicago Klandom was badly buffeted when suspicious indications of pro-Simmons sentiment led to the removal of ten Windy City Cyclopes.

In addition, Grand Dragon Palmer had to fight against disloyalty to himself as well as to Hiram Evans. One of the Grand Titans disagreed over the selection of a candidate for Springfield's legislative seat, and he and Palmer came to blows. With the local unit demanding a state convention to decide, Palmer suspended the Klavern and went to court for possession of its treasury. The eventual replacement of Palmer as Grand Dragon settled some of the lawsuits, but failed to restore the harmony and prestige of the Invisible Empire. Although the legislature turned down a law which would have made public the membership lists of secret societies, the victory had not been the Klan's doing, and the decline of its prestige and membership continued. Although downstate units remained active during the early thirties, it was the battling twenties that lingered on in men's memories. The habit of violence in Williamson County continued into the post-World War II period. The historian of *Bloody Williamson*, Paul Angle, relates that even in the late forties, men still identified each other as "Kluckers" and "anti-Kluckers."

26

BADGER GAMES IN WISCONSIN

The Ku Klux Klan in Wisconsin was like a misunderstood child. Its patriarchal grandfather in Atlanta interfered in its upbringing, and its ambitious parents exploited and drove it upward when all it wanted was to go out and play with the other children. No wonder it ended up with a nervous breakdown. This is essentially the picture painted by the historian Norman Weaver in his perceptive seminal study of the Great Lakes Klans.[1]

In Wisconsin, Weaver maintained, "Americanism" did not seem seriously under attack. With the exception of an influx of Italian construction workers into Madison's "Little Sicily" and the colonized Poles in the cut-over lumber areas in the northwestern part of the state, the ethnic issue did not seem large in the eyes of Wisconsin Klandom. In some ways this is difficult to understand. Although there were few Negroes, almost half of the people were Roman Catholics, but Weaver explained that they were not active as such in state politics. For the most part, these Catholics were of an earlier Irish and South German variety and the state itself had become accustomed to the predominance of the British, Germans, and Scandinavians. Lingering wartime suspicions of hyphenated loyalties, fears of La Follette Progressivism, and alarm over Milwaukee socialism were not a primary breeding ground for the Klan. Although Professor Weaver seemed to underestimate the extent of Badger State anti-Catholicism, the feeling was less violent there than in many other parts of the country. What Wisconsin Klansmen seemed to have wanted was a fraternal lodge for native-born white American Protestants that would offer a little ritual, a little discrimination, and a little *gemütlichkeit*. What they got was a fervent appeal to the emotions and the pocketbook that, in time, sapped the real potential of the Klan as a stable, permanent force in the Wisconsin fraternal and lodge world.

[1] Norman Weaver, "The Knights of the Ku Klux Klan in Wisconsin, Indiana, Ohio, and Michigan," unpublished Ph.D. dissertation, University of Wisconsin, 1954, Chs. 2–3.

The state's first Klan was organized in the fall of 1920 among carefully selected business and professional men in Milwaukee. After an initial meeting had been held aboard a U. S. Coast Guard cutter, they met as the Milwaukee Businessman's Club in a hall over the Pabst Theatre, and units were set up in Racine and Kenosha. Everything was done in secret and while the Milwaukee Klan No. 1 languished in its provisional status, all of the moneys flowed out into the pockets of the Kleagles and the Klan headquarters in Atlanta. The members impatiently demanded an accounting of local Klan funds, and when it was refused they walked out of the Invisible Empire. The national headquarters hastened to stem the revolt. While conceding nothing on the issue of finances, Atlanta let Milwaukee pick the new state leader, William Wiesemann, a local insurance man who was prominent in Masonic circles.

Wiesemann came in at a lucky moment. The Klan tide was on the rise in the fall of 1921, and, for the next three years, he made a good thing of it—but more for himself than the Klansmen of Wisconsin. Basking in the publicity of the congressional hearings, the Klan began to recruit earnestly. Klan thousands turned out for parades, picnics, barbecues, and rallies in Milwaukee, Oshkosh, and Racine. The Klan's advertisements read "Masons Preferred" and despite opposition from their top leaders, many Masons joined. The hostile Grand Master was eased out of power. Somewhat more surprisingly, an impressive number of Milwaukee's Socialists also crossed the portals. Closing their ears to the Klan's conservatism and their own leaders' outrage, they listened only to the blandishments of its anti-Catholicism. One successful Socialist lawyer, John Kleist, ran for the state Supreme Court as both a Klansman and a Socialist and made a better showing than anyone had ever done on the straight Socialist ticket. The Klan had more Socialists on its rolls, he informed party leaders, than they did. For the Klansmen and Klanswomen, Tri-K girls, Junior Klansmen, and foreign-born Protestant Krusaders, meeting in fraternal halls and church basements, the Invisible Empire seemed a satisfying outlet for patriotic sentiments and in-group friendliness.

The trouble was that their leaders wanted more tangible returns. Southern clerical Klansmen and local recruiters insisted that it was necessary that they hate rather than merely distrust the Jews and Catholics. King Kleagle Wiesemann liked the feel of the money flowing in and had worked out an arrangement with his subordinate recruiters by which his own share would be enlarged. What disturbed him, and his superiors in Atlanta, was the coming day when the Klaverns would have to be chartered and allowed to keep the fees from new members. Milwaukee No. 1 had been promised a charter when it reached one thousand members. When this goal seemed imminent, Wiesemann moved it back to five thousand, and as the hopeful pushed close to achieving this, he jumped the ante to ten thousand. The frustrated and angry Klansmen again withdrew from the Klan and filed suit against it. Faced with the loss of both members and secrecy, Atlanta gave in again and transferred or demoted the top state leaders. Charles Lewis was sent in from Michigan and managed to reclaim the dissidents and get the realm chartered.

From the beginning of its public life, the Klan and the politicians eyed each other warily. The mayor of Madison said, however, that he saw nothing wrong with the order and it returned the compliment, even offering the city authorities the services of the Klan's military unit, the Klavaliers. Although this was not accepted, the tendency toward wine and violence manifested by the inhabitants of Madison's Little Sicily gave the Klan a useful menace against which to operate.

When the police chief and the district attorney refused Klan aid in cleaning up "the Bush," as the area was sometimes called, the mayor used information gathered by Klan detectives and appointed Klansmen to a special liquor squad. There were a number of Klansmen on the police force and when a policeman was killed in the Bush it served to bring the police and Klan closer together.

The Klan did well in local elections in Oshkosh, Racine, Kenosha, and in Chippewa County, but most state officials remained hostile. Although he vetoed an antimask bill, Governor John Blaine denounced the Klan and refused to let it meet on state property. The Klansmen paraded through the streets of Madison to show that they were undisturbed by the governor's hostility, and they pledged themselves to see a Klan fraternity, Kappa Beta Lambda, standing for "Klansmen Be Loyal," established at the university. In addition to the opposition from the governor, and the campus, the top Masonic and Socialist leaders attacked it, and John Kleist was eventually expelled from the party. The American Legion in Wausau asked Klan organizers to leave town, and a mob stormed the Commercial Hotel in Waukesha when an organizational meeting was held there in 1924. Klan rallies and parades were heckled and on occasion broken up in Boscobel, Chippewa Falls, and Marinette, giving the Klan a chance to claim persecution by "Roman rowdies," and the governor a chance to side with the Klan's antagonists.

La Follette's Progressives were the dominant force in the Badger State, and they made no bones about their dislike of the hooded order. The Klan, on the other hand, praised the Progressives when they opposed American admission to the World Court, but generally struggled against them. In 1925, when the senior La Follette died, one of the Klan's Grand Titans, Daniel Woodward, ran against "Young Bob" for the Senate. Despite the fact that he finished a poor third, Woodward tried it again the next year when Governor Blaine moved up to the other Senate seat. With the top state post left open, the Klan had the satisfaction of seeing a friend enter the governor's mansion. The young, opportunistic Fred Zimmerman, who had combined his secretaryship of state with Klanship and anti-Catholicism, now saw his chance. Having withdrawn from the Klan, he toured Wisconsin with an entourage composed of priests and rabbis, a reversed-collar Methodist and a Negro jazz band, smiling broadly at Klansmen when he denied membership in the organization. Surprisingly enough, he won, with the votes of both Klansmen and Roman Catholics.

But even this achievement was not enough to inspire and strengthen the Klan in the Badger State. By 1924, Weaver reported, the peak had been reached and the movement had expanded as far as it was going to go. The forty thousand votes that Klansman Dan Woodward polled in his Senate race against La Follette were probably the most that it could deliver, although an estimated seventy-five thousand citizens of the Badger State at one time or another paid their ten dollars to the Invisible Empire.

Inner dissension and the struggle over the dollars of the Wisconsin Klansmen began once again to splinter the Invisible Empire. Most of the members of the Milwaukee chapter, foiled in their hopes for a bit of peaceful Protestant fellowship, dropped out for the third and final time. Dan Woodward denounced Klan intrigue and immorality and joined a schismatic Knights of American Protestantism which had splintered from the Indiana Klan and set up business in the Fox River Valley of Wisconsin. Edward Young Clarke, the national Klan's first great recruiter, drew a few unhappy Klansmen to his new orders. The rebel Minutemen, founded by the exiled Grand Dragon of Colorado, won the Dane County and Madison Klan leaders, and revivals in Oshkosh in 1925 and 1926 by itinerant anti-Catholics and fast-buck promoters left the faithful exhausted and in debt. By 1931, when ex-Emperor Simmons sent in William Wiesemann to carry the tidings of his new version of Klanlike fraternalism, Wisconsin was not even faintly interested. The next year, Weaver reported, the last Klan units had called it quits.

27

WHITE ROBES ON WOODWARD AVENUE

Michigan had a highly polyglot population in the 1920s. Half of her people were first- and second-generation Americans. To such earlier streams of Irish and Germans, Hollanders and Scandinavians, the twentieth century brought immigrants from southern and eastern Europe and from the southern part of the United States. The Hollanders had settled on the shores of Lake Michigan, and the Germans and Scandinavians had gone to the farms, and to the lumber and mining areas of the Upper Peninsula. Now the Poles and Italians, Ukrainians, Russians, Czechs and Hungarians, Negroes and Southern whites flooded into Detroit and into the industrial towns and cities across the lower part of the state.

The Ku Klux Klan in Michigan, by best estimates, never numbered more than one person in fifty, but, as elsewhere, it found that change, immigration, and ethnic diversity provided it the chance to do a little profitable business. The Klan's platform and appeal consisted mainly of the things it was against: corruption, foreigners, Roman Catholics, and Negroes. A Klan-supported candidate was elected mayor of Flint in 1924 on a "clean up the city campaign" after the incumbent was recalled from office. The Invisible Empire rallied behind a bill for the registration of all foreigners, in the hope that deportation might be the eventual next step. Klan ministers orated against the Roman Catholics. Klan office seekers looked for Catholic officeholders to run against, and the state realm pushed for a bill to outlaw parochial schools. When Hiram Evans, then only the Exalted Cyclops of Dallas Klan No. 66, visited Michigan, he made the most of anti-Catholic suspicions. Referring to somewhat unsubstantiated reports that the Pope in Rome was plotting a St. Bartholomew's Day for Detroit, Evans promised that if that time ever came, the Texas Klan would send up special trains of Klansmen, and Woodward Avenue would run knee-deep in Catholic blood instead. The trains which ran from the South, however, seemed to be bringing more Negroes than Klans-men, as Detroit's colored population tripled to 120,000 during the 1920s.

The Klan grew more slowly in Michigan, probably not approach-ing its peak of 75–80,000 members until the mid-twenties. Norman Weaver, the able historian of the Klan in the Great Lakes area offers the explanation that states like Indiana and Ohio were sufficiently lucrative initially to absorb Klan attention.[1] Until Michigan was in-corporated, the Klan recruiters operated under the name of the Na-tional Research Bureau, and when the members of the Detroit Klan got tired of waiting for formal self-government they organized an independent SYMWA club. The "Spend Your Money With Ameri-cans" patriots were absorbed into the Klan again when it got its charter to do business in Michigan, but the earlier name was highly suggestive of the motives displayed by the leaders of the Invisible Empire in the state. As Professor Weaver described it, Klansmen were solicited for contributions for a Detroit temple, a subdivision deal, a piece of choice property on Schwartz Lake in Oakland, a Klan airplane, a Klan record company to exploit records made by a Klan quartet, the purchase of the Saginaw *Star* as a Klan newspa-per, Klan welfare funds, and Klan politics. Klansmen paid and paid, Weaver related, but nothing ever materialized. One of the most prominent characteristics of the Michigan Klan was its continuous dissension over the distribution of the spoils. As expansion slowed, the struggle became more acute, and disappointed hopefuls were highly inclined to take their unhappiness to court. Altogether, Klan deals and financial squabbles did much to discredit it in the eyes of its often unhappy knights.

But despite its unrealized hopes and financial disappointments, the Ku Klux Klan was influential in Michigan, and it grew in the middle twenties. Enforcement of the Burns Anti-Mask Law, enacted in 1923, was left up to local authorities, and the Klan was not greatly troubled. It went about its usual lodge meetings, picnics, parades, barbecues, and nocturnal cross burnings. It spread through the small towns and the industrial cities of Central Michigan from Bay City and Saginaw down through Flint, Detroit, Lansing, Jackson, Kalamazoo, and up the shores of Lake Michigan from Muskegon, where the "Holland

[1] Norman Weaver, "The Knights of the Ku Klux Klan in Wisconsin, Indiana, Ohio, and Michigan," unpublished Ph.D. dissertation, University of Wisconsin, 1954, Ch. 7.

Dutch" flocked to it in large numbers. The Invisible Empire was particularly strong around Flint, Lansing, Kalamazoo, and Muskegon.

When two Klansmen ran in the 1924 Republican gubernatorial primary, they did best in those areas. The two Klan contestants were a minister from Adrian, a prosperous little college town near the Ohio border, and James Hamilton, a well-known loser in state politics. Hamilton was one of those perennial figures in American politics who come to prominence on the strength of a single issue. For Jim Hamilton it was opposition to private and parochial schools, and he sought a constitutional amendment requiring public school attendance in Michigan. In 1920 he ran for governor as the head of a Wayne County Civic Association. By 1924, he and his program had joined the Klan, and both were on the ballot, with Hamilton now heading a Michigan Public School Defense League. Neither won, and the school-law campaign was finally laid to rest when the U. S. Supreme Court struck down a similar proposition which had gotten enacted in Oregon.

In the always turbulent motor city of Detroit, where the converging streams of immigrants, Negroes, and Southern whites met head on, a Klan-endorsed candidate came so close to the runoff in 1924, that he had another try at it the next year. Race conditions were perilously explosive in Detroit, and, when well-to-do Negroes attempted to move from the crowded ghettos of Paradise Valley, they met violent resistance. The Klan took the lead in organizing various neighborhood improvement associations to stand guard against such unwanted intruders, and when trouble came, as it did on three occasions in 1925, Klansmen did their bit. The most famous was the case of Dr. Ossian Sweet, a prominent colored surgeon who had moved into a white neighborhood. When his brothers and friends helped him defend his new home from an attacking mob, it took all of Clarence Darrow's skill to save them from conviction of first-degree murder. The NAACP charged that many Detroit policemen were Klan members, and Mayor Smith put the blame on the hooded order for the outbreak of violence.

To the Klan, the mayor's hostility was simple to explain. His honor, John W. Smith, was a Roman Catholic. Having made a good showing in the previous election, the Klan went all out against Smith in 1925. Klan leaders came in from other states, reportedly as far away as North Carolina and New York, and a smoothly functioning political machine organized workers in every precinct. Reams of literature were distributed, money was made available, and cars were provided to get voters to the polls. Close to election time, Charles Bowles, the hitherto little-known Detroit lawyer, who was the beneficiary of all of these efforts, denied having any connection with the Klan. However, the bitterness of the campaign, which the Invisible Empire continued to wage for him, offended many citizens, Protestant and Catholic alike. When a Congregational pastor hotly denounced Mayor Smith for his Catholicism, and the minister's wife publicly called for the tar and feathering of all women who did not vote for the Klan, many Protestant ministers and their parishioners objected. Among them was the young minister of the Bethel Evangelical Church, Reinhold Niebuhr.

Rallied behind Mayor Smith was the unlikely combination of the Detroit Federation of Labor and the city's big industrialists. One of them was Henry Ford. Having burned his fingers before on the anti-Semitism of his Dearborn *Independent,* he was now willing to try a new tack. Dismissing the Ku Klux Klan, the Knights of Columbus, and the Masons as tools of Wall Street, he was out for Jim Smith. Faced with this turn of events, the Klan responded with ingenuity. Since Henry Ford was against him, the Klan explained to Jewish voters, Bowles was surely their friend. On Election Day, Mayor Smith polled 140,000 votes to 111,000 for Bowles, doing particularly well in the silk stocking districts in the North End and northwest sections of the city. Although Klan-supported candidates, including one Klansman, did manage to find places on the city council, the election that counted was lost.

The failure to achieve spectacular political success plus a general violence of utterance and behavior—including the arrest of Muskegon's Klan leader for killing three people with the bomb he sent to the man who had beaten him for city office—helped push the Klan into decline by 1926. Within the Klan itself, bitter internal struggles over the organization's treasure hastened the process. By 1928, the Klan was a long way from dead in Michigan but it had lost its respectability and political influence. When Bowles finally made it into the mayor's office in 1929, only to be recalled eight months later, the Klan was not in evidence.

28

NATIONAL POLITICS

As the Invisible Empire grew, it received widespread attention which soon turned into national concern. Led by the New York *World,* newspapers and congressmen demanded that Washington take action. At the same time the Justice Department received a stream of letters detailing Klan outrages and outrageous claims. Klan lecturers boasted that congressmen, senators, and high military officers belonged, so too, they said, did numerous members of the Cabinet, and someone of even higher office. Stories were told of initiations held on the steps of the Capitol and in the White House itself. The latter story was vigorously denied, and the attorney general wrote reassuringly to his U. S. Attorneys that neither he nor President Harding were Klansmen. The President conferred with Daugherty and Detective Burns, who headed the Justice Department's Bureau of Investigation in which young J. Edgar Hoover was serving.

The problem in the early twenties was whether or not the federal government had any jurisdiction. Congressman Tague, a Democrat from Massachusetts, proclaimed that the violation of the First, Fourth, Fifth, Sixth, and Thirteenth Amendments to the Constitution which promised religious freedom and prohibited improper seizure, trial, punishment, and involuntary servitude, ought to be enough. Senator David Walsh, his colleague in the upper house, wrote to the attorney general pointing out that there were laws which prohibited conspiracy to take away rights guaranteed under the federal Constitution.

The attorney general's response was that Klan activities were a state matter and therefore he had no jurisdiction. However, he saw no need for vigilante organizations and offered to help investigate the Klan if any state wanted to prosecute. Oregon and Louisiana accepted his offer, and the Bureau of Investigation supplied the evidence, even though no convictions resulted. As far as the use of mails was concerned, the decision was that only cases of incitement to murder, arson, or assassination would create federal jurisdiction. Threatening letters were apparently not considered sufficient cause, though E. Y. Clarke was later indicted for using the mails to defraud. A refusal to prosecute was not the same thing as a statement of approval, however. In addressing a Shriners' convention, President Harding attacked "misguided zeal and unreasoning malice" and drew a line between "secret fraternity" and "secret conspiracy."

The Invisible Empire commanded not only the attention of the executive branch, but of the legislature, the Supreme Court, and the state houses of the nation. The Congress was as disinclined to take action as was the Executive. The House Rules Committee investigation, in 1921, turned out to be a platform rather than a pillory for Colonel Simmons, and two senatorial-election investigations, in 1923 and 1927, failed to disturb the seats of Klan senators from Texas and Indiana.

Over the long run the Klan's record did not emerge so favorably from the Supreme Court of the United States. The high tribunal heard three cases concerning the Klan and decided against it in each instance. Oregon's Klan-supported compulsory public school bill was invalidated. The respective requirements of Kansas and New York for state chartering and for unmasking and public registration of Klansmen, were permitted to stand. In all three cases the black-robed justices had stern things to say about the white-robed knights. The Klan did not respond with the same interest in court that was to mark its oratory in the 1950s and 1960s, although it did oppose the appointment of Pierce Butler because of his Catholicism and supported the nomination of a Southerner, John J. Parker of North Carolina.

Under prompting from the New York *World,* a large number of governors initially let themselves be counted as opposed to the Klan, but as its strength increased, the occupants of the state houses became increasingly discreet. So too were most senators and congressmen who represented the affected areas. A political reporter for the Baltimore *Sun* summed up the prevailing spirit of political caution when he told the story of a poker game that took place in a midwestern newspaper office. One of the players was an influential congressman, a hearty, outgoing man whom the working press greatly liked. Someone sought to tease him by making up a story about a new congressional resolution for an investigation of the Klan. The politician suddenly became unhappily serious. "That is nothing to joke about," he said, "not even in whispers. That stuff runs like quicksilver. You can't tell when somebody is going to pick up a word, and where it will end. There are thousands of those fellows in my district. But I don't know they are there. Nobody will be able to prove to me they are there. And if I don't know they are in my district, I am not called upon to express an opinion about them. That's what I am doing. That is the only thing to do. And don't you risk queering my game by any such jokes."[1]

By the fall of 1922, discreet silence or the denial of a Klan presence and problem had become standard operating procedure for most national lawmakers. When Governor Parker appealed for federal aid in preventing open warfare in northern Louisiana, the state's congressional delegation was almost wrathful in their avowals that there was nothing untoward going on in the Pelican State. In the hotly fought 1922 election in Texas, which sent Klansman Earl Mayfield to the U. S. Senate, only Cactus Jack Garner declined to straddle the Klan issue. The defeat that year of Kansas City Congressman Phil Campbell, who had chaired the abortive congressional investigation, as well as of Jewish congressmen from Peru, Indiana, and San Antonio, Texas, seemed to indicate the wisdom of the general congressional reticence.

In 1922, the Klan helped to elect governors in Georgia, Alabama, California, and Oregon, and came close to knocking Missouri's Jim Reed out of the U. S. Senate. It was reported that perhaps as many as seventy-five members of the lower house had received help from Klan votes. An undetermined, unguessable, number of congressmen, veterans, and newcomers, had actually joined the hooded order, and E. Y. Clarke was asking the local chapters to suggest likely candidates for the future. The next year, the Klan continued to expand, with its greatest strength developing in the upper Mississippi Valley and in the Great Lakes kingdom of D. C. Stephenson.

Few things impressed the new Imperial Wizard, Hiram Evans, more than his success in electing a genuine Klan senator from Texas, and Washington began to occupy more and more room in his thoughts. There were repeated stories that Klansman Gutzon Borglum was able to arrange a private meeting for him with President Harding, and when Evans and Democratic presidential hopeful, William Gibbs McAdoo, happened to sojourn at the fashionable

Indiana resort of French Lick Springs at the same time, it inspired new rumors.

In 1923, Klan leaders had their first major taste of backstage politics in Washington as they won the contest over the seating of Texas' Senator Earl Mayfield. Herschel McCall, one-time Michigan lawyer who had moved south and become Grand Dragon of Texas, was sent as the Invisible Empire's official ambassador to the United States. During the Mayfield contest, the Klan made friends with Indiana's senior senator, Jim Watson, and picked up W. F. Zumbrunn, the Missouri-born Washington lawyer whose ways among the important people brought admiration from the unsophisticated Evans. Fascinated with his growing prestige, Evans shifted his headquarters away from the faction-ridden city of Atlanta and took up business residence at the Klan's Massachusetts Avenue offices in the nation's capital.

29

THE CHAMPIONSHIP FIGHT
IN MADISON SQUARE GARDEN

By 1924, with over two million members and a series of impressive political victories already won, the Invisible Empire exuberantly looked forward to the presidential wars. Too newly successful and inexperienced to know exactly what they wanted, the Klan's leaders were sure of one thing and that was that they meant to be counted. With its members mainly Democrats in the South and Republicans in the North and West, the Klan had a foothold in both parties. Since they had the most to gain from Klan support in contested primaries and close races, Republican leaders hoped that any Klan issue could be avoided at their national convention. A sixty-man lobby headed by Evans and his new Indiana Dragon, Walter Bossert, arrived in Cleveland to make sure that this would be the case.

But party silence was not enough; the self-confident Klan moguls wanted a triumph as well. President Coolidge was to have the top slot but the vice-presidential nomination was open for contest and the Klan had a candidate. Indiana's Jim Watson had helped seat Texas Klansman, Earl Mayfield, in the U. S. Senate and the upper chamber looked like a friendly place to the Invisible Empire. "All of our boys throughout the nation will understand only one thing," *Fiery Cross* editor Milton Elrod announced from imperial headquarters in the Statler, "and that is Senator James E. Watson for Vice President—flat." Only he could carry the Middle West, the Klan figured, and besides this would be a good way to let President Coolidge know that the senatorial group was not to be ignored. "The Senate has stood for the things the Klan believed to be right," Elrod explained. However, it was one thing to quietly cultivate the Klan and prevent intraparty strife, it was quite another to pick a man with a Klan endorsement. "My God, they have ruined me," Watson groaned when he received the news, and amid bitter recriminations, the Klan tried to withdraw its statement.

Although the Invisible Empire was not to pick a candidate, there was still the question of the party's stand on the Klan itself. R. B. Creager, the committeeman from Texas, promised to raise the subject, despite attempts to dissuade him. Feeling that the Klan was dangerous both to the society and to his party, he gave up possible ambassadorial appointment to lead the fight. The New York delegation, headed by Senator Jimmy Wadsworth and Congressman Ogden Mills, promised to support his anti-Klan plank. So did a widely publicized Committee of Notables composed mainly of college presidents and Protestant bishops, with a sprinkling of Baptists. However, their campaign was quietly buried in a short but hot fight in the resolutions committee where only New York, California, New Jersey, and Louisiana voted with the Texan. The plank that emerged made no mention of the Invisible Empire and safely affirmed "unyielding devotion to the Constitution and to the guarantees of civil, political, and religious liberty therein contained." The party professionals, happily sensing the strength of President Coolidge's candidacy, had no intention of permitting the boat to be rocked.

There was no such control when the Democrats met in New York's Madison Square Garden two weeks later. As the party of the outs, they had no unifying presidential incumbent to hold them together. Although partisanship always runs high in politics, the party was split by unusually deep divisions. East of the Mississippi River and north of the Ohio and Potomac it was most noticeably the party of the immigrant, importantly Catholic, wet, and was more than often run by big city bosses or political machines. In the South and the West the party was dry, Protestant, and old-stock American.

In 1924, the leading candidate was William Gibbs McAdoo, President Wilson's lean, compellingly able, and attractive son-in-law. McAdoo had headed Wilson's Treasury Department, handled his war financing, and directed the wartime operation of the nation's railroads. Born in Georgia, bred in Tennessee, he had built the Hudson River tubes of New York, challenged the bankers and industrialists in Washington, and finally moved to the West to don his political spurs in California. Out of deference to the ailing President he had stood aside in 1920; now he meant to have the nomination. Although he spoke out against bigotry and intolerance in a 1923 address at the University of Southern California, he remained silent on the topic thereafter, and he had never pointedly taken aim at the Klan. After some desultory rumoring that the dollar bills during his tenure at the Treasury were impregnated with pictures of the Pope, the rosary, and assorted Catholic symbols, the Democratic branches of the Invisible Empire rallied behind him. And it was no wonder. Both of the other major candidates, Al Smith and Oscar Underwood, were unfriendly to the noble experiment of Prohibition, and were otherwise unsuitable. The conservative, able Underwood, who had led his party's forces in both the House and Senate, considered the Ku Klux Klan to be the nation's Number One problem and he said so on all occasions. As governor of New York, Al Smith had shown that he wore no man's bridle and was second to none in executive ability, but he represented everything about the urban, immigrant East that the Klan feared. Besides, he was a Roman Catholic. Many Klansmen found Indiana's Senator Samuel Ralston the most friendly, but he was initially no more than a dark-horse contender. McAdoo, representing both the liberalism and the Klan forces of the South and West, was no bigot. His chief strategist, Bernard Baruch, was a Jew; his floor manager, former Senator James Phelan, was an Irish Catholic, but if McAdoo did not personally favor the Klan, he felt that he could not afford to alienate its support. His representatives solicited the Klan vote and he tacitly gave it shelter.

Early summer in New York City was hardly the best time and place to iron out so divisive an issue as the Ku Klux Klan, and so the degree that it was raised might well determine the course of the convention. The Underwood forces, struggling against the Invisible Empire in their own Alabama, and having lost the delegates to it in Georgia, considered the Klan the prime issue and meant to fight. For the Catholic leaders and the Smith partisans in the East, the Klan was a hateful antagonist, but the wisdom of raising the issue was a matter of question. The leader of the Smith forces and the man who was to place "the Happy Warrior" in nomination, Franklin Roosevelt, hoped for a compromise plank that would leave no wounds. However, with McAdoo substantially the front-runner, there might be something to be gained from fishing in the Klan-troubled waters.

As the delegates began to arrive, no one knew how important the Klan issue would be. Among the early arrivals was George Brennan, the former schoolteacher and insurance man who had helped pick the Cox-Roosevelt ticket in 1920. With the death of Tammany's Charles Murphy, Brennan was the major power in Eastern urban Democracy. Senator Underwood called upon him at the Waldorf-Astoria to urge that Brennan and the Smith forces help save the party by joining him in battle against the Klan. Brennan agreed. Led by Illinois, Ohio, Pennsylvania, New York, and Alabama, the anti-Klan forces began to coalesce.

The Invisible Empire had also arrived in strength, both among the delegates and in the person of Evans and his advisers who had taken up residence at the McAlpin and Great Northern hotels. The Klan's board of strategy included Indiana's Walter Bossert and editor Milton Elrod, Georgia Grand Dragon Nathan B. Forrest III, and convention delegates Earl Mayfield, Klan senator from Texas, and Virgil Pettie, treasurer and newly elected national committeeman from Arkansas. Greatest Klan strength was believed to be in the Georgia and Texas delegations, with additional support in Arkansas, Mississippi, Florida, Kansas, Iowa, Oklahoma, and a score of other states.

On the second day, when the convention got down to business, Forney Johnson of Alabama rose to place the name of Oscar Underwood in nomination. In his speech, he spoke of the need for a stand against secret un-American organizations, and when he named the Ku Klux Klan the convention went wild. This was no carefully planned show of strength for a presidential candidate, but a spontaneous expression of feeling. There was a shout of approval from the New York delegation and the Massachusetts standard was waved high. Delegates scrambled out of their seats and pushed into the aisles. The McAdoo supporters, in Georgia, Texas, Oklahoma, Kentucky, and California, sat stonily in their seats believing that it was all a conspiracy against their candidate. Standards swayed as demonstrators tried to carry them into the teeming aisles. There were fist fights in the Missouri and Colorado delegations but the state banners remained where they were. Parading delegates shouted "Get up, you Kleagles!" at their seated brethren whose anger rose at the taunts. For twenty-five minutes the uproar continued until the band restored order by playing "America." When Johnson finally got to name his man, the response was mild by comparison, but the cat was now out of the bag. The issue of the Klan could not be avoided.

As the nominations continued on to the third day, there were few mentions or allusions to the other struggle that was developing. Nevertheless the McAdoo men realized that they had the most to lose. Having failed at the opening of the convention to escape from the requirement of a two-thirds majority to nominate, they sought to begin voting on the candidates before the battle over the platform poisoned the proceedings. However, the delegates rejected an evening session, and the nominations continued on the fourth day. A representative from North Dakota, who was expected to second McAdoo, startled the hall by condemning the Klan "in the name of the intelligent Protestants" in his state. There was another spontaneous parade, while McAdoo men muttered angrily about betrayal, but when noise subsided, the speaker ended anticlimactically for the Californian. The galleries, packed with Smith men, became more and more raucous. They harassed McAdoo seconders with cries of "Oil! Oil! Oil!" trying to brand McAdoo, who had been an attorney for oilman E. L. Doheny with the scandals of the Harding administration. The galleries became increasingly raucous. When the New Yorkers chanted "Ku, Ku, McAdoo!" the Californian's supporters countered with anti-Smith cries of "Booze! Booze! Booze!" but they lacked the strength of numbers. It was not for nothing that Tammany had been packing meetings for more than a hundred years.

Originally the McAdoo forces had hoped to avoid the Klan issue or to pass over it with a mild statement. As the controversy became heated in the Garden and within the Resolutions Committee, it soon appeared that a majority of the delegates probably did want to condemn the Klan. To get by, without having the Klan specifically denounced by name, was clearly the best that both the Invisible Empire and the McAdoo leaders could hope for.

The testimony before the Resolutions Committee had, at times, been fiery. Congressman Harry Hawes of Missouri claimed that the life of the party was at stake. Pointing at William Jennings Bryan, sitting on the committee for Florida, he stated that Jews and Catholics had supported the party's elder statesman in the past, and it was the duty of the Democratic party to stand by them now. The anti-Klan leaders warned that if a strong plank did not emerge from the committee, they would write it in from the floor of the convention. If no such stand were taken, the stubborn Missourian promised, he would leave the party and lead a great Republican majority in his own state. The Underwood proposal was the strongest; he wanted the wording adapted from the Democratic rejection of the Know-Nothing Party in 1856, but the committee turned this down. Bryan's proposal was to reaffirm the liberties protected by the Constitution but not mention the Ku Klux Klan. Led by Senator David Walsh of Massachusetts, a number of the members vowed that the Klan had to be named. To pleas for unity and Bryan's appeal that four years hence the Klan would have been forgotten, they would not yield.

The Resolutions Committee reached the Klan issue at 1 A.M. on the morning of the twenty-fifth; at dawn on the twenty-eighth, having twice reported to the convention that the platform was not ready, they were still in disagreement. The battle was long and bitter, the members were weary and short-tempered from frustration and lack of sleep. Only Utah's Senator William King, immaculately dressed in his formal evening clothes, had remained poised and calm throughout. Judge John McCann from Pennsylvania, a Roman Catholic, asked for permission to appeal for divine intervention, and with tears running down his cheeks, he knelt and recited the Lord's Prayer. Then Bryan also recited the prayer and besought the Holy Spirit to shed light on the darkness of the committee's doubts. It was 6 A.M. The members went back to their hotels for a few hours' sleep, and at 10 A.M. Homer Cummings, who had presided over the 1920 convention and was to be the New Deal's first attorney general, went before the convention to tell them that the committee had adjourned in disagreement and prayer and would like a few more hours to try again to arrive at agreement. During the interval, Bryan and others sought a compromise to which the candidates could agree, but there was none. The Bryan Plank was adopted, with most of the New England, Middle Atlantic, and Great Lakes states, plus Missouri, Alabama, and three of the territories, dissenting.

When the delegates reassembled on the afternoon of the fifth day, the floor and galleries of Madison Square Garden were packed, and a large number of policemen stood by, ready for any trouble from the spectators. The platform took a long time to read and the weary Homer Cummings, exhausted by the committee struggle, had to be spelled by others. The delegates applauded over mention of pay raises and the League of Nations but it was the plank on the Klan for which everyone waited. The statement on religious freedom came at the end. There were cheers as the platform pledged the party to maintaining the various Constitutional freedoms and to the condemnation of "any effort to arouse religious or racial dissension." Then, suddenly, it was over. There had been no mention of the Klan.

For a moment there was silence, and then the minority reports on the League of Nations and the Klan were announced. A mass of roaring, shouting delegates exploded to their feet as William Pattangall, Democratic candidate for governor of Maine began the dissenting resolution, "We condemn political secret societies. . . ." Again for a second time the convention drowned out the chairman's cries for order when Pattangall's down-Eastern twang clipped out the words "Ku–Klux–Klan."

Newton Baker's plea for the memory of Woodrow Wilson and for the League of Nations also drew warm response. The delegates rose to their feet singing, as the band played the "Battle Hymn of the Republic" and "Onward, Christian Soldiers," but the minority resolution was voted down by almost two to one.

Now it was time to join battle over the Klan. An hour was allotted for each side. Robert Owen, senator from Oklahoma, began for the majority resolution. "This is not a question as to the Ku Klux Klan winning or losing," he said, as the delegates applauded, ". . . The only difference . . . is whether or not the Democratic National Convention shall stigmatize the Ku Klux Klan by name. . . ." Attesting to the religious egalitarianism of his own life and career, he ridiculed the Klan but discounted its menace. The galleries were initially friendly but when he brushed off the Mer Rouge murders and then went on to say "We have got laws in this country," a voice called back "They didn't do much good in Mer Rouge." "Will you say by the voice of this Convention that the membership of the Ku Klux Klan, which amounts . . . to something over a million citizens of the United States are guilty of violating the constitutional provisions?" he asked rhetorically, only to be greeted with cries of "Yes!" "Yes!" from the hall. When he ended in defense of the large number of "good citizens" who had joined the order, hisses and boos were louder than the applause.

Pattangall spoke next and demanded that the Klan be named. The force of bigotry, intolerance, and hypocrisy had crept influentially into American life, and the Democrats had to call it by its right name and denounce it throughout the country, he proclaimed. Succeeding speakers appealed again and again to the wartime sacrifices which knew not race, religion, nor national stock and demanded that their party not "quaver" nor yield to "cowardice" on the issue. As the Underwood supporters had argued, "Why draw a picture of a horse and then not name it as a horse?" Bainbridge Colby, who succeeded Bryan as Wilson's Secretary of State, echoed the theme, crying "If you are opposed to the Ku Klux Klan, for God's sake, say so." Edmund Moore led Cox's Ohio forces into the fight, claiming that it was not a religious but a political fight, for "if 343 members of the Klan who are members of this Convention can control the action of the other eight hundred, if the Imperial Wizard has got us all in his pocket, I, for one, am going to crawl out." If the delegates refused to condemn the Klan, he continued, then all Southern politicians, as many had privately told him, would have to compromise with it when they returned home. A Tennessee speaker explained the same thing more graphically, by comparing the menace of the Klan to the experience of two Negroes visiting a Memphis zoo. The city man was unimpressed with the wildcats but his country companion was more experienced; "If you were to go up in a tree some night and put your hand on one of them, thinking it was a 'possum, you would know why they call them wild."

Most forceful of all was the young editor and former mayor of Athens, Georgia, Andrew Erwin. Grandson of Howell Cobb, one-time speaker of Congress and Secretary of the Treasury under Buchanan, and son of a Confederate officer, no one could question his Southern heritage. Although he was McAdoo's campaign manager in his piedmont district, Erwin had fought the Klan. At first the galleries heckled him, assuming that he would favor the weaker plank. "I come from Georgia," he reassured them, "and we have been trying for five years to get you Yankees to talk about this proposition." Denying that the Klan was like other fraternal orders, he explained that he had never heard of the Masons or Elks mustering a highly paid staff of lobbyists and spying investigators to go from state to state to influence delegates. "And just as soon as they do," he continued, "then I favor a plank denouncing them." The Klan was an enemy to freedom of conscience and societal peace and harmony. In the name of the Confederacy's Father Ryan and Judah P. Benjamin, and of the Americans who had died in France, he called upon the convention and particularly the delegates from Georgia, to erase the stigma of the Klan. Again the hall erupted in a torrent of cheering and applause. Delegates rushed to congratulate him. A woman kissed him, and fellow Democrats hoisted him to their shoulders and paraded with him around the hall while the convention band increased the glowering discomfiture of the rest of his delegation by playing "While We Go Marching through Georgia."

Those who wished to avoid mentioning the Klan could offer nothing comparable in pyrotechnics, though they did end their case in high drama and pathos. Their arguments were defensive pleas to avoid giving undue importance to the Klan, and to respect the good intentions of those who composed its rank and file. "Are we," asked the governor of North Carolina, "to try, condemn, and execute more than a million men who are professed followers of the Lord Jesus Christ?" No one defended the Klan or spoke well of it, but the supporters of the majority plank pleaded with their listeners not to let the party be wrecked upon the rocks of the Klan issue. "We came here not to fight Democrats; we came here prepared to fight Republicans," a Louisiana speaker announced. "We want the issue to be the Green House on K Street, not Three K's."

Finally the patriarch of the party, William Jennings Bryan, closed the debate. At sixty-four, his shoulders were hunched a little forward in his ever familiar black alpaca coat. His face was deeply lined, his hair sparse, and his once-golden voice eroded by time. His mission was to heal the division in the party which had honored him and which he loved and to try yet again to make the city-dwellers of the East understand his people from the plains and prairies of the West and the red hills and deltas of the South. He spoke now to hostile galleries whose boos and hisses broke the effect of his climaxes. The great battle of distressed people against oppressing monopolies was being diverted into a party-splitting quarrel over an organization which was bound to die of itself, he argued. "We said, 'Strike out three words and there will be no objection.' But three words were more to them than the welfare of a party in a great campaign. You have listened to . . . the best Democratic platform that was ever written . . . but none of our principles, none of our pleas stirred the hearts of these men like the words 'Ku Klux Klan.' . . . I am not willing to bring discord into my party. . . . I am not willing to divide the Christian Church. . . ." More and more his words sought for the traditional religious responses: "It was Christ on the Cross who said, 'Father, forgive them, for they know not what they do.' And, my friends, we can exterminate Ku Kluxism better by recognizing their honesty and teaching them that they are wrong." Applause and catcalls greeted his conclusion. For those who had followed the Great Commoner it had been a moving experience, others, like William Allen White, who called it "an apology for expediency," remained untouched.

Throughout the vast, packed, excited hall, no tempers had been soothed. As the voting began, most of the remaining order dissolved beneath the cries of the galleries and the angry, milling delegations on the floor. Arguments flared into fist fights. Delegates struggled to get their individual wishes recorded, but the unit rule held the votes of almost a dozen states, like Louisiana, Nevada, and Washington, firm to the majority resolution. Montana's Senator Walsh, who had doggedly unraveled the Teapot Dome scandals, and who was him-self to return home to fight a Klan challenge, pounded for order in the growing melee.

The vote was going to be close, and the McAdoo managers, identifying the move to name the Klan with opposition to their candidate, calculated that every vote would count. The Georgia delegation, where the fires of Klandom burned most brightly, had cast seventeen votes "No," and "2½" for the minority plank. Struggling to disqualify proxies while they rushed missing delegates to the floor, the Georgia leaders had their delegation polled. Then the chairman, Hollins Randolph, great-grandson of Thomas Jefferson, shouted that three of the Georgians wished to change their vote. Marion Colley, the granddaughter of the Confederate Secretary of State Robert Toombs, was committed to McAdoo but had voted to name the Klan. Now she was surrounded by shouting, pleading, threatening men who told her that she was "stabbing McAdoo in the back." At first she could not get out the words, and when for a second time Senator Walsh asked how she voted, she began "I am against the Klan . . ." The presiding officer interrupted her. Under the rules of the convention she must answer only "yes" or "no." She voted no and slumped back into her chair. Another delegate changed his vote, and the chairman moved on to the Illinois delegation. Hollins Randolph turned to P. A. Stovall who had been Wilson's minister to Switzerland. "This is a direct request from Mr. McAdoo just received," Randolph told him. "Your vote may lose him the Presidency. We've stood by you, now stand by us." Without waiting for an answer, he shouted for Chairman Walsh's attention: "Mr. P. A. Stovall desires to change his vote." "I vote no," Stovall whispered. Marion Colley tearfully made her way to her unyielding fellow delegate, Andrew Erwin, who had touched off the demonstration against the Klan earlier in the evening. "That's all right, Marion," he comforted her. "Don't say a word about it. You did what you thought was best."

The "name the Klan" leaders tried desperately to free votes tied by the unit rule and to disqualify some of the votes cast against the amendment, but without avail. One of the Massachusetts delegates, Chelsea Mayor Lawrence Quigley, popped up repeatedly in various other delegations, challenging the accuracy of their votes and seeking to appeal the rulings from the chair. Finally the votes were in, and the chair announced the results: $541\frac{3}{20}$ voting "aye"; voting "no," $542\frac{3}{20}$. The amendment to name the Klan had lost by a vote—although the next day's recalculation slightly increased the margin. As the chairman proceeded to the vote on the now unchanged platform, Mayor Quigley was on his feet again, shouting "Mr. Chairman, I question the accuracy of the vote of the entire Convention." Ignoring him, Senator Walsh went on to complete the vote. Then Franklin Roosevelt, of New York, who had placed Al Smith in nomination, moved for adjournment and the stormy night was over.

The Klansmen had come to New York confident that they were too powerful to be challenged or named. They were shocked to find that they were a minority, and that no man cared to defend them publicly. Although the McAdoo forces, and those of Ambassador John W. Davis who was eventually nominated, opposed a strong anti-Klan resolution they had privately sought to compromise as much as they could on the issue. Even the Klan's more personably acceptable choice, Indiana's Sam Ralston, had disavowed favor for the Invisible Empire. The narrowly won triumph in the fight over the party platform was not one to enhearten the Invisible Empire. As for the Democrats, it embittered the convention to the extent that neither Al Smith nor William Gibbs McAdoo could win the nomination nor the Democrats the election. It took nine more days and one hundred and three ballots for the hot, weary, and almost apathetic Democrats to pick John W. Davis and William Jennings Bryan's brother, Charles, as the vice-presidential candidate. Tex Rickard, the sporting world's legendary promoter commented, as the bedraggled delegates filed out, "Of all the fights I ever pulled off in the old Garden, that was the best draw I ever saw."

30

ANTICLIMAX:
THE NINETEEN TWENTY-FOUR ELECTION

Vacationing in Maine before beginning his campaign, John W. Davis discussed the Klan with party leaders, including William Pattangall, but he declined comment and was not expected to make one. This situation was soon changed. Apparently Davis had considered taking a stand in his acceptance speech, but he hoped that the issue was closed and decided not to do so. He soon learned that this was anything but the case and he resolved to speak out. His advisers were divided, and he was warned that his decision might well cost him the votes of Ohio and West Virginia. Nevertheless he determined to make a statement and decided to do it in Ohio. A few days before the Buckeye State Democratic convention, Davis appeared at a big Democratic rally at Sea Girt, the summer capital of New Jersey, tucked down among the breezy sea airs of the Klan's Monmouth County stronghold. Governor George Silzer urged that this would be a good time to speak out on the Klan; the crowd would be large and the statement would swing New Jersey safely into the Democratic column. Davis agreed, and he told a surprised and cheering audience "If any organization, no matter what it chooses to be called, whether Ku Klux Klan or by any other name, raises the standard of racial and religious prejudice or attempts to make racial origins or religious beliefs the test of fitness for public office, it does violence to the spirit of American institutions and must be condemned. . . ."

In delivering this rebuke to the Invisible Empire, the candidate had been motivated by both principle and policy. He and his advisers had calculated that the South would remain Democratic whatever course he took. What was at stake was the presidential belt of states, stretching from New York and New Jersey, across Pennsylvania and the Middle West to Iowa, Missouri, Kansas, and Nebraska. In most of the states, the Klan was already largely committed to the local

Republican parties. It made good sense to reassure the disgruntled Smith supporters in the Eastern and Midwestern cities, and the increasing Negro vote might be a potential bonanza for the Democrats.

In his Sea Girt speech, Davis had shrewdly called upon his Republican opponent President Coolidge to also condemn the Klan and thus remove the issue from politics. The answer came the next day, but not from the White House. It was presented in Maine, where the President's running mate Charles G. Dawes had gone to help Klanbacked Owen Brewster into the governor's chair. With the Democrats running on a straight anti-Klan issue, the Maine Republican leadership had specifically ordered all candidates not to reply. The party's national chairman agreed, and local Republicans were horrified when Dawes decided to speak on the subject.

Dawes began by describing the Klan as representative of "an instinctive groping for leadership, moving in the interest of law enforcement, which they do not find in many cowardly politicians and officeholders." It was not the right way, he went on, praising the Klan's behavior in Oklahoma and Illinois, but it was correctly motivated and bravely carried out even though the results in each case were unfortunate. The Klan might appeal to adventurous youth but government could not last if this were the right way. If lawlessness had to be met by lawlessness, then it would destroy civilization. That, Dawes concluded, was why he opposed the Klan. Contrary to what many had feared, it did the party no harm. The Maine chairman told him that he had greatly helped the party there, and President Coolidge privately praised the speech. So, while the President's silence comforted the Klansmen, Dawes' Augusta speech pleased the anti-Klan Republicans.

Although the President avoided replying to the taunts and demands that he disavow the Klan, his Democratic opponent found it opportune to take the opposite tack. Emboldened by William Jennings Bryan's endorsement, Davis made anti-Klan comments a regular feature in his campaign. A carefully planted heckler would stand up during each speech and question him as to his stand on the Klan. Davis would then make a well-phrased and witty reply that always brought general applause from his audience.

Although the Klan question enlivened the campaign, it is difficult to see that it greatly changed the results. Coolidge and the Republicans were unbeatable. In the last days before the election, the Klan sent out word to its Georgia cohorts to cut the Democratic ticket. *The Searchlight* carried underlined portions of the remarks on equality regardless of race, which Davis had made to a Negro audience in Indiana. A number of Klansmen, led by McAdoo adherent M. O. Dunning, turned aside from the party of their fathers and the Confederacy. In time, Coolidge duly took note of this heroism by appointing Dunning the Federal Collector of Customs for the port of Savannah. However, with a Negro occupying a similar post in New Orleans, as well as top party offices in Mississippi, the likelihood of a Klan-led break over the race issue was not very large.

In November, it was a runaway for "Silent Cal" and the Republican party, which gathered in over 54 per cent of the vote. Apart from Wisconsin, the Progressive party candidate Robert La Follette did well only in the wheat and corn belts, west of the Mississippi River. Davis carried the South and the border state of Oklahoma. Only in Missouri, Maryland, and West Virginia did he come close, and the Klan vote may well have cost him his own West Virginia.

In Senate and governorship races, Klansmen or Klan favorites won handsomely in Indiana, Colorado, Oklahoma, Kansas, Kentucky, and probably in Iowa, while the Chicago press claimed that Klan support had helped Governor Len Small in Illinois. Al Smith was never in danger in New York, but the Klan did come surprisingly close to upsetting Senator Walsh in Montana. Although the Klan often sought to enhance its luster by endorsing a sure winner, as in the case of Kansas' Senator Arthur Capper, the 1924 elections added to the prestige of the Invisible Empire. William Allen White, who had given some stiff yanks to the shirttails of the Klan in Kansas, was convinced that the working men of the Middle West had displayed strong Klan sentiment and voted for Coolidge to "be against the Pope." Although not everyone agreed, the Richmond *Times-Democrat* summed up the belief that "Pillow slips and nightgowns have been exalted . . . the Klan did itself proud in the recent election."

31

FROM CANADA TO THE RIO GRANDE

1

In November of 1924, after the election of Calvin Coolidge and the mixed but impressive performance of Klan-backed candidates, the Imperial Wizard Hiram Evans took a month-long trip to survey and inspire his western domain. Embarking in Chicago, he traveled westward to Denver. Then, ignoring his sparse legions in Utah, Idaho, Nevada, New Mexico, and Arizona, and canceling a stop in Casper, Wyoming, he alighted in Billings, Montana. Next he crossed over to Washington for triumphal receptions in Spokane, Seattle, and Tacoma, before moving down the Pacific Coast and then entraining for Texas.

2

The successful Klan in Oregon flowed over into the neighboring state of Washington. Major Luther Powell, who had gotten things underway in Portland, was squeezed between opposition in his Portland Klavern and the rise to power of Fred Gifford as the top Klan potentate of Oregon. In the early days of Klandom there were always new frontiers waiting for its imperial salesmen, and so Powell took over the unorganized but developing territory of Washington. As King Kleagle of Washington and Idaho, he established his headquarters in the Securities Building in downtown Seattle and stirred up his colonizers.

There were, he told the Klan press, forty-two Klaverns in the state, the largest, in order of size, being Seattle, Spokane, Walla Walla, and Tacoma. With nine regional salesmen covering the territory, Klan affairs were progressing nicely. Some Klaverns met in downtown office buildings such as the Lippitt Building in Colfax, and the Realty

Building in Spokane. Others used the facilities of the fraternal lodges. The Columbia Klan No. 1 of Vancouver met every Wednesday night in the Moose Hall and every Saturday night was the Klan night at the Odd Fellows Hall in Walla Walla. The time was Tuesday night at the Odd Fellows in Olympia, and Wednesday night for the Masonic Temple in Tacoma. Some Klans, however, were busy constructing their own quarters.

When Hiram Evans came to the West during his triumphant tour of inspection in 1924, he was regally treated in Washington as befitted the head of a far-flung fraternal Empire. He banqueted with the Scottish Rite Masons in Spokane, Seattle, and Tacoma, spoke in Moose Temples, and was feted by Seattle's Chamber of Commerce. The only sour note, his national weekly commented, was the solitary opposition of William Randolph Hearst's Seattle *Post-Intelligencer.*

Major Powell had set up a weekly newspaper, *The Watcher on the Tower,* and ever looking for new lands to conquer, turned both to the foreign born and to the sea-borne. With his help, a naturalized Canadian, Dr. M. W. Rose, set up The Royal Riders of the Red Robe. This organization, later to be merged into the national American Krusaders, was a Klan affiliate for those right-minded naturalized Americans who had been unfortunate enough to be born outside of the United States. Garbed in crimson rather than white and headed by a Grand Ragon, it offered "a real patriotic organization to all Canadians, Englishmen, and other White, Gentile, Protestants." Immigrants from Greece, Italy, and the Balkans were not eligible.

The Klan's sea-borne adventure was the United States Navy. Letters were sent to naval ships in the area. The seamen from visiting vessels, such as the U.S.S. *California,* were invited to attend chapter meetings in Seattle and Bellingham, and Powell boasted that United States Navy Klan No. 1, provisional, had been set up on the U.S.S. *Tennessee.*

With things well underway, the Klansmen settled down to being Klansmen. Primarily the Klan was a social lodge, and there were always those who sought the traditional fraternal path to business success, such as the proprietor of The Klansmen's Roost, on Seattle's Westlake Avenue, "Where Kozy Komfort and Komrade Kare Kill the Grouch with Viands Rare."

K lannishness
ompels
o-operation
antankerous
abals
onstantly
apitulate

The Watcher on the Tower proclaimed. The "Kabals" as might be expected were directed by Rome. The sheriff of Seattle was a "Casey" —as Powell liked to refer to Catholics—and served as a convenient peril.

Mexicans and Greeks should also be sent back to where they came from, an Imperial Lecturer told Klansmen in the Lewis and Clark Auditorium in Spokane, in order that white supremacy and the purity of Americans be defended. At a monster celebration and naturalization of new Klansmen just outside of Seattle in July of 1923, the Klan was hailed as "the return of the Puritans in this corrupt, and jazz-mad age."

As far as its actual program was concerned, the Washington Klan mustered its klannish Americanism in defense of the public schools against illiteracy and Rome. On the national scene it supported the idea of a secretary of education in the President's Cabinet, and the restriction of immigration. Locally it placed a compulsory public school bill, modeled on the law that had been passed in Oregon two years before, on the ballot in the 1924 election.

The Klan's strength in the state of Washington was considerable, it perhaps reached thirty-five to forty thousand, and the politicians were leary of it. The race between Coolidge and the Progressive candidate La Follette, in 1924, appeared sufficiently close that neither the Republicans nor the Democrats cared to take on the Klan as well. The school-bill issue seemed to generate little public heat, however, and it was turned down in November.

In a sense this performance was typical of the Invisible Empire in Washington. The Klan was there, but it was not greatly active. It did not go in for night riding or do much for local charities or politics. It occasionally saw its members elected to local office, such as mayor of the little hops and lettuce town of Kent, south of Seattle, and it praised Congressman Albert Johnson as "a clean, loyal American," for helping push through an immigration restriction bill. It held occasional big public rallies. It went through the usual debilitating internal schisms over fees and salaries, financial accounting, national versus local decision making, and the backwash of the fight between Simmons and Evans for control in Atlanta. Luther Powell, being more of a frontiersman than a settler, moved on to prospect for Klan gold in Alaska. The Klan continued its existence into the 1930s, but it was not a major force in Washington.

3

Entering from neighboring Washington, the Klan spread down along the Snake River Valley in central and southern Idaho. The state's two Kleagles operating out of Lewiston and Boise organized Klaverns in those cities and in Caldwell, Nampa, Twin Falls, Burley, and Pocatello. Although the Klan was active as far north as the mining center of Lewiston, where an invasion of a Negro home was responsible for the police getting orders to shoot to kill any masked invaders or home molesters, it kept out of the upper part of the panhandle. Located mainly in the farming country along the Snake River, the Klan was a social club where the members from time to time sat down to worry about the foreigners and Catholics in the lumber and mining camps to the north, and the Pope in Rome. In one little town, the solitary Jewish family was included in all of the Klavern's social activities to show that the Klan was a strictly nondiscriminatory movement aimed only at outsiders.

4

In 1923, the Billings, Montana, Klavern took a large advertisement in the *Gazette* to deny that it was an anti-Negro, -Jewish, or -Catholic organization. It was simply, the ad explained, pro-American. Whatever views the Invisible Empire in Montana had on the Jews and Negroes, it certainly had its mind made up about the Catholics, and in 1924 it almost defeated the state's most noted son, Senator Thomas J. Walsh, because of his religion.

The boys were a little restless at first in the Copper State. A Warland man was whipped for mistreating his wife, and a legislator who sought to investigate the state's Prohibition-enforcement staff was threatened with tarring and feathering. Things soon settled down, however, and in September of 1923, Montana became a self-governing realm of the Invisible Empire. At the ceremony in Livingston, attended by delegates from Helena, Bozeman, Kalispell, Glasgow, Red Lodge, Butte, Lewiston, Havre, Harlowton, Missoula, Great Falls, Miles City, and Roundup, a local businessman was inaugurated as Grand Dragon. New Klansmen were initiated at a large public ceremony in Lewiston, which featured an address by Reverend E. A. Jordan of St. Paul and a rendition of "The Star-Spangled Banner" by the Klan Khoral Klub.

At the 1924 National Convention in Madison Square Garden, where the Democrats wrangled so bitterly over the Klan, Senator Walsh was widely praised for the way in which he presided over the turbulent proceedings. He had come to the Garden as a major hero of his party for having cracked open the Teapot Dome oil scandals of the Harding administration. Although Walsh was a McAdoo supporter, and the Montana delegation voted against condemning the Klan by name, his conduct in the Senate and at the convention, plus the fact that he was not only a dry but a Roman Catholic, made him attractive to the deadlocked delegates. Both sides liked him, and if the weary delegates had not decided on John W. Davis on the 104th ballot, the dapper senator from Montana might well have gotten the nod. He turned down certain nomination as Vice President, and instead went home to campaign for re-election.

Hailed though he might be elsewhere, in Montana he faced the fight of his political life. Frank Linderman, a writer and hotelkeeper from Flathead Lake, had won the Republican nomination against him. Linderman, a leader of the old anti-Catholic American Protective Association, entered the primary with Klan support and won a narrow victory. In doing so, he carried almost half the counties in the state, doing particularly well in Flathead, Lewis and Clark, Park, Toole, and Yellowstone. This left the Republicans in somewhat of a quandary; they had a real tartar on their hands, but he was a Republican and he might well win. Party leaders crossed their fingers and hoped for the best. The National Committee sent in the standard ten-thousand-dollar contribution, and the state chairman stuck to the answer that he had no knowledge as to whether or not Linderman was a Klansman.

Although Senator Walsh attacked the Invisible Empire at the state Democratic convention in September, the Klan remained an undercover, though vital issue. Linderman's supporters conducted a whispering campaign against Walsh's Catholicism and accused him of having been influenced in Washington by religious considerations. Many Republicans and many Protestants deplored Linderman's campaign, and the official Methodist newspaper, the *Pacific Christian Advocate,* condemned it. In the November election, there was much ballot splitting; though Calvin Coolidge carried Montana, Walsh defeated Linderman by eight thousand votes.

When Imperial Wizard Hiram Evans stopped off in Billings on his postelection inspection, Grand Dragon Lew Terwillinger prepared an enthusiastic welcome. The Chamber of Commerce gave a luncheon for Evans and his entourage, and that evening he addressed a meeting of Klanswomen at the First Methodist Church, following this with a major speech in the Coliseum. Praising President Coolidge for his frugal ways and for keeping his mouth shut, Evans told his listeners that only the gentile Protestants were fit to rule in America. However, in Montana, a small but decisive majority of voters had decided otherwise.

5

Evans had been scheduled to speak in Casper, Wyoming, but the local Klans were not able to provide a sufficiently large response and a meeting hall to make it worth his while. When the First Christian Church learned who was going to speak in its auditorium, the board canceled the rental, and the Imperial Wizard of the Ku Klux Klan did not alight to view so unworthy a portion of his far-flung Empire. The Klan harvested its recruits in Wyoming, convened them in the halls of the Odd Fellows and Masons. It kept them healthy on chicken dinners and picnics in the mountains, and indulged in all of the necessary components of restrictive fraternalism, but it seemingly left no mark on the state.

6

In Utah the Klan seems to have ignored both the Mormons and their Church. Rome, as usual, was the real menace, and the Klan was reported to have been the cause of a big struggle within the Masonic order in the state. There is no indication that the Klan went in for either night riding or politics. Its major coup in Salt Lake City was to take revenge for the municipal antimask law, by getting all bewhiskered Santa Clauses banned at Christmas time. That was in 1925, the year of the Klan's biggest flurry of activity. It held its first state convention north of Salt Lake City in the shadow of Ensign Peak, and lit the surrounding hills at night with its burning crosses. Another big rally, staged shortly after by the active Provo Klavern, drew several thousand Klansmen, but even this degree of interest did not last and Klan strength soon slipped away.

7

The Klan never really got started in Nevada. Perhaps its sparse population did not, in the eyes of Klan officialdom, merit a serious effort. Of the state's approximately seventy-five thousand citizens, only 20 per cent lived close enough together to be organized. However, if an aggressive Klan were organized, it might wield considerable power. This is what the Democrats and the La Follette men feared in 1924, for here as in most other Western states the Klan was Republican. The Reno Klan boasted that it had eighteen hundred members or almost 15 per cent of the total population of Nevada's largest metropolis. When the Invisible Empire advertised a big parade on Saturday night through downtown Reno, it was the subject of much nervous speculation. On the appointed October night, spectators counted less than two hundred masked marchers, including the band. The Invisible Empire, they concluded, was mostly invisible.

8

The Ku Klux Klan had been off to a quick start in Arizona although it never developed very far. Its early leader was the former managing editor and a member of the family which owned the state's second largest newspaper, the Phoenix *Gazette*. Tom Akers was the Exalted Cyclops of the Kamelback Klan No. 6 of Phoenix, and under his direction the hooded order became a little reckless. A group of Klansmen took a Phoenix school principal, whom the official courts had acquitted of immorality, flogged him, and marked his face with carbolic acid. A grand jury investigation reported that the owner of the Blue Belle Cafe and a colored bank janitor had also been whipped. Tom Akers himself was indicted for the latter episode, and Governor George Hunt sought to have him extradited back to Arizona to stand trial. When the word got out that the governor had a list of almost nine hundred Klansmen, including the owner of a furniture-manufacturing company, an investment company official, and a number of county and state officeholders, a wave of resignations from the Klan followed.

"Malign influences which have unloosed the monsters of hate, fear, prejudice and suspicion among neighbors and citizens should be destroyed as un-American," Governor Hunt reported to the legislature next spring, in recommending the passage of anti-Klan laws. During the heated debate that followed, it was claimed that members of the legislature belonged to the Klan. The Invisible Empire was condemned for the disruptive and terroristic role which it had played in Phoenix the preceding year, and a bill was passed prohibiting the public meetings of masked men and increasing the penalties for hooded misdeeds.

Tom Akers had gone off to high office in the Klan's intelligence branch in Atlanta, but he did feel it safe to return during the summer of 1923 for the installation of his successor. At a state-wide rally at Glendale, McCord Harrison of Phoenix, editor of *Arizona Klankraft* and King Kleagle, was chosen as Grand Dragon of Arizona. The realm was then split into two divisions with their headquarters at Tempe and Winslow. Among those present at the ceremony were delegations from the Klans of Glendale, Phoenix, Globe, Tempe, Winslow, Yuma, Williams, Gilbert, Prescott, Florence, Miami, and Flagstaff.

After its early night riding, Klansmen settled down to a quiet existence. In a single foray into politics in 1924, the Klan entered the Democratic gubernatorial primary. The election centered on the development of the Colorado River and on the Invisible Empire. Governor Hunt won renomination and the Klan's candidate came in third. For the most part, thereafter, Arizona Klans met to enjoy their rituals and social events, and talk about the construction of chapter houses and about the great Invisible Empire. A few built, but their members slipped away. In 1926, Arizona's whimsical U. S. Senator, Henry Ashurst (Democrat), denounced both Klan and the wets in a speech to the Knights of Columbus.

9

The story in New Mexico was drab from the Klan's point of view. Wherever it raised its head, people complained. In 1924, the state Democratic convention adopted a resolution which declared that the

Klan did violence to the spirit of American institutions. However, the next year when the Klan sought to uphold that spirit by entering its jim-dandy "Little Red Schoolhouse" float in a civic parade in Raton, it got criticized for this, too. Boasting of its success in getting members and keeping Roman Catholic teachers out of city and county schools, the Pioneer Klan No. 15 of Roswell admitted in 1931 that life was hard for a Protestant Anglo-Saxon organization, in a state whose population, the Klan reported, was 80 per cent Mexican and Roman Catholic, and a Jew was governor.

32

EVERY MAN FOR HIMSELF IN FLORIDA

The guiding maxim in Florida politics has long been said to be "Every Man for Himself," and the same principle of anarchic localism seems to have prevailed in Klan affairs. The story of the Florida Ku Klux Klan in the 1920s was not one of a mighty state-wide organization but rather that of a myriad of growing, active individual Klaverns.

The sandy soil of the Sunshine State had been prepared in advance for the sowing of the Klan seed. In the second decade of the twentieth century a virulent anti-Catholicism was preached with ever increasing success in Florida's Bible Belt. Georgia's Tom Watson touched it off with his widely circulated *Jeffersonian Magazine*. A resolution passed by the Democratic Party Executive Committee in 1916, condemning religious prejudice and secret societies, became Exhibit A in the minds of those who conjured up visions of a conspiracy to Romanize Florida. The great apostle of Florida nativism was Sidney J. Catts. A native of Alabama, the spawning ground of Klan wizards, he came to Florida as a Baptist minister, a calling which he left to become the state agent for a fraternal life-insurance company. Thus far he had followed the path of his fellow Alabaman, Col. William J. Simmons, who had disinterred the Ku Klux Klan in the twentieth century, but where the latter went into Klandom, Sidney Catts turned to politics—though with substantially the same message. And so, in 1916, while Colonel Simmons was struggling to get his fraternal order going, Sidney Catts was on his way to the governor's mansion, touring the rural back country in his Model T, sounding the warning against the encroachments of Satan. Governor Catts' widely proclaimed message of support for the American flag, Prohibition, and the little red schoolhouse against the menace of the convent, parochial school, Rome, and Africa, had already popularized the doctrines which the Klan was to preach in the Sunshine State.

The Klan entered Florida through the gateway city of Jacksonville, and rapidly spread throughout the state. From the beginning the Klan sought to keep Negroes from the polls, and in Jacksonville and Orlando open parades and covert warnings of violence were used. By 1922, the Klan had emerged as a direct participant in politics. In the June primaries of that year, the Klan made a virtual clean sweep in Volusia County, carrying Daytona, Ormond, and Deland for its ticket, which included candidates for judicial, municipal, and legislative office. Internal dissension, however, made it a short-lived victory. The mayor of Deland refused to heed the wishes of the local Klan leader, so the Klan summoned him to a meeting in the woods at which he was tried for mutiny. Despite threats, the mayor and his friends withdrew from the Klan, and many of the better citizens also started dropping out.

Local setbacks, however, did little to stem the growth of the Klan in Florida. The largest Klavern was Stonewall Jackson No. 1 of Jacksonville, but the mother Klan was soon being challenged by John B. Gordon No. 24 of Miami and Olustee No. 20 of St. Petersburg. Chapters proliferated throughout the state, mixing the names of national and Southern heroes, such as the Andrew Jackson Klan of Hastings and the Albert Sidney Johnson Klan of West Palm Beach, with descriptive bits of Floridiana, like Key West's Klan of the Keys, the Fort Gaines Klan of Ocala, and the Klan of the Palms at Fort Myers. Klansmen paraded through Jacksonville and then disappeared as all of the street lights in the business district mysteriously went dark. The Jacksonville and Levy county fairs had special Klan days. Flags and Bibles were presented at high school dedications at Largo and Clermont. Klansmen met to gobble down fried fish and barbecue at Hastings and Williston, and held memorial services for departed members at Dunnellon and West Palm Beach. Klansmen made presentations at church services in St. Petersburg and Tampa and gave a big contribution to the Y.M.C.A. building fund in the Sunshine City. Stonewall Jackson No. 1 joined other Jacksonville civic groups to protect city beaches from commercial exploitation, while St. Petersburg's Olustee Klan used her Pass-a-Grille beach for cross-lit initiations. The Lakeland Klan boasted that it was the first to have its own lodge building while that of Lake Worth, where the women of powerful George B. Baker Klan No. 70 devoted their efforts to the running of a free nursery, was to be two stories high.

In November of 1923, Orlando's Cherokee No. 9 had played host to representatives from all of the Klans in Florida to mark the in-

auguration of Florida as a self-governing realm in the Invisible
Empire. Klansmen continued to meet, initiate, feast, and march
throughout the state. In Miami the Knights of Columbus unsportingly
withdrew from the Fruit and Flower Parade when the Klan entered
a float in the civic and fraternal division. Built to depict the Klan's
fight against ignorance and superstition, the float presented a dragon,
labeled "The Enemies of American Ideals," about to attack a youth
in front of a red schoolhouse. Between the monster and his intended
prey stood three Klansmen with drawn swords. In a mountain cavern
in the rear of the float there was an altar and a fiery cross, protected
by two more Klansmen. In addition, four mounted Klansmen were
grouped at each corner of the float, which was encircled with a forty-
eight-starred banner bearing the names of the states of the Union.
It may not have been the most beautiful float but it was certainly
the busiest, and it took first prize.

The Klan was similarly busy. Klansmen in Ocala worried about
slot machines, and the Miami Klan denounced horse and dog racing
and all other forms of gambling. Speaking at the Levy County fair,
the Grand Dragon deplored the poor quality of education in the state,
and so the Invisible Empire took a proper interest in academic affairs. In Florence Villa the Klan threatened a newly built Negro
school and a white woman who had contributed to it. On the campus
of Stetson University, a Klan newspaper claimed, a unit of the Invisible Empire was operating under the name of the Fiery Cross Club.
At the University of Florida at Gainesville the Alachua Klan was
disturbed by the presence of a Roman Catholic priest who was preparing the innocent students for seduction by Rome through the device of a dramatic society which he had organized. The Klan agitated
against him and his campus privileges were withdrawn.

The Klan boasted that in Deland individual Klansmen were help-
ing the authorities uphold Prohibition, despite "harassment by cor-
rupt politicians, rum rings, and a few unscrupulous Romans." The
Klan rallied behind a bill to provide for Bible reading in the public
schools, and, when a Florida delegation went to Madison Square
Garden pledged to William Gibbs McAdoo, antagonists and the New
York *World* claimed that prominent members of the delegation were
Klansmen.

During the spring of 1923 in the little orange-growing center of
Kissimmee, three men, including the night stationman for the railroad and a local doctor, were whipped, tarred, and feathered. When
a fourth man was caught spying on a Klan meeting he was also beaten.

Late in the year there was a series of floggings in Tampa. In nearby Sumter County, the mayor of a small town wrote to the *World* that not less than a dozen of his neighbors had been taken out and lashed, primarily for political opposition to local Klansmen and criticism of the Invisible Empire. At Sanford an elderly man who had been trying to sell his insecticide spray for celery by denouncing those currently in use as poisonous, was also flogged. When a disabled Miami veteran whom his wife wanted chased out of town was flogged instead, the Klan disclaimed responsibility, but there was little question about the assailants of a Miami real estate man who was similarly treated. When a Gainesville man was severely beaten for neglecting his wife and children to chase after another woman, the mayor and chief of police declared the punishment to be a "kindness to the man and his family" and "a blessing to the city of Gainesville."

The major outbreak of reported Klan violence took place in Putnam County, west of St. Augustine. In September of 1926, Governor John W. Martin called in the county sheriff and the mayor of Palatka to discuss investigative findings that at least sixty-three floggings had taken place there in the space of a year. Every Saturday night, as many as five people had been taken out and lashed. Two of the victims had died; among the others had been several women. Klan sympathizers claimed that the violence had been directed at bootleggers and the operators of bawdy houses. The Tampa *Tribune* commented that the first few victims were probably undesirables, but that if all of those who deserved it had been thus punished they would have included 5 per cent of the victims and 100 per cent of the floggers. Other floggings had been taking place, the paper commented, from Volusia and Polk counties in the north and central parts of the state to Monroe in the south. Governor Martin spoke out forcefully. Such a situation in which "mobs formed at night to terrorize the community and citizens had to carry concealed weapons," could not continue. He characterized it as "a disgrace to Florida" and threatened to remove the sheriff and proclaim martial law if the violence continued.

However, Klan violence, in those instances when it was publicized, created little stir elsewhere in the state. Despite occasional opposition from such diverse sources as Governor Martin, the Tampa *Tribune* and the Gainesville *Sun,* the minister of Tampa's Palm Avenue Baptist Church, and the politicians and American Legion post of Deland, there was no general revulsion of feeling, political attack, or turning away from the Klan. Although the Klan campaigned for

Herbert Hoover, and his victory resulted from the kind of a campaign that the Klan liked, the hooded order does not seem to have been an important factor in his success. Unlike what had happened in most other states, however, the Ku Klux Klan continued to be active in Florida as the twenties came to an end. Whether it was because no ambitious state leader had emerged to lead the Florida Klan into an unseemly drive for political power, or because the state was too politically disorganized or too receptive to deny it, the Florida Klan held on to its members and looked forward to the thirties.

33

ATTEMPTED DOMINION IN VIRGINIA

The revival of the Deep South's cherished hero of Reconstruction days was displeasing to many Virginians. In the spring of 1921 the Richmond chapter of the United Daughters of the Confederacy petitioned the governor to prevent the organization of the Klan in the state, and the leaders of the Democratic party were never pro-Klan. The State Corporation Commission brought suit against the Klan and got it fined for carrying on unauthorized business in the state. Civic officials in Norfolk and elsewhere denounced it, and the strong plank on religious freedom adopted by the 1924 Democratic state convention was considered a direct slap at the Klan. The major newspapers in Richmond and Norfolk were anti-Klan, though, whereas the Norfolk *Virginian-Pilot* spoke out against the hooded knights, the Richmond *Times-Dispatch* and *News Leader* assumed that the best course was to refuse them publicity and mention. Bright, able young Governor Harry Byrd was busy reforming the state administrative system and consolidating the party which he had inherited from his uncle, Hal Flood. However he did not approve of the Invisible Empire, whose anti-Catholic intolerance he could not stomach, and he was no friend to night riding and lynch law.

Even without official approval, the Klan did well. It set up its first Klavern and its headquarters in Richmond where the chief of police said that he had never heard more patriotic speeches. The Klan paraded and recruited in the one-time capital of the Confederacy and in the summer primaries of 1921 managed to defeat a Roman Catholic commissioner of revenue. Several Klans were organized in and around Richmond and Petersburg. Even so, the main strength of the Invisible Empire centered elsewhere.

The prime Klan territory in Virginia was down in Norfolk, Princess Anne and Nansemond counties in the southeastern corner of the state, across the river in Newport News at the tip of the James peninsula, in the rich southern tobacco counties in the shadow of the Blue Ridges—from Halifax to Patrick County—around Lynchburg, and in the neighboring counties of Roanoke and Wythe. There was something similar about all of these areas, strung along the southern part of the state. First, the hooded knights did not gather their strength in the rural counties of southside Virginia, which contained the largest number of Negroes, or in the tidewater or in the Appalachian plateau to the west where the people were less inclined to go along with the political gentry in Richmond and the Democratic dominance of the state. The centers of Klan strength in the Old Dominion State lay in a series of growing, industrializing cities, most notably Norfolk, Newport News, Portsmouth, Lynchburg, Danville, Hopewell, and Roanoke. These cities handled the coal shipped in by railroad from the mines of Virginia and West Virginia, packed and distributed the seafood of the middle south, built ships, manufactured fertilizer, farm machinery, cotton and silk textiles, chemicals, paints, cottonseed oil, and munitions. They marketed the tobacco, made the shoes and hosiery, fired the foundries, treated the lumber, cut out the furniture, and manned the railroad shops and the cellulose factories.

Into the factories and slums of the rapidly growing, unplanned cities moved the rural folk—white and Negro—of Virginia. These Virginians were simple, proud, direct people, unused to the tempos of the world of industry and the impersonal life of the raw manufacturing town. Yet, though their world was shaken up, they were offered no broadening experience by being thrown together dependently with people just like themselves in the busy factory life. The factories and shipyards had drawn many Negroes who lived in dingy shantytowns on Princess Anne Road, near Scott's Creek, in Hell's Half Acre, or along the Blackwater Creek. Although he competed only at the level of unskilled labor, it was important that the Negro be kept in his place. Then too, in this proudly Anglo-Saxon state, where less than 1 per cent of its people were foreign born, the menace of the foreigner, particularly the Roman Catholic, was cause for all patriotic God-fearing men to remain on the alert. For the relocated rural folk living in belts around the industrial cities, the membership in the Klan became second only to church as a source of both social and ethnic expression.

Hundreds of Virginians packed Klan rallies in the Palace Theatre in Danville, the Pythias Hall in Suffolk, and the high school auditorium in Whaleyville, and paraded through Richmond, or were told in Norfolk that the Klan would control the country after the 1924 election. In 1924, the Eastern Shore was given the full treatment at its first big Klan rally at Cape Charles, with mounted Klansmen, a burning cross, fife-and-drum groups, and several thousand Klansmen from all over the state. The major Klan expansion drive that year was up through the Valley of Virginia. Its success was mixed, but it stirred up controversy in the communities into which it went. In Winchester, a Klan minister-recruiter was arrested for implying that bootleggers were tipped off about raids and favored in court, but city hall was thrown open for an organizing meeting for a women's chapter of the Klan. There was a fist fight at St. Paul's during Sunday-morning services when an Episcopal clergyman from Michigan, who had been touring Virginia for the Klan, took exception to unfavorable comments made in the local minister's sermon. In Staunton the deacons and minister of the West Main Street Methodist Church wrangled angrily when the latter spoke out approvingly of the hooded order. The Klan held a Flag Day initiation in Shenandoah Cavern, and a Front Royal Baptist minister told a Washington's Birthday service that if the father of his country were alive he would be a Klansman.

In 1925, John M. Purcell was up to succeed himself as state treasurer of Virginia. He had begun as a clerk and had worked himself up in the office and in Richmond politics until he became the city's Democratic chairman. When the treasurer died, Purcell was appointed to replace him. Now Purcell was running for office himself for the first time and on a state-wide basis. Since the party was behind him, his campaign should have occasioned no particular attention or problem, but this was not the case. Purcell was a Roman Catholic, and this mattered in Virginia in the 1920s.

His opponent in the Democratic primary had come from the old wilderness town of Wytheville and in pressing Purcell closely had carried the Roanoke-Danville portion of the state where the Klan was strong. Now his Republican, but Protestant, opponent was from the same region. John David Bassett came from one of the small, newly industrialized towns south of Roanoke on the North Carolina border. His family's chair factory formed the nucleus and had given its name to the town of Bassett. The main, and perhaps the only issue was Purcell's religion, no criticism being directed at his personal behavior or his performance in office.

Although Bassett dodged the issue of whether he himself belonged to the Ku Klux Klan, posters throughout the state hailed him as the

"100 per cent candidate." The main campaign manifesto used against Purcell, on the other hand, was the charge that he was a member of the Knights of Columbus. Among the various pieces of campaign material attacking Purcell for his Catholicism was a bogus circular under the forged letterhead of the Knights of Columbus which directed all Catholics to vote for their coreligionist, Purcell. This particular piece of ammunition fell unwittingly into Catholic hands. A Negro delivery boy forgot the address to which he was to deliver newly printed copies of the circular, and opened the package to refresh his memory. Then he dutifully delivered them to the local headquarters of the Knights of Columbus. A bitter investigation by the Democratic party and the Knights of Columbus failed to reveal the source of the circulars other than that they had been ordered by one James Esdale who could not now be traced. Perhaps it was only coincidence that a James Esdale was the Klan Grand Dragon of Alabama and Illinois and occasional trouble shooter for the Invisible Empire.

With the other offices assured to the Democrats, the Republicans were in a quandary. This was the strongest race that one of their candidates for state-wide office had made in half a century, but by the eve of the election they mustered up sufficient determination to denounce the various anonymous anti-Catholic campaign letters and circulars. On Election Day, Bassett carried Newport News plus Danville and most of its surrounding counties. He also did well around Roanoke, Norfolk, and Portsmouth, and in some of the wards in Richmond. In the Valley of Virginia, Bassett cut into Purcell's strength and the Klan picked up a scattering of offices. All of these areas were carried handily by Governor Byrd and the other Democratic candidates. Where they won by state-wide margins of over fifty thousand, Purcell's was but seventeen thousand. The Richmond *News Leader* and the *Times-Dispatch* had considered the campaign against Purcell's Catholicism shameful but had sought to contain the issue by not publicizing it. Now they expressed their distaste forcefully.

The Klan was still out to get Purcell's scalp when he came up for election again in 1928, and opposed Governor Byrd's short ballot plan which would have made several offices, including the state treasurer's, appointive. By 1928, the Klan had become so bitter that it burned a cross in protest when the governor spoke in Covington, and actually threatened him with flogging.

The animosity between the Klan and the political leadership of Virginia was to continue past the 1920s. It was, however, but a single, though major portion, of the rejection of the Klan by many of the state's business, educational, and political leaders. In 1926 the Klan attempted to organize a boycott of the A. & P. food chain in Virginia which, they claimed, had discharged Klansmen and canceled a printing contract with a Richmond printer when his Klan membership became known. There was bitter public criticism when the president of historic old William and Mary College accepted a Klan offer to present a flagpole and flag to the college. However, the sense of outrage turned to laughter when President Chandler then used the occasion to lecture to Imperial Wizard Hiram Evans and five thousand assembled Klansmen about religious freedom and the evils of mob activity. Praising Klan ideals, the William and Mary prexy told the assembled brethren that it was time to start living up to them.

More than anything else, a burst of Klan violence in the late summer of 1926 stirred up general sentiment against the Klan. A Roman Catholic priest in Norfolk, who was leading a group of Negro boys on an outing, was taken to a lonely spot in a swamp and interrogated. Elsewhere, seventy armed Klansmen seized four young white men, released one of them when he showed a Klan membership card, and flogged the others. Near Bristol on the Tennessee border, two young women were flogged, and in Wytheville an accused Negro rapist was lynched. Although the lynching was not directly the action of the Klan, the blame for the general state of affairs was placed on the begowned shoulders of the Invisible Empire. Governor Byrd, the press, the judiciary, and the Norfolk Ministerial Association expressed themselves in no uncertain terms. An antimask ordinance was passed in Norfolk and sought elsewhere.

In the election year of 1928, the Klan fought against the governor's ballot reforms and rallied its small but noisy forces against Al Smith. The Republicans didn't mind, and the Republican party chairman for Virginia, R. H. Angell of Roanoke, turned up as one of the owners of the bitterly anti-Catholic and pro-Klan *Fellowship Forum*. The Democrats felt differently, however. Representative R. Walton Moore, a long-time congressman from northern Virginia was opposed by Klansmen because he had refused to introduce Alabama's fire-eating Senator Tom Heflin to a "Klan Day" audience at the Fairfax County fair, and Governor Byrd rapped the powerful Methodist Bishop James Cannon for spreading religious prejudice during the campaign.

As the Depression decade of the 1930s began, the Ku Klux Klan was neither powerful nor absent from the state of Thomas Jefferson.

From the ever active and ever alert Balliston Klan No. 6 of Fairfax County to Bluefield, where the Klans of Virginia and West Virginia rallied, to Roanoke where the Robert E. Lee Klan No. 4, the state's largest, met in its red-brick, white-porticoed mansion on Day Street, to the Klavern of the Portsmouth Klan No. 16, at King and Middle streets, the Virginia realm of the Invisible Empire boasted and endured.

34

RIOTOUS DOINGS IN PENN'S WOODS

In the late summer and early fall of 1921, the Invisible Empire moved into the rolling farm country, mining valleys, small towns, and cities of Pennsylvania. In the east, where a dozen Klaverns were active in Philadelphia and Chester counties, progress was soon halted, for Atlantan F. W. Atkins proved disloyal to his imperial allegiance. As one of the group of Northern leaders who quarreled with Colonel Simmons and E. Y. Clarke over the right way to run the Klan, Atkins lost his job and his followers. When he consoled himself with the Klan's treasury and the destruction of his records, eastern Pennsylvania Klandom was plunged into deep and retarding confusion.

In the west, things went better for Sam Rich, the Kentucky-reared Kleagle and future Grand Dragon, as his peddlers of klannishness spread their wares through the valleys of the Allegheny, Monongahela, and Youghiogheny rivers. Particularly strong units, E. H. Loucks related in his brilliant history of the Pennsylvania Klans, grew in the industrial and mining towns of Pittsburgh, New Kensington, Homestead, Mount Pleasant, Johnstown, Altoona, Indiana, and Connellsville. Although the Klan worried about the large numbers of Roman Catholics and foreigners in the state as well as the uncertain enforcement of Prohibition, it initially confined its activities to church visits and charitable and fraternal affairs.

Although the Klan had more than 125,000 members in western Pennsylvania, by the end of 1924, it was remarkably unsuccessful in politics. It reportedly helped elect some friends, perhaps even Klansmen, to the legislature but remained apparently more of a political handicap than an aid. In 1923, a Catholic member of the Pittsburgh city council did better than ever when the Klan and the Prohibitionists came out against him. Two years later in Du Bois and Johnstown, Democrats who were opposed by the Klan won in normally

Republican areas. Yet if the Klan was not a political force, it was a major presence in the life of western Pennsylvania.

In the east, it took a while to get all of the problems straightened out. After he had skimmed off as much money as he could, the Klan's Northern mogul, D. C. Stephenson, placed the whole state in the hands of Grand Dragon Rich. It took the Pennsylvania leadership quite a while to understand the "Pennsylvania Dutch," Loucks reported. While the eastern Pennsylvanians were militantly Protestant, clannish, fraternal-minded, and anti-Catholic, they resented the manipulations and demands for obedience which state officials were accustomed to use west of the Susquehanna. However, once the Dutch were allowed a freer hand they became the most loyal of Klansmen, whose organizations survived much of the disruption and civil war of the late twenties. Reaching their peak about 1925, the eastern Klans totaled nearly a hundred thousand members. Close to a third were in Philadelphia and most of the rest centered in the mill and mining counties of Schuylkill, Luzerne, and Carbon, in the Lehigh Valley, and in the farming country south of Harrisburg.

The major continuing concern of the Klan was with education. This meant the use of the King James Version of the Bible for the ten daily passages, without comment, proscribed by law, and the display and respect for the flag. Klansmen checked up on these, donated Bibles and flags to the schools, pressed against the presence of Catholic teachers and materials. They performed such patriotic duties as the removal of Bellini's portrait of the Doge of Venice, who looked too much like a Pope, and of D. S. Muzzy's history text which unpatriotically called George Washington a rebel. There was a near riot in Luzerne County over Klan participation in a school ceremony, but in Greensburg the Klan helped passage of a bond issue for the new high school.

The Pennsylvania Klan was not as inclined to violence as some of its Southern and Western brothers were, but it soon got its share. In 1923 there was a clash with American Legionnaires in Lancaster, over a Klan wreath at the Armistice Day rites. A little girl was reportedly kidnaped from her grandparents in Pittsburgh and a Waynesboro man was flogged for failure to take care of his mother. In addition, there were Klan strong-arm squads, such as the Homestead and Harrisburg Wreckers, the Reading Night-Riders, the Venango gang, who smeared buildings with cow dung; the Everett Klansmen who discussed castrating a Negro; and the Mechanicsburg outfit which actually did have a genuine flogging. Two truckloads of hooded men fired at an encampment of Negro Boy Scouts in Upper Darby. When two policemen were shot while they investigated a masked meeting on the Haverford Campus, the Lower Merion police chief ordered his remaining men to shoot to kill. In the Pittsburgh suburb of Wilkinsburg, threatening calls over the barring of the Klan led to cancelation of a Defense Day parade.

With the Klan growing self-confident and talking constantly about the menace of lawbreakers, bootleggers, the micks and Italians, the nuns in the schools, and the Pope in Rome, an even more serious outbreak of violence was not unlikely. In the summer of 1923, there was an armed clash in the industrial town of Carnegie, just west of Pittsburgh, and more trouble narrowly averted the next week at nearby Scottdale. The next spring there was an even more serious outbreak in the town of Lilly near Altoona.

Each of the three communities was a rough industrial town with a considerable Roman Catholic population. When ten thousand Klansmen gathered on the hillside for the initiation ceremonies under the watchful eyes of their visiting Imperial Wizard, the mayor of Carnegie was frightened. No parade could be permitted, he decided. For the Klansmen, however, there would be a dangerous loss of face in backing down. The Imperial Wizard, Hiram Evans, consulted with Grand Dragon Rich and the parade marshal. "Go ahead," he decreed. The main bridge to town had been blocked with trucks and so the Klansmen approached on a different road, pushing aside a car which had been turned across their path. As the marching Klansmen started through the streets of Carnegie, a shouting crowd met them with a hail of sticks, stones, and bricks. The Klansmen in the front ranks shrank back but those behind pressed them onward into the jostling crowd which overflowed into the street. Hoods were knocked off and robes torn. As the battered marchers struggled on, a shot was fired and a young Klansman, Thomas Abbott, died with a bullet through the temple. The Klan ranks backed up and then turned around, retreating across the bridge, out of town to the hillside where Evans and Rich waited. Some of the marchers demanded that they rally and go back to mop up the town. "No," Evans told the angry Klansmen, the time was not yet ripe—though it would soon come. Grand Dragon Rich liked to say that it took a good riot to swell the ranks of the Klan, and the whole event had been an exciting one for his visiting boss. That night, Hiram Evans felt, was worth twenty-five thousand new members, and he suggested to Rich that it ought to be repeated. Americanism under attack by foreign ruffians was always a good theme and the excitement of violence acted like a tonic to recruitment. In young Tom Abbott, the Klan had gained its hero. A ninety-page booklet, *The Martyred Klansman*, was written about him, and his name was used for memorials and fund-raising whenever Keystone Klansmen met.

The Klan was spoiling for a fight and it almost got it the next week in Scottdale. A gang of toughs in the neighboring town of Everson had waylaid Klansmen and desecrated their regalia. The whole area needed a show of force. "Remember Carnegie and Come Prepared," the word went out, and the anticipation heightened. Permits were issued for the parade and its route was drawn right past the parish church. Klansman and anti-Klansman gathered arms. "No masked Klansman will get as far as Pittsburgh Street," the latter threatened, while the wearers of the robe boasted that if one of their number fell there would not be a Roman Catholic alive in Scottdale by morning. From the look of the groups of men on the housetops and the rumors of strategically concealed Klan machine guns, anything was possible. The street lights went out in one section of town and no one knew whether the man beside him on the crowded sidewalks would turn out to be his friend or enemy. It was all too much for the Exalted Cyclops of Scottdale and he wanted the whole thing called off. However, his cohorts from other Klaverns were not going to be turned back again. Finally the state police offered to lead the parade through town, if the marchers would unmask. The leaders agreed and a diminished line of Klansmen passed through the town without incident.

The violence that had thus been narrowly averted finally burst forth in the little mining town of Lilly, where the Klan had twice tried to burn crosses, early the next spring. Everyone expected trouble. Klansmen converged on Lilly by chartered trains from Johnstown and Altoona, ready "to give the micks something to think about." They donned their robes in the trains and marched through town to their meeting place. When someone pulled a plug at the electric station and the street lights went out, the Klansmen pushed on, using pocket flashlights. A mob swept to the foot of the hill where the Klansmen surrounded their blazing cross. A hooded sentry was captured, disrobed, and put on a passing train. When his robes were waved before his assembled brethren, the decision was made to cut things short and return to the station. The crowd turned nasty and began assailing the rear guard of the Klan. A fire hose was used to drench the retreating marchers. As the Klansmen reached their train, those already on board opened fire on the pursuing crowd, which shot back. The railroad got its train out quickly and sent word ahead to the police in Johnstown who took off the wounded and arrested those who had not disposed of their weapons. Four men died as a result of the adventure; others were injured and eventually eighteen Klansmen and ten residents of Lilly were sentenced to prison. Klansmen from the Indiana, Pennsylvania, Klavern had been prominent among those arrested at Lilly, and the next year someone set fire to their new $34,000 Klan building. The big city press was so unkind to the Klan after Carnegie and Lilly that the Klan had a go at its own state paper, but its demise only cost Klansmen more money.

Everything was costing the Klansmen and -women money. Klan lodge, educational, and charity work was expensive. So was the Klan Haven for orphans, for which the Klan and the state shared expenses. This was money well spent, but Klansmen felt less charitably inclined about their losses on stock in the ill-fated attempt to market a specially wrapped Klan candy and put out the short-lived Klan newspaper.

The Klan's recruiters had worked the territory as thoroughly as they could, ready to take anyone in who had the initiation fee. The yield was rich. Klan leaders spied on each other and maneuvered for a place at the trough. Everyone kept his own books. The long-suffering rank and file became increasingly aware of this, although it was difficult to say whether they most resented the financial goings-on or the imperiousness of their state and national leaders. This was not a problem for the men alone; the Women of the Ku Klux Klan went through most of the same experiences.

The historian Loucks tells how the Women of the Klan were used as a pawn in Klan power struggles. At the national level, Judge James Comer, the Arkansas Grand Dragon who helped raise Robbie Gill into power and then married her, called the tunes. At the state level, the men's organization got a cut of the initiation fees and the top Klansmen enlarged their take by getting their wives appointed Kleagles. The lands and funds of Klan Haven orphanage were attractive and so there was a big fight to take these out of the women's hands. Judge Comer and Philadelphia Klan head, Paul Winter, meddled repeatedly in the affairs of the W.K.K.K., removed the popular leader of the state organization, and turned the fourteen-hundred-member Canwin Women's Klan of Philadelphia into rebellion. Having been swindled on the profits from a jointly-sponsored boat ride down the Delaware, ignored when they sought punishment of a local Klan leader whom they accused of immoral conduct with two Klanswomen, and denied an attempt to tell their grievances to their Imperial Commander, the Philadelphia and Chester Women of the Ku Klux Klan quit. After a short, nervous life as "The Women's Christian Patriotic League," they disbanded.

After 1925 the growing discontent among the men focused on Paul Winter in Philadelphia and on Grand Dragon Rich. In the City of Brotherly Love, Paul Winter, the pugnacious little bantam who had been brought in from Reading to be Hiram Evans' field representative, became increasingly unpopular. His response was to use his new, Atlanta-approved, Triple-S Super-Secret Society, known as "the black-robed gang," to back up his position. Modeled on the Night Riders of Ohio, the Triple-S wore a skull and crossbones as well as the Klan insignia on their black regalia. They had been organized as an outlet for the restlessness among those Klansmen who had discovered that life within the Invisible Empire was primarily composed of dull rituals and wrangling meetings. Eventually Winter and the leader of the "black-robed gang" fell out over Winter's involvement with the latter's wife. Dissident Klansmen managed to bring Winter up on charges. Evans' men interfered on behalf of Winter, and the plaintiffs lacked the needed three-fourths majority. When Winter vengefully banished his remaining enemies and disbanded the Warren G. Harding Klan, many of the other Philadelphia chapters melted away.

In western Pennsylvania, similar protests mounted over Sam Rich's handling of state affairs and discipline. A delegation was sent to the Imperial Wizard, and, when nothing happened, the Klans of Allegheny County prepared to select a new Grand Dragon on their own. His hand forced, Hiram Evans delayed as long as he could and finally set up a tribunal to try Rich. Even with his friends on it, Rich lost. A temporary leader was sent in, but the local Klans now charged that he was "defiling the state office by immoral relations with his stenographer." Evans then promised them the opportunity to pass on their next leader, but at the convention called for that purpose, he had his own candidate rammed down their unwilling throats. This was Rev. Herbert C. Shaw, a Rome-hating Tennesseean who had been a Methodist minister in Erie, Pennsylvania.

Most of the Pennsylvania Klansmen hadn't wanted Shaw, and he made it rather clear that he didn't think much of them either. In addition, he was so violently outspoken about the Roman Catholics and Negroes that he embarrassed and disturbed many Klansmen. In September of 1926, they sent a delegation to the third biennial Klonvokation in Washington to tell Evans and the assembled ranks of Klandom how they felt about things. They complained about the way in which Shaw had been appointed, the lack of democracy in Klan affairs and even tried to object to the donation of a yacht to the Imperial Wizard. Rebuffed but not silenced, they continued to bombard Evans with their views about Shaw's shortcomings.

By this time Evans was rather tired of what the Klansmen in Pennsylvania thought. He banished their spokesman, John Strayer, who combined his roles as Exalted Cyclops of the Westmoreland Klan and Minister of the United Brethren Church, with membership in the state legislature. After more controversy, the charters of the Coraopolis, Manor, New Kensington, Duquesne, Homestead, Vandergrift, Jeanette, and Latrobe Klans were also revoked. When they tried to go it on their own, Evans decided to use them as a warning lesson for other Klansmen. He sought to enjoin them from using the Klan name and sued them in federal court for $100,000 damages. To his surprise, the banished Klansmen fought back. Since a plaintiff in such a case has to come into court with "clean hands," the defendants set out to see what could be done. They told all they knew—and perhaps a bit more—and collected testimony from Colonel Simmons, D. C. Stephenson, and anyone else who wanted to have his say. The resulting affidavits detailed kidnapings, floggings, torture, and stories about men ceremonially burned alive in Texas. The newspapers reported much of the testimony, and the judge decided that the Klan's hands were far from pure. The rebel groups lingered on for a while and a number of the loyal Klans continued to function, but the enthusiasm and support for the Invisible Empire was gone.

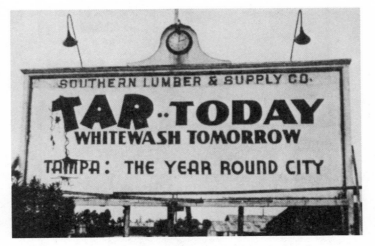

The general state of affairs in Tampa, Florida, during the 1930s

The first public announcement of the revival, drawn by "Colonel" Simmons himself and printed in the Atlanta Journal, December 7, 1915, next to the advertisement for The Birth of a Nation

Klan parade in Washington, D.C.

KURSES!

—McCarthy in the New Orleans *Times-Pi*

"Colonel" Simmons and Hiram Wesley Evans battle for the spoils

"THE GHOST WALKS"
—Memphis *Commercial Appeal.*

Evans wins

Klan parade in Tulsa, Oklahoma, 1923

Klan paraders in Long Branch, New Jersey, in the 1920s

Klansmen in Neptune City, New Jersey

Klan marchers in Washington, 1925

Dr. Samuel Green, the Atlanta obstetrician who revived the Klan after World War II

Sam Roper (second from the left, with white hood and cigar), the Georgia policeman who took over when Doc Green died in 1949

A Georgia tradition

Klansmen meet under Florida pines near Jacksonville

Klansmen rally in a field in South Carolina

The Lumbee Indians of North
Carolina celebrate their victory
over the Klan. Lumbee leader
Simeon Oxendine (on right)

E. L. Edwards, Imperial Wizard
and sometime Chevrolet paint-
sprayer in Atlanta, the top Klan
potentate of the 1950s

Imperial Wizard, Robert Shelton,
the rising Klan light of the 1960s

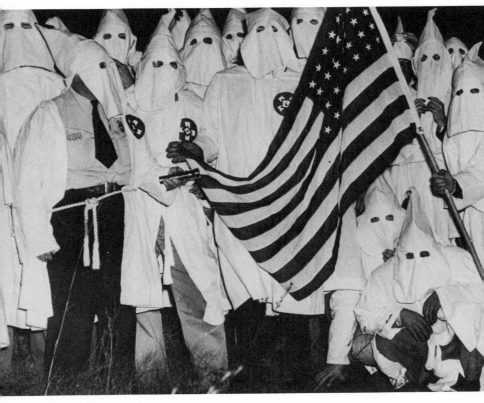

Dual loyalties in Birmingham, Alabama, in the 1960s

Police officers guard civil rights demonstrators at St. Augustine, Florida

35

METHODISTS AND MADNESS
IN THE GARDEN STATE

In most states where the Invisible Empire took root, opposition was slow in developing. Usually the Klan in politics or Klan excesses were necessary to vitalize effective resistance, or else the realm was badly damaged by internal dissension over inept leadership, and leadership and financial exploitation from Atlanta. In New Jersey the Klan met with continuous objection from almost the very beginning. It had its friends in politics but generated more opposition than it gained support. Although it occasionally threatened violence, it tended to be on the receiving end. The 1923 riots might have led to warfare similar to that in Illinois' Williamson County, if the New Jersey Klan had not been so pacific. Yet the Klan prospered and spread throughout the state, finding a particular haven in the shore towns of Monmouth County and stout champions among the Methodists and the other godly folk of the Garden State.

The Ku Klux Klan first spread to New Jersey from the neighboring states of New York and Pennsylvania early in 1921. By the end of the summer, Klan leaders claimed that they were organized from the wooded ridges of the state's northern, lake-studded highlands to the pine barrens, beaches, and tidal marshes of its southern coastal plain. Primarily, however, Klan strength centered where most of the people were, in the urban and industrial belt which girdled the center of the state. Its first strongholds were in Passaic, Bergen, Essex, Union, and Morris counties and in the area around Trenton and Camden on the Pennsylvania border. Leif Ericson Klan No. 1 of Paterson was the first major unit, but although the Klan found converts in Hoboken, Jersey City, and Newark, it soon learned that closely built-up residential towns provided a more stable base. Bloomfield in the shadow of Montclair, became particularly important and supplied the Klan its Caesar, Attorney Arthur Bell, who with his wife, was destined to rule the Klansmen and -women of the Garden State. The Klan's evangelicals next brought the good news down into receptive Somerset and Middlesex counties and found a particularly warm welcome in and about Plainfield and a rather hot one in Perth Amboy.

By 1923, the Klan had found its real home amid the bluffs, dunes, and beaches of Monmouth County. From the once-flamboyant and fashionable old resort town of Long Branch to the boarding houses of Asbury Park, the tiers, turrets and chalets of Ocean Grove's private homes, and the tent city of its famous Methodist retreat, where the Sabbath was unmarred by bathing, secular activity, or vehicular traffic, the Klan was king in the mid-twenties. Here it marched, rallied, and worshiped, and here on the grounds of the Klan's Shark River recreation park, New Jersey's Grand Dragon dwelt and the Imperial Wizard of the Invisible Empire was feted by admiring subjects. Although the Klan sortied down to Cape May at the southern tip of the state and maintained vital outposts of Empire in Pleasantville and the outskirts of Atlantic City, it felt most at home in Monmouth County.

The Klan's program in New Jersey was the standard one, which tended always to see what it was for in terms of whom it was against. New Jersey's population doubled between 1900 and 1930, with a marked influx of immigrants from southern and eastern Europe settling directly or filtering in from other states. One out of every five whites was foreign born and was probably living in one of the northern counties. The number of Negroes drawn into the industrial plants during the war and into the servants' quarters of wealthy residential areas, like those around Montclair, tripled upward to 5 per cent of the population.

Its purposes, the Klan announced, were to protect the Constitution and pure womanhood, maintain white supremacy, and the separation of Church and State, and uphold law and order. With a hang-over from the war days, the Leif Ericson Klan denounced the Steuben Society and threatened political reprisals if the teaching of the German language was restored in the Paterson schools. The problem, as the Klan saw it, was one of "German-Bolshevist-pacifist-radical-internationalist" propaganda. In 1924 the Klan blamed the silk mills strike on sovietism and foreign agitators, charging that there were almost half a million Communist agents in the United States, and agreeing with the mayor of Paterson that alien strikers ought to be deported. Although there were no substantiated reports of actual Klan violence, nocturnal crosses flamed their warnings to communities and individuals. Drunkenness, wife beating, mixed marriages, and other such transgressions were the subject of individual communications, usually suggesting that the recipient mend his ways and sojourn elsewhere.

The Klan supported efforts to segregate Negro school children in Atlantic City and identified crime in Trenton with the influx of Southern Negroes. Before an assemblage of ministers, public officials, and Klansmen in Asbury Park, Grand Dragon Arthur Bell revealed that he had learned of eighty-seven thousand cases of white girls living with Negroes and men of the yellow race. White Protestant America faced a world in which members of Negro societies pledged themselves to marry white girls, the Roman Catholics were extending their power over the armed services as a preliminary to a general take-over, and the Jews, who controlled 85 per cent of vice in the nation, were out to dominate finance and the law.

In the Asbury Park area, the Klan attempted to discourage Jewish and Roman Catholic visitors and to stem the influx of New York vacationers. This kind of business turned out to be bad business, Harold Wilson, historian of *The Jersey Shore* reported, and cost the Klan some local support. Jewish summer residents departed Long Beach in large numbers. Some Catholic inhabitants moved, and others took countermeasures, as in the case of a local Roman Catholic academy which stopped buying from their iceman when some of the nuns recognized him in a Klan parade. Apart from involvement with its ritualism and fraternalism, the primary concerns of the Ku Klux Klan in New Jersey was the preservation of the traditional American values and, as Mrs. Bell told her Tri-K girls, the return to "the teachings of our mothers." This meant stressing the virtues of Protestant fundamentalism, Prohibition, and opposition to the Roman Catholic Church. It was not surprising, therefore, that in New Jersey this often led to friendly relations and co-operation with many Protestant churches.

Particularly characteristic of the Ku Klux Klan in New Jersey was the support which it received from the ministry. Although Baptist, Presbyterian, Dutch Reformed, and Evangelical pastors and churches supplied pulpits and prestige for the Klan, its truest friends came from the Pillar of Fire Church and the Methodists. The "holy jumpers" of Bishop Alma White's religious community of Zarephath looked with favor on the Klan which they saw as a girded ally in the fight to protect the Bible Christianity against modernism and higher

criticism. Having taken their name and guiding sign from the pillar
of fire which had led the Israelites through the wilderness, there was
a certain tendency among the faithful to blur that image with the
Klan's blazing cross. Bishop White praised the Klan by book and
sermon, and predicted it would sweep the colleges, beginning with
nearby Princeton. In the venerable colonial town of Bound Brook,
nearby, a group of her followers came close to enduring martyrdom
for the Invisible Empire.

In the late spring of 1923, the Klan had pushed its recruiting drive
in the suburban towns at the base of the Watchung mountains where
the soldiers from the Continental armies had once skirmished with
the British. Oblivious of a growing muttering and protest, a widely
publicized meeting was scheduled for Bound Brook at the beginning
of May to form a Klan unit among the sober, overalled members of
the Pillar of Fire. A number gathered together in their church to hear
the Klan speakers tell them that all one-hundred-per-cent Americans
should join the Invisible Empire. No sooner had the words been uttered than a tattoo of stones crashed into the building, hurled by the
mob of obviously unpatriotic Americans which had been gathering
outside.

The small handful of state troopers who joined local police were
able to do little more than hold off the hundreds of angry townsmen
who ringed the church until early morning. By the time the police
were able to open up an avenue of escape in the direction of nearby
Zarephath, the furniture and windows of the church had been stoned
into a shambles and the autos of many of the Holy Rollers had been
similarly mistreated.

The relationship which most other Protestant churches enjoyed
with the Ku Klux Klan was somewhat less dramatic, but busy nevertheless. Klansmen appeared at friendly churches such as the Third
Presbyterian in Elizabeth, the Grace Methodist in Kearney, the First
Baptist in Bayonne, the Calvary Methodist Episcopal in Paterson,
and the Grace Methodist Episcopal in Newark. Usually by prearrangement, they entered in full regalia, sat in special sections, donated purses to the minister, delivered talks on why the Klan favored
white supremacy, the gentiles, and Protestantism, and filed out as
church choirs sang "Onward, Christian Soldiers." While the approving Klansmen and congregations listened, ministers offered special
sermons on Americanism, and quoted from Romans 12:1, the "Klan
verse" of the New Testament:

I beseech you therefore, brethren, by the mercies of God, that ye present your bodies a living sacrifice, holy, acceptable unto God, which is your reasonable service.

If some of them had reservations about Klan doctrines, the thought of Rome, the outrages against Protestant services in Ireland, and the menace of the Knights of Columbus tended to soften their doubts. In Monmouth and Ocean counties Klansmen regularly paraded through the streets of Long Branch, Asbury Park, Point Pleasant, and Lakewood on their way to Sunday-morning services. As ever, members of the cloth joined the Klan. The recruiters and speakers whom the national Klan sent into the state were often ministers, and some local pastors changed their calling to become Kleagles, while others headed Klaverns and held state or local Klan office.

Of all the denominations, the ministers of the Methodist Episcopal Church figured most often in New Jersey Klan affairs, despite warning from their senior Bishop J. F. Berry of Philadelphia. Things came temporarily to a head at the New Jersey Methodist Conference in March of 1924. Four candidates for the ministry were suddenly asked to remove their coats and vests so that Bishop Berry could see if they were wearing any Klan emblems. Then the bishop questioned them about membership in secret organizations and asked them if they considered that it was part of their duty to become "public detectives" and "ferret out transgressors."

In truth, many ministers in New Jersey felt that this was indeed a very important part of their duty, and they warmly approved of joint efforts with the Klan to carry it out. The principal objects of their concern were always immorality and hooch. In Asbury Park, the Civic-Church League and the Klan met at the First Methodist Episcopal Church to combine forces against the menace. On the report from an Anti-Saloon League detective and the affidavit of a local printer, they denounced local politicians and businessmen. Published announcements brought people flocking to the churches to hear six leading ministers tell of a veritable Belshazzar's feast which, they claimed, had featured drunkenness and dancing by nude women. Those who had attended the banquet at issue were wrathful in their denials of drinking and unclothed women. "The charge that a nude woman sat in my lap is a damnable lie," the mayor announced. There were no nude women, he went on, and no one sat in his lap. The printer who had signed the affidavit was arrested for perjury, and while the grand jury fruitlessly sifted the evidence, Klan and Civic-

Church League leaders prepared his defense and Klansmen guarded his home.

Although vice was always a matter of interest, the bond which united Klansman and churchman was a common struggle against demon rum and its minions. New Jersey was a state in which the issue of Prohibition was not formally settled. With the Democrats strongly Catholic and preferentially less than dry, there were also dangers within the Republican party. Some of its major leaders, like Senator Walter J. Edge, were willing to compromise with the absolute moral principle of a dry New Jersey. In the 1924 primaries, the drys and the Klan opposed him for renomination and took half the counties in the state, though not the sufficiently populous ones. Although a dry America was the most important article of agreement, the Klan and the faithful found other paths in common. In the spring of 1925, they filled the galleries of the state assembly chambers to witness the course of a bill to permit New Testament readings in the public schools. With the gubernatorial elections coming up that year and one of their most prominent possible choices a Roman Catholic, the dominant Republican party sidetracked the bill. After five hours of waiting and hymn singing, the disappointed spectators in the galleries quietly dispersed for home. Later that summer the Klan and the Ministerial Association of Plainfield joined in opposition to Sunday movies. Klan ministers offered as their text that the hooded order was the only hope of bringing Christians back into the fold, and the Grand Dragon promised that he would strive to return New Jersey to "the old-fashioned religion."

Over the long run, the Klan proved an embarrassingly divisive and deterrent element. In Monmouth County the pastor of the Centerville Baptist Church became uneasy over the handling of Klan fundraising drives and whether the Kleagle ought to be provided with two cars. When his protests were ignored he quit both pulpit and Klavern, turned to anti-Klan evangelism and ran for all available state offices on a KAN THE KLAN platform. Klansmen paraded around his house. He armed. They heckled his meetings and only the intervention of the state police got him away without harm. In Bloomfield, the vestry of the Episcopal Church of the Ascension disapproved of their minister's Klan associations. When they stopped paying, the Klan took up the slack for a while until he finally resigned, ascribing the whole thing to jealousy over his wife's high degree of refinement and culture. In a little village of Atco, near Camden, a minister who opposed Klan participation in the dedication of a new undenominational church was fired after the leading layman in his congregation received information in a dream that the minister was a false prophet and an advocate of free love. The minister armed and threatened to shoot any Klansmen who might be tempted to burn a cross in front of his house. When a minister left his wife and two children to run off to El Paso, Texas, with another woman and the Klan's funds, the blow-by-blow details of his subsequent apprehension and return became Topic A in the press.

It was at the 1926 Methodist Conference that the strongest statement came from within the church itself. This time it was from Bishop Edwin Hughes of Chicago, who presided. His scathing attack on the Klan brought repeated murmurs of protest from among the several hundred ministers who tended to feel that criticism of the Klan was dangerous modernism. At one point Bishop Hughes jerked off his glasses and pounded the table with his fist to silence protest. When he was interrupted a second time, he roared out at the assemblage "Hear me, despite your prejudices, for Christ's sake. If we keep on with our silly movement we will cause the black, yellow, and brown races to combine against Caucasians, and then God help the white peoples of the world."

Despite the waning of Klan fortunes, official disapproval, and, in 1927, the resignation of the Asbury Park Klan's chaplain, the somewhat shopworn relationship between Klan and cloth continued. Imperial Wizard Hiram Evans came to New Jersey to attend Klan sunrise services at Basking Ridge and Bridgewater under the auspices of the newly formed New Jersey Easter Sunday Evangelistic Society. The menace of the papal plot to make Al Smith President of the United States, helped hold together what there was left of the once-potent *entente cordiale*. Klansmen and churchmen joined to sponsor Senator Heflin at a closed rally on the old Upsala College grounds, and a Methodist minister in Paterson was arrested for the unlicensed distribution of Klan posters calling, MEN AND WOMEN, KEEP THE ROMAN MENACE OUT.

As soon as it had felt its power growing, the Klan had become involved in politics. The biggest question that brought New Jerseyites to the polls was Prohibition, and the Klan was naturally interested in such a topic. The Democratic party, with its numerous foreign-born and Roman Catholic members, wanted the sale of beer and light wines, claiming that the Eighteenth Amendment was an invasion of states' rights. And what was even worse, the Democrats denounced the Klan. Their presidential candidate, in 1924, added insult to injury by picking New Jersey's summer capital of Sea Girt, deep in the Klan's Monmouth County, to make his disavowal of the hooded order.

The Republican party, on the other hand, politely refrained from throwing any names about. The Negroes in Morristown claimed that the Republican candidates in the 1923 election were pro-Klan, and in Trenton's Mercer County the hooded knights supported the unsuccessful Republican candidate for sheriff. In Atlantic City, where the regular Republican candidates were not sufficiently dry, the Klan rallied behind unsuccessful reform Democrats. Usually, however, the Klan was reliably Republican, and in Monmouth and Ocean counties, where the Democratic governor was insolent enough to make anti-Klan speeches, it helped defeat Democratic candidates. Down in Middlesex, Monmouth, and Ocean counties the Klan discovered that Major Stanley Washburn, its favorite for the Republican congressional nomination, had a Roman Catholic as his personal secretary. When the major refused to either fire his secretary, a wartime comrade in arms, or accept the latter's resignation, the Klan switched to open attack. Together with the drys, who had some reservations about the major's candidacy, it helped bring his defeat.

Within the next few years, however, even Monmouth County turned a cold political shoulder to the Klan. The mayors of Asbury Park and Bradley Beach were overtly unfriendly. Representative Basil Bruno, who had introduced the Bible-reading bill in the legislature, was badly defeated in his effort to gain control of the grand jury selections by running for sheriff. In 1928, when Grand Dragon Bell and his staff took a hotel room in Newark and invited Republican primary candidates to come and make known their Americanism, none appeared.

Almost from the very beginning, the Klan faced overt opposition in New Jersey. Both the Newark and the state Directors of Public Safety threatened to shoot misbehaving Klansmen. Many towns refused the Klan permission to parade or take part in civic activities on the grounds that, as Jersey City boss Frank Hague put it, such demonstrations invariably provoked rioting and lawlessness. Police in the northeastern part of the state sought to arrest Klansmen who lit fiery crosses or caused disorders, and in Harrison, just outside of Newark, being a Klansman was in itself enough to get arrested.

In Atlantic City, where an extremely active Klan accused the city government of protecting vice and lawbreakers, Mayor Bader and the city council took strong steps. Klansmen were forbidden to parade or assemble in the city and the police were instructed to use their clubs on any who tried. When the call went out for the formation of an anti-Klan Vigilance Committee, four thousand people showed up at the parish hall of St. Nicholas Church. A large group of Negroes were among those present, and two of them shared the speakers' platform with ministers and the ineffable mayor who told of his plans to use sirens and flashing traffic lights when it was necessary to summon the vigilantes to action.

Naturally, Negro and Roman Catholic organizations opposed the Klan and when the Columbus Day oratory got limbered up, it was easy to see why the Invisible Empire favored the abolition of October 12 as a national holiday. Other Klan antagonists included the Elks of Atlantic City and the state Commander of the American Legion, as well the Methodist bishops.

But this was not yet the end of the list. If the Klan had had any idea that it might march unmolested through the state of New Jersey, this hope was soon chastened. A laborer named Dennis O'Connor waded into the ranks of a Klan parade in Long Branch and assaulted three Klansmen in the rear ranks. An egg-throwing episode in Bloomfield turned a Flag Day parade into a near donnybrook, and the assaults on Klansmen at Bound Brook and Perth Amboy did not enhance the Klan's prestige.

In August of 1923, several hundred Klansmen meeting in Perth Amboy's Odd Fellows' Hall were assailed by thousands of rioting townsmen. Even when reinforced by firemen and state troopers, the police could not control the raging mob. When the crowd first started getting out of control, two carloads of Klansmen made a dash for it. One of them got away, but the other car was overturned and its occupants were beaten. There was little the police could do other than try and keep the mob out of the meeting hall. The streets belonged to the mob. Rioters brushed the police away from a patrol wagon and beat the Klansmen inside. A state trooper was lifted off of his motorcycle and pinned in a nearby doorway. Helmeted police clubbed their way through to the hydrants so the firemen could connect their hoses, but the mob re-formed, broke through, and cut the hoses. A Klansman who attempted to slip into the mob was beaten unconscious and his assailants only reluctantly abandoned their attempt to drop his body down the sewer when a policeman rushed up crying "My God, don't do that! That's murder!" As the crowd grew in the early hours of the morning, the shower of bricks and stones continued to rain on the Odd Fellows' Hall and the embattled policemen. The police finally turned to tear gas but their supply was small and it seemed wise to try and get the Klansmen to safety before the effect wore off. However, as the besieged knights dashed out of the doors and down the fire escapes they were met by the mob which again was coming forward to assault the building. When one Klansman tried to draw a pistol, the police just barely managed to hide him in an adjacent stable while the pursuing townsmen searched the police station. When the state troopers arrived, an attempt was made to lead the remaining Klansmen over the roofs to waiting cars. The mob realized what was happening and caught two of the cars, wrecking them and beating the Klansmen to the ground. A patrol wagon, which had made it out of town with its cargo of Klansmen, was met on the road by incoming crowds. The terrified Klansmen were punched and mauled until they managed to escape to the woods, while their exultant punishers overturned the van.

It was not until five-thirty in the morning that the last of the Klansmen were herded to the police station, there to wait for hours more until it was fairly safe to leave. Even during the next day, suspected Klansmen were reportedly chased through the streets, their cars stoned, and two autos dumped in the Raritan River.

Although Governor Silzer deplored the rioting in Perth Amboy, he was hostile to the Klan and during earlier troubles had taken the stand that he was not interested in complaints from masked groups. Although the Klan occasionally threatened and harassed some of their fellow citizens in New Jersey, the Klan was on the receiving end and more the object rather than the doer of violence. This opposition from officials and mobs helped to shift the center of Garden State Klandom southward toward more hospitable Monmouth County.

However, internal battles probably had at least as great an impact on Klan fortunes as did external ones. Dissension was initially most strongly felt within the northern province of the New Jersey realm. This was the area which had been organized during the Imperial Wizardship of Colonel Simmons, and Klansmen in Passaic. Bergen, Essex, and Hudson counties opposed the new officials sent in by Stephenson and Evans. Klansmen in Hoboken resisted the national Klan but came close to riot when they were told that they would have to pay their initiation fees all over again to join Simmons' new substitute Knights of the Flaming Sword. The rapaciousness of national and local leaders led to splits and resignations in Camden and other areas. Even in faithful Monmouth County there was dissent and two of the leading Klan ministers resigned over the Klan's high-handed financial manipulations. With its star on the wane in the county, the national Klan unsuccessfully went to court to claim control of the valuable Shark River recreational park, which the local Klan had wisely placed, out of reach, in the name of the Monmouth Pleasure Club Association. It seemed clear by the late 1920s that, despite some successes and its continued existence, New Jersey was just not ready for the Klan.

36

THE E-RI-E WAS A-RISING,
AND THE GIN WAS GETTING LOW

New York City was the enemy capital for the Invisible Empire, but the Klan had a crack at it nevertheless. The summer of the New York *World*'s exposé, the Klan had a small sales staff at work in the city, holding regular private meetings on Central Park West and ceremonials in a room at the Chelsea Hotel. At the same time, other Kleagles were taking soundings in nearby Peekskill, Port Jarvis, Freeport, and Cold Spring Harbor. At the beginning of the year, Mayor John Hylan had set the police on the alert for the Klan with the declaration that any group which created disorder or antagonisms was out of place in New York City's uniquely diverse world. Despite bomb scares, crank extortion notes, charges and denials, Klan-organizing drives languished in the metropolis.

In the fall of 1922, the local Klan burst back into the headlines when it was claimed that Klan literature was being handed out at the city's largest Baptist church. The fiery fundamentalist pastor of the Calvary Baptist Church, John Roach Stratton, denied all charges, and it turned out that his associate evangelist was at fault. Reduced to only occasional duties, when his pulpit was absorbed by Calvary, Oscar Haywood had been lecturing on the Klan to various groups of Masons who, he claimed, provided the Klan with 75 per cent of its members. Everybody was getting mad. The Grand Master of the New York Masons angrily denied the claims. Dr. Stratton lumped "white Ku Klux Klanism" with "yellow journalism," and the "green sectarianism" of the Irish, and denounced them all.

The local American Legion and prominent speakers, such as First Presbyterian's Harry Emerson Fosdick, voiced disapproval of the hooded order. Mayor Hylan, vactioning at French Lick, Indiana, a watering spot also favored by Klan potentates, wired orders that the Klan was to be driven out of New York City. On the reasoning that the Klan belonged in the same class as anarchism, the job was turned over to the bomb squad which flushed out a Klan nest in the borough of Brooklyn. The Invisible Empire had selected the Brooklyn traffic court chambers as the safest place to hold its secret night meetings, and so Klan leader Wilson Bush had been presiding from the vacated chair of the magistrate. Although the Brooklyn district attorney upheld the right of Klansmen to assemble peacefully, elsewhere, things were getting a bit warm. The temperature continued to heat up when a cache of weapons, including hand grenades, turned up in back of Bush's home.

In the face of the swelling opposition, Dr. Haywood retreated from the scene returning to his native North Carolina to enter the legislature and eventually play an important role in the schism within the Tarheel Klan. Direction of the good work was taken over by two of his colleagues from Mississippi. While Maj. E. D. Smith organized the Klan's legions in upstate New York, Dr. William J. Mahoney, one of Klandom's most traveled national lecturers, exhorted the faithful on Long Island.

As the Klan expanded across the Island and upstate from Westchester to Buffalo's Erie County, the state assembly passed a bill designed to stem its tide. Sponsored by Jimmy Walker, the dapper state senator and future mayor of New York, the bill slipped through the assembly by an unexpectedly narrow margin. Exempting labor, the Masons, and benevolent organizations, the Walker Law denied the Klan the right of the mask, the mails, a role in politics, and the secrecy of its membership lists. A howl of anger went up from the Klan. A score of defiant midnight initiation meetings were scheduled from Niagara Falls to Eastport, Long Island.

Although all over the state initiates were kneeling before its altars, promising to obey the Klan and keep its secrets under pain of disgrace, dishonor, and spiritual death, the hooded order sought means of getting around the law. It managed to get incorporated as a benevolent society, under the name of Alpha Pi Sigma, Inc., but then was caught changing its name back to the Ku Klux Klan before filing the papers. A welter of charges, countercharges, injunctions, and suits followed. However, it was not until late in 1928 that the U. S. Supreme Court upheld the law, pointing out that the Invisible Empire had been behaving in a way that was certainly neither fraternal nor benevolent.

The Klan suffered temporary setbacks upstate during the summer of 1923, when attempted organizational meetings and parades in

Elmira led to street fights, but it flourished on Long Island. As Freeport was the center of Klan activity in Nassau County, Bayshore became its bastion in Suffolk. In the two counties, the Klan burned its fiery crosses, drew its thousands to its rallies, and participated actively in community affairs. At the Lynbrook firemen's tournament, the Klan's female auxiliary carried off the prize as the most popular organization in Nassau County, and the next year the Klan donated the trophy at Huntington. The Island saw Klan weddings, christenings, church visits, and special services. The only open opposition seemed to come from the American Legion which consistently objected to the Klan taking part in Memorial Day parades. The Klan's particular concern was that the Bible should be a part of the public school life and that Roman Catholicism must not. Al Smith and Tammany represented all that was wrong in society, and the names of those who had supported the Walker Law gave clear indication as to who the enemy was.

One of those was John G. Peck, a dry, Baptist, Republican assemblyman from Suffolk County. A little more than a week before the election, the Klan organized an Independent party, represented by an encircled "A"—standing for America. Pamphlets were circulated claiming that he had voted to repeal Prohibition and it was whispered about that he was pushing for money for the parochial schools. Peck just managed to squeak through in a race in which the Democrats ran third. In the other Suffolk County contests in Islip, Brookhaven, Oyster Bay, and particularly in Babylon, the Klan-endorsed candidates swept the day, and Major Smith, on horseback, led a mile-long victory parade through Bayshore.

By the beginning of 1924, one out of every seven people in Suffolk was reportedly a member of the Klan. Led by the county's other assemblyman, the Klan faction took control of the Republican county committee. Klansmen accused the sheriff of being soft on the rum-runners, and they took to patrolling the highways at night, stopping and searching suspicious-looking automobiles. Ministers praised the Americanism of the Klan. The W.C.T.U. listened approvingly to its exhortations and the federal Prohibition agents on occasion worked with it. Religious animosities became sharper. Hicksville's war dead had all been Roman Catholics, but fist fights broke out when Knights of Columbus paraders tried to remove a Klan wreath from the memorial. A Jewish druggist, accused of making advances toward a child, was threatened, kidnaped, and finally forced out of town. When a member of the liquor patrol was killed, the Klan flashed the news across the Island, and hundreds of armed men turned out to blockade the highways in search of his assailant. To a degree, at least, the Klan had become the unofficial government.

The Klan was active, though not uniformly as successful, elsewhere in the state. When crosses blazed on the hitherto quiet hillsides of Ithaca, the Cornell students took it as a lark, and the wrestling team announced its plan to grapple with any Klan invaders. On Morningside Heights things struck a more serious note. When students in Columbia University's Furnald Hall realized that the Negro whom they passed in the halls was not a janitor but a resident in their dormitory, a cross was burned on campus and he was threatened and harassed. He refused to leave; the dean backed him up, and no troops were needed on the Columbia campus.

The center of the upstate Klan was in Binghamton, where Major Smith the King Kleagle for New York had made his home. Despite the refusal of a parade permission the previous year, the Klan had had highly placed friends in Binghamton and the surrounding towns and counties. It took an option on the four-story Knickerbocker Building, which they planned to make into a Klan temple with business offices and a large auditorium for meetings. However, when Klansmen from all over the state were invited for a big three-day camp-out and rally to celebrate the Fourth of July, the turnout was disappointing. Only a tenth of those expected actually arrived at Stowe Park, and rain, mosquitoes, and random, hostile fusillades of bricks and gunshots served to send the faithful home ahead of schedule.

The Klan could never gain the degree of community approval in upstate New York that marked its establishment on Long Island. Klansmen got in trouble for making a liquor raid on the Central Hotel in Marathon and for the beating of two Geneva men, and the reports that a Rochester insurance man had been branded by New England Klansmen, were bad publicity. In Poughkeepsie members of a hostile crowd sprinkled tacks on the road outside an Exposition Hall meeting, and in Endicott an attempt to put Klansmen on the school board ended in both a riot and the rejection of the Klansmen. The state American Legion came out against the Klan and the Rochester lodge of the Odd Fellows pressed for an anti-Klan declaration from an unwilling state convention.

Nineteen twenty-four was the year for conventions and the Klan generally took a buffeting. The Democratic and Socialist state conventions predictably condemned the Klan, and the one bit of sus-

pense came over what the Republicans would do. The month before
the convention an explosion rocked the Invisible Empire in the western part of the state. The fuse had been lit six months before when
the ministerial leaders of an antivice campaign charged that Mayor
Frank K. Schwab of Buffalo had been protecting the evildoers. Naturally this did not please the mayor and when a West Side taxpayers'
organization, which he was asked to address, turned out to be a group
of hostile Klansmen, he was furious. He denounced the minister of
the United Presbyterian Church as a Klansman and told the police
that he wanted the hooded order investigated. A policeman new to
the force was able to join the Klan and work his way into its inner
circle. One night someone made off with the files from Klan headquarters in the Calumet Building and they eventually and mysteriously passed into the hands of Mayor Schwab. When the Klan's
records and correspondence were published it made fascinating if
not ennobling reading. Some of it dealt with the Klan's efforts to replace public officials, such as the sheriff of Erie County, and U. S.
Senator Royal Copeland, whose secretary the Klan did not like. Some
of it dealt with local law-enforcement efforts and the connections
between the Klan and local ministers. As always, much of it related
to quarrels over money. The important part of the material now in
the mayor's hands was the names of some four thousand local members of the Invisible Empire. The Protestant chief of police refused
to make them public, as the mayor hoped, and the press said that it
was fearful of libel suits. The list finally appeared in a pamphlet
hawked on the streets for from fifty to seventy-five cents. Its effect
in Buffalo was devastating. Most of the leaders in Buffalo's Protestant
minority were among those listed. They included schoolteachers, ministers, directors of insurance companies, city officeholders, café owners, mechanics, laborers, and farmers—a cross section of the life of
the community. The name of the minister who had attacked the
mayor, was there. So too was that of the regional director of the Anti-
Saloon League. One of the top lodge men in Buffalo, a big, bluff man,
given to sonorous oratory, had told his fellow fraternalists that if
any of them could prove that he was a member of the sheeted order,
he would never cross their threshold again. The next day his name
was on the list, and he killed himself. Houses and shops were marked
at night with the Klan initials. Businesses were boycotted. The dairy
owned by a Buffalo state assemblyman and revealed Klansman received a flood of cancellations. One of the crusading antivice
clergymen was arrested in a car with a woman and sentenced for

misconduct. He claimed persecution, and Klansmen were undergoing just that, despite appeals from both press and pulpit that the civic strife be ended.

But even this was not all there was to the affair. The story which was first carried in the press was that several Klansmen had shot each other as a result of the quarrel. Then it turned out that one of those dead was the policeman who had worked his way into the Klan just before the records were stolen. The Klan had brought a detective up from North Carolina, and a police captain let slip the information that the suspected patrolman was a Roman Catholic. Klansmen had shadowed the young policeman until the fatal night, when they had tried to seize him. He pulled out his revolver and they theirs. Shots exploded in the dark night and both the policeman and the Klan investigator fell dead on the pavement. George Bryant, the leader of the Buffalo Klan was wounded. The charge of murder against Bryant did not hold and so he was tried for having violated the Walker Law which required registration of the Klan. Bryant had been one of those who had tried to incorporate the Klan as a benevolent fraternal order, and now Klan lawyers came up from Washington to help. The case finally reached the U. S. Supreme Court, which ruled in 1928 that organizations such as the Klan had no constitutional right to secrecy. The Buffalo *Evening News* anticipated the court's sentiment in its response to the ministers and others who had written in that the Klan was no different from other fraternal groups. Was it possible to imagine men being shot, the *Evening News* asked, for revealing the membership lists of the Masons or the Knights of Columbus?

When the state Republicans met late in September of 1924, the Klan was the hottest issue. The New York City delegation demanded that the hooded order be condemned while the representatives from Long Island as well as many upstate leaders were strongly opposed to doing so. After a bitter fight, the anti-Klan plank was carried by one vote in the Resolutions Committee and the chairman gaveled it through the convention. With the selection of an anti-Klan candidate in Theodore Roosevelt, Jr., many local leaders feared that this might cost the Republicans the election. The national Republican committee responded to these fears by scheduling Maine's Governor-elect Owen Brewster to campaign for the party on Long Island and in the southern tier, to keep the Klan vote from becoming disaffected. Roosevelt joined the Democratic candidate Al Smith in attacking the Klan, but at least he was a Protestant and a Republican. Though it could muster little enthusiasm, the Klan supported his unsuccessful candidacy.

The Klan remained an active part of the social and political life of Suffolk and Nassau counties during 1925. All over the Island, Klansmen met for rallies, parades, and karnivals. At Manhasset, the Klan rented the high school auditorium under the name of the Nathan Hale Association, but usually no cover was deemed necessary. The first big rally of the year was held in Port Washington. A Klan parade, beginning a week-long muster at Roosevelt, featured floats representing the Declaration of Independence, the Pilgrims, Betsy Ross, and the importance of Bible reading in the little red schoolhouse. A minister from Binghamton told Klan thousands in Freeport that the Roman Catholics were trying to start a religious controversy by protesting against discrimination in the Rockaway school system. The Klan's ceremonial traffic was so heavy that the Merrick Road had practically become a Klan highway, and in Patchogue, the city fathers suggested that the Klan seek its parade permit for a Sunday rather than disrupt the Saturday shopping. In Suffolk's fall elections, the Klan rallied behind two Protestant candidates for the legislature and picked the police chief of Amityville to run for sheriff. Though a former Klansman ran a bitterly anti-Klan campaign on the Democratic ticket, the Republicans carried the country.

By the following year, however, Klan strength was on the wane on Long Island. Although Klansmen still marched and rallied, the people were obviously becoming tired of hooded harangues and community conflict. Anti-Klan Democrats won the village presidencies of Babylon and Greenport, and in Freeport, a Klan write-in campaign was not able to turn back a Catholic trustee candidate. Later in the year, the annual klorero of the New York realm drew only a thousand kluxers to the Mineola fairgrounds. When a car carrying New Jersey Klansmen to a Saturday-night rally in Freeport had a blowout in the Queensbridge Plaza, a jeering mob of young ruffians pelted it with fruit and stones.

It was not in New York City, but upstate, that the condition of Klan affairs really mattered. At the time of its peak strength, perhaps 10 per cent of the members were from Long Island. The others, for the most part, had come from the lower Hudson Valley, the southern tier of counties around Binghamton, and along the Mohawk Valley. The New York *Times* estimated that in 1923 its members numbered around two hundred thousand. In the middle twenties the Klan was an active force in many communities but it had not been able to create a successful state-wide organization.

Although its strength was on the decline, upstate Klansmen remained on the moral alert. The Peekskill Klansmen were still shaky over the doings of Daddy Browning but they rallied enough to warn a local man against marrying a girl of "mixed blood" and they drove away a band of gypsies by a dawn attack on their encampment. At the new Klan Haven Home in Mannsville, south of Watertown, Klan orphans were trained in farming and domestic science, and "one-hundred-per-cent gasoline" was dispensed by a Ku Klux Klan filling station in Painted Post. In Binghamton the Klan took part in raids on suspected bootleggers, and kluxers from six counties met in nearby Endicott to discuss ways of repealing the Walker Law. The big rallies that year were in Peekskill—always a major Klan center—Trumansburg, at the Klan-owned Wellsville fairgrounds in Allegheny County, and in Elmira where the Chemung Klavern, with its famous Klan band, hosted a five-day Independence Day rally. But despite the Klan's many activities, its fortunes were not encouraging. In Binghamton, Republican regulars beat back an attempt to take over the county committee, and a Klan campaign to rally the church folk and the drys to elect the saloon-raiding Commissioner of Public Safety as mayor, also failed.

While political defeat and external attack were a bitter experience for the Klan, much of its trouble, as always, came from within. In Ulster County, where the Klan boasted of fifteen thousand members, a deep schism had taken place over financial exploitation and strong-arm tactics of the leadership. The Kleagle was too fond of patting his pistol holster and talking of violence when there was opposition to his wishes, and when a meeting was arranged to discuss Klan finances, he failed to show up at all. Klansmen who pressed embarrassing questions were suspended. So were those who protested such actions. Finally the whole Ulster Park chapter was suspended from the Klan and roughly barred from its accustomed room in the Odd Fellows' Hall. Klansmen grumbled over not being permitted to make their own robes, and it was calculated that if the membership figures were correct, $225,000 had been drained out of the community for initiations and regalia. Two schismatic organizations, Dr. Galen Locke's Minutemen and the Indiana-born Independent Klan of America solicited disillusioned members. This in turn caused great heartache to local politicians, who had become accustomed to making arrangements with one Klan but felt helpless in the face of three, when alignment with one meant exposure by the others.

Although there were large upstate rallies near Syracuse, in Penn Yan, and Rochester in 1926, it betokened no gain in power. The Klan's activity around the Flower City, on the banks of the Genesee, was in part caused by Klan unhappiness over the prospect of a congressional election waged between candidates of the Jewish and Roman Catholic faiths. When the Citizens' League, the defender of a dry America, failed to field a threatened third candidate the Klan was forced to remain a feeling without a party.

The Rochester rallies were the only real show of strength the western Klan put on. Not only had the Klan been blitzed in Buffalo but it had been all but decimated in the neighboring counties. The causes had been the usual ones: internal dissension and exploitation. The destruction of the Batavia Klavern, the year before, was probably not untypical. After a series of quarrels, George Bryant, the Buffalo leader and Grand Titan of western New York, had narrowly escaped being assaulted when he had had to tell a Batavia meeting that moneys, which forty-nine members paid for their robes, had been misused. This, according to the local policeman who told the story, had been the end of the Klan in Batavia.

Still, in 1926 the Klan did muster what strength it could to protect the Republican party. It had been bad enough to have 1924's unrepentant Republican gubernatorial candidate, Colonel Roosevelt, attack the Klan before a wildly cheering state meeting of the American Legion. Now the party was preparing to return an upstate Judas to the U. S. Senate. Led by the national *Fellowship Forum*, New York Klansmen called for the defeat of the patrician Senator James Wadsworth. He was the tool of big business, the Klan charged, who was seeking to destroy the Immigration Act of 1924 in order to flood the nation with alien immigrants. Worst of all, he was only a shaky dry. For at least a year the Klan had been seeking strength to prevent his renomination, with its efforts, so Wadsworth's manager claimed, reaching from St. Lawrence County in the north to Binghamton's Broome County on the Pennsylvania line. The drys made a fight against Wadsworth at the nominating convention, but as it became clear that the Republicans were picking revisionist candidates to balance a dry platform, talk of revolt grew. The Klan-supported drys found a candidate in state Senator Franklin W. Christman from Herkimer, who entered the lists as an independent. As Wadsworth passed through the southern tier on his way to Herkimer, the large letters K.K.K. on the sides of barns testified to the strength and nature of his unavailing opposition.

The years 1927 and 1928 were ones of momentous problems for New York Klandom, but from the amount of time and emotional energy committed the main problems seemed to be how to get the Klan into the Queens Memorial and Independence Day parades and how to keep Al Smith out of the White House. May 30, 1927, was a day of violence. In Manhattan, riots between fascisti and antifascisti resulted in two deaths. In Jamaica, Queens, where fourteen hundred white-robed Klansmen and -women waited their turn to march in the Memorial Day parade, things took on the appearance of a Keystone Cops comedy.

When the G.A.R. gave the Klan a place in the parade, the Knights of Columbus and the Boy Scouts withdrew. The police felt that it would be better for all concerned if the Klan did likewise. A police inspector backed by fifty men, ordered the Klansmen not to march. When the Klansmen protested, the police formed a line across the road. The Klan band struck up "Onward, Christian Soldiers" and the Klansmen broke through the police line and joined the marchers. The police then twice halted the parade while they tried to persuade the white-robed contingent to disband. The Klansmen refused, and the inspector let a stream of traffic in from a side street to cut them off. However, the resolute Klansmen double-timed through the stream of surprised motorists and overtook the rest of the parade. Next, the police tried to block off the mounted leader of the hooded marchers with the use of more automobiles. He got away and the seemingly unstoppable Klansmen were disappearing down the avenue leaving the police discredited before a jeering crowd of spectators. Seeing that there was not a moment to lose, the inspector commandeered a bus still partially filled with a group of Negro picnickers on their way to the Rockaways and took off, zigzagging among the other marchers, in pursuit of the sheeted invincibles. By this time, the Klansmen had already passed the reviewing stand, and as the police finally forced them out of the parade the street became a seething mass of struggling policemen, Klansmen, and volunteer participants from the crowd. From a spectator point of view the parade had been a grand success, but the Klan, some of the other marchers—through whose ranks the chase had run, and an investigating grand jury were not amused.

With Klan ranks somewhat depleted in many parts of the Empire, Klan leaders converged on New York during the summer of 1927.

The Imperial Wizard, himself, was scheduled to speak in Syracuse, and the Klansmen of his loyal satrapies of Peekskill and Long Island hoped that he could be induced to grace their own elaborately planned festivities. Alabama's fire-eating, Rome-hating Senator Heflin addressed the assembled thousands of the United Protestant Alliance of Queens, meeting at the Klan's Triangle Ballroom in Richmond Hill. Paul Winter, Philadelphia's former Klan entrepreneur, was calling the signals for the Queens corner of Klandom, and Charles B. Lewis, the trouble-shooting Grand Dragon from Michigan and Wisconsin, had assumed control of New York State affairs. Imperial Women's Commander, Robbie Gill Comer, was a speaker at Freeport that summer. So was Arthur Bell, who with his wife, Leah, often represented the New Jersey Klansmen and -women before their New York neighbors. Mingling with these distinguished visitors and emigrees were the Klan's military and police orders—the uniformed Klavaliers and Empire State Troopers, leaders of Klan-front groups and friends, Klan juniors and girls—answering to kradle roll calls and junior pep rallies, and ordinary Klansmen and -women. Since the accord between Mussolini and the Vatican, antifascist Italian Protestant clergymen had begun to appear on Klan platforms, and the Krusaders added the willing, alien-born, Nordic Protestant one hundred percenters to their ranks. Though long-established elsewhere, the Krusaders were a comparatively recent arrival on the Long Island scene, parading through the streets and potato patches that a decade later would ring to the brass bands and marching boots of the German American Bund.

Although much less active, the Klan was not out of politics. Whether or not the Klan was backing one of the candidates became a central issue in a municipal court election in the Ridgewood-Glendale section of Queens and many people disagreed when the borough sheriff said that there was no special significance in his appointment of Klan organizer Paul Winter as a special deputy. The next year, a group of sewer contractors, under indictment for attempted bribery, claimed that Queens' first Republican borough president was a former member of a Klan affiliate. Their chief witness was a Jamaica real estate dealer who combined the additional occupations of Exalted Cyclops and Republican district leader.

Despite such recurring charges and connections, and the large crowds that turned out near Syracuse and Albany in 1928 to hear Senator Heflin predict Al Smith would fail in his attempt to tie the United States presidency to "the tail of the Roman Catholic kite," the Klan was slipping. Someone burned out the clubhouse in Port Washington and the Triangle Ballroom in Jamaica was up for sale. When Klan chief Hiram Evans unmasked his subjects in the late winter of 1928, swords, helmets, and an emphasis on military formations failed to make up for the lost hood and mask, and the Invisible Empire's declining prestige. The Klan was still on the scene by the beginning of the 1930s, but power and its importance were gone. It had never been a dominant force in the life of New York State, but from Freeport to Buffalo it had expressed the way a good many people felt about life in the 1920s.

37

DEFENDING THE PURITAN FATHERS

1

In New England, what the Klan feared had come to pass. The newly arrived waves of immigrants had poured over the countryside until, by the 1920s, the sons and daughters of the Puritans were being reduced to a minority. Naturally the Klan had a go at organizing the defense of the values and virtues of old-stock America. The Invisible Empire never garnered the mass support that it did in many other parts of the nation, but it was still sufficiently important to become a local issue in parts of Connecticut and a state-wide one in Maine. In Vermont, Klansmen raided a Roman Catholic church. In Rhode Island part of the klannish National Guard had to be disarmed, and in Massachusetts the Invisible Empire might well have had use for such arms, as Klan meetings touched off a string of hostile riots during the spring and summer months of 1924 and 1925.

2

When flaming crosses on the Connecticut hillsides first announced the Klan's presence in the state, most people refused to take it seriously. Governor Everett Lake called its midnight initiations "comic operas," whose initiators were "sharp artists" out to collect "a little easy money from some foolish people," and most mayors refused the Klan parade permits. Nevertheless, the Klan became a factor to consider in the Nutmeg State. By the summer of 1925, it had an estimated eighteen thousand members.

The Invisible Empire was most active in New Haven, New Britain, and Stamford. Its largest congregation was in New Haven, where Italian-Americans, Jews, and Irishmen occasionally rubbed shoulders with aristocratic young men from Yale. The way to handle the Klan came up in the conversation, one day, of two professors. One of them, Wilbur Cross, the dean of the Yale Graduate School, who would later be a three-term governor of the state, remembered years afterwards how the discussion had gone. His companion had jestingly suggested a campaign platform on which they could both run for office. What is to be our attitude toward the Ku Klux Klan? the future governor asked. Don't worry about the Ku Kluxers, his colleague told Cross. "You can go ahead and rip them up the back. I will say nothing for or against them publicly. All I have to do is to tell their leaders privately that they have nothing to fear from Cross if he is elected. They will understand. They will line up for you."

In the hardware city of New Britain, with its large Italian and Ukrainian population, the Klan opposed Mayor Paomessa, and there was a near mutiny on the police force when word spread that one of the members was a Klansman. In neighboring Berlin the Klan hopefully announced that a wrecking crew was being formed to jail politicians, preferably Jews and Catholics, who flouted the Klan's influence.

Nineteen twenty-four was a big year for the Klan around Stamford and in Connecticut politics generally, as the hooded knights held large meetings on the old Havemeyer estate and on Webbs Hill in North Stamford. With Grand Dragon Harry Lutterman of Darien directing local arrangements, Klansmen by the thousands turned out for the North Stamford meet. Traffic backed up on the roads and local constables co-operated with Klan guards to handle the jam. The town buzzed with rumors and there were reports of boycotts against local merchants. The Republican state convention turned down an anti-Klan plank, but the Democrats were delighted to run against the Klan, which they described as "the most un-American thing in America." All of the candidates on the local Democratic ticket signed a political advertisement in the Stamford *Advocate* attacking the Klan, while their Republican opponents kept an uncomfortable silence. The Klan's answer didn't help things any. The reaction in town to the Klan's emphasis on the "foreign" names on the Democratic ticket was so unfavorable that the hooded knights belatedly claimed that the Democrats themselves had been responsible for the ad. Hardly had this quieted down when the Grand Dragon was unsuccessfully suing the Stamford *Sentinel* for the theft of Klan documents, and this was followed by the revelation that the local Lincoln Republican Club was in reality a front for the Invisible Empire.

Dissidents in the club had made this news public, and the Klan's major troubles came, as always, from within. In the summer of 1924, the national Klan stopped sending out financial reports to its chapters, and protests, at least from the New Haven chapter, brought no satisfactory reply. In January of 1926, the mother Klavern of Connecticut decided to disband. Its leader, Arthur Mann, publicly denounced the national Klan for its corrupt pursuit of the almighty dollar. Things had been different under Colonel Simmons, Mann claimed, but with Evans autocratically at the helm, the money had poured out, the wrong kind of recruits had been dumped in, and an unpopular official from Michigan had been forced on them. The Klan, the departing Klansmen announced, was not only anti-Jew and anti-Catholic, it was anti-American and anti-Protestant as well.

The desertion of the faithless Klansmen of the New Haven Klavern was a blow to the Klan whose fortunes were on the decline in Connecticut. However, Klansmen still turned out in large numbers for events like the Klan field days in Greenwich or speeches in Bridgeport and Sterling by Imperial Wizard Evans and Senator Heflin. Into the early thirties the Klan continued to meet in the fields, chapels, and banquet rooms of the Nutmeg State. New chapters such as the Elihu Burritt Klan of New Britain were still to be born and staunch oaks like the Israel Putnam Klan of Stamford offered leadership to other Klaverns functioning in Groton, New London, Caanan, Norwalk, and Danbury, but by the end of the twenties, Klandom in Connecticut was going no way but down.

3

The Rhode Island Klan probably never held more than twelve to fifteen thousand members. The usual crosses were burned and the imperial orators stressed the accustomed values of home and Church, the Bible, Constitution, school, and flag, and successful rallies drew thousands of members to the fairgrounds at Foster Center and Greenville.

The Klan was apparently not very active in Rhode Island politics. In the presidential year of 1924, Rhode Island Democrats whooped it up for Al Smith in Madison Square Garden while the state Republicans specifically denounced the hooded order. In denying the Klan the use of Providence's Benefit Street Armory for further "religious" meetings, Governor William Flynn flayed the Invisible Empire as "vicious" and out of place in a state founded by a seeker after religious liberty. The Klan apparently found no incongruity, for its major Klavern proudly bore the name of Roger Williams.

After 1925, Klan strength declined below the thousand mark. By 1928 it was composed of nine hundred Klansmen, plus a few women's auxiliary units, divided among Klaverns in Providence, the south counties, and Newport. However, the Klan's greatest local fame was still ahead. On St. Patrick's Day in 1928, the Providence *Journal* broke the story that the Klan had taken over three companies of the state militia. The historic 1st Light Infantry, a privately re-cruited but officially chartered portion of the militia, had fallen upon bad times. The ranks were depleted and disbandment was being con-sidered. Then, suddenly, Companies E, F, and H turned out smartly for drill in the Cranston Street Armory, over two hundred strong. Not only did they shoulder new Springfield rifles, but their armament included a shiny new machine gun. The other militiamen, envious but puzzled over the privately acquired armaments, watched the new units make uniformed appearances at local churches. When the Ku Klux Klan turned up, handling the arrangements at a military dance, they felt they knew the answer.

Investigations by the adjutant general and the legislature revealed most of the story. The Klan, like the chartered militia companies, had been in need of members. Why not use one to fill the other. The Klan's militant Klavaliers, who had tired of drilling with spears at their West Friendship Street headquarters, joined the Light Infantry. All new recruits for the militia were thenceforth required to join the Klan first at fifteen dollars per man. The rifles and the machine gun were paid for by private subscription from patriotic and usually un-suspecting donors. With the United States, as the Klan saw it, in the midst of its continuing "Roman crisis" and a religious war impending, the 1st Light Infantry would be but the first step toward control of the nation's militia and armories.

However, with the plan revealed and the authorities acting with unpatriotic haste, the Klan was struck yet another blow. As always seemed to happen, a disaffected Klansman was ready to step forward and testify. Klansmen had been told, he related, that both President Coolidge and Alabama's Senator Heflin were members, although he personally did not believe the report on the former. The Rhode Is-land Klan, he continued, had devoted its efforts to such tasks as in-vestigating the marital problems of one of its own officers as well as the case of a minister unfrocked by the Methodists. When he identi-fied two state senators as Klansmen, they both denied it, despite the fact that during the Klan's 1927 crusade against interracial marriage, one of them had sponsored the bill in the legislature.

Tall, affable J. W. Perry, the Grand Dragon of Rhode Island and Connecticut, failed to clear up any of these points when he testified before the legislative committee, but he was cleared of perjury charges at his trial the next winter. No crime had been committed in the attempted Klanization of the 1st Light Infantry, but the state had the Klansmen give up their arms and the militia was watched more carefully. By 1930, Klan membership was below one hundred.

4

The men of the Bay State have always taken their politics and history more strongly than most, and so the story of the Ku Klux Klan in Massachusetts was more traumatic than that in Connecticut. And it was more violent, even though there was no attempt to bring the National Guard into it all. Massachusetts generally tried to give an appearance of unfriendliness toward the Klan. Mayors and district attorneys denounced it. So did the grand master of the Masons, and it was denied the use of Springfield's High School of Commerce.

However, things were more hospitable in Worcester, which soon became the center of Klan activity in the state. Although there was protest when the news leaked out, permission was given for the use of the Shrine building and a visiting national officer was invited to address the Exchange Club. What with the spread of alienism, bolshevism, and Catholicism in Massachusetts, there was much for the Klan to do. It took the noted New England author, Lothrop Stoddard, to put everything in the proper perspective and the Klan quoted approvingly his warning that "the white race will be absorbed and fused with those of darker color, unless precautionary measures are taken." These fears he had confided in his book, *The Rising Tide of Color,* which was popular among those who fearfully visualized racial mongrelization. The staunchest defenders of the white race, his fellow racial theorist Madison Grant had helped him realize, were the Nordics. Their purity and leadership had, in turn, to be protected against the kind of dilution that was brought by the wave of immigration from southern and eastern Europe. The Klan looked like his kind of organization to Lothrop Stoddard, and he became the Exalted Cyclops of Provisional Klan No. 1 of Massachusetts. At least this is what *Hearst's Magazine* claimed, despite Stoddard's denials, with supporting evidence.

Given the nature of the Klan, there were always members who felt that the best way to purify America was through direct action, or at least the threat of it. Warnings, specific and general, were sent out in Lynn, Woonsocket, and Fall River, where the mayor was told that he had better clean up the local dance halls, and Lawrence.

The shrewd Svengali of Boston politics, Mayor James Michael Curley, saw the signs of the times, and arranged to receive similar threats against the lives of his children. If there was political hay to be made, Curley was going to make it, and the next year when he ran for governor, he made the Klan one of his chief issues. And it was a live one in the Bay State. In 1923 the Massachusetts House passed a resolution saying that the Klan was dangerous to American rights. When the state conventions met the following year, the Klan was important enough for the Democrats to condemn it by name in their platform and for the Republicans, while deploring prejudice, to avoid doing so. When the Republican National Committee arranged to have Ralph Brewster—the Klan-supported governor of Maine—campaign in Massachusetts, local Republicans objected and got the plans canceled.

Within the city of Boston the Invisible Empire could hardly have expected a friendly reception from Mayor Curley. He warned the Klan that it could not meet in his city, even on private property, and he was true to his word. His method was quite simple. Whenever the Klan sought to meet, they found that an intensive inspection by police, building, and fire inspectors was just in the process of discovering violations. When any were found the police would order the whole building vacated, even though on one occasion it also meant evicting the Knights of Columbus. As a result, no one dared rent space to the Klan.

Critics, such as the *Nation* and the American Civil Liberties Union, were not happy over the use of such tactics against the Klan, and they saw their fears confirmed when Mayor Curley proceeded to treat the birth-control crusader, Margaret Sanger, in the same way. When the ACLU attacked the bans on Klan and birth-control meetings and sought to repeal the mayor's power to decide who had the right to speak on the Boston Common, Mayor Curley derided the ACLU leaders as "parlor bolshevists and soda-water revolutionists."

Where the mayor used the law against the Klan in Boston, there were others who were less concerned with the legal niceties. During the summer and fall of 1924 and the spring and summer of 1925, Klansmen and anti-Klansmen clashed in a series of bloody battles in eastern and middle counties of the state. Most of the riots took place in Worcester County, "the heart of the commonwealth," but Norfolk, Middlesex, and Essex also got their share. In most cases the pattern was the same. Anywhere from several hundred to ten thousand Klansmen would assemble for a meeting, often with visiting kluxers coming in from other states. Local crowds would gather on the edge of the Klan field or guarded perimeter, milling about, straining to catch a glimpse of what was going on within the hooded circle, muttering derisive and hostile comments and threats. Then, when a burning cross flamed against the dark sky to mark the end of the meeting, the crowd would surge forward. Amid a shower of stones, sticks, and often bullets, a general melee would ensue.

On one July night more than fifty people were injured during battles in Spencer and Lancaster, and in the latter town two hundred Klansmen were besieged for nine hours before the police were able to lead them away from the jeering crowd. The next night saw three men in the hospital with buckshot wounds and twenty-one in jail after a Klan initiation in Groveland led to a similar brawl. Two days later, with all police leaves canceled and state troopers disarming Klansman and townsman alike, a number of Shrewsbury rioters ended up in jail. To further fuel the growing passions, a newspaper reporter turned up claiming the Klan had branded him on the arm and forehead. Even when ten thousand Klansmen rallied in the multinational college and mill town of Worcester, their numbers did not prevent trouble. On the first day a plane rented by the Klan was brought down by a rifleshot, and early the next morning gangs of local boys and young men stoned cars and beat up Klansmen leaving at the end of the meeting.

When spring again warmed the spirits of the Massachusetts men and made outdoor meetings possible, the Bay Staters picked up where they had left off. Toward the end of April, one hundred and fifty Klansmen were besieged on a field in Northbridge, by rock-throwing adversaries who also roughed up one of the policemen who tried to restore order. Three weeks later it was the Klansmen's turn as they beat up two antis and turned over several cars, after another Northbridge meeting. In the little agricultural town of Berlin, Klansmen and anti-Klan exchanged fusillades of stones, and in Gardner, home of the Boston rocker, three hooded horsemen who led a Klan parade were stoned by gangs and then arrested by the police for not having a permit. In Burlington, where the walls of the old meeting house had been shaken by the firing of artillery during the siege of Boston, a Klan rally was punctuated by the now usual riot. A score of men were hurt in a riot near Westwood as rock-throwing hostiles besieged Klansmen in an old farmhouse.

When Klansmen from Sudsbury, Wellesley, Newton, and other Middlesex and Worcester towns gathered with their brethren from Framingham on the old muster ground of the state militia, they were prepared for trouble. As the usual anti-Klan forces gathered, five men were cut down from ambush by a blast of buckshot. While an angry mob milled about outside the Framingham police station, the some seventy-nine arrested Klansmen surrendered a private arsenal of clubs, rifles, pistols, and shotguns. Upon being questioned about the steel helmet which he was wearing under his peaked hood, one Klansman explained that he had been at Klan meetings before.

Nothing daunted, the next night they were at it again on a field two miles from the center of Reading. With the violence growing and the participants turning from their primitive missiles to the more civilized use of firearms, many people were coming to view the situation with growing alarm. The president of the Law and Order League of Massachusetts asked Governor Alvan Fuller to prevent the growing incitement to violence by prohibiting all Klan meetings. The plea was pigeonholed and in mid-September, Klan and anti-Klansmen rounded out the 1925 season with a battle in the streets of North Brookfield.

Klansmen turned out in respectable numbers during the perilous spring and summer of 1925, despite what the Klan's *National Kourier* described as a "foreign mob" brutally attacking "Americans." However, the prospect of being beaten, stoned, or perhaps even shot, did not fan the ardor of Massachusetts Klansmen, who seemed on the whole more pacific than their antagonists. The fact that the Klan was continually coming off second best, plus the disappointment of its hopes for power, including the failure of its candidate in the Boston municipal elections, drained off enthusiasm and members. When President Coolidge's close friend, Senator William Butler, was defeated, the support of the Klan and the Anti-Saloon League was reckoned to have been more of a handicap than an aid.

Both the violence and Klan ambitions had been toned down after 1925, and the Klan found that at least in and around Springfield it could meet in peace. Thousands of Klansmen showed up for a four-day Klonklave in suburban Agawam in September of 1926, and the following June, Klansmen from all over New England gathered in the metropolis of western Massachusetts to hear the Roman Catholic Church denounced. When the assembled Klansmen were asked to show who was willing to fight against Al Smith and Massachusetts' newly elected Senator David Walsh, thousands of hands were raised skyward. In the eastern part of the state, anti-Americanism was still rampant, for when Senator Heflin arrived in Brockton the next year to tell the truth about Mussolini, the Pope, the Knights of Columbus, Roman Catholics, and immigrants in general, hostile crowds outside of Vasa Hall greeted him with jeers and catcalls. Mud and stones were thrown at his auto, and at a second meeting a bottle struck one of his police guards, an un-American gesture that Heflin discussed at length in the Senate when he got back to Washington.

5

While fiery crosses blazed on the hillsides of Connecticut and central Massachusetts, a tall, lanky, former Salvation Army bandsman named Eugene Farnsworth was beating the drums for the Invisible Empire in the traditionally Republican states of Vermont, New Hampshire, and Maine. In the shadows of the Green and the White mountains the Klan mixed practical lodge work with opposition to the Catholic tide from French Canada and that old enemy of New England, demon rum. Though the Klan prospered best in Vermont's northern regions, it was not important in the life of the state despite impressive rallies in Morrisville and Montpelier in the mid-twenties. And the Klan could have very well done without its biggest piece of publicity for this came when one of its organizers was arrested for robbing St. Mary's Cathedral in Burlington. In New Hampshire the Klan was strongest in the eastern slope industrial town of Rochester, on the Maine border. There, Farnsworth's successor the Hoosier Klansman Dr. E. W. Gayer established his tristate headquarters and tried his hand in local politics.

The most prosperous portion of Dr. Gayer's inheritance was the imperial satrapy of Maine. In that rural, Protestant, church-going state, with a tradition of high tariff, dry Republicanism, the hooded knights found what they lacked elsewhere in New England: a chivalrous knight-errant behind whom they could rally. Ralph Owen Brewster probably never joined the Klan, but he and the Invisible Empire formed an alliance by which he lent his rising political prestige in return for its votes. The issue that seems to have brought them together was the question of state aid to parochial schools, although the two most probably would have met anyway. Within the safe walls of the Republican party the Maine farmer had been by tradition a nonconformist, a "constitutional kicker," Frederic Collins described him for *Collier's,* and the Klan was often of the same frame of mind. There was no real race problem down east, but over the years French Canadians and Irishmen had been moving into mill towns like Lewiston and Biddeford. It was not bad enough that they voted Democratic, but most of them were Roman Catholic as well.

The controversy over the schools had begun several years before, when the bishop of Portland asked the legislature to permit Maine towns to use part of their funds to aid parochial schools. There hadn't been much support for the idea, but it presented something good to oppose. Brewster, a Maine-born, Mayflower-descended, and Harvard-trained, war-hero lawyer, enthusiastically took his stand. His proposed constitutional amendment to prohibit public funds for parochial schools narrowly missed out in the legislature but the Klan took careful note.

The first Maine unit of the Klan was in Bangor, but its largest Klavern and its home and its heart came to reside in Portland, where Eugene Farnsworth set up headquarters in a $60,000 estate out on Forest Avenue. The Klan emerged in the public eye and the political arena when it threw its support on the side of municipal reform in Portland and helped—though some said hindered—the adoption of a city-manager form of government. Being on the winning side meant not only permission to demonstrate against the Knights of Columbus on Columbus Day, and a membership which grew to an estimated 2700 in Portland, but also enlarged prestige throughout the state. In the spring elections of 1923, Klan-endorsed tickets, headed by "one-hundred-per-cent Americans" broke the traditional Democratic hold on the towns of Sacco and Rockland. In many parts of Maine, townsmen who had always skeptically opposed the increased levies requested by the school boards, eagerly laid out the money to protect the little red schoolhouses of America through joining the Klan.

Although Klan strength probably never reached much beyond the fifteen-thousand mark, this meant, with the votes of the Klansmen's wives included, control of more than one out of every ten votes likely to be cast. The very secrecy of the Klan made its possible power seem even greater, and concentrated as it was within the dominant Republican party, it meant that the Invisible Empire might well hold the power to pick the eventually successful candidates.

This is what happened in 1924. The president of the state Senate, Frank Farrington, had fought the Brewster school amendment on the grounds that many private academies served as the local high schools in their communities. Those Republicans, who opposed Brewster's rising, pushy star, rallied behind Farrington and many Democrats invaded the Republican primary to vote for him. After a bitter campaign and a recounted vote, Brewster emerged as the party's candidate. To run against him, the hopeful Democrats picked William Pattangall, also a Mayflower Maine Yankee, a Protestant, Mason, and former attorney general of the state, who had been their candidate two years before. Pattangall had led the anti-Klan forces in the wild fight in Madison Square Garden. His issue was the Klan and he intended to push it for all it was worth against what he hoped would be a badly divided Republican party. If anything could carry a Democrat into the state house this ought to be it. During the primary, Brewster denied both membership in the Klan and seeking its support, but further than this he did not go. Although he was not charged with being a Klansman himself, the Democrats did not let the state forget that the Grand Dragon Farnsworth, who had sold Klandom to the Pine Tree State, had campaigned for Brewster in the primary and openly boasted that he would pick the next governor.

With Maine's election scheduled two months earlier than the rest of the country, what went on there drew national attention and the Republican party was somewhat concerned. Leading anti-Klan Democrats came to speak for Pattangall, and the Republican vice-presidential candidate, Charles Dawes, made a speech in Augusta in which he praised the Klansman while rejecting the Klan way of solving things.

Many Republicans, including the outgoing Governor P. P. Baxter, opposed the Klan, and the state's top Negro leader, William Lewis, turned to the Democrats, but Brewster did not seem seriously endangered. Nevertheless he issued a last-minute statement unfavorable to the Klan. On Election Day, the Republican voters, many holding their noses as the state Republican chairman privately put it, gave Brewster the usual comfortable margin.

Although Brewster had been nominated by the Klan, he had been elected by the people of the Pine Tree State—however reluctantly— and apart from occasional charges of favoritism to his Klan friends, the Klan issue did not dog his first administration. For many Maine citizens, the very maverick nature of Governor Brewster's political life constituted the attraction. An early supporter of woman suffrage and always a big favorite with the Prohibition and Church vote, he appeared to many as a reform leader who was being opposed by the machines, bosses, and aristocratic elements within the party. His support of commission government in Portland, utility regulation, and his fight against aid to parochial schools solidified that impression. His connection with the Klan did not weaken his position.

By 1926, William Pattangall who had fought him on the Klan issue two years before had accepted appointment to the state Supreme Court, and Brewster himself was easily re-elected in a relatively quiet campaign. It was in the race for the U. S. Senator that the noise came, and it was considerable. The Republican nominee was Arthur Gould, a self-made millionaire from the potato belt of Aroostook, who had worked his way up from a farm laborer to a railroad magnate. On the face of things, Arthur Gould appeared not to be a surprising or unsuitable Republican candidate, but there were a number of disqualifying aspects to his victory. In the first place he had won nomination over the new state Senate president whom the Klan supported. In the second, his wife was a Roman Catholic, and finally, he was from the wrong part of the state. According to Maine tradition, the state's two senators should not come from the same area. With the incumbent Senator Frederick Hale representing Portland, Brewster had moved his residence upstate in order to improve his position when he ran for the U. S. Senate in 1928. Now with an Aroostook man unexpectedly on his way to Washington, Brewster's calculations were upset. The big population centers down east would certainly not hold still for two north country senators.

In the last days before the special election, a prominent Klan minister from the little residential town of Randolph, accused Gould's supporters of having spent too much money during the primary and Governor Brewster announced that he could not in good conscience support a man so morally if not legally tarnished. The Democratic candidate, or so Gould's lawyer claimed, had met with Klan leaders in Pittsfield only a few days before and promised them that if he were elected he would support Klan principles and Brewster for senator in 1928. What was more, the lawyer continued, the whole case had been cooked up at a special conference in Washington between Brewster, the new Grand Dragon for Maine, DeForest Perkins, and Imperial Wizard Hiram Evans. This, Governor Brewster denied. True, he had been in Washington for an executive committee session of the Governors' Council, but Grand Dragon Perkins' courtesy call had lasted no more than ten minutes and Brewster had of course received him courteously as he would any citizen of his state. Only this and nothing more.

The excessive expenditures charged against Gould were dismissed, and Maine's Republican leader denounced "the unholy alliance" of the Democratic party, the Klan, and the Republican governor.

In the election Gould won handsomely, supported not only by the leaders and rank and file of his own party but by many anti-Klan Democrats as well. He carried every town in the state, including such normally Democratic centers as Lewiston, Biddeford, and Rockland, as well as the reputed Klan stronghold of Randolph. Even the Klan strength in the rural districts seemed not to have been deliverable to the Democratic candidate.

After the Gould fiasco, Klan strength reportedly fell off rapidly in the legislature, in Portland, and in the state at large. Probably partially due to this receding wave, Brewster suffered his first major setback when he went ahead with his plans to try for the Senate in 1928. Amid charges of Klandom and corruption from former Governor Baxter, Brewster was turned back in the primary. The next year, Portland denied the Klan use of city hall for an address by Tom Heflin the peripatetic anti-Catholic senator from Alabama. The Klan, in Maine, no longer counted, and Ralph Owen Brewster's rise upward would have to proceed in the future without its help.

38

THE KLAN INTERNATIONAL

During the days of his early success, E. Y. Clarke, the Klan's chief salesman, dreamed of extending the Klan's dominion to include all Anglo-Saxon, Germanic, and Scandinavian portions of the globe. It was only a passing fantasy, however, for the Klan had enough fat to fry at home to keep it busy. Apart from the establishment of branches in Alaska and the Canal Zone, the Klan did little foreign business. This did not keep others from trying their hand, however. During the 1920s, stories filtered in from time to time reporting the establishment of Klan chapters in Hawaii, New Zealand, Shanghai, Lithuania, Czechoslovakia, England, Cuba, and Mexico. There is no way to judge the truth of these reports, but it does not matter much, for there is no indication that any such chapters operated actively or long endured.

Only in Germany were there any reports of headway. Several naturalized Americans returned to the fatherland in 1925 and organized *Der Deutsche Orden des Feurigen Kreuzes* in Berlin composed of some three hundred merchants, mechanics, clerks, and laborers. In true Klan style, internal conflict soon broke out. The original organizers were expelled and the whole affair ended up in the newspapers. The German press poked fun at the Klan and no one seemed inclined to be alarmed. The Vienna *Neue Freie Presse* commented that Germany was "full of such groups of ill-balanced and romantic youths," with their secret meetings, their stores of arms, and their military posturings. They were "silly rather than dangerous," it felt.

Only in the fair Dominion of Canada to the north did the call of the Klan evoke a substantial answering response. Naturalized ex-Canadians in Oregon and Washington joined the Riders of the Red Robe which the Klan had created for foreign-born, but otherwise eligible, right-thinking people. North of the border there were continuous rumors of hooded expansion, and when a series of incendiary fires ravaged Roman Catholic churches, including the historic old Quebec Cathedral, the Klan was blamed. However, not until 1926 was a church bombing, that of St. Mary's in Barrie, Ontario, successfully pinned on the Invisible Empire.

Hiram Evans disclaimed any connection with the Canadian Klan, which had established its headquarters in Toronto. Even so, to make certain that their business venture utilized the latest techniques, Canadians recruited their top salesmen from the United States. The great battlefield turned out not to be the environs of the Imperial Palace in Toronto but on the western prairies of Saskatchewan. With the former South Bend Cyclops, jolly Pat Emmons, who had caused Hiram Evans so much trouble, lending an experienced hand, the imported Kleagles and their Canadian employers made a killing.

Until the mid-twenties the Anglo-Saxon farmers of Saskatchewan had contentedly occupied themselves with raising wheat and voting for the Liberal party. Then, a change in the kind of immigrant coming into the province began to cause considerable alarm. The newcomers were from southern and eastern Europe, mainly Poles, Ukrainians, and Russians. The Conservatives opposed the Roman Catholic textbooks and the special school privileges permitted the new arrivals, as well as the general principle of unrestricted immigration. They lashed out at the Liberals for permitting the English language and character of the province to be endangered by this wave of "non-preferred Continentals."

Under these conditions, the Klan's anti-Catholicism had considerable appeal. Starting from the railroad center of Moose Jaw, near the United States border, the flames spread rapidly, fanned by ministerial support. Within two years the Klan claimed more than forty thousand members out of a total provincial population of some three quarters of a million people. With this great a strength, local Klansmen could not understand why their chapter treasuries were always empty. Seeing the signs of the times, the Klan's salesmen made one final sweep through the province and decamped for other climes. When Pat Emmons was indicted for misappropriation of Klan funds, he returned voluntarily and won acquittal by showing that his contract, in effect, gave him the right to keep all the money he could get his hands on. The disappointed Knights of Saskatchewan picked their own leader and resolved henceforth to operate independent of any other group, but the Invisible Empire was already on the decline.

39

MARCHING ON WASHINGTON

It is difficult to say when the Klan reached the peak of its power. By
the time of its election successes of 1924, it was already on a greased
slide downward in the Southwestern states of Texas, Oklahoma, and
Arkansas which had been its first bastions of power. Its Louisiana
realm was a shambles, California was long since past its early exuber-
ant pinnacle, and Oregon was already out of its grasp. Klan power
in Georgia had leveled off and the citizens of Atlanta were not completely unhappy to see the imperial potentates fold their robes and
ship their valises off to Washington. In Kansas, William Allen White
and the state charter board were cramping the Klan's regal style.
While there was much power and many members still to be reaped
in the Midwest and elsewhere within the Empire, the great spectacular spurts of growth that marked its progress in Illinois, Indiana, and
Ohio, were over. The Hoosier realm was divided in uneasy balance
between the Stephenson and Evans forces, and internal disruption
was gnawing away at many state realms and local chapters.

The Klan had never seriously considered creating its own political
party, and in the light of the history of third parties in America this
was not an unwise decision. Despite temporary liaisons with the Republicans in Texas, Oklahoma, and Georgia during the 1924 elections, the Southern Klans were mainly composed of Democrats. Apart
from occasional maneuvers in Oregon, Iowa, Ohio, and Maine, the
Invisible Empire was Republican in the North and West.

The Northern Klansmen were unhappy enough already over
Southern rule and were hardly inclined to abandon their traditional
political allegiance for the opposing faith or for a new untried venture. Most Southern Klansmen were no more willing. The Klan did
facilitate some interparty movement, particularly from the Democratic to the Republican ranks among the Oklahoma and southern
Indiana Baptists, and the Invisible Empire usually had strength in

both camps. For the most part, however, the organization had enough trouble trying to unite its cohorts behind a fellow wearer of the robe, and it could not be counted on to deliver its vote, when it meant crossing party lines. Throughout its history, the Klan tended to muster its greatest strength in voting against people rather than for them.

Given the nature and rigidities of the Klan, what were its political possibilities and future? Ambitious politicians joined it. Others compromised with the Klan in order to survive in areas where it was strong. It commanded and secured congressional as well as strictly local patronage. The Klan became tangled in the presidential hopes of William G. McAdoo as well as in the plans of Indiana Senators Ralston and Watson. D. C. Stephenson dreamed of using the Klan as a means to ride a Republic elevator to the presidency. The Klan mystery man, Gutzon Borglum, had a vision of the Klan as the instrument of a pro-farmer, anti-tariff, Anglo-Saxon progressivism expressing the "minds of the villagers and agrarians" without foreign ideologies and in opposition to the alienism of New York and the eastern cities. However, though his ideas interested Stephenson, whose Republicanism could not allow him to consider a lower tariff, Borglum did not represent the Klan's mind and heart.

Since the Klan talked so urgently about its own vital effort in defending an endangered nation, the future of the Klan itself depended at least in part on its ability to achieve something nationally. Its role was that of a pressure and veto group. In general terms, there were three facets of the Invisible Empire apart from its unofficial function as a money-making machine for its owners. The Klan operated as a fraternal order, as a local vigilante organization, and as a resistance movement. The third role was that of defending the values of one-hundred-per-cent Americanism and was intertwined with the other two. Consciousness of oneself as a native-born, white, Protestant American was not only the major bond of cohesion, it was a call to action. The reality of the un-American menace and the success of the Klan's leadership were vital questions which inevitably drew the Klan into the national political arena and demanded performance. To fail of accomplishment would doom the Invisible Empire more to invisibility than imperium.

Although the Klan enjoyed the telling of horror stories about how Woodrow Wilson's evil secretary, Joseph Tumulty, filled the government with Roman Catholics, Harding and Coolidge stirred few such fears. Nor was the Congress itself dangerous or imperiled. The Klan's own congressional roundup for 1923 listed:

HOUSE OF REPRESENTATIVES

Republicans: 215 Protestants (180 of them Masons)
7 Roman Catholics
2 Jews
1 Mormon
1 Unknown

Democrats: 168 Protestants (120 of them Masons)
30 Roman Catholics
5 Jews

SENATE

Republicans: 48 Protestants (29 of them Masons)
1 Mormon

Democrats: 39 Protestants (31 of them Masons)
5 Roman Catholics
1 Mormon

In total, hardly a menace and more than likely a friend. Although President Coolidge was to speak out unnecessarily strongly to the American Legion in favor of toleration, diversity, and opposition to race prejudice, he had given Dunning the Savannah appointment and picked a judge in Oregon who favored the compulsory public school bill.

The Klan's leaders were jubilant over their successes in the 1924 elections. The Imperial Wizard boarded his private railway car and made a triumphant tour of his western dominions, while Southern Klansmen gathered in Atlanta for a big Thanksgiving Day parade and a dedication ceremony on top of Stone Mountain. At the beginning of the new year, Klan potentates, joined by Senator Mayfield and Tennessee's Senator Kenneth McKeller gathered in Dyersburg, to celebrate the marriage of Klan lobbyist W. F. Zumbrunn to a Tennessee girl.

In February of 1925, the Imperial Wizard hailed the elections and the passage of the new immigration-restriction law as the Klan's most recent and important triumphs. No one represented more clearly the dominant American attitude on immigration than did the Klan. As the historian Oscar Handlin has summed it up, the philosophy that underlaid the laws of 1917–24 was that "the national origin of an immigrant was a reliable indication of his capacity for Americanization." The Klan simply made the dividing line absolute. Those who did not stem from the white, Protestant, Nordic stock were not just inferior in their capacity for Americanization, they lacked the capacity. The Klan praised Albert Johnson, the energetic Washington congressman who spearheaded the drive for the restrictive law, and it pushed a letter-writing campaign in support of the bill. Pleased as it was with the "anti-polyglot-ism" of the new Johnson Act, the Klan felt that its major weakness was the absence of a program of deportation, a feeling in which Congressman Johnson concurred. "Every signer of the Declaration of Independence was white," the Klan's *National Kourier* proclaimed, and patriotism meant keeping things that way.

Elsewhere in the field of foreign relations, the Klan felt a growing disenchantment with Mussolini and a feeling of protective warmth for the new Calles government in Mexico. Naturally, the machinations of the Pope lay at the bottom of both attitudes. Mussolini stood high in the eyes of Klan orators until he patched up Church-State relations in Italy. From that point on, the Klan's basic suspicion of all things Italian added him and the renegotiation of Italian war debts to its blacklist. On the other hand, the Invisible Empire saw in the anti-Catholicism of Mexico's new President Calles, a blow for the kind of religious liberty that it appreciated. When American Catholics became upset over the developing campaign against clerical control of education in the volatile sister Republic to the south, Klan leaders praised the Mexican Government and rhetorically offered to protect Mexico from subversion or attack. The chief plum that the Klan expected as reward for its contribution to Coolidge's election was the ambassadorship to Mexico. Klan lobbyist Zumbrunn, who hoped to be appointed, was beside himself with rage when the President disappointed him.

The Klan's other major legislative concerns were the creation of a National Department of Education and blocking American membership in the World Court. Friendly legislators in states, such as Washington, Oregon, and Michigan, introduced bills making priestless public schooling compulsory. Local Klans kept vigilant watch on their schools and sought control of the boards. For half a decade in Washington, the Klan pressed for passage of the Towner-Sterling bill which would lead to a federal strengthening and control of the entire school system. What the Klan sought, with some aid from the National Education Administration and the Southern Scottish Rite Masons, was a Cabinet-level department which would spend liberally to advance teacher training and salaries, educate aliens and illiterates, and promote physical education—in short, federal aid to education. President Coolidge and other States' rights advocates feared the centralizing tendencies of such a law, and the Klan's enthusiastic advocacy badly hurt its chances of passage. Its opponents rallied against it and managed to sidetrack the bill.

The Klan's chieftains were also concerned about the possibility that the United States would join the Permanent Court for International Justice. For those who lamented the nation's failure to become a member of the League of Nations, the World Court seemed to be the next-best step. Most Americans probably mildly favored the step. Not so the Ku Klux Klan. Its leaders saw the World Court as a "back door" means of involvement in the League, as well as a place where America's interests would be placed in the hands of foreigners. They conjured up pictures of the World Court overruling immigration restriction in order to pour papist aliens into the country. It was all a clever plot to embroil the United States in the Old World's troubles.

As the fight reached its Senate climax in the spring of 1926, the Klan put forth what was probably its greatest national veto effort. Evans himself took charge of the campaign. While the now-depleted ranks of the faithful were urged to flood Washington with letters, Evans and his officials openly pressed senators for their votes. By this time, the Klan's political power had been so diluted by scandal and internal dissension that it no longer commanded the fear and respect that it once had. Arkansas' Senator Joseph Robinson, who had been accustomed to keep judiciously quiet, bitterly assailed Missouri's Senator Jim Reed for marching side by side with the Klan, and Kentucky's Senator Richard Ernst resisted the personal entreaties of the Imperial Wizard. Claiming that he spoke in the name of a quarter of a million Protestant men and women of the Buckeye State, the Grand Dragon of Ohio demanded that Senators Simeon Fess and Frank Willis reject the court. However, even though the Klan had aided their election, both declined. So too did Colorado's two Klan-elected senators, both up for re-election later in the year. On the vote which accepted the World Court the Invisible Empire was probably responsible only for the negative ballots of the four senators from Indiana and Oklahoma. When President Coolidge later undercut the ratification which he himself had urged, it was not because of the Klan.

Once the congressmen and Klan lobbyists had ceased their labors for the summer, the Imperial Knights of the Ku Klux Klan found yet a different use for the nation's capital. To raise their flagging spirits and membership, the legions of the Klan massed on the parade grounds of Washington and trod the avenues of presidents and heroes in solemn processional. The Klan announced that it would request the President to review its 1925 parade. Since he had once addressed the Catholic Holy Name Society, he owed them at least that; after all, hadn't they been responsible for his election in the first place? Wherever possible, President Coolidge handled demands from Klan and anti-Klansmen with an equanimous silence. The White House announced that the President would be at the summer White House in Swampscott, Massachusetts, during the month of August, and it later turned out that no one at Klan headquarters had actually remembered to send him an invitation. To the demands that he denounce the parade, however, he made no comment.

The District of Columbia commissioners refused to prevent the parade, giving the Klansmen permission to march if they did so unmasked. The only notice taken by the federal government was the special-detail of blue-jacketed, white-trousered marines, who in unspoken tribute to the leaders of the Klan, guarded the Treasury Department. Downtown Washington buildings wore no flags or ornaments of welcome.

By Friday night, the seventh of August, endless caravans of dusty cars were pouring into the city, and the first count of charter trains included fifteen from Pennsylvania, two from Cleveland and Akron, Ohio, five from New Jersey, and others from Long Island, Buffalo, Erie, Columbus, Toledo, Pittsburgh, and Jacksonville, Florida. The streets of Washington were alive with crawling, swarming vehicles, flying the American flag, or carrying signs, painted or chalked on their sides. Klan Headquarters was hastily moved to the New Willard Hotel while the rank and file found shelter where they could. White-sheeted Klansmen met the trains at Union Station to pass out information. Hotels and boarding houses were filled. Klansmen settled down for the night in large camps which were set up at Fifteenth and H streets, N.E., Bethesda, and on the side of the Baltimore Pike. Many Klansmen had come prepared for an outing, like the Elmira, New York, contingent which set up its headquarters tent at the "one-hundred-per-cent-American camp" in northeast Washington, and the Freeport, Long Island, contingent which had brought along four trucks loaded with food and cooking equipment. Others slept in their cars or under the trees.

From midafternoon until dusk on Saturday, a great avalanche

rumbled through the Washington streets, channeled by walls of spectators as some forty thousand uniformed Klansmen and -women paraded down Pennsylvania Avenue to Fifteenth Street, where they wheeled left to the grounds of the Washington Monument.

The Klan legions marched in close, well-drilled formations, sixteen to twenty abreast, with their arms folded across their chests. Most wore their regular white robes with their masks folded upon the hoods. Contrasted with them were the bright capes and uniforms of special drill teams, costumed American heroes, bands, banners, and occasional horsemen. Sometimes they marched silently, but usually the bands blared patriotic anthems or hymns such as "Onward Christian Soldiers" and *"Adeste Fideles."* Leading the parade were a masked horse and rider carrying the national emblem, then the male and female color guard, the police, and the potentates of the Invisible Empire. The Imperial Wizard, Hiram Evans, wearing a flowing royal-purple robe, trimmed in gold, and surrounded by the rich-colored garments of his Dragons, Klokards, and Kleagles, bowed continuously to. applause from the crowd. After him marched the small flag-carrying District of Columbia delegation, followed by a token representation from the Lone Star realm. Then, for more than an hour, the Pennsylvania Klansmen and -women passed in review. There were more than two thousand from Pittsburgh alone, followed by the Philadelphia contingents. A dozen brass bands, several fife-and-drum corps and two bagpipe contingents set the tempo. From time to time, the hooded Pennsylvanians sang "Maryland, My Maryland" and "Keep the Home Fires Burning," and waved banners proclaiming their devotion to the little red schoolhouse. Intersticed among the white-garbed marchers were the sky-blue capes and caps of the Altoona ladies and the olive-drab uniforms and helmets of the Montgomery County Klansmen.

Next came the New Jersey Klansmen with the large Mercer County contingent in the lead, file after file, representing all of the counties and most of the cities of the state. There followed a second prolonged wave of Keystone patriots, mainly from the eastern portion of the realm. Their garb was more varied than the others, with the women from Chester County wearing wide-brimmed white-canvas hats and the members of Philadelphia's Liberty Klan No. 1 dressed in military uniforms with steel helmets and policemen's sticks.

It took two hours for the Pennsylvania and New Jersey units to parade by, and then the New Yorkers swung onto the avenue, led by the red-caped and hatted knights of Chemung County. No banners identified their bearers as representatives of the great metropolis, but all the upstate counties were there, as well as practically every town and hamlet of Long Island. One Nassau banner called attention to Revelations, Chapter 7, wherein the Bible told of the white-robed of all nations standing before the throne of God.

From time to time the Klansmen raised their right arms, palms downward in a fascistlike salute, and whenever anyone on the sidelines did it, the marchers responded. Second in size only to the Pittsburgh columns were the one-hundred-per-cent Americans from Akron, Ohio, who offered the only massed glee club in the line of march. Niles and Daytona each sent large formations, and the Ohio legions helped those from Pennsylvania, New Jersey, and New York form the bulk of the procession. Virginia's Kluxettes carried two 75-by-40-foot flags, stretched across the avenue to collect donations, and Maryland also sent several hundred marchers. There were a few Klansmen from Florida, North Carolina, West Virginia, and Kentucky, but there was no sign of the expected hooded veterans from battle-scarred Massachusetts and war-torn Indiana.

As the Klansmen and -women finished, they sprawled wearily on the slopes of the Washington Monument awaiting the evening ceremonials on the stage of the outdoor Sylvan Theatre. The hot summer day, which had taken its toll among the marchers now threatened to dissolve into a thunder shower. The Reverend Dr. John Gilledge, from Columbus, was the main speaker but before the proceedings were well launched, the climax arrived unwanted. "Don't leave," host Kleagle L. A. Mueller cried. "It will not rain! God won't let it." But the heavens opened up and drenched him as he spoke.

On Sunday, Klansmen laid wreaths on the tombs of the Unknown Soldier and William Jennings Bryan, and after burning an enormous cross on the Arlington Horse Show grounds, speeches, and the singing of "America" to a new, native American tune, the remaining Klansmen went home.

For all the troubles which plagued the Invisible Empire and the reports of its growing decline, its first national parade was an impressive display of numbers, enthusiasm, and organization. Hiram Evans' Dallas homecoming and D. C. Stephenson's coronation in Kokomo's Melfalfa Park had drawn greater numbers of Klansmen but neither had produced an organized parade of comparable proportions. The feeling among the Klan's leaders was one of elation and there was much talk of making the parade a regular yearly reunion.

By the time that the Klan got around to its second national parade a year later, Klan ranks and enthusiasm had decidedly lessened. The United States Senate ratified the World Court, and the Klan's genuine one-hundred-per-cent Senator Rice Means had just been defeated in Colorado's Republican primaries. The wet, Catholic Senator Edwin Broussard won renomination in Louisiana, and Klan favorites were being closely pressed in Indiana, Ohio, Oklahoma, Kentucky, and Massachusetts. Only Alabama and Oregon offered election cheer to the Invisible Empire.

Initially the pattern was the same as that of the previous year: the dusty cars with their chalked slogans or their red K.K.K.'s in the windows, the special trains, and the tourist camp and parking-lot encampments. The appearance of countless red skullcaps, bearing the white Klan letters, marked 1926 as a year for new and more splendid uniforms. The Imperial Wizard's party was more spectacularly be-gowned than ever. Evans himself wore a great gold star on his hood and members of his cabinet had silver ones on theirs. There were even more women and girls than last time, when they had numbered perhaps one out of four among the marchers, and they too were often colorfully dressed. A nattily attired Zouave band wore blue capes, caps with fezzes on them, and reddish-brown knickers. And at the head of the New York delegation marched a platoon dressed after the fascist style in dark army shirts, knickers, puttees, and wearing alpine hats with flowers. Two floats added another touch of color. The one from Paterson, New Jersey carried a pretty "Miss 100-per-cent America," holding an open Bible, and her court, while the Lemoyne, Pennsylvania, Klansmen had turned to the dependable "Little Red Schoolhouse" as their inspiration.

But despite its spectacle, the Klan was not concealing the fact that the ranks were not much more than half of what they had been the year before. Where they had marched as platoons, twenty abreast, they now formed columns of fours, with wide gaps between formations. Again, the Northern Klans supplied almost all of the strength. As had been the case the year before, Pennsylvania and New Jersey were the largest, with delegations coming from all of the counties in the Garden State. Only the Virginia delegation, with more than a thousand marchers, showed signs of growth.

On the following day, the leaders of Klandom met in the District Auditorium for their third biennial Klonvokation. Here at least the disintegration that had been taking place within the Klan made no inroads on the assembled enthusiasm of its officials. To a cheering throng, Evans proclaimed that the Klan was ready to defend Mexico if any European nation should "set an armed force on the soil of the Western Hemisphere," and he warned the League of Nations to keep hands off. He denounced foreign entanglements and the World Court, and asked the nation to reaffirm its neutrality and isolation. On the domestic front, he expressed the ire of the Klan over the priestly administration of the last sacraments to the movie hero Rudolph Valentino, and called for the creation of a public attitude which would legislate against the restrictive marriage practices and claims of the Church. When he thundered that the only platform on which he would consent to re-election was one of "aggressive warfare against Romanism, alienism, Bolshevism, and anti-Americanism of all kinds," his wildly shouting followers rushed the stage and carried him around the hall on their shoulders.

Turning to important internal matters, the Klonvokation authorized their Imperial Wizard to continue to occupy bridal suites in hotels and otherwise maintain a standard of living in keeping with the dignity of the Klan. When Evans told his followers, "Boys, I've been strutting myself. I am going to leave it to you whether I shall continue to do so," they roared their approval. Finally, with the decision to present a "hands off Mexico" resolution to President Coolidge's Secretary of State, and a binding oath taken by all Klan officials that they would attend Protestant Church every Sunday, the third general convention of the Klan came to a close.

True to his promise, Evans launched his campaign against Romanism and Catholic-marriage practices. In the spring of 1927, Klan publications heralded the effort, while friendly lawmakers introduced Klan-drafted bills into their state legislatures. The proposed laws sought to punish any criticism of civil marriage, prohibited prenuptial pledges concerning the religion of children born of interfaith marriages, and barred interracial unions. For good measure, an additional bill sought the outlawry of the iniquitous Knights of Columbus. None passed, for the Klan was far past the days when it could honestly hope to deliver.

40

DECLINE

In the mid-twenties the Invisible Empire exercised dominion over more than three million subjects. By 1928, no more than several hundred thousand remained. How is this to be explained?

The dark soil within the American heart in which the roots of the Klan had found sustenance was still fecund. Part of the Klan's success had come from the moment of the 1920s, but there were other more enduring doorways in American life which had opened to the Klan's knock of destiny. Anti-Catholicism lay close below the surface, ready to emerge upon call when other conflicting traditions weakened their vigilance, and were not ready to do battle against it. The private enforcement of law and the social order was also a basic American way of doing things, a traditional instrument against evil and the weapon of a mass in-group society against corruption, immorality, the outsider, and change. Time was chipping away at the traditional religious and moral values of a small-town America. Evolution still stalked fundamentalist Christianity. The trucks of the bootleggers rumbled along the American highways after dark, and the younger generation still pulled over to the side of the road to take a nip from the flask. They smooched and petted a bit on the back seat or got out of the car to go into speak-easies, blind tigers, and motel cabins, and sometimes just took the back seat out of the car with them. Crime prospered and so did city and state officials, substantially in excess of their official incomes. The same conditions, which had created indignation in the breasts of the good burghers of Tulsa and Muncie, persisted after more than half a decade of the Invisible Empire. The upright citizens, led by their ministers, were just as accessible to the vision of the city of God as being inhabited exclusively by white Anglo-Saxon, native-born Protestants, as they had been only a few years before.

During the mid-twenties, the Klan had been a national power, from lodge and state halls to the cloakrooms of Congress and the floors of the national-party conventions. In 1928, one of the Klan's greatest fears had come to pass: a Roman Catholic sought the presidency of the United States. He was beaten back, at least partly by the spirit of American nativism of which the Klan had made itself the leading exponent. And yet at this juncture of peril and triumph, the Klan had earned none of the laurels. How is this sudden collapse to be explained?

In part klannish power declined because many of the fears which it represented had faded. "That dago of the Tiber," as Klan periodicals liked to call the Pope, had been a symbolization of all the things that distressed a considerable portion of the American people. By the late twenties, most Americans had settled down from the restlessness and disappointment that the war and its uncertain peace had bred. No Negro rebellion had taken place on the cotton farm or in the urban ghetto. The gates had been closed to the immigrant hordes. Times were better and looking up for most of urban America, and the farms had never supplied the real strength of the Klan. If the Bishop of Rome still appeared overly interested in what was going on in Italy, Mexico, and the United States, at least the Bolshevik revolution seemed to be settling down to destroy itself by internal struggles or become sensibly capitalist under the New Economic Policy.

Along with nativism and the vigilante use of force to preserve the status quo, fraternalism was a third part of the complex of attitudes which made the Klan possible. America has long been a nation of joiners, of men bound together for companionship and community purposes. American fraternalism has often been a path to assimilation and Americanization of a heterogeneous society, but as often as not, the concept of fraternity has often stood for exclusion. This was the path of the Invisible Empire.

Colonel Simmons and many of his best organizers had grown up within the fraternal world and so, initially, did the Ku Klux Klan itself. E. Y. Clarke recruited his Kleagles from among the Masons, and the future Imperial Wizard Hiram Evans attracted notice in Atlanta when he intrigued for the Klan in the Lodges of Texas. The Klan allied with the Orange Lodges and Scottish Rite Masons in Oregon and elsewhere in a struggle against Catholic parochial schools and the touch of Rome in the public ones. Although the grand masters of the Masons furiously denounced the Invisible Empire and forbade it to their brethren, they could no more keep their rank and file out of the Klan than could the Socialists of Wisconsin. And so the Klan fed upon the exclusiveness of the Woodmen of the World and the Junior Order of Mechanics, the anti-Catholic suspicions of the Masons, and the fraternalism of the Elks, the Knights of Pythias, and the Odd Fellows, signed up their members and held its meetings in their temples and halls.

Not only were the lodge halls of America generally open to the Klan, so were many of the vestries and chapels. The Protestant pulpits supplied the respectability, the orators, and a good part of the local leadership. A recent student of the Klan and the churches in Mississippi has written that the secret of its success was gregariousness "sanctified by the spiritual language which the Klan employed."[1] This did not mean general denominational approval, for with the exception of Bishop Alma White's Holy Rollers, no Episcopal or Methodist bishop, church convention, or religious periodical praised the Klan. A Southern Baptist newspaper might well remain silently neutral or condone the aims—though not the methods—of the Klan, but the conventions of the Baptist and Methodist Churches condemned lynching and masked outrages. In the North, and sometimes in the South, the stand was often stronger.

On the whole the Presbyterian, Episcopal, Lutheran, Universalist, and Congregationalist ministry was unfavorably disposed toward the Klan. Most of the support from the cloth was offered by Baptists, Methodists, and Disciples of Christ. Probably the Methodists, possessing the strongest bent toward social action, supplied the largest number of ministerial Klansmen. The Klan in New Jersey, for example, was distinctly Methodist. In Warren County, Mississippi, a Methodist minister later estimated that 10 per cent of his denominational brethren in the county had been enthusiastic Klansmen and another 15 per cent had joined under social pressure. Of the rest, perhaps a quarter mildly approved but never joined, while another quarter were actively opposed to the hooded order.[2] All over the country, ministers joined, or approved or accepted the Klan's hooded offerings during Sunday-morning services, while others actively rejected and denounced the Invisible Empire. A Methodist minister in Jackson, Mississippi, preached that the Klan was "unnecessary, un-American, and certainly un-Christian." The Methodist bishops were everywhere hostile. Bishop E. H. Hughes, for example, reminded his New Jersey

[1] Laura Bradley, "Protestant Churches and the Ku Klux Klan in Mississippi During the 1920's," unpublished Master's thesis, University of Mississippi, 1962, p. 25.
[2] Ibid., p. 59.

Convention that "It is not Anglo-Saxon blood but the blood of Jesus Christ that has made us what we are."

The clerical tone of the Klan cannot be satisfactorily explained in terms of donations or free memberships, although Klan lectureships often proved attractive to chronically underpaid ministers. Some joined under pressures from their vestry and parishioners, and others fell prey to the Klan's promise to fill the benches of their churches. However, the real lure of the Klan was its anti-Catholicism and its promise to fulfill the puritan creed. The Klan, in short, appeared to be doing what the Church talked about. It promised to bring Christian righteousness to society, to make it dry and' moral. Here were the good folk of a minister's congregation asking only that he join them and make the community as it ought to be. At last, that to which he had given his heart and his life had become something that others cared about and were willing to do something about. How could he refuse them his guidance? Those who formed the Klan, in the early days of its success in particular, were the better citizens as well as the law-enforcement officers of his community. How could he deny them and his calling as well? How difficult it was to remember that not all of those who cried "Lord, Lord," would enter the gates of Heaven, when so few really cried "Lord, Lord" at all. And when so many deserved punishment in this world and were surely going to get it in the next, it was sometimes possible to forget that if St. Paul had been a flogger, it was before, not after, his conversion.

As the ministry was often in an equivocal position when dealing with the Invisible Empire, so was the press. Clearly, the Klan thrived on publicity. The Klan was news and editors demanded more stories. Even the initial exposés, like those of the New York *World* and the *Journal-American,* actually helped the Klan grow, despite the accounts of rapaciousness, intrigue, immorality, and violence. There have always been two philosophies on how to handle organizations and movements like the Ku Klux Klan. One school of thought said ignore it and it would die. The other maintained that the press had a duty to present all news and that the Invisible Empire could not stand full exposure. The 1920s lent support for all positions. Surely the New York City newspaper campaign against the Klan only strengthened it in the hinterland, for New York City and the Klan's America were not the same.

The hard-core Klansman, who read one of the some several score Klan newspapers and periodicals, was probably satisfied with what he found there. For the most part the county weeklies and the small local papers kept quiet. What the Klan did elsewhere was not news; what it did locally was hardly fit to print. To talk about it would be to offend good people, or advertisers or subscribers, or bring bad publicity to one's town, or perhaps even threats of violence. Existence was too financially precarious to be risked through ill-considered crusades. So the country editor kept his peace. So did many of his city brethren. You couldn't have told from reading the press of Oregon that the Klan had become the prime power figure in the state or from the Montana papers that Senator Walsh might well be defeated for re-election because he was a Roman Catholic.

Some papers, like the Norfolk *Virginian-Pilot,* the New Orleans *Times-Picayune* and the Raleigh *News and Observer,* printed what went on. When the Klan scandals broke in California and Colorado, the Los Angeles *Examiner* and the Denver *Post* had a field day. Some courageous small-town papers, such as the *Midway Driller* of Kern County, California, and Indiana's Muncie *Post-Democrat,* reported the news and said what they thought, and William Allen White's Emporia *Gazette* socked the Klan hard in Kansas.

There were those papers, such as the Wichita Falls *Times,* and the Amarillo *News,* which sometimes supported the Klan's political efforts, and when Tom Adams of the Vincennes *Commercial* started turning up material harmful to the party, the Republican Editorial Association, which had authorized his investigation, turned against him.

In total, the American press was bold, cautious, cowardly, sensationalistic, partisan, conscientious, and heroic when it came to reporting the Klan. On the whole, the press explained it partially and poorly, and often not at all; but the New York *World;* Memphis *Commercial Appeal;* Columbus, Georgia, *Enquirer-Sun;* Montgomery, Alabama, *Advertiser;* and Indianapolis *Times* received Pulitzer prizes for their coverage of the Klan story in the 1920s, and half a dozen others equally merited the same award. During the Klan's early years, nothing the press could have done, would have stayed its spread, and all mention, of whatever kind, helped. After the initial explosive success of the Invisible Empire, everything the press reported and said about it probably helped bring on its decline.

The downfall of the Invisible Empire was clearly not caused by the actions of its enemies. In part, the Klan declined because it appealed to negative, defensive feelings which, though strongly rooted in the American life, did not prove sufficient to long sustain a major movement. The society, even of the American village, was too heterogeneous and too optimistic to fit within the Klan mold for any long period of time. The forces of change were too powerful to be held back. On the whole, the Klan just could not deliver. The sociologist John M. Mecklin, writing before the Klan had even reached the peak of its power in the middle twenties, diagnosed its problem.

Were the Klan more closely organized and animated by a more definite and comprehensive program it might become a force to be reckoned with in national life. There is, however, little danger that the Klan as a whole will ever be able to utilize all its strength in a political or social program. This is due to the essential local nature of the Klan, its singular lack of able and statesmanlike leaders, its planless opportunism, and, above all, its dearth of great unifying and constructive ideals. In the language of Freudianism, the Klan is essentially a defense mechanism against evils which are more often imaginary than real. It is for this reason negative rather than constructive in its influence.[3]

In the long run, Mecklin was right.

Apart from a certain skill in merchandising, its leadership was as uninspiring as its program. The leaders were out for money even more than power, and they ruled irrationally and dictatorially in its pursuit. The fight over the spoils plus the aristocratic and exploitative nature of the Invisible Empire, wrecked the organization in nearly every state and practically every community. The individual Klans, everywhere, were almost always in revolt against the higher leadership. Some members just quit, while others seceded to form short-lived local organizations copied after the Klan. Discontented Klansmen could seldom gain satisfaction, or even a hearing, within the Invisible Empire.

Almost invariably internal disputes brought a flurry of charges and countercharges in the press and in the courts. Not only was it harmful to the Klan to have its dirty linen always being washed in public, but the spectacle of a secret, terrorist organization settling its internal problems in court was not one to inspire fear or respect.

The very terrorist tendencies of the Klan eventually contributed mightily to its demise. The Ku Klux Klan was oriented toward and structured for violence and in the 1920s it went in for this kind of action on a large scale. The Klan was a secret, masked, nocturnal

[3] John M. Mecklin, *The Ku Klux Klan* (New York, 1924), pp. 32–33.

organization, with a tradition of direct action. Klansmen were oath-bound to protect their fellow wearers of the robe. The adherence or caution of public officials and peace officers gave it important areas of local immunity. The Klan's self-appointed role as the defender of the essential values of society placed upon it the imperative to take steps against sins and evil, and therefore against the sinners and evil-doers of society.

Klansmen talked incessantly of violence, and they could not even discuss most ordinary subjects without resorting to violence of utterance. Indeed, talk of action was one of the early selling points of the Klan in the South and West, and one of the ways to banish lethargy during the later days in the East.

Whether it was Colonel Simmons unloading his armaments upon the speakers' podium in a little Georgia town, or E. Y. Clarke in Tulsa, Oklahoma, talking about the "third degree" for those who liked a little "rough stuff," or Evans telling the Grand Dragon of Pennsylvania that a riot like Carnegie was worth twenty-five thousand members, its leaders counseled violence. Many Klan realms and units had their specially recruited strong-arm squads who wore black robes and special insignia, and who were ripe and ready for action. "There are lots of fellows who come to me in an anxious sort of way and want just a little of the rough stuff," E. Y. Clarke told a meeting in Tulsa. "They want the man who is honest-to-God 100 per cent, who would be just tickled to death to have his liver cut out and just to have a little rough stuff . . . and if you crave any of this rough stuff be sure that you get qualified to go up into the third degree."

Much like its Reconstruction ancestor, the Klan was a curiously set up society, undemocratic in organization and decision, and uncontrollable in local action. The national leaders could not have controlled its excesses even if they had wished to, something which Hiram Evans seems to have occasionally considered. The very dynamics of the Klan dictated violence.

And so it threatened, boycotted, banished, tarred and feathered, flogged, mutilated, and on occasion murdered. The actual numbers of victims can never be known, for in many cases the survivors left town or suffered in silence fearing to report their injury. Often, as in the cases of Georgia and Alabama in the late twenties, what seemed to be a sudden outbreak of terror was in reality but a break in the walls of silence which guarded what had been going on all the time.

The number of actual assault victims in Texas and Oklahoma may well have been over a thousand. There were over a hundred cases each in Florida, Georgia, and Alabama, more than a score in the North Carolina piedmont, possibly dozens in California, several in Arizona and Oregon, and scattered incidents through the Midwest and Mountain States. Open warfare rent "Bloody Williamson" County, Illinois, and riots marked the presence of opposition in South Bend, Indiana; Ohio's Mahoning Valley; and Carnegie and Lilly, Pennsylvania. Sometimes the Klansmen were clearly on the receiving end. Klansmen and anti-Klansmen fought on summer nights in New Jersey cities, and Irishmen battled Klansmen across central Massachusetts, during the summers of 1924 and 1925. In those areas where the Klan had things its own way, it was rarely the Negro, Jew, or Roman Catholic who felt its lash, but rather its fellow white, native-born Protestant, Anglo-Saxon fellow countryman—a fact which may well throw extra light upon the reality of the alien menace which the Klan fought, as well as the uses to which the hooded organization was put.

While the bravado and violence of the Klan initially brought respect and members, in time they created revulsion. The Texas floggings, the Elduayen affair in Inglewood and the Kern County tortures, the murder of Captain Coburn, Madge Oberholzter's death at the hands of D. C. Stephenson, the Georgia and Alabama lashers, and a dozen other stories stayed in the headlines for weeks. The Mer Rouge murders placed the dark bayous and the white-robed knights of Louisiana on the nation's front pages for over six months. People read about it, legislators talked about it, and it did the Klan no good.

In 1927, a group of long-rebellious western Pennsylvania Klansmen, led by their ministers, seceded from the Invisible Empire. Hiram Evans' response was to sue them for $100,000 damages. By this move he not only sought to get his hands on their regalia and treasury and keep them from using the Klan name, but also to use the case as a warning to all fractious Klaverns. Since this was an equity case, the defendants had only to prove that the plaintiff national Klan had come into court with sullied hands and reputation. And they set about it with a vengeance. For days, in sharp courtroom battle, witnesses paraded to the stand to describe Klan secrets, Klan intrigues, Klan dissensions, and Klan horrors. D. C. Stephenson sent his affidavit from the Michigan City penitentiary and Colonel Simmons told the details of his own betrayal. The nation's press carried stories ranging from the kidnaping of a small girl from her grandparents in Pittsburgh to reports that a Colorado Klansman was beaten to death when he tried to drop the order. Descriptions of whippings and floggings were commonplace and witnesses disagreed over how many men had died at the hands of the hooded Empire. One account, which denials never quite offset, told of how a man in Terrell, Texas, had been doused with oil and burned to death before several hundred assembled Klansmen. In a verdict blazing with indignation, the judge threw out the Klan's case on the grounds that it had come into court with very unclean hands indeed.

Long before this, the affluent and civic-minded in most communities had come to realize what a divisive force the Klan really was. They had had many opportunities to see the violence it had done not only to individuals but to Church and communal harmony practically everywhere it existed. The goodly came more and more to realize that the Klan was not. Terror went too far; the extremists ranted too loudly and the leaders were too immoral and uninspiringly inept. Probably if the Klan had grown more slowly and more carefully, free from excessive exploitation and misdirection from on top, it might have found an enduring place in the world of American in-group fraternalism. All of the necessary resources had been there. The failure of the Ku Klux Klan to anchor itself as a successful feature in American life was due more to its own ineptness than any other cause or combination of factors. The decline of the Klan as a mass movement in America was its own fault, nobody else's.

41

NINETEEN TWENTY-EIGHT,
A YEAR OF PERILS AND PROMISES

The Klan saw 1928 as a year of desperate perils and of a great opportunity. It was an election year, and unless something miraculous were done, the Democrats would nominate Al Smith. To the Eastern big-city strongholds of the party, Smith was both a hero and a sacred cause. This was their man, the first born of the new urban immigrant America and of the faith of their masses. To party regulars elsewhere in the nation, he was an able, ingratiating leader who was inescapably going to be nominated and who might even wrest the election away from the Republicans by winning key states such as Massachusetts, New Jersey, and New York.

The long, bitter struggle at the 1924 convention had pulled much of the poison out of Al Smith's candidacy. The regulars were agreed that the party was not to risk destroying itself with another great Civil War. The memory of the fight over the Klan and of the 104 ballots that finally nominated John Davis was enough to last a lifetime. Not so for the Klan. Al Smith's election would be a catastrophe for America, and a crusade against him might be the remaking of the Invisible Empire. The Klan was going to fight Smith's candidacy, Evans announced, because he was the representative of alien, Catholic, boss-ruled, wet, nullificationist Eastern Democracy, with priests instead of consciences. Taking credit for having beaten Davis four years before, and, more justifiably, for having forced the retirement of Alabama's Senator Oscar Underwood, he lined the Klan up on the side of the native, American-minded Protestant, dry Democracy of the South and West. However, although it had a cause, the Invisible Empire lacked a political paladin and an army to rally behind him.

William Gibbs McAdoo was not a candidate. Alabama's Catholic-baiting Tom Heflin, who was the Klan's only true friend in national life, had no following. The desperation of the Klan was apparent in its covert consideration of two men whom it had once bitterly opposed and almost defeated for re-election: Missouri's Jim Reed and Montana's Thomas Walsh. Neither was friendly to the Klan and both had decided drawbacks. Senator Reed was a Protestant and an isolationist, but he was a wet. Senator Walsh was safely dry but distressingly Roman Catholic. Among the candidates who were in any way possibly acceptable, only they seemed to have some slight chance of success.

Senator Heflin traveled about the country assuring Klan rallies, at $150 to $250 an oration, that Smith would never be nominated. In Georgia, Florida, Mississippi, Oklahoma, and Texas, the Klan sought delegates to the Democratic convention and in Alabama it experienced some success.

The Republican convention in Kansas City picked "the great engineer," Herbert Hoover. His outlook was too internationalist, the Klan felt, but at least he was Protestant, of a sort, and safely dry. When the Democrats assembled in Houston late in June, Smith's nomination was certain, and what there was of a hot time came from the weather rather than the convention. The Klan did throw what weight it could behind the dry plank in the platform which Smith, upon his nomination, proceeded to repudiate. Convention Chairman Joe Robinson, from the once-proud Klan state of Arkansas, spoke out strongly against stirring up a religious issue, and for this un-American point of view Evans and his chief counsel William Zumbrunn tried to prevent his nomination for Vice President.

In the months between the convention and the November election, the Klan did what it could to defeat the ticket of Smith and Robinson. The question was what it could contribute. In Georgia and Florida the demand for pledges to vote against Al Smith brought further depletion of Klan ranks. The former Exalted Cyclops of the Blue Ridge Georgia Klavern returned anti-Smith material, with the farewell: "So good-by, Mr. Grand Dragon, good-by Klan. I desire to walk in the ways of my fathers of the South who were Democrats"; and in Miami, Florida, the former sheriff resigned from the Klan when ordered to stand trial for supporting the Democratic ticket. Some prominent Klan friends, such as Hanibal Goodwin, the Klan's North Carolina attorney, and Dr. John Hawkins, former Solebury, Pennsylvania, Exalted Cyclops, publicly supported Smith. The Klan, then, was unable to muster a show of solidarity against Al Smith; to what degree was it able to influence the election?

Major issues in the campaign were Al Smith's religion, his immigrant and Tammany background, and his opposition to Prohibition. It was on these things the Klan felt most strongly, and it wasn't the only one concerned about them. Democrats in Maine were divided over the election, as were those in North Carolina and many other states. In Al Smith's own New York, thousands of Democrats split their tickets to make Hoover President and Franklin Roosevelt governor, Protestants both, against the Catholic Smith and the Republican candidate for governor who was Jewish. Nor was a vote against Al Smith necessarily a vote for prejudice and bigotry. The influence of Smith's Catholicism upon his actions as President would naturally be a question until effectively put to the test. Many people felt most strongly about the necessity of Prohibition, and Al Smith's nasal drawl, and New York accent, together with his derby and pinstriped suit, managed to convey something less than a presidential impression.

Klan speakers and periodicals said their worst about the Democratic candidate. Scores of thousands of copies of the ever popular "Knights of Columbus Oath" were put in circulation, which the Democrats sought to counter by passing out close to a hundred thousand copies of a congressional report that the oath was a fake. The prime anti-Smith instrument was the Klan-lining fraternal weekly *The Fellowship Forum,* published in Washington, D.C., by an expansive drugstore impresario, James S. Vance. In preparation for the 1928 election, he had also set up a radio station, which bore his initials, financed in part by contributions gathered from the Klan faithful, and which was eventually purchased by CBS as its outlet in the nation's capital.

Copies of *The Fellowship Forum,* with headlines reading ROMAN CATHOLIC CLERICAL PARTY OPENS BIG DRIVE TO CAPTURE AMERICA FOR THE POPE, greeted Smith when his train arrived in Kansas. Week after week, it was the same. While Klan circles tried to raise money for an Election Eve mailing throughout the South, the Republicans and Democrats traded charges. Democratic headquarters claimed that the Republicans had directed a woman seeking anti-Smith material to *The Fellowship Forum* and that the Republican leaders had sent anti-Catholic "hot stuff" into North Carolina. The Republican National Committee replied that the woman had been "a plant." It denied as best it could that its state chairman in Virginia and its candidate for governor in West Virginia were part owners of *The Fellowship Forum,* one of whose representatives was touring the country with Hoover. As many worried drys and Protestants were swinging toward the Republican column, many Negro voters, led by the *Afro-American* and the Chicago *Defender*, edged toward the Democrats.

From the beginning, the Democrats had seized upon the Klan issue, despite Herbert Hoover's call for religious toleration and freedom of worship. The Klan did exist, and to millions of Americans the Imperial Wizard in Washington was an even less-pleasing image than the Pope in Rome. Smith started off his campaign by going to Oklahoma City, where the Klan was noisily active, to speak out on religion, while Franklin Roosevelt opened his own campaign for governor on the same tack in New York's southern tier. In New Jersey, former Ambassador Henry Morgenthau called the election a battle between Al Smith and the Klan, and the Democratic candidate expressed something of the same sentiments during his Madison Square Garden finale.

In the end, the old-stock native America and prosperity were too much for the Irish boy from the Lower East Side. The Republicans were still the nation's major party, and times were good. In 1928, probably no Democrat could have won. The Democrats lost Florida, Texas, Oklahoma, North Carolina, Tennessee, Kentucky, and Virginia, and carried only Massachusetts and Rhode Island outside the South. However, the Klan did not deserve any important share of the credit other than having helped condition the American people to such campaigns. Despite the call to its Midwestern Klansmen to rally in Washington for Herbert Hoover's inauguration, the Ku Klux Klan had not gained from the election.

42

THE DEPRESSION DECADE, 1929-39

With the growing misery of the Depression, the Klan ranks throughout the nation became thinner. Many of the remaining thousands melted away, unable or unwilling to spend their meager resources to maintain their membership in the shrunken Invisible Empire. Depletion also set in in the ranks of the leaders. Lodges of sorrow marked the passing of Klan stalwarts such as Gen. Nathan Bedford Forrest III, former leader of the Confederate veterans who had lent his soothing skills and his grandfather's name to the twentieth-century Klan, and other one-time potentates now departed in search of more profitable business connections. Imperial Wizard Hiram Evans was on the move more than ever before, rallying the far-flung outposts of his once mighty domain, and that deadly enemy of papal intrigue, Senator Tom Heflin, was always available for paid orations. For the next half decade, Evans lectured to Klansmen in San Diego, supped with the Boston Tea Party Klan of Massachusetts, rallied with his provincial aides in Fort Worth, and banqueted with the politicians as the guest of the Capitol Klan of Columbia, South Carolina. Distinguished speakers were in short supply in the thirties, although Toledo's escaped nun and ex-priest were available for hire when there was call for them. Mainly Klansmen entertained themselves within their Klaverns and visited each other for ceremonies and socials.

For the most part, the Klans tended to keep their depleted ranks out of the public eye, but there were occasional Fourth of July parades in Greenwich, Connecticut; Saginaw, Michigan; on Long Island, and in northern Virginia. Klansmen in the Rocky Mountain States delighted in encampments, and picnics were always in style anywhere. Klans in neighboring states often met together, and occasionally a cross would be burned or a big rally would be hosted by Kokomo's Nathan Hale Klan, or by Ohio's Tuscarawas County Klan on the spacious grounds of its Klan home near New Philadelphia. In

Georgia, a shrewd, able organizer, named Samuel Green, was working his way to the top of the state realm, where Klansmen still paraded as they had done during the flush days of the 1920s. The states where the Invisible Empire still held its greatest strength were New Jersey, New York, Pennsylvania, Michigan, Ohio, Indiana, Wisconsin, Illinois, Kentucky, California, Virginia, Florida, and Georgia.

Despite continual membership drives, the Klan was still declining, even though its total strength was probably still close to a hundred thousand. Old friends, like Charles Bowles in Detroit, might finally get elected to office, and proven enemies such as Nebraska's maverick Senator George Norris faced Klan opposition, but the Invisible Empire had few bastions of power. Tom Heflin's blatant anti-Catholicism had not only antagonized his fellow U. S. Senators but also a growing number of his fellow Alabamans. The state Democratic Executive Committee used his support of Herbert Hoover in 1928 to refuse him approval and he was beaten for re-election. Twice again he tried to return to the Senate, once with the help of the Republicans and always with the support of the Klan, but the people of Alabama said no. However, it was not until Lister Hill had beaten him for the seat relinquished by the new Supreme Court Justice Hugo Black, that the Klan would formally admit that Heflin had long been one of its own.

The Klan of the 1930s was primarily a social organization, stressing the fraternal side of its nature which had been its main appeal in countless communities during its better days. But even though there were Klansmen about and keeping busy, there was no disguising the hard times that had hit the Invisible Empire. Where "TWK" (Trade With a Klansman) signs had blossomed out in store windows in the 1920s, now the urging of Georgia's Grand Dragon was to "Trade With a Klansman in Good Standing," and there was somehow, something wistful about the New Year's greeting in the *Kourier* for January 1931:

> And here's hoping
> That you keep
> Smiling Thru
> 1931 With—Ku Klux Klan

As far as a proposed solution for the gnawing pangs of the Depression itself, the Klan had no comprehensive plan. However, two things seemed clear. The first was that nothing could be done as long as foreigners crowded into the country to take jobs away from the

Americans. Not only must the gates be even more firmly barred, but those who were here and did not belong must be deported. Then there would be jobs for all. This meant the removal of all aliens, whom the Klan estimated at three and one-half million.

Secondly, Klansmen must be very careful to avoid unpatriotic action. It was laudable, for instance, for the York, Pennsylvania, Klavern to organize two enormous meat and bean soup dinners for the victims of the Depression. However, direct action by labor or the unemployed received no Klan approval. Ohio's destiny-bound Grand Dragon, James Colescott, sent out strong instructions to all Klansmen to stay out of "such lawlessness" as unemployment demonstrations and to contribute to the Red Cross instead. An official of his Akron Klavern used the Klan's national magazine to denounce those who took part in a hunger march on the state capital as "Negroes, Hunks, Dagoes, and all the rest of the scum of Europe's slums."

When the textile workers at the Florence Mills in Forest City, North Carolina, went on strike for an increase in their fifteen-dollars-a-week wage, the state's Grand Dragon, Dr. Amos Duncan, urged them to return to work. In the early thirties the National Textile Workers Union came to the Klan's Greenville, South Carolina, stronghold. When a biracial unemployment council began to lead the jobless in a series of protests, this was obviously a case for the police and the Klan. Considering the left wing affiliations of the Union, the demands for free house rent, abolition of chain gangs, and ten-dollars-a-week work relief, were relatively moderate. However, the existence of an unrest that brought demonstrating veterans to the home of an antibonus bank president and which failed to draw the line between black and white, required action. When a delegation from the unemployment council appeared before the West Greenville town council, robed and masked Klansmen stood silent witness in the hall. Since the protestors had apparently missed the message, a hundred masked Klansmen raided a council meeting two nights later and beat up the Negroes present, plus those whites who tried to protect them. According to the local press, the police, who had refrained from interfering, felt that the Klan would thus put a stop to "Communist" organizations in Greenville. However, the police canvassed the colored section of town warning against any more meetings, and the Klan paraded to underline the message.

The major battle cry of the thirties developed into a demand that the American Constitution be protected from the strange things going on in Washington. In 1930, according to the Klan's semiofficial history, Klan leaders now back in Atlanta had become enthusiastic over the presidential chances of Franklin Roosevelt. Although he had led the Smith forces at both the 1924 and 1928 conventions and shared the ticket with him in the latter election, Roosevelt had managed to emerge with few enemies, even within the Invisible Empire. And besides, his many visits to Warm Springs had made him a favorite in Georgia. Surely he would be better than the Catholic Al Smith and the hard-drinking, long-time anti-Klan leader of the House of Representatives, John Nance Garner. Klansmen took part in the founding of the Roosevelt Southern Clubs and Paul Etheridge, the Klan's top lawyer, headed the organization. In addition, the Klan claimed, it supplied some of the expense funds and the office furniture. A break apparently developed prior to the National Convention when it turned out that the clubs were expected to raise money for the cause rather than receive money from it. A parting of the ways took place and the Klan "discovered" that Roosevelt's campaign manager, Jim Farley, was a Roman Catholic.

The Klan was soon in opposition to F.D.R. and had their fears justified once he took office, for he appointed the sinister Mr. Farley as Postmaster General and started bringing "too many Jews and Catholics" into Washington. A Virginia meeting attacked the New Deal for having "honeycombed Washington with Communists." Over a thousand Klansmen and -women at an Annapolis rally were told that a wave of communism was sweeping the land and that the Depression would not be ended until the nation returned to fundamental principles. The York, Pennsylvania, Klan denounced "brain trusters" leading the nation to revolution. A Westchester rally in a wooded glen, near the Hudson River, praised Hitler and was critical of the New Deal and the "communism of F.D.R. and the Jews."

In the summer of 1934, Imperial Wizard Hiram Evans called upon Klansmen to help preserve constitutional government from sovietism, communism, fascism, and all other isms, but the real menace seemed to be coming from an unexpected direction. The biennial Klonvokation that summer devoted most of its attention to the dictatorial behavior and radical economics of Huey Long. In closed session the Klan considered condemning him for undermining constitutional republican government, but decided against any formal stand. "You don't get in an open contest with a polecat," the Imperial Wizard explained. Rather the Klan would go after Huey in a quiet way and join with the "decent people" of Louisiana in opposing him at the next election.

Armed with reports from Atlanta, newspapermen rushed to see what response they could get from Long, for the Kingfish was never one to turn the other cheek. Standing in the back of the Statehouse watching his legislature in action, he responded, "You tell that tooth-puller that he is a goddam lying sonuvabitch! I know him personally. This isn't secondhand information and it isn't confidential!" With Huey talking like a Klansman, the Klan tried taking the high-sounding path, hoping to be able to rally its now long-defunct legions which had once numbered some two-score thousand in the Pelican State. Apparently, however, the only thing the new campaign stirred up was the Kingfish, who graphically threatened to have Hiram Evans lynched if he ever set foot in the state.

When the Klan potentates next gathered in solemn assembly, two years later in Philadelphia's City of Brotherly Love, the Kingfish was dead and the Invisible Empire had turned its attention back to the safer enemy in Washington. In reviewing its past history, the Klan took credit for having controlled immigration, kept the country out of the World Court, and warded off entangling alliances with Europe. In 1927 it had prevented sinister business and ecclesiastical elements from plunging the nation into war with Mexico to restore oil lands and Church property. In 1928 the Klan had kept Al Smith out of the White House, and, in 1930 and 1935, had again prevented United States involvement in the World Court. Now, in 1936, the great menace was communism, particularly in the schools, and the threat to constitutional government. There were aliens, Reds, and treason in high places. Radical rats, like Felix Frankfurter, John Dewey, and Rexford G. Tugwell, were gnawing away at the Constitution, and to underline their feeling about "That Man" in the White House, Atlanta Klansmen paraded along the announced route of his prospective visit.

Despite his antagonism to the growing power in Washington being used against anyone other than Reds and aliens, Hiram Evans did have one major job for the federal government. That was to stamp out the Black Legion. Late in the spring of 1936, the body of a young WPA worker, named Charles Poole, was found on a lonely suburban road near Detroit, shot in the head. Two detectives, combing his background and his associations for a clue, came up with practically a regiment of them. First, they discovered "The Wolverine Republican Club," which turned out to be part of a Klan-like organization that called itself the Black Legion. The Black Legion had apparently grown up from a small self-help, social club among the marginal workers in Detroit in the early 1930s. The members were primarily immigrants from the hill country of Mississippi, Kentucky, and Tennessee. They were, for the most part, ill-adjusted to the monotony and the discipline of factory life, and were too uneducated and too unskilled to hope for anything other than insecure, low-paid seasonal employment. The Legion had been organized as a good-time club and as a place where the members could exchange leads on jobs.

That they soon turned to violence was not too surprising. Perhaps the members had learned it directly from the Ku Klux Klan. Some had surely been members; there were reports that only former Klansmen were eligible and in time there were Klansmen in the top leadership. As a secret, masked organization, operating in former Klan territory and with the Klan's heritage about them, the dynamics of their organization followed the same pattern. Its first success came when two of the members lost their jobs and their former employer was taken to a meeting of the Black Legion and threatened with flogging or execution if he did not take them back.

Word spread, and members flocked in. Lodges were formed in the industrial cities around Detroit and in Indiana and Ohio, where the old Klan had been strong. V. F. Effinger, an electrical contractor from Lima, Ohio, who had been active in high Klan circles as late as 1931, took over as brigade commander. According to the records seized by the Michigan police, Dr. William J. Shepard, city health officer of Bellaire, Ohio, was also one of the leaders. Dr. Shepard denied any connection. Back in 1925, he had gotten tired of the long klannish rituals and had gotten together a group of Klansmen who dyed their robes black and formed a company of night riders. When they showed up at a big rally at Buckeye Lake, other Klansmen had been envious. The Grand Dragon objected to his innovation, Shepard explained, and he withdrew from the Klan, but his night riders had made an impression. "Pretty darn soon the darn thing grew by leaps and bounds. Everyone around here wanted to be one of my blacks, and everyone started organizing black groups, and then there were a lot of wildcat outfits." The Black Legion was obviously one of them. "You have to have mystery in a fraternal thing to keep it alive," he went on, "the folk eat it up."

Unlike its Klan mother, the Black Legion was not initially an exploitive organization. Its dues started out at ten cents a month and what profit there was came from sale of the regalia. Its leaders lived modestly. The bulk of its members were factory workers, public em-

ployees, and ambitious petty politicians. Once the movement seemed
to be going somewhere the political hopefuls flocked in, but even
when the legion first turned to violence, scant word of its presence
leaked out to the general public. Apparently without the knowledge
of some of its more respectable members, the legionnaires tried their
hand at flogging, bombing, and finally murder.

A movement has to go somewhere. Several of the Michigan regiments were in friendly communication with Silver Shirt leader William Dudley Pelly, the would-be American *Führer*. A delegation from
Pontiac went down to Asheville, North Carolina, to talk to him, but
recommended nonaffiliation. Where next? "You can't go on with
only night meetings forever," Effinger told one of his Michigan lieutenants, "you've got to go into politics." And so the Black Legion set
out to see what it could do about creating a better Michigan. Like its
spiritual father the Klan, the Legion was anti-Catholic, -Negro, and
-Jew, and its goal had become political power. By the mid-thirties it
was well on its way to success in several Lower Michigan towns and
counties. It did best in Pontiac and surrounding Oakland County
where close to a hundred public officials belonged, including the city
treasurer, a member of the legislature, and top police, fire, municipal,
and judicial officers.

Although its political importance was growing, the Legion still re-
sorted to violence against its enemies, reluctant members, and political opponents. When the ritualistic execution of luckless Charles
Poole blew the whistle on the Legion, some of its members were
planning the murder of the municipal president of Ecorse and a
Highland Park newspaper publisher because they opposed candidates
whom the Black Legion wanted elected. Once the news about the
Legion was out, its life was forfeit. Close to a hundred members were
removed from the Oakland County payrolls amid bitter public recrim-
ination against them, and in the fall of the year eleven legionnaires
were convicted of the murder of Charles Poole.

Although the Klan commonly disclaimed any of its members who
ran afoul of the law, there was no question about the sincerity with
which the Klan leaders and Hiram Evans disowned the Black Legion.
With the horror with which any true believer regards a deviation
within its own ranks, the Klan called for punishment of the Legion.
The following year when Warner Brothers used Klan insignia in the
filming of a motion picture called *The Black Legion,* the Klan filed
suit for damages.

However, what was going on in Florida was unquestionably the real Klan. Its membership has been estimated at approximately thirty thousand and the figure does not seem unreasonable, for in the early 1940s, the Imperial Wizard was to tell a closed session of the House Un-American Activities Committee that Florida was the largest realm in the nation. And so, during the Depression years, the Florida Klans continued to meet, add new chapters, and occasionally hold state-wide rallies, like the one sponsored by the Cherokee Klan of Orlando, to let the people know "that there are Klansmen everywhere and that this is still a white-man's country." Klan activity, however, tended to be centered in three areas: Jacksonville, Miami, and the citrus belt from Orlando to Tampa in the center of the state. Jacksonville, where Grand Dragon George Garcia held court, was its imperial city. In Miami, the powerful John B. Gordon Klan was ever on the moral alert. It sought to keep a Negro choir from taking part in a white revival service and threatened two Filipino members of the U. S. Coastguard who had "married white women." In 1937, with tacit approval of the Dade County sheriff, the Klan raided a night club and roughed up some of the help and entertainers. The Klan put pressure on Miami strip joints, private clubs, and gambling, and a municipal officer, whom it denounced for not keeping Miami's Negro popula-tion "under control," lost his job.

It was in central Florida, however, that the Klan rode most freely and most often. Less secretive, according to reports, than the 1920s, it still sought to regulate the behavior of the Negroes and prevent their voting. It punished wayward officials, unfaithful married people, and indiscreet single ones, and closed places of vice. In Gainesville, to the north, the Klan burned down the houses of prostitution so that the students at the university would not be distracted from their studies. Many public officials and office seekers joined the Klan. Communism had, as elsewhere, become the object of special atten-tion, and it was widely defined. In the eyes of many, anyone sus-pected of unorthodoxy, from labor agitation to nudism, deserved no protection from the law. In some areas, people lived in fear of night riders and kept their weapons handy.

Although the Klan operated primarily as a social organization, there were some topics which stirred the hooded knights into action. One of them was organized labor. "The CIO is a subversive, radical, Red organization," a Bartow lawyer-Klansman asserted, "and we'll fight fire with fire." And fight the unions with fire they did. In the citrus counties, many people considered the Klan to be a protector of the societal and economic well-being. "Citrus growing is a hundred-million-dollar industry," people would point out, which could not afford to pay higher wages. Union organization had to be prevented, by force if necessary. An organizer who was working among citrus workers in Lakeland responded to a call for help one night and was never seen again, and there were boasts that other bodies had been dumped in swamps and in abandoned water-filled phosphate mines.

In 1935 a local political group called the Modern Democrats got caught in the middle of the struggle between the city and county forces for control of Tampa's lucrative vice and political spoils. The Modern Democrats, led primarily by Socialists, sought labor organization and municipal reform The Klan was strong among city employees, and a city fireman joined the reform organization to keep the police informed. They raided a meeting of the Modern Democrats, booked and questioned several of the insurgents and then turned them over to Klan floggers brought in from Orange County. One victim, Joseph Shoemaker, was flogged, castrated, caked with tar, and had his leg plunged into the boiling-tar bucket. When he died after nine days of intense pain, it was a national issue.

The outburst of indignation over the torture of Shoemaker, contrasted with the indifference which greeted most such cases. The American Civil Liberties Union offered a reward for conviction of the floggers. The mayor of Tampa and the board of aldermen each ordered investigations, and the local Central Trades and Labor Council, the American Legion, and Veterans of Foreign Wars all condemned the affair. The Socialists and the I.W.W. added their protest, and a National Committee for the Defense of Civil Rights in Tampa was organized with such members as the ACLU, the Negro Labor Committee, and the ILGWU. Norman Thomas became national chairman, and the pastor of Tampa's First Congregational Church assumed local leadership. The governor, the Tampa Bar Association, and the American Federation of Labor, whose national convention was scheduled for the city, joined in the cry. At the request of the Tampa Ministerial Association, the mayor called for a period of public mourning, and ministers from all of the major Protestant faiths took part. The Tampa chief of police conducted a personal investigation and declared all of his men innocent, but when the grand jury handed down its report, Chief Tittsworth himself was among those indicted.

A top lawyer was provided by someone. The local cigar manufacturers put up bail. The venue was changed and the best "jury picker" in the county taken on as assistant defense counsel. Supporters of the defense and the prosecution held mass meetings. Norman Thomas and the director of Governor Eugene Talmadge's Georgia Veterans' Bureau traded charges. Patriotism and opposition to "communists like Norman Thomas," were made the issue. A crucial witness "committed suicide." The background and beliefs of the victims rather than their flogging received primary attention. Despite damaging testimony by the Tampa chief of detectives and other policemen, the judge directed the acquittal of former Police Chief Tittsworth and another defendant. The courts ruled that kidnaping meant only "intent to secretly confine," and though it took two trials, and a reversal by the Florida Supreme Court, the defendants went free.

From time to time during the 1930s, the name of the Ku Klux Klan bounced momentarily back into the headlines as former members sought to return to public life, and were greeted with storms of protest. In 1930 it was William Baldwin whom Senator Nye had picked as chief aide to the Senate Election Expenditures Committee. In 1937, Tom Heflin ran the gantlet when he and another alleged Klansman were appointed special assistants to the U. S. Attorney General. The next year the California Republicans brought forth what they claimed was a lifetime Klan membership card made out in the name of William G. McAdoo, who was seeking re-election to the U. S. Senate. In 1938, Indiana's former Grand Dragon, Walter Bossert, made an unsuccessful bid for the Republican senatorial nod. The next year the Senate sought to withdraw its approval of Elmer Davies, a newly appointed federal judge in Tennessee, when his former Klan connections came out. In 1944, Robert Lyons had to give up his new post as Republican national committeeman from Indiana, and Los Angeles radio commentator Hal Styles lost out in his congressional bid when he was identified as the former leader of the Klan in Jamaica, New York.

Nineteen forty-four was a good year for bringing up past Klan connections, and in the fall of the year the Hearst papers broke the story that the Democratic vice-presidential candidate, Senator Harry Truman, had taken part in a 1922 Klan ceremony in a pasture south of Independence, Missouri. In 1952, Walter Winchell brought the story out again. On both occasions, Truman denied the charge maintaining that he and the Klan had been antagonists both in the political and Masonic life of Missouri.

All of these were matters of flickering or local interest. Only one case made the national headlines and lingered there. This was the nomination of Senator Hugo L. Black to the Supreme Court of the United States. The Alabama senator had been one of the leaders of the liberal wing of the Democratic party, who pushed President Roosevelt in the direction of New Deal reform. In 1937, when the first vacancy opened up on the Supreme Court, Roosevelt named Senator Black to it. There had long been rumors of Black's one-time Klan connections, rumors which anyone in the know in Alabama could have substantiated, but the Senate refused to take them seriously. However, hardly had the nomination been approved, with the usual courtesy which the Senate traditionally extends to its own, when the whole story came tumbling out. Hugo Black had joined in September of 1923, as one of almost two thousand Alabamans, who were initiated in the spectacular city-center ceremony by which the Robert E. Lee Klan No. 1 of Birmingham, celebrated its anniversary as one of the first families of Klandom. Black had remained in the Klan until 1925 when he withdrew, with the Klan's agreement, to run for the Senate. Black's predecessor, Oscar Underwood, had been one of the most honored and respected leaders of the Senate, but he had chosen to fight the Klan, and that meant political death in Alabama during the middle twenties. Black's resignation from the Klan was a purely political maneuver, so that no embarrassing questions might be raised during the election. After his election he appeared at a victory celebration at the Klavern on South Twentieth Street in Birmingham, along with the Klan governor-elect, Bibb Graves. Amid much hilarity punctuated by praise for the Anglo-Saxons and verbal assault on the "niggers" and Roman Catholics, Black rose to thank the Klansmen for making his election possible and accepted a gold-engraved Grand Passport to the Invisible Empire from the hand of the Imperial Wizard. All of this was now carefully set forth and documented in a Pulitzer prize-winning series in the Pittsburgh *Post-Gazette*.

As soon as he was confirmed, Black had gone off on vacation in Europe, and now as public protest mounted he returned, close-mouthed, refusing to make any comment to the press. He was saving his words for the coast-to-coast radio audience that leaned forward toward their sets on October 1, 1937, to hear how he was going to explain his way out of that one. His remarks were short; the explanation did not come. Yes, he had joined the Klan but he had resigned before he became senator and had never rejoined. The Imperial Passport which Evans had given him was unsolicited and had no meaning. He had not associated with the Klan since that time. That was all he had to say. To the nation's editorial writers, it was less than satisfactory. Only a disproof or his resignation would have been sufficient and he offered neither.

Hugo Black was born in the small Alabama market town of Ashland, the birthplace of Imperial Wizard Hiram Evans. The practice of medicine seems to have been the dream of young boys in the depressed farming areas of Alabama, for both boys considered becoming doctors, as had their neighbor, William J. Simmons. Where Evans chose dentistry, Black turned to the law. With opportunity greatest in the growing cities of America, Evans went off to practice his art in Dallas, and Black soon moved to Birmingham. The clients of a poor struggling young lawyer are such as he can find, but lawyer Black seemed to have an affinity for the underdog. He represented a carpenters' union, striking Alabama miners, and a number of Negroes, winning a victory on one occasion for a colored client who had been held in jail too long. As a police court judge, he was considered colorful and fair, and a Negro appearing in Judge Black's court found that his testimony counted the same as a white man's. As a lawyer, Black was not above the emotional appeal to men's prejudgments, but, most of all, he was a poor man's advocate. As prosecutor of Jefferson County, he ended the fee system for paying jailers and sheriffs, prosecuted those who used the third degree, and won the enmity of the coal and insurance companies by challenging their respective policies of shortchanging those with whom they did business. Squeezed into resigning from office, he worked up a flourishing personal-injury practice.

He was in politics and ambitious, and he was a joiner in a world in which this was the nature and necessity of a politician. With the Invisible Empire the rising force in Alabama politics, it was not surprising that he added a Klan card to his collection of memberships in the American Legion, Knights of Pythias, Masons, Civitans, Odd Fellows, Moose, and Pretorians. Although lodgeman Hugo Black was made of leadership stuff, his association with the Klan was apparently in the back ranks, and a student of the whole episode maintains that the future justice's generally mild Anglo-Saxonism was more phraseology than ideology.[1] Still, Hugo Black's Klan was stained with blood in Alabama and elsewhere, and braver men like Senator Underwood, stood up against it. In Alabama in the mid-twenties,

[1] Daniel M. Berman, "Hugo L. Black: The Early Years," *Catholic University Law Review*, VIII (1959), 103–116.

they did so at a political price and perhaps it was this lesson that Judge Black had foreseen.

The Klan was not pleased when he was appointed to the Supreme Court. In 1928 he had given Al Smith at least nominal support and two years later led the fight that defeated the Klan's more dependable friend, Tom Heflin. Senator Black's prolabor stand in Washington was not at all the Klan's dish of tea, and his advocacy of Negro rights under New Deal wages and hours laws was downright unforgivable. Alabama Klansmen supplied much of the material for the *Post-Gazette*'s story of Black's Klansmanship in the twenties, but once the scandal was on, the Klan naturally supported his fitness and tried to use the publicity for recruitment. Justice Hugo Black's staunchest supporters, under fire, turned out to be organized labor, with John L. Lewis and the CIO in the fore.

And the Klan was no friend to labor in the mid-thirties. As the Klan had discovered the communists in the early thirties, it now found organized labor. Although Klansmen demonstrated against Negro voting and continued to enforce basic morality, the unions were the big issue. Organizers were told to lay off the Roman Catholics, Jews, and Negroes, and concentrate on the invasion of the South by the Steel and Textile Workers Organizing Committees. Evans asserted that the CIO "was infested with Communists," and "led by aliens," who sought to destroy civil rights, undermine the social order, and instigate "industrial war." A campaign of posters, warnings, cross burnings, and floggings were being carried on in the industrializing piedmont. In Florida, Klansmen paraded through Winter Haven, Lake Alfred, and Auburndale during the citrus packing-house strikes of 1937, with signs warning STRIKERS AND RADICALS WILL NOT BE TOLERATED. Klan organizers were threatened in Columbus, Georgia; Chattanooga, Tennessee; and Greenville, South Carolina. Klan headquarters moved into a new office in downtown Atlanta. Money now seemed available; organizers were engaged and old rolls canvassed. Union leaders in some areas of the North were jittery. The Klan denounced sit-down strikes, and Klan chief of staff, Jimmy Colescott, arrived in strike-bound Akron to push recruiting. "We're going to break up those damn unions," Klansmen boasted as they flogged a union representative who had attempted to organize the workers at the Georgia Savings Bank and Trust Company's Scottdale Mills, in suburban Atlanta.

The attempted revival of the Klan as an antiunion instrument was in the hands of James Colescott, a former veterinarian from Terre

Haute, Indiana. Now in his forties, Colescott had been a lieutenant to "The Old Man," D. C. Stephenson, in the early days and had lasted through to head the Klan in the Midwest during the Depression years. In 1937, he was called to Atlanta and elevated to chief of staff.

The Imperial Wizard Evans was in the general process of retirement from active control of Klan affairs. Most of the Klan's real estate had been liquidated but Evans had an imposing house in the good section of town and was personally doing very well. The Klan helped the election of Georgia Governor E. D. Rivers, a former Klan lecturer, and Evans had been a lieutenant colonel on his staff. He was obviously on the in, for he got a share of the state printing as well as a monopoly on the sale of asphalt for the state highways. He was not in the latter business himself, but rather acted as agent for those who wanted their bids seriously considered. The state attorney general, Ellis Arnall brought suit and Evans got off with a $15,000 fine. He had to return some of the printing money, and he and ex-Governor Rivers had to wriggle a bit to get out of a mail-fraud case the next year.

When his appointed officials had last re-elected him, Evans announced that it would be his final term. As it drew to a close, there were rumors of dissension. The actual handling of Klan affairs had fallen more and more into Colescott's willing hands. In 1936, an insurance company purchased the old Imperial Palace on Peachtree Street and in turn sold it to the Roman Catholic Church. The sacred ground, where once the white-robed defenders of Protestant America had trod, was being turned into a rectory for the new Cathedral of Christ the King. And then Bishop Gerald O'Hara thought of a master stroke. Why not, he told the Atlanta *Constitution*'s Ralph McGill, invite the Imperial Wizard of the Ku Klux Klan to the dedication. Evans was in a box. Whether he accepted or not, the bishop's invitation made a good yarn for the press. No better way could have been picked to announce to Klansman and alien alike that the Church of Rome now lived in the former Imperial Palace of the Invisible Empire. The joke was on the Klan. Evans put the best face he could on the situation and showed up for the ceremony, but other Klansmen were furious. It was all very well for Evans to announce, as he had done earlier in the year, that the Klan had subordinated "racial and religious matters" in order to oppose "communism and the CIO," but he had no business trying to practice it. Evans wanted out anyway, and the Klan was willing. There was talk about a payment of $220,-

000—for the Klan was a valuable piece of property—but no substantiation is available. In June of 1939, in a ceremony in the Dixie Ball Room of the Henry Grady Hotel, James A. Colescott was elevated to the Imperial Wizardship.

43

ALL DRESSED UP BUT NOT GOING ANYWHERE: THE COLESCOTT ERA

Jimmy Colescott was a short, stocky man, bald and round-faced, who gave the impression that he did not deny himself at the table. He possessed neither the juicy flowering phrases of Colonel Simmons nor the hail-fellow quality of Evans, but during his almost two decades of Klan activity he had been a dependable lieutenant and able organizer. Although he made the usual public disavowal of violence, Colescott announced that his administration would be one of action. Recruitment was pushed with much use of newspaper advertisements, and claims were made of substantial membership increases. The old "nightshirt factory" in Buckhead was reopened, and the new Imperial Wizard undertook a series of inspirational trips through the North, Midwest, and Florida. Delegates from most West Virginia cities attended a state meeting in Charleston, and Klansmen from Yonkers and Binghamton Klaverns joined those from Brooklyn and Jamaica for a New York City rally. Pennsylvania Klansmen got together in Germantown; Wilmington No. 7 was still active as were such New Jersey Klaverns as No. 4 of Bloomfield, the Unity Klan of Linden-Rahway, and the Dr. Hiram W. Evans Klan No. 70 of Hackensack. The Klan claimed that it had units operating in Dayton and Akron, Ohio, and outside of Cincinnati to the south. The Michigan Klan, aided by a regular weekly radio program pushed its recruitments among the factory works of Detroit, while the loyal Nathan Hale Klan of Kokomo, Indiana, remained spasmodically alive, and a new organization was struggling to get going in Lake County. In southern Indiana, which had once been prime Klan country, the Klan had been damaged "pretty severely" by the "Stephenson matter," Colescott told congressional probers, and only a single, small Klavern still existed. The Invisible Empire was doing better next door in Rockford, Illinois, with some activity in Chicago, Champaign-Urbana, and to the north.

Missouri Klans met in St. Louis and Hannibal, and when Colescott paused to deliver his pep talks to the brothers of Joplin Klan No. 3, they gathered to meet him in their famous, mysterious Klan cave. There were Klan stirrings in Oklahoma and Colorado, but an Omaha, Nebraska, recruiter did the Invisible Empire no good when it turned out that a nudist organization, which he also headed, shared the Klan's post-office box. He explained that the two organizations were completely separate, however, as some of the church folk might not be too keen on nudism, but his considerate sense of propriety did not spare the Klan from wry comment by the press. With the exception of the Aberdeen, Washington, Klansmen, whose stones rattled the windows of the town's union halls, the only active realm in the West was California. Although Grand Dragon Earl Snelson operated out of Long Beach and his Klansmen occasionally popped up in Azusa and Glendale and made protest appearances in Los Angeles itself, the center of renewed activity seemed to be in the San Joaquin Valley around Tulare. At the other end of the country, the realm of Florida, which the Fiery Cross boasted had been "long a stronghold of the Ku Klux Klan," everything was bustling. Colescott spoke at Klan meetings in his two major centers, Tampa and Orlando, and later returned to be feted in Daytona and in Avon Park, and to salute his paraders from the courthouse steps of Live Oak. Although his Empire recorded its greatest gains in Michigan, Colescott later told the congressional probers it was strongest in the Sunshine State.

And so the followers of Imperial Wizard Colescott carried out his administration of action. Negro voters were threatened in Miami, Florida, and Greenville, South Carolina. Jews were denounced in Mattituck, New York, and Rosedale, New Jersey. Papism and Romanism were attacked in Jersey City. The Klan expressed its alarm over "Mr. Roosevelt's sellout to the Roman Catholic Church" when he sent an envoy to the Vatican, but nationally the Klan didn't like Wendell Willkie any better, for he had fought the Klan during his Democratic days, both at the 1924 National Convention and over the school board in Akron, Ohio.

The Klan itself admitted that its membership rose and fell in response to events around it, but what with the ever present Negro and the growth of organized labor, things in South Carolina had reached a permanent crisis situation. Colescott denied that the Klan was fighting the CIO, but The Fiery Cross and klannish activity indicated otherwise. As though the unions weren't bad enough, the CIO was going in for race mixing. CIO WANTS WHITES AND BLACKS ON SAME

LEVEL, *The Fiery Cross* headlined, describing it as an organization of Communists trying to fool people into thinking it a labor union. The press reported that the businessmen were saying that if the Klan wanted to run the CIO out of the South, they were for the Klan and they knew plenty of other good men who felt the same way they did. Klansmen boasted that the Invisible Empire was active from the mountains of the piedmont to the waters of the Great Pee Dee and the lowlands of Charleston. Klaverns were organized or organizing in Aiken, Hartsville, Darlington, Chester, Pamplico, and Great Falls. However, though it rode in various parts of the state, it was strongest in the western textile centers of Anderson and Greenville counties. In Anderson, the night riders spied on the unions and flogged both the organized and unorganized whose moral behavior they found excuse to question. As it had been throughout the thirties, Greenville was the Klan's stronghold. Armed Klansmen twice raided the county National Youth Administration (NYA) camp at Fountain Inn, robbing and beating some of the young Negroes and tacking up a sign reading NIGGERS, YOUR PLACE IS IN THE COTTON PATCH. Negroes were assaulted in Greenville and nearby Simpsonville, and the police cooperated with the Klan in a joint campaign of arrests and harassment to turn back a Negro-voter-registration campaign. Backed by concern from the press and pulpit, Governor Burnett Maybank sent his police into Anderson after a white garage mechanic was flogged. Klan records were seized, Klansmen arrested, and some of them eventually jailed.

Klan night riding in Georgia turned out to be even more extensive. Whenever there was nothing else to do, Klansmen could always don their hoods and flowing robes and demonstrate before the Atlanta *Constitution* building, wherein dwelt their prime chronicler and mortal enemy, Ralph McGill. However, for several years Klan floggers had been at work in and around patient, long-suffering Atlanta. Their "crusade for better living" coincided with the CIO's organizing drive and an increase in Negro-voter registrations, but their victims were recruited from the general public. In March of 1940, an East Point barber, who liked to take a nip or two on a cold night, was whipped and left to die in the frost-covered woods. The resulting grand jury investigation revealed that some fifty other Georgians had been worked over during the preceding two years. They included a white owner of a Negro theater in Decatur, a fundamentalist minister whose meetings made too much noise, and a young Atlanta couple who had been beaten to death in lovers' lane. Eventually eight floggers, including several deputy sheriffs, landed in prison—to wait the later clemency of Eugene Talmadge. The popular outcry and the resulting police action brought crises within the Klan in South Carolina and Georgia. It retrenched, disclaimed, and—for the record—unmasked.

These were just not lucky days for the Klan and the next serious bit of trouble came over the German-American Bund. Not that the Bund and the Klan were antagonists—far from it. During the late thirties there was a prolonged flirtation between the Klan and a growing proliferation of fascist organizations. The names of William Dudley Pelly, Mrs. Leslie Fry, James Edward Smythe, Col. E. N. Sanctuary, Gen. George Van Horn Mosley, and many other "front" leaders turned up with Klan associations. Some had gotten their start in the Klan. *X-Ray* editor Court Asher was once D. C. Stephenson's lieutenant in Indiana. White Shirt leader George W. Christians had been a Klansman. So had George Deatherage, founder of the Knights of the White Camellia, who claimed that the Nazis had copied their anti-Jewish policy and their salute from the Klan and who suggested to his followers that they now shift to burning swastikas. Deatherage did his best for the Nazi cause in America; so did Colonel Sanctuary who organized the company that published the Klan's semiofficial history. Mrs. Leslie Fry had slipped back into Germany, but testimony before the House Un-American Activities Committee claimed that she had made Hiram Evans a $75,000 offer for possession of the Invisible Empire.

Southern Klansmen and *The Fiery Cross* were generally hostile to the German-American Bund, but things were somewhat more friendly elsewhere. Two Klan leaders, one a New Yorker and the other from the West, reportedly wanted to support Hitler. *Bundesführer* Fritz Kuhn later told Ralph McGill that there had been negotiations with representatives from the Michigan and New Jersey Klans, with what he expansively claimed was the understanding that the Southern Klans would go along.

Things had certainly reached a far cry from the early 1920s when Klansmen in Paterson, New Jersey, had protested against the Steuben Society and the teaching of German in the schools. On August 18, 1940, several hundred robed Klansmen shared the grounds of the Bund's Camp Nordlund, near Andover, with a similar contingent of uniformed Bundsmen. Clad in yellow robes, Arthur H. Bell, the Bloomfield lawyer, who had led the New Jersey Klansmen in the 1920s, attacked the singing of "God Bless America," which he described as a Semitic song fit only for the Bowery taverns and brothels.

Edward James Smythe, Protestant War Veteran head, who had organized the meeting, lauded Bund leader Kuhn. Then the Camp Director and Deputy *Bundesführer* stepped to the front of the platform. "When Arthur Bell, your Grand Giant, and Mr. Smythe asked us about using Camp Nordlund for this patriotic meeting, we decided to let them have it because of the common bond between us. The principles of the Bund and the principles of the Klan are the same," he proclaimed.[1] At this point, Klan leader Bell grasped the hand of the Bundsman. After the speeches were over and a message from Imperial Wizard Colescott had been read, a Klan wedding was performed beneath a fiery cross. When the neighboring residents gathered outside the fence chanting "put Hitler on the cross" and singing the "Star-Spangled Banner," the Bund band struck up and drowned them out.

The midsummer's idyl at Camp Nordlund indicated no immediately prospective merger of the two patriotic organizations, but the resulting publicity and response were so unfavorable that Colescott repudiated the meeting. Arthur Bell and Rev. A. M. Young, the New Jersey Klan secretary were unceremoniously ousted from the Klan despite their long years of dedicated service. *The Fiery Cross* became more outspokenly hostile to the Bund. Although local Klans remained busy in the face of unionization attempts in Alabama and central Florida, the war brought a decided limitation of Klan activity. Klonvokations were suspended to conserve gasoline. Accompanied by the state's attorney general, Imperial Wizard Colescott journeyed up to Washington to see if one of the Florida senators could arrange for B'nai B'rith and the Knights of Columbus to join the Klan in patriotic programs. Although the Klan had been attempting to bore from within the labor movement in the North, there is no evidence that it was directly involved in the great Detroit race riot and the Philadelphia transit strike.

In 1944, the U. S. Bureau of Internal Revenue struck a body blow against the Invisible Empire when it filed a lien for back taxes of over $685,000 on profits earned during the 1920s. "It was that nigger-lover Roosevelt and that Jew Morgenthau who was his Secretary of the Treasury who did it!" Colescott later explained from his retirement in Miami. "I was sitting in my office in the Imperial Palace in Atlanta one day, just as pretty as you please, when the Revenuers knocked on my door and said they had come to collect three-quarters

[1] John Roy Carlson, pseud., *Under Cover* (New York, 1943), p. 153.

of a million dollars that the government just figured out the Klan owed as taxes earned during the 1920s. . . . We had to sell our assets and hand over the proceeds to the Government and go out of business. Maybe the Government can make something out of the Klan—I never could."[2]

[2] Stetson Kennedy, *I Rode with the Ku Klux Klan* (London, 1954), p. 87.

44

THE HOODED WORLD OF DR. GREEN

With the end of the larger war in Europe and Asia, there were those who were willing to try where Colescott had not been successful. In October of 1946, the first cross since Pearl Harbor was burned on Stone Mountain, and stamped over the old application blanks was a new name, THE ASSOCIATION OF GEORGIA KLANS. Its leader was a mild-appearing, bespectacled, fifty-five-year-old Atlanta obstetrician with a small, sandy, toothbrush mustache. An articulate and shrewd organizer, Dr. Samuel Green, had been a Klansman since the early 1920s. When others departed during the lean Depression days, Green had stayed on. In the early thirties he became Grand Dragon of Georgia and later Colescott's right-hand man. Slowly rising up the ladder of succession, he had grasped the leadership of the Klan when the Internal Revenue Service jarred it out of Colescott's uncertain hands. Although the Invisible Empire had supposedly disbanded to escape the long arm of the Treasury Department, he had kept together an informal association of local Klans in Georgia, South Carolina, Tennessee, Florida, and Alabama.

The times seemed generally right to make a serious attempt to get Klandom going again. The extension of the wartime Fair Employment Practices Committee came up before Congress, and, in January of 1946, the Southern senators began their effort to talk it to death in Washington. Atlanta Klaverns asked their members to send dollars to Senators Walter George and Richard Russell and to Mississippi's Theodore G. Bilbo and Congressman John Rankin to beat back the FEPC. Former Klansmen felt the old stirrings and new recruits were coming in. There were indications of strong Klan efforts being made in California, Kentucky, Tennessee, and Alabama, as well as reports that the Invisible Empire was by no means dead in New York, New Jersey, and Pennsylvania. Evangelists preached the doctrines of Jesus and the Klan at rallies in east Tennessee and in

Knoxville. In Chattanooga, repeated cross burnings forced a Jewish woman to close the store she had opened in suburban Red Bank, and J. B. Stoner, one of the rising young men of postwar Klandom, was pushing sales of *The Protocols of Zion*. A member of the Chattanooga Board of Education brought a Klansman to a discussion of pupil absenteeism and the Klan launched a campaign of threats and beatings to urge parents to improve the situation.

In purpose and action it was the old Klan, although it was growing increasingly parochial. It would concentrate on character development and klannishness, defined as mixing with those who have the same ideas. As usual it was to protect the home, the chastity of white womanhood, the United States, its Constitution and flag. A special pitch was made to returned, restless servicemen faced with the danger of similarly restless former Negro servicemen and with "the niggahs who got all the good jobs while you were in uniform." "I'll tell you this," the Grand Dragon announced to an interviewer, "no CIO or AFL carpetbagging organizers, or any other damned Yankees are going to come into the South and tell Southerners how to run either their businesses or their niggahs." President Truman's FEPC was a troublemaker, so were the Jews and increased Negro voting, as well as the unions. "We won't tolerate any alliance between niggahs, Jews, Catholics, and labor organizers either," he warned.

By the spring of 1946, Doc Green's Invisible Empire was swinging into high. In a Southland torn by a spate of lynchings and mob violence, Georgia's Gene Talmadge and Mississippi's hard-bitten Theodore Bilbo warned against a black invasion of the voting booth. Back fees were paid for the period of 1943 to 1946 and the old Klan charter was reactivated. Klansmen received instructions to get their robes laundered for a major initiation ceremony on Stone Mountain, and exclusive picture rights were sold to *Life* magazine. In West Virginia, Robert Byrd, still a decade away from the U. S. Senate, urged the need of a revival in the Mountaineer State upon the willing Samuel Green.

Almost immediately, the Klan ran into serious opposition. U. S. Attorney General Tom Clarke, President Truman's courtly Texas friend, announced that he would use every law on the books to break the Klan before it got going again. In response to the numerous complaints during the summer of 1946, the Justice Department and the FBI were looking for cases where Klansmen had broken federal laws or joined with state officials to interfere with the exercise of civil rights. The government studied charges that Florida officials had co-operated with the Klan in keeping Negroes out of housing projects and that Georgia Klansmen had fired into Negro homes as a warning against voting. Although investigations carried on in seven states led to no court action, the knowledge that the FBI was delving into one's affairs was a sobering thought and one which was to remain in the Klansmen's minds. The following year the Ku Klux Klan joined its dire enemy the Communist party on the attorney general's list of subversive organizations.

A number of states were inclined to go even further than the national government. When the California Klan tried to get going again, state Attorney General Robert W. Kenny went to court to get it outlawed, and Los Angeles police put pressure on its organizers. The governor of Pennsylvania asked the FBI to aid his state agents. Michigan and Ohio also conducted investigations and Kentucky joined Indiana and New Jersey in seeking to keep the Klan from doing business in their states. In New York City there had been more than a dozen units clinging to life in the various boroughs until 1944 when they were consolidated into four Klaverns, one each for Brooklyn, Queens, the Bronx, and Staten Island. A state undercover agent worked his way into the Klan and obtained a list of eleven hundred names which were turned over to the FBI. The Klan itself was banished from the state and one-time incorporator Horace Demarest, now a GOP leader in Queens, lost his job as Deputy State Motor Vehicle Commissioner.

All of these buffetings on the frontiers of the Invisible Empire were of minor importance. Georgia was the heart of the Empire and there the struggle was vital. As Doc Green's rejuvenated Klansmen found self-expression through violence, Governor Ellis Arnall, who as attorney general had forced Hiram Evans to disgorge some of his state asphalt profits, set out to revoke the Klan's charter. According to the charter, the Klan was to be a nonprofit, charitable, benevolent, eleemosynary society for the promotion of pure Americanism. According to the state of Georgia, it was a profit-seeking, politically motivated organization which notoriously violated both the criminal laws of the state and the civil rights of Georgia's citizens. The legal resources of the state were thrown into the case and Assistant Attorney General Daniel Duke was given charge. A dynamic young lawyer, Duke, had gone after the Atlanta Klan in 1940 and had broken the back of its violence with the conviction of eight Klan floggers. When the Klan pulled strings to get them pardoned, he had fought the issue out with Governor Talmadge in a scene which

Life magazine made famous from coast to coast. Under the caption
THE GOVERNOR OF GEORGIA REMEMBERS THAT HE WAS ONCE A
FLOGGER HIMSELF, *Life* described the exchange:

> On a table in front of Governor Eugene Talmadge were two
> leather man whips that might have come straight from a Gestapo
> cellar in Poland. Also on the table were clemency petitions for
> six Ku Klux Klansmen now in prison for flogging pro-union
> mill workers. Assistant Solicitor Dan Duke, fighting the peti-
> tions, shook a whip in the Governor's face and shouted: "These
> are whips you could kill a bull elephant with." Gene Talmadge
> . . . stared straight at the whip. Then he announced that he was
> sorry for the floggers, would take their pleas under considera-
> tion. He recalled that he had once helped flog a Negro himself.
> "I wasn't in such bad company," he said. "The Apostle Paul
> was a flogger in his life, then confessed, reformed and became
> one of the greatest powers of the Christian Church. That proves
> to me that good people can be misguided and do bad things."[1]

This was December 1941. After Pearl Harbor, Dan Duke enlisted
in the Marines and the governor, over newspaper and Church protest,
pardoned the floggers. Now Dan Duke was back on the job racing
hard, for Gene Talmadge was again waiting in the wings.

Ellis Arnall had taken over after Talmadge and now in the fall of
1946 Old Gene staged a comeback, with the aid of the Klan and the
county unit system of voting, and would again assume office in January of the new year. While the Klan could not be killed by the
revocation of its charter, such a censure could embarrass and compli-
cate its operations. Dan Duke went North to seek information from
the legal officers of New York and New Jersey. When it was finally
drawn up, the state's case rested upon two major points. One was the
Klan's various flirtations with the German propagandists, the Bund,
and various domestic right-wingers, including a continuing relationship with Gerald L. K. Smith, through Kentucky's Continental League
for Christian Freedom. The other was the Klan's intent to "organize
police officers, cab drivers, truck drivers, and others in key positions"
to seize parts of the state government.

The atmosphere was not made easier for the Klan by the successful
prosecution of an Atlanta-based neo-Nazi terrorist organization
named the Columbians. Dan Duke labeled the brown-shirted Co-

[1] *Life,* 11 (December 8, 1941), 40–41.

lumbians as the "juvenile delinquents of the Klan." The most notable of the Columbians' Klan connections was Rev. A. C. Shuler, who served as a Klan lecturer before turning to the greener pastures of the Florida Citizens Councils in the 1950s. An Atlanta jury needed only twenty-nine minutes to find the widely publicized Columbians guilty and when Old Gene's luck and life ran out just before his inauguration, Doc Green gave up the old national Klan's charter.

Now describing itself as a purely local organization, the Association of Georgia Klans continued to operate. It hurt Doc Green's pride not to be able to call himself the Imperial Wizard but there were compensations. In his capable hands the Invisible Empire grew, particularly in Georgia. As ever, many law officers joined, giving the Klan areas of local immunity. City councilmen belonged and the Klan made a particular effort to bring in all of the cab drivers of Atlanta. "When the word comes," Grand Dragon Green announced mysteriously in closed meeting of Atlanta Klavern No. 1, "every cab in Atlanta will be needed!" In 1948, Klan-intimidation campaigns did much to keep Negroes from the polls and secure the triumph of young Herman Talmadge as governor. The Klan had been happy to work for Old Gene's son and as a token of appreciation, he appointed Doc Green a lieutenant colonel and aide-de-camp on his staff.

In keeping with the times, the Klan undertook a public-relations program to improve its public image. A hooded Klansman dressed up as Santa Claus, presented a radio to a 107-year-old Negro; food was distributed among the needy, and twenty suits of underwear stamped K.K.K. were donated to the old folks' home in Atlanta. But violence was still the Klan way and Klansmen talked incessantly of killing. The Klan had its own Klavalier Klub whipping squad, and Doc Green had to banish an extracurricular group who called themselves "the Black Raiders," after they were arrested. To prevent such unfortunate occurrences in the future, Klansmen were cautioned to remove the AGK (Association of Georgia Klans) stickers on their windshields.

But the secret life of their Invisible Empire was becoming something of juicy public scandal. The Klan seemed to have no secrets from Drew Pearson, Walter Winchell, and Ralph McGill's Atlanta *Constitution*. Mainly through the efforts of a slight but fiery-willed young writer named Stetson Kennedy, who had smuggled himself into the Klan ranks, everybody was reading about what went on in Klan meetings. Kennedy's employer the Non-Sectarian Anti-Nazi League was discreetly passing along his information, and the children of America were turning on their radios to hear Bud Collyer, as

Superman, defeat the hooded legions of the Klan. The Klansmen didn't like being made fun of, and it was a hard experience after staying up late defending Americanism to be awakened by your children arguing outside your bedroom window over whose turn it was to play Superman and beat up the Klansmen today. And it was upsetting listening to them shout the new secret password which had been revealed to you in solemn secrecy only after the payment of twenty-five cents.

Klaverns worried about their security systems, announced the uncovering of fictional traitors, and swore that radio and newspaper columnist Drew Pearson would be silent tonight. The Klan had had its chance to "get" Drew Pearson, for in 1946 he demanded an opportunity to broadcast from the Invisible Empire's holy Stone Mountain. All its owners could think to do was to close the mountain until after the state election. Pearson spoke, unmolested, on the steps of the capitol building in Atlanta, revealing Old Gene's secret campaign promise to appoint an Atlanta Cyclops as head of the Georgia Bureau of Investigation. Since the leakage of Klan secrets seemed to be continuing unabated, the leaders decided that it would be unwise for members of the city police force to appear conspicuously or in uniform at meetings. This caused unrest among the undertakers who feared their reputation was equally at stake, and others stirred uneasily.

But the Klansmen still continued to meet and to talk like Klansmen.

Meeting of Atlanta Georgia, Klavern No. 1
November 1, 1948
125 present
10 new applicants
1 reinstatement

The Grand Dragon, Dr. Green, has had all of his teeth pulled, and consequently was not feeling well. He came but didn't stay long. He let R— act, as Exalted Cyclops, in his place.

Rev. H—, an old railroad engineer, made a long talk on a visit he had with Senator Russell, who promised that he would have Congress pass Federal laws to prohibit intermarriage between black and white. H— made a religious talk that in God's sight it is no sin to kill a nigger, for a nigger is nothing more than a dog or a beast. Russell told him he had one of his books, and he was going to use his book and the same scripture passages to pass the bill against intermarriage.

H—— is to preach to-morrow (Wednesday) night at East Point and it is to be broadcast and all Klansmen are invited to listen in or attend.

Jimmy H——, the city detective, spoke about a white man who was shot by a nigger last Friday—or perhaps it was by two niggers. He said they knew who and would arrest them. He also spoke of a Negro and a white man arrested in Carrollton, Georgia, for the murder of a white boy . . . whose body was found in some bushes. The boy was trying to protect the girl whom he was going with from being attacked by a mask-wearing man. The girl said she was sure it was a colored man. H—— said this was about the fourth attack lately in that vicinity and it looked like the Klan was going to have to do something around there. He said about 1,000 people were milling around the jail in Carrollton yesterday, trying to take the nigger out and lynch him.

B——, the Grand Titan, talked. He said this showed how great the need was to have a Klavern in every community, because of such attacks.

A policeman named C—— got up and made a long talk along the same lines.

Trigger N——, also a policeman, got up and made a talk and said he hoped he wouldn't have all the honor of killing the niggers in the South and he hoped the people would do something about it themselves; and that Carrollton had some good Klansmen in it who were able to handle the situation—but maybe they needed some help from the outside and if some went up (from No. 1) to put on a parade or demonstration it might help things out.

R—— and V—— (head of the Klavalier Klub) reported on Videlia. Said 300 attended and they were met by the Chief of Police, the Assistant Chief, and the Sheriff of the County (all of whom gave their assistance). Everyone of the city officers are Klansmen, except the Mayor who is opposed. The Klan has said that it will have a new Mayor after the next election. They are going to work on him. Dr. Green made a speech (from Videlia) and it was broadcast throughout South Georgia.

In the West End, where there has been trouble with the Negroes buying property and moving in, a fellow named H—— reported colored people buying up real estate and moving in on Glenn Street and around Candler Warehouse. R—— said he would have the Klavalier Klub investigate.

R—— said Drew Pearson did not have anyone in the Klavern

Hall to give out information, any more. He commented on Drew
Pearson quoting Dr. Green's urging all Klansmen to vote for
Thurmond. Also, he said, the man who gave out that information
was out of the Klan for good. He referred to this man as "a bald-
headed bastard."

R—— urged all Klansmen to get out and get the vote in Tuesday morning and to work like they did in the last primary—when
working for Talmadge—for Thurmond.

V—— spoke about the Black Legion trial. . . . All except one
of these were members of the Klan at one time, they tried to run
things their own way and couldn't and so started this up.

It was announced there is to be a big chicken supper on Nov.
13. All members in Atlanta are invited. It is to be the No. 1
Klavern.

. . . Big preparations for the December meeting in Macon,
and all in the State are urged to go to it.

R—— said that new Klaverns are being established now, on the
average of one a week throughout the country. It is surprising,
he said, how the Northern States are taking to the Klan. He
spoke particularly of Detroit, Chicago, New Jersey, Indiana,
Maryland, Pennsylvania, and New York State. The Klan is
really growing in these states.

So the Klan carried on, officially and unofficially, its warnings,
night raids and floggings, its parades and cross burnings, its oyster and
chicken pilau suppers, and its Klonvokations and mystic initiations
on Stone Mountain. The Klan whooped it up for Dixiecrat candidate Strom Thurmond when he came to speak at Wildwood, Florida,
and Birmingham Klansmen warned that they stood ready to enforce
segregated seating when Henry Wallace addressed a rally there. Although the hooded order's program of parades and cross burnings
had helped Herman Talmadge through the Democratic primary by
keeping down the Negro vote in Georgia, not even the Klan itself
claimed to have influenced the national election. However, it was a
busy year for the Peach State Klan nevertheless.

Mississippi editor Hodding Carter, keeping watch over his South
like a father with a difficult child, wrote that the Invisible Empire was
"sloshing over like an overfull cesspool from its Georgia stronghold"
into neighboring states. Although in 1949 Doc Green claimed 140
Klaverns in Georgia, twenty in South Carolina and fifteen each in
Florida, Alabama, and Tennessee, federal tax investigators estimated

the number of Klansmen at not over ten thousand. Twice that seems a more likely guess. And the Klan was beset by opposition as never before. The charter revocation suit had harassed it in Georgia and the federal tax suit loitered in the wings. The governors of Southern states were showing an increased inclination to take action against the order, and grand juries pressed it more closely even though petit juries were still reluctant to convict. The Southern press was more inclined to speak out against the Klan as was the ministry. In South Carolina, for instance, the Baptist State Convention warned its members against joining the Klan and asked for enforcement of laws against the hooded order.

Although the Georgia legislature turned down an antimask law in January of 1949, the vote for it was impressive. A growing list of cities led by Wrightsville and Macon, where the Klan had held its 1948 convention, outlawed the public wearing of the mask and Columbus banned cross burning. In neighboring Alabama, Governor "Big" Jim Folsom was pressing his antimask laws through the legislature. In ordering the arrest of any driver who covered up his license plates, the governor announced that "mobs, hooded or unhooded, are not going to rule Alabama." When a cross burning took place near Suffolk, Virginia's Governor William Tuck proclaimed that he would "not allow any of our people of any race to be subjected to terrorism or intimidation in any form by the Klan or any other organization . . . based on terror."

After a Klan motorcade drove through Tallahassee, Florida, in January of 1949, Governor Fuller Warren, himself a former Klansman, asked the legislature for action, stating that "the hooded hoodlums and sheeted jerks . . . made a disgusting spectacle, these covered cowards who call themselves Klansmen." Although his request that the mask be banned and the Klan outlawed was initially buried in committee, many cities passed their own antimask laws. American Legion posts supported the governor's stand and the Tampa *Tribune*, which the Klansmen bitterly called "The red Trib," and applauded "hit 'em another lick, Guvner!" If outlawry was unconstitutional, as a number of lawmakers claimed, then why not require public registration, the paper asked, proclaiming that Florida should require "Open parades, openly marched in." Those with nightshirts, the *Tribune* philosophized, should be subject to the same laws as the men who wore pants.

In many states anti-Klan laws had been on the books since Reconstruction days and one of them was used against a Klan leader in

Tennessee. These old statutes were of little use, however, for they required that a specific intent to use intimidation to interfere with civil rights had to be proven to the jury. The new laws and ordinances now made the public use of the mask, whatever its wearer's intent, sufficient for conviction. The Anti-Defamation League circulated model state and municipal ordinances and at least eighteen states, including many in the South, had such laws on their books by mid-1948. Some made exceptions for Halloween and Mardi Gras, while others upgraded the penalties for masked misdeeds.

Two particular characteristics of the postwar Klan emerged clearly. The first was the open pattern of resistance in numerous communities where the Klan was active. The second was that while the Klan could still commit violence and inspire terror, the organization itself gained little prestige. Jeers and laughter, from Negro as well as white, greeted many a Klan speech, parade, and cross burning. In Greenville, Georgia, Negroes lined the road for a Klan parade; giggling children drumming on kitchen pots and pans followed the marchers and an old woman called out to Klansmen, "Send us your sheets, white folks, we'll wash 'em." When the Grand Dragon, Samuel Green himself, spoke in Columbia, South Carolina, white students from the university heckled him and tossed stink bombs. In Talladega, Alabama, a twelve-year-old boy kicked down a blazing Klan cross and an armed group of men went out in search of the Klansmen. During the summer of 1950, students at all-Negro Atlanta University were asked to answer a detailed questionnaire about violence and security in their communities. Half of those questioned said the Klan was operating in their areas, although more than two thirds of those living in rural districts and small towns reported no. The city police were believed to be increasingly, though not generously, likely to take action against the Klan, as were responsible members of the Negro and white communities. Fifty per cent of those from rural areas indicated that the Klan was feared, but more than two thirds of the small-town and city dwellers said that it was not. Hodding Carter commented in 1949 that while the Klan of the 1920s had been politically powerful and an overawing organization in the 1920s, the South was not willing to permit that to happen again.

45

THE DEATH OF THE DRAGON

In August of 1949, disaster overtook the Invisible Empire. The hand of Providence reached out to the rose garden of Grand Dragon Samuel Green's Atlanta home and unceremoniously inducted him into membership in a rather different sheeted aggregation. During the postwar years, Sam Green had held together a Klan movement which was not attracting many men of his ability and professional respectability.

The Invisible Empire was already plagued by dissidents, "Bolshevik Klans," Doc Green had called them. Now it splintered badly. The new leader of the Association of Georgia Klans was Sam Roper, a slow-speaking former Atlanta policeman who headed both Herman Talmadge's Georgia Bureau of Investigation, and the Oakland City Klan No. 297. Roper was unable to hold the factions together, and independent Klans proliferated. New Klans sprang up in Georgia, Alabama, Florida, the Carolinas, and Tennessee. Not a Klan for each, but Klans galore. They engaged in endemic violence. Grand Wizard William Morris of Alabama and Grand Dragon Tom Hamilton of North Carolina ended up in jail. So did many of their followers. While external pressures mounted, those business firms which had favored the Klan's antiunion path found it increasingly difficult to get the Klansmen to attend to business.

During 1949, even before the unexpected departure of Doc Green, there had been a wild and furious outbreak of Klan violence in Alabama, Tennessee, and Georgia. South of what Klansmen liked to call the Smith and Wesson line, burning crosses lit the dark countryside. Klansmen fired bullets into the houses of unfriendly lawyers and threatened hostile editors in Gastonia, North Carolina, and Milledgeville, Georgia. In Tennessee a pack of Klansmen assaulted two Chattanooga men who refused to kneel in tribute before a blazing cross, and another herd invaded the Little Holiness Church of Dolly Pond and blackjacked six men for not looking after their families. It was even dangerous for Tennesseeans to go visiting. When seven Chattanooga Negroes had a few too many in the little town of Hooker, Georgia, Dade County Sheriff John M. Lynch turned them over to a Klan flogging party for proper sobering up. Although the American Legion, labor, the pulpit, and the press bitterly pounded the Klan, the degree of official police action usually depended on a reading of local sentiment. Thus, in Soperton, Georgia, the next year, the sheriff did not bother to investigate when four men were flogged, while the sheriff of nearby Dodge County couldn't look into an incident there because he was busy—baby sitting. Too often a shooting "in the line of duty" or the aggressive "questioning" of a prisoner in his jail cell obviated any need for Klan intercession.

On the other hand, the mayor of Iron City, Georgia, and a posse of friends shot it out with fleeing Klansmen who escaped over the Alabama border after a hundred-mile-an-hour chase, and Sheriff Lynch and one of his deputies were convicted in federal court of violating the civil rights of the prisoners whom they had turned over to the Klan. Generally, the Southern Regional Council tended to feel, the police were beginning to enforce the laws a little more evenhandedly and there was a somewhat greater likelihood of getting juries to convict accused Klansmen.

Across the state line from Georgia a bald, heavy-set, multichinned, roofing contractor named William Morris had incorporated his Federated Ku Klux Klans of Alabama, and they rode into violent action in the late spring and early summer of 1949. A woman who reportedly "rented rooms" to high school students was dragged from her house and threatened with burning at the stake. A mother was flogged for encouraging one of her daughter's suitors whom the Klan did not like. So were the suitor and two friends. A Navy veteran was worked over for not supporting his family to the Klan's satisfaction, and an unsegregated café was raided. Governor Folsom went on the air to tell the people of Alabama "Your home is your castle; defend it any way necessary," and the state-wide antimask law was easily passed through the legislature. After several Klan jurymen were excused, almost a score of night riders were indicted and Bill Morris went to jail for refusing to produce a list of Klan members. When he was let out on bail to get the list, he announced that it had been "stolen," and so back to prison he went. And there he sat in the Birmingham jail for sixty-seven hot summer days, feuding with his subordinates over lines of authority and whether the Klan should unmask.

Many of his followers resigned lest their Grand Wizard decide to unmask them individually. Finally Morris ended his unrewarding martyrdom by re-creating a list from memory which satisfied the judge, even though not the state's attorney general.

While Morris' Klansmen were undergoing trial in Birmingham, violence flared again. Charlie Hurst, a rural storekeeper in Pell City, west of Birmingham, was shot by a group of hooded night riders. One of the band committed suicide, placing the blame for the killing on Rev. Alvin Horn who had been representing the Georgia interests in Alabama. Although civic pressure forced the Pell City Klavern to disband, the charge against Reverend Horn did not stick, leaving his Klan future undimmed.

Even in Georgia the Klan star seemed to be on the wane, and the evidence came from the Talmadge camp. Up through 1951 all efforts at a state antimask law had been beaten back, though with narrowing margins, but the word which reached the governor was that the Invisible Empire was becoming more of a liability than an asset. Imperial Wizard emeritus Hiram Evans, who had faded away into comfortable retirement, commented that you couldn't start a fire in wet ashes. So in the winter session of the 1951 legislature, Herman Talmadge's boys took over the lead and pushed through the laws they had hitherto opposed. Less than two months later, Governor Jimmy Byrnes of South Carolina signed a similar bill, prohibiting adult maskers and intimidatory cross burnings.

Nevertheless, Tom Hamilton, the plump, bespectacled, sportily dressed former wholesale grocer from Atlanta did not get the message. An alumnus of Doc Green's old Association of Georgia Klans, Tom Hamilton had moved to the little South Carolina town of Leesville where he bought a fine colonial-type mansion with white columns and carried on his grocery and Klan businesses. When the latter prospered, he felt it his duty to give it his full attention. Although unaffiliated Klaverns still remained active in traditional Klan towns like Greenville and Anderson, Tom Hamilton's domain lay a good 150 miles away, in the rich tobacco, cotton, peanut, and sweet-potato country along the North Carolina border.

In the summer of 1950, motorcades and cross burnings in Horry and Columbus counties heralded the arrival of the Klan. Then came the recruiting drive and the need to provide the boys with a little action. Visiting orators like Florida Klan entrepreneur Bill Hendrix might point out the dangers of the Jews, Jay-cees who met with nigras and didn't believe in segregation, and the communist-lining University of North Carolina, but the real need for the Klan lay right there in Horry and Columbus counties. Too many people were drinking too much. Men were becoming lazy, beating their wives, forgetting to take care of their mothers, missing church, running around, and engaging in immoral cohabitation. And so the floggings began. The call from a "distressed" motorist, or the man who appeared at your door at night and asked to use the telephone, might be decoys for mayhem-minded Klansmen. In the period of two years, at least thirteen men and women, usually white, were taken from their homes and flogged. People bolted their doors at night and stood their rifles and shotguns at the sides of their beds. On the North Carolina side of the border, the Columbus County sheriff reported, "My deputies are afraid to go to anybody's house at night to carry out even routine duties—people down here are in the mood to shoot first and ask questions later."

On the other side of the border, however, Horry County Sheriff C. E. Sasser raided Klan headquarters after the hooded knights kidnaped the proprietor of a Negro dance hall and left one of their own number, a Conway police constable, dying in the exchange of gunfire that followed. Despite the attentions of local sheriffs, both Carolina governors, a pair of Pulitzer prize-winning editorial campaigns by the little Tabor City *Tribune* and Whiteville *News Reporter,* and the FBI, it took almost two years to put a checkrein on Tom Hamilton and his hooded followers. When the sheriff's deputies arrested Klansmen at a revival service at the Cane Branch Baptist Church, the pastor and his congregation had the deputies arrested. Even though the deacons and stewards of the other Conway churches got together to make the deputies' bond, it looked as though Grand Dragon Hamilton was right when he boasted that the Klan was too powerful to be stopped. Occasional Klansmen were arrested but the most that anyone could get Hamilton on was carrying a battery-operated cross on his car which the state claimed was a violation of its law against cross burnings.

Finally, early in 1952, the Klansmen of the "Southlands Sportclub of Fair Bluff" carried their sporting a little too far. To be precise, they pulled a man and woman out of bed and took them across the state line into South Carolina. The Klan moralists stretched them across a car fender and laid on with a machine belt nailed to a cut-down ax handle, to convince them of the need to live better lives. The trip across the state line made it a federal offense, and the FBI at last was free to act. By the time all the court cases were over, fifty-eight Klansmen had been fined, and more than a score went to jail for an average of three years. Grand Dragon Hamilton himself was in for four. The "Tarheelias *Führer* of the meat counter and vegetable bins," had received his comeuppance, the Greensboro *Daily News* chortled.

In the splintering of Klandom which took place with the death of Samuel Green in the summer of 1949, there emerged a variety of would-be entrepreneurs who hoped to pick up the fragments. Some of the efforts were of short duration like that of the bumbling old Lycurgus Spinks who somehow managed to get tapped to "Meet the Press" on coast-to-coast radio and television. Doc Spinks had given most things a try during his career, including the ministry, politics, and embezzlement, and had won his doctorate as a sex lecturer for "men only" with special "ladies only" matinees. He made an impressive picture with his long white, flowing hair and a chest full of medals, but his Klan following was nonexistent and when he no longer had a national audience he soon tired of the sport. "Grant may have taken Richmond," an amused Mississippian commented, "but old Spinks sure took Washington."

The most peripatetic operator in the new anarchic Klandom, its most assiduous Horatio Alger, was a Florida plumbing contractor named Bill Hendrix. When a schismatic group of Klansmen split off from the Association of Georgia Klans and organized the Original Southern Klans, Inc., in southwestern Georgia, Bill Hendrix took over as their Florida agent. Despite Governor Warren's denunciation of the hooded order, Hendrix got a Florida charter, as well as a place on the attorney general's list of subversive organizations. When the home office in Columbus, Georgia, folded, Hendrix was in business for himself.

Selecting the more expansive name of Northern and Southern Knights of the Ku Klux Klan, Hendrix sought to build his new empire outward from the Tallahassee area. The riot which greeted the Paul Robeson concert in Peekskill, New York—a favored Klan territory during the 1920s—gave Hendrix a chance to claim far-flung Northern support, but his world was still confined to a limited following in Florida. After a secret Klonvokation in Jacksonville, he announced the election of a short-lived "Permanent Emperor Nathaniel II," titled after the first Imperial Wizard of the Reconstruction Klan and generally believed to be the local Democratic county chairman. Changing the name again, this time to the Southern Knights of the Ku Klux Klan, he entered into a coalition with William Morris' Federated Klans of Alabama and Tom Hamilton's Association of Carolina Klans. Their program was to wage war on "hate movements," such as B'nai B'rith, the Federal Council of Churches of Christ, the NAACP, the clerical hierarchy of the Roman Catholic Church, and the communist-oriented progressive educationists.

While Morris and Hamilton sought to pacify their own realms, Hendrix focused his attention on the Sunshine State. When Palm Beach officials criticized a salesman for the Association of Georgia Klans, who were working the territory south of Fort Pierce, Hendrix charged into the act. Palm Beach's evil joints and dives had placed it on the Lord's blacklist, he announced, and would surely be destroyed. Burning crosses illuminated the night skies of Hialeah and Miami Shores as the members of the long-lived George B. Gordon Klan divided between the Roper and Hendrix organizations. With his newly found Carolina ally by his side, Bill Hendrix toured northern Florida speaking against the communistic welfare state, people who lived in adultery, and the Jews. An invitation to the Florida legislature to join him at a Live Oak rally on the courthouse steps brought no takers, however, and it was the opposition rather than the Klan ranks that seemed to be growing. The angry city fathers of Palm Beach passed an antimask ordinance. So did Orlando after Klan use of the public parks drew criticism from Drew Pearson, and Orlando citizens took up a collection for a Negro veteran whose new home had been set afire by members of the hooded order.

With the press and civic groups firmly behind it, an antimask bill was reintroduced in the legislature in the spring of 1951. Similar laws had just been placed on the books in Georgia and South Carolina, and the bill encountered little serious trouble, even though Hendrix registered as a lobbyist in order to testify against it. It passed unanimously in the lower house and by a thirty-one-to-six margin in the Senate. One of those to vote against outlawing public wearing of the mask was Senator Charlie Johns who was later to win fame as a relentless investigator and critic of the quality of the Americanism at the state universities.

A summer of cross burnings, from Miami and Fort Myers to Jacksonville and the panhandle, touched off by Klan sneak squads, proved an ineffectual rejoinder. At Tampa, Miami, and Bartow meetings the turnout was poor. Some new sort of device was needed, and the ever resourceful Grand Dragon came up with one: he would run for governor of Florida. This way he would have legitimate access to public parks and platforms; the newspapers would report what he said, and who knew but that lightning might indeed strike if all white men would get together and vote as they should. It was a fine idea and most Klansmen happily approved. Some trouble did come from Bill Griffin, the Tampa private detective and Grand Titan for central Florida. Griffin mistakenly assumed that there was now a vacancy at the top of the Klan, and that he himself would make a far more suitable leader. The ultimate result was that Hendrix and Griffin parted company amid a welter of charges and countercharges, having laid the foundation for a long and bitter animosity that was to bear unexpected fruit in the 1960 national presidential election.

While Hendrix was touring northern Florida seeking votes and members, a different campaign was being waged to the south. When a blast was touched off at Miami Negro Carver Village housing project, the chief of police reported that he had reasons to believe that the Reds were responsible. However the Dade County Property Owners Association and the members of the John B. Gordon Klavern had been actively opposed to an expansion of Negro housing. "Yes sir, ladies and gentlemen," a hooded speaker announced from a loudspeaker "this is the Ku Klux Klan! Whenever the law fails you just call on us! We're going to see to it you don't have to sleep with niggers like they do over in Miami Beach." Bombs were set off at a Jewish school and a synagogue, and sticks of dynamite were found on the steps of a Catholic church. On Christmas Eve, 1951, a dynamite blast in Mims, near Cape Kennedy, killed the state NAACP leader, Harry Moore, and his wife. Although no convictions resulted, a federal grand jury reported that there had been a whole series of floggings in Orange County and that the floor plan of Harry Moore's house had been displayed and discussed at Klan meetings.

Such events hardly disturbed gubernatorial candidate Bill Hendrix. He held forth on a program of opposition to such "isms" as the FEPC, the UN and the Jews—a program which, except for the last item, was indistinguishable from the local Democratic party platform in his imperial city of Jacksonville. While Hendrix orated, his Kleagles passed out application blanks for the Klan. Hendrix got eleven thousand votes, but few members, and his success as honored speaker to the Florida Sheriffs' Association was balanced by conviction in federal court of sending pornographic postcards to his political opponents. It was all right to tell the applauding peace officers that the murdered Negro leader Harry Moore was a communist and a troublemaker, two terms which the Klan tended to consider synonymous, but there was some danger in speaking about live antagonists. On one of his cards, Hendrix had addressed Fuller Warren as "the scalawag perverted governor," and for Drew Pearson's benefit he had sent a crude cartoon of a toilet bowl, labeled AMERICAN POT FOR COMMUNISTS AND STOOGES, into which a figure marked as the columnist was disappearing. Hendrix was fined $700 and received a year's suspended sentence. On the same day, his one-time confederate, William Morris was arraigned for mailing "obscene, lewd, lascivious, filthy and indecent" pamphlets, and only four months before, Tom Hamilton had been fined $1000 for mailing defamatory material. "It looks like I'm out of the mailing business," Hendrix commented after the verdict, and his Alabama and Carolina associates probably felt the same way.

Of course, Carolina Grand Dragon Tom Hamilton was soon out of the business entirely, and in the spring of 1952 was on his way to jail as his Association of Carolina Klans toppled before the FBI and the federal courts. It had been a cold winter and spring for the anarchic world of Klandom, which had also seen Charles Klein the Number Two man of the Sam Roper's Association of Georgia Klans go to prison for dynamiting the home of an Atlanta Negro. The cumulative publicity made things difficult for all good Klansmen trying to turn a dollar and save America. Bill Hendrix had been making plans with Carolina Klan mogul Hamilton to reactivate the Klan in the Old Dominion State of Virginia. Governor John Battle, backed up by the Junior Chamber of Commerce promised to curb any such revival and Klansman Hendrix reluctantly retreated. "All that trouble in North Carolina hurt," he said. "People want to forget all that beating and bloodiness." However coursing through the veins of the stocky forty-one-year-old plumbing contractor was some of the same stubborn entrepreneurial spirit which had made the nation great. Despite bitter protest from the Sons of Confederate Veterans, he next projected a nationwide American Confederate Army. It would be a maskless combination of all-white, Christian, anticommunist organizations, to be clad in the gray uniforms of the heroes of the South's most glorious hour. Already, he boasted, he had a good sixty to seventy colonels recruited. Here again, though, the touch was not quite right. For the time being at least, he decided being a Klan leader was just not sufficiently rewarding. He withdrew from the world of Klandom but could not resist founding, along the way, a "White Brotherhood" which would not use violence unless it was absolutely necessary.

46

LAISSEZ FAIRE, VIOLENCE, AND CONFUSION IN THE LATE FIFTIES

It was the Supreme Court decision against public school segregation on May 17, 1954, that gave the Invisible Empire a new impetus and environment for action. In a South marked by growing hysteria, the Klans burst into activity. The ever ready knight, Bill Hendrix, charged into action and a resurgent proliferation of would-be leaders galloped about the landscape seeking support from old Klans and new Klansmen. In Florida particularly, the picture remained anarchic, and a secret gathering of northern Florida leaders, held in the woods northwest of Jacksonville, brought no peace.

Shortly after the school decision, a red-haired, bespectacled paint sprayer at GM's Fisher Body plant in Atlanta, named Eldon Edwards, revitalized the Klan in Georgia. With old Doc Green's son Sam Junior acting as lawyer, he got the state to charter his "U.S. Klans, Knights of the Ku Klux Klan," which absorbed what was left of the old Association of Georgia Klans. Compared to the others, the U.S. Klans did well, partially because Edwards talked tough and partially because he did not particularly practice it. Controlling a reasonably unfragmented kingdom in Georgia, he directed his primary efforts to expanding the frontiers of his domain. In competition with at least seven other would-be Klan organizations, Edwards' U.S. Klans reached a peak membership of between twelve thousand and fifteen thousand followers early in 1958. No other leader could, at best, claim more than several thousand.

Discipline and relative restraint were not what many Klansmen wanted, however. Cross burnings, parades, motorcades, and verbal violence were not quite enough. There were those who thirsted for a bit of the real thing, and there were others who took careful note of the increasing personal fortunes of Eldon Edwards. Rivals reached out for Klan money and Klan power. Jesse B. Stoner, late of Chattanooga, and Horace Sherman Miller of Waco, Texas, were loners. J. B. Stoner, thirty years old at the time of the Supreme Court decision, had been an active Klansman for a dozen years. He had roamed through the world of Klandom, now signing up recruits, now running for Congress, or picketing the White House, one day opposing integration at Miami's Orchard Villa School, and the next arranging to become head of a new Klan in Virginia—if only anything could be gotten going there. Wherever he was, J. B. Stoner filled the mails with pleas to do away with the Jews, through joining whatever his present klannish enterprise happened to be. Finally by the 1960s, he had settled down in Atlanta, sharing an office with the scion of a distinguished old Peach State Klan family and owner of the sacred pastures of Stone Mountain, James Venable. For probably as long as he has ever stayed in one place and tended to one task, J. B. Stoner handled the affairs of the bitterly anti-Semitic National States Rights party, which in turn had drawn its inspiration from Adolph Hitler, whose SS symbol it bears.

Because of his World War I disability, Horace Miller necessarily lived a stationary life. He traveled instead on the wings of the post-office department which carried his often unintelligible newsletter and the application blanks of his mail-order Klan. When Klan material turned up in far portions of the globe among the neofascists in England or Austria, it usually began its journey from Waco, Texas.

The Bryant brothers, Arthur and Joseph, of Charlotte, North Carolina, were arrested in 1955 for sending their unsigned anti-Catholic and anti-Semitic literature through the mails. What turned up was not only that they had dynamite and a rifle mounted over a truck windshield, but also a pair of not unimpressive criminal records, extending from larceny and bad-check passing, to juvenile rape and senior solicitation for prostitution.

When it came to talking tough, and maybe doing something about it, Alabama's Asa Carter's name ranked high on the list of Klan enterprisers in the mid-fifties. "Ace" was an Alabama farm boy who went off into the Navy and, unlike most Klansmen, got a touch of college, studying journalism at the University of Colorado. He worked as a radio announcer and eventually found his way back home again. He made something of a reputation for himself around Birmingham panning rock-'n'-roll music, and when he went into the Klan business he took with him a BE-BOP PROMOTES COMMUNISM sign to put up on his office wall in the dingy ex-movie house out on

Bessemer Road where he made his headquarters. When he was fired for attacking the Jews on his broadcasts, it confirmed what he knew about them anyway and he was ripe for action. Sam Engelhardt, a big planter down in heavily Negro Macon County, was signing up businessmen, planters, bankers, and lawyers for the Alabama White Citizens Councils, but this left out the common man—and Asa Carter. So Ace began organizing the mechanics, farmers, and storekeepers into a Klanlike White Citizens Council, to the ire of Sam Engelhardt, into a new Ku Klux Klan of the Confederacy.

Where the Councils elsewhere decried physical violence and Eldon Edwards generally tried to keep his Klansmen satisfied with strong talk and minimal night riding, Ace's followers eschewed moderation. One of his boys hit the headlines and the police blotters by leaping up on the stage of the Birmingham Municipal Auditorium to assault singer Nat "King" Cole, while four others got twenty years in jail for the turpentine-soaked castration of a helpless Negro kidnaped for a sacrificial initiation ceremony. It was also some of Ace's boys who went up to Tuscaloosa to help welcome Negro coed Autherine Lucy to the University of Alabama. Early in 1957 at a meeting in his moviehouse auditorium, two of his Klansmen objected to Asa Carter's one-man way of running things and asked for an accounting of the finances. Under such provocation there was nothing that Ace could do but draw the revolver that he liked to wear strapped around his waist and let them have it. Both wounded insurgents recovered and the attempted murder charges against Carter were dismissed, but his dim star had just about flickered out.

Another brief stellar luminary in the world of Klandom during the late 1950s was Frederick John Kasper. Kasper gave an Ivy League, intellectual note to Klan affairs. He was a slender, well-groomed young man from a good middle-class family in New Jersey. After leaving Columbia University, he ran a small bookstore in Greenwich Village and idolized the aging literary hero and wartime propagandist for Mussolini's Italy, Ezra Pound. Kasper dated a Negro girl and had a good time in the free, and mixed, world of pseudobohemia, but this wasn't getting him anywhere. Ezra Pound told him that to become famous a man had to "DO SOMETHING," to take sides, no matter what the side was. Kasper picked white supremacy and stocked his new bookstore in Washington, D.C., with anti-Semitic literature and the writings of Ezra Pound.

Admiral John Crommelin was a masterful war hero who had been shot down when he bucked the Eisenhower-administration brass to save the Navy's aircraft carriers. When he launched a new career by running for the U. S. Senate to save Alabama and America from the Jews, John Kasper came down to help. There he met Ace Carter and the two informally teamed up later that summer to see what they could do to keep the schools of Charlottesville, Virginia, and Clinton, Tennessee, segregated. In a pamphlet entitled "Virginians Awake," Kasper used his best Pound-like style to sum up the nature of the problem they faced, and offered a few suggested solutions.

> Jail the NAACP! Hang the Supreme Court Swine! Destroy the Reds! Save the White! Now damn all race-mixers . . . they stink: Roose, Harry & Ike. God bless Jeff/Jax & John Adams, also Abe. Loathe carpetbag, despise scalawag. Hate mongrelizers (pink punks, flat-chested high-brows, homos, perverts, freaks, golf-players, poodle dogs, hot-eyed Socialists, Fabians, scum, mould on top of the omelette). Myerization of News, liars for hire; the press-gang, degenerate liberals crying for petrefaction of putrefaction, complainings—used to be blacker and richer. Social democrats, new dealers, Said Ben: Better keep 'em out or yr/grand children will miss you . . .

> Death for Usurers, money monopolists, obstructors of Distribution (international finance, World Bank and Bunk, Unesco currency, Federal Reserve racket, Barney Baruch's check book, Schiff and Warburg finance Bolshevik refolooshun 1917, Lehman finances Newhouse $$ Birmingham News).[1]

Clinton was John Kasper's great moment. As a result of a week of door-to-door canvassing and haranguing he turned the little four-thousand-person community into a raging, seething mob town that only the Tennessee National Guard could quiet. Clinton juries twice acquitted him of incitement to riot, but eventually a federal judge sentenced him to a year in prison for contempt.

John Kasper never joined the Klan, but the hooded knights took him to their hearts as one of their own. While he appealed his several court sentences, he was a much sought-after attraction on the Klan circuit, particularly in central Florida. However, when an investigating committee of the Florida Legislature offered testimony, including pictures, that Kasper had consorted with Negroes at mixed-race parties in New York City, a reaction set in. Many of his former Klan friends

[1] Seaboard White Citizens Council pamphlet "Virginians Awake," quoted by James Rorty, "John Kasper's Moment of Glory," *ADL Bulletin,* December 1956.

disowned him, although the newspapers in central Florida were to still receive occasional letters from mothers and fathers who testified that that well-dressed young fellow with such nice manners stood for what America was really all about. When John Kasper was released from jail, a small group of friends including Ace Carter and Admiral Crommelin sought to prepare a small welcome ceremony, but his moment was past.

Of the Klan unsuccessfuls who splashed its name across the headlines in the post-school-decision fifties, the most woebegone was the Rev. James W. "Catfish" Cole of Marion, South Carolina. In 1956, Imperial Wizard Eldon Edwards had commissioned him to organize North Carolina, but Cole soon came to feel that it would be a shame to have to divide the spoils and power with anyone else. Where the newly self-styled Grand Wizard made his fatal error, however, was in his decision to carry Klandom into Robeson County, North Carolina. The Klan had operated there against "errant" whites and Negroes in the early fifties until the county solicitor and the FBI caught some of them for carrying victims over the state line, and the solicitor, Malcolm Seawell, let the rest know that any more night riding meant a first-degree burglary prosecution which carried the death penalty. Now, in 1958, Reverend Cole had a new wrinkle. The population of Robeson County was fairly evenly divided between three groups: whites, Negroes, and the Lumbee Indians. In order to accommodate each of them, the county had a complete system of three-way segregation in schools, rest rooms, and other places of public use. The Lumbees were a proud and prosperous people who have never lived a reservation life. Many people believe that they were the descendants of the lost colonists of Roanoke. Some of them had blue eyes and many of them carried old English family names such as Drinkwater and Oxendine. For a number of years they were known as "Croatans," after the single word found carved on a doorpost of the "lost colony."

Most of the Lumbees were farmers but some had gone into business or served in city office. The town of Pembroke was largely Indian. While the Lumbees were unhappy over their own second-class status, there was one thing about which they felt most strongly, and that was the importance of setting themselves apart from the Negroes. It was into this community that Catfish Cole's Klansmen brought their flaming crosses as a warning against Indians mingling with whites, and in which they planned a big outdoor rally.

Although warned against it, Cole went ahead with his plans. On the appointed chill January night some half a hundred Klansmen found themselves gathered in the center of a field near Maxton while hundreds of armed Lumbees watched impassively from the road and the surrounding fields. Several of the Indians had streaked their faces with lipstick war paint, one was wearing a souvenir war bonnet with advertising printed along its side. At eight-thirty when the meeting was supposed to begin, the Lumbees converged on the Klansmen who clustered fearfully beneath a single light bulb suspended from a pole. The few bits of Klan regalia were quickly shucked by their owners. An enormous Indian reached out and broke the bulb with the barrel of his rifle. The darkness was immediately lit by repeated bursts of light as Indians fired their guns in the air and the photographers flashed away. The Klansmen, trusting to wisdom rather than valor, fled. There were a scattering of injuries and automobile tires riddled by shotgun pellets. A few bits of regalia, a Klan banner, and the P.A. system were left in the hands of the Lumbees. After the battle was over, the state highway patrolmen moved in, arrested an armed and intoxicated Klansman whom they found lying in a ditch, and suggested that it was time for the jubilant Lumbees to go home. Reportedly, Sheriff Malcolm McLeod dispersed them with the warning that if they didn't hurry, they would miss seeing "Gunsmoke" on television.[2] Grand Wizard Cole was soon extradited to North Carolina and went to jail for incitement to riot. The press and magazines carried the story and pictures from coast to coast, and everybody laughed, except the Klan. The Kaspers, Coles, and Carters were doing it no good.

And so, in the highly competitive world of free-enterprise Klandom, nearly a score of nonaligned Klans pranced across the landscape from Texas and Arkansas to the Carolinas. However, even in a Southern world of federal court decisions and token integration, they failed to grow and prosper. Part of this was the fault of the kind of leadership which the Klans drew. On the whole it was appallingly bad. Most Wizards and Dragons, like Bill Hendrix, were concerned with the Klan as a money-making organization. Many, like the Bryan brothers in North Carolina, had considerable criminal records. Some, like Ace Carter, were emotionally unstable and prone to sudden violence. Few, as shown most notably by Rev. Alvin Horn of Alabama, were not inclined to practice the morality that they publicly preached. Most, like Reverend James Cole who took on the Lumbee Indians, were

2 Ben Haas, *KKK* (Evanston, Illinois, 1963), p. 126.

prone to the unforgivable fault of bad judgment. Although they dreamed big, they thought small.

The leadership potential in the South entered the battle for segregation through more favored and subtle instruments such as the White Citizens Councils, Federations for Constitutional Government, anticommunist crusades, and regular party politics. Economic and political pressure were espoused more readily than violence, which many embattled segregationists opposed for moral as well as policy reasons. The Klan leadership tended to come from people who might well be described as marginal fanatics and mercenary opportunists.

Alas for the latter, and for all sincere Klansmen, money was in short supply. It was obviously not going to come from the nonaffluent membership of the Klan itself. The business community did not support the Klan. A Klan sheriff usually meant the absence of law and order and the probability of a red-light district, gambling, drunkenness, absenteeism, and bad publicity. Businessmen in Clinton and Little Rock, were frightened by the kind of men and passions attracted by racial violence.

And in the late fifties and early sixties, violence remained the way of the Klan. In 1959 the Friends' Service Committee, National Council of Churches of Christ, and the Southern Regional Council published a report on the first four years after the Supreme Court's school decision. It listed some 530 cases of overt "racial violence, reprisal and intimidation" and generally opined that law and order had been deteriorating in the South. The list of cases was a vastly mixed bag, and the various formations of the Ku Klux Klan were far from responsible for all of them, but there was instance after instance of the Klan's involvement in threats, cross burnings, floggings, and bombings. An admittedly partial list of overt violence, much of it the work of the hooded knights, included:

6 Negroes killed;

29 individuals, 11 of them white, shot and wounded in racial incidents;

44 persons beaten;

5 stabbed;

30 homes bombed; in one instance (at Clinton, Tenn.) an additional 30 houses were damaged by a single blast; attempted blasting of five other homes;

8 homes burned;

15 homes struck by gunfire, and 7 homes stoned;

4 schools bombed, in Jacksonville, Nashville, and Chattanooga, and Clinton, Tenn.;

2 bombing attempts on schools, in Charlotte and Clinton;

7 churches bombed, one of which was for whites; an attempt
made to bomb another Negro church;

1 church in Memphis burned; another church stoned;

4 Jewish temples or centers bombed, in Miami, Nashville,
Jacksonville, and Atlanta;

3 bombing attempts on Jewish buildings, in Gastonia, N.C.,
Birmingham, and Charlotte;

1 YWCA building in Chattanooga and an auditorium in
Knoxville dynamited;

2 schools burned;

In addition, 17 towns and cities were threatened by mob
action.[3]

In view of the fact that society and government strongly disapproved of any such violence and juries were increasingly prone to
indict and convict, it was an impressive total. Part of the explanation
probably lay in the general improvement of the methods of finding
out about and recording instances of violence. But it was more than
this. Race relations were uncertain, changing—the heat was on. To
strike back—and to strike out violently was a traditional response.
When the politicians pledged resistance and officials and community
leaders practiced it both covertly and openly, by noncompliance and
organized economic pressure, the example was there. Society seemed
really to be saying "go ahead" at the same time it told the Klans that
they had better behave.

These were the mixed signals which the banker, the lawyer, and
the businessman, the middle classes, and "all of those people who
were putting on airs but who were no better than anyone else" were
sending out. Such communication within society was at best only
partial, for the Klan's natural constituency did not listen to what the
upper class and business leaders of society had to say. The people
who could send their children to private schools, move to a more expensive all-white neighborhood, who never ate at the lunch counters,
and weren't likely to have to confront Negroes at their country clubs,
offered no competition to the Klan's Cyclopes and Dragons.

And so, while the Southern attorney generals and governors
condemned the Klan which had not had a look-in in a Southern

[3] *Intimidation, Reprisal and Violence in the South's Racial Crisis*, p. 15.

Statehouse since the Grand Dragon addressed Strom Thurmond's applauding South Carolina legislature in 1948, the Klan's sporadic cross burnings, beatings, and floggings continued. There was one new feature, and that was the use of the dynamite. Between January 1, 1956, and June 1, 1963, at least one hundred and thirty-eight bundles of dynamite sent clouds of smoke rising upward above the scarred racial frontiers between the Negro and white worlds. Negro homes, churches, the newly purchased house in a white neighborhood, the residences of white moderates or sympathizers, newly integrated schools, the YWCA in Chattanooga and the Knoxville auditorium, and synagogues in Miami, Jacksonville, Gadsden, and Nashville collapsed into rubble or bared their wounds.

Although the general response to the bombings was one of shock and condemnation, the dynamiter, Klansman or racial extremist, was outside of the ordinary community and not affected by its feeling.

A special police intelligence organization, the Southern Conference on Bombing (SCB), was set up in 1958 under the sponsorship of the then staunchly segregationist Mayor Haydon Burns of Jacksonville, to co-ordinate the efforts of Southern law-enforcement agents, but bombers were difficult to track down and even harder to convict. Would-be dynamiters were convicted in Charlotte, North Carolina, but a pair of Klan practitioners in Montgomery were acquitted, despite a signed confession. In Atlanta, Attorney James Venable successfully defended a group of National States Rights party men against similar charges, with the aid of character witnesses including Klan Wizard Eldon Edwards and an alibi provided during a period of "temporary lucidity" by an inmate of a state mental institution. Although police efforts were not particularly successful, explosives did leave fingerprints behind for the trained expert. Careful police work and a growing co-operation among the states and with the FBI, which had carefully infiltrated the most prominent fringe groups, promised some measure of control if only by promoting caution among the bombers. Only a portion of the dynamitings, though a large one, had been carried out by organized-resistance groups such as the Klan. A rough distribution of responsibility would probably credit the Klan with individual house bombings and place the institutional variety, such as schools, churches, and synagogues, at the door of other groups.

The attention given to the synagogue is particularly characteristic. One of the most pronounced aspects of the present Klan has been its violent anti-Semitism. While this has long been a Klan theme, it has become increasingly strong. Without the resources to turn out their own propaganda, the Klans found a ready, inexpensive supply of literature available from professional anti-Semites such as Conde McGinley and Gerald L. K. Smith, and other propagandists on the Citizens Council lists. The tone was right and the words soon became their words. As the Klan turned more and more to anti-Semitic arguments and inspiration, the leadership of the two movements became more and more intertwined. Integration was denounced as a "Communist-Jewish conspiracy plotting to overthrow white-Christian mankind." Temple and synagogue bombings were described as attempts on the part of the Jews to gain sympathy; Eichmann didn't really do it—and good for him if he did. Hitler had the right idea. Arrested Klansmen were victims of Jewish persecution, and the "Jew-N" was to blame for the troubled state of the world. A nazilike salute was used in South Carolina rallies; Asa Carter's Klansmen dressed in pseudo storm trooper outfits, and the Klan's friend, the violently anti-Semitic National States Rights party used this insignia

which they inherited from the Third Reich by way of the Columbians.

The success of anti-Semitism stemmed from the patness of the explanation it offered for the Klansman's anxieties: his fear of racial mixing, his financial and social insecurity, and his xenophobia. He experienced some difficulty in picturing the hitherto docile Negro, to whom he was accustomed, as being in intense revolt. The explanation of a Jewish conspiracy proved most illuminating, and Klan speakers found that it often took such a note to warm up their audiences. When Southern governors denounced the Negro revolt as the product of communism and troublemaking outsiders, surely the Klansman was justified in adopting similar theories of his own.

The composition of the Klan ranks as the decade of the 1950s drew to a close was a major factor in the receptivity to pat explanations, racial antagonisms, and violence. The Sunshine State of Florida was a good illustrative example. By the end of the 1950s the remaining strength of the Klan in Florida had coalesced in the northeastern corner of the state. In Jacksonville, torn between the polar roles of a modern expanding metropolis and the capital of crackerdom, the political and social outlook was predominantly conservative. With Mayor Haydon Burns preparing to bridge the two and cross over that bridge into the governor's mansion, the citizens acquiesced at the polls to rural small-county control of state affairs and usually sent like-minded representatives to the legislature. While this meant no augmented strength for the various Klans, it did create a world in which they could hold on to a marginal existence and occasionally score successes, such as on "Ax-handle Saturday" in August of 1960. Although the five would-be Klan empires which eked out a competitive existence in Jacksonville, totaled less than a thousand members, they attempted to follow their separate paths.

The most active Florida representative in the world of Klandom was the Florida Ku Klux Klan, whose major Jacksonville unit, like so many Klans elsewhere, met under an assumed name. In this case it was a Fellowship Club, convening in its rented hall on King Street or in the barn owned by one of its members, and occasionally sponsoring meetings in the Duval County Auditorium, or joining other Klan outfits in rallies, institutes, and cross-burning recruitments. Although its numbers probably ran more than a hundred, only a dependable score or two were regulars. They gathered together on meeting nights, milling about informally engaging in the usual Klan small talk of guns and killing. When the meetings were brought to order, the discussion turned to the various menaces to the national well-being, recruitment drives, and the plans to build the new Klavern. The hard-core membership included a retired minister or two, a chiropractor, a plumber, local car and jewelry salesmen, a high school student, an occasional former politician, and several now-pastured associates of Gerald L. K. Smith.

Meeting with other Klan-front groups organized as historical societies, Democratic Women, States' Rights associations, and Progress and Better Government movements, the Fellowship Club sponsored a poorly attended local armory speech by George Deatherage, one of the would-be American *Führers* of the 1930s. Usually the Klaverns worked better when they could get down to local business. Members might differ in their alarm about the Jews, the international bankers, Mrs. Roosevelt, or Nelson Rockefeller, but the pressures of Negro integration gave them a point of common concern. When the wave of Negro lunch-counter sit-ins spread to Jacksonville, the time for action was ripe. On the morning of August 28, 1960, people all over the world picked up their morning papers to read of the first of the riots between Negroes and whites which wracked Jacksonville for three hot summer days. Initially directed at the Negro sit-in demonstrators at big downtown department and dime stores, it encompassed the unruly elements looking for something to happen: for trouble, for a fight, for a chance to strike out at the not particularly friendly world around them.

In a dangerously excited town, it was the Florida Klan which deserved a good share of the credit for starting things off. It was decided that as many Klansmen as possible would go downtown on Saturday morning and see if anything might be done. The word was passed around. In the confused, angry atmosphere that had developed in the second city of Florida, there was a run on the hardware stores and when the crowds formed in front of Rich's Department Store and Woolworth's on the morning of August 27, there were so many ax handles in evidence that when someone described the day's events as "Ax-handle Saturday" the name stuck. The word had been out that the Klansmen and trouble were coming, but with the mayor inactive and the chief of police disconcertingly out of town, once the first blow was struck the last was yet to come.

In an excellent study of the typology of the Klansman,[4] the sociologist James Vanden Zanden, has pointed out that the Klan could best be understood more as a status than a resistance movement. The bulk of the wearers of the white robe occupied an ambiguous and insecure position in society. The Klansman was usually a day laborer, a mechanic, or an industrial worker. His leader probably owned a one-pump gas station and general store, or was a deputy sheriff, an unemployed lightning-rod salesman, or sold storm windows. He stood at the juncture of the middle and working classes, with middle-class identification but without its prestige occupations and status. He and his followers had probably been drawn into the larger city from the farm or small town, and were still partially uprooted and only partially assimilated. Their path to self-prestige was through emphasis on differentiation between themselves and the Negro—with whom they often found themselves in economic competition—and organized overconformity to the institutionalized caste patterns of the South and to one-hundred-per-cent Americanism. Rather than being a direct reaction to and defense against the im-

[4] Paper delivered to the American Sociological Association, September 1959, and partially printed as "The Klan Revival," *American Journal of Sociology*, 65 (1960), 456–62.

mediate possibility of integration, the Klan was generally centered in areas which were not, through the end of the 1950s, directly so threatened. It was almost absent from the rural, Black Belt area of the South. The Klan was a town phenomenon and, with the exception of isolated chapters in such places as Baton Rouge, Shreveport, Waco, and Little Rock, it was centered in the piedmont area of Alabama and the Southeastern United States.

DATE	ALABAMA	ARKANSAS	FLORIDA	GEORGIA	LOUISIA
1956 JANUARY	Montgomery— home of Martin Luther King				
MARCH				Atlanta—Negro home in a mixed neighborhood	
JULY				Atlanta—Negro home in predominantly white neighborhood	
AUGUST	Montgomery— home of Negro minister				
1957 JANUARY	Montgomery— 4 churches, 3 houses			Americus— Koinonia Farm	
FEBRUARY					
MARCH	Mobile—home in mixed neighborhood				
APRIL	Bessemer—2— Negro church and home				
MAY					
JULY	Birmingham— Negro home				
AUGUST					
;EPTEMBER					

SSISSIPPI	NORTH CAROLINA	SOUTH CAROLINA	TENNESSEE	TEXAS	VIRGINIA
			Clinton—5 different dyna- mite blasts in Negro section		
				Beaumont— 2 Negro homes	
			Knoxville— auditorium		
				Beaumont— 3—truck, home, church of white "moderates"	
			Chattanooga— Negro home in white neighborhood		
			Jersey— Negro home		
			Nashville— integrated school		

DATE	ALABAMA	ARKANSAS	FLORIDA	GEORGIA	LOUISIAN
OCTOBER					
NOVEMBER	Bessemer— Negro home			Ringgold— Negro home	
DECEMBER	Birmingham— 5 Negro homes				
1958 JANUARY		Little Rock— home of NAACP official			
FEBRUARY					
MARCH			Miami— synagogue		
APRIL	Birmingham— synagogue (attempted)		Jacksonville—2— Negro school and synagogue		
MAY	Bessemer— Negro home				
JUNE	Birmingham— Negro church				
JULY	Birmingham— Negro home			Columbus— Negro home	
AUGUST					
OCTOBER				Atlanta— synagogue	
1959 AUGUST				Ringgold—3 homes, 2 Negro, 1 white Roscoe— Negro church	
SEPTEMBER		Little Rock—3— school board office, fire chief's car, business office of mayor			
DECEMBER					
1960 FEBRUARY		Little Rock— Negro home			

358

SSISSIPPI	NORTH CAROLINA	SOUTH CAROLINA	TENNESSEE	TEXAS	VIRGINIA
	Greensboro—Negro home		Chattanooga—2 Negro homes		
	Charlotte—synagogue (attempted)	Gaffney—home of white "moderate"	Chattanooga—Negro home		
		Cowpens—Negro home			
			Chattanooga—YWCA		
	Gastonia—synagogue (attempted)		Chattanooga—school		
			Nashville—synagogue		
				Beaumont—white home	
			Memphis—Negro church		
			Clinton—school		
				Houston—playground	
			Chattanooga—Negro home		

359

DATE	ALABAMA	ARKANSAS	FLORIDA	GEORGIA	LOUISIANA
MARCH	Gadsden— synagogue				
APRIL				Atlanta— Negro home	
MAY				Ringgold— Negro home	
JUNE			Miami— Negro home		
JULY		Little Rock— school warehouse, college dormitory (attempted)			
AUGUST			Jacksonville—3 Negro businesses		
SEPTEMBER				Atlanta—car	
OCTOBER		Little Rock— car of Citizens Council member			
NOVEMBER				Atlanta— 4 homes	
DECEMBER.				Atlanta— school	
1961 JANUARY				Douglasville— Negro home	
FEBRUARY				Cobb County— Negro home Mableton— Negro home	
APRIL				Cobb County— home white union official	
MAY				Atlanta—2 Negro homes Lakewood— mixed revival meeting	
JUNE				Atlanta—2— car, restaurant	

360

MISSISSIPPI	NORTH CAROLINA	SOUTH CAROLINA	TENNESSEE	TEXAS	VIRGINIA
					Chesterfield County— 2 Negro homes
			Nashville— Negro home		
			Nashville— Negro home		
			Chattanooga— 5 Negro homes and white realtor		
			Memphis— Negro home		
				Austin— house	

DATE	ALABAMA	ARKANSAS	FLORIDA	GEORGIA	LOUISIANA
JULY				Atlanta—4 Negro homes in mixed area	
AUGUST				Atlanta— Negro home	
SEPTEMBER				Atlanta— Negro home in disputed neighborhood	
OCTOBER			Miami— union building	Atlanta— drive-in cafe	
1962 JANUARY	Birmingham— 4—3 Negro churches, 1 Negro home				
FEBRUARY					Shreveport- home of Ne leader C. C Simpkins
APRIL					Shreveport- Negro Maso Lodge
MAY					Shreveport- Simpkin's summer hon
JUNE					
SEPTEMBER				Valdosta— Negro church	Shreveport- home white integrationis
OCTOBER					
DECEMBER	Birmingham— Negro church				

MISSISSIPPI	NORTH CAROLINA	SOUTH CAROLINA	TENNESSEE	TEXAS	VIRGINIA
Biloxi— sheriff's car					
Wiggins— airplane					
			Kingston— car—white labor official		
	Durham— mixed meeting				
		Bishopville— Negro home			Norfolk County— first Negro home in white area
		Lake City—taxi (only one owned by Negro)			
Oxford— Negro home					
Biloxi—2— Negro home and gas station Columbus— home V. chmn. Miss. Adv. Comt. on Civil Rights					

DATE	ALABAMA	ARKANSAS	FLORIDA	GEORGIA	LOUISIANA
1963 FEBRUARY		Pine Bluff— Negro church			
MARCH	Birmingham— Negro homes				
APRIL				Macon— mayor's mailbox	
MAY	Birmingham—2— A. D. King's home, Gaston Motel				Baton Roug LSU camp

[5] Barbara Patterson, "Defiance and Dynamite," *New South*, 18 (May 1963), 8–11.

MISSISSIPPI	NORTH CAROLINA	SOUTH CAROLINA	TENNESSEE	TEXAS	VIRGINIA
Clarksdale— Aaron Henry's home					
Holmes County— NCC Worker's home					
Clarksdale— Aaron Henry's store					
Jackson— home of NAACP official					
Oxford—Ole Miss dormitory					

47

THE NEW FRONTIERS
OF THE NINETEEN SIXTIES

After tapering off in 1958 and 1959, the Klans sprang into action with the Negro lunch-counter sit-ins, freedom rides, and massed demonstrations of the early 1960s. All of these offered an impetus and occasion for the type of direct violence in which the Klan excelled. By creating the specter of a Negro menace they gave the Klan a degree of approval in some localities that it had lacked for many years.

In Florida the particular kind of prestige, which "Ax-handle Saturday" had conferred on the whole movement, initially tended to bring recruits for all of the Klan units. Despite continuing rivalries, there was much talk of possible mergers among the fragments of Florida Klandom. The new momentum toward unity and growth was soon exhausted, however, and rivalry as usual wracked the Invisible Empire at all levels. The death of Eldon Edwards, in the summer of 1960, brought only increasing uncertainty and competition within the power structure. On the local level in Jacksonville the Fellowship Club made some desultory efforts to place a friend on the Board of Control of the state's universities and ran favorites for the legislature and the city commission. All efforts were lost, amid bitter accusations that the factional Bedford Forrest Klan had given the plot away by putting out a handbill of endorsement.

One of the casualties of the intramural wars among the Florida Klans may well have been the presidential hopes of Richard Milhous Nixon. In September of the presidential year of 1960, Bill Hendrix, the hardened veteran of many Klan wars, announced that he was for Arkansas Governor Orval Faubus, the unwilling candidate of the National States Rights party. Since the bitterness between Hendrix and his fellow would-be Dragon, W. J. Griffin, was well known, the press went to see what Griffin thought of things. This put the Tampa private detective in an embarrassing position. Hendrix had gotten Faubus first, and to tag along behind his rival was too bitter a pill for Griffin to take. He swallowed hard, cleared his throat, and proclaimed that he was for Nixon.

On October 13, in the third of their crucial TV debates, John Fitzgerald Kennedy was questioned about the claims made by some of his prominent supporters that "all bigots will vote for Nixon." Kennedy replied, "Well, Mr. Griffin, I believe, who is the head of the Klan, who lives in Tampa, Florida, indicated in a statement, I think, two or three weeks ago that he was not going to vote for me, and that he was going to vote for Mr. Nixon." Having delivered his shaft, he went on to say that it was absurd to think that Nixon did anything but strongly disapprove of any such endorsement, a sentiment that Nixon was glad to echo from Los Angeles. "I don't give a damn what Nixon said," Griffin retorted the next day, "I'm still voting for him." And in an election in which John Kennedy's narrow victory depended so heavily on the overwhelming margins piled up in Negro precincts in cities such as Chicago, perhaps W. J. Griffin's words helped make the difference.

When Eldon Edwards was struck down by a heart attack his successor was already waiting impatiently in the wings. Where Edwards had talked tough but sought to avoid going very far out on the limb with actual violence, Robert M. Shelton appeared to be a man of action, and he seemed to be a real comer both within and outside of the Klan ranks. He was a good organizer, he seemed to have friends in high places, and he was lucky. His luck came most primarily from the fact that his chief competition in Alabama Klan affairs, the Reverend Alvin Horn, had no luck at all.

Back in 1950, Reverend Horn and a group of Klansmen had gone after a Pell City storekeeper, Charlie Hurst, who was shot when he struggled to get away. Horn was eventually acquitted, but it was bad publicity and the episode didn't indicate much control over things. Then his wife, depressed over an operation, killed herself. As the father of six children it was natural that Horn should seek a new helpmate for himself, but when in 1957 he finally found her, there was a terrible public to-do. The trouble was that the Reverend Alvin Horn was forty-six and his runaway bride was only fourteen. The police brought her back and lodged Horn in jail for contributing to the delinquency of a minor. Her parents planned to annul the marriage on the grounds of nonconsummation. When it turned out that that ground would obviously not stand up, they let the marriage stand. All of this did not appear to be quite the moral standards which the Klan claimed it represented, and Robert Shelton, a young rubber worker from Tuscaloosa, replaced Reverend Horn as Grand Dragon of Alabama. The ambitious Shelton soon quarreled with Edwards, was expelled, and formed his own Alabama Klan. Then, in 1958, he again was Johnny on the spot and his stroke of good fortune came with Alabama's gubernatorial election. John Patterson, who had signed the Southern attorney generals' resolution against the Ku Klux Klan, was in the race. His campaign manager was banker Charles Meriwether, who had managed the Crommelin campaign which first brought John Kasper and Ace Carter together. Candidate Patterson was induced to make an appeal for support to Shelton's constituency, and with Patterson victorious, Shelton's star was in the ascendancy. He was appointed state sales agent for Goodrich Tire Company for whom he managed to land a $1,600,000 contract from the state.

In time, relations cooled between Shelton, his friends, and his employer. Governor Patterson came out in early support of John Kennedy's presidential hopes and Shelton told a Tuscaloosa Courthouse convention of Alabama Klansmen that they "should stay away from Kennedy and keep an eye on John Patterson and Charles Meriwether," whom he claimed were tools of the Jews. While many other Alabama politicians were to later roundly attack the Kennedy administration, Charles Meriwether, from his new post on the Export-Import Bank, obviously was not too dissatisfied. Shelton however was soon separated from the Goodrich Tire Company, in what they described as a reduction in force and he denounced as political persecution.

The heart of Klan affairs lay in Georgia and Alabama, but there was still life elsewhere. In Florida, the Fellowship Club concentrated its interests on local politics, opposition to integration, and the construction of a meetinghouse. Work was started on the Klavern and the county obliged with a piece of road, under the mistaken belief that the structure was to be a church. A raffle for a pistol and a rifle added money to the building fund. In June of 1961, representatives of the various Florida Klans met in Orlando to discuss ways of making integrated use of lunch counters unpleasant, and cards reading A NEGRO HAD THAT SPOON IN HIS MOUTH were printed up to be left on the counters. The general feeling in Florida Klandom was that violence had been shown to be unprofitable and dangerous, and so true Americans ought to adopt the kind of pressure tactics which they felt had proven so successful for the NAACP and other Negro organizations. When the protest marches reached their peak in Ocala during the summer of 1963, KKK stickers rather than Klansmen turned up all over town to encourage the resistance of the city fathers. In Chattanooga, which had ignored the Klan during Reconstruction and cradled it in Tennessee ever since the 1920s, the Invisible Empire neither substantially gained nor lost during the early sixties. This was the home of the splinter Dixie Klans, Inc., chartered in 1956 by a retired Chattanooga accountant, and the Georgia Invisible Empire usually found a responsive ear here. Chattanooga is a manufacturing and transportation hub. It combines a large industrial working class and a substantial, affluent population, but for a city of its size and development the ordinary middle class is remarkably small. Klan membership was not very impressive but its following and feeling were something that was kept in mind in city politics. The Klan's strength was to be found in the East Lake and Highland Park sections of the city, which stretch along the foot of Missionary Ridge from Rossville, Georgia, north to the Tennessee River.

By 1962, Chattanooga, aided by an intensive program of segregation through urban renewal, was prepared for the inevitable beginning of public school integration. Most of the city's leaders had agreed that the step must be taken peacefully, and the Klan quietly observed the transition. However, in the 1962 congressional elections, with a New Frontiersman running on the Democratic ticket, things had become a little too much for even the Klan to bear. Although the Republican businessman had been a party to the smooth school transition, at least he was otherwise more sound. A few nights before the election, the Klan spokesman was put on television to help do his bit and the more conservative Republican went off to Washington.

With the exception of Mississippi, where the White Citizens Councils and the state government seemed to have local affairs well in hand, the Klans continued to eke out existence in most of the South during the early 1960s. They had gotten permission but few members in Virginia and drew small but dependable crowds to their North Carolina rallies, and better ones in the western parts of neighboring South Carolina. There were at least three organizations each in Texas and Arkansas, and although Klansmen claimed to be staging a revival in northern Louisiana, the Klan had long kept an eye open for signs of racial unorthodoxy among Shreveport schoolteachers and the professors of Centenary College.

It was in Georgia and Alabama that the real fortunes of a Klan revival in the early sixties rested. When Eldon Edwards died in August of 1960, his boyish young protégé, Georgia Grand Dragon Robert Lee "Wild Bill" Davidson, succeeded him. Unfortunately, Davidson's nickname, which he had earned with the attraction-getting buckskin jacket that he wore as an insurance salesman, was more indicative of appearances than performance. Wild Bill was too nervous and high strung for an organization such as the Klan. His inherited box-salvage plant in Macon wasn't doing well, and his rejection of both Shelton and the National States Rights party as too fanatical, indicated that his reign was going to be a pale copy of Eldon Edwards. The fact that he appointed Alvin Horn as his Alabama lieutenant was a commentary on the quality of talent available to him. After an explosive meeting early in 1961, his second in command, Calvin Craig, took the slim Georgia legions over to Bob Shelton. Since Mrs. Edwards was disinclined to relinquish her hold on the copyrights of the U.S. Klans, Shelton continued to style his "only authentic" organization, as the United Klans of America.

During the postwar forties and fifties, the Klan had talked of resistance but it had been mainly a status movement for its members, operating primarily in areas that were not faced with the prospect of imminent integration. Merely by joining the Klan and participating in its verbal defiance and occasional sporadic violence, the Klansman satisfied the urges that carried him toward membership. In the sixties, however, Negroes entered the colleges of South Carolina, Georgia, Alabama, and Mississippi; public school integration ground inexorably on its laggard way, Negro voting registration increased, and Negro demonstrations put pressure on the segregated public facilities and life all over the South.

All of this presented the Klan with a great challenge and a great opportunity. This was the chance to gain the active role and the increasing membership that had so long eluded it. At the same time what could the Ku Klux Klan do about the rising wave of the Negro-rights movement? And could it afford to be able to do nothing? Georgia and Alabama Klansmen laid their work aside and grabbed their pamphlets and guns to dash off to the bus stations of Birmingham, Montgomery, and Gadsden and the campuses at Oxford, Athens, and Tuscaloosa. They occasionally got a few good licks in and some good publicity. When the police let opposition to the "freedom rides" in Alabama erupt into violence, Shelton and Horn were federally enjoined against further trouble and Judge

Frank Johnson in Montgomery announced, "If there are any more such incidents as this again, I am going to put some Klansmen, some city officials, some city policemen and some Negro preachers in the Federal penitentiary." There was certainly nothing wrong with good publicity like that, and the judge's charge that Klansmen had conspired to bring about the bus riots in Montgomery, Birmingham, and Anniston was at least generally correct. After all, what was the harm of a few arrests for incitement to riot and some fines? Surely, with Jimmy Venable to handle the defense and a Klansman on the jury, no serious harm was likely to result.

The Klan had picketed Negro sit-ins in Atlanta department stores, and when the NAACP was insolent enough to hold its 1962 convention right in Atlanta, naturally Klansmen did a little bit of counterprotesting. At nearby Stone Mountain, nazi-style armbands mingled with red and white Klan robes, as the National White Americans party and James Venable's Defensive League of Registered Americans joined the Klan for a Fourth of July protest.

The following Saturday, the Klan hosts, some three hundred strong, rallied again in Jimmy Venable's pasture at the base of Stone Mountain. A small detachment of state troopers and county police stood by to prevent the demonstration spilling over onto state property on the mountain itself. After Grand Dragon Craig and other speakers had worked the Klansmen to the correct emotional temperature, they set out anyway. There was a struggle between the Klansmen and the outnumbered troopers who struck out with their clubs and responded to a rock barrage by lobbing tear gas into the crowd. When a Klansman called out, "Let's go up the mountain, women and children first," the troopers entered into a parley with Craig and his leaders. It was agreed that twenty Klansmen would be allowed to ascend the mountain for a "religious ceremony," but as the troopers stood aside the whole mass of Klansmen and spectators swept forward up the slopes. The press generally accounted it as a victory, though a minor one, for the Klan over an irresolute and outmanned state patrol. Governor Eugene Vandiver was considerably distressed; "I can assure you it won't happen again," he promised.

From the slopes of his granite tabernacle, Grand Dragon Craig had had a few words to say about what was going to come next in Georgia. The politicians had better "get right with the K.K.K." or they would have a hard row to hoe, he warned. A few months later at the biggest Peach State rally in more than a decade, a few miles outside of demonstration-torn Albany, Imperial Wizard Robert M. Shelton himself had come to present the Klan line. "We don't want no violence," he announced, "but we ain't gonna let the niggers spit in our face either." The future, he promised, would be one of bloodshed and victory. Calvin Craig, speaking next, laid it on the line. His listeners should fire all Negroes who worked for them and vote to put former Governor Marvin Griffin back in charge of things. In Georgia, at least, despite a somewhat increased interest in the Klan and a touch of arson, dynamite, and shotgun pellets, there was little violence and less victory. The universities, a bit of Atlanta, and the first public schools desegregated. Marv Griffin did not make it to the governor's mansion, and when a Negro woman in the little town of Dallas, Georgia, opened fire on a band of Klansmen who tried to break into her house, it was the Klansmen who went to jail.

The Klan was clearly going to live on in Georgia and Jimmy Venable had organized his own National Knights Federation, but national attention was focused on Imperial Wizard Robert M. Shelton and Alabama. For the most part the Klan had not been active in the real Black Belt counties of Alabama, where the Negroes make up most of the population and seldom vote. It was in the center of the state, however, that the Klans rode more freely than perhaps anywhere else in the South. If a rough four-sided figure were to be drawn to include Tuscaloosa, Birmingham, Anniston, and Montgomery, the major area of Klan activity would have been enclosed. Ringed in would be the major civil rights arena in Alabama, containing Montgomery where Martin Luther King and the bus boycott first made headlines, the battlegrounds of the freedom rides, beatings, bus burnings, and bombings, the Talladega home of Reverend Horn and the Tuscaloosa site of the University of Alabama and Robert Shelton's headquarters. Within this field wherein the Klan had sown its dragon's teeth, lay the one-time stronghold of Eugene "Bull" Connor. From 1958 until his 1963 defeat at the polls and in the courts, the tough Birmingham police commissioner came close to making his own law. In its simplest form Bull Connor's law read that Negroes and whites were not equal, either in the eyes of society or the police. By his violent tactics and his tacit acceptance of those private operators who followed his example, encouragement was held out to Birmingham's Klansmen. Some six hundred thousand people lived in Birmingham's Jefferson County, and constituted one out of every five people in the state. Forty per cent were Negroes. In the bustling steel centers of Birmingham and nearby Bessemer, the Negro was a possible economic competitor of the working-class white, and the Bessemer highway came to be as close as there was to a Klan highway in America. When it came down to bombings and beatings, the Negroes of Birmingham claimed, it was sometimes difficult to distinguish between the Klansmen and the deputies. Also within the Klan's charmed geographical quadrilateral was the governor's mansion in Montgomery where Alabama Governors John Patterson and George Wallace refrained from giving the impression that pro-segregation violence was completely distasteful.

Despite the fertile soil and degree of tacit permissiveness and occasional approval which the Klan received in central Alabama, the law was tightening up on Klan night riding. The press was not their friend, and the community leaders and "big mules," those giant out-of-state businesses such as U. S. Steel who have the biggest word on things in Birmingham, mildly bestirred themselves to incline toward racial moderation. Altogether, Klan ranks did not climb out of the low thousands.

Nor had the craggy-faced, young Imperial Wizard Bob Shelton found the magic formula. As Admiral Crommelin repeatedly discovered, anti-Semitism and opposition to fluoridated water and mental health as Communist-inspired can carry one only so far in the South. The crusades against kosher cookery launched by Shelton's former public-relations director, Wally Butterworth, who was once the big-time "Vox Pop" radio announcer, had little organizational punch.

The Klan's solution to the Negro-rights movements in the turbulent summer of 1963 was primarily imitative. The image-conscious Klan leaders cried out to their audiences: "Let's be nonviolent . . . we've got to start fighting just like the niggers." Klansmen were told that they must stage marches, registration drives, boycotts, and sit-ins. When Negro demonstrators shoved and shouted, Klansmen did the same. Georgia Dragon Calvin Craig explained to his listeners in the university city of Athens how to treat the local branch of a desegregated cafeteria chain: "You good white folks . . . just go in there and get you a glass of water and just sit." While Governor Wallace lingered briefly in the schoolhouse doorway of the University of Alabama, the public-relations-oriented Shelton and his Klansmen kept the newspapermen supplied with free sandwiches. It was perhaps ironic that Bob Shelton's almost miraculous survival from the crash of the plane in which he was flying northward to protest the Negro "March on Washington," was pushed to the inside pages while civil rights demonstrators captured the headlines and blanketed the press and television.

48

THE LONG HOT SUMMER

By the spring of 1964, as the marchers again began to fill the streets of southern cities, the Klan's response was no more certain or original, and now a touch of Islam tinged its flowing robes. For several years Klan leaders had bitterly pointed out that it was the Klansmen, not the "moderate" civic leaders, who actually end up living in an integrated world. At cross-lit nocturnal rallies in rural areas, Klan speakers echoed this note of desperation. They called upon all white men to strike back by refusing to employ Negroes in their homes or businesses, but such pleas were not particularly successful because most of their listeners couldn't afford to have anyone working for them in the first place. Finally at a big daylight meeting in Atlanta's Hurd Park, with local Black Muslim leader Jeremiah X in attendance and singled out for praise, Bob Shelton and his top lieutenants presented an explanation of how the Invisible Empire proposed to escape from integration. Perhaps unwittingly like the Black Muslims, the Klan would seek its long discussed goal of creating a racially private world of its own. Incorporated Caucasian communities with their own houses, schools, churches, and business organizations would enable the faithful to escape court-ordered contamination. Like the old days of the twenties the Klan had mobilized its talents to sell its members insurance, but this time, under Bob Shelton, the money seemed headed back into Klan affairs. By the fall of the year the United Klan's Imperial Wizard could announce, somewhat vaguely, that land had already been purchased in Alabama.

The serious, never-smiling young Shelton, now an air-conditioner salesman, had come to represent the more conservative button-down-collar wing of Klandom. This meant no lessening of antagonism against the Negro, whom he saw as a depraved savage not far removed from the beast and the jungle, but in practice it did lead to a slight diminution of verbal and actual violence.

With his old units, plus associated groups such as the Dixie Klans, the Improved Order of Klans, the Association of Georgia Klans, and newly recruited formations in southwestern Mississippi and north-eastern Louisiana, Shelton had a loosely disciplined empire stretch-ing from Ocala, Florida, to Chattanooga, Tennessee, and Baton Rouge, Louisiana. Far outnumbering all rivals, Shelton felt no need to compromise with other Klan groups, even though his repre-sentatives attended the secret unity conventions in Biloxi, Mis-sissippi, and the Dinkler Plaza and Henry Grady hotels in down-town Atlanta.

The main impetus for such meetings came not from Shelton and his United Klans and affiliates, but from the more chaotic followings of Atlanta Attorney Jimmy Venable. Lacking Shelton's ability to organize things well, Venable opted for variety. In addi-tion to his own National Knights, he had his Defensive League of Registered Americans, Inc., his Committee of One Million Cau-casians to March on Washington, and his anti-Semitic boycotters, the Christian Voters and Buyers League. Most of the Klans that did not work with Shelton belonged to Venable's Federation of Klans.

The major problem that continued to face and baffle the hooded knights was what to do about integration. The Klansman was sworn to resist it. He had pledged himself, in mystic oneness with his fellow Klansmen and in the mirror of his own self-respect, to suc-ceed, by whatever means. Having thus emotionally crossed over the threshold of violence, the Klansman was highly likely to turn to action. When he did, he was particularly vulnerable. Whether his violence was spontaneous or carefully planned, the police and the greatly respected FBI knew where to look. Usually there were too many Klansmen in on the secret, and, as has been the way since the days of Klan trials in Reconstruction South Carolina, Klansmen under pressure told on each other.

The Klans, therefore, successfully turned to violence only where popular and police sentiment granted them a high degree of local immunity. During the long hot summer of 1964, Klansmen found such places as Madison County, Georgia, and St. Augustine, Florida.

The preceding fall, at a Klan rally just outside the ancient Florida city, Connie Lynch, the Klan's string-tie, traveling evangelist, had successfully heated up his audience with cries for blood. "I'll tell you something else," he had said. "You've got a nigger in St. Augustine ought not to live . . . that burr-headed bastard of a dentist. He's got no right to live at all, let alone walk up and down your streets and breathe the white man's free air. He ought to wake up tomorrow morning with a bullet between his eyes. If you were half the men you claim to be," he harangued his listeners, "you'd kill him before sunup." After his oratory had moved everyone more than an hour closer to sunup but without producing any blood, Connie turned the platform over to his Jacksonville Klan host and the crowd started to drift away. Suddenly there were cries from the woods of "Niggers! Niggers!" and four Negroes, including the dentist R. N. Hayling, who had been trying to spy on the meeting, were dragged forward at gunpoint. As the Klansmen began to beat the Negroes and cry for their mutilation and death, a spectator in the crowd slipped away and called the sheriff, who arrived in time to rescue the captives and arrest four Klansmen. Local juries found the Klansmen innocent of assault and battery, but convicted the Negroes for attacking the Klansmen. In a right-thinking community like this, a useful organization such as the Klan might have a real future.

There was, however, a serious problem. Since the 1920s one of the patriotic duties of the Klan had been to protect America from Roman Catholic subversion, and rural Klan fundamentalists still occasionally preached the anti-Catholic evangels from Klan platforms. The old Spanish town of St. Augustine was primarily Catholic, which would on the surface have made it an unlikely field for the sowing of the Klan seed. However St. Augustine faced a greater peril in the upward push of the Negro. This in itself was distasteful, and the citizens of St. Augustine had learned from years of education by the John Birch Society, the Dan Smoot Report, the Florida Coalition of Patriotic Societies, and a succession of patriotic speakers that communism lay behind the civil rights movement. It was not without justification that the mayor could boast that there was "more awareness of communism" in his community than in the rest of Florida.

In the face of this more serious menace, Jacksonville Klansmen closed ranks with young Catholics from St. Augustine's Minorican colony. The local activists, belonging to what an observant newspaperman called "the shirt-tail and mud-flap school of social expression" were led by Holsted "Hoss" Manucy, whose curly sideburns, black cowboy hat, and impressive brawny girth were to become as famous symbols of resistance as Connie Lynch's jutting jaw and string tie and Birmingham Commissioner "Bull" Connor's police dogs. The city of St. Augustine, on the eve of its quadricentennial celebration, drew its life from the tourists who came to view the preserved and re-created buildings and monuments of its Spanish origins. In many ways, St. Augustine, with at least token integration of its schools, public and commercial facilities, political life, and civic employment, permitted a greater degree of racial intermingling than hundreds of other Southern towns. Having gone this far, however, the white community was determined that it would go no further. The Negroes, led by Dr. Hayling, were resolved that there was further to go. The former refused to meet with Negro leaders and talk things over. The mayor refused to appoint a biracial commission on the grounds that St. Augustine had no racial problems, despite the fact that the Florida Advisory Committee of the U. S. Civil Rights Commission reported that with the breakdown in communication between the communities, conditions were "considerably worse than in most, if not all, other cities in the state."

Negro organization and demands brought threats of violence, economic pressure, beatings, and cries of police brutality. Shots were fired into Dr. Hayling's home and a young member of Hoss Manucy's Ancient City Hunting Club was shot and killed as he rode with friends, shotguns in hand, through the Negro district. St. Augustine was beginning to make the newspapers. When a mixed group of integrationists, including Mrs. Malcolm Peabody, the wife of a retired Episcopal bishop and mother of the governor of Massachusetts, was arrested for seeking service in a segregated restaurant, St. Augustine hit the headlines a little earlier than the planners of the city's quadricentennial had anticipated. Sheriff L. O. Davis went down to the Negro district to announce that he wasn't in the market for any colored votes. "I used the word 'nigger' so they would know I meant it," he explained. Negro leaders turned from the NAACP to the Southern Christian Leadership Conference and asked Martin Luther King to come and take charge of things.

By the latter part of May there were nightly speeches and prayers in the Negro churches, after which columns of singing protesters formed to march on the Plaza de la Constitution in the center of town. Sit-ins began at the big downtown motor lodge on Bay Street. Klansmen from Jacksonville's tough militant knights turned up for

active duty. So did long-time Klansman-lawyer J. B. Stoner, whose
skills as an organizer and in defending dynamiters gave him particular prestige in Klan circles. Stoner was not much of an orator,
but Connie Lynch was among the best. Ever on the move from coast
to coast and organization to organization, with an uncanny sense of
where his services might be needed, he arrived in his pink Cadillac
to help prepare the defenses against "Martin Lucifer Coon" and the
"Jew-conspiracy" of race mixing. Demonstrators who violated undesirable guest and trespass laws in local restaurants and churches were
carted off to jail, penned out in the broiling June sun during the day
and often locked in a sweatbox cell at night, while Southern Christian
Leadership officials scoured the ranks of its members and friends to
find new waves to fill the jails.

Negro marchers, exhorting themselves and each other to refrain
from striking back, formed ranks to face barrages of bricks, clubs,
acid, and blows from Klansmen and Manucy's raiders gathered in
the plaza. Receiving no orders to the contrary from St. Augustine's
business leaders, Sheriff Davis' officers refrained as long as possible
from interfering. Angry segregationists turned their particular attention to white marchers, and the attacked was more likely to end up
under arrest than the attacker. News photographers and cameramen
complained that policemen and their dogs were no respecters of the
freedom of the press. Town officials, police, integration lawyers, and
state officials wrangled before Federal District Judge Bryan Simpson
as to whether nighttime processions should be banned or permitted.
Judge Simpson pressed the sheriff to maintain law and prevent violence. Inspecting a list of the sheriff's new deputies, the judge exploded
when he came to the name of Holsted R. Manucy, whose civil rights
had been forfeited when Judge Simpson had previously sentenced
him for bootlegging.

Martin Luther King's forces, having been defeated in Albany,
Georgia, needed to win a victory. They called for help from supporters outside of St. Augustine. Responding individuals and groups
filtered in from Birmingham and Boston—rabbis and ministers, white
college professors, and Negro teen-agers. Ex-deputy Manucy's raiders
tailed out-of-state cars and exchanged reports through civilian band
radios. Sentinels were stationed at St. Augustine Beach and when
integrationists arrived, carloads of reinforcements came roaring down
the beach, confederate flags flapping, and club-wielding whites
plunged into the surf after the racial interlopers. When Klansmen

and segregationists paraded through the colored district, Negroes lined the sidewalks singing "I love everybody." Curious spectators turned out nightly to watch Klan and Negro meetings, but the tourists, upon whom St. Augustine depended for its economic life, had practically disappeared. Despite the newspapermen and state police officials who piled into the motels, business was suffering badly.

The scene of the daily conflicts shifted from the old shedlike slave market in the plaza to the Monson Motor Lodge, to the surf of St. Augustine Beach, and then back again. The governor's police maintained order for a few days until the Klansmen and raiders discovered that arrested attackers were turned over to Sheriff Davis, who seldom booked them and rarely set bonds above twenty-five dollars. Bail for those participating in sit-ins ran into the thousands of dollars, and J. B. Stoner and his Klansmen lounged about on the front steps of the jail. As the assaults on marchers and wade-ins reached the peak, the Klansmen and raiders broke through police lines. Beatings and injuries became more severe. Women, children, and occasionally an infuriated state trooper faced the blows. Martin Luther King, arrested at the Monson Motor Lodge, was removed to jail in nearby Jacksonville because his life was believed to be in danger in St. Augustine. He was bailed out in order to receive an honorary degree at Yale, and then returned to St. Augustine again.

When five Negroes and two white integrationists jumped into the swimming pool of his motel, Monson Motor Lodge manager James Brock could take it no longer. "I can't stand it, I can't stand it," he wept. Indeed, Brock and many of the other small businessmen were trapped in the middle. Although a convinced segregationist, Brock had expressed his willingness to open up his establishment if required by law or requested by business leaders. He dared not be first. As he later explained it, "If I integrated, there wouldn't be more than one Negro a month registered at the motel, but the first night I integrated, all my windows would be busted in." Community leaders who had been willing to countenance violence against Negroes and integrationists found that they were now unable to control it or turn it off, and state officials publicly agreed that St. Augustine businessmen must share the blame for it all.

Appearing on national television with Lynch and Stoner, a prideful Holsted Manucy was asked whether he thought that the trouble would continue in St. Augustine. In a booming voice that must have sent shivers down the spines of local businessmen, "Hoss" happily replied, "Oh yes, there is going to be trouble for a l-o-n-g time!"

After a painfully bloody and highly publicized month, the inter-cession of the governor and the passage of the civil rights law man-aged to bring an uneasy peace to the nation's oldest city, although only the stern hand and careful guidance of Judge Simpson prevented more than sporadic violence. Even so, early one morning a fire bomb was touched off in the restaurant of James Brock's motel.

Klansmen J. B. Stoner and Connie Lynch were arrested for illegal cross burning, and the court ordered Stoner to withdraw his imported National States Rights party pickets from in front of integrated es-tablishments. Hoss Manucy managed to stay in the news as a result of having clued the police in on a Ku Klux Klan bomber, in the mis-taken belief that he was turning in, for a reward, the man who had dynamited the tracks of the strike-bound Florida East Coast rail-road. Facing the courts yet again in the fall, Hoss changed his mind after an hour's meditation in jail and supplied a list of the members of his Ancient City Hunting Club.

Little more than a week after things began to settle down in St. Augustine, Lt. Col. Lemuel Penn and several companions were re-turning home from summer training at Fort Benning, Georgia. Colo-nel Penn, who was Director of Adult and Vocational Education for the District of Columbia, had come safely through World War II in the Pacific, but he was a Negro and conditions were unsettled in Madison County, Georgia. The three Klansmen in the car behind the Negroes on the dark road had noted the Washington license plates and decided that this was part of a rumored civil rights invasion. The Klansmen pulled alongside and emptied their shotguns. Colonel Lem-uel Penn's luck had run out.

For a while it looked as though that of the Klansmen would fol-low suit. FBI men moved in and offered rewards. Klansmen talked, and the driver of the car confessed. Conviction turned out to be an-other thing. The federal government could only prosecute for viola-tion of civil rights, and so the state of Georgia undertook the murder trial. The state did its best, but it was perhaps asking too much for a jury from a rural Georgia county to decree the execution of their neighbors for the killing of a Negro. The defense attorney made the most of this, telling the jury that the President had sent hordes of federal men swarming into Madison County ordered to bring back "white meat." Never let it be said, he continued, "that a Madison County jury converted an electric chair into a sacrificial chair on which the pure flesh of a member of the human race was sacrificed—

to the savage revengeful appetite of a raging mob." The jury found the Klansmen innocent, and the sheriff stepped up to offer his congratulations. The best that the government could do was to hope that the lesser charge might stick in the federal court.

The long hot summer of 1964 stretched tautly on. The Ku Klux Klan appeared regularly in the headlines and on the editorial pages. Negro marchers lingered in the streets. After a spring and summer of debate and prophecy, the Civil Rights Act had passed and seemed to be met by compliance, but with murder done thrice in Mississippi and violence not yet over, no one dared predict peace. The summer was just as hot on Harlem's 134th Street as it was in Mississippi. It was hot also in Rochester, New York, and in South Chicago, Philadelphia, Elizabeth, Paterson, and Jersey City. It was easier to register Negroes in Madison County, Florida, than in Neshoba County, Mississippi, but threats, beatings, and arrests were not to be avoided. August is always a good month for assaults and muggings in Washington, D.C., and in Phoenix, Arizona. It was hot ninety miles away from Florida in Castro's Cuba, and ten thousand miles away in Vietnam not even the rainy season quieted the outbursts of gunfire in the outskirts of Saigon. In North Carolina where Grand Dragon J. Robert Jones' United Klan had been growing over the summer, Elm City's Negro First Presbyterian Church accepted an offer from white students to help with a new coat of white paint. Grand Dragon Jones objected, but the students went to work anyway, and two men were arrested by the police when they attempted to burn the church.

While North Carolinians thus contended over their divergent plans for church remodeling and Colonel Lemuel Penn was being buried with full honors at Arlington National Cemetery, the Republican National Convention met in San Francisco's Cow Palace to nominate Barry Goldwater. There was no real uncertainty about the decision of the convention. Senator Goldwater's victory in the California primary added to the efforts of his devoted followers in the precinct and county, and state conventions had all but ensured his victory. The essential beginning of his hope to win the national election in November was the support of a Southern electorate disaffected over the civil rights law and agitation. After seeing the more liberal wing of the Republican party capture the nomination with Willkie, Dewey, and Eisenhower, and with Richard Nixon's "sell out" of their support and of the election of 1960, the Republican conservatives were not to be turned back from power. It was not the John Birch Society which booed New York Governor Rockefeller and voted down the windy platform amendment by which the moderates would have condemned extremism and the Klan. The conservatives correctly recognized the amendments as a desperate last-minute attempt to split Senator Goldwater's supporters and deny him the nomination. They saw the maneuvers of the Eastern Republican leadership in the same light that the McAdoo supporters had seen the attempt to condemn the Klan at the Democratic convention of 1924, forty years before. It was a political thrust, garbed in moralistic clothing, aimed at depriving them of the victory they had earned. The delegates booed Governor Rockefeller and cheered attacks on television and the press which they felt to be their enemies. They swept aside the amendment to name the Klan along with other extremists, and thundered their approval as Senator Goldwater, in the most eloquent speech of his campaign, told them that extremism in the defense of liberty was no vice and moderation in the pursuit of justice was no virtue.

While seeing the political uses to which the attack on extremism had been hopefully put, the sense of power that came with victory blinded the Republican standard bearer and his exultant followers to the moral questions that were also involved. Dean Burch, the new national party chairman, and the vice-presidential candidate, William Miller, both expressed willingness to accept the votes of the Klan. It remained for Barry Goldwater himself to formally reject Klan support after a Gettysburg meeting with President Eisenhower and Richard Nixon.

The Ku Klux Klan had little to offer Barry Goldwater, but when the governor of Alabama was prevailed upon to withdraw from the race, Klansmen reluctantly scraped WALLACE stickers off of their bumpers and turned to the Arizonan. The opportunity of supporting John Kasper and J. B. Stoner on the National States Rights party ticket held no positive appeal to Bob Shelton and his United Klans. Following his Georgia Grand Dragon in endorsing the Republican senator, Imperial Wizard Shelton shrugged off Senator Goldwater's rejection of the Klan. "That's his privilege," Shelton commented, and his Georgia Dragon Calvin Craig explained that he was a Goldwater Democrat, not necessarily because of the senator himself but because he offered the only real choice in the battle to protect states' rights and constitutionalism from socialism.

Shelton's Alabama Dragon, Robert Creel, was more forthright in his support. Governor Wallace and Senator Goldwater could do only so much by themselves. "They need our help," he told a rural Alabama Klan meeting. The Klan, Creel continued, was the representative of the majority of the people of Alabama who hated "niggerism, Catholicism, Judaism, and all of the isms of the whole world." This did leave it with what might have appeared to be a difficult problem, for as the Republican vice-presidential nominee William Miller later pointed out, Goldwater was half Jewish, while he, Miller, was "all Catholic." This was a puzzle that the Klan for the most part was not interested in facing, although in the last weeks of the campaign, pro-Johnson forces in some portions of Georgia occasionally unkindly raised the question. In dealing with the Democratic standard bearers, the hooded potentates encountered no such dark alleys. When the Democratic platform denounced the Klan by name, Shelton commented that it was "an honor."

After the initial miscues at the top, the Republican party evidenced no interest in the Klan's support for their candidate, even when the Klan engaged in get-out-the-vote drives around Atlanta and in anti-Johnson areas of southwestern Georgia. There was no doubt that many white Southerners were angry over the Negro demands and the civil rights law. Moderate candidates were pressed hard in the Georgia primaries, and Shelton's Grand Dragon Calvin Craig drew forty per cent of his district's vote when he ran for the state Senate. Although using the Klan as the vehicle for anger didn't mean the same thing as hopping aboard a hooded bandwagon, the Klans did add between five and ten thousand members, and money was a little more plentiful.

The particular areas of Klan growth were in North Carolina, Jacksonville, Florida, and southwestern Mississippi around the railroad and mill town of McComb. Although the Klan had been accustomed to set one night aside each year for a string of cross-burnings across northern Louisiana and southern Mississippi, the emergence of organized Klandom in Mississippi represented an expansion into territory which had not seen any meaningful Klan strength since the 1920s. With some public officials and the hitherto intransigent Citizens Council acquiescing to creeping integration in Mississippi, the Klan has stepped into the void created by what it scornfully considered to be the timidity of businessmen and politicians. In southwestern Mississippi, the machine shops of McComb and the state highway patrol supplied a substantial increment of membership for the Klan.

Nevertheless, a reaction was mounting against it, and the aroused concern of state governors and federal agents had become enough to make the Klan jittery. Mississippi Governor Paul Johnson began sending his special investigators into violence-troubled parts of his state and sternly pressed members of the highway patrol to quit the Klan if they didn't want to be dropped from the force. The governors of Florida and Georgia offered no words of welcome to the Klan, and FBI men watched its footsteps to see if they led to violence. While Deep South juries were reluctant to convict for major or capital crimes in state court, federal indictments and trials threatened to jail for lesser crimes. As the Invisible Empire's second century dawned, Klansmen feared that President Lyndon Johnson would celebrate his landslide with repressive measures against the Klan.

49

DECLINING POWER

By the mid-1960s, the history of the hooded Knights of the Ku Klux Klan had come full circle. The Klan had begun a century before as a resistance movement against political rights and social opportunity for the newly freed Negro, and it had done its work well. Now it could again create fear and produce isolated pockets of violence and murder, but it could not halt the much more extensive revolution that was taking place. After the Civil War, the freedmen were neither educationally nor psychologically prepared to assert and maintain their rights, and the war-weary North was not, for the most part, willing to maintain a garrison state and fully support social revolution.

After a hundred years, many changes directly affected the Negro. Reaction against Nazi racism, anti-imperial revolutions and the rise of the non-Caucasian world, competition with communism, the new sciences of ethnology and anthropology, growing national wealth, the Negroes' urban migration, and rising standards of Negro life all influenced their position. Equally important were their increasing demands to participate in the mainstream and the material benefits of American life. Now, at last, the necessary middle-class leadership had developed within the Negro community. The national government, long active elsewhere in the economy and society, had become an instrument for racial change, and the student generation, black and white, had forcefully prompted its hand. It is axiomatic that racial problems can be solved only in an expanding economy, where there is room and opportunity, and in the 1960s, the American economy grew steadily at a rate unequalled in national history. And so, a hundred long years after the abolition of slavery, the larger American society was committed, however fitfully, to creating a true biracial, or perhaps even nonracial, society.

The Negro, even in the South, lived in a society that was rapidly becoming urban, but the forces of change and equality clashed with traditional caste inferiority, ignorance, fear and apathy, social disorganization, and a still potent racial restriction. Although meaningful integration proceeded slowly and unevenly, its progress was shown by the changes in the leadership of the opposition. By the early 1960s, Southern politicians were no longer loudly saying "NEVER." For a brief period in the mid-1960s, it was the turn of the Southern police officers such as Eugene "Bull" Connor in Birmingham and Sheriff Jim Clark of Selma. Their use of force served only to advance, rather than retard, integration, and they were soon out of favor and out of office. As political and economic pressure and legal restrictions failed to contain the Negro revolution, overt and noisy opposition passed almost solely into the hands of the Ku Klux Klan, which had long been calling for racial war.

Who responded? Within a cycle of growth and decline, the membership in the various Klans, including the ladies' auxiliaries, reached its maximum at about fifty thousand. The hard core, i.e., those who lived their lives completely in a Klan world, numbered no more than ten thousand. This was not a large group. An extremist movement in almost any society, propelled by dreams of blood and battle, could probably draw an equal number. Outside the deep South, the Klan recruited intensively in North Carolina and established itself in a small way in Virginia and Delaware. It had outposts in California and in the Chicago police force, scattered pickets elsewhere, and a few successful colonies in southwestern Ohio. Its memberless leaders in states such as Pennsylvania, New Jersey, and New York came from neo-Nazi would-be putschists.

The explanation of Klan violence is a complex one. As Edgar Z. Friedenberg has written, most men "accept violence if it is perpetrated by legitimate authority," and during wartime there are almost no limits to its legitimization. Society has historically been inclined to regard violence as acceptable if it is devoted to protecting the existing order against would-be disrupters.[1] This kind of vigilante justification in particular cloaked the Klansman in the sanctified robes of approval, in his own eyes and in those of at least a portion of his society.

[1] "A Violent Country," *New York Review of Books*, October 20, 1966, p. 3.

Although he lacked the wide communal support that he had during Reconstruction, the Klansman believed that he was meant to defend the ultimate values of his society from hideous attack. His symbol for those values was "white womanhood," realized, of course, in his wife-daughter. He lived in a two-layered world which he saw as divided between Klansmen and aliens. His outlook was a paranoid feeling of persecution with himself as the central object of an apocalyptic conspiracy. In reality, he was at war with the increasing complexity and impersonality, of which the Negro revolution was but one part. The Klansman explained change as a plot directly undertaken, as Imperial Wizard Bobby Shelton liked to describe it, by "beatniks, sex perverts, and tennis shoe wearing communists," and he found his example almost exclusively in that traditional symbol of the frustrated, the Jew, now turned communist, who gave meaning to the otherwise puzzling assertiveness of the Negro.

The Klansman did not believe that he hated, but his style was characterized by aggressiveness, part of the training of a rural, caste-ridden society, in which the young and the unsuccessful are trained to achieve self-respect through aggressiveness. The Klansman's world was one of guns and the talk of violence—a merger between a life-style and a solution to the problem of race.

Given this willingness to use violence as a means of personal expression and social solution, what could the Klansman hope to accomplish? The Klans might have developed their own strategy or attempted to react to that of the Negro revolution. Having no greater plan than striking back blindly and forcefully, the Klan became the captive of its enemies.

For the Negro leaders, each year meant a combination of old and new problems, of which the Klan, though dangerously violent, was one of the least. Nineteen sixty-four was the year of the civil rights law banning restriction in public accommodations. In the view of much of white America it was time to relax and let tempers and tensions cool, to follow things up slowly, to consolidate.

Negro leaders saw it differently. There were still many rights that needed protection. The ordinary Negroes were often apathetic. Even if they were interested in registering and voting, they were not at all convinced that they would be allowed to do so in some portions of the rural South. They needed greater protection against violence, not only from vigilantes and Klansmen, but often from police officers and local judges and juries. In the North particularly, Negroes were concerned about access to housing, the quality of schooling, police treatment. The concern about jobs, however, was not limited to any one area of the country; it affected Negroes everywhere. The Negroes' choices, as they saw them, were to appeal to black and white cooperation or to black separateness.

In 1964, the appeal was to cooperation, and the Reverend Martin Luther King, Jr., was its leader. He had to appeal to black pride and white consciences. "We must be ready for a season of suffering," he announced. His plan, however, was simpler than his path. He would bring his marchers out into the streets until someone cracked somewhere—in Selma, Alabama, in the state house in Montgomery, in Washington, D.C.—perhaps even in the Klaverns of the Ku Klux Klan. If would-be Negro registrants could not get on the voting books, then they must approach the ballot by way of public demonstrations. "We are going to bring a voting bill into being in the streets of Alabama," King told his followers.

There was no Klan in Selma, Alabama, birthplace of one-time Birmingham Police Commissioner Eugene "Bull" Connor, and of the first Citizens Council in Alabama. However, there were Sheriff Jim Clark's mounted posse, Colonel Al Lingo's state troopers, and George Wallace in the governor's mansion. They and local officials and white citizens agreed that the Negroes must be kept in their place.

And so for more than two months, beginning in January of 1965, Selma Negroes gathered in front of Brown's Chapel Methodist Church and Beulah Baptist Church to march on City Hall—or wherever else their human petition was most likely to gain attention. Soon there were ten times more Negro names on the police blotter than on the voting rolls. One Negro had been killed, and the barricade, the billy, and the prod had become standard forms of police response.

Although more than a month of demonstrations brought headlines and volunteers, there was no sign of a breakthrough, so a march on the state capitol at Montgomery was announced. On Sunday, March 7, a flying wedge of police and troopers followed by a mounted posse waded into the marchers. With teargas, clubs, canes, and ropes they routed the petitioners and sent more than twenty-five to the hospital. Sheriff Clark, Governor Wallace, and their men had done what Martin Luther King had not been able to do: they had scored a breakthrough for the Negroes.

With a promise from the President for a strong voting bill, troops, federal marshals, and an okay from the courts, the success of the march to Montgomery was assured. The gathering in front of the state capitol, with Governor Wallace watching through binoculars from behind the blinds of his office, symbolized to a large degree the victory the marchers felt was sure to be theirs. However, the cost of that victory was the lives of a black woodcutter and a white Boston clergyman, and there would be one more.

Among the thousands of students, newspapermen, ministers, priests, rabbis, nuns, FBI and Justice men, and citizens who poured into Selma after "Bloody Sunday" was a young mother from Detroit, Michigan, Mrs. Viola Gregg Liuzzo. A member of the transport committee, she was assigned to drive carloads of marchers back to Selma. On her second trip to Montgomery for passengers, she had just crossed Big Swamp Creek in rural Lowndes County where the demonstrators had spent the third night of their march, when a car swept past her on a curve of U.S. 80. Two shots were fired, and Mrs. Liuzzo slumped forward as her green Oldsmobile swerved off the road into a barbed-wire fence.

Just after noon the next day, President Lyndon Johnson announced over national radio and television that Klansmen had been arrested for the murder. Describing the Klan as a "hooded society of bigots" disloyal to the United States, he declared war on the Invisible Empire. He praised Viola Liuzzo's sacrifice and promised to fight the Klan, as his father had done in Texas during the 1920s. Even Alabama Governor Wallace felt that things had gone too far. "Life simply should not be that cheap," he commented.

Finding the Klan suspects was not difficult for the FBI men who quickly fanned out to check the highway and interview witnesses. The black educator Lemuel Penn had died in the same manner the summer before in northeastern Georgia. Night patrolling had long been a Klan routine, particularly in Alabama where the Bessemer-Birmingham road occasionally came close to becoming a Klan highway. The FBI knew where to look, for this time one of its undercover informants had been in the car with Mrs. Liuzzo's murderers. Three members of the United Klan's Birmingham chapter were quickly arrested.

Despite widespread public anger, the violent death of Mrs. Liuzzo was initially helpful to the Klan, which drew its membership almost exclusively from that resentful portion of society which looked on physical resistance as the necessary and suitable expression of beleaguered white manhood. The Klan also had a wider pool of nonparticipating supporters who saw them as the only organization that did anything to counter the Negroes' push into their lives. Others were fearful of being firm toward the Klan lest they be accused of being soft on the Negro question, and there were always those for whom silence advances from cautious policy to become an article of faith.

The Klan's chaotic reaction to the black revolution in the mid-1960s resulted in at least a dozen murders. Half of them were committed by Mississippi's newly formed, independent, and extremely violent White Knights of the Ku Klux Klan. Despite national pressure and the federal government's success in gathering evidence, for a while it seemed more difficult than ever to gain convictions. Where racial murder might well have brought punishment before, civil rights murder gained an initial aura of being a resistance movement and received temporary immunity. Judges obstructed and dismissed indictments, juries refused to convict, and Alabama's Governor Wallace, whose parole board released convicted Klansmen, declined to help his Attorney General investigate the Klan. Although all of the violence did not originate with Klansmen, they benefited from it, and from the immunity that seemed to cloak it. And yet, despite increasing membership, stirrings of growth and power within the Klan were merely illusory.

It is not possible under American law to forbid the existence of an organization such as the Klan. Only overt misdeeds by individuals, not organizations and opinions, are punishable. In the American system of divided powers, most acts of violence, including murder, were under state jurisdiction. In those communities where the citizens and police were willing to act, Klansmen went to prison, and support for the night riders melted away. Only where state and local leaders talked fiercely about resistance to integration and refused to support law and order was the Klan able to function as a terrorist group. The list of such communities was not long, but names such as St. Augustine, Birmingham, Selma, Philadelphia, Macomb, and Bogalusa became painfully well known in America in the 1960s.

Even so, the tide was turning. Southern resistance and violence shocked and angered the nation, which, led by the President, pressed for new laws. Police brutality in Birmingham, Alabama, helped pass the 1964 statute forbidding discrimination in public accommodations. Conflict in Selma produced the 1965 voting rights law. Southern politicians became noticeably more cautious as the number of black voters soared.

By mid-decade Washington was finally willing to try to punish Klan violence where local prosecutors and juries would not. Federal Bureau of Investigation agents and informers infiltrated the Klan. Klansmen, always inclined to talk too much about their deeds, found their boasts being used against them. Others, recoiling from violence or jittery over FBI surveillance and questioning, confessed. Since the days of the first Reconstruction Klan, there has almost always been a Klansman to "tell all" in court.

The reputation of the FBI helped to hold down Klan membership and activity. Local police officials in Bogalusa, Louisiana, were ordered by the courts to protect civil rights workers. The federal government brought out a vague law against conspiracy, passed in 1870 to curb the first Klan of Reconstruction days, and used it against the murderers of Mrs. Liuzzo, Colonel Penn, and the Mississippi civil rights workers. The Supreme Court upheld its use to protect interstate travelers, and broadly hinted approval for any law making civil rights violence a federal crime. President Johnson promptly presented such a bill, which Congress enacted after the murder of Martin Luther King, Jr.

Much of the public's anger and the federal government's action was the result of the brutal murders of three young civil rights workers in Mississippi. Early in 1964, a young social worker and his wife arrived in Meridian, Mississippi, to run a Negro community center for the Congress of Racial Equality (CORE). In addition to the perilous nature of trying to open up jobs and the voter rolls for Mississippi Negroes, he faced other disadvantages. He was white, a New Yorker, and a Jew. He lived in the Negro quarter when he could find a place and usually dressed in blue jeans, a sweat shirt, and sneakers. He also had a beard. As respectable Mississippians liked to say after his death, what else could be expected "when someone with a name like Schwerner comes down from New York to stir up things?" The power structure and the better informed people of Mississippi did not favor violence; in the larger cities they generally tried to prevent it. They looked down on the hooded knights; but if the Klan was trash, a nigger was a nigger, and the Mississippi way of life was under assault. So out-of-state "mixers," presumptuous Negroes, and incautious moderates were likely to be spit at, shot at, beaten, burned, and bombed.

According to testimony at his trial, Sam Holloway Bowers, owner of the Laurel, Mississippi, Magnolia Consolidated Realty Company and the Sambo Amusement Company (distributor of vending machines) and Imperial Wizard of Mississippi's White Knights of the Ku Klux Klan, had Michael Schwerner marked for elimination. When Schwerner was joined at the community center by a young Meridian Negro named James Chaney, and Andrew Goodman, a white New York college student, they too were included in the White Knights' final solution for Schwerner. On June 21, during the 1964 "Mississippi Summer" of the associated civil rights organizations, the three drove out to Nashoba County to view the remains of a Negro church that had been burned by the Klan. As his trial later established, the deputy sheriff from the county seat of Philadelphia, Cecil Price, was tipped off that the civil rights workers were there. He arrested Chaney for speeding and Schwerner and Goodman "for investigation." Holding them in jail long enough to work out the necessary plans, the deputy let them pay their way out after dark, stopped them again once they were out of town, and turned them over to a group of his waiting fellow Klansmen. Schwerner, Goodman, and Chaney were shot and their bodies buried in an earthen dam. The charred remains of their blue Ford station wagon were found and reported two days later by Indians from the nearby Choctaw reservation.

While most Mississippians watched, scoffed, joked, and lamented their state's crucifixion, police, the FBI, and some four hundred sailors from the Meridian Naval Auxiliary Air Station searched for the missing men. Forty-four days after their disappearance, the FBI, armed with warrants and heavy earth-moving equipment, appeared at the dam and quickly dug down to the bodies.

The trial of the accused slayers was not held for three more years. A local grand jury had refused to return an indictment. State officials maintained, with some basis, that the FBI had refused to aid fully their efforts. For their part, the federal representatives were perhaps equally justified in their mistrust of the state officials. Since the state apparently was not going to try the Klansmen, the federal government brought charges under the old Conspiracy Act of 1870, as it had with the killers of Lemuel Penn and Viola Liuzzo. Obstructed if not harassed by the federal referee and federal district Judge W. Harold Cox, both segregation-minded Mississippians, the government could not get indictments and a trial until 1967. In reality, the trial and ultimate conviction, which neither Mississippi nor a national audience expected, were probably made possible only by the delay. In 1964 it was not likely that a Mississippi judge and jury would have produced a guilty verdict. By 1967 the federal case had been tightened against procedural error, and local feeling was changing. An all-white, working-class jury, drawn from an integrated panel, listened soberly and attentively to the confessions of three Klan participants and to the low-keyed, evidence-packed presentation of U.S. Assistant Attorney General John Doar. The defense offered character and alibi witnesses, but none of the defendants took the stand.

When the jury initially reported itself deadlocked, Judge Cox sent them back again, telling the dissenters that although they ought not to yield in their own convictions, they should consider the position of the majority. This instruction, which lawyers and reporters traditionally have called the "dynamite charge," worked. When the jury convened the next morning, it quickly brought in a decision. Klan Wizard Sam Bowers, Nashoba Deputy Sheriff Cecil Price, and five other Klansmen were pronounced guilty. Deputy Price and another Klansman, who had commented within earshot of the judge that they might give the jury a dynamite charge of their own, were denied bail while the judge considered the sentencing. The Mississippi press greatly praised both judge and jury, and the Klansmen eventually went to prison for a maximum of ten years, although parole eligibility promised earlier freedom. For Imperial Wizard Bowers, however, there were still more indictments to face.

The key elements in the Penn, Liuzzo, and Mississippi convictions were a growing local feeling against extreme violence, combined with Klan informers and confessions, and forceful efforts by the federal government. With state leadership more outspoken in most cases, the FBI digging up the facts, and the U.S. Attorney General's staff lawyers presenting them in court, the hooded knights complained about being terrorized themselves. Federal juries, still drawn from the South but selected from larger, regional areas, were becoming more likely to convict for racial violence than those drawn exclusively from small, ingrown communities. Juries had been integrated, and broader jury selection was under way.

During the winter of 1965–66, the Klan had further bad luck, this time in the form of a congressional investigation. As the Southern-led House Committee on Un-American Activities probed deeply into the secret order, United Klan leader Robert Shelton told the press, "I'll be there with my boots on." However, not only did he remain silent in the hearing room as the subcommittee exposed the details of Klan operations and profiteering, but he was cited and sentenced for contempt for his newfound reticence. Throughout the South a growing local refusal to permit it to ride freely restrained the Klan as a vestigial doer of racial violence. Only a limited number of communities, whether through fear or approval, countenanced its night riding. In others, law was enforced and distaste for the Klan openly expressed. In the little town of Hemingway, South Carolina, the mayor and local businessmen protested that Klan rallies nearby gave the false impression that the town approved of the hooded knights. High school students erected signs along the highway with slogans such as "Stamp Out Boll Weevils, Tobacco Worms, and the KKK," and a sketch of a hooded Klansman captioned "Picture of a Nut." When the house of a North Carolina Negro leader was burned down, his fellow townspeople, white and black, contributed money and labor to rebuild it. In Anniston, Alabama, civic and business leaders signed a letter to the newspapers announcing that the Klan was not wanted in their community; they offered a $20,000 reward, which led to solution and conviction in a local racial murder.

In Mississippi, where a rural, frontier, exploitative, caste society lingered more strongly than in other states, leaders in many middle-sized cities denounced Klan violence. It is significant that when Imperial Wizard Sam Bowers was again arrested and this time indicted for murder with another group of his White Knights, it was the result of a combined effort by the FBI, the Mississippi state police, and the local sheriff and his men. For the first time in such a case, a local jury brought first-degree murder convictions.

No one expects the Ku Klux Klan to disappear from American life. Congressional investigations, contempt citations, community rejection, and criminal convictions cannot wipe out an organization whose existence is an expression of—and often a solution to—its members' own problems of personal and social definition. Klan violence, traditionally the instrument of the few rather than the masses, would always be possible. Despite continuous defections, contritions, and confessions, the paranoia of the average Klansman is too firmly rooted in his personality to be dispelled.

In the latter half of the 1960s, confusion over the seeming endlessness of the Vietnam War mounted, and "black power" stressed black pride and assertion rather than white conscience. An $850 billion economy seemed to be bypassing the growing urban ghettos, and many people felt they saw a weakening of the national will to be moved toward equal citizenship. In reality, what had passed was the utopian optimism and excitement the young integrationists had felt when the movement first marched out into the Southern streets and countryside. The path ahead would be difficult; mass demonstrations and new laws would not result continually in spectacular gains. On black campuses as well as in urban slums, impatience and social unrest were growing. So, too, was white alarm over rioting and lawlessness. But this shift in phase promised neither a cessation of change nor a greatly enlarged opportunity for the hooded knights. It is an often demonstrated truth that the degree of violence practiced is directly proportionate to the helplessness of the victim. The power of the Klan over the Negro has depended on the latter's impotence and subjection. By the latter part of the 1960s, the black was no longer powerless, and the actual role of the Ku Klux Klan as his oppressor was receding beyond recall.

50

BAD TIMES IN THE 1970s

The 1970s appeared to be an age of decline for the Klans. During the civil rights movements of the 1960s, the various Klans seemed no more effective a force against the advance of black equality than had the politicians, White Citizens Councils, and the sheriffs. Congress passed a public accommodations law in 1964, a voting rights act in 1965, and housing and protection laws in 1968. The FBI, both within and without the law, was putting pressure on the Klans, and juries brought in guilty verdicts. Black majorities were building and were beginning to elect black councilmen, legislators, and sheriffs. In much of the deep South, beatings and deaths at the hands of the Klans had been the direct cost of each of these steps, but by the 1970s, the costs were being shared.

Into jail went the killers of Colonel Lemuel Penn in Athens, Georgia, and of Viola Liuzzo in Lowndes County, Alabama, seven of the murderers of the three civil rights workers in Philadelphia, Mississippi, and four of the men who firebombed a house and killed Mississippi black leader Vernon Dahmer. Klansmen were arrested for plotting the murder of the new black mayor of Fayette, Mississippi, Charles Evers. Byron de la Beckworth, whom earlier juries failed to convict for the sniper murder of Medgar Evers, the civil rights leader and brother of Charles, went to jail for a planned bombing attempt in New Orleans. So did Tommy Tarrants, after a shootout killed the attractive young teacher Kathy Ainsworth, as she and Tarrants attempted to bomb the house of a prominent Jewish businessman in Meridian, Mississippi. South Carolina Grand Dragon Robert Scoggins and the United Klans' Imperial Wizard Robert Shelton served time in federal prisons for refusing to provide records to congressional investigators. The Grand Dragon of Michigan and four of his followers went to jail for bombing school buses in Pontiac, Michigan. Each conviction and imprisonment sapped the energy of Klansmen and the strength of their organizations. Although federal juries were more likely to convict than state juries, local and state police often stepped in to control or arrest Klansmen.

The FBI was particularly active and must have seemed a terrorist organization to many Klansmen. Until John and Robert Kennedy and Lyndon Johnson succeeded in redefining the role of the FBI, Bureau agents in the South were white Southerners working closely with local police forces that were often sympathetic if not infested with Klan members. Neither they nor their director seemed interested in civil rights or the Klan. J. Edgar Hoover had complained to an earlier Attorney General that the Bureau should not be giving so much attention to "investigating murders, lynchings, and assaults, particularly in the Southern states." It only stirred up agitation, he explained. While freedom riders and an Assistant Attorney General of the United States were beaten to the ground by Klansmen at the Birmingham and Montgomery bus stations, FBI men watched from across the street but did not interfere. Although the Bureau did have resident agents in Mississippi, it was not until the disappearance of the three civil rights workers during the summer of 1964 that a field office was opened in the state.

Once committed, the FBI was willing to go more than halfway. From 1964 onward, the FBI took an active role in securing the evidence and testimony that sent Klansmen to jail, although as later events would reveal, J. Edgar Hoover's whims could be costly to justice. But there was more. In 1956, the FBI had begun a program of surveillance and sabotage against dangerous left wing groups, which from Hoover's viewpoint came to include not only the Communist party and the Trotskyites, various radical terrorists, and the New Left, but also Martin Luther King, Jr., and the women's liberation movement. In the summer of 1964, the Ku Klux Klan was added to the list. With Hoover's approval, the program set out to "take advantage of our experience with a variety of sophisticated techniques successfully applied against the Communist party, U.S.A."

The Bureau now added seventeen Klans and six other hate groups to the "disrupt and neutralize" efforts of its covert Internal Security Counterintelligence Program, known by the acronym, COUNTERINTELPRO. The "sophisticated techniques" included not only the use of informers and theft of Klan records, but also all manner of planted newspaper stories, rumors, and anonymous letters and postcards revealing Klan membership and accusing Klan leaders of everything from drunkenness, adultery, and misuse of funds to being informers for the FBI itself. By the 1970s, the Bureau claimed that one out of every six Klansmen worked for the FBI. This included at least one state leader, and there was talk of attempting to depose the United Klans' Imperial Wizard Robert Shelton and replacing him with an FBI informant.

Though the program was successful, Director Hoover feared that its illegal operations might become known to the public. In 1971, the year before his death, he closed down COUNTERINTELPRO. Four years later an NBC reporter, Carl Stern, heard mention of the program and used the Freedom of Information Act to find out more about it. A U.S. Senate investigation revealed something of COUNTERINTELPRO's extent, and a new Freedom of Information suit by a group of reporters made public some fifty-two thousand censored pages of the Bureau's records and began a long battle over access and preservation of FBI records.

Sharing the headlines with the wiretapping and the FBI campaign to discredit Martin Luther King, Jr., was the portly figure of the Bureau's one-time top Klan informant, Gary Thomas Rowe, Jr. Of the Bureau's more than one thousand "domestic intelligence informants," Gary Rowe was the star. Recruited in 1960, he had surfaced five years later to finger the Klansmen who had gunned down Viola Liuzzo on a lonely Alabama road between Selma and Montgomery. Rowe had been a passenger in the killers' car, and his testimony sent two brother Klansmen to the penitentiary. Wearing a head and face mask that resembled a torn paper bag, Rowe told the congressmen that he had been in on almost everything, from beating the interstate bus riders of the early 1960s to an FBI-ordered campaign to disrupt Klan units by having sexual relations with the wives of fellow Klansmen. And there was more, including beatings, perhaps a murder and—the word was to come later from the Birmingham police—possible involvement in the 1963 bombing of Birmingham's Sixteenth Street Baptist Church.

Between 1960 when he was first recruited by the FBI and 1965 when he broke cover to testify in the Liuzzo trial, Rowe was paid more than twenty thousand dollars by the Bureau, first for information and then to relocate with a new identity (hence the mask). Although his cover was destroyed by his testimony, Rowe profited from the exposure; Bantam Books reportedly paid him and his ghost writer $25,000 for his slim paperback autobiography titled *My Undercover Years with the Ku Klux Klan.* The book is characterized by the kind of writing that fills the pages of magazines for men; it is replete with verbs and virile conversation but lacks any sort of modifying description or understanding. According to the book's testimony, Gary Thomas Rowe had bested—and outwitted—his brother Klansmen of Birmingham's fearsome Eastview 13 Klavern in drinking, fighting, and sexual conquests for half a decade.

Before concern began to mount about the nature of the violence Gary Rowe had perpetrated himself, Columbia Pictures added $25,000 to his take for the rights to film his life for NBC-TV. With football broadcaster and former Dallas Cowboy quarterback "Dandy" Don Meredith playing Rowe as a rough but well-meaning battler for the law, NBC swallowed hard and presented its somewhat tarnished drama, *The Freedom Riders,* in the fall of 1979. Meanwhile, the Justice Department was being forced to face the question of whether Rowe had been an agent provocateur. Had he actually instigated the incidents of violence, and had the FBI approved and covered up his actions? Rowe claimed that they had and that he was told that J. Edgar Hoover approved.

No one loves an informer, including the police officers who employ him, but without him the hands of justice would often be tied. Contrary to the heroic image put forth by motion pictures and television, it is seldom the police officer who infiltrates. Rather it is the member who informs, whether out of patriotism, morality, revenge, a desire to escape prosecution himself, or a need for money. It was informers such as Rowe, plus the testimony of frightened or penitent Klansmen, and painstaking investigative work that combined to produce the FBI's successes against the Ku Klan Klan.

Of the many killings that marked the struggle of the 1960s, the deaths of four black teenagers in the bombing of Birmingham's Sixteenth Street Baptist Church remained the chief unsolved crime. Within days after the bomb went off against the wall of the church, federal agents were sure they knew who had set it. However, the problems of surveillance and gathering evidence were soon overtaken by the need to protect that evidence from misuse. Alabama Governor George Wallace had taken as strong a stand as anyone against integration, but the church bombing murders were hardly the kind of publicity he was counting on to launch his campaign for President. Martin Luther King's telegraph message, "The blood of our little children is on your hands," was sure to discourage voters with weak stomachs. After an unsuccessful effort to somehow pin the bombing on "unknown black perpetrators," the governor's investigators arrested the FBI's prime suspects. The best the state could do was to charge Ku Klux Klansman "Dynamite Bob" Chambliss with illegal possession of dynamite. The charge did not hold, but the prime suspects were now warned and the bombing went into the "unsolved" file. Gary Rowe later claimed that this was where the Alabama State Police and the Klan intended it to rest.

Murder has no statute of limitations in Alabama, and a rising young lawyer named William Baxley kept this in mind. He had first heard the news of the bombing at his Kappa Sigma fraternity house on the University of Alabama campus in nearby Tuscaloosa. It made him sick to his stomach and he did not eat that day. Son of a prominent state judge from Dothan and a mother deeply involved with her church, Baxley's sense of justice and morality did not condone racism or unpunished murder. Baxley was a born prosecutor, as his career attests. With his law school classmates helping him organize his statewide campaign, he rose from being a local state's attorney to Attorney General of Alabama by the time he was thirty. As the state's chief law officer, he went after corrupt sheriffs and legislators. When he came up for reelection in 1974, no one thought it worthwhile to run against him.

After his first election, Baxley reportedly wrote four names on his state telephone credit card. They were Cynthia Wesley, Denise McNair, Carol Robertson, and Addie Mae Collins, the four young girls who had been changing into their choir robes after hearing a sermon on "The Love That Forgives." Denise McNair was eleven and the others fourteen years old when they died in the bomb blast. That was eight years before, but Baxley had not forgotten them, and now he saw their names whenever he used his card. It took four more years and threats of newspaper publicity before the FBI would make at least some of their files available. Not without justification, the FBI had been hesitant about revealing its evidence and informants to the Alabama police; Baxley's sincerity, however, impressed them.

Of at least equal importance was the fact that J. Edgar Hoover had died in 1972. Hoover had rescued the Bureau from the ill repute of its Harding era but had plunged it into even deeper scandal in the 1950s and 1960s. Shortly after the bombing of the

Sixteenth Street Baptist Church and some fourteen years before Alabama Attorney General Baxley would bring one of the bombers to trial, the FBI had cracked the case and had strong testimony against Chambliss and at least three other men who helped set the dynamite. Hoover had twice refused the FBI's Birmingham office permission to seek prosecution and cautioned against letting the Justice Department suspect how much the FBI knew. Unbeknown to the Bureau's chief Klan informant Gary Rowe, the FBI hired what it regarded as an even more violent, assassination-minded Klansman, John Wesley Hall (now dead), whom they had reason to believe might have been involved in the bombing.

After going through the files, Baxley believed that there had been enough evidence to go to trial within weeks of the bombing, though Hoover may well have been correct in his assumption that in 1963 the all-white juries of Birmingham were not likely to convict, even for such a heinous crime as this. By 1977 some of the participants were dead, including the man believed to have made the bomb. Baxley's staff pressed their investigation. In September of 1977, an Alabama grand jury indicted Robert Edward Chambliss on four counts of first degree murder.

Baxley hoped that Gary Rowe would strengthen the case against Chambliss and others involved in the bombing, but Rowe's lie detector tests produced disturbing results. When questioned about the bombing, Rowe's polygraph reading indicated "strong and consistent unresolved deceptive responses." Rowe, it seemed, was telling less than all he knew. Baxley's investigators began to suspect that Rowe might have been in the car that carried the bombers to the church. At the very least, the trial would have go to on without Rowe as a witness for the prosecution.

The trial was held before three black and nine white jurors. Most of the latter were middle-aged, working-class housewives. The evidence was circumstantial but powerful. Chambliss' niece by marriage, now a Methodist minister in Birmingham, testified that Chambliss, whom she called "a racial fanatic," was angry over integration of the Birmingham schools. He had told her that he had "enough stuff put away to flatten half of Birmingham." He had said, "You just wait until after Sunday morning, and they will beg us to let them segregate." Another witness had wandered into a room in Chambliss' house and had seen his store of dynamite, piled "like oversized firecrackers." A Birmingham policeman remembered Chambliss describing how to make a "drip bomb" in which a fishing float would complete the circuit and set off the explosives when enough water had dripped out of a leaking bucket. An FBI explosives investigator testified that small, light objects frequently survived explosions and that such a fishing float had been found in the wreckage of the Sixteenth Street Baptist Church. Chambliss was identified as having been sitting in a parked car across the street early in the morning of the explosion. Chambliss' niece told of her uncle watching a TV program about the bombing and protesting, "It wasn't meant to hurt anybody; it didn't go off when it was supposed to."

Robert Chambliss did not take the stand, but his attorney, Arthur Haynes, Jr., whose father had been mayor of Birmingham in 1963 and who was sharing the defense case, argued that the charges were not proven. Everyone "talked rough" in those days, he explained. Baxley's summation for the prosecution lasted ninety minutes and brought many of the jurors to tears. "You've got a chance to do something," he told them. "Let the world know this is not the way the people of Alabama felt then or feel now."

The decision was not easy for the jury, the foreman related, and it had taken nearly all of the evidence to convince them. After six hours they brought in a verdict of guilty of murder in the first degree. Chambliss' life sentence meant ten years in prison before he would be eligible for parole. "This is a terrible thing to do to a seventy-three year old man," he complained.

Attorney General Baxley repeatedly stated that Chambliss had not acted alone and promised additional arrests for the more than fifty bombings that had shaken Birmingham during the 1960s. The grand jury that had named Chambliss also indicted National States Rights Party lawyer J. B. Stoner for another of the bombings. No one had as many connections in the Klan world as Stoner, who once commented that Hitler had been "too moderate." For more than three decades, Stoner carried his message of hatred for Jew and Negro to the Klaverns of the hooded knights and defended their members when they got into trouble.

Aware of the propaganda opportunities that arise during elections, Stoner had repeatedly run for office, often gaining a respectable number of votes. During one gubernatorial race in Georgia, Jerry Ray, the brother of Martin Luther King's assassin, had managed his campaign. Facing extradition to Alabama, where placing a bomb against an inhabited dwelling constituted a capital crime, Stoner had an even greater incentive to be elected. As governor of Georgia he could certainly claim to be fully within his rights in refusing to extradict himself to stand trial in Alabama. When the Federal Communications Commission ruled that it was also within his rights to say what he wanted in his campaign, he infuriated many Atlantans with TV spots denouncing integration as "a nigger plot" to take over white women. "You cannot have law and order and niggers too," his advertisements proclaimed. However, the man elected governor was not J. B. Stoner, who had to face instead the new breed of law and order in Birmingham, Alabama, which proceeded to convict him.

Denise McNair's father was now an elected member of the Alabama legislature. A black lawyer whose house had been bombed was a member of the Birmingham City Council. In the fall of 1979, the voters elected a black man mayor of Birmingham. At the Sixteenth Street Baptist Church, where the stained glass window of the sanctuary depicted a black Christ hanging on the cross, a memorial plaque contains pictures of Denise McNair, Cynthia Wesley, Carol Robertson, and Addie Mae Collins smiling. The inscription reads, "May men learn to replace bitterness and violence with love and understanding."

51

CONFRONTATION, POOR-BOY POLITICS, AND REVIVAL

The 1970s did not seem very promising. Although Klansmen might have the weapons and the will for "a little action," the chances of being caught were becoming much too high and the behavior of judges and juries was downright discouraging. Still, the various competing, though shrunken, hooded empires, peopled by Klansmen and FBI informants, continued to rally and parade in Walker, Louisiana; Pensacola, Florida; Macon and Stone Mountain, Georgia; Aurora, Illinois; and Chenango County, New York; to burn occasional crosses in New Jersey and even school buses in Pontiac, Michigan. Attempts were made to project a better image. Klansmen would "light up" a cross, rather than "burn" one, because that sounded more respectful. Lawyer Venable's National Knights and David Duke's Knights dropped their bans against Roman Catholics. Duke, a young Louisiana State University history graduate, carried his message to the college campuses and told working-class listeners in South Boston that the Klan would help them "protect, preserve, and advance the white race." A real celebrity, the lovely woman jockey Mary Bacon made the TV evening news and lost most of her contracts for endorsements by revealing her Klan membership. "We are not just a bunch of illiterate southern nigger killers," she reassured her fellow Klanspeople. "We are good white Christian people, hard-working people working for a white America." She added, "When one of your wives or one of your sisters gets raped by a nigger maybe you'll get smart and join the Klan."

The newly elected Grand Dragon of a splinter Texas Klan attributed his success to a Dale Carnegie course, and an Indiana Grand Dragon complained about Klansmen showing up at rallies out of uniform: "If you join the Shrine you buy a fez, or the 40 & 8, you get a chapeau. . . . If you can't afford a robe," he sputtered, "you can't afford to belong to the Klan." The Klans survived but their ranks seemed destined to remain depleted. There was almost a melancholy note to the Florida Grand Dragon's explanation that the Klan existed because "the white people has rights just like anybody else."

And then, at the end of the 1970s, something happened. There was a dramatic increase in the number of cross-burnings, rallies, marches, confrontations, and shootings. Klan ranks grew. The Anti-Defamation League of B'nai B'rith, which for a generation has known at least as much about the Klans as the Klans themselves, first called it "a minor renaissance" in 1978. By the next year, the ADL reported not only an increase in visibility but also impressive proportionate gains in membership. Since mid-decade, Klan membership had increased from some 6500 to 10,000. Perhaps more significant, Klan approval and support appeared to have grown substantially. In the media, TV commentators and editorial writers announced "the Klan revival" and talked of "the New Klan" and "the amazing rebirth." The wire services and the press reported, "Klan hasn't folded up its sheets," "Klan's growing militancy reminiscent of sixties," and "Klan rises again in the South."

What had really happened? Ten thousand Klansmen and women were not a large number out of the two hundred and twenty million Americans or even of some seventy million Southerners. They did not compare in power with the several hundred thousand Reconstruction era Klansmen, the millions of the second Klan during the 1920s, or even the several score thousand that the third Klan period mustered during the civil rights battles of the 1960s. Since Doc Green's death in 1949, no one had been able to unite the Klans and rule an undivided empire as Green, Hiram Evans, Colonel William J. Simmons, and General Nathan Bedford Forrest had done. Revival did not mean unity, and Klan ranks remained thin.

The "fourth period" revival of the Klans was a matter of place, confrontation, and economic anxiety. Its home was in the towns and smaller Southern industrial cities. The confrontations that took place in northern Mississippi and Alabama—Tupelo, Holly Springs, Byhalia, Lexington, Corinth, Okolona, Elkmont, Moulton, Courtland, Huntsville, Cullman, Tarrant City, Fairfield, and Decatur—were not of the old pre-1960s variety. Although the fading Klan entrepreneur of Stone Mountain, Jimmy Venable, might complain about "niggers calling white girls by their first names," the day of punishing the "uppity" black was gone.

In bygone times, the Klan patrolled the borders of race relations in the South. Now the erosion of those borders had produced a limited, but potentially deadly, Klan revival as an expressive form of poor-boy politics. Its essence was the inability of the rural-minded Southern working-class white to either prevent or accept racial change. It was this powerlessness that caused the revived Klans to play the game of violence as an expressive alternative to actual power for controlling larger events. In the renewed world of Klandom at the end of the 1970s, Bill Wilkinson's Invisible Empire was the most militant.

What happened was actually a version of the standard scenario. Police violence and questions about the quality of justice meted out to black people would produce a protest, which would grow to include issues of jobs and poverty. An organization would then be formed and its members would take to the streets to march on City Hall and perhaps boycott downtown merchants. A Bill Wilkinson would come to town to encourage white resistance and Klan recruitment. Black and Klan demonstrators would jostle each other in the streets. Crosses would be burned. Nighttime rallies would draw applauding spectators and new members for the Klan. Since everyone was armed, there would be incidents in the streets and on country roads, and shots would be fired into the homes of black and sometimes white leaders.

As downtown business suffered, mayors would say, "Why us? We've always gotten along so well!" Klansmen from neighboring counties, civil rights marchers from Atlanta, and agents from the Justice Department in Washington would arrive. Efforts to ban marches would be declared in violation of the First Amendment to the Constitution. At high cost to municipal budgets, riot police with bulletproof vests and shotguns, aided by state troopers and an occasional patrol helicopter, would keep blacks and Klansmen apart and marches separate. With the help of civil rights lawyers, now often black and federally funded, the black protesters would usually win the courtroom battles. The Justice Department's Community Relations Service would help city commissions not only make rules for marches and public meetings, but write laws banning the carrying of weapons by marchers or spectators. With mediation, compromises, some arrests and convictions, and numerous suspended sentences, confrontation would simmer down to a hostile standoff and ultimately an uneasy peace.

Black men killed by police officers, testimony of rape and beatings in county jails, a "suicide" found hanging in his cell with hands and feet bound, and the refusal of local government and juries to act moved black protest into the streets of northern Mississippi. Alfred "Skip" Robinson had begun to organize his United League of Mississippi in the mid-1960s. It had remained a 1960s-type civil rights organization; its members wore T-shirts reading "Justice for all," not "Black power." Robinson, a brick mason and contractor in Holly Springs, was a stubborn man who had dedicated his life to organizing his people and, said his white detractors, seeking office and political power. The United League was anchored in the black churches, and Robinson spoke to them in the language they understood. "My knees won't bend," he told them, and they cheered him.

To their demands that the police officers accused of beating black prisoners be fired, the United League added that city governments and white merchants must hire more black people. Marches for justice and boycotts for black jobs damaged business in Okolona and Tupelo, raised community tempers, and brought in the Klan and the national media. Local and state politicians denounced the Klan as "a bunch of hoods covered up with a sheet" and not representative of the people of Mississippi, but the crowds at Imperial Wizard Bill Wilkinson's rallies grew, and they cheered as he promised to "restore this government to the white people." Klansmen attacked black marchers in Tupelo and Okolona, and shot at cars on the highways outside town at night. In many Mississippi towns there were token black councilmen and school board members, and the politicians and merchants were inclined to seek compromise with the black demands. However, neither action nor inaction was likely to satisfy the United League and the Klansmen. As a city councilman commented, Tupelo was a stage on which a potentially violent drama was being acted out.

It was Alabama that gave Bill Wilkinson's Invisible Empire its biggest chance. A young retarded black named Tommy Lee Hines was accused of robbing and raping three white women. Many members of the black community felt Tommy Hines, whose I.Q. was only 39, to be incapable of such actions as driving the car involved in the abduction. The Reverend R. B. Cottonreader's organized protest marches and "Justice City" tent community camp-in on the Decatur city hall lawn brought Klan leader Wilkinson to town. His aggressive rhetoric drew crowds of five thousand and then ten thousand people to the biggest rallies that anyone could remember since the great days of the 1920s. Wilkinson seemed to have discovered the way to build Klan power and he meant to make the most of it. In a trial that had been moved to nearby Cullman, an all-white jury found Tommy Hines guilty, and he was sentenced to thirty years in jail. A reversal on appeal for Hines plus other trials coming up meant a prolonged season of protest and counterprotest. However, the confrontation was moving beyond Tommy Lee Hines.

Imperial Wizard Wilkinson's style was one of tough talk and a display of the ordnance. Although he might look benign with his large, "mod," Gloria Steinem glasses and slightly rotund figure dressed in a three-piece blue suit, his belted and booted, uniformed bodyguards, with their pistols, rifles, shotguns, and Thompson submachine guns, looked anything but peaceful. As one Alabaman described him, Bill Wilkinson was a "gun-toting, cigar-chewing, cow-pasture Klansman, a man unafraid of action," proud to be a red-neck.

Klansmen and black demonstrators clashed in the parking lot outside a supermarket where a black man had been arrested for shoplifting. Having already banned tent cities from the lawn, the Decatur city council forbade the carrying of weapons at a demonstration. The Klan responded with a nighttime motorcade of pickup trucks, past the mayor's house, with the drivers waving their rifles. "If the mayor wants our guns, he'll have to come and get them," a Klan leader proclaimed.

Black demonstrators, led by Southern Christian Leadership Conference President Joseph Lowery, came up from Atlanta to support the Reverend Mr. Cottonreader. A thousand blacks who marched through downtown Decatur found their route blocked by 250 Klansmen with lead pipes, ax handles, and baseball bats, who shouted, "Niggers, that's as far as you go!" In the melee that followed, the Decatur police tried to keep the groups apart. There was a pistol shot in the direction of the Klansmen followed by a general exchange of fire in which the police also joined. When the police finally cleared the streets, four people had been wounded, but no one had been killed. The SCLC promised to return, and the club-carrying Klansmen in the Municipal Building hallways, stamped their feet and shouted, "White Power;" the summer of 1979 was launched in northern Alabama.

Weekends meant cross-burnings and rallies, and Klansmen stopped cars on the roads at night to collect donations "to fight the niggers." State and FBI investigations led to conviction of Klansmen for shooting into homes of black leaders and interracial couples as the violence spread to the central part of the state. Nighttime potshooting was becoming a part of life, but heavily armed police managed to keep peace as Klansmen and black protesters paraded separately through Decatur.

The state of Alabama passed a law forbidding firearms within a thousand feet of a public demonstration. When in August of 1979 Wilkinson's Invisible Empire decided to repeat Martin Luther King's famous march from Selma to Montgomery, the police were waiting at the Montgomery line to meet them. If the Klan ranks, which had swelled to over 170, were somewhat less in number than the 10,000 who had marched into Montgomery with Dr. King, they made up for it in armament. The pile of weapons confiscated by the police at the entrance to the Klan's campsite included pistols, rifles, chains, knives, bayonets, brass knuckles, and a submachine gun. When the marchers crossed the city line the next day and were arrested for parading without a permit, their weapons had been reduced to mace, knives, and the ax handles on which they carried their posters.

How had the Klansmen felt when their march took them past the spot where Viola Liuzzo died fourteen years before? No remorse, apparently. Imperial Wizard Wilkinson replied that "she was doing an unsanctimonious thing, helping those niggers." What had been the purpose of the Klan march? "To protect the civil rights of white people." Martin Luther King's marchers had been permitted to rally on the capitol steps, but Wilkinson's demonstrators were arrested for parading without a permit. The difference in treatment symbolized what the Klans were protesting. The Klan's working-class constituency believed that a reversal had taken place in America, i.e., that the black man had been elevated and the white man had taken his place in the hole. The root cause for this belief was preferential treatment by the government, and it gave a long felt neglect its particular urgency. Imperial Wizard Bill Wilkinson summed up the theme sounded on every Klan platform when he attacked government programs, saying, "I for one am sick of Negroes and other minorities being given jobs I deserve."

Bill Wilkinson had served his apprenticeship as principal lieutenant and editor of David Duke's *Crusader* before breaking away in 1975 to build his own empire. Now Duke found his Knights of the Ku Klux Klan in competition with Wilkinson's new Invisible Empire as well as senior Klan leader Robert Shelton's somewhat more numerous but slightly fading United Klans. Duke claimed lack of interest in what he called the "illiterate, gun-toting, redneck" image of Bill Wilkinson's cow-pasture Klandom. Although his message emphasized the same economic uneasiness, Duke sought a broader audience—and one that was better informed. "We're not just a bunch of fools running around in bed sheets," he explained. "We believe that white people in America face discrimination in employment, promotions, scholarships, college entrance, and union admission."

In the media of the 1970s, David Duke had become a real celebrity; he was paid to speak on college campuses and was welcome on radio and TV interview and talk shows. Through these, he began to win at least a hearing from middle-class America. Wilkinson decided he could do better in the Klan's traditional recruiting ground, the "good old boy" world of bourbon and coke and pickup trucks with the rifle on the rack. He and Duke parted with the usual bad feelings and dispute over money that traditionally mark the emergence of entrepreneurs in the competitive Klan world. Wilkinson was practically an illiterate, Duke commented disparagingly, "A man who has never read anything."

David Duke was a reader, a new kind of Klansman, the smoothest talking salesman since Indiana's ambitious Grand Dragon of the 1920s, D. C. Stephenson. But there was a difference: David Duke had convictions. As a boy, Duke had developed a fascination with Adolf Hitler, World War II, and the Jews, and it led him into the tangled world of the American Nazi movement and remained with him on the Louisiana State University campus and in the Ku Klux Klan.

His attempt to appeal to a more educated middle-class America required that Duke live a divided life. While other Klan salesmen could freely offer their rural audiences the Nigger-and-Jew litany that pervades the world of Klandom, Duke had to take the path of reasonableness before the media and still manage to hold onto the traditional Klan constituency. This was a paradoxical situation, for none of the other Klan leaders was as deeply focused on the "Jewish menace" as Duke or as well read in history, the racial literature, and the story of Nazi Germany. Although all of the various Klan leaders considered the root of the nation's problems to be the Jewish-communist menace and were in touch with the various anti-Semitic groups on the right, they considered Duke's Nazi fixation to be extreme.

Off camera, Duke was not to be "out-niggered." On the platform, he had the orator's skill so generally lacking in the Klan world. In interviews and on TV, he was poised, articulate, low-key, and sincere. Tall, slim, blond, with razor-cut, blow-dried hair and stylish clothing, David Duke's youthfulness, and articulateness, set him off from the rest of the Klan world. In 1975, when he ran for the Louisiana Senate in a wealthy district of Baton Rouge, he drew a respectable one-third of the votes. Was this a vote for the Klan? "Right wing," snapped the distinguished Louisiana State University historian and Huey Long biographer, T. Harry Williams. "They got rich and are afraid of someone taking it away from them." To many of the 11,000 in Louisiana's Sixth District who voted for him, Duke was that nice young man who campaigned door-to-door and was opposed to busing, gun control, taxes, criminals, discrimination against white people, and all that regulation and interference from Washington.

Duke counted literally hundreds of radio and TV appearances. Each college lecture earned him more than a thousand dollars, as well as a chance to spread his message and win converts. Only in his public television PBS interview for a 1978 special, *The New Klan*, did he come a cropper. This time he was up against *New York Times* star Southern reporter Wayne King; unlike most of Duke's other interviewers, King had the evidence:

> WAYNE KING: You sell things. You pass out things called "Nigger Huntin' Licence" . . .
>
> DAVID DUKE: No, we do not. I do not pass out—I do not . . .
>
> WAYNE KING: You do not, but your lieutenants do. Maybe you do. It came from Louis Beam. . . .
>
> DAVID DUKE: Well, I don't . . .
>
> WAYNE KING: He's your Grand Dragon, isn't he?
>
> DAVID DUKE: No. He's a Great Titan.
>
> WAYNE KING: It says, "HAVING PAID THE LICENSE FEE (somebody's name) IS HEREBY LICENSED TO HUNT AND KILL NIGGERS," in caps, "DURING THE OPEN SEASON IN TEXAS." This is beautiful, David . . .
>
> DAVID DUKE: Well, it is a joke. Yes, it is satire.
>
> WAYNE KING: For a guy who says you don't belittle other

races—I mean this is really pretty scurrilous stuff, and pass yourself off as a New Klansman. Here's another one. There's very violent rhetoric in there, and some very—some of the alleged Jewish—"Ratstein" pictures of . . . who look like rats.

DAVID DUKE: Now that, I think is excellent satire. . . .

WAYNE KING: You really do?

DAVID DUKE: It's humor.

(In his calm, slow spoken way, Wayne King bored in.)

WAYNE KING: (Showing Duke a picture of a young man in a Nazi uniform holding a sign saying, "Gas the Chicago Seven"): You may remember this. That's you.

DAVID DUKE: Yeah, that's me. Okay.

WAYNE KING: That's amazing, David. "Gas the Chicago Seven"?

DAVID DUKE: It's not amazing. I was young.

WAYNE KING: You still sell the Nazi literature.

DAVID DUKE: Well, I sell books on all sorts of subjects, but I don't sell Nazi literature as such.

WAYNE KING: You don't?

DAVID DUKE: No.

WAYNE KING (showing a book list): *The Nameless War, Mein Kampf, Hitler Was My Friend, Germany's Hitler, The Testimony* (sic) *of Adolf Hitler.*

DAVID DUKE: Now, wait a second . . .

WAYNE KING: *The Hitler We Loved and Why, UFO's: Nazi's Secret Weapon, My Part in Germany's Fight, Dr. Joseph Goebbels* . . .[1]

Duke's media hosts and questioners on the networks were seldom as well prepared. Duke's message was low-keyed, thoughtful, polite, and winning. He had no animosity toward any other race. He was only for the rights of white people. The Chicanos had *La Rasa*, Blacks had the NAACP, the Jews had their organizations. No one ever complained about all-black fraternities. He was not

---

[1] *The New Klan: Heritage of Hate,* PTV Publications, Broadcast by PBS, November 19, 1978. Duke complained afterwards that, from a two-hour interview, the only portions used were brief selections that made him look bad. In other media interviews, he explained, it was not a matter of questioners being ill-prepared; his positions and philosophy held up because they were informed and consistent. Duke, who, under various pen names, wrote on health, nature, and environmental subjects, was extremely knowledgeable. Of all of the United States presidential candidates in 1980, David Duke was probably the most widely read.

against black people. He was *for* white people. Jesse Jackson and the Reverend Ralph Abernathy debated him; Carl Rowan confronted him; Tom Snyder, Barbara Walters, Jack Nelson, and scores of others interviewed him. *Oui* and *Playboy* profiled him, Candice Bergen photographed him, but none pressed him as Wayne King had done, and many found him sincere and impressive. Listeners phoned in, polls favored him, and his mail grew.

Being a Klan leader and organizing the revival is a demanding, all-consuming business. It involves continuous travel, speaking to small groups as well as large, and the constant threat of physical attack. David Duke dropped the Klan's traditional bars against Roman Catholics and turned away from the usual ladies' auxiliary path, integrating Klanswomen into his ranks instead. Both he and Wilkinson had a particular interest in recruiting high school students for the Klan youth corps, but Duke's efforts had a broader range. He distributed leaflets calling upon white students to fight for white power against the "black, Chicano, and Yang criminals who break into your lockers and steal your clothes and wallets." He and his lieutenants worked the high schools in cities such as Buffalo, Chicago, Los Angeles, and San Diego. The young men in the armed services were another quarry. Although he won no more than a handful of recruits, the publicity payoff was enormous when black and white marines fought in Camp Pendleton or crosses were burned at sea or black and white sailors clashed on Charleston- and Norfolk-based supply ships and aircraft carriers.

While the Klan revival was limited, it represented a lingering racism in American society. It sprang from an unwillingness to accept the changing role of black people in American society and from the conditions and conflicts that were the result. Confrontation over justice and jobs in northern Mississippi and Alabama produced the kind of racist response that gave impetus to the upswing in the cycle of Klan membership. Behind the clashes in Tupelo and Decatur was the old populist resentment and suspicion that times were not going to be good and that jobs and promotions were going to somebody else. That that somebody was black was too much to accept. Integration, welfare, affirmative action, hard times, and the Reverend R. B. Cottonreader's tent city blacks camped out on the city hall lawn and throwing beer cans into the shrubbery because a black man was convicted for raping a white woman were more than a man should be asked to bear, they felt. There was enough racism in enough people so that when David

Duke or Bill Wilkinson or Bobbie Shelton called out, the following exchange took place:

"What do we want?"
"White Power!"
"What?"
"White Power!"
"WHITE POWER!"

52

DEATH IN GREENSBORO

Greensboro is a middle-sized industrial city of 160,000 people in the North Carolina Piedmont. Despite its five colleges, the first response of North Carolinians when asked to describe the city is "blue collar." In addition to P. Lorillard tobacco and Vicks chemicals, there are the textile mills—Burlington, J. P. Stevens, and Cone Mills—which each year produce enough denim to more than cover the entire state of North Carolina. The approaches to Greensboro are thick with the typical fast food restaurants, gas stations, used car dealers, and suburban shopping centers that usher one into most American cities. The aging downtown buildings of the immediate post–World War II boom, none higher than eight stories, do not give a distinctive skyline or feeling.

Greensboro's main claim to fame is that General Nathanael Greene turned back the British there at the battle of Guilford Courthouse and started General Cornwallis on his retreat to Yorktown and the surrender that assured American independence. Such history is favored by most city boosters, for the distant past tends not to offend. However, the name of Greensboro more recently has joined those of Montgomery, Oxford, Albany, Birmingham, Selma, Memphis, and the other Southern cities where the racial history of America has been rewritten and is not yet finished.

North Carolinians like to say that "moderation" has been the keynote of relations between whites and blacks in their state. By the 1950s, Greensboro had already elected a black city councilman and there was a black member on the school board. When Governor Luther Hodges spoke to the black student body of North Carolina Agricultural and Technical State University, he urged them to keep things cool by following a policy of voluntary segregation. Generally, state legislators saw token integration as the way to maintain separation of the races.

Dr. Martin Luther King, Jr., and the black bus boycotters had walked to victory in Montgomery, Alabama, in the mid-1950s, but civil rights did not become a mass movement until four nervous but determined black freshmen from A & T sat down at a Woolworth lunch counter on February 1, 1960. David Richmond, Franklin McCain, Joseph McNeil, and Ezell Blair, Jr., had hatched the idea during a dormitory bull session the night before. It had been stimulated, however, by nights of such talk at NAACP youth group meetings, a growing awareness of black history, the Montgomery example, a Martin Luther King, Jr., speech at A & T, and the fact that Joseph McNeil had been refused service at the Greensboro Trailways Bus Terminal lunch counter.

The sit-ins spread across the South. They flowed into the freedom rides, into the streets of Albany, Birmingham, St. Augustine, Selma, onto the back roads of Mississippi, into the public accommodation and voting rights bills. They set in motion the movement of black people into the politics and the mainstream of Southern life. With it all came the decline of the Ku Klux Klans. Once black people became a factor in Southern politics, white politicians toned down their rhetoric, white sheriffs began to be somewhat more restrained, and some black legislators, policemen, and sheriffs began to appear among the white ones. A promising young black minister turned congressman, from Atlanta, named Andrew Young, summed it up:

When not many black people could vote, the politicians used to talk about the "niggers." When we got 10 to 15 per cent voting, they called us "nigra." When we got up to 25 per cent, they learned how to say "Nee-grow." Now that we have 60 to 70 per cent registered and voting, they say how happy they are to see "so many black brothers and sisters here tonight."

On February 1, 1980, twenty years after the Woolworth sit-in, there was a civic ceremony in Greensboro, North Carolina. With the mayor looking on, David Richmond, Franklin McCain, Joseph McNeil, and Jibreel Khazan (formerly Ezell Blair, Jr.) were welcomed at the lunch counter by Woolworth's black manager, and historical markers were unveiled outside.

Even so, it had not been easy in Greensboro. "Moderation" meant maintaining things as they were. Although kept out of the national headlines, under pressure from the students at A & T,

Bennett College for Women, and occasionally the white colleges, Greensboro suffered a decade of sit-ins, demonstrations, mass arrests—and confrontations with the Ku Klux Klan. On the day that the Woolworth sit-in was honored, a memorial to a student who had been shot during a National Guard sweep of the campus in 1969 was unveiled at A & T. In the mid-1960s, the student leader at A & T was Jesse Jackson. During the even more difficult times later in the decade, an Air Force veteran named Nelson Johnson occupied that position. It was not until 1971 that the Greensboro public schools were integrated; they were among the last holdouts in the South. Jesse Jackson had gone off to Chicago. Nelson Johnson remained, working with the poor in Greensboro.

Across the nation on February 1, 1980, the media retold the story of the original sit-in that had touched off the civil rights movement of the 1960s. People spoke with pride of the racial progress that had resulted. The next day, February 2, in a twist of plot that might have intrigued Greensboro's famous native son, the writer O. Henry, more than five thousand angry people, black and white, took to the streets in a new racial protest. They had come from Chicago and Detroit, from the Eastern seaboard cities, and from the South to protest the killing of four white men and a black woman in the streets of Greensboro by a band of Klansmen and American Nazis.

Shortly before noon on Saturday, November 3, 1979, a nine-car caravan worked its way into the narrow streets of Greensboro's black district where an anti-Klan rally was forming in front of the Morningside Homes at Everitt and Carver Streets. There were shouted insults. Demonstrators in the street pounded on the cars with sticks and clubs. Someone in a lead car fired a pistol into the air. Then, as TV news camera teams filmed away, half a dozen men climbed out of a sedan and a yellow van in the rear of the procession, opened the trunk of the sedan, and took out rifles and shotguns. With cigarettes dangling from their lips, they leaned over the hood of the car and opened fire on a shrieking, scattering crowd of men, women, and children at a distance of no more than twenty-five feet. Within seconds, the wounded and dying lay bleeding in the street. Of the dead and dying, one was a Duke University computer operator and three were doctors, graduates of Duke and the University of Chicago and Virginia medical schools. The black woman had been student body president at Bennett College.

With the occasional exception of the Ku Klux Klan, there are no large-scale, meaningful left or right wing groups in America, but there are many fragments at both ends of the political spectrum. Two of them had met violently in the streets of Greensboro.

For several years, a devoted Maoist group, who called themselves the Workers Viewpoint Organization, had been attempting to organize the Greensboro textile mills. Working part-time in clinics and hospital emergency rooms or hiding their educations and professions in order to get jobs in the Cone Mills or at J. P. Stevens, they sought to lead "the struggles of the oppressed people" and the coming anticapitalist revolution. One of the doctors killed in the shooting had been president of his textile union; another was a shop steward who had been running for president of his union. The leader of the group, who went untouched by the Klan bullets, was the integrationist battler of the 1960s, Nelson Johnson.

Like radical idealists of times past, the WVO members had given up promising careers to work and live among the poor. They saw the working classes as the essential revolutionary element and had gone to the mills to reach and radicalize them. They had been turned off by "the system." In their study groups, reading and discussions had convinced them that the revolutionary moment was at hand. For them, the capitalist system was violent, and therefore the struggle against it could not be nonviolent. In Durham and Greensboro, they worked with the black poor, the university and hospital service workers, and in the mills. It would be difficult, but the working class would rise, they believed.

By the summer of 1979, the WVO was having trouble in the mills. Despite the heat, the deafening noise, and the fiber-filled air that caused brown lung disease, the management position was strong. No one had yet organized the Southern mills, even for trade union goals. The WVO were well liked, but they were caught between management and the national union. The Amalgamated Cotton Textile Workers Union did not wish to share the labor movement, slim though it was, with the revolution. The National Labor Relations Board upheld WVO member Dr. James Waller's dismissal for omitting his degree from his job application at the Cone Mills, and the national ACTWU had taken over direction of the Cone Mills locals on the grounds that the elected officers did not properly represent all the workers in the mills.

Squeezed between capital and labor, the WVO seemed very much in need of a change in tactics. They changed the name of their organization to the Communist Workers Party and challenged the Ku Klux Klan. The newly emerged CWP clashed with the Klan at nearby China Grove, burned a Klan banner, and disrupted its showing of the film *The Birth of a Nation.* A "Death to the Klan" march was scheduled for November 3 and was well advertised. Open letters to the leaders of the White Knights of Liberty and to the Federated Knights of the Ku Klux Klan announced that Klan cowardice would be further exposed by the march. The Communist Workers Party would "physically smash the racist KKK wherever it rears its ugly head. Death to the Ku Klux Klan."

There were at least five competing Klans in North Carolina, and those Klansmen who didn't find the various Invisible Empires active enough often wound up in one of the even smaller National Socialist, or Nazi, parties. The Klansmen and Nazis who drove into Greensboro in the caravan that Saturday morning were mainly mill workers and laborers, in their thirties, from around Winston-Salem and small towns in Lincoln County on the South Carolina line. Concerned about "saving America" from race-mixing and communism and such, many of them were new to Klandom. As the *New York Times'* Wayne King described it, "These guys are not what you'd call real successful."

When Joe Grady, leader of the White Knights, chose not to accept the CWP invitation to "face the wrath of the people," rival Klan leader Virgil Griffin decided that this was his chance. His Invisible Empire had been meeting with the National Socialists to work out a United Racist Front, and he brought some of his Nazi allies along with him. There was enough racism in both groups to show the Communists that they were not going to let anyone call them cowards.

A third party to it all, though not consulted, was the neighborhood of the black housing project where the rally was to begin. A fourth party was the police. The anti-Klan marchers had promised not to carry weapons, filed the route of the parade, and had been given a permit. The CWP had publicized its rally and march. When a Klansman asked for the route plan, the city attorney ruled that it was a public document and he was given a copy. Twenty-six men under the direction of a black officer were assigned to keep things orderly, and the police had an informant among the Klansmen and Nazis who came in that morning on the Interstate. As the starting time approached, the police found rallies going on in two different places. No one would give any information to the sergeant who checked out the Morningside Homes site, and the crowd added a "fascist pig" chant to their denunciations of the Klan. The police were split between the two locations, and the sergeant decided to avoid provocation and keep his men at a distance from the Morningside housing project. With the warning to be on post by half an hour before the start of the march, some of the men were given permission to go for food.

There were thirty to thirty-five Klansmen and Nazis. Having come to town early, they had been standing around and were eager to get started. Although the police had been informed that their intent was to heckle, some of them had weapons. According to the police report afterward, there had been no legal grounds for stopping and detaining them. Some eight cars started out and a ninth joined them. It was forty minutes before parade time, and a number of the police officers had not yet come back from eating. The Klansmen claimed that they had intended to leave their rifles and shotguns behind in the trunk of Ray Caudle's Ford sedan. This would have left them armed only with the six dozen eggs they had bought on the way. One of the Klansmen took the Ford and went off for food, but the rest were impatient so someone got on the citizens band radio and called him back. The Klan caravan started out, and the Ford sedan with the weapons in its trunk joined at the end of the line. "Jack Fowler got hungry so five people died," a Klan attorney sought to explain it.

By the time the police caught up with Jack Fowler's friends, four people were dead, one was dying, and the wounded were scattered on the street outside Morningside Homes. It took less than two minutes for the police to arrive, and the ambulances followed soon after. The yellow van was stopped and twelve Klansmen and Nazis arrested. Murder charges were eventually placed against fourteen of the assailants. Presumably on the informant's report that the shooting had not been planned in advance, no conspiracy charges were placed, and the people in the other Klan cars were not arrested. Four days later, the editor of the Greensboro *Daily News* summed it up:

> As the fifth victim, a medical doctor turned textile worker died in a Greensboro hospital, his alleged murderers sang 'Onward, Christian Soldiers' and 'My Country 'Tis of Thee' in a Greensboro jail.

It was both "puzzling," he said, and "tragic."

There was a sense of disbelief and horror in white Greensboro and anger in black communities across the country. For black people in the American South, the Ku Klux Klan is a never-ending symbol of racial oppression. The grieving CWP survivors blamed the deaths on the police as a "pig-Klan assassination conspiracy." President Carter ordered the FBI to investigate. The Southern Christian Leadership Conference, locked in conflict with Klansmen in northern Mississippi and Alabama and Georgia, had already met in Norfolk with representatives of more than thirty organizations to work out a national anti-Klan campaign. Now the SCLC called a major planning session for Atlanta in December.

"The Klan is for real," SCLC President Joseph Lowrey stated, adding that it did not exist in a vacuum. Neither did the anti-Klan protest. The conflict in the streets represented larger social problems and conflict. CWP blood had been shed in a black neighborhood by white racists. The police had knowingly permitted the armed convoy of Klansmen and Nazis to drive into the Morningside Homes area and were not there when the shooting took place. Now "the press and the establishment" were talking about "provocation" and were trying to pass it all off as a shootout between radical fringe groups, and CWP leaders as well as Nazis and Klansmen were under arrest. The problem for black churches and organizations was how to share the protest over Greensboro and opposition to the Klan without becoming too closely associated with the Communist Workers Party's dangerous martyrs and survivors. One could not fail to be moved by Dale Sampson's quiet, dry-eyed description of her husband's death, but few civil rights leaders wished to join the call for a communist revolution in the streets of Greensboro.

An interfaith memorial service filled Greensboro's AME Bethel Church with an interracial crowd of politicians and concerned citizens, but it was carefully timed to keep it separate from the funeral march for the slain activists. The larger national memorial, which took place three months later on February 2, was marked by the same ambivalence. The December planning meeting in Atlanta had focused on the march as a major undertaking for its new national Anti-Klan Network. Endorsement, support, and marchers were energetically recruited around the country, but until the last moment, there was a struggle to pledge the Communist Workers Party *not* to carry weapons during the procession.

During the march, the CWP contingent pushed forward toward

the head of the line, lofting their AVENGE THE CWP 5 and DEATH TO THE KLAN signs as they chanted anti-police slogans at the heavily armed parade escorts. Contingents of protesters bused in from New York, Ohio, Pennsylvania, Virginia, Tennessee, West Virginia, and Georgia swelled the number of marchers to close to seven thousand, but the absence of many national black and civil rights organizations and leaders indicated that the anti-Klan world was perhaps as divided as that of the Invisible Empire.

53

THE ENDURING KLAN

After the Civil War, the hooded Knights of the Ku Klux Klan paraded and struck on horseback. During the 1920s, they came to cross-burnings, parades, and beatings in Model T motorcars. Today, as in the 1970s, they arrive at rallies in Executive Campers, and their media celebrity, David Duke, travels around the country by jet to take part in TV talk shows. But although their means of transportation have changed with the times, the Ku Klux Klan has been for more than one hundred years—in fits and starts—a secret, terrorist society dedicated to maintaining white rule in the United States.

The Klan has been a vigilante organization, a national liberation front, a revitalization movement, a secret order, a fraternal lodge, a status society, a bastion of poor-boy politics and, in the twentieth century, a money-maker for its leaders. Its method has been violence.

There have been four major periods in the Klan's history. The first Klan rode during the troubled times after the American Civil War. The second Klan emerged just before World War I, reached its peak in the mid-1920s, and then suffered a long decline until World War II, gas rationing, and back taxes forced its adjournment altogether. Revived again after the war, the fragmented Klan has not enjoyed the unity and moments of triumph known by its predecessors. It was deadly but not effective in counteracting the civil rights movement of the 1960s. The rise of black political power in the South, along with changing racial attitudes and the expanded police role of the national government created formidable barriers to the violence of the Klan night riders. However, after encountering ill fortune for most of the 1970s, economic uncertainty, black-white confrontation, and new leadership produced a sporadic renewal of Klan violence and something of a revival.

Throughout its history, the Klan has been a conservative, not a revolutionary, organization. As a vigilante, it has sought to uphold "law and order," white dominance, and traditional morality. To do this it has threatened, flogged, mutilated, and, on occasion, murdered. The main purpose of the Klansmen, Kligrapps, Kludds, and Night Hawks, Cyclopses, Titans, Dragons, and Wizards assembled in their Dens, Klaverns, and Klonvokations, rallying in rented cow pastures, and marching in solemn procession through city streets, has been to defend and restore what they conceived as traditional social values. The Klan has basically been a *revitalization movement*. The noted anthropologist Anthony F. C. Wallace divides such movements into two kinds, *revivalism* and *nativism*. Revivalism seeks to "bring back previous conditions of social virtue," and nativism attempts to "purge the society of unwanted aliens." Together these have been the sacred missions of the Klan.

During Reconstruction, the Klan opposed the Northerners and former slaves who threatened the power of those who had traditionally ruled the South and the status (and thereby the self-opinion) of those who had traditionally followed. In the 1920s, the Klan, bred out of legend as the savior of a downtrodden people during Reconstruction, sought to protect and revitalize the small-town, gregarious, xenophobic culture against immorality and change. "Colonel" William J. Simmons, who revived the Klan, called it "comprehensive Americanism."

Colonel Simmons reported having had the kind of vision that so often characterizes revivalist movements. It had come to him during an illness. "On horseback in their white robes they rode across the wall in front of me," he related. "As the picture faded out, I got down on my knees and swore that I would found a fraternal organization that would be a memorial to the Ku Klux Klan." The enemy was the outsider-alien as symbolized particularly by Roman Catholicism and personified by the Pope, whom Klansmen liked to call "that dago on the Tiber"; the foreign-born; Jews (though minor at first, their importance—as demons—in Klan ideology greatly increased later in the century); and, of course, blacks. Today's Klansman gives himself the status and prestige that society has otherwise denied to members of his working-class and precarious lower middle-class strata by appointing himself defender of the traditional American symbols: flag, Constitution, Bible (King James Version), white womanhood, and racial separation.

One of the Klan's main appeals in the twentieth century has been the fellowship of like-minded people. Like other ancient, mystic, and noble orders which dot the American fraternal landscape, the Klan has its robes, rituals, hierarchies, secrets, and sacred ceremonials that pass the would-be member from the world of "aliens" to that of "patriotism and Klannishness." Public rallies are often toned down for public relations purposes. Imperial Wizards are more likely to appear in three-piece suits or leisure suits, cut to the prevailing fashion. Long hair, the trademark of the hippies of the 1960s and early 1970s, has been rescued from the recent past and integrated into the Klan's system of American values, but it is the old ways that still count. It is uniforms and guns—boots, belts, and insignia, the pistol on the hip, the rifle, and the sawed-off shotgun (carefully cut no shorter than eighteen legal inches)—and the tears shed for the imperiled little blue-eyed, blonde-haired girl, and the talk of "apes and niggers" that make Klannishness fulfilling. No one has understood this better than Bill Wilkinson, the former electrical contractor from Denham Springs, Louisiana, who has made the Thompson submachine gun the symbol of his rising Invisible Empire.

Although the Klan is basically an order of men, as secret societies are wont to be, it learned early the great truth of American fraternalism: no organization succeeds without a ladies' auxiliary. The women of the Reconstruction Klan stayed home and sewed robes and disguises. The great Klan of the 1920s had its Klanswomen, Junior Klansmen and Klanswomen, and Tri-K organizations. As in the 1920s, the women's auxiliaries today are mostly composed of wives and girl friends of Klansmen, but an occasional Klanswoman does surface. David Duke's innovative realm, which also recruits Roman Catholics, has merged with his Klanswomen and even has a woman who is skilled in the martial arts as head of security.

Combined with Klandom's sense of mission is an overwhelming awareness of powerful enemies; today that enemy is the spreading "Jew-Communist race-mixing conspiracy." This, together with a heritage of violence—the cherished possibility of "rough stuff"—adds to the sense of danger and excitement. For this Klansmen pay their initiation fees, kneel in prayer, and swear obedience, secrecy, and fidelity to the mysterious Invisible Empire.

By 1980, a major shift had taken place in the Klan's historic role. As the Klansmen saw it, they were not so much fighting to protect white dominance in America as they were to regain it. The confrontations and Klan growth in northern Mississippi and Alabama produced by Skip Robinson's United League boycott and marches and the trial of Tommy Lee Hines had their roots in the belief that white people were being squeezed and their livelihood threatened. The black poor still might be terribly poor and black unemployment high, but as the big national companies like General Motors, General Electric, and Monsanto moved into Decatur and other Tennessee Valley towns, there was growing talk about special treatment for blacks with respect to hiring, training, and promotions. Everybody had a story about someone who had reportedly lost his or her job because a black had to be hired to fill it. With the nation drifting powerless against the Russians, Iranians, and inflation, Klan spokesmen shouted out their "Bakke," "Weber," and "Affirmative action" catechism and signed up new members. In many ways, it is surprising that there were so few of them.

It is not easy to organize a Klavern in most states outside the South, for Klannishness is basically Southern. Those who attempt to do so are more likely to be strange than earnest. The North and West have forgotten the hooded legions that paraded through their streets in the 1920s, but a few Klan memories linger on in Indiana. Anything will grow at least a little in California, and New York and New Jersey are exotic enough to contain at least a flickering presence.

Measured against other sporadic efforts, Marion, Indiana's Grant County Unit 10 of Robert Shelton's United Knights was a comparative success story. Its forty members, mostly young workers at the Fisher Body Plant, met regularly in someone's flag-bedecked den to talk about how white people have to protect their racial heritage. On the other hand, an open meeting such as Dale Reusch's 1977 Fourth of July rally on the steps of Ohio's capitol building in Columbus was likely to be attacked by ill-mannered protesters and saved from mayhem only by police protection.

On the East Coast, where public identification subjects Klansmen to attack and loss of employment, Klan promoters are usually more noticeably at odds with their society than the working-class midwestern Klansmen. Most Midwesterners are members of the undemanding Confederation of Independent Orders of the Invisible Empire. If the Midwesterners are secessionists from major Southern Klan organizations, the East Coast members are splinters from splinters, floating in and out of each other's Klans and confederations, and various Nazi groups. Their followings are miniscule, uniformed, armed, and fiercely anti-Semitic. Civil rights groups and the press practically tingle over their existence, and this has probably added to the excitement of belonging. They were an unusual lot. A Pennsylvania Grand Dragon lost an eye in a barroom fight, and a New York Grand Dragon was a teacher of the mostly black inmates at a state penitentiary. Many of the Northern Klan leaders came from German backgrounds, and several Klan and Nazi potentates were revealed to be Jewish, leading to the suicide of one high-ranking New Yorker in what psychiatrists saw as a peak in self-hatred.

The history of the Eastern Klans has usually been marked more by publicity and travail, than by success. The story of Edwin Reynolds' short-lived but busy Klan career is a good example. According to the *New York Times,* Reynolds, a twenty-three-year-old unemployed machinist, had been an effective organizer but had been dismissed by the Pennsylvania Grand Dragon for adultery, misuse of drugs, misuse of Klan funds, and "being a member of an anti-Christian cult." "He set aside our oath," his former Grand Dragon indignantly related, "and substituted his own, requiring everyone to swear allegiance to Hitler." With his faithful following reduced to nine after he and a comrade were arrested for the rape of a young woman who had spied on them for the equally non-pacific Jewish Defense League, Reynolds advised his followers to turn to David Duke as "the future of the Klan and the white race." A Duke rally in New Jersey had drawn around twenty people. As to the rape charge, Reynolds responded, "I will say only that I am innocent, and Heil, Hitler." In disbanding his unit, he summed up its career. "The White Knights of the New Jersey Ku Klux Klan, after a twenty-two month history of television shows, countless newspaper and magazine interviews, street demonstrations, intense recruitment, and court injunctions, will proudly disband for the best interest of the Klan movement in New Jersey." According to the Anti-Defamation League, the estimated total membership of all the various Klan factions in New Jersey was eighty persons!

Only the American South provides fertile soil for the Klan seed. Whatever their impact in the 1920s, memory of the Klan does not linger in other parts of the country. Even in the South, the activities of the 1920s are seldom mentioned. However, though it is hardly necessary to speak well of the current Klans, they occasionally receive credit for being part of a great tradition. One of the many letters that appeared in the Greensboro *Daily News* columns for months after the November 1979 shootings spoke for that tradition. Although disavowing membership in or support for the Klan, the writer replied to President Carter's condemnation of the Klan:

> For all the undesirable things the Klan has stood for in the past, Mr. Carter should be aware of the reasons for its existence and the right things for which it has stood.
>
> The Klan was born in the South when the South was thrust under Yankee oppression, ruled by illiterate and dishonest carpetbaggers. The South had been defeated in war and was economically bankrupt. Determined to regain control of their government, their rights and their property, many southern whites found in the Klan a solution.

In the South, people speak with understanding and perhaps pride about their great-grandfather having belonged to the Klan. For a small-town, blue-collar mill worker or truck driver, upset over integration, busing, and job pressures, the Klan is meaningful because it speaks to his concerns. Membership may not result in a lifetime commitment. Like the Klansmen themselves, the various Klans come and go, but in times of trouble, there is usually a Klan available. If one is a joiner or is overwhelmed with racial concern and anxious for action, a lodge membership or a franchise can be secured. The Klan is an *available* Southern tradition.

Klansmen and former Klansmen run for office in the South and in many places can expect to win a reasonable number of votes—though they will not be elected—for anything from school board member to lieutenant governor. In particular, a slight Klan shadow seems to hang, like a wisp of smoke, over Alabama politics. In 1958 George Wallace tried to take advantage of his Klan-supported opponent, John Patterson, by taking a bed along with him on the campaign trail. "Where is John Patterson?" he would ask his audiences. Then he would lift up the covers, peer inside, and call out, "Who is down there between the sheets with you, John? Are you in bed with the Ku Klux Klan?" Patterson won, however, and rewarded United Klan Wizard Robert Shelton with the state automobile tire contract. Wallace resolved not to be "outniggahed" again and made friends with the Klan. His Lieutenant Governor Jere Beasley spoke at Shelton's 1970 Klonvokation and Senator John Allen sent a friendly telegram. Although it is difficult to prove causality, the two Alabama Attorney Generals who attacked the Klan, Richmond Flowers in the 1960s and William Baxley, who successfully prosecuted the bomber of the Birmingham Sixteenth Street Baptist Church in the 1970s, both missed election to the governor's mansion.

In addition to "How did it get started in the first place?" three questions are usually asked about the Klan: What was the origin of the burning cross? Why do people do things like that? What next?

The birth of the Klan during the troubled times in the post–Civil War South has already been described. The fiery cross came later. It seems to have emerged from the fertile imagination of Thomas Dixon, author of *The Clansman,* who attempted to ground it in fact by claiming that the original Klansmen had inherited the tradition from their Scottish highland ancestors. It is not surprising that the story was accepted without question. Colonel William J. Simmons adopted it to help revive the Klan in the twentieth century. Ever since, Klansmen have used the blazing cross, usually a tall telegraph pole and its crosspiece, wrapped in burlap, which is bound by wire and soaked in kerosene. Set alight at the climax of rallies, it is ritual, warning, and advertising.

Ted Gurr, co-chairman of one of President Lyndon Johnson's National Violence Commission task forces, has written that "the capacity, but not a need, for violence appears to be biologically inherent in men." Is it possible that man, as psychoanalysts and ethnologists suggest, does have inherent aggressive drives? If this is so, then the Ku Klux Klan ought to be a natural mobilizer and vehicle for this aggressiveness. The history and rationale of the Klan are characterized by intimidation tactics and bodily harm. It is a secret, oath-bound society that draws its members from rural and working-class strata, or subcultures, which are socialized to establish reputation, social space, and often personality by fighting.

The Klansman sees a world divided between his own kind and "aliens." Within the Klavern, special action squads often exist and the talk is continually of guns and killing. At public rallies, speakers on flat-back trucks beneath blazing crosses often balance the blandness of their new public relations images with an implied threat of violence with the reminder, "This is the Klan speaking!" The language that draws the greatest response is tough talk, especially references to "niggers." With violence so heavily implied, it is surprising how little there actually is.

Most Klan violence took place during Reconstruction, when the Klan was acting as a guerrilla force, a national liberation army attempting to overturn what it saw as illegal rule by oppressive outsiders. During the 1920s when the Klan numbered in the millions nationwide, whipping was the most common kind of Klan violence, and was used most frequently to settle old scores and punish local misbehavior. Although there was a considerable amount of violence, particularly in Texas, Oklahoma, Alabama, and Georgia, it was remarkably sporadic. In other parts of the nation, where tens of thousands of Klansmen rallied from Maine to California, despite tough talk and a sense of masked immunity and power, Klans and Klansmen held back.

In the 1950s and 1960s, Klansmen bombed churches, assaulted integration-minded bus riders, and shot civil rights workers in Mississippi because they felt they could get away with it. Perhaps a kind of territoriality exists on a psychological level in the human species and prompts men to defend not only their homes and neighborhoods but also their threatened prestige and status in society. In addition, the excitement of inflicting pain has always held a psychic reward for Klan floggers. Nevertheless, Klan violence clearly has been triggered by social and cultural values, rather than instinctive ones. Historically police passivity rather than Klan aggressiveness has determined whether violence will occur. It would seem, therefore, more useful to apply the cultural term "hostility" rather than the biological term "aggression" to describe the relationship between Klansmen and the world of aliens outside the Invisible Empire.

The best way to view the recent Klans is as a status movement. This has much to do with the answer to the question, "What next?" Today's Klansmen are not only unhappy over the social politics of America's post-industrial, pluralistic society, they feel left out. Since the 1960s, studies by the Anti-Defamation League, Vander Zanden, the political scientist William Moore, and my own studies for the National Violence Commission have found the typical Klansman to be in his twenties to middle thirties with no more than a high school education. He has usually been a skilled blue-collar worker (carpenter, bricklayer, mechanic, truck driver), a small independent businessman (the owner-operator of a barber shop, gas station, or repair shop), a small-town policeman, or a part-time minister. He lives in a rural area or in a small- to middle-sized town. Whatever his place in the class structure, the Klansman resents his lack of recognition and prestige in society.

Klan members feel threatened about their jobs and beset by a society and a federal government that they believe are hostile to them and their values. They believe that the government and the national media are controlled by the Jew-Communists. New York, not Washington or Moscow, is seen as the center of the "communist conspiracy." The initials FBI really stand for the "Federal Bureau of Integration," Klan speakers explain, and the Department of HEW means "nigger Health, nigger Education, and nigger Welfare." A Klan song laments:

You have to be black to get a welfare
check and I'm broke.
No joke.
I ain't got a nickel for a coke.
I ain't black you see,
so Uncle Sam won't help poor nigger-hating me.

Lacking influence, Klan politics take an expressive form. As Klansmen, and therefore defenders of one-hundred-per-cent Americanism, the white race, school, neighborhood, and way of life, Klan members confer on themselves the prestige that society has otherwise withheld from them. Membership in the Klan is very satisfying in itself and may well lessen the need for overt action. However, although secrecy and the traditional aura and talk of violence that generally pervade Klandom may lead to sporadic acts, in the post-1960s' South, the community approval and the police permissiveness necessary for a campaign of violence have declined significantly.

There is also the matter of the Federal Bureau of Investigation. By the middle 1960s, presidential pressure had prompted the FBI into action, and it moved with dispatch. Although there are questions as to the degree to which informants were involved in violent episodes, they did enable the FBI to solve the civil rights murders of the 1960s. In addition, the agency undertook the same kind of disruptive action against the Klan that it had practiced against left wing groups. It simply adopted the methods employed by many secret societies. The FBI's Counterintelligence Program: Internal Security, Disruption of Hate Groups operation, known as COUNTERINTELPRO, sought to disrupt the Klan internally by spreading rumors of financial and sexual corruption, and also breached security within the Klan. The FBI sent Klansmen anonymous postcards covered with crude cartoons captioned, "Which Klan leaders are spending your money tonight?" "Someone knows who you are," and "Is your job safe even after everyone finds out you're a Klansman?"

Postcard messages sent anonymously to Ku Klux Klansmen by the FBI in the 1960s.

Made available by the Freedom of Information Act.

Although a Klansman might have the weapons and the will for "a little action," the chances of being caught were so strong as to be very dissuasive by the 1970s.

When the FBI and Southern juries started being less polite to Klansmen, Klansmen became more polite to outsiders and aliens. And then for a while it seemed that this might all come to an end. The J. Edgar Hoover scandals over what the FBI had been doing to disrupt the Klans and the lives of others on its lists and what the FBI had *not* been sharing with the Justice Department ostensibly weakened its Klan surveillance. As Congress considered whether the new restraints on the FBI were too loose or too tight, FBI agents complained that they could react to but no longer anticipate Klan violence. It was by no means certain, however, that all of the FBI's close observation had really ended, and it was clear that law enforcement agencies, as in the case of the Greensboro, North Carolina, killings, were still infiltrating the Klans.

Beyond the recruitment of Klansmen and the surveillance by police, there was yet another player in the Klan game, and that was the black community. The Ku Klux Klan continued to be a very important factor in the lives of black people. The hooded and robed Klansman in the street was more an object of derision than fear although the danger of violence, while diminished, was still real. More important, the Klan was a prime symbol. It represented past oppression and suffering and the obstacles that lay ahead for black people in America. Slavery seemed too distant, too difficult to really identify with, too aberrant an experience. The Klan was a present—and future—reality. Even if the Klan itself was not the problem, black leaders easily slipped into talking about "Klan-mindedness" in the behavior of the white world.

In the late 1970s, there were Klansmen in the streets of northern Mississippi and Alabama, and the Southern Christian Leadership Conference clashed with them during protest marches. There were beatings, and shots were fired and people wounded. In the confrontations with the Klan, the SCLC had discovered a cause. Fighting against the Klan might revive the flagging civil rights movement in the black communities and give the SCLC the purpose, unity, and community leadership that had been ebbing since the death of Martin Luther King, Jr.

The march in Decatur, "three thousand strong," had been exhilarating for the SCLC, the first time they had placed their bodies on the line since the 1960s. It had been decided at meetings in Jackson, Mississippi, and Norfolk that they would form a nationwide network to fight the Klan. When the killings took place in Greensboro, a major conference was called in Atlanta in December, 1979, to plan a protest march in Greensboro and a strategy for legal, political, and "direct" nonviolent action.

For the "left and progressive forces," black and white, church and labor, which met in Daddy King's Ebenezer Baptist Church under the auspices of the SCLC and IFCO (the Interreligious Foundation for Community Organization), the Klan represented the racial cutting edge of fascism in America. Reports described Klan recruitment in the colleges, in the armed services, on the assembly lines, in prisons, and in police forces. They were all linked together, SCLC President Joseph Lowery explained, "colonialism, imperialism, racism, and Klanism." Ann Braden, who with her husband Carl had begun interracial labor organizing in Kentucky before many of the conference representatives had been born, described how the conference saw the Klan revival. Each previous period of Klan power, during Reconstruction and the 1920s, had also been one of social and economic upheaval—and repression. Conversely, when there were strong popular mass movements, as in the 1930s and 1960s, the Klan had been weak. Now, at the beginning of the 1980s, there was another period of turmoil; society was falling apart. Schools, cities, and the economy were in trouble, and the Klan represented the threatening path toward a repressive, big business, police-state society.

The anti-Klan Network drew together the talent of the social activists as well as an unstable consortium of left-wing ideological splinter groups (as the conflict with the Communist Workers Party over the Greensboro memorial march was to reveal). Within the Network, anticapitalist rhetoric vied with the anti-Klan purpose for central place. The conference in Atlanta and the subsequent Greensboro march were significant for the absence of national black leaders and more moderate support. Even the black mayor of Atlanta made no token appearance, and other traditional allies were strangely absent.

The nation's prime Klan-watcher (at least, outside of the FBI) had long been the Anti-Defamation League, but it was not involved in the Network. If the sight of black leaders singing "We Shall Overcome" with the Palestine Liberation Organization had seemed strange to Jewish civil rights supporters, then the behavior of the American Civil Liberties Union also must have struck them as peculiar. Given the choices that must be made in the commitment of limited resources, the ACLU's cases involving the firing of the

Klan prison teacher and guards in New York, the disciplining of Klan marines in Camp Pendleton, California, and the anti-mask law in Pensacola, Florida, seemed somewhat surprising.

The Greensboro episode posed dual problems for the leaders of the anti-Klan Network. Cooperation with the various communist groups, Moscow or Peking, Maoist, Trotskyite, or others, could be very dangerous. That communist blood had been spilled in a black neighborhood by white racists might well give them a foothold in the black communities. Organizations such as the SCLC knew well the problems of trying to work with the true believers of the left, but also were reluctant to appear less militant. The enemy was supposed to be the Ku Klux Klan, and the anticapitalist rhetoric was not likely to be reassuring to the potentially much larger number of moderate supporters. As Stokely Carmichael had maneuvered Martin Luther King into endorsing black power, in Greenwood, so Greensboro represented a potential entrapment of the left, which the SCLC did not find completely unappealing.

Perhaps as difficult as dealing with the Klans and the Communists was the relationship with the police. The black experience had been that the police were often more violent than the Klans and that, in the South, membership historically tended to overlap. Although the Klan might be a fearsome experience, its presence was episodic; the police were an unavoidable fact of life. Charges of police brutality touched off the protest marches of the late 1970s as they had the urban riots of the 1960s.

Marches in Okolona, Tupelo, Decatur, and Birmingham against beatings and shooting by the police had produced the Klan revival in northern Mississippi and Alabama. In the opinion of many black people, lax police protection had been responsible for the shootouts in Decatur and Greensboro. At a Klan rally, police and sheriff's dispatchers from Baldwyn and Tupelo revealed their membership, and the other policemen, whom the United League was trying to have fired because of jailhouse beatings, were honored guests. A Sylacauga policeman was among those indicted for shooting into homes of Alabama blacks. The Marshall County sheriff thanked the Klan for its contribution to law and order, and the police chief of Gadsden estimated that perhaps a dozen of his men were also Klansmen. The sergeant in charge of the riot squad in strife-ridden Pensacola complained about the press coverage of his remarks. He had only been joking when he told reporters that his deputies had a new game at the jail called *Selma*. "You grab a club and hit a nigger. . . . Now I don't want you to think I'm a racist," he had said, "I like black folks. In fact I'd like to have two of them in my backyard for the dogs to play with. Niggers are better than milk bones."

The white middle class' knowledge of jail comes mainly from books and television. Many will remember Fannie Lou Hamer's sobbing testimony to the Credentials Committee at the 1964 Democratic Nominating Convention in Atlantic City:

> They beat me and they beat me with the long flat blackjack. I screamed to God in pain. My dress worked itself up. I tried to pull it down. They beat my arms until I had no feeling in them. After a while the first man beating my arm grew numb from tiredness. The other man who was holding me was given the blackjack. Then he began beating me. . . . All of this on account we want to register. . . .

Many will also remember the Justice Department's confirmation of FBI informer Gary Rowe's account of the Alabama Highway Patrol and the Birmingham Police calling in Klansmen to beat the 1960 freedom riders and telling them to do what they wanted as long as they were out of the Greyhound station in fifteen minutes. Police Commissioner "Bull" Connor excused the absence of the police for those fifteen minutes on the grounds that they had been home visiting their mothers for Mother's Day. In most black communities, police courtesy and violence were not learned from television and books.

Policing is a dangerous job in a violent world. Safety comes from aggressive patrolling, particularly in high crime areas, which are usually poor and black. From the police point of view, force establishes necessary "respect." Police resistance to the firing of fellow officers accused of mistreating black prisoners is a matter of protective solidarity not unknown in other professions. As to the charges of negligence in preventing violence between Klan and demonstrators, the CWP in Greensboro had tried to have it both ways, first rejecting police protection and then complaining that it had not been provided. Crowd policing traditionally tends to be reactive. The first clash often takes the police by surprise; consequently, for the next march the area is flooded with officers in riot gear and helicopters overhead, at not inconsiderable cost to municipal budgets.

This still leaves unsettled the role of the police and the question of what to do when policemen are—or start behaving like—Klansmen. The number of black police and state troopers (often the result of court orders to integrate) was small but growing, as was the number of black sheriffs. "Bull" Connor was gone. Selma's ex-Sheriff Jim Clark was sentenced to two years in prison on a marijuana-smuggling conviction. Birmingham elected a black mayor in 1979 as did Atlanta in 1977 and New Orleans in 1978. In 1979, most of the nation's black mayors were in the South.

Mississippi Governor Cliff Finch denounced the Klan as "a hate organization" and denied that it represented race relations in the state. So did local chambers of commerce, newspapers, and the Tupelo councilman who called Bill Wilkinson's patriots "a bunch of hoods covered up with a sheet." Perhaps Decatur, Alabama, represents as clearly as anyplace the changes, resistances, and ambiguities that beset race relations in the South of the 1980s. Decatur sat out the civil rights struggles of the 1960s and escaped the overt conflict that earned its mid-state, industrial big brother the nickname of "Bombingham." Mayor Bill Dukes protested that he was not "Bull" Connor and Decatur was "no Birmingham," arguing that the clashes over Tommy Lee Hines were not a civil rights matter. This was nothing like the sixties, he complained. There were blacks on the city's major boards. Only one of Decatur's sixty policemen was black, but Decatur was trying. "Decatur doesn't deserve this," he lamented. "We've gotten caught in a crossfire."

The Reverend R. B. Cottonreader, the local SCLC leader, saw it differently. "The Klan's been in Decatur all along," he said. "The only thing is they hadn't been dressed out. We pulled off the scab and discovered the cancer."

"I never say we're nonviolent," Imperial Wizard Bill Wilkinson explained, disdaining David Duke's "new Klan" image. "I suppose the average Klansman is apt to be more violent than the normal person. That's because we feel so strongly about our beliefs."

No two communities are exactly alike. Racial change came more slowly to some parts of the South than to others. When the economy is slow or times bad, conflicts often sharpen. In time, both the black demonstrators and the Ku Klux Klan will march away from the streets of Decatur, but the problems will continue, as will the history of the Klans. As Klansmen boast:

Yesterday, Today, Forever,
Since Eighteen Hundred and Sixty-Six,
the KU KLUX KLAN
has been riding and will
continue to do so as long as
the WHITE MAN LIVETH.

ACKNOWLEDGMENTS

This work has been made possible only by many kindnesses and much help from people both within and outside of the academic profession. In dealing with a secret organization such as the Ku Klux Klan, where internal records and correspondence are generally unavailable, the working press of America has proven to be an impressive instrument of knowledge. The New York *Times*, with its expert coverage and its priceless index, is the essential starting point for the study of the twentieth-century Klan. The files of the Journalism Library and the Pulitzer prize collection at Columbia University are helpful, and the clipping books of the American Civil Liberties Union are of great value. I benefited from the use of the clipping files of the Tampa *Tribune* and the Los Angeles *Times,* and I want to particularly thank Alfred Friendly and Jack Burness for access to and aid with the files of the Washington *Post and Times-Herald.* It would have been difficult to do without the Newspaper Room of the Library of Congress and the Inter-Library Loan microfilm exchange.

The Gutzon Borglum Collection of the Library of Congress, the Stetson Kennedy Papers in the Schomburg Collection of the New York Public Library, the ACLU archives, the Department of Justice files in the National Archives, and the records of the Non-Sectarian Anti-Nazi League and the Florida branch of the Anti-Defamation League were invaluable. I am appreciative of the courtesy, aid, and collections of the New York Public Library, the Library of Congress, and the University of Florida Libraries, where Mr. Ray Jones and Mrs. Margaret Duer have been extremely helpful.

I am particularly indebted for aid given me by Bernard Bellush, Manning Dauer, Anthony Di Biase, Frank N. Elliott, Justin Finger, Sherman Harris, Harold Hyman, Melville Kahn, Robert W. Kenny, Joseph A. McGowan, Herbert F. Margulies, Robert S. Morris, Nathan Perlmutter, Frank A. Quinn, Samuel Proctor, Wilson Record, Irwin Schulman, James Sheldon, Arthur Spiegel, Eckard V. Toy, Jr., James W. Vanden Zanden, Richard Vowles, Charles Walden, Fuller Warren, Hy Weinberg, Donald Williams, and Michael Wolfson. Rembert Patrick, Samuel Proctor, Justin Finger, D. Allen Williams, George Cunningham, Robert Greenwood, Kenneth Harrell, Selden Henry, Seymour Lipset, C. J. Reuter, Bill Lazar, Charles Lowery, Brandt Ayers, Dawn Stephens, Sam Vaughan, and Will Davison.

In the first serious study of the Ku Klux Klan,[1] the historian Walter L. Fleming closed his Note of Acknowledgment with the following sentence, which I would like to echo: "There is still much that is obscure about the Ku Klux Klan and I shall be glad to obtain additional information in regard to the order, and also to receive notice of mistakes and errors in this account."

DAVID M. CHALMERS

[1] J. C. Lester and D. L. Wilson, *Ku Klux Klan, Its Origin, Growth and Disbandment*. Walter L. Fleming, ed. (New York, 1905).

BIBLIOGRAPHY

Chapter 2. The Klan Rides, 1865–71

GENERAL: **W. J. Cash,** *The Mind of the South* (New York, 1960), pp. 3–147. **C. H. Coleman,** *The Election of 1868* (New York, 1933), Chs. I, XI, XIII. **E. Merton Coulter,** *The South During Reconstruction* (Baton Rouge, 1947). **Homer Cummings** and **Carl McFarland,** *Federal Justice* (New York, 1937), Ch. 12. **William A. Dunning,** *Reconstruction, Political and Economic, 1865–1877* (New York, 1962). **John Hope Franklin,** *Reconstruction* (Chicago, 1961). **Robert S. Henry,** *First With the Most* (New York, 1944), Ch. XXVII. **Stanley F. Horn,** *Invisible Empire: The Story of the Ku Klux Klan, 1866–1871* (Boston, 1939). **Mark M. Krug,** "On Rewriting of the Story of Reconstruction in the U. S. History Textbooks," *Journal of Negro History,* XLVI (1961), 133–53. **J. C. Lester** and **D. L. Wilson,** *Ku Klux Klan, Its Origin, Growth, and Disbandment,* **W. L. Fleming,** ed. (New York, 1905). **Otis A. Singletary,** *Negro Militia and Reconstruction* (Austin, 1957). **Allen W. Trelease,** "Who Were the Scalawags?" *Journal of Southern History,* XXIX (1963), 445–68. U. S. Congress, *Report of the Joint Select Committee to Inquire into the Condition of Affairs in the Late Insurrectionary States* (Washington, 1872), 13 vols. **Bernard A. Weisberger,** "The Dark and Bloody Ground of Reconstruction Historiography," *Journal of Southern History,* XXV (1959), 427–47. **T. Harry Williams,** "An Analysis of Some Reconstruction Attitudes," *Journal of Southern History,* XII (1946), 469–86.

STATE STUDIES: **T. B. Alexander,** "Kukluxism in Tennessee, 1865–1869," *Tennessee Historical Quarterly,* 8 (1949), 195–219. **E. Merton Coulter,** *Georgia* (Chapel Hill, 1947), Chs. XXVI–XXVII. **W. W. Davis,** *The Civil War and Reconstruction in Florida* (New York, 1913), Chs. XXII–XXIII. **J. E. Dovell,** *Florida* (New York, 1952), Vol. II, Ch. XIV. **Walter L. Fleming,** *Civil War and Reconstruction in Alabama* (New York, 1905). **John G. Fletcher,** *Arkansas* (Chapel Hill, 1947). **James W. Garner,** *Reconstruction in Mississippi* (New York, 1901), Chs. 5–11. **Ernest P. Landers, Jr.,** *A History of South Carolina, 1865–1960* (Chapel Hill, 1960), Ch. 1. **H. T. Lefler** and **A. R. Newsome,** *North Carolina* (Chapel Hill, 1954), Chs. 34–35. **M. C. McMillan,** *Constitutional Development in Alabama, 1798–1901* (Chapel Hill, 1955), Chs. VII–XI. **V. L. Wharton,** *The Negro in Mississippi, 1865–1890* (Chapel

Hill, 1947). **W. C. Nunn,** *Texas under the Carpetbaggers* (Austin, 1962), Ch. 12. **Otto H. Olsen,** "The Ku Klux Klan: A Study in Reconstruction Politics and Propaganda," *North Carolina Historical Review,* XXXIX (1962), 340–62. **James W. Patton,** *Unionism and Reconstruction in Tennessee, 1860–1869* (Chapel Hill, 1934), Chs. IV–X. **R. L. Peak,** "Lawlessness in Florida, 1868–1871," *Florida Historical Quarterly,* XXX (1962), 164–85. **Dunbar Rowland,** *History of Mississippi* (Chicago, 1925), Vol. II, Chs. XXV–XXVI. **Herbert Shapiro,** "The Ku Klux Klan During Reconstruction: The South Carolina Episode," *Journal of Negro History,* XLIX (1964), 34–55. **Francis B. Simkins,** "The Ku Klux Klan in South Carolina, 1868–1871," *Journal of Negro History,* XII (1927), 618. **F. B. Simkins** and **R. H. Woody,** *South Carolina During Reconstruction* (Chapel Hill, 1932). **W. S. Simkins,** "Why the Ku Klux Klan?" *The Alcade,* IV (1916), 734–48. **Thomas S. Staples,** *Reconstruction in Arkansas, 1862–1874* (New York, 1923). **Millard Thompson,** *Reconstruction in Georgia* (New York, 1915), Ch. XIV. **Albion W. Tourgee,** *A Fool's Errand,* **J. H. Franklin,** ed. (Cambridge, 1961).

CHAPTER 3. THE BIRTH OF A NATION

Atlanta *Constitution,* December 17, 1917. Atlanta *Journal,* November 28, December 7, 1915. **Raymond A. Cook,** "The Man Behind 'The Birth of a Nation,'" *North Carolina Historical Review,* 39 (1962), 519, 540. **Thomas Dixon, Jr.,** *The Leopard's Spots* (New York, 1908); *The Clansman* (New York, 1905); *The Traitor* (New York, 1907). **Eric Goldman,** *Rendezvous with Destiny* (New York, 1953), 227–29. **Richard Griffith** and **Arthur Mayer,** *The Movies* (New York, 1957), 23–25. **Theodore L. Gross,** "The Negro in the Literature of Reconstruction," *Phylon,* 22 (1961), 5–14. **Lewis Jacobs,** *The Rise of the American Film* (New York, 1930), Ch. XI; *Literary Digest,* 50 (1915), 608–9. **Milton MacKaye,** "The Birth of a Nation," *Scribner's,* CII (November 1937), 40–46, 69. *The Nation,* 111 (1920), 519. *New Republic,* 2 (1915), 185. New York *Times,* November 28, 1905; January 23, 1923; April 4, 1946. *Outlook,* 109 (1915), 854. **C. Van Woodward,** *Origins of the New South, 1877–1913* (Baton Rouge, 1951).

CHAPTER 4. THE KLAN REVIVAL, 1915–21

Atlanta *Journal,* December 7, 1915. **Robert L. Duffus,** "Salesmen of Hate," *World's Work,* 46 (May 1923), 31–38. **Henry P. Fry,** *The Modern Ku Klux Klan* (New York, 1922). **Edgar I. Fuller,** *The Visible of the Invisible Empire* (Denver, 1925). **Ward Green,** "Notes for a History of the Klan," *American Mercury,* 5 (1925), 240–43. **C. Winfield Jones,** *Knights of the Ku Klux Klan* (New York, 1941). *Literary Digest,* 68 (February 5, 1921), 42, 45, 46. **Emerson H. Loucks,** *The Ku Klux Klan in Pennsylvania* (Harrisburg, 1936), Ch. X. **John M. Mecklin,** *The*

Ku Klux Klan (New York, 1924). **Marion Monteval** (pseud.), *The Klan Inside Out* (Chicago, 1924). New York *Times,* 1919–21. New York *World,* September–October 1921. **Arnold S. Rice,** *The Ku Klux Klan in American Politics* (Washington, 1962), Ch. 1. **William G. Shepherd,** "How I Put Over the Klan," *Collier's,* 82 (July 14, 1928), 5–7, 32, 34–35; "Ku Klux Koin," 82 (July 21, 1928), 8–9, 38–39. *The Nation,* 113 (1921), 285–86. **William J. Simmons,** Deposition. Case No. 1897 in Equity, U. S. District Court for Western Pennsylvania (1927–1928). U. S. Congress. House Committee on Rules, Ku Klux Klan Hearings, October 11–17, 1921, 67th Congress, First Session (Washington, 1921).

CHAPTER 5. THE EYES OF TEXAS

Charles C. Alexander, "Invisible Empire in the Southwest: The Ku Klux Klan in Texas, Louisiana, Oklahoma, and Arkansas, 1920–1930," unpublished Ph.D. dissertation, University of Texas, 1962; "The Ku Klux Klan in Texas, 1920–1930," *The Historian of the University of Texas,* I (1962), 21–43; "Secrecy Bids for Power: The Ku Klux Klan in Texas Politics in the 1920's," *Mid-America,* 46 (1964), 3–28. American Civil Liberties Union Files (New York), 1924. **Max Bentley,** "The Ku Klux Klan in Texas," *McClure's,* 57 (May 1924), 11–21. *Catholic World,* 116 (1922), 440–41. *Dawn,* 1923. **Robert L. Duffus,** "Salesmen of Hate: The Ku Klux Klan," *World's Work,* 46 (May 1923), 31–38. *Fiery Cross,* May 1923. Ku Klux Klan Files, Department of Justice (National Archives), 1921–22. "The Ku Klux Klan in Politics," *Literary Digest,* 73 (June 10, 1922), 15; "Ku Klux Victory in Texas," *ibid.,* 74 (August 5, 1922), 14; "Quaint Customs and Methods of the Ku Klux Klan," *ibid.,* 44–52; "Klan Victories in Oregon and Texas," *ibid.,* 75 (November 25, 1922), 12–13. **Reinhard H. Luthin,** *American Demagogues* (Boston, 1954), Ch. 7. **S. S. McKay,** *Texas Politics, 1906–1944* (Lubock, 1952). **O. F. Naille,** *The Fergusons of Texas* (San Antonio, 1946). *The Nation,* 112 (1921), 905; 113 (1921), 137, 285; 116 (1923), 325; 118 (1924), 698. *National Kourier,* November 1925. *New Republic,* 40 (1924), 3, 384–85. New York *Times,* 1921–30. New York *World,* June 11, 1922, August 20, 21, 22, 1924. "Klan as an Issue," *Outlook,* 138 (1924), 5. **Arnold S. Rice,** *The Ku Klux Klan in American Politics* (Washington, 1962). Richmond *Times-Dispatch,* September 1924. **Ralph W. Steen,** *Twentieth Century Texas* (Austin, 1942). **Bascom N. Timmons,** *Garner of Texas* (New York, 1948), Ch. VI. U. S. Senate, Senator from Texas, Hearings before a Subcommittee on Privileges and Elections, 68th Congress, 1st and 2nd sessions (1924).

CHAPTER 6. MAYHEM AND MARTIAL LAW IN OKLAHOMA

Charles C. Alexander, "Invisible Empire in the Southwest, the Ku Klux Klan in Texas, Louisiana, Oklahoma, and Arkansas, 1920–1930," unpublished Ph.D. dissertation, University of Texas, 1962. ACLU Files,

1921–23. **Aldrich Blake,** *The Ku Klux Kraze* (Oklahoma City, 1924). *Current Opinion,* 75 (1923), 521–23. *Dawn,* October, 1923. *Hearst's Magazine,* 45 (1924), 46–49, 148–50. "The Masked Floggers of Tulsa," *Literary Digest,* 78 (September 22, 1923), 17; "Oklahoma's Uncivil Civil War," *ibid.* (September 29, 1923), 10–11; "Constitution Week in Oklahoma," *ibid.,* 79 (October 13, 1923), 12–13; " 'Jack, the Klan-Fighter' in Oklahoma," *ibid.* (October 20, 1923), 38, 40, 42, 44. **Edwin C. McReynolds,** *Oklahoma* (Norman, 1954), 347–55. *The Nation,* 116 (1923), 324; 117 (1923), 74, 239–40, 311. *New Republic,* 36 (1923), 86, 163–64, 202–5. New York *Times,* 1922–28. *Outlook,* 135 (1923), 133, 395–96, 438–40, 492–95, 530–31. *Survey,* 51 (1923), 73–75. **Howard A. Tucker,** *A History of Governor Walton's War on the Ku Klux Klan* (Oklahoma City, 1924).

CHAPTER 7. THE RAZORBACK KLAN

Charles C. Alexander, "Invisible Empire in the Southwest: The Ku Klux Klan in Texas, Louisiana, Oklahoma, and Arkansas, 1920–1930," unpublished Ph.D. dissertation, University of Texas, 1962; "White-Robed Reformers: The Ku Klux Klan Comes to Arkansas, 1921–1922," *Arkansas Historical Quarterly,* XXII (1963), 8–23; "White Robes in Politics, 1922–24," *ibid.,* 195–214; "Defeat, Decline, Disintegration," *ibid.,* 311–31. ACLU Files, 1922–23. American Guide Series, *Arkansas* (New York, 1941). *Dawn,* 1922–23. **John G. Fletcher,** *Arkansas* (Chapel Hill, 1947). **V. O. Key, Jr.,** *Southern Politics* (New York, 1949), Ch. 9. Ku Klux Klan File, Department of Justice (National Archives), 1922–23. *The Nation,* 117 (1923), 74, 311. New York *Times,* 1922–28. **Arnold S. Rice,** *The Ku Klux Klan in American Politics* (Washington, 1962), pp. 49–51.

CHAPTER 8. LOUISIANA: BLACK SHEETS AMONG THE BAYOUS

Charles C. Alexander, "Invisible Empire in the Southwest: The Ku Klux Klan in Texas, Louisiana, Oklahoma, and Arkansas, 1920–1930," unpublished Ph.D. dissertation, University of Texas, 1962. ACLU Files, 1923–24. **Max Bentley,** "Let's Brush Them Aside," *Collier's,* 74 (November 22, 1924), 21–22. **Leonard L. Cline,** "In Darkest Louisiana," *The Nation,* 116 (1923), 292–93. *Dawn,* December 1922. **W. E. B. DuBois,** *North American Review,* 223 (1926–27), 291–304. **R. L. Duffus,** "How the Ku Klux Klan Sells Hate," *World's Work,* 46 (1923), 174–83. *Fellowship Forum,* 1923. Ku Klux Klan File, Department of Justice (National Archives), 1922–23. "The Murders of Mer Rouge," *Literary Digest,* 76 (January 13, 1923), 10–12; "Mer Rouge Murders Unpunished," *ibid.* (March 31, 1923), 10–12. New Orleans *Times-Picayune,* May–June 1924, December 1924. New York *Times,* 1922–28. Shreveport *Times,* August 1924, December 1924. **Allen P. Sindler,** *Huey Long's Louisiana, State Politics, 1920–1952* (Baltimore, 1956), pp. 38–55.

CHAPTER 9. MISSISSIPPI: FIERY CROSSES ON THE LEVEE

ACLU Files, February 1923. **Laura Bradley,** "Protestant Churches and
the Ku Klux Klan in Mississippi During the 1920's," unpublished M.A.
thesis, University of Mississippi, 1962. Federal Writers' Project, *Mississippi* (New York, 1938). **V. O. Key, Jr.,** *Southern Politics* (New York,
1949), Ch. 11. Knights of the Ku Klux Klan, *Mississippi Realm Official Monthly Bulletin,* June 1927–January 1928. Ku Klux Klan File,
Department of Justice (National Archives), August 1921. **Reinhard H.
Luthin,** *American Demagogues* (Boston, 1954), Ch. 3. *National Kourier,*
1923. New York *Times,* 1923–28. **William Alexander Percy,** *Lanterns on
the Levee* (New York, 1941).

CHAPTER 10. GEORGIA: THE KLAN TABERNACLE

ACLU Files, 1922–23. **Thomas Boyd,** "Defying the Klan," *Forum,*
76 (1926), 48–56. **E. M. Coulter,** *Georgia, A Short History* (Chapel Hill,
1947). Columbus *Enquirer-Sun,* December 1925. **E. I. Fuller,** *The Visible
of the Invisible Empire* (Denver, 1925). **John Hohenberg,** *The Pulitzer
Prize Story* (New York, 1959), pp. 69–70. Ku Klux Klan File, Department of Justice (National Archives), 1922. *Kourier Magazine,* 1925–36.
"The Ku Klux in Politics," *Literary Digest,* 73 (June 10, 1922), 15. *The
Nation,* 115 (1922), 8–10; 117 (1923), 311; 125 (1927), 173. New York
Times, 1920–28. **Arthur Raper,** *Tenants of the Almighty* (New York,
1943), 178–79. **Arnold Rice,** *The Ku Klux Klan in American Politics*
(Washington, 1962), Ch. V. Washington *Post,* May 11, 1955.

CHAPTER 11. THE HEART OF DIXIE

ACLU Files, 1922–23. **Daniel M. Berman,** "Hugo L. Black: The Early
Years," *Catholic University Law Review,* VIII (1959), 103–16; "Hugo
Black, Southerner," *American University Law Review,* 10 (1961), 35–
42. Ku Klux Klan File, Department of Justice (National Archives),
1921. "Alabama's Floggers," *Literary Digest,* 95 (October 29, 1927),
11–12. Montgomery *Advertiser,* August 1927. *The Nation,* 113 (1921),
232; 125 (1927), 173, 218, 311–16. *Newsweek,* September 20, 1937.
New York *Times,* 1920–30. *Outlook,* 147 (1927), 261, 457. **R. A. Patton,** "A Ku Klux Klan Reign of Terror," *Current History,* 28 (April
1928), 51–55. **Hugh D. Reagan,** "The Presidential Campaign of 1928
in Alabama," unpublished Ph.D. dissertation, University of Texas, 1961.
Arnold S. Rice, *The Ku Klux Klan in American Politics* (Washington,
1962), Ch. V. **W. G. Shepherd,** "The Whip Hand,"' *Collier's,* 81 (June
7, 1928), 8–9; "The Whip Wins," *ibid.* (June 14, 1928), 10–11, 30, 32.
Writers' Program, *Alabama* (New York, 1941).

CHAPTER 12. OREGON: PURITANISM REPOTTED

ACLU Files, 1922–23. *Dawn*, 1922–23. **R. L. Duffus**, "The Ku Klux Klan in the Middle West," *World's Work*, 46 (1923), 363–72. *Fiery Cross*, May 11, 1923. Ku Klux Klan File, Department of Justice (National Archives). "The Ku Klux Klan in Politics," *Literary Digest*, 73 (June 10, 1922), 15; "Klan Victories in Oregon and Texas," *ibid.*, 75 (November 25, 1922); "Wiping Out Oregon's School Law," *ibid.*, 81 (April 26, 1924), 33–34. **John M. Mecklin**, *The Ku Klux Klan: A Study of the American Mind* (New York, 1924). *The Nation*, 113 (1921), 233; 116 (1923), 6, 325. *National Kourier*, April 1925. New York *Times*, 1922–26. **Pierce**, Governor of Oregon, *et al.* v. The Society of the Sisters of the Holy Name, 268 U.S. 510 (1925). **Waldo Roberts**, "The Ku-Kluxing of Oregon," *Outlook*, 133 (1923), 490–91. **Lawrence J. Saalfeld**, "Forces of Prejudice in Oregon, 1920–1925," unpublished M.A. thesis, Catholic University of America, 1950. *Survey*, 49 (1922), 76–77. **Eckard V. Toy, Jr.**, "The Ku Klux Klan in Tillamook, Oregon," *Pacific Northwest Quarterly*, 53 (1962), 60–64.

CHAPTER 13. SUCCESS AND SCHISM IN THE TARHEEL STATE

ACLU Files, 1922–23, 1925. Federal Works Agency, *North Carolina* (Chapel Hill, 1939). **V. O. Key, Jr.**, *Southern Politics* (New York, 1949), Ch. 10. Ku Klux Klan File, Department of Justice (National Archives). *The Nation*, 116 (1923), 82, 325. *National Kourier*, November 1924; January, April 1925. New Orleans *Times-Picayune*, May–June 1924. New York *Times*, 1922–28. **Elmer L. Puryear**, *Democratic Party Dissension in North Carolina, 1928–1936* (Chapel Hill, 1962). Raleigh *News and Observer*, September 15, 1921, February–March 1923; February–April 1927. **Arnold S. Rice**, *The Ku Klux Klan in American Politics* (Washington, 1962), p. 44. Tampa *Tribune*, May 26, 1924.

CHAPTER 14. KLANSMEN IN THE CAROLINA PIEDMONT

Columbia *State*, January–February 1923, June 19, 1925. **James F. Byrnes**, *All in One Lifetime* (New York, 1958). *Fiery Cross*, May–July 1923. **Ernest M. Lander**, *A History of South Carolina, 1865–1960* (Chapel Hill, 1960), Ch. 3. *The Nation*, 115 (1922), 514; 123 (1926), 497. *National Kourier*, December 1924, April, June, November 1925. New York *Times*, February 15, November 19, 1923. **David D. Wallace**, *South Carolina, A Short History* (Chapel Hill, 1951), Ch. LXIII.

CHAPTER 15. THE PRICE OF SUCCESS

ACLU Files, 1923. **Edgar A. Booth,** *The Mad Mullah of America* (Columbus, 1927). **Gutzon Borglum** Ms. (Library of Congress, Washington), 1923–24. Case No. 1897 in Equity, U. S. District Court for Western Pennsylvania (1927). *Dawn,* 1922–24. **R. L. Duffus,** "Salesmen of Hate," *World's Work,* 46 (1923), 31–38, 574. **Ward Greene,** "Notes for a History of the Klan," *American Mercury,* 5 (1925), 240–43. **C. Winfield Jones,** *Knights of the Ku Klux Klan* (New York, 1941). **Henry P. Fry,** *The Modern Ku Klux Klan* (Boston, 1922). **Edgar I. Fuller,** *The Visible of the Invisible Empire* (Denver, 1925). Ku Klux Klan File, Department of Justice (National Archives). Ku Klux Klan, Hearings before Committee on Rules, House of Representatives, 67th Congress, 1st Session, 1921. "The Clash in the Klan," *Literary Digest,* 77 (April 21, 1923), 13; "Colonel Simmons and $146,000, From K.K.K. to K.F.S.," *ibid.,* 80 (March 8, 1924), 36, 38, 40. **Emerson H. Loucks,** *The Ku Klux Klan in Pennsylvania* (Harrisburg, 1936), Chs. II, IV, X. *Minutes of the Imperial Kloncilium of the Knights of the Ku Klux Klan* (Atlanta, 1923). **Marion Monteval** (pseud.), *The Klan Inside Out* (Ardmore, 1924). *The Nation,* 115 (1922), 8–10; 118 (1924), 270–71. New York *Times,* 1921–24. New York *World,* June, September–October 1921; November 1, 1923; June 16, 1924. **Arnold Rice,** *The Ku Klux Klan in American Politics* (Washington, 1962), Chs. I–II. **William G. Shepherd,** "How I Put Over the Klan," *Collier's,* 82 (July 14, 1928), 5–7, 32, 34, 35; (July 21, 1928), 8–9, 38–39; (July 28, 1928), 8–9, 47–49. **William J. Simmons,** *The Klan Unmasked* (Atlanta, 1922); *America's Menace* (Atlanta, 1926). U. S. Senator from Texas, Hearings before a Subcommittee on Privileges and Elections, 68th Congress, 1st and 2nd sessions (1924). Washington *Post,* December 29, 1959.

CHAPTER 16. THE TEN-DOLLAR SPECIAL

Frank Bohn, "The Ku Klux Klan Interpreted," *American Journal of Sociology,* XXX (1925), 385–407. **Sam H. Campbell,** *The Jewish Problem in the United States* (n.d.). **Robert Coughlan,** "Klonklave in Kokomo," *The Aspirin Age,* **Isabel Leighton,** ed. (New York, 1949). *Dawn,* 1923. **R. L. Duffus,** "The Klan Sells Hate," *World's Work,* 46 (1923), 182–83. **Hiram W. Evans,** "The Klan's Fight for Americanism," *North American Review,* 223 (1926), 33–63. **Stanley Frost,** *The Challenge of the Klan* (Indianapolis, 1923). **Henry P. Fry,** *The Modern Ku Klux Klan* (Boston, 1922). **Norman Hapgood** and **Louis Glavis,** "The New Threat of the Ku Klux Klan," *Hearst's International,* XLIV (January 1923)–XLV (April 1924). **John Higham,** *Strangers in the Land* (New Brunswick, 1955), Ch. 8. Knights of the Ku Klux Klan, *The Practice of Klannishness* (Atlanta, 1924). *The Ku Klux Klan Katechism* (Columbus, 1924). "Quaint Customs and Methods of the Ku Klux Klan,"

Literary Digest, 74 (August 5, 1922), 45–52; "The Klan as a National Problem," *ibid.*, 75 (December 2, 1922), 12–13; "A Defense of the Ku Klux Klan," *ibid.*, 76 (January 20, 1923), 18–19; "The Klan's Challenge and the Reply," *ibid.*, 79 (November 17, 1923), 31–33. **E. H. Loucks,** *The Ku Klux Klan in Pennsylvania* (Harrisburg, 1936), Chs. 2, 3, 4, 8. *The Martyred Klansman* (Pittsburgh, 1925). **John Mecklin,** *The Ku Klux Klan: A Study of the American Mind* (New York, 1924); *My Quest for Freedom* (New York, 1945), 246–52. **Marion Monteval** (pseud.), *The Klan Inside Out* (Claremore, 1924). *National Kourier,* 1925. New York *Times*, 1920–30. **Arnold Rice,** *The Ku Klux Klan in American Politics* (Washington, 1962). **Frank Tannenbaum,** "The Ku Klux Klan: Its Social Origin in the South," *Century,* 105 (1923), 873–82. **Norman Weaver,** "The Knights of the Ku Klux Klan in Wisconsin, Indiana, Ohio, and Michigan," unpublished Ph.D. dissertations, University of Wisconsin, 1954.

CHAPTER 17. GOLD-RUSH DAYS IN CALIFORNIA

ACLU Files, 1923. **R. L. Duffus,** "The Ku Klux Klan in the Middle West," *World's Work,* 46 (1923), 371–72. **E. I. Fuller,** *The Visible of the Invisible Empire* (Denver, 1925), 67. Ku Klux Klan File, Department of Justice (National Archives), 1922. *Kourier Magazine,* December 1921, May–June 1929. Los Angeles *Examiner,* May–June 1921. Los Angeles *Times,* March–May 1922. **Sharon Lybeck,** "The Ku Klux Klan in California," unpublished paper, University of California at Los Angeles, 1961, in possession of Professor Harold Hyman, University of Illinois. **Donald J. Merlino,** "Sacramento's Cloak of Secrecy," unpublished paper, Sacramento State College, 1961, in possession of Professor Joseph McGowan, Sacramento State College. **Michael L. Sellick,** "The Ku Klux Klan in Sacramento," unpublished paper, Sacramento State College, 1961, *ibid. National Kourier,* December 5, 1924, April–December 1925. *New Republic,* 38 (1924), 110. New York *Times,* 1921–30.

CHAPTER 18. PIKES PEAK OR BUST

R. L. Duffus, "The Ku Klux Klan in the Middle West," *World's Work,* 46 (1923), 363–72. **E. I. Fuller,** *The Visible of the Invisible Empire* (Denver, 1925). **Ben B. Lindsey** and **Harvey J. O'Higgins,** *The Beast* (New York, 1911). *The Nation,* 120 (1925), 81; 122 (1926), 22; 123 (1926), 284. *New Republic,* 41 (1924), 121. New York *Times,* 1921–29; March 27, 1943. New York *World,* September 9, 13, 1924. *Rocky Mountain News,* September–November 1924; January, May–August 1925; September–November 1926; May 1932. *Survey,* 54 (1925), 75–76, 271–74, 319–21, 426–27; 55 (1926), 473; 57 (1927), 623; 58 (1927), 468. *Time,* 41 (April 5, 1943), 78. Washington *Post,* September 12, 1926.

CHAPTER 19. IN DEFENSE OF INLAND AMERICA

MISSOURI. ACLU Files, 1923–24. *Dawn,* December 1922. *Fiery Cross,* March–June 1923. *The Nation,* 113 (1921), 286; 116 (1923), 325. *National Kourier,* December 1924; November 1925. New Orleans *Times-Picayune,* June 16, 1924. New York *Times,* 1921–28. New York *World,* June 4, 24, 1924; August 6, 1924. **Alfred Steinberg,** *The Man from Missouri* (New York, 1962), pp. 63–64, 78–85, 118, 224. *Watcher on the Tower,* June 1923.

NEBRASKA. **R. L. Duffus,** "The Ku Klux Klan in the Middle West," *World's Work,* 46 (1923), 363–72. **Alfred Lief,** *Democracy's Norris* (New York, 1939), Chs. XIV–XV. *National Kourier,* November 1925. New York *Times,* 1924–28. **Richard L. Neuberger** and **Stephen B. Kahn,** *Integrity, The Life of George W. Norris* (New York, 1937), Ch. XIV. **George W. Norris,** *Fighting Liberal* (New York, 1945), Ch. 28. Omaha *World Herald,* August 1926.

IOWA. ACLU Files, 1923–24. *Dawn,* 1922–23. Des Moines *Register,* January–March 1923; June 1964. *Fiery Cross,* April–June 1923. *The Nation,* 113 (1921), 286. *National Kourier,* 1925. New York *Times,* 1923–28. New York *World,* June 3, 1924; July 25, 1924. **P. J. Orn,** *The Nightshirt in Politics* (Minneapolis, 1926). U. S. Senate, Senatorial Campaign Expenditures, 69th Congress, October 25, 1926.

NORTH AND SOUTH DAKOTA. ACLU Files, 1923. *Fiery Cross,* May 1923. Grand Forks *Herald,* January–February 1923. *National Kourier,* June 1925. New York *Times,* 1922–27.

CHAPTER 20. TWISTING THE KLAN'S SHIRTTAIL IN KANSAS

ACLU Files, 1923. **John D. Bright,** *Kansas, The First Century* (New York, 1956), II, 72, 79, 82, 386, 431–33. **Frank C. Clough,** *William Allen White of Emporia* (New York, 1941), Ch. XIV. *Dawn,* 1924. **R. L. Duffus,** "The Ku Klux Klan in the Middle West," *World's Work,* 46 (1923), 363–72. *Fellowship Forum,* February 13, 1926. **David Hinshaw,** *A Man From Kansas* (New York, 1945), Ch. 7. **Walter Johnson,** *William Allen White's America* (New York, 1947), Ch. 17. Ku Klux Klan File, Department of Justice (National Archives). State of Kansas Ex. Rel. Charles B. Griffith Attorney-General, plaintiff v. The Knights of the Ku Klux Klan *et al.* (1924). "Why Kansas Bans the Klan," *Literary Digest,* 75 (November 11, 1922), 13; "William Allen White's War on the Klan," *ibid.,* 83 (October 11, 1924), 16. *The Nation,* 116 (1923), 325; 122 (1926), 525. *National Kourier,* 1924–25. *New Republic,* 41 (1924), 95. New York *Times,* 1922–27. Topeka *State Journal,* February–March 1925. *Watcher on the Tower,* June 1923. **William F. Zornow,** *Kansas* (Norman, 1957), Ch. 18.

CHAPTER 21. BAD LUCK IN MINNEAPOLIS

ACLU Files, 1923–24. *Dawn*, 1923. **A. I. Harris**, "The Klan on Trial," *New Republic*, 35 (1923), 67–69. **George Mayer**, *Floyd B. Olson* (Minneapolis, 1951). Minneapolis *Tribune*, May–June 1923. *National Kourier*, June 1925; July 1930; February 1931. New York *Times*, May 1923. U. S. Senate, Senatorial Campaign Expenditures, 69th Congress, October 25–26, 1926.

CHAPTER 22. BORDER-STATE KLANS

KENTUCKY. ACLU Files, 1922–24. *Fiery Cross*, 1923. *Kourier*, 1923. *National Kourier*, 1925. New York *Times*, 1921–26. **Arnold S. Rice**, *The Ku Klux Klan in American Politics* (Washington, 1962). *Watcher on the Tower*, 1923.
TENNESSEE. ACLU Files, 1923. *Dawn*, 1923. *Fellowship Forum*, 1926. *Fiery Cross*, 1923. **Henry P. Fry**, *The Modern Ku Klux Klan* (Boston, 1922). *National Kourier*, 1925. New York *Times*, 1922–25. *Outlook*, 133 (1923), 742. **Arnold S. Rice**, *The Ku Klux Klan in American Politics* (Washington, 1962).
WEST VIRGINIA. **C. H. Ambler**, *West Virginia* (New York, 1950). ACLU Files, 1923–24. *The Nation*, 117 (1923), 18. *National Kourier*, April 10, November 21, 1925. New York *Times*, 1921–28.
DELAWARE. ACLU Files, 1922–23. New York *Times*, 1922–24. Wilmington *Evening Journal*, September 1923; September 1924.
MARYLAND. ACLU Files, 1922–23. Baltimore *Sun*, October 28–November 7, 1923; June 24–29, 1927. *Dawn*, 1923. *Fiery Cross*, 1923. *National Kourier*, June 12, 1925. New York *Times*, 1922–26.

CHAPTER 23. KLAN CASTLES IN INDIANA

ACLU Files, 1923–24. **Max Bentley**, "The Ku Klux Klan in Indiana," *McClure's*, 57 (May 1924), 23–33. **Gutzon Borglum** Ms., Box 61 (Library of Congress, Washington). **Robert A. Butler**, *So They Framed Stephenson* (Indianapolis, 1940). **Robert Coughlan**, "Klonklave in Kokomo," *The Aspirin Age*, **Isabel Leighton**, ed. (New York, 1949). *Dawn*, 1923. **R. L. Duffus**, "The Ku Klux Klan in the Middle West," *World's Work*, 46 (1923), 369–72. *Fiery Cross*, March 16, 1923. **Morton Harrison**, "Gentlemen from Indiana," *Atlantic Monthly*, 141 (1928), 676–86. Indianapolis *Times*, 1927. "The Klan 'Backs' a College," *Literary Digest*, 78 (September 15, 1923), 43–45; "A Klan Shock in Indiana," *ibid.*, 81 (May 24, 1924), 14; "A Klan Senator from Indiana," *ibid.*, 87 (November 14, 1925), 16–17; "Fight for Freedom of the Press," *ibid.*, 90 (August 14, 1926), 99. **James B. Martin**, *Indiana, An Interpretation* (New York, 1947), Chs. 14–15. **Powell A. Moore**, *The Calumet Region* (Indianapolis,

1959), 457–70, 553–58. **Samuel T. Moore**, "A Klan Kingdom Collapses," *Independent*, 113 (1924), 473–75, 517–19, 534–36. *The Nation*, 116 (1923), 421; 118 (1924), 271, 698; 123 (1926), 387; 125 (1927), 81–82. *National Kourier*, April 1924. New Orleans *Times-Picayune*, June 18, 1924. *New Republic*, 36 (1923), 35–36. New York *Times*, 1922–30; May 28, 1938; December 22, 1956. New York *World*, June 29, July 2, August 10, 1924. **William G. Shepherd**, "Indiana's Mystery Man," *Collier's*, 79 (1927), 8–9, 47–49. Deposition of **D. C. Stephenson**, Case No. 1897 in Equity, Federal District Court for Western Division of Pennsylvania, 1927. **E. M. Thornbrough**, "Segregation in Indiana during the Klan Era of the 1920's," *Mississippi Valley Historical Review*, XLVII (1960), 594–618. U. S. Senate, Senatorial Campaign Expenditures, 69th Congress, October 18–22, 25, 27, 1926. **Norman F. Weaver**, "The Ku Klux Klan in Indiana," unpublished M.A. thesis, University of Wisconsin, 1947; "The Knights of the Ku Klux Klan in Wisconsin, Indiana, Ohio, and Michigan," unpublished Ph.D. dissertation, University of Wisconsin, 1954, Chs. 4–5.

CHAPTER 24. MIGHTY OHIO

ACLU Files, 1923–24. *Dawn*, 1923. **Embrey B. Howson**, "The Ku Klux Klan in Ohio after World War I," unpublished M.A. thesis, Ohio State University, 1951. Ku Klux Klan Files, Department of Justice (National Archives), 1921, 1923. *New Republic*, 37 (1924), 20, 178. New York *Times*, 1921–27. *Outlook*, 138 (1924), 396. **Norman F. Weaver**, "The Knights of the Ku Klux Klan in Wisconsin, Indiana, Ohio, and Michigan," unpublished Ph.D. dissertation, University of Wisconsin, 1954, Ch. 6.

CHAPTER 25. THE FIGHTING ILLINI

ACLU Files, 1923–24. **Paul M. Angle**, *Bloody Williamson* (New York, 1952). *Dawn*, October 1922–December 1923. **R. L. Duffus**, "The Ku Klux Klan in the Middle West," *World's Work*, 46 (1923), 363–72. *Fiery Cross*, February 1923–January 1924. Ku Klux Klan File, Department of Justice (National Archives), 1924. " 'Bloody Herrin' Again," *Literary Digest*, 82 (September 13, 1924), 9; "Klan Victories and Defeats," *ibid.*, 83 (November 22, 1924), 16; "Gun-Play and Sudden Death in Herrin," *ibid.*, 84 (February 21, 1925), 34, 36, 38, 40; "The Reformation of Herrin," *ibid.*, 86 (August 1, 1925), 28–29. *National Kourier*, 1925. **Agnes Wieck**, "Ku Kluxing in the Miners' Country," *New Republic*, 38 (1924), 122–24. New York *Times*, 1921–28. New York *World*, June 6, 1924. *Outlook*, 138 (1924), 110.

CHAPTER 26. BADGER GAMES IN WISCONSIN

ACLU Files, 1923–24. *Dawn*, 1922–24. **Herbert F. Margulies,** "Anti-Catholicism in Wisconsin Politics, 1914–1920," *Mid-America*, 44 (1962), 51–57. Milwaukee *Journal*, April 8–17, 1928. *The Nation*, 118 (1924), 270–71. *National Kourier*, 1925. New York *Times*, 1921–26. New York *World*, September 6, 1924. **Norman Weaver,** "The Knights of the Ku Klux Klan in Wisconsin, Indiana, Ohio, and Michigan," unpublished Ph.D. dissertation, University of Wisconsin, 1954, Chs. 2–3.

CHAPTER 27. WHITE ROBES ON WOODWARD AVENUE

ACLU Files, 1922–23. *Dawn*, 1923. Detroit *Free Press*, August–September 1924; October–November 1925. "Detroit's Murderous Election Climax," *Literary Digest*, 106 (August 9, 1930), 9–10. *National Kourier*, 1925. *New Republic*, 63 (1930), 361–63. New York *Times*, 1921–28. New York *World*, September 12, 1924. *Outlook*, 138 (1924), 109; 155 (1930), 535. **Mary Ovington,** *The Walls Came Tumbling Down* (New York, 1947), 198–200. **Norman Weaver,** "The Knights of the Ku Klux Klan in Wisconsin, Indiana, Ohio, and Michigan," unpublished Ph.D. dissertation, University of Wisconsin, 1954, Ch. 7.

CHAPTER 28. NATIONAL POLITICS

Edgar Allen Booth, *The Mad Mullah of America* (Columbus, 1927). **Gutzon Borglum** Ms., Box 61 (Library of Congress, Washington). **E. I. Fuller,** *The Visible of the Invisible Empire* (Denver, 1925). Ku Klux Klan File, Department of Justice (National Archives). "The Ku Klux in Politics," *Literary Digest*, 73 (June 10, 1922), 15; "The Klan as a National Problem," *ibid.*, 75 (December 2, 1922), 12–13; "The Klan's Political Role," *ibid.*, 79 (November 24, 1923), 13–14. *The Nation*, 117 (1923), 570. **John W. Owens,** "Does the Senate Fear the Ku Klux Klan?" *New Republic*, 37 (1923), 113–14. New York *Times*, 1921–24. New York *World*, 1921–24. The People Ex. Rel. Bryant v. Zimmerman, 278 U.S. 63 (1928). **Pierce,** Governor of Oregon, *et al.* v. The Society of the Sisters of the Holy Name, 268 U.S. 510 (1925). **Charles E. Rice,** *Freedom of Association* (New York, 1962).

CHAPTER 29. THE CHAMPIONSHIP FIGHT IN
MADISON SQUARE GARDEN

Charles C. Alexander, "Invisible Empire in the Southwest: The Ku Klux Klan in Texas, Louisiana, Oklahoma, and Arkansas, 1920–1930," unpublished Ph.D. dissertation, University of Texas, 1962. **Lee N. Allen,**

"The McAdoo Campaign for the Presidential Nomination in 1924," *Journal of Southern History*, XXIX (1963), 211–28. **Gutzon Borglum** Ms., Box 61 (Library of Congress, Washington). **David B. Burner**, "The Democratic Party in the Election of 1924," *Mid-America*, 46 (1964), 92–113. **Frank Freidel**, *Franklin D. Roosevelt: The Ordeal* (Boston, 1954), Ch. X. **Frank R. Kent**, *The Democratic Party* (New York, 1928), XXXIII–XXXV. "The Klan and the Democrats," *Literary Digest*, 81 (June 14, 1924), 12–13; "The Klan Enters the Campaign," *ibid.*, 82 (July 12, 1924), 9–10. New Orleans *Times-Picayune*, June 28, 1924. *The Nation*, 118 (1924), 698. New York *Times*, January–August 1924. New York *World*, June–July 1924. *Official Report of the Proceedings of the Democratic National Convention* (New York, 1924). Providence *Evening Bulletin*, June–July 1924. **Arnold Rice**, *The Ku Klux Klan in American Politics* (Washington, 1962), Ch. VI. **Michael Williams**, *The Shadow of the Pope* (New York, 1932), Ch. X.

CHAPTER 30. ANTICLIMAX: THE NINETEEN TWENTY-FOUR ELECTION

ACLU Files, 1923. **David B. Burner**, "The Democratic Party in the Election of 1924," *Mid-America*, 46 (1964), 92–113. *Current Opinion*, 77 (1924), 418–22, 683. **Charles G. Dawes**, *Notes As Vice President* (Boston, 1935), Ch. I. *Independent*, 113 (1924), 141. **Walter Johnson**, *William Allen White's America* (New York, 1947), Ch. 17. "The Klan and the Candidates," *Literary Digest*, 82 (September 6, 1924), 10–11; "Klan Victories and Defeats," *ibid.*, 83 (November 22, 1924), 16. **Emerson H. Loucks**, *The Ku Klux Klan in Pennsylvania* (Harrisburg, 1936). *New Republic*, 36 (1923), 4; 40 (1924), 3. New York *Times*, 1924. *Outlook*, 138 (1924), 392.

CHAPTER 31. FROM CANADA TO THE RIO GRANDE

WASHINGTON. ACLU Files, 1924. *Dawn*, 1922–24. *Fellowship Forum*, September 25, 1926. *Fiery Cross*, May 25, 1923. *The Nation*, 118 (1924), 271. *National Kourier*, November 28, 1924; December 5, 1924. New York *Times*, 1922–26. *Watcher on the Tower*, 1923.

IDAHO. *Dawn*, 1923. New York *Times*, September 18, 1923; August 18, October 28, 1924. *Watcher on the Tower*, 1923.

MONTANA. ACLU Files, 1923. **J. Leonard Bates**, "Senator Walsh of Montana, 1918–1924," unpublished Ph.D. dissertation, University of North Carolina, 1952. Great Falls *Tribune*, September–November 1924. *Fiery Cross*, March 1923. *The Nation*, 117 (1923), 570. *National Kourier*, November 28, 1924. New York *Times*, 1924. *Watcher on the Tower*, September 15, 1923.

WYOMING. Casper *Daily Tribune*, November 6, 1924. *Dawn*, 1923. *Fiery Cross*, June 1923. Great Falls *Tribune*, November 12, 1924. New York *Times*, October 18, 1924. New York *World*, October 12, 1924. *Wyoming State Tribune and Cheyenne State Leader*, November 6, 1924.

UTAH. National Kourier, 1925. New York *Times,* December 4, 1925. *NEVADA.* New York *Times,* October 20, 30, 1924. *NEW MEXICO. National Kourier,* May 1925. New York *Times,* 1923–24. New York *World,* September 18, 1924. *ARIZONA.* ACLU Files, 1923. Arizona Legislature, Journal of the House, February 1923. *The Arizona Republican,* May–June 1922. *Dawn,* 1923. New York *Times,* 1922–26.

CHAPTER 32. EVERY MAN FOR HIMSELF IN FLORIDA

ACLU Files, 1922–23. Alachua Klan No. 64, "Floridians Take Your Stand," University of Florida. **William G. Carleton,** "The Popish Plot of 1928," *Forum,* 112 (September 1944), 141–47. **David Chalmers,** "The Ku Klux Klan in the Sunshine State: The 1920's," *Florida Historical Quarterly,* XXXXIII (1964), 209–15. *Dawn,* March 1923, 1925. **H. J. Doherty, Jr.,** "Florida and the Presidential Election of 1928," *Florida Historical Quarterly,* XXVI (1947), 174–86. **J. E. Dovell,** *Florida,* Vol. II (New York, 1952), Ch. 18. *Fellowship Forum,* February 1927. *Fiery Cross,* May 25, 1923; February–March 1925. Gainesville *Sun,* January 18–23, March 18, 1923. **Charles H. Hildreth,** "A History of Gainesville, Florida," unpublished Ph.D. dissertation, University of Florida, 1954, pp. 227–29. "Reign of the Tar-bucket," *Literary Digest,* 70 (August 27, 1921), 12–13. Ku Klux Klan File, Department of Justice (National Archives), 1922–23. Miami *Daily News,* November 3, 1928. *The Nation,* 113 (1921), 285–86. *National Kourier,* November 1924–May 1925. *New Republic,* 25 (1921), 195–97. New York *Times,* 1920–28. New York *World,* June 25, 1924. Tampa *Tribune,* November 2, 1920; February 19, November 2–5, 1923; June 25, 1924; September 14, 1926.

CHAPTER 33. ATTEMPTED DOMINION IN VIRGINIA

ACLU Files, 1924. *Fellowship Forum,* 1928. *Fiery Cross,* April–May 1923. *The Nation,* 123 (1926), 388. *National Kourier,* March–May 1925. New York *Times,* 1922–30. Raleigh *News and Observer,* February 23, 1927. **Arnold S. Rice,** *The Ku Klux Klan in American Politics* (Washington, 1962). Richmond *News Leader,* November 1925. Richmond *Times-Dispatch,* September–October 1924; November 1925; September 1926. Virginia Writers Project, *Virginia* (New York, 1941).

CHAPTER 35. METHODISTS AND MADNESS IN THE GARDEN STATE

ACLU Files, 1923–24. *Dawn,* 1923. Ku Klux Klan Files, Department of Justice (National Archives), 1924–25. **William M. Kunstler,** *The Minister and the Choir Singer* (New York, 1964), Ch. 29. *National Kourier,* March 13, 1925. New Jersey Federal Writers Project, *New*

Jersey (New York, 1939). New York *Times*, 1921–28. **Harold Wilson,** *The Jersey Shore* (New York, 1935).

CHAPTER 36. THE E-RI-E WAS A-RISING, AND THE GIN WAS GETTING LOW

ACLU Files, 1923–24. *Dawn*, 1923–24. *World's Work*, 46 (1923), 574. *Fellowship Forum*, September 18, 1926. *Fiery Cross*, June 1, 1923. *Independent*, 113 (1924), 54. Johnstown *Democrat*, September–October 1924. Ku Klux Klan Files, Department of Justice (National Archives), 1922–23. "New York's Anti-Klan Outburst," *Literary Digest*, 75 (December 23, 1922), 31–32; "The Klan Defies a State," *ibid.*, 77 (June 9, 1923), 12–13. *The Nation*, 118 (1924), 698. *National Kourier*, June, November 1925. *New Republic*, 38 (1924), 191. New York *Times*, 1920–30. New York *World*, September 1921; November 1923; July–September 1924. The People Ex. Rel. Bryant v. Zimmerman, 278 U.S. 63 (1928). Providence *Evening Bulletin*, July 2, 1964. Writers Project, *New York* (New York, 1940).

CHAPTER 37. DEFENDING THE PURITAN FATHERS

CONNECTICUT. ACLU Files, 1923. **Wilbur L. Cross,** *Connecticut Yankee, An Autobiography* (New Haven, 1923). *Fellowship Forum*, February 27, 1926. *Independent*, 116 (1926), 58–59. *National Kourier*, October 1929. New Haven *Journal-Courier*, January–February 1926. New York *Times*, 1921–26. New York *World*, October 5, 1924.

RHODE ISLAND. *Fiery Cross*, March 1933. *National Kourier*, November 21, 1925. New York *Times*, 1923–29. New York *World*, June 7, 1924. Providence *Evening Bulletin*, June 9, 1924; March 17, 29, 1928. Report of the Adjutant-General to the General Assembly About Chartered Commands (Providence, March 20, 1928).

VERMONT. *Dawn*, December 1922. *Fellowship Forum*, February 1926. *National Kourier*, May–June 1925. New York *Times*, 1924.

NEW HAMPSHIRE. Boston *Advertiser*, January 26, 1923. Boston *Transcript*, June 13, 1925. New York *Times*, 1924. New York *World*, September 27, 1924.

MASSACHUSETTS. ACLU Files, 1923–25. Boston *Advertiser*, January 26, 1923. Boston *Evening Transcript*, June 13, 1925. Boston *Globe*, June 11, 1925. Boston *Herald*, June 26, 1925. *Dawn*, October 1922; April, 1923. Great Falls *Tribune*, October 19, 1926. **Joseph Martin,** *My First Fifty Years in Politics* (New York, 1960). *The Nation*, 115 (1922), 514; 118 (1924), 270–71. *National Kourier*, 1925. New York *Times*, 1921–29. New York *World*, August 1, 1924; April 29, September 20, 1925. Richmond *Times-Dispatch*, October 18, 1924.

MAINE. ACLU Files, 1923. **F. L. Collins,** "Way Down East with the Ku Klux Klan," *Collier's*, 77 (December 5, 1923), 12. *Dawn*, 1923. *Current Opinion*, 77 (1924), 419–22. **Charles G. Dawes,** *Notes As Vice*

President (Boston, 1935), pp. 23–28. Detroit *Free Press,* September 7, 8, 1924. *Fiery Cross,* April 1923. **Lane Lancaster,** "The Democratic Party in Maine," *National Municipal Review,* 18 (1929), 744–49. *The Nation,* 117 (1923), 311. *New Republic,* 36 (1923), 87. New York *Times,* 1922–26, December 26, 1961. New York *World,* August 1, September 5, 7, 1924. *Outlook,* 138 (1924), 77. **William R. Pattangall,** "Is the Ku Klux Un-American?" *Forum,* 74 (1925), 321–32. Washington *Post,* December 26, 1961.

CHAPTER 38. THE KLAN INTERNATIONAL

Canadian Forum, 10 (1930), 233. *Canadian Magazine,* 66 (October 1926), 31. *National Kourier,* April 1931. "The Ku Klux Klan in Saskatchewan," *Queen's Quarterly,* 35 (1928), 592–602. "Canada's 'Keepout' to Klanism," *Literary Digest,* 76 (February 3, 1923), 20–21. *Living Age,* 327 (1925), 128. New York *Times,* 1922–30. New York *World,* September 25, 1921; August 24, 1925.

CHAPTER 39. MARCHING ON WASHINGTON

Gutzon Borglum Ms., Box 61 {Library of Congress, Washington). *Current History,* 28 (1928), 51–55. *Dawn,* 1923. Deposition of **D. C. Stephenson,** Case 1897 in Equity, Federal District Court of Western Pennsylvania, 1927. *Independent,* 116 (June 19, 1926), 718–19, 726. Knights of the Ku Klux Klan, *Mississippi Realm Official Monthly Bulletin,* June 1927–January 1928. *Kourier Magazine,* December 1924–December 1928. "The Klan Walks in Washington," *Literary Digest,* 86 (August 22, 1925), 7–8. **Emerson H. Loucks,** *The Ku Klux Klan in Pennsylvania* (Harrisburg, 1936), Ch. 7. *National Kourier,* November 21, 1924–May 22, 1925; September 1926. *New Republic,* 45 (1926), 310. New York *Times,* 1920–30. **Arnold S. Rice,** *The Ku Klux Klan in American Politics* (Washington, 1962), Ch. 2. Richmond *Times-Dispatch,* September 14, 1926. Washington *Post,* August 1925; September 1926. Washington *Star,* August 1925; September 1926. *World's Work,* 55 (1928), 243–52, 399–407.

CHAPTER 40. DECLINE

ACLU Files, 1922–26. **Paul M. Angle,** *Bloody Williamson* (New York, 1952), Chs. 8–11. **Laura Bradley,** "Protestant Churches and the Ku Klux Klan in Mississippi During the 1920's," unpublished M.A. thesis, University of Mississippi, 1962. Case No. 1897 in Equity, U. S. District Court for Western Pennsylvania, 1927. **Tom Clark,** *The Southern Country Editor* (Indianapolis, 1948). **T. M. Conroy,** "The Ku Klux Klan and the American Clergy," *American Ecclesiastical Review,* 70 (1924), 47–58. **Robert Coughlan,** "Klonklave in Kokomo," *The Aspirin Age,*

Isabel Leighton, ed. (New York, 1949). *Dawn,* 1922–23. *Fiery Cross,* May 26, 1923. *Fellowship Forum,* April 10, 1926. **Edgar I. Fuller,** *The Visible of the Invisible Empire* (Denver, 1925). *Literary Digest,* 1921–28. **Emerson H. Loucks,** *The Ku Klux Klan in Pennsylvania* (Harrisburg, 1936). **Robert S. Lynd and Helen M. Lynd,** *Middletown* (New York, 1929), Ch. XXVIII. **John M. Mecklin,** *The Ku Klux Klan: A Study of the American Mind* (New York, 1924). **Robert M. Miller,** *American Protestantism and Social Issues, 1919–1939* (Chapel Hill, 1958), Chs. IX–X. **Marion Monteval** (pseud.), *The Klan Inside Out* (Claremore, 1924). *The Nation,* 113 (1921), 285–86. *National Kourier,* November 14, 1924; March 6, 1925. *New Republic,* 45 (1926), 310–11; 46 (1926), 29; 52 (1927), 330–32; 53 (1927), 33–34. *New York Times,* 1920–29. *New York World,* September–October 1921. *The Pulitzer Prizes, Plan of Award,* Columbia University. **E. F. Stanton,** *Christ and Other Klansmen, or Lives of Love, The Cream of the Bible Spread upon Klanism* (Kansas City, 1924). **Frank A. Quinn,** "The Ku Klux Klan: An American Social Movement," unpublished paper, University of California, 1949, in possession of the author. **Frank Tannenbaum,** "The Ku Klux Klan: Its Social Origin in the South," *Century,* 105 (1923), 873–82. *U. S. Senator from Texas, Hearings before a Subcommittee on Privileges and Elections, 68th Congress, 1st and 2nd session.* (1924). **Norman Weaver,** "The Knights of the Ku Klux Klan in Wisconsin, Indiana, Ohio, and Michigan," unpublished Ph.D. dissertion, University of Wisconsin, 1954. **Michael Williams,** *The Shadow of the Pope* (New York, 1932).

CHAPTER 41. NINETEEN TWENTY-EIGHT, A YEAR OF
PERILS AND PROMISES

Charles C. Alexander, "Secrecy Bids for Power: The Ku Klux Klan in Texas Politics in the 1920's," *Mid-America,* 46 (1964), 3–28. *Atlanta Constitution,* November 1928. **William G. Carleton,** "The Popish Plot of 1928," *Forum,* 112 (September 1949), 141–47. **Carl N. Degler,** "American Political Parties and the Rise of the City: An Interpretation," *Journal of American History,* LI (1964), 41–59. **H. J. Doherty, Jr.,** "Florida and the Presidential Election of 1928," *Florida Historical Quarterly,* XXVI (1947), 174–86. *Fellowship Forum,* 1926–28. **Frank Freidel,** *Franklin D. Roosevelt: The Ordeal* (Boston, 1954), Ch. XVI. Knights of the Ku Klux Klan, *Mississippi Realm Official Monthly Bulletin,* 1927–28. *Kourier Magazine,* 1927–28. **S. S. McKay,** *Texas Politics, 1906–1944* (Lubock, 1952). **Edmund A. Moore,** *A Catholic Runs for President* (New York, 1956). *New York Times,* 1928. **Roy V. Peel and Thomas C. Donnelly,** *The 1928 Campaign: An Analysis* (New York, 1931). **Hugh D. Reagan,** "The Presidential Campaign of 1928 in Alabama," unpublished Ph.D. dissertation, University of Texas, 1961. *Washington Post,* 1928. **Arnold S. Rice,** *The Ku Klux Klan in American Politics* (Washington, 1962), Ch. VII. **Michael Williams,** *The Shadow of the Pope* (New York, 1932).

CHAPTER 42. THE DEPRESSION DECADE, 1929–39

Daniel M. Berman, "Hugo L. Black: The Early Years," *Catholic University Law Review,* VIII (1959), 103–16; "Hugo Black, Southerner," *American University Law Review,* 10 (1961), 35–42. **Hazel Hertzberg,** "The Shoemaker Case, The Social Forces Which Produced and Carried It Forward," unpublished paper, City University of New York, 1961, in possession of Professor Bernard Bellush, City University. **Edwin D. Hoffman,** "The Genesis of the Modern Movement for Equal Rights in South Carolina, 1930–1939," *Journal of Negro History,* XLIV (1959), 346–69. **Morris Janowitz,** "Black Legions on the March," *America in Crisis,* Daniel Aaron, ed. (New York, 1952). **Stetson Kennedy,** *Southern Exposure* (New York, 1946). *Kourier Magazine,* 1929–36. Los Angeles *Times,* 1936–39. **Ralph McGill,** *The South and the Southerner* (Boston, 1963), Ch. X. *The Nation,* 145 (1937), 278, 311–12, 365–66, 367–69. *Newsweek,* 10 (September 20, 1937), 9–12. New York *Times,* 1929–39. *Outlook,* 155 (August 6, 1930), 539. **Arnold S. Rice,** *The Ku Klux Klan in American Politics* (Washington, 1962), Ch. VII. Tampa *Tribune,* 1931–39. Washington *Post,* 1933–39.

CHAPTER 43. ALL DRESSED UP BUT NOT GOING ANYWHERE: THE COLESCOTT ERA

Ellis Arnall, "My Battle Against the Klan," *Coronet,* 20 (October 1946), 3–8. Atlanta *Journal,* June 4, 1944. **John Roy Carlson** (pseud.), *Under Cover* (New York, 1943). *Fiery Cross,* July 1939–October 1942. **Theodore Irwin,** "The Klan Kicks Up Again," *American Mercury,* 50 (1940), 470–76. **Winfield Jones,** *Knights of the Ku Klux Klan* (New York, 1941). **Stetson Kennedy,** *I Rode with the Ku Klux Klan* (London, 1954); *Southern Exposure* (New York, 1946). Los Angeles *Times,* 1939–45. **Ralph McGill,** *The South and the Southerner* (Boston, 1963), Ch. X. *New Republic,* 99 (1939), 186–87. *Newsweek,* 15 (January 29, 1940), 15. New York *Times,* 1939–45. Special Committee of the House of Representatives on Un-American Activities (Dies Committee), Executive Hearings Made Public, 6 (1942), 2912–47. Washington *Post,* 1939–45.

CHAPTER 44. THE HOODED WORLD OF DR. GREEN

Anti-Defamation League of B'nai B'rith, *Unmasking the Klan* (New York, n.d.); "The Citizens Councils and Anti-Semitism," *Facts,* II (January 1956), 69. **Harry T. Brundidge,** "The Klan Rides Again," *Cosmopolitan,* 121 (August 1946), 27, 124–28. **James Burt,** "Columbians Incorporated," unpublished paper, University of Florida, 1960, in possession of Professor David Chalmers. **Arnold Forster,** *A Measure of Freedom*

(New York, 1950). New York *Heràld Tribune*, April 1957. Stetson Kennedy, *I Rode With the Ku Klux Klan* (London, 1954); *Southern Exposure* (New York, 1946). Grady R. Kent, *Flogged by the Ku Klux Klan* (Cleveland, Tennessee, 1942). Ku Klux Klan File, Schomburg Collection (New York Public Library). Kendrick Lee, "Ku Klux Klan," *Editorial Research Report*, July 1946. *Life*, 11 (December 8, 1941), 40–41, 20 (May 27, 1946), 42, 44. Los Angeles *Times*, 1946–48. Harold Martin, "The Truth about the Klan Today," *Saturday Evening Post*, 222 (October 22, 1949), 17–18, 122–26. Ralph McGill, *The South and the Southerner* (Boston, 1963), Ch. X. Alexander F. Miller and Mozell Hill, *Safety, Security, and the South* (Atlanta, n.d.). *The Nation*, 163 (1946), 691–94. New York *Times*, 1945–49. Non-Sectarian Anti-Nazi League Files (New York). Tampa *Tribune*, 1946–49. Washington *Post*, 1945–48.

CHAPTER 45. THE DEATH OF THE DRAGON

ADL, *Facts*, 1949–54. James Byrnes, *All in One Lifetime* (New York, 1958), 407. Arnold Forster, *A Measure of Freedom* (New York, 1950). Jay Jenkins, "Again, the Klan: Old Sheets, New Victims," *Reporter*, 6 (1952), 29–31. *Life*, 32 (March 31, 1952), 44–46. Harold Martin, "The Truth About the Klan Today," *Saturday Evening Post*, 22 (October 22, 1949), 17–18, 122–26. Miami *Daily News*, May 10, 1950. Miami *Herald*, March 3, 26, 27, 1953. *The Nation*, 173 (1951), 82, 254–56; 174 (1952), 215; 175 (1952), 267. New York *Herald Tribune*, September 27; December 3, 1950; April 15, 1957. New York *Times*, 1949–54. *Newsweek*, 39 (February 25, 1952), 30; 40 (August 11, 1952), 24. Hugh D. Price, *The Negro in Southern Politics* (New York, 1957), 42–51. Tampa *Tribune*, 1949–54. *Time*, 59 (February 25, 1952), 28; 60 (August 11, 1952), 21. Washington *Post*, 1949–54.

CHAPTER 46. LAISSEZ FAIRE, VIOLENCE, AND CONFUSION IN THE LATE FIFTIES

American Examiner, September 25, 1958; July 30, 1959. American Friends Service Committee, *et al.*, *Intimidation, Reprisal and Violence in the South's Racial Crisis* (1959). American Jewish Committee, *Bigotry in Action* (New York, 1958); "Review of Ku Klux Klan Activities," *For Your Information*, June 1959. Amsterdam *News*, February 21, 1959. ADL, *Bulletin; Facts*, 1954–59; Files (Miami, Florida). Atlanta *Journal*, October 15, 1958. Charles Craven, "The Robeson County Indian Uprising Against the KKK," *South Atlantic Quarterly*, 57 (1958), 433–43. Wilma Dykeman and James Stokely, *Neither Black Nor White* (New York, 1957). Gainesville *Sun*, January 20, 1957; January 22, 1958. Ben Haas, *KKK* (Evanston, 1963). John Kasper, *Segregation or Death* (n.d.). Fletcher Knebel and Clark Mollenhoff, "Eight Klans Bring New Terror to the South," *Look*, 21 (April 30, 1957), 59–60. Ernest P. Lander, *History of South Carolina, 1865–1960* (Chapel Hill, 1960). Los Angeles

Times, 1955–60. **James B. Martin,** *The Deep South Says "Never"* (New York, 1957). Miami *Herald,* 1955–60. **Robert J. Murphy,** "The South Fights Bombing," *Look,* 23 (January 6, 1959), 13–17. New York *Herald Tribune,* April 14–28, 1957. New York *Post,* 1955–60. New York *Times,* 1955–60. N. M. **Newton,** *Crusade for Democracy* (Ames, 1961). **Howard H. Quint,** *Profile in Black and White* (Washington, 1958). St. Petersburg *Times,* January 20, 1958. Southern Regional Council, *New South,* 1955–60. Tampa *Tribune,* 1955–60. **James Vanden Zanden,** "The Klan Revival," paper delivered to the American Sociological Association, September 1959, partially printed in *American Journal of Sociology,* 65 (1960), 456–62. Washington *Post and Times-Herald,* 1955–60.

CHAPTER 47. THE NEW FRONTIERS OF THE NINETEEN SIXTIES

ADL (Miami, Florida), Files and publications, 1960–63. Atlanta *Constitution,* July 9–10, 1962; September 4, 1962. Atlanta *Journal,* July 3, 1962. Charlotte *Observer,* September 1, 1963. Cincinnati *Enquirer,* June 10, 1963. **James G. Cook,** *The Segregationists* (New York, 1962), Ch. III. Daytona Beach *Morning Journal,* September 20, 1963. **Wilma Dykeman and James Stokely,** *Neither Black Nor White* (New York, 1957). Florida Council on Human Relations, *Newsletter,* October–November 1963. Gainesville *Sun,* July 16; September 9, 19; November 5, 1963. **Ben Haas,** *KKK* (Evanston, 1963), Ch. XI. **Bill Hendrix,** "Campaign Platform of a White Man," Spring 1960. New York *Herald Tribune,* March 24, 1961. Jacksonville *Times Union,* July 9, September 7, 1962. Miami *Herald,* January 2, 9; February 22, 1960; September 15, 1961; July 10, September 30, 1962; August 28, September 21, November 2, 1963. National Knights of the Ku Klux Klan, Inc., misc. letters and publications. New York *Courier,* January 12, April 9, May 7, June 18, August 13, 1960. New York *Post,* January 12, March 15, 1960. New York *Times,* 1960–64. *New South,* 1960–64. *Newsweek,* September 17, 1962; August 26, 1963. **Drew Pearson,** Miami *Herald,* April 30, 1960; April 23, October 19, November 5, 1962. Pittsburgh *Courier,* March 19, 1960. St. Augustine *Record,* September 19, 1963. St. Petersburg *Times,* September 17, 1961; May 13, July 10, 1963. *Southern School News,* March 1962. Tampa *Times,* June 7, 1960. Tampa *Tribune* and Files, 1960–63. *Time,* LXXVII (June 2, 1961), 14–18. United Klans of America, Inc., Knights of the Ku Klux Klan, misc. letters and publications. "What the 'Sit-ins' are stirring up," *U.S. News and World Report,* XLVIII (April 18, 1960), 52–56. **James R. Venable,** "History of the Ku Klux Klan," n.p., n.d. **Donald E. Williams,** "Protest Under the Cross," *The Southern Speech Journal,* XXVII (1961), 43–55.

CHAPTER 48. THE LONG HOT SUMMER

ADL (Miami, Florida), Files, 1964. **Trevor Armbrister,** "Portrait of an Extremist," *Saturday Evening Post,* 237 (August 29, 1964), 80–83.

Atlanta *Constitution*, 1964. **Mary Ellen Blaisdell**, "The National States Rights Party," unpublished paper, University of Florida, 1964, in possession of the author. **Rev. Irvin Cheney**, "St. Augustine Ku Klux Klan Meeting," unpublished report, Florida Council on Human Relations, September 1963. Florida Council on Human Relations, *Newsletter*, September 1963. Florida Legislative Investigation Committee, "Background Information on the National States Rights Party," Tallahassee, 1964. Gainesville *Sun*, 1964. **Juanita Green** and others in the Miami *Herald*, 1964. **Sherman Harris**, "Present Status of the Klans," unpublished report, ADL (Atlanta, Georgia), October 1964. **John Herbers** and others in the New York *Times*, 1964. **George McMillan**, "The Klan Scourges Old St. Augustine," *Life*, 56 (June 26, 1964), 21. St. Augustine *Record*, 1964. Tampa *Tribune* and Files, 1964. **Martin Waldron** and others in the St. Petersburg *Times*, 1964. **Pat Waters**, "The American Middle Ground in St. Augustine," *New South* (September 1964).

CHAPTER 49. DECLINING POWER

ACLU, monthly and annual reports, 1965–1968. ADL files (Miami, Florida), reports and publications, 1965–1968. **Stewart Alsop**, "Portrait of a Klansman," *Saturday Evening Post*, April 9, 1966, pp. 23–37. Atlanta *Constitution*, 1965–1968. Detroit *Times*, April 24–28, 1967. FBI, Annual Report to the Attorney General for 1967. **Richmond M. Flowers**, Preliminary Results of Investigation of the United Klans of America, Inc., October 18, 1965. University of Houston, *Proceedings of the Sixth Annual Intergroup Conference, The Radical Right*, 1967. **William B. Huie**, *Three Lives for Mississippi* (New York, 1965). Committee of the U.S. House of Representatives on Un-American Activities, Activities of Ku Klux Klan Organizations in the United States, Hearings, Report, Contempt Citations, and Bills, 1965–1967. *Life*, 1965–1968. *Newsweek*, 1965–1968. New York *Times*, 1965–1968. New York *World-Telegram and Sun*, May 1965. St. Petersburg *Times*, 1965–1968. Tampa *Tribune* and files, 1965–1968. *Time*, 1965–1968.

CHAPTER 50. BAD TIMES IN THE 1970s

ACLU, *Civil Liberties* (November 1978). **Bill Cornwell**, "The Birmingham Bombers, 1963–1976," *Nation* (September 4, 1976). FBI, COUNTERINTELPRO documents, 1964–1971 (available under the Freedom of Information Act). "The Ku Klux Klan & Similar Terrorists," *Facts on File*, 1975. **Jack Nelson**, "Informer: FBI Allowed Klan Violence," Los Angeles *Times* Service, November 30, 1975. **Gary Thomas Rowe, Jr.**, *My Undercover Years with the Ku Klux Klan* (1976). **Arthur M. Schlesinger, Jr.**, *Robert Kennedy and His Times* (1978), Ch. 14–16. U.S. Senate Select Committee on Intelligence Activities (1975), Vol. VI, pp. 888–950. **Patsy Sims**, *The Klan* (1978), Ch. 13. "Terrorism Today:

An Interview with Thomas Tarrants," *Christianity Today* (September 22, 1978). *New York Times,* August–November 1977, February 17–18, 1980, particularly articles by Wayne King and Howell Raines. Birmingham *News,* September–November 1977.

CHAPTER 51. CONFRONTATION, POOR-BOY POLITICS, AND REVIVAL

Atlanta *Journal and Constitution,* 1975–1980. Community Relations Service, *Annual Reports.* David Carlson in the Marion (Indiana) *Chronicle Tribune,* June 1979. Harry Crews, "The Buttondown Terror of David Duke," *Playboy* (February 1980). *The Crusader,* 1977–1979. *Facts on File,* 1979, pp. 864–66. Tom Gordon, "Still with Us after All These Years . . ." Anniston (Alabama) *Star,* June 7, 1979. Judy Klemesrud, "Klansladies," *New York Times* Service, 1975; *Los Angeles Times,* January 29, 1979. Ron Deaton, "Klan Revival," *Progressive* (June 1975). Guy Martin, "Ain't Nothin' You Can Do but Join the Klan," *Esquire* (March 1980). Aryeh Neier, "Mississippi Relives its '60s," *Nation* (September 23, 1978). Adisa Douglas, *IFCO News,* Spring/Summer 1979. Patsy Sims, *The Klan* (1978). Fredric Tulsky, "Standing Up to Fear in Mississippi," *Southern Exposure* (Fall 1978). David Duke Interview (May 2, 1980).

CHAPTER 52. DEATH IN GREENSBORO

William Chafe, "The Greensboro Sit-Ins," *Southern Exposure* (Fall 1978). ———, *Civilities and Civil Rights, The Fruits of Moderation: Greensboro, North Carolina and Civil Rights* (1979). Greensboro *Daily News,* November–March 1980, particularly the writings of Mae Israel, Dwight Cunningham, Lindsey Gruson, Charles Babington, Steve Berry, and Jack Scism. *New York Times,* August 1979–March 1980, particularly the writings of Wayne King and Anthony Lewis. Hall Gulliver, "The Killers Are Riding Again," Atlanta *Constitution,* November 16, 1979. Robert Watson, "Media Martyrdom: The Greensboro Shoot-out," *Harper's* (March 1980), and the reply by Signe Waller, "The Shootings and After: A CWP Response," Greensboro *Daily News,* March 30, 1980. Greensboro Police Department, "An Administrative Report of the Anti-Klan Rally," November 3, 1979. National Conference on New Strategies to Counter the Ku Klux Klan, Atlanta, December 14–15, 1979, and the journals of the CWP (*Workers Viewpoint*), SOC (*Southern Fight-Back*), ERC (*The Southern Advocate*), RCP (*Revolutionary Worker*), and *The Guardian.*

CHAPTER 53. THE ENDURING KLAN

Anti-Defamation League of B'nai B'rith, "The Ku Klux Klans, 1978," *Facts* (March 1978), "The U.S. Neo-Nazi Movement: 1978," *Facts* (March 1978), "The Ku Klux Klan Tries for a Comeback," *Facts* (November 1979). **Wayne Greenhaw,** *Watch Out for George Wallace* (1976). **Patsy Sims,** *The Klan* (1978). **William V. Moore,** "Status Politics and the American Right: The Contemporary Ku Klux Klan," presented at the SPSA, 1975, and the articles of **Wayne King** and **Tom Wicker** in the *New York Times,* **Susan Harrigan** in the *Wall Street Journal,* **Michael Kelly** in the Bergen *Record,* **Willard Rose** in the Miami *Herald,* **Jack Nelson** in the Los Angeles *Times,* **Brandt Ayers** in the Anniston *Star,* and **Bill Hladky** in the Ft. Lauderdale *Sun-Sentinel.*

A growing concern about civil rights and with both the diversity and the fault lines of American society has increased scholarly interest in the Klan. **Charles C. Alexander's** *The Ku Klux Klan in the Southwest* (1965) is a model study. **Kenneth T. Jackson's** *The Ku Klux Klan in the City, 1915–1930* (1967) is an able piece of work with an outstanding essay on sources, in spite of errors in emphasizing the uniqueness of the urban dimension. **Allen W. Trelease's** *White Terror: The Ku Klux Klan Conspiracy and Southern Reconstruction* (1972) presents the full story of the first Klan. **Patsy Sims'** *The Klan* (1978) has the skilled reporter's talent for recreating personality and place.

For further bibliography and comment, see my article "The Ku Klux Klan in Politics in the 1920s," *The Mississippi Quarterly,* XVIII (1965), 234–47; "The Politics of Violence: Race and the Twentieth Century South," *Gulf Coast Politics in the Twentieth Century,* Ted Carageorge, ed. (1973); reviews in the *American Historical Review,* October 1962, January 1966, and July 1968; and articles on the first and second Klans in *American History Illustrated,* January and February 1980.

World interest in the Ku Klux Klan has always been high. It is exciting when the mighty stumble, and American race relations is a well-reported subject. The foreign press picks up Klan stories; the German edition of *Playboy* commissioned its own article; recent books on the Klan have been written in French, Italian, Polish, and Russian; and this volume appears in French and Spanish as *l'Amerique en cagoule* and *Los Americanos Encapuchados.*

INDEX

Abbott, Thomas, 238, 239
Adams, Tom, 173, 295
Addams, Jane, 26
Affirmative Action, 427
AFL, 326; Tampa Shoemaker case, 312
Ainsworth, Kathy, 397
Akers, Tom, 222, 223
Alabama, 6, 16, 78–84, 305, 368; anti-mask law, 336; Birmingham, 79, 80, 390, 391, 398; Sixteenth Street Baptist Church bombing, 400–404, 436, 438; Decatur, 408–10, 414, 434, 436, 438; disbandment, 19; Huntsville, 15; influence, 80; investigations, 83; leadership, 367–68; membership, 80; "muzzling bills," 81, 82; night riders, 81; 1960s, 370, 372–73; late 1970s revival, 406–10, 414–15, 436; opposition, 79, 81–82; politics, 163, 200, 289, 314; press, 16, 81; Reconstruction, 12; Selma, 389, 391; supporters, 79, 82–83; United Klans, 6; violence, 298, 335, 336; White Citizen's Councils, 345. See also Black, Hugo L.; Patterson, John; Wallace, George; Baxley, William; Shelton, Robert
Alabama Conference, 29
Alaska, 279
Alexander, Thomas, 11
Allen, Henry, 143, 144, 167
Allen, John, 429
Allen, Rev. Keith K., 91
Ambrose, Rev. F. Halsey, 141, 142
American Civil Liberties Union (ACLU), 50, 271; Tampa Shoemaker case, 312; 435–6
American Confederate Army, 342
Americanism, 57, 70, 115, 162, 165, 176, 218, 282; defense of, 32–33; ministers on, 246–47
American Krusaders, 217
American Legion, 95, 118, 138, 139, 192, 228, 237, 251, 254, 256, 257, 336; Tampa Shoemaker case, 312
American Protective League, 31, 149, 220

American Unity League, 183, 184
Angell, R. H., 234
Angle, Paul, 188, 189; Bloody Williamson, 185, 189
Anti-Catholicism, 3, 5, 33, 34, 66–67, 71, 73–74, 78–79, 85, 86, 110–12, 113, 114, 123, 131, 152, 156, 162, 176, 194, 225, 227, 230, 245, 291, 377; Klan lure, 294; Oklahoma, 55
Anti-Defamation League, 334, 406, 428, 431, 435
Anti-Klan Network, 422, 434–36
Antimask legislation, 64, 65, 333. See under name of state
Anti-Saloon League, 43, 47, 65, 155, 164, 247, 258, 273
Anti-Semitism, 5, 6, 71, 73–74, 78, 79, 110, 197, 343, 346; present-day, 351–52, 411–13, 425, 426, 428
Arizona, 222–23; Klankraft, 223
Arkansas, 3, 10, 16; activities, 56–58; decline, 281; disbandment, 19; Little Rock, 57, 58; membership, 57; politics, 57; power, 59
Arnall, Ellis, 317, 327, 328
Asher, Court, 322
Ashurst, Henry, 223
Association of Georgia Klans (AGK), 325, 329, 335, 337, 339, 342, 343
Atkins, F. W., 236
Atlanta University, 334

Bacon, Mary, 405
Bader, Mayor, 250
Badger State. See Wisconsin
Baker, George, 90
Baker, Newton, 208
Baldwin, William, 313
Baltimore, 112; Sun, 60, 199
Barnette, W. C., 65
Barton, Bruce, 163
Baruch, Bernard, 204
Bassett, John David, 232–33
Battle, John, 342
Baxley, William, 401–403, 430

Baxter, P. P., 276, 278
Bay State. *See* Massachusetts
Beall, Frank H., 159, 160–61
Bearse, Hiram, 167
Beasley, Jere, 429
Bell, Arthur, 243–44, 245, 250, 264, 322–23
Bellamy, James R., 98
Benjamin, Judah P., 209
Berry, J. F., 247
Beveridge, Albert J., 167
Bilbo, Theodore G., 69, 325, 326
Birmingham Sixteenth Street Baptist Church bombing, trial (Birmingham), 399–404
Birth of a Nation, The, 2, 25–27, 28, 29, 32, 420
Bitzer, Bill, 25
Black, Hugo L., 5, 78, 79, 80, 84, 305, 314–16; background, 315; Supreme Court appointment, 314, 316
Black Insurrection, 17
Black Legion, 308–10
Black Legion, The (motion picture), 310
Black Muslims, 375
Blaine, John, 192, 193
Blease, Cole, 98
Bluegrass State. *See* Kentucky
B'nai B'rith, 340
Bolshevism, 110
Borglum, Gutzon, 31, 106, 169, 200, 282
Bossert, Walter, 169, 170, 173, 202, 205, 313
Bourbons, 22–23
Bowers, Sam Holloway, 393, 394, 395
Bowles, Charles, 197
Braden, Ann, 435
Brady, Matthew, 25
Brennan, George, 204–5
Brewster, Owen, 3, 214, 259, 271, 274–78
Brookhart, Smith W., 139
Broussard, Edwin, 65, 289
Brown, Thad, 181
Browning, Daddy, 261
Brownlow, William G., 11
Bruno, Basil, 250
Bryan, Charles, 212, 348
Bryan, William Jennings, 206, 207, 208, 210, 214, 288, 348
Bryant, Arthur, 344
Bryant, George, 259, 262
Bryant, Joseph, 344
Buckeye State. *See* Ohio
Burbank, W. J., 139
Burch, Dean, 383
Burns, Haydon, 351, 353
Bush, Wilson, 255
Business, boycott of, 180, 234
Bus riots, 370–71
Butler, Pierce, 199
Butler, William, 273

Butte, George, 47
Butterworth, Wally, 373
Byrd, Harry, 230, 233, 234
Byrd, Robert, 326
Byrnes, James F., 99, 337

California, 3, 85, 88, 305, 320; decline, 281; Gold Rush, 119–25; Inglewood affair, 120–21, 122, 124; opposition, 120–21, 327; politics, 124–25, 200; press, 122; reign of terror, 121–22; supporters, 119, 121, 123; Taft, 3
Calles, President (Mexico), 284
Camp, "Colonel," 66, 67
Camp Pendleton, 414, 436
Campbell, Philip, 38, 145, 200
Campbell, Rev. Samuel, 184
Campbell, William, 151
Canada, 279–80; membership, 280; public education, 88
Canal Zone, 279
Cannon, James, 234
Capper, Arthur, 215
Carlson, John Roy, 323n
Carpenter, Rev. C. N., 138
Carpetbaggers, 20
Carter, Asa, 6, 344–47, 348, 352, 368
Carter, Hodding, 332, 334
Carter, James E., 429
Catholics, 47; in Congress, 283; politics, 139; Roosevelt, 307; Smith, Al, 301–2 (*see* Smith, Alfred E.), *See* Anti-Catholicism
Catts, Sidney J., 225
Caudle, Ray. *See* Greensboro murders
Chambliss, Robert, 401–403
Chaney, James, 393
Christ, 136, 163, 325
Christians, George W., 322
Christman, Franklin, 262
Church: Klan and, 60, 62, 68, 75, 76, 86–87, 91, 111, 293–94; nuns, 159, 165, 179; opposition from, 167. *See* Ministry
Church-State separation, 180, 244
CIO, 5, 311, 316, 326; Klan and, 320–21
Citizens' Alliance, 149
Citizens' Bureau of Investigation, 31
Citizens' League, 262
Civil rights; 326; Act, 384, passage, 382; movement, 377
Civil War, 2, 8, 10, 12; post-confusion, 17
Clansman, The, an historic romance of the Ku Klux Klan, 24–25, 27, 93
Clark, Jim, 387, 389, 438
Clarke, Edward Y., 31–36, 52, 70, 73, 101, 104–5, 107, 193, 200; ambition, 279; fraternalism, 292; indictment, 199; opposition, 236; reputation, 105; retirement, 107; Tyler, 100; violence, 297

Clarke, Tom, 326
Clayton, Powell, 13
Cline, Leonard, 60
Clinton, 349
Cobb, Howell, 209
Coburn, William S., 73, 107, 120
Colby, Bainbridge, 208
Cole, Nat "King," 345
Cole, Rev. James "Catfish," 6, 347–49
Colescott, James, 5, 181, 306, 319–24; action, 319, 320; German-American bund, 323; Green, Dr., 325; Imperial Wizard, 318–24; unions, 316–17
Colley, Marion, 211
Collier, John W., 68
Collins, Addie Mae, 401, 404
Collins, Frederic, 275
Collyer, Bud, 329–30
Colorado, 3, 126–34; crime, 131–32; Denver, 4, 126, 133; Doers Club, 126 (See Lindsey, Ben); opposition, 127–28, 129, 132, 133; politics, 126–30, 131, 163; popularity, 131; Riders of the Red Robe, 131
Columbians, 328–29, 352
Columbia University, 257, 345
Columbus Day, 275
Comer, James, 57–58, 101, 102, 104, 106, 240
Comer, Robbie Gil, 58, 264
Committee of Notables, 203
Committee of Thirteen, 149
Common Sense, 6
Communism, 5, 307, 311, 352, 377
Communist party, 316; subversive list, 327
Communist Workers Party. See Greensboro murders
Community Relations Service, 407
Congressional Reconstruction Act, 11
Connally, Tom, 48
Connecticut, 266–68; dissension, 268
Connor, Eugene "Bull," 372, 387, 389, 437, 438
Conspiracy Act of 1870, 392, 393
Continental Congress, 8
Coolidge, Calvin, 45, 72, 75, 107, 127, 129, 133, 137, 155, 170, 176, 178, 202, 203, 214, 221, 269, 282; education, 285; election, 1924, 215; Klan, 214, 283, 286; World Court, 285
Copeland, Royal, 258
Cornell University, 257
Cottonreader, R. B., 408–409, 438
Courts: family, 128; juvenile, 128, 129, 130; Klan, 59 (see Juries)
Cox, W. Harold, 393
Craig, Calvin, 370, 371–72, 383
Creager, R. B., 203
Creel, Robert, 383–84
Crommelin, John, 345–47, 368

Cross, Wilbur, 267
Cummings, Homer, 207
Curley, James M., 271

Dahmer, Vernon, 397
Dale, George, 167
Daniels, Josephus, 27, 93, 94
Daniel, Watt, 61–62, 63, 64
Darrow, Clarence, 196
Dartmouth College, 112
Davidson, Robert Lee "Wild Bill," 370
Davidson, T. W., 45
Davies, Elmer, 313
Davis, John W., 47, 157, 212, 213, 215, 220, 300; nomination, 212; Sea Girt speech, 213, 214
Dawes, Charles G., 214, 276
Dawn, The, 2, 184, 185
de la Beckworth, Byron, 397
Dean, Colonel, 145, 147
Deatherage, George, 322, 353
Delaware, 158–59
Demarest, Horace, 327
Democratic party, 57, 74, 167, 202; election, 1964, 384; Klan, 281; national convention: 1924, 4, 203–12, 220, 300, 1928, 301; Reconstruction, 11, 21
Denver University, 130
Depression, the Great, 4, 5, 234, 304–18, 325
Der Deutsche Orden des Feurigen Kreuzes, 279
Dewey, John, 308
Dewey, Thomas, 382
Dixie Klans, Inc., 369, 376
Dixon, Thomas, 2, 23–25, 26, 27, 93, 430
Doar, John, 394
Donahey, Vic, 178, 179, 180
Duke, Daniel, 327–29
Duke, David, 405, 410–15, 424, 426, 428, 438
Dukes, Bill, 438
Duncan, Dr. Amos, 306
Dunning, M. O., 72, 75, 215
Durham, Baxter, 97
Duvall, Mayor, 174

Economic discrimination, 180, 234
Edge, Walter J., 248
Education, 14–15, 180; compulsory public, 180, 284; federal aid, 284–85; Klan, 237; parochial, 194, state aid to, 275, 276, progressivists, 340; public school law, 196, 199, 218 (see under Oregon); school segregation decision, 343, 349; university, 168. See also Schools and under name of university
Edwards, Eldon, 343, 345, 347, 351; death, 366, 367, 370
Effinger, V. F., 309, 310
Eichmann, Adolf, 352

Eighteenth Amendment, 249
Eisenhower, Dwight D., 382, 383
Elduayen, Fidel, 120, 121
Election: *1924,* 213–15; *1928,* 300–3
Elks, 209, 251
Elliott, Charles, 26
Ellis, Dr. A. D., 40
Elrod, Milton, 150, 202, 205
Emancipation, 18
Emmons, Pat, 173, 280
Employment, 305–6
Emporia College, 144
Engelhardt, Sam, 345
Equal-rights movement, 6
Ernst, Richard, 285
Erwin, Andrew, 74, 209, 211
Esdale, James, 80, 81, 82, 83, 233
Etheridge, Paul, 30, 71, 106, 307
Evangelists, 325
Evans, Dr. Hiram W., 3, 5, 39, 40, 42,
  44, 45, 54, 55, 57, 64, 70, 73, 75, 78,
  80, 95, 96, 97, 99, 132, 157, 184, 202,
  277, 319; anti-Catholicism, 221; Black,
  Hugo L., 315; Black Legion, 308–9,
  310; Canadian Klan, 280; Chicago,
  189; convention, *1924,* 205; Dallas
  homecoming, 288; fraternalism, 292;
  Fry, Mrs. Leslie, 322; headquarters,
  101, 201; Illinois, 185; Imperial Wizard, 104, 108; Indiana, 173; inspection
  tour, 216, 217, 221; Klonvokation
  (3rd), 290; labor, 316; lecturer, 304;
  Long Huey, 307, 308; Michigan, 194;
  New Jersey, 249, 252; North Carolina,
  92; Pennsylvania, 238–39, 241–42, 298;
  platform, 290; politics, 169; power,
  105, 107; retirement, 317–18; Simmons, 92, 105–7, 138–39, 189, 219;
  Smith, Al, 300; Stephenson, 164, 165,
  168–71, 172, 175, 281; supporters,
  101–3, 106; unmasking, 265; violence,
  297; Washington parade, 287–89;
  World Court, 285
Everett, R. O., 93
Evers, Charles, 397

Farley, James, 307
Farnsworth, Eugene, 274, 275, 276
Farrington, Frank, 276
Faubus, Orval, 366, 367
FBI, 6, 326, 338, 342, 347, 351, 376,
  390, 392, 393; COUNTERINTELPRO,
  398–99, 400–402, 432–34
Federal Council of Churches of Christ,
  340
Federal Force Act, 19
Federations for Constitutional Govern-
  ment, 349
Fellowship Forum, 157, 234, 262, 302
FEPC (Fair Employment Practices Com-
  mittee), 325, 341

Ferguson, James, 43, 46–47, 48, 112
Ferguson, Miriam Amanda, 46, 47, 48
Fess, Simeon, 285
Fifth Amendment, 36
Fiery Cross, 150, 202, 320–21, 322, 323
Finch, Cliff, 438
First Amendment, 36
Fleming, Walter, 19
Florida, 5, 13, 15, 225–29, 305, 320; anti-
  mask law, 340; Citizens Councils, 329;
  Fellowship Club, 352, 368; intramural
  wars, 366; Jacksonville sit-ins, 353–54;
  1930s, 311–13; *1950s,* 343ff; opposi-
  tion, 228; politics, 226; St. Augustine,
  376–81; supporters, 352ff; violence, 16,
  227–28, 234, 298, 340–41, 366. *See*
  Hendrix, Bill; 391
Flowers, Richmond, 430
Flynn, William, 268
Folsom, "Big" Jim, 333, 336
Ford, Henry, 197
Foreign affairs, 284, 290, 308
Foreigners, fear of, 110, 231. *See* Xeno-
  phobia
Forrest, Nathan Bedford III, 2, 9, 15,
  18–19, 39, 73, 76, 106, 205; death, 304;
  disbandment order, 19; on Klan, 20–21
Fosdick, Harry Emerson, 254
Fourteenth Amendment, 11
Fourth Amendment, 36
Fowler, Jack. *See* Greensboro murders
Fox, Phil, 73, 107
Frank, Leo, 71
Frankfurter, Felix, 308
Franklin, Benjamin, 8
Fraternalism, 292–93, 299; mystery, 309
"Fraternity," 30–31, 32
The Freedom Riders, 400
Freedom rides, 366, 370–71
Friedenberg, Edgar Z., 387
Friends' Service Committee, 349
Fry, Henry P., 35
Fry, Mrs. Leslie, 322
Fuller, Alvan, 273
Fuqua, Henry, 64

Galligan, George, 186, 188
Garcia, George, 311
Garfield, James A., 66
Garner, John Nance, 44, 200, 307
Gayer, Dr. E. W., 274
George, Walter, 76, 325
Georgetown University, 111
Georgia, 3, 5, 6, 16, 70–77, 305, 368; an-
  timask law, 333, 337, 340; Atlanta, 3,
  34, 35, 70, 73, 78, 153; *Constitution,*
  73; charter revocation, 327–28, 333;
  Columbus *Enquirer-Sun,* 74–75; con-
  servatives, 11–12; decline, 281, 337; dis-
  bandment, 19; heart of Klan, 327;
  Macon, 73; Nashville Convention, 15;

Georgia (cont'd)
  night riders, 76; 1950s, 343ff; 1960s,
  370; opposition, 73, 74, 327–29; poli-
  tics, 71–72, 163, 200; Reconstruction,
  16; Roosevelt, 307; Stone Mountain,
  30, 70, 283, 325, 330, 344, 371; sup-
  porters, 71–72, 73–74, 329; vigilante
  role, 71; violence, 76, 298, 321–22, 335,
  336, 381
German-American Bund, 5, 264; Klan,
  322–23, 328
Germany, 279; language, 244
Gifford, Fred, 87–88, 89, 90, 216
Gill, Robbie, 240
Gish, Lillian, 26
Godwin, H. L., 96
Goldman, Eric, Rendezvous with Des-
  tiny, 27n
Goldwater, Barry, 382–84
Goodman, Andrew, 393
Goodwin, Hanibal, 301
Gordon, George W., 15
Gordon, John B., 15
Gould, Arthur, 277–78
Governors' Conference (1922), 87
Grady, Henry A., 92, 94–95, 97, 102
Grady, Joe, 420
Graham, Royal, 127, 133
Grant, Madison, 270; The Passing of the
  Great Race, 110
Graves, Bibb, 80, 82–83, 84, 314
"Graves-Klan Muzzling Bill," 81, 82
Greeks, 218
Green, Dr. Samuel, 5, 305, 325–34; death,
  6, 335, 339
Green, Samuel Jr., 343
Griffin, Marvin, 372
Griffin, Virgil. See Greensboro murders
Griffin, W. J., 366
Griffith, C. B., 147
Griffith, D. W., 2, 25–26, 28, 30
Gurr, Ted, 430

Hague, Frank, 250
Hale, Frederick, 277
Hall, Grover Cleveland, 81–82
Hamilton, James, 196
Hamilton, Tom, 335, 337–40, 342
Hamlin, Clarence C., 127
Hammer, Fannie Lou, 437
Handlin, Oscar, 283
Hanson, Victor, 81
Harding, Warren G., 36, 62, 111, 179,
  198, 199, 200, 220, 282
Hardwick, Thomas W., 71, 74
Harold, Dr. C. L., 175
Harreld, J. W., 55
Harris, Julian, 74–75
Harris, William J., 72
Harrison, McCord, 223
Harrison, Pat, 68, 69

Harrison, Rev. William E., 123
Harwood, Brown, 43, 175
"Hate movements," 340
Haverford College, 238
Hawes, Harry S., 137, 206
Hawkins, Dr. John, 301
Hayes, Rutherford B., 22
Hayling, Dr., 378
Haynes, Arthur Jr., 403
Haywood, Oscar, 95, 96, 254, 255
Hearst, William Randolph, papers, 217,
  271, 313
Heflin, Tom, 97, 142, 234, 249, 264, 269,
  278, 305, 313; attack on, 274; Klan,
  300–1
Hendrix, Bill, 339–42, 343, 348, 366–67
Henry, R. L., 43
Hill, Lister, 305
Hines, J. K., 76
Hines, Tommy Lee, 408–409, 427
Hitler, Adolph, 307, 344, 352; Klan, 322
Hoosier State. See Indiana
Hoover, Herbert, 55, 69, 97, 156, 229;
  nomination, 301; platform, 303
Hoover, J. Edgar, 198, 398–402
Horn, Rev. Alvin, 348, 367–68, 370
Horn, S. F., 9; Invisible Empire, 9n
Howson, Embrey B., 176, 176n, 180
Huffington, Joe, 163, 169
Hughes, Edwin, 249, 293–94
Humphries, J. H., 157
Hunt, George, 222, 223
Hylan, John, 254, 255

Idaho, 219
Illinois, 4, 33, 183–89, 281, 305; Chicago,
  189; membership, 185; notoriety, 185;
  opposition, 183, 184; Williamson
  County, 185–89, 243, 298
Immigration, 112, 113, 141, 156, 176; Act
  of 1924, 262; Canada, 280; Klan, 218,
  283–84; Massachusetts, 270; New
  England, 266; restriction law, 283
Independent Klan of America, 261
Indiana, 3, 5, 162–74, 195, 281, 285, 305;
  autonomy, 169; Indianapolis Times,
  174; investigations, 199; membership,
  164; Muncie, 33; opposition, 167, 327;
  politics, 139, 163, 166–67, 170; power,
  175; schism, 167; vigilantes, 166, 427
Integration, 6, 352, 353–54, 380; Klan,
  376. See St. Augustine under Florida
Investigations, 36–38, 198, 199
Invisible Empire. See Wilkinson, Bill
Iowa, 138–40; Des Moines, 139–40, Register, 138; opposition, 139, 140; politics, 139
Italy, 284
I.W.W., 51, 125; Tampa Shoemaker case,
  312

Jackson, Ed., 170, 172, 173, 174

Jackson, Helen, 159, 179
Jackson, Jesse, 418
Japanese, 124–25, 141
Jayhawker State. *See* Kansas
Jefferson, Thomas, 211, 234
Jeffersonian Magazine, 225
Jenny, John, 140
Jeremiah X, 375
Jews, 32, 33, 47; in Congress, 283; power, 245; Roosevelt, 307; scapegoat theory, 110. *See* Anti-Semitism
John Birch Society, 382
Johns, Charlie, 340
Johns Hopkins University, 23, 63
Johnson, Albert, 218, 284
Johnson, Andrew, 10, 11
Johnson, Forney, 205
Johnson, Frank, 371
Johnson, Hiram, 124
Johnson, Jack, 156
Johnson, Lyndon, 384, 385, 390
Johnson, Nelson, 418–19
Johnson, Paul, 385
Johnson, Rivers, 93, 95
Johnson Act, 284
Jordan, Rev. E. A., 220
Juries, 121, 126, 150, 333, 350, 377, 381–82; convictions, 336; Klan, 52, 63, 73, 76, 83; Klansmen on, 184
Jurisdiction, federal, 198–99
Juvenile court, 128, 129, 130

Kamelia, 105, 106, 107
Kansas, 143–48, 199; Charter Board, 281; decline, 281; opposition, 143, 144; politics, 144–45; supporters, 144, 145
Kasper, John, 6, 345–47, 368, 383
Kennedy, John F., 367, 368, 381
Kennedy, Stetson, 329
Kenny, Robert W., 327
Kentucky, 154–56; Continental League for Christian Freedom, 328; opposition, 327; politics, 139, 155
Kimbro, George B. Jr., 40
King, Martin Luther, 372, 378, 379, 380, 389, 392, 398, 400, 403, 410, 417
King, Wayne, 412–13, 420
King, William, 207
Klan Haven orphanage, 240
Klan Krest, 35
Klan University, 70, 105, 168
Kleagles, 33–34, 35
Klectoken (initiation fee), 33–34
Klein, Charles, 342
Kleist, John, 191
Kludd (chaplain), 34
Knight Hawk, The, 107
Knights of Columbus, 95, 111, 138, 149, 233, 247, 256, 259, 275, 290; "oath," 111, 302
Knights of the Air, 35

Knights of American Protestantism, 193
Knights of the Flaming Sword, 252
Knights of the Ku Klux Klan. *See* David Duke
Knights of the White Camelia, 16
Know-Nothing party, 206
Kubli, K. K., 89, 90
Kuhn, Fritz, 322, 323
Ku Klux Klan: achievements, 308; activities, 10, 18, 33; affiliates, 217; anti-laws, 333–34; anti-policy, 282; appeal, 114–15; biggest year, 221; Black Legion, 310; Cabinet, 106; center, 355; characteristics, 40; chartering policy, 98; composition, 352ff; control, fight for, 100–8; Constitution, 9, 105; Constitutional violations, 36; decline, 281, 291–99, 304ff, causes, 295ff; defeats, 149; demise (1871), 2; Democratic National Convention (1924), 202–12; disbandment policy, 19; dissension, 92, 108, 169, 189, 252, 281, 296, 335 (*see under* states); divisive force, 299; *1865–71*, 8–21; economic grievances, 18; education level, 344; elections: *1924*, 215, *1928*, 300–3; enemy (*see* Anti-Catholicism); ethnographic pattern, 112–13; fascist organizations, 322; fears, 292, 352; federal jurisdiction, 198; finances, 160, 165, 282, 343, 348; First Annual Klonvokation, 101–5; folk legend, 2, 20, 23; founding, 2, 8ff; fraternalism, 2, 5, 30, 180; free-enterprise, 343ff, 348; future, 282; Grand Dragons, 15; growth, 109, 112; headquarters, 40, 42, 65, 75, 143, 201; hierarchy, 116–17; historical theme, 70; Imperial Palace, 106 (*see* Atlanta *under* Georgia); in-group, 115; initiation fee, 32, 33; international, 279–80; investigations, 61, 73; Kalendar, 117; Klannishness, 5; Klonvokations, 101–5, 289–90; language, 117–18; leadership, 18–19, 70, 104–5, 106, 135–36, 252–53, 282, 296, 299, 317–18, 325, 348–49, 367 (*see* Clarke, Colescott, Evans, Green, Dr. Samuel, *and* Simmons); lecturers, 34, 329, 339, 377, 378, 379; lobbyists, 209, 283; local autonomy, 4; membership, 4, 5, 9–10, 18, 19, 30, 31, 33, 35, 160–61, 202, peak, 291, standard, 110; methods, 169; militant order, 264, 269; motivation, 114; *1920s*, 4, 334; *1930s*, 304ff; *1949*, 332–33; *1950s*, 343ff; *1960s*, 366ff; name, 9; national opinion of, 212; national phenomenon, 3; national politics, 160; national struggle, 89; negativism, 296; oath, 9, 44, 115–16; objectives, 114; opposition, 5–6, 42ff, 138, 243, 305, 326ff, 333ff, 350–51 (*see* Press *and* White, William

Ku Klux Klan (cont'd)
Allen); organization, 2, 3–4, 9, 15, 33–34, 90, 98, 103, 151 (see Simmons); party affiliations, 281; politics, 4, 15–16, 47, 68–69, 72, 75–76, 79–80, 95, 202, 222, 282; power, 5, 291–92, 343; peak, 281, 296; pressure tactics, 368–69; prestige, 334; problem, 296; program, 32–33, 78, 85, 93, 119, 143–44, 284–85; psychic value, 115; publications, 2, 16, 35, 76, 106, 125, 150, 157, 184, 202, 273, 284, 294, 302 305; public image, 7; in public life, 313; purposes, 9, 14, 40–41; Radical governments, 11; rebirth, 2, 70; Reconstruction, 2, 4; recruitment, 32, 33; reputation, 108; revival, 6, 28–38, 98, 99; role, 282; salute, 288; secrecy, 9, 31, 275, 329–30; self-destructiveness, 4; social gatherings, 304–5; social grievances, 18; Southern rule, 281; Southern view of, 20–21; splintering, 339; status movement, 354–55, 370; Stone Mountain (see under Georgia); subversive list, 327; success, 19, 100–8, 291; summer (1964), 376ff; supporters, 75 (see under states); tax status, 140, 159, 323–24 (see U.S. Internal Revenue Service); titles, 4; unmasking, 265; violence, 2, 4–5, 9, 10, 13–14, 18, 296–99, 349ff; women, 240–41, auxiliary, 57, 58, 104–6 (see Kamelia); post World War II, 325ff, 334; "Young Men's Democratic Clubs," 15; young Turks, 101–2. See Simmons, Stephenson, and under name of states; Revitalization movement, 425; Fourth period revival, 406–15, 424–27, 435

Labor, 5, 156–57, 306, 320; Klan, 51, 145, 155, 311–12, 316, 323, 336
Ladies of the Golden Mask, 164
LaFollette, Robert, 139, 215; Progressives, 190, 192–93
Lake, Everett, 266
Land of the Thousand Lakes. See Minnesota
Lange, Otto, 45
Lanterns on the Levee, 66
Law-enforcement, 350–51
Leach, George E., 149, 150–51
League of Nations, 136, 207, 208, 285
Legislation: antimask, 64, 65, 333 (see under name of state); compulsory school bill, 126, 199, 218, 283; Klan interests, 95, 284–85; juvenile, 128; Walker Law, 255, 256, 259, 261
Leopard's Spots, The, 24
Lewis, Charles, 192, 264
Lewis, John L., 316

Lewis William, 276
Life magazine, 326, 328
Lincoln, Abraham, 10, 111, 163
Linderman, Frank, 220–21
Lindsey, Ben B., 4, 127, 128–30, 131, 133–34
Lingo, Al, 389
Little Rock, 349
Liuzzo, Viola Gregg, 390, 392, 393, 394, 397, 399, 410
Locke, Dr. John Galen, 127, 130–31, 132, 133, 261; resignation, 132
Long, Huey, 64, 65, 307–8
Loucks, E. H., 38, 114, 236, 237, 240
Louisiana, 4, 59–65, 200; Bogalusa, 391, 392; decline, 281; federal investigation, 198; Mer Rouge, 93, 138, 141, 185, 298; Morehouse Parish, 59–60, 65; notoriousness, 59; politics, 64; Shreveport, 59; violence, 298. See Long, Huey
Louisiana-Arkansas Law Enforcement League, 56
Lowery, Joseph, 409, 422, 435
Loyal Leagues, 10, 13, 15, 17
Lumbee Indians, 347–48
Lutheran University Association, 168
Lutterman, Harry, 267
Lynch, Connie, 377, 378, 379, 380, 381
Lynch, John M., 336
Lynchings, 49, 71, 109–10, 234, 326
Lyons, Robert, 313

McAdoo, William Gibbs, 72, 200, 203–5, 206, 209, 210, 211, 212, 220, 227, 282, 313, 383
McCall, Charles C., 80 81, 83
McCall, H. C., 42, 101, 104, 201
McCann, John, 207
McCray, Warren, 170
McGill, Ralph, 317, 321, 322; Atlanta Constitution, 329
McGinley, Conde, 6, 352
McKeller, Kenneth, 283
McKinley, William, 66, 111
McKoin, Dr. B. M., 61, 63
McNair, Denise, 401, 404
McNary, Charles, 90
McNaught, Dr. C. E., 151
McRae, Thomas C., 57
Magnolia State. See Mississippi
Mahoney, Dr. William J., 255
Maine, 3, 266, 274–78; politics, 275–78
Mann Act, 105, 172
Mann, Arthur, 268
Manucy, Holsted, 377–78, 379, 380, 381
Martin, John W., 228
Martyred Klansman, The, 239
Maryland, 159–61
Masons, 34, 66, 138, 149, 191, 209, 254, 259, 292; Klan, 42; in Congress, 283

Massachusetts, 3, 270–74; opposition, 270, 271; politics, 271; riots, 266, 272–73
Maybank, Burnett, 321
Mayfield, Earl B., 39, 43–44, 46, 48, 172, 200, 201, 202, 205, 283
Means, Rice, 127, 132, 133, 289
Mecklin, John M., 112, 114, 115, 296
Mencken, H. L., 1
Mer Rouge, 93, 138, 141, 185, 298
Meredith, Don, 400
Methodists, 3, 293; in N.J., 243, 244, 245, 247
Mexico, 43, 284, 290, 308; people, 112, 218, 224
Michigan, 88, 194–97, 305, 397; Burns Anti-Mask Law, 195; finances, 195, 197; National Research Bureau, 195; platform, 194; politics, 196–97. See Black Legion
Militia, 12, 13
Miller, Horace S., 344
Miller, William, 383
Milliken, Carl S., 133
Mills, Ogden, 203
Miner, Roy, 150
Ministry, 135–36, 138, 141, 154, 165, 176, 180, 184, 185–86, 197, 241, 242, 249, 293–94; anti-Klan, 183, 197, 248–49, 333, 336; Canada, 280; N.J., 245–47
Minnesota, 149–51
Minutemen, 193, 261
Miscegenation, 27, 245, 270; law against, 95
Mississippi, 10. 15, 16, 66–69; disbandment, 19; Greenville, 66, 67, 68; integration, 384–85; Meridian riot, 14; 1960s, 369, 392–94, 397; 1970s revival, 406–408, 414–15, 436
Mississippi Civil Rights murders, 392–94
Missouri, 135–37, 313. See Truman, Harry S.
Montana, 219–21
Moody, Dan, 45–46, 48
Moore, Edmund, 208
Moore, Harry, 341
Moore, R. Walton, 234
Moore, William, 431
Morality, 114
Morgenthau, Henry, 303, 323
Morley, Clarence J., 127, 129, 130, 131
Mormons, in Congress, 283
Morris, William, 335, 336–37, 339–40, 342
Mosley, George Van Horn, 322
Motion picture industry, 25
Mountain State. See West Virginia
Mueller, L. A., 288
Murphy, Charles, 204

Mussolini, Benito, 274, 284; Vatican accord, 264

NAACP, 167, 196, 340, 341, 369, 378; Atlanta Convention (1962), 371
Nalls, L. A., 83
Nathan, George Jean, 1
Nation, 271
National Council of Churches of Christ, 349
National Education Administration, 284
National Guard, 3, 269
National Kourier, 125, 157, 273, 284, 305
National States Rights party, 343, 351, 352, 366, 381, 383; insignia, 352
National White Americans party, 371
National Youth Administration, 321
Nativism, 110, 111, 113, 124, 225, 292
Nazis, 322, 328, 352, 411, 413, 420–22, 428. See German-American Bund and Hitler
Nebraska, 137–38
Neff, Pat, 44, 45
Negroes, 5; post Civil War, 17; credulity, 9; demonstrations, 370; Detroit, 195, 196; disfranchisement, 23; education, 14; emancipation, 10; freedom rides, 6; Klan, 2, 10, 41; leaders, 14; lunch-counter sit-ins, 6; majority, 17; militia, 13; N.J., 245; planters, 16; politics, 12, 163; population, 176; protest marches, 6; resistance, 13–14; rights movement, 6, 370, 373; segregation, 23; sit-ins, 6; Smith campaign, 303; strikebreakers, 143; suffrage, 13
Nevada, 222
New Deal, 5, 207, 307
New England, 266ff; Catholics, 275
New Hampshire, 274
New Jersey, 3, 114, 243–53, 289, 305; Methodists, 293; Monmouth County, 244, 248, 252; opposition, 243, 250–52, 327; politics, 249–50; purposes, 244; Sea Girt, 250; strongholds, 243–44; supporters, 245–46, 247, 428
New Mexico, 223–24
New Republic, The, 168
New York, 3, 4, 114, 199, 255–65, 305; dissension, 261, 262; finances, 261; Long Island, 256–57, 259, 260; membership, 260; opposition, 256, 327; politics, 256, 259, 262–63, 264; supporters, 258; violence, 263
New York City, 112, 141, 254–55; riots, 382
New York Journal American, 294
New York Times, 73, 80, 147, 153, 182, 260
New York World, 35–36, 38, 42, 71, 74, 198, 199, 227, 228, 254, 294

Newman Club, 86
Niebuhr, Reinhold, 197
Night riding, 20, 44–45, 73, 76, 81, 119–20, 321; origin, 16–17
Nixon, Richard M., 366, 367, 382, 383
Norris, George W., 138, 305
North Carolina, 10, 16, 18, 92–97; disbandment, 19; opposition, 92–93; Raleigh, 93, 94, 97; role, 92; segregation, 347; White supremacy, 23; Greensboro, 416; lunch counter sit-ins, 417; murders, 418–23, 435, 437
North Carolina A & T, 416–17; lunch counter sit-ins, 417–18
North Dakota, 140–42, 151
Notre Dame University, 167
Nunn, W. C., 16
Nutmeg State. See Connecticut
Nye, Gerald P., 313

Oberholtzer, Madge, 171–72; death, 298
O'Connor, Dennis, 251
O'Donnell, Pat, 183–84; Tolerance, 183
O'Hara, Gerald, 317
Ohio, 3, 112, 175–82, 195, 281, 305; finances, 181; Knights of the Flaming Circle, 177, 179; leadership, 175, 181–82; membership, 175, 176, 180–81; Night Riders, 241; opposition, 177; platform, 176; politics, 177–80; tactics, 180; vigilantes, 166
Oklahoma, 3, 49–55, 88, 285; activities, 51–52; antimask bill, 54; atmosphere, 49–50; decline, 281; membership, 49, 50, 54; politics, 50–51; power, 59; Tulsa, 33, 52; violence, 52, 298
Oklahoma A & M, 51
Oklahoma Farmer-Labor Reconstruction League, 50, 51, 53
Olcott, Ben, 87, 88, 89, 90
Old Dominion State. See Virginia
Olson, Floyd B., 150
Orbison, Charles, 106, 173
Oregon, 3, 85–91, 112, 216, 279; decline, 281; dissension, 90–91; federal investigations, 198; Federation of Patriotic Societies, 85, 88; opposition, 87, 91; pattern, 86; politics, 87–90, 91, 200, 289; Portland, 87; press, 91; public school bill, 126, 199, 218, 283
Original Southern Klans, Inc., 339
Osborn, Clyde W., 176, 178, 181
Owen, Robert, 208

Paine, Rowlett, 153
Palmer, Charles G., 185–86
Palmetto State. See South Carolina
Parades, 34, 39–40, 304, 305; Washington, D.C., 286–88, 289
Parker, John J., 199

Parker, John M., 59, 62–63, 64
Parochial schools, 3
Patriotism, 109
Pattangall, William, 207, 208, 213, 276, 277
Patterson, John, 368, 429
Paulen, Ben, 145, 146, 147
Peabody, Mrs. Malcolm, 378
Pearson, Drew, 329, 330, 340
Peay, Austin, 153
Peck, John G., 256
Peddy, George, 43–44
Pelican State. See Louisiana
Pelly, William Dudley, 310, 322
Penn, Lemuel, 381, 382, 390, 393, 394, 397
Pennsylvania, 3, 236–42, 289, 305; Carnegie riot, 297; finances, 236, 240; membership, 237; opposition, 327; politics, 236–37; Triple-S, 241; violence, 237–40
Percy, LeRoy, 4, 66, 67, 68
Percy, William Alexander, Lanterns on the Levee, 66
Perkins, DeForest, 277
Perry, J. W., 270
Pettie, Virgil, 205
Phelan, James, 204
Phipps, Lawrence, 127, 133
Pierce, Walter, 88, 89
Pine Tree State. See Maine
Pine, W. B., 54
Police, 52, 59
Politics: Alabama, 163, 200, 289, 314; Arkansas, 57; California, 124–25, 200; Colorado, 126–30, 131, 163; Florida, 226; Georgia, 71–72, 163, 200; Indiana, 139, 163, 166–67, 170; Iowa, 139; Kentucky, 139, 144–45, 155; Klan in, 39, 47, 68–69, 72, 75–76, 79–80, 95; Louisiana, 64; Maine, 275–78; Maryland, 159–60; Massachusetts, 271; Michigan, 196–97; Minnesota, 149–51; Missouri, 136–37; Negroes, 163; New Jersey, 249–50; New York, 256, 262–63, 264; Ohio, 177–80; Oklahoma, 50–51; Oregon, 87–90, 91, 200, 289; Pennsylvania, 236–37; Tennessee, 152, 153; Texas, 43–44, 45–48, 200, 201; Virginia, 232–34; West Virginia, 156–57; Wisconsin, 192
Pomerene, Atlee, 181
Poole, Charles, 308, 310
Populists, 11, 22–23, 71
Pound, Ezra, 345
Powell, Luther, 86, 90, 216, 217, 218, 219
Press, the, 32, 74–75, 138–39, 141–42, 167, 198; Alabama, 81–82; Black, Hugo L., 314; California, 122; exposés, 294–95; Georgia, 73; Klan, 18, 35–36,

Press, the (cont'd)
38, 108, 217, 228, 230, 233, 294–95, 313, 333, 336; Klan University, 168; North Carolina, 93; Oregon, 87, 91; Stephenson case, 173
Price, Cecil, 393, 394
Progressive party, 215
Prohibition, 45, 56, 85–86, 98, 114, 160, 248, 249; agents, 256
Protestantism, 112, 113–14; divisiveness, 180
Protestants, in Congress, 283
Protocols of Zion, The, 326
Public school bill, 88–89, 126, 199, 218, 283
Pulaski, Count Casimir, 8
Pulitzer prize, 75, 82, 152, 174, 295, 314
Purcell, John M., 232–33

Quigley, Lawrence, 211

Race relations, 71, 350, 351; fears, 162; mores, 18
Race riots, 10–11; Carnegie, 297; Detroit, 323; Jacksonville, 354; New York City, 382; Oklahoma, 49; Reconstruction, 13; World War I, 109–10
Radicals, 12, 14
Ralston, Samuel M., 167, 170, 172, 204, 212, 282
Ramspect, Robert, 30
Randolph, Hollins, 211
Randolph, Ryland, 16–17, 19
Rankin, John, 325
Rawsey, H. C., 101
Rawsey, Kyle, 104
Ray, Jerry, 403
Razorback State. See Arkansas
Reconstruction: Congressional, 11, 20; courts, 9; Klan, 297, 339; Negro role, 20; presidential programs, 10–11; radical governments, 11, 12, 13, 17, 19–20
Redburn, Rev. W. A., 123
Reed, James, 136, 200, 285, 301
Republican party, 14, 167, 202, 222; elections: 1924, 215, 1964, 383–84; Klan, 2, 15–16, 55, 281; national convention: 1928, 301, 1964, 382; Reconstruction, 11
Reusch, Dale, 1977
Rhode Island, 3, 266, 268–70
Rich, Sam, 236, 237, 238, 241
Richards, Tom, 61–62, 63
Richardson, Friend W., 124
Rickard, Tex, 212
Riders of the Red Robe, 88, 91, 131; purpose, 279
Ridley, Rev. Caleb, 75, 106
Riots, 10–11, 298; Carnegie, 297; Detroit, 323; Jacksonville, 354; Klan, 272–73 (see Violence); New York

City, 382; Robeson concert, 339; summer (1964), 382
Rising Tide of Color, The, 270
Ritchie, A. C., 159–60
Rittenhouse, D. M., 106–7
Rivers, E. D., 107, 317
Robertson, Carol, 401, 404
Robertson, Felix D., 46, 47, 48
Robeson, Paul, 339
Robinson, Alfred "Skip," 408, 427
Robinson, James, 172
Robinson, Joseph, 58, 285
Rockefeller, John D., 23
Rockefeller, Nelson, 353, 383
"Roman crisis," 269. See Anti-Catholicism
Roosevelt, Franklin D., 204, 211–12, 302, 323; Black, Hugo L., 314; governor, 302, 303; Klan, 307
Roosevelt, Theodore Jr., 259, 262
Roper, Sam, 335, 342
Rose, Dr. M. W., 217
Rowbottom, Harry, 170
Rowe, Gary Thomas, 399–402; My Undercover Year, with the Ku Klux Klan, 400, 437
Royal Riders of the Red Robe, The, 217
Russell, Richard B., 72, 74, 76, 325
Ryan, Father, 209

Saalfeld, Lawrence J., 87, 91
St. Mary's of the Woods, 167
Sampson, Dale. See Greensboro murders
Sanctuary, E. N., 322
Sanger, Margaret, 271
Savage, Fred, 101, 102–3, 104
Scheible, Mayor, 178
Schools: compulsory public (see under Oregon); integration, 369, 370; issues, 139–40; segregation, 14–15, 346, decision (1954), 6, 343, 349; teachers, 14, 156. See Education
Schwab, Frank K., 258
Schwerner, Michael, 392, 393
Scoggins, Robert, 397
Scopes trial, 74
Searchlight, 76, 106, 214
Searchlight Publishing Co., 35
Seawell, Malcolm, 347
Segregation, 14–15, 346, 349
Shank, Lou, 167
Shaw, Rev. Herbert C., 241–42
Shelton, Robert, 6, 367–68, 370, 372, 373, 383; United Knights, 375–76; 389, 394–95, 397, 399, 415, 427, 429
Shepard, Dr. William J., 179, 309
Shields, John, 153
Shoemaker, Joseph, 312–13
Shriners, 148, 149
Shuler, Rev. A. C., 329
Sieber, Joseph, 178

Silzer, George, 213, 252
Simkins, Francis, 13
Simmons, Bessie, 106
Simmons, William J., 2, 28–38, 39, 42–
  43, 63, 70, 71, 78, 98, 159, 164, 319;
  background, 225, 315; betrayal, 298;
  Clarke, 100; decline, 57, 73, 101, 104;
  Evans, 92, 105–7, 138–39, 189, 219;
  fraternalism, 292; Grady, 92; House
  investigation, 199; Klan University,
  169; immigration, 113; lawsuits, 169;
  opposition to, 101–4, 236; organiza-
  tion, 116; retirement, 107; supporters,
  106, 189; violence, 297, 425, 430
Simpson, Bryan, 379, 381
Sit-ins, 353–54, 366, 371, 378, 380
Sixth Amendment, 36
Skipworth, J. K., 60–61, 62, 63, 65, 106
Small, Len, 184, 215
Small town, society of, 113–14, 291, 295–
  96
Smart Set, 1
Smith, Alfred E., 47, 48, 58, 69, 76–77,
  84, 97, 99, 142, 157, 204, 206, 212, 214,
  215, 234, 249, 256, 259, 264; Klan, 55,
  300–3
Smith, E. D., 255
Smith, George W., 154
Smith, Gerald L. K., 328, 352
Smith, John W., 188, 196, 197
Smith, William, 12
Smith and Wesson Line, 335
Smythe, James E., 322, 323
South: biracial political attempts, 11–12;
  Black Belt area, 355; "black codes,"
  10; Congressional Reconstruction, 12;
  cotton areas, 16; fears, 17–18, 21; fin
  de siècle, 23; heritage, 28, 71; Klan:
  concentration, 5; Whites, 9; 1960s,
  369ff; occupation of, 19–20, 22; political struggle, 11; post-war(s) society,
  17, 326ff; Radical Reconstruction, 11,
  12, 13, 19–20; school segregation deci-
  sion, 343; violence, 349ff
South Carolina, 10, 11–12, 15, 16, 18,
  98–99, 320–21, 352; antimask law, 337,
  340; disbandment, 19; militia, 13; purpose, 13; Hemingway, 395
South Dakota, 142, 151
Southern Christian Leadership Conference, 378, 379, 409, 434–35
Southern Conference on Bombing (SCB),
  351
Southern Publicity Association, 31–32,
  70, 183
Southern Regional Council, 336, 349
Southern Scottish Rite Masons, 284
Spanish-American War, 29
Spinks, Lycurgus, 339
Stanley, A. O., 155
Stapleton, Ben, 127, 132

Steck, Daniel, 139
Steiwer, Frederick, 91
Stephens, Thaddeus, 24
Stephens, William, 123
Stephenson, David C., 3, 5, 101–4, 162–
  65, 166, 167–70, 173–75, 200, 298;
  ambition, 171; Colescott, 317; coro-
  nation, 288; Evans, 281; imprisonment,
  172, 174; Klan position, 237; New
  Jersey, 252; One Hundred Years of
  Health, 171; presidency, 282
Stern, Carl, 399
Stetson University, 227
Steuben Society, 244, 322
Stoddard, Lothrop, 270–71; The Rising
  Tide of Color, 110, 270
Stoner, J. B., 326, 343–44, 379, 380, 381,
  383, 403–404
Stovall, P. A., 211
Stratton, John Roach, 254
Strayer, John, 242
Strikebreakers, 143
Strikes, 145, 157
Styles, Hal, 313
Subversive organizations, 327
Suffrage, Negro, 10, 11, 17, 18, 370
Sunday, Billy, 91, 165
Sunshine State. See Florida
Sweet, Dr. Ossian, 196

Talmadge, Eugene, 107, 313, 322, 326,
  327–29
Talmadge, Herman, 329, 332, 337
Tammany, 204, 256
Tarheel State. See North Carolina
Tarrants, Tommy, 397
Taylor, Gilbert, 181
Teapot Dome scandals, 210, 220
Tennessee, 8, 9, 10, 15, 16, 152–53; Con-
  servatives, 11–12; disbandment, 19;
  Nashville Convention, 11; 1960s, 369;
  opposition, 152; politics, 152, 153; Re-
  construction, 11; supporters, 152; vio-
  lence, 335
Terrall, Tom J., 57
Terwilliger, Lew, 221
Texas, 3, 10, 16, 39–48, 88, 112; activi-
  ties, 41–42; anti-Klan, 39, 42; Dallas,
  3, 40, 41, 44, 45, 48, press, 47, 48; de-
  cline, 48, 281; Forth Worth, 40, 48;
  Houston, 39–40, 41, 42, 48; investiga-
  tions, 45, 199; membership, 40, 126;
  politics, 43–44, 45–48, 200, 201; power,
  44, 59; San Antonio, 40, 48; supporters, 41, 47; violence, 44–45, 175, 298;
  Waco, 40, 41
Texas Rangers, 45, 48
Thirteenth Amendment, 36
Thomas, Norman, 312–13
Thompson, Ira, 83
Thurmond, Strom, 332, 351

Tillman, Ben, 98
Toombs, Robert, 211
Towner-Sterling bill, 284
Truman, Harry S., 136, 313, 326
Tuck, William, 333
Tugwell, Rexford G., 308
Tully, Wynn, 154
Tumulty, Joseph, 74, 282
Tyler, Elizabeth "Bessie," 31–36, 73; Clarke, 100; resignation, 101, 104

Underwood, Oscar W., 72, 79–80, 204, 205, 208, 300, 314
Union Leagues, 10, 13, 14, 17
Unions. *See* Labor
United Confederate Veterans, 39
United Daughters of the Confederacy, 230
United Klans, 383. *See* Shelton, Robert
United League of Mississippi. *See* Robinson, Alfred
United Mine Workers, 54, 155, 156, 167
United Nations, 341
United Protestant Alliance, 264
University of Alabama, 345
University of Colorado, 344
University of Florida, 227
University of Georgia, 74
University of Illinois, 185
University of Minnesota, 149
University of North Carolina, 337–38
University of Oklahoma, 50
University of Oregon, 86
University of Texas, 43, 47
University of Wisconsin, 192
Upsala College, 249
Upshaw, William D., 38, 71
Urban areas, 114–15, 156
U.S. Congress, 38, 199, 282–83; investigations, 36, 100; reticence, 199–200
U.S. Constitution, 198, 306, 308
U.S. House of Representatives, 57, 283; investigations, 71; Rules Committee, 36; Un-American Activities Committee, 394–95
U.S. Internal Revenue Service, 6, 36, 323–24, 325, 333
U.S. Justice Department, 36, 59, 61, 62, 87, 198; investigations (1946), 326–27
U.S. Klans, 343, 370
U.S. Navy, 217, 346
U.S. Senate, 126, 172, 202, 283, 313; Klan, 39, 44, 80; traditions, 314; World Court, 289
U.S. Supreme Court, 5, 91, 134, 148, 199, 255; anti-Klan ruling, 259; public school law, 196; school segregation decision (1954), 6, 343. *See* Black, Hugo L.
U.S.S. *California*, 217
U.S.S. *Tennessee*, 217

Utah, 221–22

Valparaiso University, 167, 168
Vance, James S., 302
Van Cise, Philip S., 127, 128
Vander Zanden, James, 354, 431
Vandiver, Eugene, 371
Vardaman, James K., 68
Vatican, 264, 320
Venable, James, 343, 351, 371, 376, 405, 406
Vermont, 266, 274
Veterans of Foreign Wars, 312
Vienna *Neue Freie Presse*, 279
Violence, 4–5, 22, 141, 153, 169, 227–28, 234, 263, 272–73, 296–99, 329, 335–37, 387–88, 390–94, 397–99, 400–03, 407–10, 418, 421, 426, 431, 436–38; dynamite, 351; economic, 180; Georgia, 71, 76; increase in, 35; *1950s–60s,* 349ff; Oklahoma, 52, 71; Pennsylvania, 237–40; press, 35–36; recruitment, 239; Texas, 42, 44–45, 71; war, 109, 327; Williamson County, 185–89. *See also* Black Legion
Virginia, 230–35, 289, 305; opposition, 233–34; politics, 232–34
Volstead Act, 105, 159

Wallace, Anthony F. C., 425
Wallace, George, 389, 390, 400, 429
Waller, James. *See* Greensboro murders
Walsh, David, 198, 206, 274
Walsh, Thomas J., 219, 220–21, 301
Walton, Jack, 50–51, 52–54
Washburn, Stanley, 250
Warren, Earl, 6
Washington, 88, 216–19, 279
Washington, Booker T., 26
Washington, D.C., 4, 70; headquarters, 75, 201; Klan, 132, 285–90; parade, 286–88
Washington, George, 8, 232
Waterman, Charles W., 133
Watson, James, 172–73, 201, 202–3
Watson, Tom, 23, 71, 225
WCTU, 86, 256
Weaver, Norman, 112, 190, 190n, 193, 195
Wesley, Cynthia, 401, 404
West Virginia, 156–57
White, Alma, 245–46, 293
White Citizens Councils, 6, 345, 349, 369, 384
White Knights, 391, 395
White Supremacy, 22, 30, 32, 39, 74, 98, 218, 270, 385
White, William Allen, 144, 145–47, 148, 210, 215, 281; Emporia *Gazette,* 4, 144, 145–46, 295
Wilkinson, Bill, 407–10, 415, 426, 438

William and Mary College, 234
Williams, T. Harry, 412
Willis, Frank, 181, 285
Willkie, Wendell, 320, 382
Wilson, Woodrow, 23, 26–27, 72, 74, 79, 136, 203, 211, 282
Winchell, Walter, 313, 329
Winter, Paul, 240, 241, 264
Wisconsin, 3, 190–93, 305; finances, 191–92; opposition, 192; politics, 192
Wobblies, 49
Women, 21, 151, 264; in Klan, 240–41, 289
Woolwine, Lee, 120, 124
Workers Viewpoint Organization. *See* Greensboro murders

World Court, 76, 181, 193, 284, 285, 289, 308
World War I, 49, 109, 111, 209, 292; Klan, 31
World War II, 5, 323
Wyoming, 221

Xenophobia, 352

Yale University, 266–67, 380
Young, Andrew, 417
Young, S. Glenn, 186–88

Zanden, James Vanden, 354
Zumbrunn, W. F., 132, 139, 201, 283, 284, 301

ABOUT THE AUTHOR

DAVID CHALMERS is Professor of American history at the University of Florida. A native of Washington, D.C., and a graduate of Swarthmore College and the University of Rochester, he has served in the army, has worked for the government, and has taught at Ohio University, the City College of New York, and Carleton College. He has been exchange professor at the Universities of Sri Lanka, Tokyo, the Philippines, and Tel Aviv, and has lectured in Vietnam, Korea, and Cyprus. He is author of five books, and has received many teaching awards including the University of Florida Teacher-Scholar of the Year. He has also headed the local American Civil Liberties Union chapter, and was a member of the "Group Protest and Demonstration" Task force of President Johnson's National Violence Commission.